W9-BGQ-748

Chris Spollen

Special thanks to

All the incredibly creative—and skilled—*artists* listed on the next page, whose illustrations appear in the color insert. In order to show Illustrator's range, we chose artists whose work represents a wide variety of styles and venues: maps, book covers, magazine covers, greeting cards, advertisements, medical illustrations, editorial illustrations, self-promos, logos, and more. We hope their work inspires you.

Nancy Aldrich-Ruenzel, Publisher, Peachpit Press; *Marjorie Baer,* Executive Editor; *Lisa Brazieal,* Production Coordinator; *Nathalie Valette,* cover designer; *Gary-Paul Prince,* Publicist; *Keasley Jones,* Associate Publisher; and the rest of the folks at Peachpit Press. They are truly a pleasure to work with.

Cary Norsworthy, our wonderful Editor at Peachpit Press.

Victor Gavenda, careful and clever Technical Editor at Peachpit Press.

Mordy Golding, Ted Alspach, Lubomir Bourdev, Pierre Louveaux, and *Marcus Chang* at Adobe Systems, Inc., for their technical support.

Mies Hora of Ultimate Symbol, for the Design Elements CD (www.ultimatesymbol.com).

Nathan Olson and *Suzanne Thomas,* freelance writers.

Stephen Dampier, for testing the keyboard shortcuts.

Leona Benten, William Rodarmor, and *Haig MacGregor,* proofreaders (goof-finders).

Steve Rath, indexer (sneak a peek at the 38-page index!).

Conrad Chavez, for drafting and laying out the Student and Instructor sections of this book.

Peter from *Elaine* and *Elaine* from *Peter*—the ultimate symbiotic relationship. Finished another book, and we're still talking to each other!

The Artists

Peter Fahrni
Voice 212-472-7126
fahrni@infohouse.com
www.oscillochrome.com
204, 205

Barbara Friedman
Voice 212-533-9535
batbf@aol.com
color section

Yoshinori Kaizu
2-14-4, Kugahara
Ohta-ku, Tokyo 146-0085
Japan
Voice +81 3-3755-8704
Fax +81 3-3755-2186
y@kaizu.com
www.kaizu.com
color section

Diane Margolin
41 Perry Street
New York, NY 10014
Voice 212-691-9537
dimargolin@erols.com
57, 77, 78, 106, 120, 126, 134,
160, 166, 262, 263, 266, 274,
275, 320, 380, 389, 406

Led Pants
10 Paseo de San Antonio
Santa Fe, NM 87507
505-955-0799
led@ledpants.com
www.ledpants.com
color section

Chris Spollen

Daniel Pelavin
80 Varick Street, #3B
New York, NY 10013
Voice 212-941-7418
Fax 212-431-7138
www.pelavin.com
iii, iv, v, vi, ix, x, xii, xv, xvi, 63,
64, 65, 167, 341, color section

Marti Shohet
32 West 83rd Street, #6
New York, NY 10024
Voice/Fax 212-362-9082
mshohet@mindspring.com
www.theispot.com/artist/mshohet
color section

Jim Spiece
Spiece Graphics
6636 Quail Ridge Lane
Ft. Wayne, IN 46804-2876
Voice/Fax 219-436-9549
sggraphics@earthlink.net
www.theispot.com/artist/jspiece
color section

Chris Spollen
Moonlightpress Studio
362 Cromwell Avenue
Staten Island, NY 10305-2304
Voice 718-979-9695
cjspollen@aol.com
http://www.spollen.com
iii, iv, 1, 55, 65, 105, 137, 307,
509, color section

Nancy Stahl
470 West End Avenue, 8G
New York, NY 10024
Voice 212-362-8779
nancy@nancystahl.com
www.nancystahl.com
443, color section

Mark Stein
Mark Stein Studios
73-01 Juniper Valley Road
Middle Village NY 11379
Voice 718-326-4839
steinstudios@worldnet.att.net
247, color section

Bart Vallecoccia,
medical illustrator
164 Manitoba Street
Toronto, ON, M8Y 1E3
Canada
Voice 416-255-7499
bartv@interlog.com
bartv@sympatico.ca
www.interlog.com/~bartv
color section

Artists Directory

INTRODUCTION i

Welcome to the Student Edition for *Illustrator 10 for Windows and Macintosh: Visual QuickStart Guide*. This edition offers exercises and review material to help you get up and running with Adobe Illustrator 10.

At the end of each chapter of *Illustrator 10 for Windows and Macintosh: Visual QuickStart Guide* you'll find a special study guide section. Each section is divided into four parts:

■ **Learning Objectives** list the main points you should learn from a chapter.

■ **Get Up and Running Exercises** are projects to help you synthesize and practice what you've learned. The exercises are based on techniques introduced in a chapter.

■ **Class Discussion Questions** help you review a chapter with your class or study group. You can explore concepts introduced in the book and in class and compare and contrast tools and techniques covered in a chapter.

■ **Review Questions** will enable you to evaluate how well you've learned key details in a chapter. Each chapter contains a set of multiple choice, fill-in-the-blank, and definition questions.

In this book you'll find everything you need to learn, and confidently work with, Adobe Illustrator 10.

Have fun!

TABLE OF CONTENTS

Note! New features, substantially changed features, and additions to the book are listed in **boldface**.

Daniel Pelavin

Chapter 1: **Illustrator Interface**

See the Student Edition pages at the end of each chapter.   **vii**

See the Student Edition pages at the end of each chapter.

Daniel Pelavin

Table of Contents

Table of Contents

Chapter 8: ## Reshape

Daniel Pelavin

Table of Contents

Daniel Pelavin

Chapter 9:   **Fill & Stroke**

          See the Student Edition pages at the end of each chapter.

Table of Contents

Daniel Pelavin

Table of Contents

Chapter 12: Create Type

Chapter 13: Style & Edit Type

See the Student Edition pages at the end of each chapter.

Daniel Pelavin

See the Student Edition pages at the end of each chapter.

Table of Contents

Chapter 16: **Symbols**

Daniel Pelavin

Table of Contents

See the Student Edition pages at the end of each chapter.

See the Student Edition pages at the end of each chapter.   **xix**

See the Student Edition pages at the end of each chapter.

See the Student Edition pages at the end of each chapter.

Chapter 22: Effects and filters

See the Student Edition pages at the end of each chapter.

Chapter 23: Precision Tools

Chapter 24: Actions

Chapter 25: Preferences

Chapter 26: Output/Export

Outputting files

Exporting files

See the Student Edition pages at the end of each chapter.

Table of Contents

Chapter 27: Web

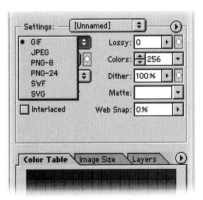

Table of Contents

        See the Student Edition pages at the end of each chapter.

ILLUSTRATOR INTERFACE

This chapter is an introduction to Illustrator's tools, menus, palettes, and measurement systems.

Note: If you'd like to glance on screen at the features discussed in this chapter as you read, launch Illustrator and create a new document (see pages 37–39).

Chris Spollen

Hide/show

Tab	Hide/show all currently open palettes, including the Toolbox
Shift-Tab	Hide/show all currently open palettes except the Toolbox

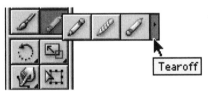

1 *Drag a pop-out menu away from the Toolbox by choosing the **tearoff** bar.*

2 *A **tearoff toolbar** is created.*

Tools

Using the Toolbox

The Toolbox contains **76 tools** that are used for object creation and modification. If the Toolbox is hidden, choose Window > Tools to display it. To move the Toolbox, drag the top bar. Click once on a visible tool to select it. Press on any tool that has a tiny arrowhead to choose a related tool from a pop-out menu. Double-clicking some tools opens an options dialog box for that tool.

To create a standalone **tearoff toolbar** **1**–**2**, release the mouse when it's over the vertical tearoff bar on the far right side of any tool pop-out menu. Move a tearoff toolbar by dragging its top bar. To restore a tearoff toolbar to the Toolbox, click its close box.

To access a tool quickly, use its letter **shortcut** (see the boldface letters on the next two pages). Some tools can be accessed using a toggle key (e.g., pressing Cmd/Ctrl accesses the Selection tool when the Pen tool is chosen). You'll learn more toggles later.

To turn tool pointers into **crosshairs** for precise positioning, check Use Precise Cursors in Edit > Preferences > General. Or press Caps Lock to turn a tool pointer into a crosshair temporarily.

➤ You'll probably want to leave Disable Warnings unchecked in Edit > Preferences > General, at least if you're new to Illustrator. With this option unchecked, an alert prompt will appear when a tool is being used incorrectly.

The Toolbox 10.0!

Note: To assign your own shortcuts for tools, use the **Keyboard Shortcuts** dialog box (see pages 529–530).

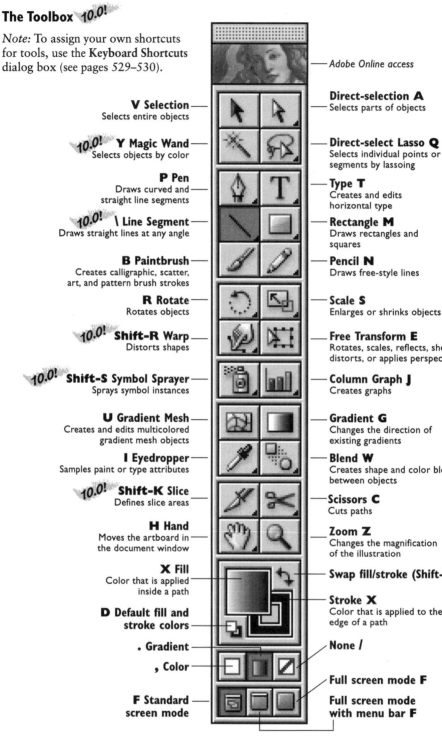

Adobe Online access

V Selection
Selects entire objects

Direct-selection A
Selects parts of objects

10.0! **Y Magic Wand**
Selects objects by color

Direct-select Lasso Q
Selects individual points or segments by lassoing

P Pen
Draws curved and straight line segments

Type T
Creates and edits horizontal type

10.0! **\ Line Segment**
Draws straight lines at any angle

Rectangle M
Draws rectangles and squares

B Paintbrush
Creates calligraphic, scatter, art, and pattern brush strokes

Pencil N
Draws free-style lines

R Rotate
Rotates objects

Scale S
Enlarges or shrinks objects

10.0! **Shift-R Warp**
Distorts shapes

Free Transform E
Rotates, scales, reflects, shears, distorts, or applies perspective

10.0! **Shift-S Symbol Sprayer**
Sprays symbol instances

Column Graph J
Creates graphs

U Gradient Mesh
Creates and edits multicolored gradient mesh objects

Gradient G
Changes the direction of existing gradients

I Eyedropper
Samples paint or type attributes

Blend W
Creates shape and color blends between objects

10.0! **Shift-K Slice**
Defines slice areas

Scissors C
Cuts paths

H Hand
Moves the artboard in the document window

Zoom Z
Changes the magnification of the illustration

X Fill
Color that is applied inside a path

Swap fill/stroke (Shift-X)

D Default fill and stroke colors

Stroke X
Color that is applied to the edge of a path

. Gradient

, Color

None /

F Standard screen mode

Full screen mode F

Full screen mode with menu bar F

Toolbox

The tear-off toolbars

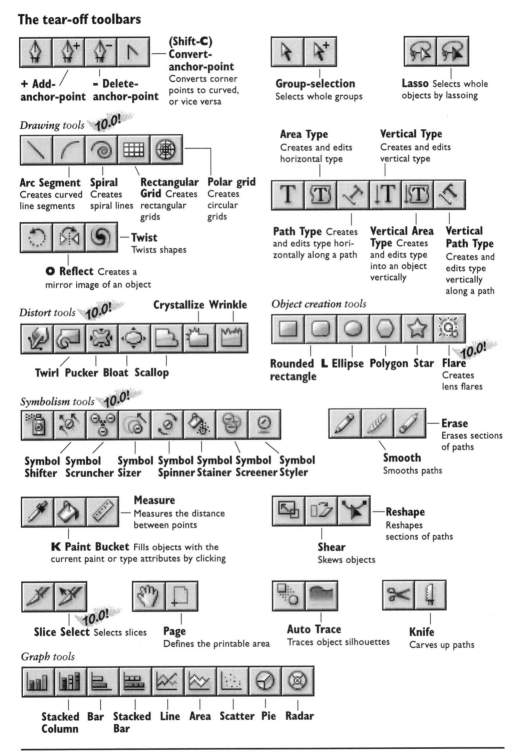

(Shift-C)
Convert-
anchor-point
Converts corner points to curved, or vice versa

+ Add-
anchor-point

- Delete-
anchor-point

Group-selection
Selects whole groups

Lasso Selects whole objects by lassoing

Drawing tools **10.0!**

Arc Segment
Creates curved line segments

Spiral
Creates spiral lines

Rectangular Grid Creates rectangular grids

Polar grid
Creates circular grids

Twist
Twists shapes

O Reflect Creates a mirror image of an object

Area Type
Creates and edits horizontal type

Vertical Type
Creates and edits vertical type

Path Type Creates and edits type horizontally along a path

Vertical Area Type Creates and edits type into an object vertically

Vertical Path Type
Creates and edits type vertically along a path

Distort tools **10.0!**

Crystallize Wrinkle

Twirl Pucker Bloat Scallop

Object creation tools

Rounded rectangle **L Ellipse** **Polygon** **Star** **Flare** **10.0!**
Creates lens flares

Symbolism tools **10.0!**

Symbol Shifter **Symbol Scruncher** **Symbol Sizer** **Symbol Spinner** **Symbol Stainer** **Symbol Screener** **Symbol Styler**

Erase
Erases sections of paths

Smooth
Smooths paths

Measure
Measures the distance between points

K Paint Bucket Fills objects with the current paint or type attributes by clicking

Reshape
Reshapes sections of paths

Shear
Skews objects

Slice Select **10.0!** Selects slices

Page
Defines the printable area

Auto Trace
Traces object silhouettes

Knife
Carves up paths

Graph tools

Stacked Column **Bar** **Stacked Bar** **Line** **Area** **Scatter** **Pie** **Radar**

Toolbox

On the screen

The Illustrator screen: Mac OS

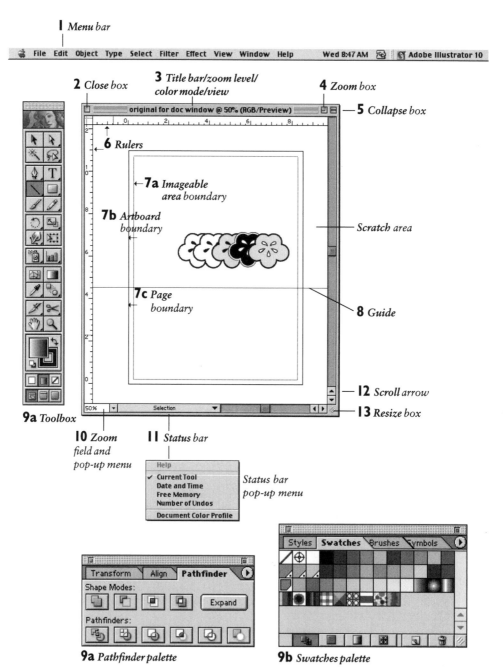

1 *Menu bar*

File Edit Object Type Select Filter Effect View Window Help   Wed 8:47 AM   Adobe Illustrator 10

2 *Close box*

3 *Title bar/zoom level/ color mode/view*

4 *Zoom box*

original for doc window @ 50% (RGB/Preview)

5 *Collapse box*

6 *Rulers*

7a *Imageable area boundary*

7b *Artboard boundary*

Scratch area

7c *Page boundary*

8 *Guide*

12 *Scroll arrow*

13 *Resize box*

50%   Selection

9a *Toolbox*

10 *Zoom field and pop-up menu*

11 *Status bar*

Help
✓ Current Tool
  Date and Time
  Free Memory
  Number of Undos
  Document Color Profile

Status bar pop-up menu

Transform Align **Pathfinder**
Shape Modes: Expand
Pathfinders:

9a *Pathfinder palette*

Styles **Swatches** Brushes Symbols

9b *Swatches palette*

Illustrator Screen (Mac OS)

Key to the Illustrator screen: Mac OS

1 *Menu bar*
Use the menu bar to open dialog boxes or palettes or choose commands.

2 *Close box*
To close a document or a palette, click its close box.

3 *Title bar/zoom level/mode/view*
The illustration's title, zoom level, color mode (CMYK or RGB), and view (Preview, Outline, Pixel Preview, or Overprint Preview) are displayed on the title bar.

4 *Zoom box*
Click a document window zoom box to enlarge the window. Click again to restore the window to its previous size. (Click a palette zoom box to shrink the palette or restore it to its previous size.)

5 *Collapse box*
Click the collapse box to shrink the document window to just the title bar. Click the collapse box again to restore the document window to its previous size.

6 *Rulers*
The current position of the pointer is indicated by a marker on the horizontal and vertical rulers. Ruler increments can be displayed in a choice of seven different measurement units.

7a–c *Imageable area, artboard boundary, and page boundary*
The imageable area within the margin guides is the area that will print on the paper size currently selected in File > Page Setup. The artboard is the user-defined work area and the largest possible printable area. The non-printing page boundary matches the current paper size. Objects located in the area

beyond the artboard will save with the file, but they won't print.

8 *Guide*
Drag from the horizontal or vertical ruler to create a guide. Guides are only used for aligning objects; they don't print.

9a–b *Palettes*
Pathfinder and Brushes are five of 28 moveable palettes that open from the Window menu. The Toolbox contains 76 (yes, 76!) drawing and editing tools, as well as color controls and screen mode buttons.

10 *Zoom field*
Enter a new zoom percentage in this field or choose a preset zoom percentage from the zoom pop-up menu.

11 *Status bar*
Depending on which category you select from the pop-up menu, the Status bar displays the name of the Current Tool, the current Date and Time from the Mac OS Control Panel, the amount of Free Memory (RAM) available for the currently open file, the Number of available Undos/Redos, or the Document Color Profile (RGB or CMYK). Option-press on the Status bar pop-up menu to learn the Moon Phase, Shopping Days 'til Christmas, and other vital statistics.

12 *Scroll arrow*
Click the downward-pointing scroll arrow to move the illustration upward in the document window. Click the upward-pointing scroll arrow to move the illustration downward in the document window.

13 *Resize box*
To resize a document window, drag its resize box diagonally.

The Illustrator screen: Windows

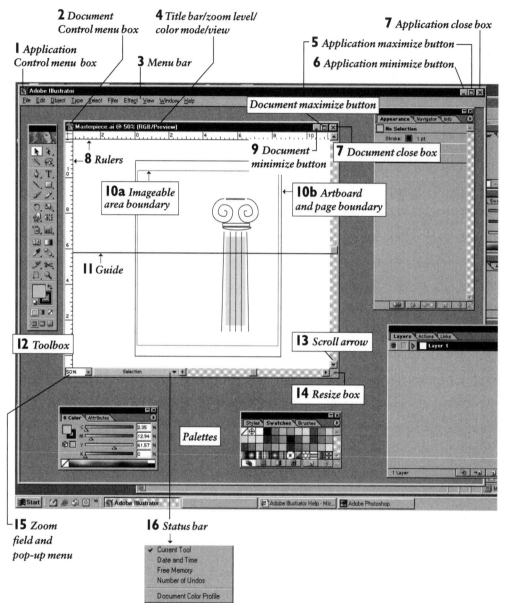

1 *Application Control menu box*

2 *Document Control menu box*

3 *Menu bar*

4 *Title bar/zoom level/ color mode/view*

5 *Application maximize button*

6 *Application minimize button*

7 *Application close box*

Document maximize button

7 *Document close box*

8 *Rulers*

9 *Document minimize button*

10a *Imageable area boundary*

10b *Artboard and page boundary*

11 *Guide*

12 *Toolbox*

13 *Scroll arrow*

14 *Resize box*

Palettes

15 *Zoom field and pop-up menu*

16 *Status bar*

✓ Current Tool
Date and Time
Free Memory
Number of Undos

Document Color Profile

Status bar pop-up menu

Illustrator Screen (Windows)

Key to the Illustrator screen: Windows

1 *Application Control menu box*
The Application Control menu box commands are Restore, Move, Size, Minimize, Maximize, and Close.

2 *Document Control menu box*
The Document Control menu box commands are Restore, Move, Size, Minimize, Maximize, Close, and Next.

3 *Menu bar*
Use the menu bar to open dialog boxes or palettes or choose commands.

4 *Title bar/zoom level/color mode/view*
The illustration's title, zoom level, color mode (CMYK or RGB), and view (Preview, Outline, Pixel Preview, or Overprint Preview) are displayed on the title bar.

5 *Maximize/restore button*
Click the Application or Document Restore button to restore that window to its previous size. When a window is at the restored size, the Restore button turns into the Maximize button. Click the Maximize button to enlarge the window.

6 *Application minimize button*
Click the Application minimize button to shrink the application to an icon on the Taskbar. Click the icon on the Taskbar to restore the application window to its previous size.

7 *Close box*
To close a document or a palette, click its close box.

8 *Rulers*
The current position of the pointer is indicated by a marker on the horizontal and vertical rulers. Ruler increments can be displayed in a choice of seven different measurement units.

9 *Document minimize button*
Click the Document minimize button to shrink the document to an icon at the bottom left corner of the application window. To restore the document to its previous size, double-click the icon or click the Restore icon.

10a–b *Imageable area, artboard boundary, and page boundary*
The imageable area within the margin guides is the area that will print on the paper size currently selected in File > Print Setup. The artboard is the user-defined work area and the largest possible printable area. The non-printing page boundary matches the current paper size. Objects outside the artboard save with the file, but don't print.

11 *Guide*
Drag from the horizontal or vertical ruler to create a guide. Guides are used only for aligning objects; they don't print.

12 *Toolbox*
The Toolbox contains 76 drawing and editing tools, as well as color controls and screen mode buttons. It is one of the 28 moveable palettes that open from the Window menu.

13 *Scroll arrow*
Click the downward-pointing scroll arrow to move the illustration upward in the document window. Click the upward-pointing scroll arrow to move the illustration downward in the document window.

14 *Resize box*
To resize a window, drag its resize box diagonally or drag the edge of the window.

15 *Zoom field*
Enter a new zoom percentage in this field or choose a preset zoom percentage from the pop-up menu.

16 *Status bar*
Depending on which category you choose from the pop-up menu, the Status bar displays the name of the Current Tool, the current Date and Time from the computer's internal clock, the amount of virtual memory (RAM) available for the currently open file, the Number of available Undos/Redos, or the Document Color Profile (RGB or CMYK). Alt-press on the Status bar pop-up menu to learn the Moon Phase, Shopping Days 'til Christmas, and other vital statistics.

Illustrator Screen (Windows)

7

The Illustrator menus 10.0!

File menu

File

New...	⌘N
Open...	⌘O
Open Recent Files	▶
Revert	
Close	⌘W
Save	⌘S
Save As...	⇧⌘S
Save a Copy...	⌥⌘S
Save for Web...	⌥⇧⌘S
Place...	
Export...	
Manage Workgroup	▶
Scripts	▶
Document Setup...	⌥⌘P
Document Color Mode	▶
File Info...	
Separation Setup...	
Page Setup...	⇧⌘P
Print...	⌘P
Quit	⌘Q

Edit menu

Edit

Undo Copy	⌘Z
Redo Move	⇧⌘Z
Cut	⌘X
Copy	⌘C
Paste	⌘V
Paste in Front	⌘F
Paste in Back	⌘B
Clear	
Define Pattern...	
Edit Original	
Assign Profile...	
Color Settings...	
Keyboard Shortcuts...	⌥⇧⌘K
Preferences	▶

(Manage Workgroup is not available in Windows, and the Exit command replaces Quit.)

Illustrator

About Illustrator...	
About Plug-ins...	
Preferences...	▶
Services	▶
Hide Illustrator	
Hide Others	
Show All	
Quit Illustrator	⌘Q

*Note: In Mac OSX, the Preferences and Quit commands are on the **Illustrator** menu.*

Object menu

Object

Transform	▶
Arrange	▶
Group	⌘G
Ungroup	⇧⌘G
Lock	▶
Unlock All	⌥⌘2
Hide	▶
Show All	⌥⌘3
Expand...	
Expand Appearance	
Flatten Transparency...	
Rasterize...	
Create Gradient Mesh...	
Slice	▶
Path	▶
Blend	▶
Envelope Distort	▶
Clipping Mask	▶
Compound Path	▶
Crop Marks	▶
Graph	▶

Type menu

Type

Font	▶
Size	▶
Blocks	▶
Wrap	▶
Fit Headline	
Create Outlines	⇧⌘O
Find/Change...	
Find Font...	
Check Spelling...	
Change Case...	
Smart Punctuation...	
Rows & Columns...	
Show Hidden Characters	
Type Orientation	▶
Glyph Options	▶

(Glyph Options is not available in Windows.)

Select menu

Select

All	⌘A
Deselect	⇧⌘A
Reselect	⌘6
Inverse	
Next Object Above	⌥⌘]
Next Object Below	⌥⌘[
Same	▶
Object	▶
Save Selection ...	
Edit Selection ...	

Filter menu

Filter

Apply Pucker & Bloat	⌘E
Pucker & Bloat...	⌥⌘E
Colors	▶
Create	▶
Distort	▶
Pen & Ink	▶
Stylize	▶
Artistic	▶
Blur	▶
Brush Strokes	▶
Distort	▶
Pixelate	▶
Sharpen	▶
Sketch	▶
Stylize	▶
Texture	▶
Video	▶

Effect menu

Effect

Apply Ellipse	⇧⌘E
Ellipse...	⌥⇧⌘E
Document Raster Effects Settings...	
Convert to Shape	▶
Distort & Transform	▶
Path	▶
Pathfinder	▶
Rasterize...	
Stylize	▶
SVG Filters	▶
Warp	▶
Artistic	▶
Blur	▶
Brush Strokes	▶
Distort	▶
Pixelate	▶
Sharpen	▶
Sketch	▶
Stylize	▶
Texture	▶
Video	▶

View menu

View

Outline	⌘Y
Overprint Preview	⌥⇧⌘Y
Pixel Preview	⌥⌘Y
Proof Setup	▶
Proof Colors	
Zoom In	⌘+
Zoom Out	⌘-
Fit in Window	⌘0
Actual Size	⌘1
Hide Edges	⌘H
Hide Artboard	
Hide Page Tiling	
Show Slices	
Lock Slices	
Hide Template	⇧⌘W
Show Rulers	⌘R
Hide Bounding Box	⇧⌘B
Show Transparency Grid	⇧⌘D
Guides	▶
Smart Guides	⌘U
Show Grid	⌘"
Snap to Grid	⇧⌘"
✓ Snap to Point	⌥⌘"
New View...	
Edit Views...	

Window menu

Window

New Window
Actions
Align
Appearance
Attributes
Brushes
✓ Color
Document Info
Flattening Preview
✓ Gradient
Info
✓ Layers
Links
Magic Wand
✓ Navigator
✓ Pathfinder
Stroke
Styles
SVG Interactivity
Swatches
✓ Symbols
✓ Tools
Transform
Transparency
Type ▶
Variables
Brush Libraries ▶
Style Libraries ▶
Swatch Libraries ▶
Symbol Libraries ▶
✓ jUNK.ai @ 136% (CMYK/Preview)

(Window > Cascade, Tile, and Arrange Icons are only available in Windows.)

Help menu

Help

About Balloon Help...
Show Balloons
Illustrator Help...
Top Issues...
Downloadables...
Corporate News...
Registration...
Adobe Links ▶
Adobe Online...
System Info...

Help > About Illustrator and About Plug-ins are available only in Windows. Balloon Help is only available in the Mac OS.

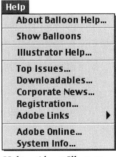

The Menus

9

Using dialog boxes

Dialog boxes are like fill-in forms with multiple choices. They are opened from the menu bar or via shortcuts.

In Windows: To activate a menu, type Alt-[underlined letter], then release Alt and type the underlined letter on the submenu.

Some modifications are made by entering a number in an entry field. Press **Tab** to highlight the next field in a dialog box. Hold down **Shift** and press **Tab** to highlight the previous field. Press on a pop-up menu to choose further options.

Click **OK** or press **Return/Enter** to accept modifications and exit a dialog box. To cancel out of a dialog box, click Cancel or press Esc.

Many Illustrator dialog boxes have a **Preview** option that when checked will apply the effect while the dialog box is open. Take advantage of this great timesaver.

Illustrator dialog boxes, like all the other features in the program, function the same way in the Mac OS as in Windows, though they look slightly different because each operating system has its own graphic interface.

*In Windows, you can type an **underlined** letter to activate that field (e.g., "U" for "Uniform"). If a field is already highlighted, type Alt plus the underlined letter.*

A **Windows** dialog box

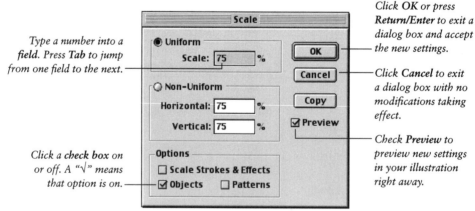

*Type a number into a field. Press **Tab** to jump from one field to the next.*

*Click a **check box** on or off. A "√" means that option is on.*

*Click **OK** or press **Return/Enter** to exit a dialog box and accept the new settings.*

*Click **Cancel** to exit a dialog box with no modifications taking effect.*

*Check **Preview** to preview new settings in your illustration right away.*

A **dialog box** in the Mac OS

Using the palettes

There are 28 moveable palettes that are used for creating artwork, and they are all opened from the **Window** menu. To save screen space, the palettes are joined into these default **groups**: Appearance/Navigator/Info; Color/Attributes; Document Info; Flattening Preview; Transparency/Stroke/Gradient; Styles/Swatches/Brushes/Symbols; Magic Wand; Layers/Actions/Links; Transform/Align/Pathfinder; SVG Interactivity/Variables; Character/Paragraph; MM Design; Tab Ruler; and Tools (toolbox). The palette name you choose from the Window menu will appear in front in its group when the group opens.

You can compose your own groups or separate a palette from its group. To **separate** a palette, drag its tab (palette name) away from the group **1**–**2**. To **add** a palette to any group, drag the tab over the group.

➤ When you compose a palette group, start with one of the resizable palette windows.

To **dock** (hook up) one palette to the bottom of another palette or palette group, drag the tab to the bottom of the other palette, and release the mouse when the thick black line appears **3**. To un-dock, drag a palette tab away from the dock group.

To **display** an open palette at the front of its group, click its tab. Palettes with an up/down arrow on the tab (such as the Color palette) have more than one **panel**. Click this arrow or the tab name to cycle through the palette configurations: tab only, two option panels, or one option panel. Another way to display a full palette is to choose Show Options from the palette menu. To shrink a palette group to just the tabs in the Mac OS, click the palette zoom box in the upper right corner; in Windows, click the minimize/maximize box. Click the same box again to restore the palette's previous size.

➤ Press Tab to **hide/show all** currently open palettes, including the Toolbox. Press Shift-Tab to hide/show all open palettes except the Toolbox.

Palettes that are open when you quit/exit Illustrator will reappear in the same location when the application is relaunched.

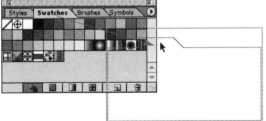

1 To *separate* a palette from its group, drag the tab (palette name) away from the group.

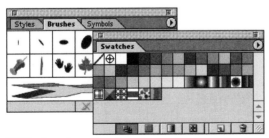

2 The Swatches palette is on its own.

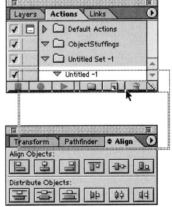

3 To *dock* palettes together, drag the tab name of one palette to the bottom of another palette, and release the mouse when the thick black line appears.

Using the Palettes

The color controls

The current fill and stroke colors display in color squares on the Toolbox **1** and on the Color palette **2**. The **Color** palette displays the color model and breakdown of the fill or stroke in the currently selected object or objects, and it's used to choose Web-safe colors or process colors and to adjust global process or spot color tints.

The **Stroke** palette displays the weight and style of the stroke in the currently selected object or objects, and is also used to change those attributes. If no object is selected, then changes made on the Color or Stroke palette will apply to subsequently drawn objects.

Whichever box (Fill or Stroke) is currently active (is on top on the Color palette or the Toolbox) will be affected by changes on the Color palette.

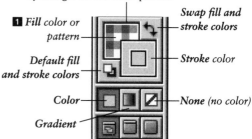

1 *Fill color or pattern*

Default fill and stroke colors

Color

Gradient

Swap fill and stroke colors

Stroke color

None (no color)

Color palette

The Color palette is used for mixing, choosing, and switching between fill and stroke colors. Choose a color model for the palette from the palette menu. Quick-select a color, black, white, or None from the bar at the bottom of the palette.

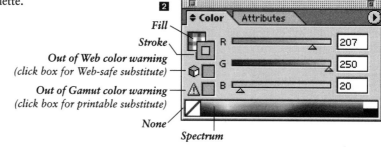

2

Fill

Stroke

Out of Web color warning (click box for Web-safe substitute)

Out of Gamut color warning (click box for printable substitute)

None

Spectrum

Stroke palette

The Stroke palette is used for editing the stroke weight and style on the currently selected object, and for creating dashed lines.

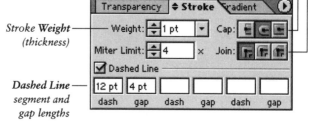

Join (bends) styles

Cap (ends) styles

Stroke Weight (thickness)

Dashed Line segment and gap lengths

Swatches palette

The Swatches palette is used for storing and choosing default and user-defined colors. If you click a swatch, it becomes the current fill or stroke color, depending on whether the fill or stroke box is currently active on the Toolbox or the Color palette.

Drag from the Fill or Stroke color box on the Toolbox or the Color palette to the Swatches palette to save that color as a swatch in the current file. Merge swatches and perform other tasks via the palette menu.

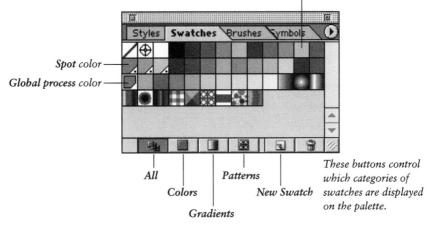

Non-global process color

Spot color

Global process color

All

Colors

Patterns

Gradients

New Swatch

These buttons control which categories of swatches are displayed on the palette.

Gradient palette

The Gradient palette is used to create a new gradient or edit an existing gradient. Move a color by dragging its square; or click a square and use the Color palette to choose a different color; or click below the Gradient slider to add a new color; or move a midpoint diamond to adjust how adjacent colors are distributed.

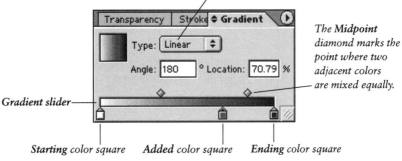

The gradient Type: Linear or Radial

The Midpoint diamond marks the point where two adjacent colors are mixed equally.

Gradient slider

Starting color square

Added color square

Ending color square

Character palette

The Character palette is used to apply type attributes: font, size, leading, kerning, tracking, vertical scale, horizontal scale, and baseline shift, as well as various foreign language options. To apply an attribute to currently highlighted text, choose a value from the pop-up menu; or click the up or down arrow; or enter a value in the field and press Return/Enter.

10.0! Character and Paragraph palettes

The Character, MM Design, Paragraph, and Tab Ruler palettes are opened from the Window > **Type** submenu. Or use one of these shortcuts:

Character palette Cmd-T/Ctrl-T
Paragraph palette Cmd-M/Ctrl-M
Tab Ruler palette Cmd-Shift-T/Ctrl-Shift-T

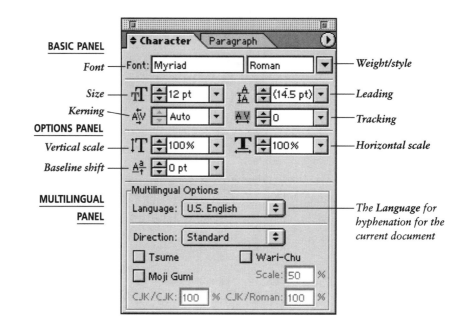

BASIC PANEL
Font
Size
Kerning
OPTIONS PANEL
Vertical scale
Baseline shift
MULTILINGUAL PANEL

Weight/style
Leading
Tracking
Horizontal scale
The *Language* for hyphenation for the current document

Multiple Masters Design palette

The Multiple Masters Design palette is used to edit the Weight and Width of multiple master fonts. Each edited multiple master font is called an instance. Instances are saved in the document in which they're created.

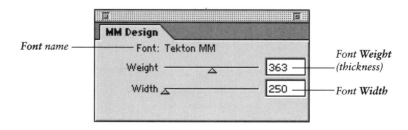

Font name
Font Weight (thickness)
Font Width

Paragraph palette

The Paragraph palette is used to apply specifications that affect entire paragraphs, including horizontal alignment, indentation, space before paragraph, word spacing, letter spacing, hyphenation, and hanging punctuation.

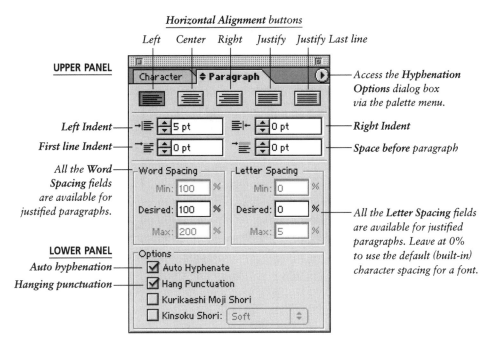

Horizontal Alignment buttons

Left   Center   Right   Justify   Justify Last line

UPPER PANEL

*Access the **Hyphenation Options** dialog box via the palette menu.*

Left Indent — *Right Indent*

First line Indent — *Space before paragraph*

*All the **Word Spacing** fields are available for justified paragraphs.*

*All the **Letter Spacing** fields are available for justified paragraphs. Leave at 0% to use the default (built-in) character spacing for a font.*

LOWER PANEL

Auto hyphenation

Hanging punctuation

Tab Ruler palette

The Tab Ruler palette is used to insert, move, or change the alignment for custom tab markers, which are used to align columns of text.

*The **Snap** function makes a tab marker snap to the nearest ruler tick mark as you insert or drag it. Ruler increments display in the currently chosen ruler units (Document Setup or Preferences).*

Left-, Center-, Right-, and Decimal-Justified buttons

*The **Alignment** box aligns the Tab Ruler with the left edge of the currently selected text.*

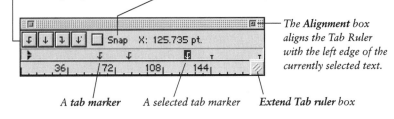

*A **tab marker***   *A selected tab marker*   ***Extend Tab ruler** box*

Paragraph Palette; Tab Ruler Palette

Layers palette

The Layers palette is used to add or delete layers or sublayers in a document. The palette is also used to select; restack; hide/show; lock/unlock; change the view for; create a clipping set for; target; or dim (for tracing) a layer, sublayer, group, or individual object. When your illustration is finished, it can be flattened into one layer or the objects can be released to separate layers for export to an animation program.

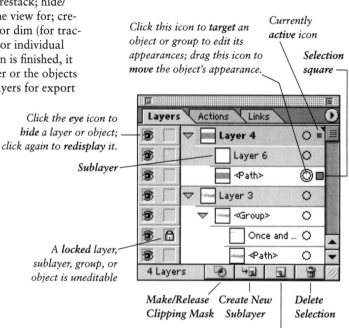

*Click this icon to **target an** object or group to edit its appearances; drag this icon to **move the object's appearance.***

Currently active icon

Selection square

*Click the **eye** icon to hide a layer or object; click again to **redisplay** it.*

Sublayer

*A **locked** layer, sublayer, group, or object is uneditable*

Make/Release Clipping Mask   *Create New Sublayer*   *Delete Selection*

Create New Layer

Info palette

If no object is selected in the current document, the Info palette shows the horizontal and vertical location of the pointer in the illustration window. If an object is selected, the palette displays the location of the object on the page and the object's width and height. If a type tool and type object are selected, the palette displays type specifications. The Info palette automatically opens when the Measure tool is used, and displays the distance and angle calculated by that tool.

Horizontal (X) and Vertical (Y) location of the currently selected object

*Object **Width** (W) and **Height** (H)*

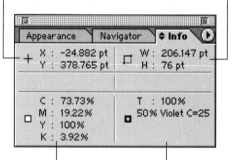

Fill info (color breakdown, or pattern or gradient name)

Stroke info (color breakdown, or pattern or gradient name)

Align palette

The Align palette is used to align or distribute two or more objects along their centers or along their top, left, or bottom edges, or to equalize (distribute) the space between three or more objects.

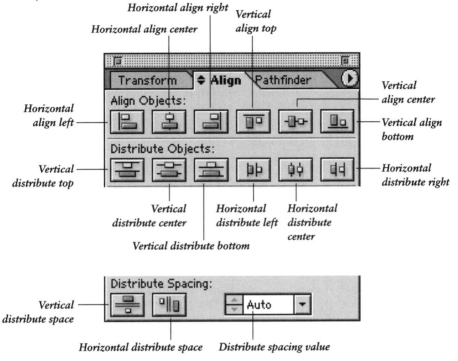

Horizontal align right
Horizontal align center
Vertical align top
Vertical align center
Horizontal align left
Vertical align bottom
Vertical distribute top
Horizontal distribute right
Vertical distribute center
Horizontal distribute left
Horizontal distribute center
Vertical distribute bottom

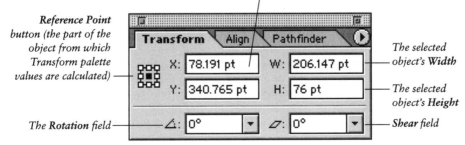

Vertical distribute space
Horizontal distribute space *Distribute spacing value*

Transform palette

The Transform palette displays location, width, and height information for a selected object. The palette is also used to move, scale, rotate, or shear a selected object or objects.

The x and y axes location of the currently selected object. Change the values to move the object.

Reference Point button (the part of the object from which Transform palette values are calculated)

The selected object's Width

The selected object's Height

The Rotation field

Shear field

Actions palette

The Actions palette is an automation tool. You record a series of commands or steps as you create or edit an illustration, and then replay those commands on any object or file. The Actions palette can also be used to create and access shortcuts.

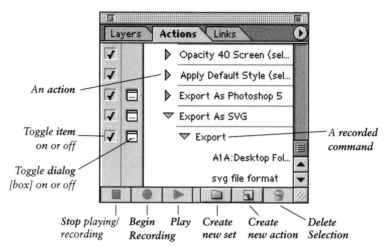

An action

Toggle item on or off

Toggle dialog [box] on or off

A recorded command

Stop playing/ recording   *Begin Recording*   *Play*   *Create new set*   *Create new action*   *Delete Selection*

Navigator palette

The Navigator palette is used for moving an illustration in its window and for changing the magnification of an illustration.

*Drag the **view box** to **move** the illustration in the document window or **click** the illustration **thumbnail** to display that area of the illustration.*

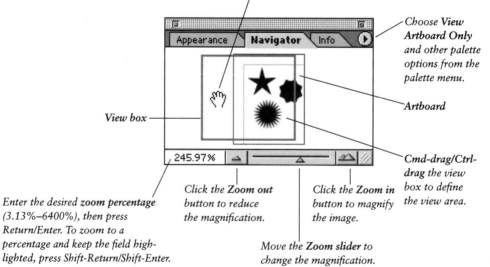

*Choose **View Artboard Only** and other palette options from the palette menu.*

Artboard

View box

Cmd-drag/Ctrl-drag the view box to define the view area.

*Enter the desired **zoom percentage** (3.13%–6400%), then press Return/Enter. To zoom to a percentage and keep the field high-lighted, press Shift-Return/Shift-Enter.*

*Click the **Zoom out** button to reduce the magnification.*

*Click the **Zoom in** button to magnify the image.*

*Move the **Zoom slider** to change the magnification.*

Links palette

A linked image is an image from another application that is placed into an Illustrator file without being embedded into the file. The Links palette lets you keep track of and update linked images, modify a linked image in its original application, and convert a linked image to an embedded image.

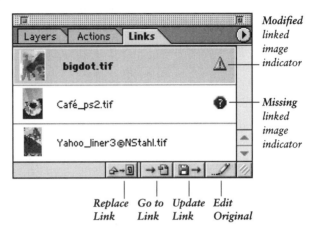

Modified linked image indicator

Missing linked image indicator

Replace Link *Go to Link* *Update Link* *Edit Original*

Pathfinder palette 10.0!

The shape mode buttons on the top row of the Pathfinder palette create new, editable, flexible compound shapes from selected objects. The Expand button converts a compound shape into either a path or a compound path, depending on how the objects originally overlapped. The pathfinder buttons on the bottom row of the Pathfinder palette create flattened, cut-up shapes from selected objects.

Expand compound shape

Exclude overlapping shape areas

Intersect shape areas

Add to shape area

Subtract from shape area

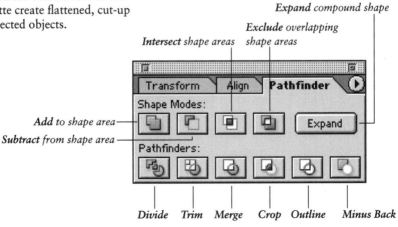

Divide *Trim* *Merge* *Crop* *Outline* *Minus Back*

Links Palette; Pathfinder Palette

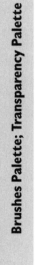

Brushes palette

The four varieties of brushes on the Brushes palette—calligraphic, scatter, art, and pattern—are used to apply brush strokes to paths. There are two basic ways to apply brush strokes. You can either choose the Paintbrush tool and a brush and then draw a shape or you can apply a brush stroke to an existing path that was drawn using any tool. The brushes that are currently on the Brushes palette save with the document. To personalize your brush strokes, you can create your own brushes.

To change the contour of a brush stroke, you can use any tool or command that you'd normally use to reshape a path (e.g., Erase, Reshape, Pencil, Smooth, Add-anchor-point, Convert-anchor-point). If you modify a brush that was applied to any existing paths in a document, you'll be given the option via an alert dialog box to update those paths with the revised brush.

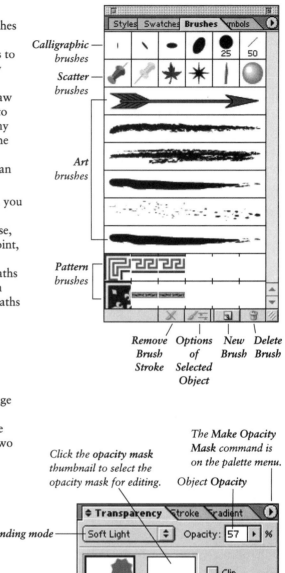

Calligraphic brushes

Scatter brushes

Art brushes

Pattern brushes

Remove Brush Stroke *Options of Selected Object* *New Brush* *Delete Brush*

Transparency palette

The Transparency palette is used to change the blending mode or opacity of a layer, group, or individual object. It can also be used to generate an opacity mask from two selected objects.

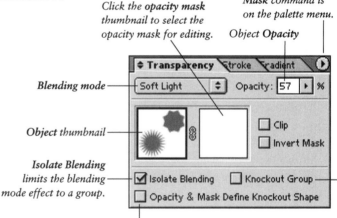

Click the opacity mask thumbnail to select the opacity mask for editing.

The Make Opacity Mask command is on the palette menu.

Object Opacity

Blending mode

Object thumbnail

Isolate Blending limits the blending mode effect to a group.

This option allows nested objects in a knockout group to show through transparent areas of an opacity mask.

Knockout Group prevents objects in a group from showing through each other.

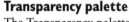

Styles palette

In Illustrator, styles are sets of attributes that are used to quickly change an object's appearance. Among the multiple attributes that a style can contain are multiple solid color or pattern fills and strokes, transparency and overprint settings, blending modes, brush strokes, and effects. Using styles standardizes object styling and also makes object styling faster.

Style thumbnail and names   *New Style*   *Delete Style*

Break Link to Style

Appearance palette

The Appearance palette lists in minute detail the individual attributes that are applied to the currently targeted layer(s), group(s), or object(s). It's used for editing, adding, or removing those attributes and for editing the attributes of a style in conjunction with the Styles palette. The palette is also used to apply multiple fills and/or strokes to a layer, group, or object, and to quickly access the palettes and dialog boxes that were used to apply those attributes.

New Art Has Basic Appearance   *Reduce to Basic Appearance*   *Delete selected item*

Clear Appearance   *Duplicate selected item*

Styles Palette; Appearance Palette

SVG Interactivity palette

The SVG Interactivity palette is used to attach interactivity to an Illustrator object for viewing in a Web browser. First you choose from a list of common JavaScript events on the Event pop-up menu. Then you add or enter a JavaScript command that will act on the object when that event occurs in the browser.

Attributes palette

The Attributes palette is used to specify overprint options for an object, show or hide an object's center point, reverse the fill of an object in a compound path, or change an object's fill rule. You can choose a shape for the image map area from the Image Map menu. In the URL field, you can enter a Web address for an object to designate it as a hot point on an image map. Click Browser to launch an installed Web browser.

Document Info palette

Like the Info palette, the Document Info palette isn't interactive. It's used solely for reading information about the current Document, or individual Objects, Styles, Brushes, etc.

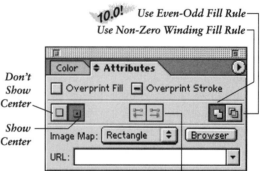

The Reverse Path Direction Off and Reverse Path Direction On buttons switch a shape's fill between color and transparency in a compound path.

Magic Wand palette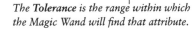

The Magic Wand tool is used to select objects of the same or similar fill color, stroke color, stroke weight, opacity, or blending mode to that of the currently selected object. Parameters are chosen for the tool using the Magic Wand palette. The Tolerance is the range within which the tool will select a particular attribute. For example, if you check Opacity and choose a Tolerance of 50% for that attribute, the tool will find and select all objects whose stroke color is similar to or matches that of the object you click on, within a range of 50%.

Symbols palette

Any Illustrator object can be stored on the Symbols palette for potential reuse in any document. To place one symbol onto the artboard, all you have to do is drag it out of the Symbols palette. A placed symbol is called an instance. The Symbol Sprayer tool is used to place multiple instances of a symbol in a document. Multiple instances form what is called a symbol set. Using symbols lets you create complex art quickly and easily.

Using any of the other symbolism tools (Symbol Shifter, Scruncher, Sizer, Spinner, Stainer, Screener, or Styler), you can change the closeness (density), position, stacking order, size, rotation, transparency, color tint, or style of multiple symbol instances in a symbol set, while still maintaining the link to the original symbol. If you edit the original symbol, any instances of that symbol in the document will update automatically.

Notes: For a very brief synopsis of what the **Variables** palette does, see page 508. For more information about this advanced feature, refer to the Illustrator documentation or *Real World Adobe Illustrator 10* by Deke McClelland (Peachpit Press).

The **Flattening Preview** palette is an optional plug-in. To install it, drag it from the Adobe Illustrator 10 > Utilities > Flattening Preview folder into the Adobe Illustrator 10 > Plug-ins folder. Read about this palette in the Adobe Illustrator 10 *Flattening Guide,* which is included with Illustrator 10.

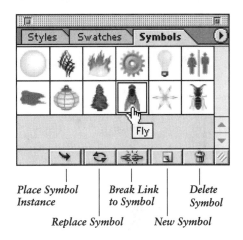

*The **Tolerance** is the range within which the Magic Wand will find that attribute.*

Place Symbol Instance

Break Link to Symbol

Delete Symbol

Replace Symbol

New Symbol

Magic Wand Palette; Symbols Palette

Mini-Glossary (A quick introduction to some of the terms that you will encounter as you proceed through this book.)

Objects

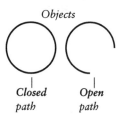

Closed path   *Open path*

Direction line

Anchor point   *Curve segment*

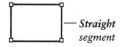

Straight segment

Selected object

Selected anchor point

Object undergoing a scale transformation

Path (Or "object") Any individual shape that is created in Illustrator. A path can be open (a line) or closed (no endpoints). Paths are composed of smooth and/or corner anchor points. Smooth anchor points have direction lines. Anchor points and segments can be modified to reshape any path.

Anchor point A corner point or smooth point that joins two segments of a path.

Curve segment The segment between two smooth points or between a corner point and a smooth point.

Straight segment The segment between two corner points.

Direction lines The pair of antennae that stick out from every smooth point. To reshape a curved segment, rotate, lengthen, or shorten a direction line.

Select Highlight an object in the document window for editing. Only selected objects can be modified. When a whole object is selected, its anchor points are solid (not hollow). The Selection tool is used to select whole objects or groups; the Group-selection tool is used to select nested groups; and the Direct-selection tool is used to select parts of objects.

Layer A stack of objects that is in front of or behind other objects. An illustration can contain multiple top-level layers and numerous sublayers. The actual objects that make up an illustration (paths, type, mesh objects, etc.) are nested within top-level layers or sublayers.

Group Two or more objects that are united via the Group command so they can be moved or modified in unison.

Transform To rotate, scale, reflect, or shear an object or create a blend between two objects.

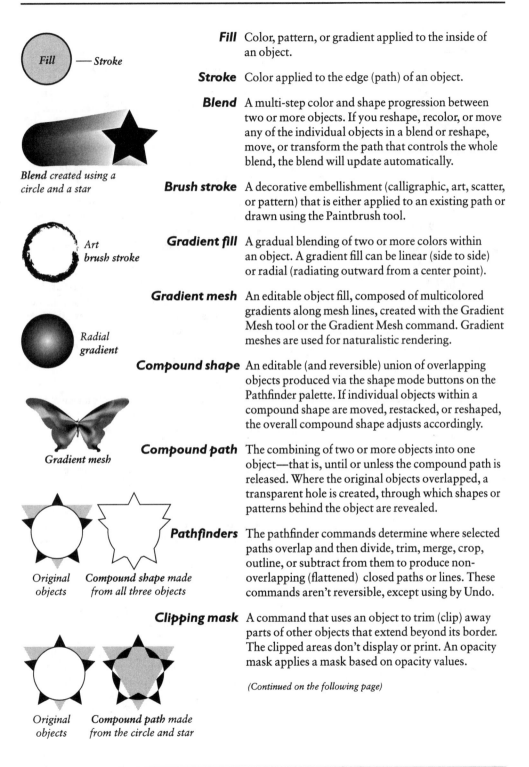

Fill   Color, pattern, or gradient applied to the inside of an object.

Stroke   Color applied to the edge (path) of an object.

Blend   A multi-step color and shape progression between two or more objects. If you reshape, recolor, or move any of the individual objects in a blend or reshape, move, or transform the path that controls the whole blend, the blend will update automatically.

Brush stroke   A decorative embellishment (calligraphic, art, scatter, or pattern) that is either applied to an existing path or drawn using the Paintbrush tool.

Gradient fill   A gradual blending of two or more colors within an object. A gradient fill can be linear (side to side) or radial (radiating outward from a center point).

Gradient mesh   An editable object fill, composed of multicolored gradients along mesh lines, created with the Gradient Mesh tool or the Gradient Mesh command. Gradient meshes are used for naturalistic rendering.

Compound shape   An editable (and reversible) union of overlapping objects produced via the shape mode buttons on the Pathfinder palette. If individual objects within a compound shape are moved, restacked, or reshaped, the overall compound shape adjusts accordingly.

Compound path   The combining of two or more objects into one object—that is, until or unless the compound path is released. Where the original objects overlapped, a transparent hole is created, through which shapes or patterns behind the object are revealed.

Pathfinders   The pathfinder commands determine where selected paths overlap and then divide, trim, merge, crop, outline, or subtract from them to produce non-overlapping (flattened) closed paths or lines. These commands aren't reversible, except using by Undo.

Clipping mask   A command that uses an object to trim (clip) away parts of other objects that extend beyond its border. The clipped areas don't display or print. An opacity mask applies a mask based on opacity values.

(Continued on the following page)

Blend created using a circle and a star

Art brush stroke

Radial gradient

Gradient mesh

Original objects

Compound shape made from all three objects

Original objects

Compound path made from the circle and star

Mini-Glossary

Drop shadow effect

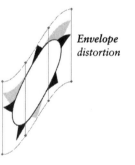

Symbol

Symbol set

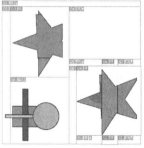

Illustration divided into slices

Appearances Editable and removable attributes, such as multiple fills, strokes, effects, blending modes, transparency values, patterns, and brush strokes.

Style A set of appearance attributes that is saved to, and can be retrieved from, the Styles palette.

Effects Commands on the Effect menu that modify the appearance of an object without actually changing its path. Effects can be edited or removed at any time.

Symbol An object that is stored on the Symbols palette. A placed symbol is called an instance. Multiple instances form what is called a symbol set. Symbolism tools are used to modify instances.

Liquify Seven tools—Warp, Twirl, Pucker, Bloat, Scallop, Crystallize, and Wrinkle—that are used to reshape an object or objects. By pushing and pulling on an object's edges with one of these tools, you can reshape the object like you might sculpt a piece of clay. Many of the Illustrator effects also produce distortion.

Envelope A special kind of container that is used to produce distortion. When you distort an envelope, the object(s) within the envelope conforms to the distortion. Both an envelope and the object(s) it contains are fully editable.

Action A recorded sequence of editing events that can be replayed on any document or object.

Optimization The process in which file format, storage size, and color parameters are chosen for an image in order to maximize its quality, yet still enable it to download and display quickly on the Web.

Slicing The division of areas in an illustration. When exporting an illustration using Illustrator's Save for Web dialog box, you can choose different optimization formats and settings for each slice in order to achieve faster download speeds. A separate export file is generated for each slice, containing the object or objects within it. Three types of slices can be created in Illustrator: object slices, text slices, and user slices.

Envelope distortion

Mini-Glossary

Division the easy way

Let's say you want to reduce an object's width by 25%. Select the object, highlight the **entire** W field on the Transform palette, type "75%", then press Return/Enter. The width will be reduced to three-quarters of its current value (e.g., 4p becomes 3p). You could also click to the right of the current entry, type an asterisk (*), type a percentage value, and press Return/Enter.

Symbols you can use

Unit	Symbol
Picas	**p**
Points	**pt**
Inches	**" or in**
Millimeters	**mm**
Centimeters	**cm**
Q (a type unit)	**q**
Pixels	**px**

Points 'n' picas

12 pts = 1 pica

6 picas = 1 inch

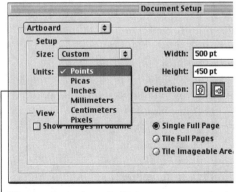

1 *Choose Units via a context menu...*

2 *...or choose from the Units pop-up menu in the Document Setup dialog box.*

Measuring up

The current ruler units are used in most palettes and dialog box entry fields, and of course on the rulers. You can choose a unit of measure for an individual document (instructions below) that differs from the default unit of measure that is currently chosen for the application in Edit > Preferences > Units & Undo.

You can enter numbers in dialog boxes or on palettes in any of the units of measure used in Illustrator, regardless of the default general units. If you enter a number in a unit of measure other than the default units, the number will be translated into the default units when you press Tab or Return/Enter. If you enter the symbol for subtraction (-), addition (+), multiplication (*), division (/), or percent (%) after the current value in any field, Illustrator will do the math for you.

➤ To enter a combination of picas and points, separate the two numbers by a "p". For example, 4p2 equals four picas plus 2 points, or 50 pt. Be sure to highlight the entire entry field first.

Follow the instructions below to change the ruler units just for the current document. Choose a unit of measure for the **current** and **future** documents in Edit > Preferences > Units & Undo.

To change the units for the current document:

Control-click/Right-click on either ruler in the illustration window and choose a unit from the context menu **1**.

or

Choose File > Document Setup (Cmd-Option-P/Ctrl-Alt-P); choose Artboard from the pop-up menu; choose Units: **Points, Picas, Inches, Millimeters, Centimeters,** or **Pixels 2**; then click OK.

➤ The current location of the pointer is indicated by a dotted line on both rulers. The higher the zoom level, the finer the ruler increments.

Units of Measure

Multiple undos

To undo an operation, choose Edit > Undo (Cmd-Z/Ctrl-Z). To undo the second-to-last operation, choose Edit > Undo again, and so on. To reverse an undo, choose Edit > Redo (Cmd-Shift-Z/Ctrl-Shift-Z). Or Control-click/Right-click on the artboard and choose either command from the context menu. You can undo or redo after saving your document, but not after you close and reopen it.

You can undo up to 200 operations, depending on currently available memory. If Illustrator requires additional RAM to perform illustration edits, the number of available undos will be reduced to the value entered in the Minimum Undo Levels field in Edit > Preferences > Units & Undo.

Context-sensitive menus

Context-sensitive menus allow you to choose a command from an on-screen menu without having to mouse to the menu bar or even to a palette. To open a context menu, Control-click (Mac OS) or Right-click (Windows) on the artboard.

Context menu offerings change depending on which tool is selected and whether any objects are selected in your illustration **1**–**3**. Not all of the commands that appear on a context menu may be applicable to, or available for, the currently selected objects.

And don't forget

Use **tool tips** to help you identify palette buttons, swatch names, tool names and shortcuts, and other application features. Just rest the pointer without clicking on a button, swatch, or icon and a tip will pop up **4**.

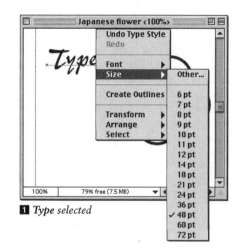

1 *Type selected*

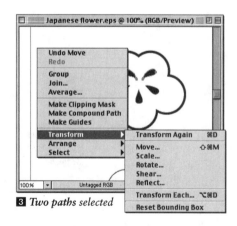

2 *Nothing selected*

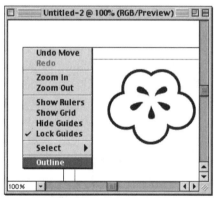

4 *A tool tip*

3 *Two paths selected*

Chapter 1: Illustrator Interface ◆ Study Guide

Learning Objectives

- Locate and identify all tools on the toolbox—including tools on the pop-out menus.

- Identify, operate, and customize the Illustrator workspace.

- Recognize which controls, menu, buttons, and options (lists, buttons, palette menu, thumbnail size...) are common to most palettes.

- Be familiar with the basic purpose of each palette (Layers, Pathfinder...).

- Use context menus.

Get Up and Running Exercises

- Given all the different ways you can arrange the workspace, what's one way you would maximize your work area? How might you adjust your workspace for a small screen, such as a laptop?
- How might you arrange the palettes for the following tasks?
  - ▲ Freeform illustration
  - ▲ Technical illustration
  - ▲ Web design
  - ▲ Layout production

Class Discussion Questions

- What is Illustrator for? Who uses Illustrator?
- Why are some commands duplicated in palettes? (For example, Layer > New Layer has the same function as the Create New Layer button on the Layers palette.)
- What is each palette for?
- Why are there so many keyboard equivalents for tools and controls? How can typing on a keyboard be helpful for a visual activity like drawing or layout?

Review Questions

Multiple choice

1. Which palette lets you rotate an object using a specific side or corner as a reference point?

   A. Info palette

   B. Transform palette

   C. Align palette

   D. Pathfinder palette

2. Which menu can you use to show or hide palettes?

   A. File menu

   B. Effect menu

   C. View menu

   D. Window menu

3. How do you set the default unit of measure for future documents?

   A. Choose Artboard in the Document Setup dialog box and change the Units value.

   B. Choose Edit > Preferences > Units & Undo, then change the General Units value.

   C. Right-click (Windows)/Ctrl-click (Mac OS) the ruler and choose a unit of measure from the context menu.

   D. Type a different unit's suffix (e.g., "in" or "mm") after a value on the Transform palette.

4. Where can you store specific colors for a document?

   A. Color palette

   B. Color picker

   C. Appearance palette

   D. Swatches palette

5. Where can you view the name of the color profile assigned to the current document?

   A. Color Settings dialog box

   B. Color palette

   C. Status bar (pop-up menu)

   D. Info palette

Fill-in-the-blank

1. To interrupt an operation in progress, press the _____ key.

2. If an object at the edge of the artwork doesn't print or is cut off, it might not be completely positioned inside the _____.

3. To automate repetitive tasks, use the _____ palette.

4. To hide all palettes instantly, including the Toolbox, press the _____ key.

5. Choose options related to a palette from a palette's _____.

6. To see the effect of dialog box settings without applying them, check the _____ option in the dialog box.

7. You can find hidden tools on the _____ .

8. Some of the commands relevant to the selected object are available on _____ menus so you don't have to find them on the menu bar.

Definitions

1. What's a path?

2. What's an anchor point?

3. What's a layer?

4. What's a fill?

5. What's a stroke?

6. What's an appearance?

7. What's a Pathfinder?

HOW ILLUSTRATOR WORKS 2

In this chapter you will learn the basic differences between object-oriented and bitmap applications and you'll get a broad overview of how objects are created and modified in Illustrator.

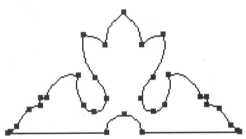

1 *Object-oriented graphics are sharp and crisp.*

2 *Objects in an object-oriented program are mathematically defined paths (this object is selected).*

Vectors and rasters

There are two main types of picture-making applications: bitmap (or "raster") and object-oriented (or "vector"), and it's important to know their strengths and weaknesses. Bitmap programs are ideal for creating soft, painterly effects, whereas object-oriented programs are ideal for creating sharp, smooth shapes and typographic designs (logos and the like).

Drawings created in an **object-oriented** program like Adobe Illustrator or Macromedia FreeHand are composed of separate, distinct objects or groups of objects that are positioned on one or more **layers**. Objects are drawn using drawing tools, and are mathematically defined. An object drawn in Illustrator can be recolored, resized, and reshaped without diminishing its sharpness or smoothness, and it can be moved easily without disturbing any other objects. An object in an object-oriented drawing will look smooth and sharp regardless of the size at which it is displayed or printed **1**–**2**.

Object-oriented files are usually relatively small in storage size, so you can save multiple versions of these files without filling up valuable hard drive space. And object-oriented drawings are resolution independent, which means the higher the resolution of the printer, the sharper and finer the printed image.

An image created in a **bitmap** program, such as Photoshop, on the other hand, is composed of one or more layers of tiny squares on a grid, called pixels. One pixel layer can be stacked above or below another pixel layer. If you paint on a bitmap image, you'll recolor just that area of pixels, not an entire, independent object. If you zoom way in on a bitmap image, you'll see a checkerboard of tiny squares **1**–**2**. Bitmap files tend to be quite large, and the printout quality of a bitmap image is dependent on the resolution of the image. Bitmap programs, however, are ideal for creating subtle color gradations, digital paintings, montages, or photorealistic images, and for editing photographs.

Though your Illustrator images will mostly consist of vector shapes, you can place or open a raster image in Illustrator and perform some operations on it. And you can **rasterize** a vector object, which means convert it into a bitmap image, and then apply filters or effects to it.

How objects are made

In Illustrator, the key building blocks that you will be using to compose an illustration are Bézier objects, type, and placed bitmap images. Bézier objects are composed of **anchor points** connected by **curved** or **straight** segments. The edge of an object is called its **path**. A path can be open (with two endpoints) or closed and continuous. You can close an open path by joining its endpoints or open a closed path using the **Scissors** tool. You can draw shapes "from scratch" or you can create a simple geometric object, such as a triangle or circle, and then reshape it.

Some Illustrator tools—such as the **Rectangle, Ellipse, Polygon, Star, Rectangular Grid, Polar Grid,** and **Flare**—produce complete, closed paths simply by clicking on the artboard. The number and position of anchor points on these paths is determined automatically.

Other tools—like the **Pencil** and **Pen**—produce open or closed paths by clicking or dragging with the mouse. The **Pencil** tool creates open freeform lines. The **Paintbrush** tool **3** can be used with its four categories of brushes to create **calligraphic, scatter, art,** or **pattern** brush strokes. You can use

1 *A **bitmap** image*

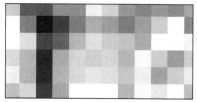

2 *Extreme closeup of a **bitmap**, showing the individual **pixels** that make up the image*

3 *Strokes drawn using the **Paintbrush** tool, using various **brushes***

10.0!

How Illustrator Works

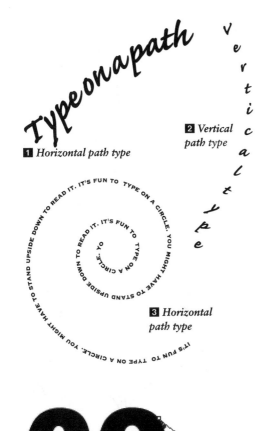

1 *Horizontal path type*

2 *Vertical path type*

3 *Horizontal path type*

4 *After type characters are converted to **outlines**, they can be reshaped like any other Illustrator objects.*

Illustrator's brushes or create your own. To draw straight lines quickly, you can draw with the **Line Segment** tool, or to draw partial curves, use the **Arc Segment** tool. *10.0!*

And last but not least, using Illustrator's most versatile tool of all—the **Pen**—you can create as many corner or curve anchor points as you need to form an object of any shape. If you want to use a scanned image as a starting point, you can place it onto a standard layer or a template layer in an Illustrator file, and then trace it manually with the Pen tool or trace it automatically using the Auto Trace tool.

The written word

Illustrator has six tools for creating **type**, a smorgasbord of features with which type can be styled and formatted, and many word processing features. Type can be free-standing, it can flow along the edge of an object (path type) **1**–**3**, or it can fill the inside of an object of any shape (area type). Depending on which tool is used to create it, type can flow and read vertically or horizontally. It can be repositioned, edited, restyled, recolored, or transformed.

If you want to personalize your type characters, you can convert them into paths, called **outlines**, and then reshape or modify them as you would any standard Illustrator path **4**.

Editing tools

An object must be **selected** before it can be modified, and there are six tools that do the job (**Selection, Direct-selection, Group-selection, Lasso, Direct-select Lasso,** and **Magic Wand**) as well as a host of useful Select menu commands. *10.0!*

Obects are modified using menu commands, filters, dialog boxes, palettes, and tools. There are 76 tools to choose from and 28 movable palettes! The palette groups include Appearance/Navigator/Info; Color/Attributes; Document Info; Flattening Preview; Transparency/Stroke/Gradient; Styles/Swatches/Brushes/Symbols; Magic Wand; Layers/Actions/Links; Transform/Align/Pathfinder; SVG Interactivity/Variables;

How Illustrator Works

How Illustrator Works

Character/Paragraph; MM Design; Tab Ruler; and Tools. For fast access, leave most of the palettes open while you work. To save screen space, dock them together in groups and shrink down the ones you use infrequently.

How it all shapes up

An object's contour can be reshaped by moving its anchor points or segments or by converting its curve **anchor points** 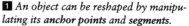 into corner anchor points (or vice versa). A curve segment can be reshaped by rotating, lengthening, or shortening its **direction lines**. Since it's so easy to reshape a path, you can draw a simple shape first and then develop it into a more complicated form later on.

Some tools are specifically designed for modifying paths, such as the **Add-anchor-point** tool, which adds points to a path; the **Delete-anchor-point** tool, which deletes points from a path; the **Scissors** tool, which splits a path; and the **Convert-anchor-point** tool, which converts corner points into curve points, and vice versa.

Some tools are used like sculptors' utensils to change the contour of an object. The **Knife** tool carves out sections of an object. The **Smooth** tool removes points to create smoother curves. The **Erase** tool removes whole chunks of a path. And the **Pencil** and **Reshape** tools reshape an object by pushing or pulling on its contour.

The **shape modes** buttons on the Pathfinder palette produce an editable compound shape from selected, overlapping objects. The **pathfinders** buttons on the same palette divide areas where objects overlap into separate objects 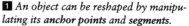.

And there are other Illustrator commands that combine objects. The **Compound Path** command, for example, cuts a hole through an object to reveal underlying shapes. Or an object can also be used as a **clipping mask** to hide parts of other objects that extend beyond its edges.

Other modifications can be made using the **transformation** tools. The **Scale** tool enlarges

10.0!

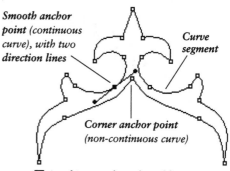

Smooth anchor point (continuous curve), with two direction lines

Curve segment

Corner anchor point (non-continuous curve)

1 *An object can be reshaped by manipulating its anchor points and segments.*

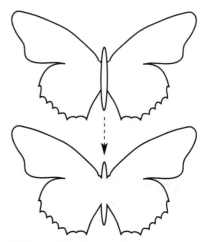

2 *The Add to shape area shape mode command combines multiple shapes into a compound shape.*

1 *Illustrator objects are very elastic: They can be rotated, reflected, sheared, or, as in this case, scaled.*

The original formation

2 *And after applying the Transform Each command*

3 *The airplane distorted using the Scallop tool*

or shrinks an object **1**; the **Rotate** tool rotates an object; the **Reflect** tool creates a mirror image of an object; the **Shear** tool slants an object; and the **Blend** tool or command transforms one object into another by creating a series of transitional shapes. Multiple transformations can be performed at once using the **Free Transform** tool, the **Transform Each** command **2**, or the **Transform** palette.

If you like more extreme distortions, you'll enjoy using the **Warp, Twirl, Pucker, Bloat, Scallop 3, Crystallize,** or **Wrinkle** tool to mold or twist existing objects. Or put an object or objects into an **envelope** and then manipulate points in the envelope mesh to reshape the object(s) inside it.

And don't fret about making a mistake: Illustrator has a **multiple-undo** capability. If you want to repeat a series of operations, on the other hand, you can save them as an **action** and then replay the action on any object or file.

Coloring

You can **fill** the inside of an open or closed object with a **solid** color, a **gradient** (a smooth gradation of two or more colors), or a **pattern** of repeating tiles. Patterns and gradients can be produced right in Illustrator. If you have a painter's touch, you'll enjoy using Illustrator's **gradient mesh** features, which create multicolored, editable gradient mesh objects. As for an object's contour, you can apply a solid color **stroke** to the edge of any object in a plain or dashed style.

A stroke or fill color can be from a matching system, like PANTONE, or it can be a CMYK, HSB, or RGB color that you mix yourself. In Illustrator, you can mix, apply, and save colors in either **RGB** or **CMYK Color** mode (not both). This means that each color will be consistent for its model—whether it's a CMYK color being color managed for color separation or a **Web-safe RGB** color chosen for display in a browser.

The **Transparency** palette lets you assign **opacity** levels to any type of object (even a

10.0!

How Illustrator Works

placed raster image or an individual type character) ; apply **blending modes** to control how objects and layers interact; or use an object as an **opacity mask** to control the transparency of other objects.

How it all stacks up

The **Layers** palette shows the complete stacking configuration of every top-level layer, sublayer, group, and object in an illustration . The palette is used to select objects; target layers, groups, or objects for appearance changes; restack objects within the same layer; move or copy objects between layers; and turn lock, display, template, and print options on and off for individual layers, sublayers, groups, and objects.

Keeping up with appearances

Attributes listed on the **Appearance** palette change an object's appearance without changing its actual underlying path 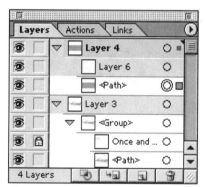. Appearance attributes that can be applied include multiple fills and strokes, transparency settings, blending modes, brush strokes, and Effect menu commands. Appearances, bless them, can be reedited, restacked, or removed at any time.

Whole sets of object attributes can be applied quickly using **styles**. Styles are stored on the Styles palette, but are edited using the Appearance palette. A style can include just about any command that you would apply to a path, such as effects, fill and stroke attributes, opacity values, blending modes, and brush strokes.

On the **Effect** menu you will find commands that change an object's appearance without changing its actual path, such as Feather, Drop Shadow, Inner Glow, and Outer Glow, as well as effect versions of most of the commands that are also on the **Filter** menu. The vector filters and effects randomly distort an object's shape or modify its color; the bitmap filters and effects add artistic, painterly touches or textures. The Filter menu commands permanently alter an object, whereas effects can be edited or removed from an object without causing the object to become

1 *Various **opacities** and **blending modes** applied to individual type characters*

2 *Layers palette*

3 *Appearance palette*

1 *Preview view*

2 *Outline view*

✓ AutoCAD Drawing (DWG)
AutoCAD Interchange File (DXF)
BMP (BMP)
Computer Graphics Metafile (CGM)
Enhanced Metafile (EMF)
JPEG (JPG)
Macintosh PICT (PCT)
Macromedia Flash (SWF)
PCX (PCX)
Photoshop (PSD)
Pixar (PXR)
Targa (TGA)
Text Format (TXT)
TIFF (TIF)
Windows Metafile (WMF)

3 *Formats available in Illustrator's* *Export dialog box*

permanently changed—only the object's appearance changes. There's even a Convert to Shape effect that allows you to change an object's contour without actually reshaping it. If you're a Web designer, you can create resizable buttons for type using this feature.

On the screen

You can draw shapes "by eye" or you can use a variety of Illustrator features to help you work with more precision, such as **Smart Guides, rulers, guides, grids,** the **Measure** tool, the **Move** dialog box, or the **Align** palette.

You can zoom in on an illustration as you work to facilitate editing and reduce eyestrain to work on a small detail or zoom out to see the overall scheme. Illustrator does everything but squint for you. If a drawing is magnified, you can move it around in the document window using the **Hand** tool or the **Navigator** palette.

An illustration can be displayed and edited in **Preview** view **1**, in which all the fill and stroke colors are displayed. Or to speed up editing and screen redraw and to make it easier to select anchor points, you can display your illustration in **Outline** view **2**, where objects are displayed as wireframe outlines. **Pixel preview** mode allows you to see how your vector objects will look when they're rasterized for the Web.

When all is said and done

There are many options for outputting your Illustrator artwork. It can be **color separated** right from Illustrator or printed on an output device, such as a laser printer or imagesetter. Or if you want to **export** your Illustrator file to a page layout application (e.g., Quark-XPress or InDesign), or to an image editing application (e.g., Photoshop), you can save it in a wide assortment of file formats, including Photoshop, EPS, TIFF, and WMF/EMF **3**.

When it comes to **Web** output, the goal is to make your page look as good as possible while minimizing its download time. For efficiency's sake, explore Illustrator's **slicing** tools. First you define slice areas in a document **1**, then you can choose different optimization (output options) for each slice.

Another way to make Web pages more efficient is by using **symbols**. Repetitive instances of an object are placed into a document via a button on the Symbols palette or using the Symbol Sprayer tool; yet on the Web page, the original object is only loaded once. The other symbolism tools (Shifter, Scruncher, Sizer, Spinner, Stainer, and Screener) are used to modify symbol instances.

Illustrator's **Save for Web** dialog box offers an impressive collection of features for optimizing graphics for the Web **2**. Here you can optimize a file, save it in an appropriate file format, such as GIF, JPEG, or PNG, and then preview it in a browser. You also have the option to assign a URL to an object to create an image map, and then export the file for use as a clickable element on a Web page.

And in addition to now standard output options mentioned above, you also can choose **SVG**, a vector file format based on XML. This format allows for interactivity and scalability; stores shapes, paths, text, and SVG filter effects; and preserves color quality, all in a small, efficient file size.

Other Web options include saving multiple layers in a document as **cascading style sheets** (CSS) to control how they're organized and displayed on the Web page. Or using the **Release to Layers** command to release groups and objects to individual layers, which can then be exported to Adobe LiveMotion or Macromedia Flash for use in Web animations.

Well, now that you have a taste of what's come, it's time to start drawing!

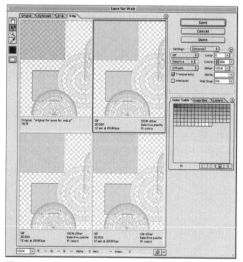

1 An illustration divided into *slices*

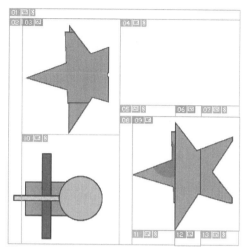

2 This is the *Save for Web* dialog box with the *4-Up* tab chosen. The original illustration is shown in the upper left corner; different optimization settings preview in the other windows.

Chapter 2: How Illustrator Works ♦ Study Guide

Learning Objectives

- Be able to describe the difference between object-oriented (vector) art and raster art.
- Understand how objects are created in Illustrator.
- Know how shapes are edited.
- Be aware of how layers can organize a document.
- Understand how to change the way an object looks.
- Know the view options available in the document window.
- Be aware of Illustrator's output options.

Get Up and Running Exercises

- Observe the difference between vector and bitmap graphics. Choose the Ellipse tool and draw an oval or circle with it. Choose the Zoom tool and zoom in to maximum magnification. Then choose Object > Rasterize, and click OK. How does the object change? You may want to examine the change more closely by choosing Edit > Undo Rasterize and Edit > Redo Rasterize.
- Try a few ways to create objects.
  - ▲ In the previous exercise, you created an object using a basic-shape tool (the Ellipse tool).
  - ▲ Try drawing a path by dragging the Pencil tool. When you release it, observe how, as with the Ellipse tool, it creates a path with points on it.
  - ▲ If you're using a pressure-sensitive stylus, choose the Paintbrush tool and drag while varying the pressure on the stylus. How is the resulting path different from the ones you drew with the other tools?
  - ▲ Create a text object. Choose the Type tool, drag a rectangle with it, and type some characters.

Class Discussion Questions

- What is the difference between object-oriented art and bitmap art?
- What are some tools for creating objects in Illustrator?
- What are the parts of an object drawn in Illustrator?
- What are some forms that type can take?
- What are some tools for selecting shapes?
- What are some tools for editing shapes?
- What are some ways to color objects?
- What are some ways to create output from Illustrator?

Review Questions

Multiple choice

1. Which one of the following is most likely to be bitmap art?
   - A. A line drawn with the Pencil tool.
   - B. A shape drawn using the Arc Segment tool.
   - C. A paragraph created using the Area Type tool.
   - D. An image imported from Photoshop.

2. Which one of the following is a selection tool?
   - A. Lasso tool
   - B. Reshape tool
   - C. Polar Grid tool
   - D. Polygon tool

3. In what kind of type can you alter the actual shape of each character?
   - A. Area Type
   - B. Type converted to outlines
   - C. Path type
   - D. Freestanding type

4. Which feature lets you instantly create a new object from multiple overlapping objects?
   - A. Clipping mask
   - B. Convert-anchor-point tool
   - C. Pathfinder palette buttons
   - D. Reshape tool

5. Which feature lets you apply a saved set of fills, strokes, and effects to an object?
   - A. Appearances
   - B. Blending modes
   - C. Layers
   - D. Styles

Fill-in-the-blank

1. You can change document magnification by using the _____ palette.

2. The fastest way to prepare an Illustrator file for a Web site is to use the _____ command.

3. You can approximate how your artwork will look at Web resolution by switching the view to _____ mode.

4. You can create a mirror image of an object by using the _____ tool.

5. To convert an Illustrator object into a bitmap, _____ it.

6. Illustrator's most versatile drawing tool is the _____ tool.

7. You can change the opacity level of an object by using the _____ palette.

Definitions

1. What does it mean when a graphic is resolution-independent?

2. What are anchor points?

3. What does it mean to make a selection?

4. What is a blending mode?

5. What is Outline view?

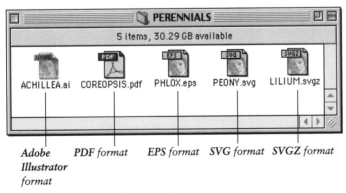

STARTUP 3

In this chapter you will learn how to launch Illustrator, create a new illustration, define the working and printable areas of a document, save an illustration in three different file formats, open an existing illustration, close an illustration, and quit/exit Illustrator.

1 Click the Illustrator **application** icon on the **Launcher**...

Creating new files

Note: A new document window doesn't appear automatically when you launch Illustrator. To create a new document after launching, see the instructions on page 39.

To launch Illustrator (Mac OS):

Open the Adobe Illustrator 10 folder on the desktop, then double-click the Illustrator 10 application icon.
or
Click the Illustrator application icon on the Launcher (on the Dock in OSX) **1**.
or
Double-click an Illustrator file icon **2**.

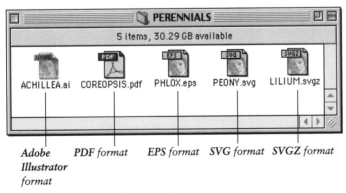

| Adobe Illustrator format | PDF format | EPS format | SVG format | SVGZ format |

2 ...or double-click an Illustrator file icon.

Note: A new document window doesn't appear automatically when you launch Illustrator. To create a new document after launching, see the instructions on the next page.

To launch Illustrator (Windows):

Open My Computer, then double-click the hard drive icon where you installed Illustrator (the default is C:). Follow the path "Program Files\Adobe\Illustrator 10," and finally, double-click the Adobe Illustrator 10 icon to start the program.

or

Double-click an Illustrator file icon **1**.

or

Click the Start button on the Taskbar, choose Programs, then click the Adobe Illustrator 10 shortcut **2**.

1 *Double-click an Illustrator file icon.*

2 *Click the Start button, then locate and click the application.*

Templates

You'll learn more about tracing on pages 203–206, but here's a sneak preview. To trace over a bitmap image, create or open an Illustrator document, then use File > **Place** to import a TIFF, PICT, or EPS with the **Template** box checked. Then, on another layer, use the **Pen**, **Pencil**, or **Auto Trace** tool to produce path shapes above the placed image.

To convert an existing layer into a template layer, click the layer name on the Layers palette, then choose Template from the Layers palette menu or double-click a top-level layer name, click Template, then click OK. On a template layer, image objects are dimmed and all objects are uneditable.

To create a new document:

1. Choose File > New (Cmd-N/Ctrl-N).

2. Type a Name for the new document **1**.

3. In the Artboard Setup area, choose dimensions for the document:

   Choose a preset size from the Size pop-up menu: 640 x 480, 800 x 600, or 468 x 60 for Web output or choose Letter, Legal, Tabloid, A4, A3, B5, or B4 for print output.

   or

   To enter custom dimensions, first choose a measurement unit from the Units pop-up menu (use Pixels for Web output), then enter Width and Height values.

4. Click a Color Mode for the document: CMYK Color for print output, RGB Color for video or Web output.

5. Click an Orientation: Portrait (vertical) or Landscape (horizontal). This can be changed later.

6. Click OK. A new document window will open, at the maximum zoom level for your monitor.

Create New Document

New Document

Name: First try

OK

Cancel

Artboard Setup

Size: Custom   Width: 500 pt

Units: Points   Height: 500 pt

Orientation:

Color Mode
● CMYK Color   ○ RGB Color

1 *In the New Document dialog box, type a Name, choose dimensions for the Artboard, and choose a Color Mode.*

In the center of every Illustrator document is one non-movable artboard work area **1**. The default artboard area is 8½ inches wide by 11 inches high.

The printable page size is the Paper [size] currently chosen in File > Page Setup/Print Setup. Letter size, for example, is 8½ x 11. You're not limited to an 8½ x 11 artboard or to the portrait format; the artboard doesn't have to match the Paper size. And if need be, you can tile (subdivide) an oversized illustration into a grid so it can be printed in sections on standard-size paper, and you can create a landscape artboard.

To change the artboard dimensions:

1. Choose File > Document Setup (Cmd-Option-P/Ctrl-Alt-P).

2. Choose Artboard from the topmost pop-up menu.

3. Choose a preset size from the Setup: Size pop-up menu (**2**).
   or
   Enter Width and Height values in any unit of measurement (Custom will then become the selection on the Size pop-up menu). The maximum work area is 227 x 227 inches. For the current document, the Units chosen in this dialog box override the Units chosen in Edit > Preferences > Units & Undo.
   or

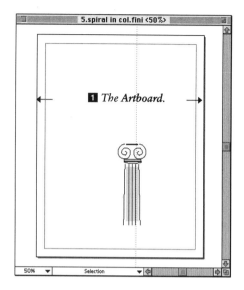

1 *The Artboard.*

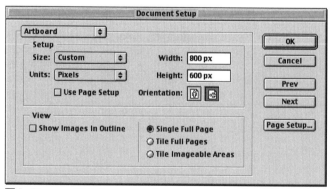

2 *In Document Setup, you can choose a preset Size; or you can enter custom Width and Height values; or you can check the Use Page Setup/Use Print Setup box to use the Paper size currently chosen in the Page Setup/Print Setup dialog box.*

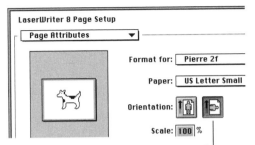

1 *Click the landscape* **Orientation** *icon in the Page Setup dialog box (Mac OS).*

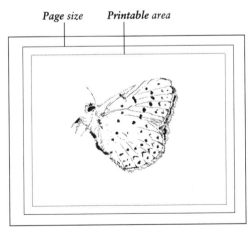

2 *Click* **Orientation:** *Landscape in the Page Setup dialog box (Windows).*

Page size   Printable area

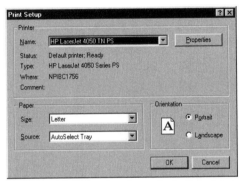

3 *The printable page in* **landscape** *Orientation*

Check the Use Page Setup/Use Print Setup box to make the artboard dimensions match the Paper size currently chosen in Page Setup/Print Setup. (Click Page Setup/Print Setup in the Document Setup dialog box to view that setting.) *Note:* Use Page Setup/Print Setup will become unchecked automatically if you choose an Artboard size that differs from the current Page Setup/Print Setup size (however, the page size will still match the current Page Setup/Print Setup size).

4. Click OK.

➤ Objects (or parts of objects) outside the artboard will save with the illustration, but they won't print.

➤ If the Page Setup/Print Setup Scale percentage is other than 100%, the page size and artboard will resize and the illustration will print proportionately smaller or larger. If Use Page Setup/Use Print Setup is unchecked in the Document Setup dialog box, the artboard will match the Artboard Setup: Size option, but the page size will match the current Page Setup/Print Setup size. If Use Page Setup/Use Print Setup is checked, the artboard dimensions can only match the Page Setup/Print Setup printout size.

You can switch the printable area of an illustration from a vertical (portrait) to a horizontal (landscape) orientation. Then you'll need to make the artboard conform to the new orientation.

To create a landscape page:

1. Choose File > Document Setup (Cmd-Option-P/Ctrl-Alt-P).

2. Mac OS: Click Page Setup, then choose Page Attributes from the topmost pop-up menu.

   Windows: Click Print Setup.

3. Click the landscape Orientation icon/button **1**–**2**.

4. Click OK.

5. Click OK to close the Document Setup dialog box **3**.

To reposition the printable area on the artboard:

1. Choose the Page tool (it's on the Hand tool pop-out menu).

2. Drag in the document window. *Note:* Areas of a page that extend outside the artboard won't print.

➤ Double-click the Page tool to reset the printable area to its default position.

➤ Double-click the Hand tool to display the entire artboard in the document window.

To create a landscape artboard:

1. Choose File > Document Setup.

2. Click the landscape Orientation icon, if it isn't already highlighted.

3. Click OK (see the tips above).

4. If the entire page isn't visible on the artboard ■, reopen Document Setup, then enter new Width and Height values to enlarge the artboard to accommodate the new orientation. And remember, objects outside the artboard area won't print.

By default, a new document consists of one page, but you can turn it into a multi-page document. If you turn on the Tile Full Pages option, as many full page borders as can fit within the current artboard dimensions will be drawn. Changing the artboard size will then increase or decrease the number of page borders.

To divide the artboard into multiple pages:

1. Choose a zoom level of 50% or smaller from the Zoom pop-up menu at the bottom of the illustration window.

2. Choose File > Document Setup.

3. Choose Artboard from the topmost pop-up menu.

4. Enter a new Width that's at least double the existing single-page width.

5. Click View: Tile Full Pages ■.

6. Click OK.

■ *The artboard in landscape Orientation. The printable page, which is in portrait Orientation, doesn't extend beyond the artboard.*

■ *Click **Tile Full Pages** in the Document Setup dialog box.*

Parts of objects that fall within this "gutter" area won't print.

1 *The artboard divided into two pages.*

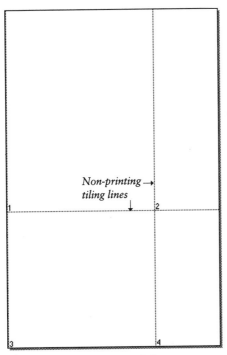

Non-printing → tiling lines

2 *An oversized illustration tiled into sections for printing (see page 448).*

7. *Optional:* Choose the Page tool ▢ (it's on the Hand tool pop-out menu), then click or drag near the left edge of the artboard. New page borders will be drawn **1**. (If the tile lines aren't showing, choose View menu > Show Page Tiling.)

➤ You can also tile full pages in landscape mode by clicking the landscape Orientation icon in the Document Setup dialog box and in the Page Setup/Print Setup dialog box and choosing Artboard Size: Tabloid. Then, if necessary, click with the Page tool near the top or bottom of the artboard to cause the new page borders to be drawn.

➤ To tile an entire artboard page into the printer's paper size, create an artboard size that's large enough to hold several print paper sizes, and then click Tile Imageable Areas in the Document Setup dialog box **2**.

➤ If you're going to need trim, crop, or registration marks, make the artboard larger than the page.

Divide the Artboard

Saving files

There are five options for saving a file from Illustrator: Adobe Illustrator document (simply "IllustratorAI" in Windows), Illustrator EPS (EPS), Adobe PDF (PDF), SVG (SVG), and SVG Compressed (SVGZ). These formats can be reopened and edited in Illustrator. If you're going to print your file directly from Illustrator, you can stick with the Adobe Illustrator format (.ai). Also, since this format is based on the PDF format, Adobe Illustrator files can also be opened in other applications that read PDF files.

If you're going to export your file to another application (e.g., a layout application for print or Web output), you'll need to choose one of the other options, as not all applications can read native Illustrator files. Other export formats are discussed on pages 47–52 and pages 454–462. Saving as SVG is discussed on page 504.

To save a file in Adobe Illustrator (.ai) format:

1. If the file has never been saved, choose File > Save (Cmd-S/Ctrl-S). If the file has already been saved in a different format, choose File menu > Save As.

2. Enter a Name (Mac) **1**/ File Name (Win) **2**. For Mac OSX, see **1**–**2**, next page.

3. Mac OS: Open the disk and/or folder in which you want to save the file. Or to create a new folder, choose a location in which to save the new folder, click New, enter a name for the folder, then click Create.

   Mac OSX: Choose a folder or disk from the Where: pop-up menu.

   Windows: Use the Save in pop-up menu to navigate to the folder in which you want to save the file.

4. Mac OS: Make sure "Adobe Illustrator® document" is chosen as the Format.

   Windows: Choose Save as Type: Illustrator (*.AI).

5. Click Save.

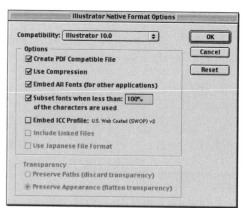

1 *The Mac OS Save As dialog box*

2 *The **Windows Save As** dialog box*

3 *Choose a **Compatibility** option (Illustrator version) and check other **Options**, if applicable, in the **Illustrator Native Format Options** dialog box. The Transparency buttons are available only if transparency is used in the file and you save to Illustrator 8 or earlier.*

Save in Adobe Illustrator Format

The Save shortcuts

	Mac OS	Windows
Save	Cmd-S	Ctrl-S
Save As	Cmd-Shift-S	Ctrl-Shift-S
Save a Copy	Cmd-Option-S	Ctrl-Alt-S

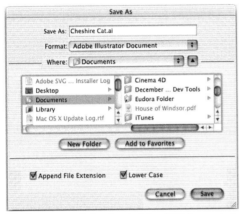

1 *The Save As dialog box in Mac OSX (expanded)*

2 *The Save As dialog box in Mac OSX (small)*

6. Choose a Compatibility option **3**. Keep in mind that early versions of Illustrator don't support all the current features, such as layers, appearances, and transparency. We recommend using Save a Copy to save a copy of the file in an earlier version instead.

7. Under Options, you can check:

   Create PDF Compatible File to save a PDF-compatible version of the file for use in other Adobe applications. Checking this option increases the file storage size.

   Use Compression to compress vector data and PDF data (if included) in order to produce a smaller file storage size.

   Embed All Fonts to save all fonts used in the illustration as part of the document. Embedded fonts will display and print on any system, even when they aren't installed. This option increases the file storage size. If not all the characters in a particular font were actually used in your artwork, you can choose to embed just a subset of characters to help reduce the PDF file size. To do this, with Embed All Fonts checked, check "Subset fonts when less than [%] of the characters are used," then enter a percentage.

   At a setting of 50%, for example, the entire font will be embedded if you use more than 50% of its characters in the file; the Subset option will be used if you use fewer than 50% of its characters in the file. *Note:* Adobe recommends not using the "Subset fonts..." option for TrueType fonts. If you do so, those fonts will be substituted if the PDF file is reopened in Illustrator.

   If a profile was chosen in Edit > Assign Profile, check **Embed ICC Profile** to embed that profile into the file in order to color manage the file.

   Include Linked Files to save a copy of any linked files in the illustration. (Read about linking on pages 254–258.)

(Continued on the following page)

Save in Adobe Illustrator Format

8. When saving in Illustrator Version 8 or earlier, click Transparency: **Preserve Paths** (discard transparency) to reset all objects to 100% opacity and discard all transparency effects (e.g., blending modes, opacity masks).
or
Click Transparency: **Preserve Appearance** (flatten transparency) to flatten the artwork while preserving the appearance of transparency. Transparency attributes will no longer be editable.

9. Click OK.

The prior version of a file is overwritten when the Save command is executed. Don't be shy—save frequently! And create backups, too.

To save an existing file:

Choose File > Save (Cmd-S/Ctrl-S).

You can use the Save As or Save a Copy command to save an existing file in a different format (e.g., Adobe Illustrator/Illustrator document, Acrobat PDF, or Adobe EPS) or to convert a file to an earlier version of Illustrator.

➤ If you use **Save As**, the new version will stay open on screen. The original file will close, but it will be preserved on disk.

➤ If you use **Save a Copy**, the original version will stay open on screen, and a copy of the file will be saved to disk.

To save a copy of an existing file:

1. Choose File > Save A Copy (Cmd-Option-S/Ctrl-Alt-S).

2. Follow the instructions starting on the previous page to save the file in the native Illustrator format. Other file formats are discussed on pages 47–52 and 454–462.

To revert to the last saved version:

1. Choose File > Revert.

2. Click Revert.

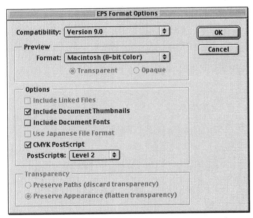

1 *Choose Format:* Illustrator EPS (EPS), *then click Save.*

2 *Choose* Compatibility *and other* Options *in the* EPS Format *dialog box.*

Not all applications can read native Illustrator files, and no preview options are available for that format. To prepare an Illustrator file for export to a page layout application or another drawing application, you should save it in either the Illustrator EPS format or the PDF format. First, EPS.

The EPS (Encapsulated PostScript) format saves both vector and bitmap objects and it is supported by most illustration and page layout programs, so it is a good choice if your file is going to be used for print output from another application. EPS files can be reopened and edited in Illustrator.

To save a file as an EPS:

1. If the file has not yet been saved, choose File > Save (Cmd-S/Ctrl-S). If the file has already been saved in a different format, choose File > Save As or Save a Copy (see the previous page).

2. Choose Format/Save as Type: Illustrator EPS (EPS) **1**.

3. Click Save.

4. Choose from the **Compatibility** pop-up menu **2**. Keep in mind that early versions of Illustrator don't support all the current features, such as layers, appearances and transparency. The earlier the Illustrator version you save to, the more drastically the illustration could change.

5. Choose a Preview Format:
   None—no preview. The EPS won't display on screen in any other application, but it will print.

   TIFF (Black & White)—black and white preview.

   TIFF (8-bit Color)—color preview.

   Mac OS: **Macintosh (Black & White)**—black and white preview (in PICT format).

   Mac OS: **Macintosh (8-bit Color)**—color preview (in PICT format).

   Note: Regardless of which preview option you choose, color information will be saved with the file and the illustration

(Continued on the following page)

Save as EPS

will print normally from Illustrator or any other application into which it's imported.

If you chose the TIFF (8-bit Color) format, click **Transparent** to save the file with a transparent background or click **Opaque** to save it with a solid background. *Note:* Choose Opaque if you're going to import the file into a Microsoft Office application.

6. *Check any of these optional boxes:*

   Include Linked Files to save a copy of any linked, placed files with the illustration (see the sidebar).

   Include Document Thumbnails to save a thumbnail with the file for previewing in Illustrator's Open or Place dialog box.

   Include Document Fonts to save any fonts used in the document as a part of the document. Only individual characters used in the font are saved, not the whole character set. Included fonts will show and print on any system, even where they aren't installed. Be sure to check this option if your Illustrator file contains type and you're going to import it into a layout application.

   CMYK PostScript to enable RGB files to print from programs that output only CMYK color. RGB fills will be preserved if the EPS file is reopened in Illustrator.

7. Choose a **PostScript** level that conforms to your printing device from the pop-up menu. Levels 2 and 3 are the preferred choices, with Level 3 being the best option for printing gradient meshes. If your file contains gradient meshes and it will be output to a Level 3 printer, choose PostScript Level 3. Level 1 is not available for Illustrator Version 9 or 10, and it produces a significantly larger file size.

8. When saving in Illustrator Version 8 or earlier, click Transparency: **Preserve Paths** (discard transparency) to reset all objects to 100% opacity and discard all transparency effects (e.g., blending modes, opacity masks).
   or

Include linked files?

If you check **Include Linked Files** in the EPS Format Options dialog box for an Illustrator file that contains a linked, placed EPS image, you won't need that original EPS image if you print the file from another program (e.g., QuarkXPress or InDesign), You will still need the original EPS image to print the file from Illustrator, though.

If your Illustrator file contains linked, placed images and you *don't* check the Include Linked Files option when saving, you'll get a second chance to save with placed files, because an alert box will open. Just say yes.

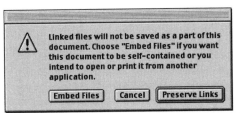

1 *This prompt will appear if you didn't check **Include Linked Files** in the EPS Format Options dialog box and your file contains placed, linked images. Here's your second chance to include those placed files.*

Click Transparency: **Preserve Appearance** (flatten transparency) to flatten the artwork while preserving the appearance of transparency. Transparency attributes will no longer be editable. Even in version 10 or 9.0 files, transparent areas will be flattened—but only when the EPS file is opened in another application.

9. Click OK. If you didn't check the Include Linked Files box and your file contains placed, linked images, an alert prompt will appear. Click Embed Files or Preserve Links **1**.

Note: If your illustration is in CMYK mode (File > Document Color Mode > CMYK Color) and it contains a placed, drag-and-dropped, or rasterized RGB image, you'll get a warning prompt if you save it as an EPS **2**, whether the CMYK PostScript option is checked or not. RGB color objects are saved as RGB in an Illustrator EPS file.

Images that are drag-and-dropped from Photoshop to Illustrator are converted to RGB automatically (don't be fooled by the linked or embedded image type that's listed on the Document Info palette). To prevent this color mode change in a CMYK Illustrator file, save it in Photoshop in CMYK Color mode and in the TIFF or EPS format, then place it into Illustrator.

> This file contains RGB images that may not separate properly if saved in an EPS file. It is suggested that you convert the images to CMYK before continuing.
>
> [Continue]   [Cancel]

2 *This prompt will appear if you save, as EPS, a CMYK Illustrator file that contains RGB images from other applications or objects with applied RGB colors that were rasterized in Illustrator.*

Save as EPS

49

Use the Adobe PDF (Portable Document Format) to prepare an Illustrator file for display on the Web or for transfer to another application or another computer platform that reads PostScript-based Adobe PDF files. The only software users will need to view your PDF file is the free Acrobat Reader (they don't need the Illustrator application), and the artwork will look as it was originally designed. The PDF format preserves all object attributes, groups, fonts, text, and layering information, and it saves RGB colors as RGB and CMYK colors as CMYK. A PDF file can also be edited using Acrobat. The PDF format also supports document text search and navigation features.

You can open one page of a multi-page PDF file in Illustrator, edit vector graphics or bitmap images on the page, if you like, and then resave the page in PDF format. If you save an Illustrator file as PDF and then reopen or place it in Illustrator, you'll still be able to edit individual objects as usual.

To save a file as an Adobe PDF:

1. If the file has never been saved, choose File > Save (Cmd-S/Ctrl-S). If the file has already been saved in a different format, choose File > Save As or Save a Copy (see page 46).

2. Type a Name/File Name, choose a location in which to save the file, choose Format/Save as Type: Adobe PDF (PDF), then click Save.

3. Choose a PDF **Options Set** (the dialog box will reconfigure automatically):

Default for print output **1**. All fonts are automatically embedded, Compression is ZIP, Quality is 8 bit, and custom color and high-end image options are preserved. This set produces the highest image quality, but the resulting file size is larger than with Screen Optimized (discussed next).

Screen Optimized for on-screen display. The document color mode and any images are converted to RGB color; fonts are embedded; and transparency, appearances, effects, opacity masks, and

Reopening a PDF

PDF is now the basis for the native Illustrator file format. If you save a file in Adobe PDF format and then reopen it in Illustrator 10, all object attributes will be preserved and be fully editable, and image links will also be preserved.

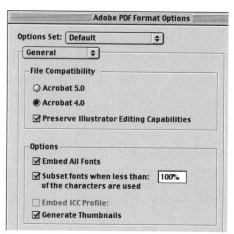

1 *General options for the Default PDF Options Set*

Save as PDF

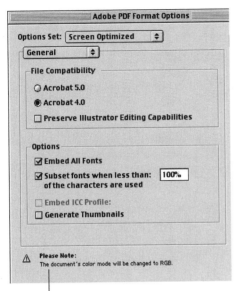

This warning will appear if you save a CMYK document as Screen Optimized.

■ The General options for the Screen Optimized PDF Options Set

other attributes are removed. The image resolution is 72 ppi, with the resulting file size being the smallest possible.

Note: If you're satisfied with the preset settings, skip to step 8. If you want to manually change any of the settings, proceed with the remaining steps.

4. Choose **General** from the second drop-down menu ■.

5. Check File Compatibility: **Acrobat 5.0** or **Acrobat 4.0.** The Acrobat 5.0 format preserves transparency, editable text, and spot colors in the illustration. The Acrobat 4.0 format requires that the PDF file be flattened during the save operation in order to preserve the appearance of transparency. *Note:* Not all applications currently can read Acrobat 5.0 files. Check **Preserve Illustrator Editing Capabilities** if you want the option to reopen and edit the file in Illustrator.

6. Check **Embed All Fonts** to have the fonts used in the file be embedded in the file. If not all the characters in a particular font were actually used in your artwork, you can choose to embed just a subset of characters to help reduce the PDF file size. To do this, with the Embed All Fonts option checked, check "Subset fonts when less than [%] of the characters are used," then enter a percentage.

If you enter 50%, for example, the entire font will be embedded if you use more than 50% of its characters in the file; the Subset option will be used if you use fewer than 50% of its characters. *Note:* Adobe recommends not using the "Subset fonts..." option for TrueType fonts. If you do so, those fonts will be substituted if the PDF file is reopened in Illustrator.

If a Profile was chosen in Edit > Assign Profile, check **Embed ICC Profile** to embed that profile into the file.

Check **Generate Thumbnails** to save a thumbnail of the file (or the page).

(Continued on the following page)

Save as PDF

7. Choose **Compression** from the second pop-up menu.

8. On the whole, the preset compression settings for the Default set **1** and the Screen Optimized set **2** are acceptable choices for PDF files. If you're satisfied with the preset settings, click OK. If you want to enter custom settings, do the following:

Check all the Average Downsampling at [ ] ppi boxes and enter your own value for the final resolution of color and grayscale bitmap images in the file.

For screen output, keep the value at 72 ppi (the default for the Screen Optimized set).

For print output, ask your print specialist how much lower than the 300 ppi default you should downsample your images. Downsampling reduces the image resolution by averaging nearby pixels and combining them to form one pixel. If an image is downsampled too much, its quality will become too low for print output.

For compression methods, choose Automatic from the pop-up menus to have Illustrator choose the appropriate compression and quality settings for your file. (For information on the individual compression methods, read pages 344–346 in the Illustrator User Guide.)

Leave Compress Text And Line Art checked to have the ZIP compression method be used on all text and line art in the file.

9. Click OK.

1 *The* **Compression** *options for the* **Default** *PDF Options Set*

2 *The* **Compression** *options for the Screen Optimized PDF Options Set*

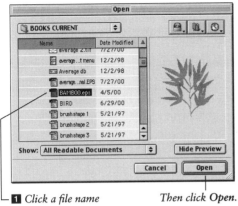

1 Click a file name (this is Mac OS). Then click **Open**.

Opening files

Follow these instructions to open an Illustrator file. Follow the instructions on page 249 to open a non-Illustrator file in Illustrator.

To open a file from within Illustrator:

1. Choose File > Open (Cmd-O/Ctrl-O).

2. Mac OS: Check Show Preview to display a thumbnail of the illustration (the file must contain a preview that Illustrator displays and QuickTime must be installed).

3. Mac OS: Choose Show: All Readable Documents to list only files in the formats Illustrator can read.

   Windows: Choose Files of Type: All Formats.

4. Locate and highlight a file name **1**–**3**, then click Open or double-click a file name. *Note:* If you get an alert dialog box about a linked file, see page 251.

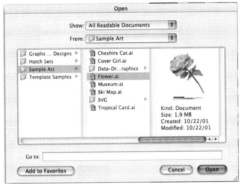

2 The Open dialog box in Mac OSX

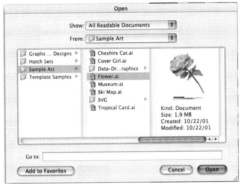

3 The Open dialog box in Windows

Ending a work session
To close a file:
Mac OS: Click the close box in the upper left corner of the illustration window (Cmd-W). In OSX, click the red button.

Windows: Click the close box in the upper right corner of the illustration window (Ctrl-W).

If the illustration was modified since it was last saved, an alert dialog box will appear 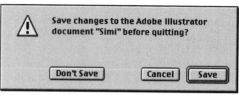. You can close the file without saving (click Don't Save); save the file (click Save); or cancel the close operation (click Cancel).

➤ Hold down Option/Alt and choose Close (or Option/Alt click the close box) to close all currently open files.

To quit/exit Illustrator:
Mac OS: Choose File > Quit (Cmd-Q).

Windows: Choose File > Exit (Ctrl-Q).

All open Illustrator files will close. If changes were made to any open files since they were last saved, an alert dialog box will appear. Save the file(s) or quit/exit without saving.

Save changes to the Adobe Illustrator document "Simi" before quitting?

Don't Save   Cancel   Save

1 *If you try to close a picture that was modified since it was last saved, this prompt will appear.*

Chapter 3: Startup ◆ Study Guide

Learning Objectives

- Launch Illustrator.
- Create new files.
- Adjust the artboard, paper size, and orientation.
- Save files.
- Open files.
- End an Illustrator work session.

Get Up and Running Exercises

- Create a new Illustrator document with a white background, sized at 6 inches wide by 4 inches high, for output to a printing press. When you're done, save it as an Illustrator file; you'll need it for other exercises in this section.
- Start with the document you created in the previous exercise. How can you change both the paper and page size to 11 inches wide by 8.5 inches high by entering the dimensions in only one dialog box?
- Create a second Illustrator document sized at 800 by 600 pixels high, for a Web page.
- Suppose you have a client that needs a complete identity design, consisting of letter-size stationery, a #10 envelope, and a business card. How might you set up the artboard to handle multiple pieces of a project?
- In the document you created at the beginning of this section, add a few objects using any tools you want. If you know how, you can add elements created outside Illustrator. Save the file. How would you create EPS and PDF versions of the file?

Class Discussion Questions

- Are there things you can set up to make it easier to launch Illustrator than in the methods described in the chapter?

- How does the Document Setup dialog box interact with the Print Setup/Page Setup dialog box?

- What determines the printable area? What does it mean when the printable area is a different size or orientation than the artboard (for example, let's say the artboard is horizontal and the printable area is vertical)?

- Why is Illustrator one of the few applications that can save directly to PDF?

Review Questions

Multiple choice

1. Which one of the following represents the work area of the document?
   A. Artboard
   B. Template
   C. Page size
   D. Paper size

2. Which one of the following represents the size of the output medium in the Print Setup/Page Setup dialog box?
   A. Artboard
   B. Page size
   C. Paper size
   D. Printable area

3. Where can you adjust the orientation of the printable area?
   A. Document Setup dialog box
   B. Page Setup dialog box
   C. New dialog box
   D. Open dialog box

4. Which one of the following file formats won't allow objects in the file to be edited in Illustrator as path objects?
   A. EPS
   B. PDF
   C. SVG
   D. TIFF

5. What determines the size of the imageable area boundary?
   A. The Artboard Setup: Size setting in the Document Setup dialog box
   B. The PPD selected in the Separation Setup dialog box
   C. The printer chosen in the Page Setup/Print Setup dialog box
   D. The area defined by the Crop Marks command

Fill-in-the-blank

1. To print a document that's larger than the largest sheet of paper your printer can print (without changing its scale), use the _____ feature.

2. For Web output, choose the _____ Color Mode.

3. The filename extension of an Illustrator document is _____.

4. If you're saving as PDF and you want all of the fonts you used to be included in the PDF document, _____ them.

5. To create a duplicate of the currently open document while leaving the currently open document open on screen, choose the File > _____ command.

6. To save a file with a small preview that will appear in the Open or Place dialog box of applications such as Illustrator, check the _____ option in the Save As dialog box.

Definitions

1. What is the artboard?

2. What is tiling?

3. What is the Page tool?

4. What are linked files?

5. What is downsampling?

VIEWS 4

In this chapter you will learn how to change zoom levels, change views (Preview, Outline, or Pixel Preview), create custom view settings, change screen display modes, and move an illustration in its window.

Change views

To use the Navigator palette to change the zoom level of an illustration:

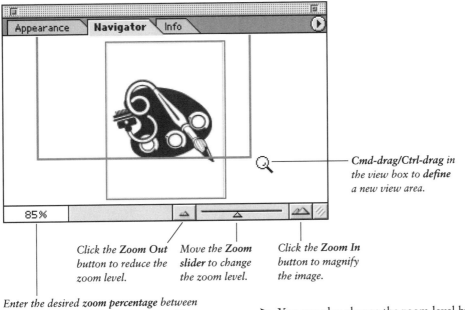

*Cmd-drag/Ctrl-drag in the view box to **define** a new view area.*

*Click the **Zoom Out** button to reduce the zoom level.*

*Move the **Zoom** slider to change the zoom level.*

*Click the **Zoom In** button to magnify the image.*

*Enter the desired **zoom percentage** between 3.13% and 6400%, then press Return/Enter. To zoom to a percentage and keep the field highlighted, press Shift-Return/Shift-Enter.*

➤ You can also change the zoom level by double-clicking the zoom field in the lower left corner of the document window, typing the desired zoom percentage (up to 6400%), and then pressing Return/Enter.

➤ To separate the Navigator from its palette group, drag its tab (palette name).

Within the document window, you can display the entire artboard, an enlarged detail of an illustration, or any zoom level in between. The zoom level (3.13%–6400%) is indicated as a percentage both on the title bar and in the lower left corner of the document/application window. 100% is actual size. An illustration's zoom level has no bearing on its printout size.

To choose a preset zoom level:

Choose View > Zoom In (Cmd-+/Ctrl-+). Repeat to magnify further.
or
Choose View > Zoom Out (Cmd--/Ctrl--). Repeat, if desired.
or
Make sure no objects are selected, Control-click/Right-click on the image, then choose Zoom In or Zoom Out from the context menu .
or
Choose a preset percentage from the zoom pop-up menu in the lower left corner of the document/program window 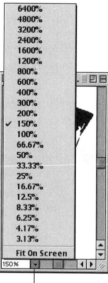. Or choose Fit On Screen from the pop-up menu to make the artboard fit within the current document window size.
or
Double-click in the Zoom field in the lower-left corner of the document/program window, type in the desired magnification, then press Return/Enter.

➤ Choose View > Fit In Window (Cmd-0/ Ctrl-0) or double-click the Hand tool to display the entire artboard in the document window.

➤ To apply a new Zoom value without exiting the Zoom field, press Shift-Return/ Shift-Enter.

1 *Make sure no objects are selected, then Control-click/ Right-click on an image and choose Zoom In or Zoom Out from the context menu.*

2 *Choose a **preset percentage** from the Zoom pop-up menu in the lower left corner of the document/ program window.*

Preset Zoom Levels

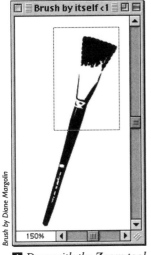

Brush by Diane Margolin

1 *Drag with the Zoom tool.*

2 *The illustration is magnified.*

To change the zoom level using the Zoom tool:

1. Choose the Zoom tool (Z). 🔍

2. Click on the illustration in the center of the area that you want to enlarge or drag a marquee across an area to magnify that area **1**–**2**. The smaller the marquee, the greater the degree of magnification. (To move the illustration in the document window, see pages 61–62.)

   or

   Option-click/Alt-click on the illustration to reduce the zoom level.

   or

   Drag a marquee, then without releasing the mouse, press and hold down Spacebar, move the marquee over the area you want to magnify, then release the mouse.

➤ To display an illustration at Actual Size (100%), double-click the Zoom tool or choose View > Actual Size (Cmd-1/Ctrl-1). *Note:* If you double-click the Zoom tool when your illustration is at a small zoom level, the white area around the artboard may appear in the document window instead of the illustration. Use the Navigator palette or the Hand tool to reposition the illustration in the document window.

➤ You can click to change the zoom level while the screen is redrawing.

This is the method to master for speedy picture editing.

To change the zoom level using the keyboard:

To magnify the illustration with any tool other than Zoom selected, Cmd-Spacebar-click/Ctrl-Spacebar-click or -drag in the document window.

or

To reduce the zoom level, Cmd-Option-Spacebar-click/Ctrl-Alt-Spacebar-click.

Zoom Tool; Zoom Shortcuts

An illustration can be displayed and edited in four different views: Preview, Outline, Pixel Preview, or Overprint Preview. In all views, the other View menu commands—Hide/Show Page Tiling, Edges, Guides, and Grid—are accessible, and any selection tool can be used. (Overprint Preview view is discussed on page 510.)

To change the view:

From the View menu, chooose Preview (Cmd-Y/Ctrl-Y) to display all the objects with their fill and stroke colors as well as all placed images or choose Outline (Cmd-Y/Ctrl-Y) to display all the objects as wire frames with no fill or stroke colors. The screen redraws more quickly in Outline view.
or
Make sure no objects are selected (click in a blank area of the artboard), then Control-click/Right-click and choose Outline or Preview from the context menu.
or
Choose Pixel Preview (Cmd-Option-Y/Ctrl-Alt-Y toggle) to turn on a 72 ppi display. Use this view for Web graphics work.

➤ Let's say you've got a large file on a slow machine and you start to Preview it in all its glory—nah, on second thought, you decide to preview it later. Cmd-. (period)/Esc to cancel the preview.

➤ You won't learn much about layers until you get to Chapter 11, but just to give you a little hint, you can Cmd-click/Ctrl-click an eye icon for a layer on the Layers palette to toggle between Preview and Outline views just for that layer.

It's a snap

In **Pixel Preview** view, you can get a good inkling of what your vector graphics will look like when they're rasterized for the Web (choose View > Actual Size first). But Pixel Preview is more than just a preview. When you choose this view, View > **Snap To Pixel** is turned on automatically, causing the edges of objects to snap to the nearest pixel edge. Also uncheck **Use Preview Bounds** in Edit > Preferences > General. Snap To Pixel reduces the need for anti-aliasing and thus helps keep edges crisp. (Anti-aliasing adds pixels along the edges of objects to make them look smoother, but it also can diminish their crispness.)

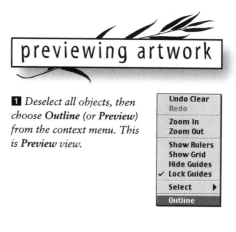

1 *Deselect all objects, then choose* **Outline** *(or* **Preview***) from the context menu. This is* **Preview** *view.*

2 *Outline view*

3 *Pixel Preview view*

1 *Type a Name for the view setting in the New View dialog box.*

2 *Choose a custom view setting from the bottom of the View menu.*

3 *In the Edit Views dialog box, highlight a view, then change the Name or click Delete.*

You can define and save up to 25 custom view settings that you can switch to quickly using an assigned shortcut, and you can specify whether your illustration will be in Preview view or Outline view for each setting that you define.

To define a custom view setting:

1. Choose a zoom level for your illustration and choose scroll bar positions.

2. Put your illustration into Preview or Outline view (Cmd-Y/Ctrl-Y).

3. Choose View > New View.

4. Type a descriptive name for the new view in the Name field, as in "40% view" **1**.

5. Click OK.

To choose a custom view setting:

Choose the view name from the bottom of the View menu **2**.

➤ You can switch views at any time. For example, if your illustration is at a custom view setting for which you chose Outline view but you want to display your illustration in Preview view, choose View > Preview.

To rename or delete a custom view setting:

1. Choose View > Edit Views.

2. Click the name of the view you want to change **3**.

3. Change the Name.
   or
   Click Delete to delete the view setting.

4. Click OK. The View menu will update to reflect the changes.

➤ If you want to rename more than one view setting, you have to click OK, then reopen the dialog box.

The number of Illustrator documents that can be open at a time is limited only by the amount of RAM (Random Access Memory) currently available to Illustrator. To activate a currently open window, you can either click in it or choose the document name from the list of open documents at the bottom of the Window menu **1**.

To facilitate editing, an illustration can be displayed simultaneously in two windows. You could choose a high zoom level for one window (such as 200%) to edit small details and a lower zoom level for the other so you can see the whole illustration. Or in one window you could hide individual layers or display individual layers in Outline view and in another window you could Preview all the layers together.

Note: The illustration in the window for which Preview view is selected will redraw each time you modify the illustration in the window for which Outline view is chosen. In this case you won't save processing or redraw time when you work in the Outline window.

To display an illustration in two windows:

1. Open an illustration.

2. Choose Window > New Window. A new window of the same size will appear on top of the first window, and with the same title followed by ":2" **2**.

3. Mac OS: Reposition the new window by dragging its title bar so the original and new windows are side by side, and resize one or both windows.

   Windows: You can choose any of these Window menu commands: Cascade to arrange the currently open illustrations in a stair-step configuration; Tile to tile open windows side by side; or Arrange Icons to move the minimized windows to the bottom of the application window.

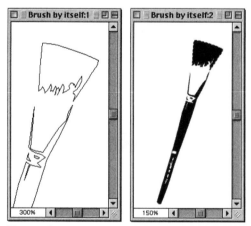

1 *The **currently open** documents are listed at the bottom of the Window menu.*

2 *One illustration displayed in **two windows.***

One Illustration in Two Windows

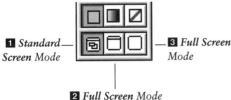

1 *Standard Screen Mode* — **3** *Full Screen Mode*

2 *Full Screen Mode with Menu Bar*

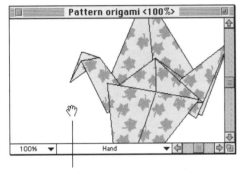

4 *Spacebar-drag in the document window to move the illustration.*

To change the screen display mode:

Click the **Standard Screen Mode** button at the bottom of the Toolbox to display the image, menu bar, and scroll bars in the document window **1**. This is the default mode.

or

Click the **Full Screen Mode with Menu Bar** (second) button to display the image and the menu bar, but no scroll bars **2**. The area around the image will be white.

or

Click the **Full Screen Mode** (third) button to display the image, but no menu bar or scroll bars **3**. The area around the image will be white.

➤ Press "F" to cycle through the three modes.

➤ Press Tab to hide (or show) all currently open palettes, including the Toolbox; press Shift-Tab to hide (or show) all the palettes, leaving the Toolbox.

➤ Choose View > Hide Artboard. Choose the command again to redisplay the artboard.

Get around

To move an illustration in its window using the Hand tool:

Click any of the scroll arrows on the edge of the document window.

or

Choose the Hand tool (H) ✋ (or hold down Spacebar to turn any other tool into the Hand tool temporarily), then drag the illustration to the desired position **4**.

➤ Double-click the Hand tool to fit the entire artboard in the document window.

Screen Display Modes; Move the Illustration

To move the illustration in its window using the Navigator palette:

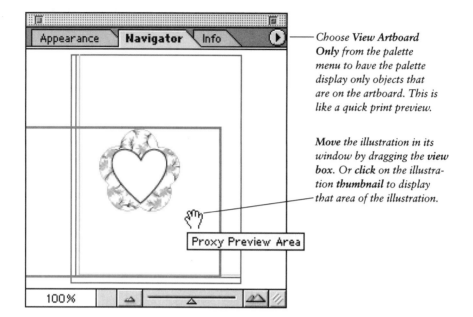

*Choose **View Artboard Only** from the palette menu to have the palette display only objects that are on the artboard. This is like a quick print preview.*

*Move the illustration in its window by dragging the **view box**. Or **click** on the illustration **thumbnail** to display that area of the illustration.*

➤ To change the color of the view box frame from its default red, choose Palette Options from the Navigator palette menu, then choose a preset color from the Color pop-up menu or double-click the color swatch and choose a color from the Color Picker. Check "Draw dashed lines as solid lines" if you want dashed lines to display as solid lines on the palette.

➤ The proportions of the view box match the proportions of the document window. Resize the document window and you'll see what we mean.

➤ The Navigator palette will display multiple pages, if any, and tiling of the imageable area.

➤ To halt a slow screen redraw on Mac OS, press Cmd-. (period). On Windows, press Esc. The display will change to Outline view. Choose View > Preview (Cmd-Y/ Ctrl-Y) to restart the redraw.

Move the Illustration

Chapter 4: Views ♦ Study Guide

Learning Objectives

- Change zoom levels.
- Change views.
- Create custom view settings.
- Change screen display modes.
- Move an illustration in its window.

Get Up and Running Exercises

- Open an Illustrator document and practice navigating in the document. Try zooming in and out, then try changing the view to the left or right, and up or down. Use the various navigation methods (tools, commands, the Navigator palette) introduced in the chapter. Which methods do you find most convenient for the types of projects you work on?

- In an Illustrator document, such as the one you opened in the previous exercise, work with custom views:

  ▲ Create a custom view that shows a document at 100% in Preview mode.

  ▲ Create a custom view that shows a document at 200% in Outline view.

  ▲ Create a custom view that is zoomed into a specific area of the illustration away from the center (for example, a detail in the lower-right corner).

  ▲ Rename or delete one of the views.

- Suppose you are preparing to show artwork to a client. How can you change Illustrator's workspace options to present the image alone on the screen?

Class Discussion Questions

- Where are the two places where you can change the zoom level by typing a percentage?
- What are other ways to zoom in and out?
- What are the ways to move an illustration within the document window?
- Why might it be useful to view the same document in two windows?
- How can Full Screen mode be useful when you aren't drawing?

Review Questions

Multiple choice

1. Which view makes the most screen space available to Photoshop while preserving easy access to commands?

   A. Full Screen Mode with Menu Bar

   B. Outline view

   C. Preview view

   D. Standard View

2. Which view is particularly helpful for Web graphics work?

   A. Full Screen mode

   B. Pixel Preview view

   C. Preview view

   D. Standard mode

3. What happens when you double-click the Zoom tool on the toolbox?

   A. The document displays at actual size.

   B. The document displays at Fit in Window size.

   C. The document is magnified to the next zoom level.

   D. The document switches between Preview and Outline views.

4. Which palette or window doesn't contain document view controls?

   A. Document window

   B. Navigator palette

   C. Appearance palette

   D. Toolbox

Fill-in-the-blank

1. To halt screen redraw, press _____.

2. To display the same document in an additional window, choose the _____ command.

3. To create a preset of display options, choose the _____ command.

4. To zoom so that a specific area of an illustration is both magnified and centered, _____ .

5. To show the document without the document page size border, choose the _____ command.

Definitions

1. What is a custom view?

2. What is Pixel Preview view?

3. What is Outline view?

4. What is Preview view?

5. Where and what is the view box?

OBJECTS BASICS 5

In Illustrator, paths (objects) are composed of anchor points connected by straight and/or curved line segments. Paths can be open or closed. Rectangles and ovals are closed paths (they have no endpoints); lines are open paths. As you'll learn in Chapter 8, any path can be reshaped.

In this chapter, first you will learn how to delete objects, for future reference. Then you will learn how to create objects quickly using the Rectangle, Ellipse, Rounded Rectangle, Polygon, Star, Flare, Line Segment, Arc Segment, Spiral, Rectangular Grid, and Polar Grid tools. And finally, you will learn how to draw in a freehand style using the Pencil tool. Once you've learned the basics in this chapter, don't miss these other important chapters: 6, Select/Copy; 7, Transform; 8, Reshape; and 9, Fill & Stroke.

Artist and designer Danny Pelavin builds crisp, effective illustrations using basic geometric shapes.

Daniel Pelavin

Deleting objects

You'll be creating lots of different shapes in this chapter, and your artboard may start to get crowded with junk. To remove an object that you've just created, Undo (Cmd-Z/Ctrl-Z). To remove an object that's been lying around, follow these instructions.

To delete one object:

1. Choose the Selection tool (V), ![cursor] then click on the object you want to delete.
   or
   Choose the Lasso tool, ![lasso] then drag around the object you want to delete.

2. Press Delete/Backspace or Del or choose Edit > Clear or Cut.

➤ If you're using the Direct-selection tool and only some of the object's points are selected, press Delete/Backspace twice.

To delete a bunch of objects:

1. Marquee the objects you want to remove using the Selection tool (V) ![cursor] or use any of the other methods for selecting multiple objects that are described in the next chapter.

2. Press Delete/Backspace or Del.

Drawing geometric objects

To create a rectangle or an ellipse by dragging:

1. Choose the Rectangle tool (M) ▢ or the Ellipse tool (L). ⬤
2. Drag diagonally **1**. As you drag, you'll see a wire frame representation of the rectangle or oval. When you release the mouse, the rectangle or oval will be selected, and it will be colored with the current fill and stroke settings (Preview view).

➤ To create a series of perfectly aligned, equal-size rectangles, create and select a rectangle, then use Type > Rows & Columns (see page 238).

To create a rectangle or an ellipse by specifying dimensions:

1. Choose the Rectangle tool (M) ▢ or the Ellipse tool (L). ⬤
2. Click on the artboard where you want the object to appear.
3. In the Rectangle or Ellipse dialog box, enter dimensions in the Width and Height fields **2**. To create a circle or a square, enter a number in the Width field, then click the word Height (or vice versa)— the value in one field will copy into the other field.
4. Click OK.

➤ Values in dialog boxes are displayed in the measurement units currently chosen from the Setup: Units pop-up menu in File > Document Setup.

Extras

Draw a rectangle or oval from its center	Option-drag/Alt-drag
Move a rectangle or ellipse as you draw it	Spacebar-drag
Draw a square with the Rectangle tool or a circle with the Ellipse tool	Shift-drag

Recoloring: sneak preview

You'll learn all about Illustrator's fill and stroke controls in Chapter 9, but here's a sneak preview. Select an object, activate the **Fill** or **Stroke** box (square) on the **Toolbox** or the **Color** palette, then click a swatch on the **Swatches** palette or click the color bar on the **Color** palette.

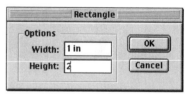

1 *Drag diagonally.*

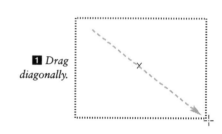

2 *Enter **Width** and **Height** values in the Rectangle (or Ellipse) dialog box. The dimensions of the last-drawn object will display when the dialog box opens.*

Circles, rectangles, and polygons (triangles)

Daniel Pelavin

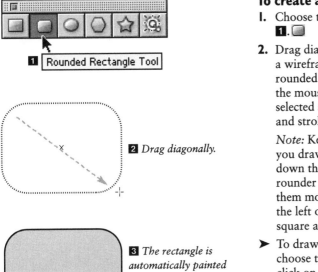

1 Rounded Rectangle Tool

2 *Drag diagonally.*

3 *The rectangle is automatically painted with the current fill and stroke colors.*

Chris Spollen

*A **great** use of rounded rectangles!*

Daniel Pelavin

To create a rounded rectangle:

1. Choose the Rounded Rectangle tool **1**. ▢

2. Drag diagonally. As you drag, you'll see a wireframe representation of the rounded rectangle **2**. When you release the mouse, the rounded rectangle will be selected and colored with the current fill and stroke colors (Preview view) **3**.

   Note: Keep the mouse button down as you draw the rectangle and press or hold down the up arrow to make the corners rounder or the down arrow to make them more square. Press (don't hold) the left or right arrow to toggle between square and round corners.

➤ To draw a rectangle of a specific size, choose the Rounded Rectangle tool, click on the artboard, then enter Width, Height, and Corner Radius values.

➤ The current Corner Radius value in Edit > Preferences > General, which controls how curved the corners of a rectangle will be, is also entered automatically in the Corner Radius field in the Rectangle dialog box, and vice versa.

Rounded Rectangle Tool

Here's a quick introduction to one of the many Illustrator filters: Round Corners. For other ways to reshape objects, see Chapter 8, Reshape.

To round the corners of an existing object:

1. Select the object.

2. Choose Filter > Stylize > Round Corners (on the top portion of the filters menu).
   or
   Choose Effect > Stylize > Round Corners to create an editable appearance (not a permanent change to the object). You'll learn lots more about effects in Chapter 22.

3. Enter a Radius value (the radius of the curve, in points). For an effect, you can check Preview, then make adjustments.

4. Click OK .

1 *Top row: the original objects; second row: after applying the Round Corners filter (30pt).*

There are a number of tools, such as Polygon, Star, and Spiral, that make light work of drawing geometric objects. All you have to do is draw a marquee in the artboard or enter values in a dialog box. The current fill and stroke colors are applied automatically (see Chapter 9).

To create a polygon by clicking:

1. Choose the Polygon tool 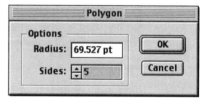.

2. Click where you want the center of the polygon to be.

3. Enter a value in the Radius field (the distance from the center of the object to the corner points) .

4. Choose a number of Sides for the polygon by clicking the up or down arrow or by entering a number. The sides will be of equal length.

5. Click OK 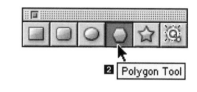. A polygon will appear where you clicked on the artboard.

2 Polygon Tool

3 *In the Polygon dialog box, enter a Radius distance and choose a number of Sides.*

4

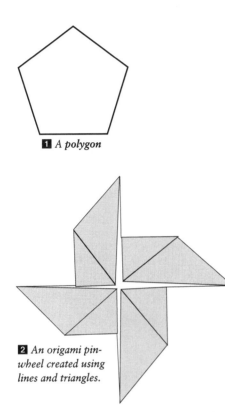

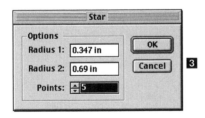

1 *A polygon*

2 *An origami pinwheel created using lines and triangles.*

4 *On the left, a classic, five-point star. On the right, after putting circles on top of the points and then clicking the Add to Shape Area button on the Pathfinder palette to join the shapes.*

To create a polygon by dragging:

1. Choose the Polygon tool.
2. Drag on the artboard, starting from where you want the center of the polygon to be **1**–**2**.

   While dragging, do any of the following:

   Drag away from or toward the center to **resize** the polygon.

   Drag in a circular fashion to **rotate** the polygon.

   Hold down Shift while dragging to **constrain** the bottom side of the polygon to the horizontal axis.

   With the mouse still held down, press or hold down the up or down arrow key to **add** or **delete sides** from the polygon.

   Hold down Spacebar and drag to **move** the polygon.

3. When you release the mouse, the polygon will be selected and it will be colored with the current fill and stroke settings.

➤ To align a new object with an existing object as you draw it, use Smart Guides (see pages 88–89).

To create a star by clicking:

1. Choose the Star tool.
2. Click where you want the center of the star to be.
3. Enter a number in the Radius 1 and Radius 2 fields **3**. Whichever value is higher will become the distance from the center of the star to its outermost points. The lower value will become the distance from the center of the star to the innermost points. The greater the difference between the Radius 1 and Radius 2 values, the thinner the arms of the star will be.
4. Choose a number of Points for the star by clicking the up or down arrow or entering a number (3–1000).
5. Click OK **4**.

➤ To rotate the completed star, see page 98 or page 103.

To create a star by dragging:

1. Choose the Star tool.

2. Drag on the artboard, starting from where you want the center of the star to be ▌1▐.

   While dragging, do any of the following:

   Drag away from or toward the center to **resize** the star.

   Drag in a circular fashion to **rotate** the star.

   Hold down Shift while dragging to **constrain** one or two points to the horizontal axis.

   With the mouse still held down, press the up or down arrow key to **add** or **delete points** from the star.

   Hold down Spacebar while dragging to **move** the star.

   Hold down Option/Alt to make the shoulders (opposite segments) **parallel** to each other ▌2▐.

   Hold down Cmd/Ctrl and drag away from/towards the center to increase/decrease the **length** of the **arms** of the star, while keeping the inner radius points constant.

3. When you release the mouse, the star will be selected and it will be colored with the current fill and stroke settings ▌3▐–▌4▐.

➤ Hold down "~" while dragging with the Star or Polygon tool to create progressively larger copies of the shape ▌5▐. Drag quickly. Apply a stroke color to distinguish the different shapes. Try using the Twist tool to twirl the shapes around their center (see page 125).

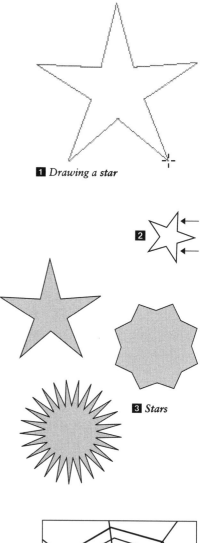

▌1▐ *Drawing a star*

▌2▐

▌3▐ *Stars*

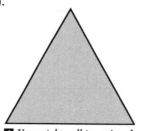

▌4▐ *You might call it a **triangle**, but actually it's a three-point star!*

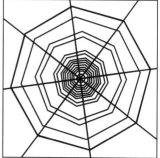

▌5▐ ***Multiple** polygons drawn with the **Polygon** tool with "~" held down.*

Star Tool

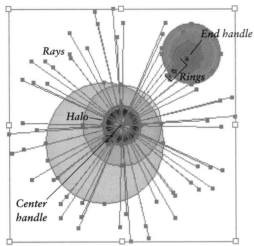

1 *A selected flare*

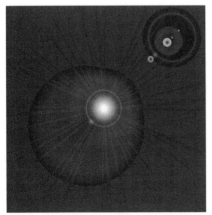

2 *Choose **Center, Halo, Rays,** and **Rings** options for a flare in the **Flare Tool Options** dialog box.*

The Flare tool creates soft glow circles that consist of four components: a center, a halo, rays, and rings **1**, like a camera lens flare. The components are filled automatically with the Fill color at different opacity settings and are fully editable. Creating flares probably won't be your top priority as an Illustrator, but the instructions are here if and when you need them.

To create a flare by entering values:

1. Choose the Flare tool (it's on the Rectangle tool pop-out menu).

2. Click on the artboard where you want the flare to appear. The Flare Options dialog box will open **2**.

3. Choose the Diameter, Opacity, and Brightness values for the Center portion (inner circle) of the flare.

4. Choose the Growth (radius) of the halo as a percentage of the overall size, and choose or enter a Fuzziness value for the halo.

5. *Optional:* Check Rays, then specify the Number of rays, the length of the Longest ray as a percentage of the average ray, and the Fuzziness of the rays.

6. *Optional:* Check Rings, then specify the overall length of the flare Path, the Number of rings, the Largest ring as a percentage of the average ring, and the Direction (angle) of the rings.

7. Click OK. Put your flare on top of a dark object—it will show up better **3**.

➤ To choose default values for the Flare tool, Option/Alt click Reset in the Flare Tool Options dialog box.

To create a flare using the current Flare Options settings:

1. Choose the Flare tool.

2. Option-click/Alt-click where you want the flare to appear (no dialog box will open).

3 *It's not easy to print a flare in this type of book.*

Flare Tool

10.0!
To create a flare by dragging:

1. Choose the Flare tool. 📷

2. Drag on the artboard where you want the center handle of the flare to appear, then drag. The further you drag, the larger the center and the halo will be.

    Before releasing the mouse, you can do any of the following:

    Move in a circular direction to change the angle of the rays.

    Press Shift to constrain the rays to the nearest 45° angle.

    Press up arrow to add rays.

    Press down arrow to remove rays.

    Hold down Cmd/Ctrl to keep the center of the flare constant.

    Press ~ (tilde) to redraw the rings in a different random configuration.

3. Drag again in another spot to create the end handle and rings for the flare.

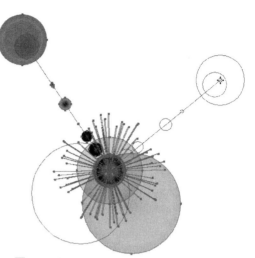

1 *Drag the* **end** *or* **center handle** *to change the* **length** *of the overall flare.*

10.0!
To edit a flare:

To change the length of the overall flare or move its rings, select the flare, choose the Flare tool, 📷 click either the center or end handle of the flare **1**, then drag the handle. This is a little tricky, and Smart Guides won't help you.

or

To edit any of the components of a flare using its options dialog box, select the flare, double-click the Flare tool on the Toolbox, then change any of the settings in the Flare Options dialog box (see the previous page). The Preview option will be checked. Press Tab to force the preview, if necessary.

or

To edit the individual components of a flare, you first have to expand it into individual objects. Once a flare is expanded, however, it can't be edited using the Flare tool or the Flare Options dialog box. Choose the Selection tool, select the flare, choose Object > Expand, check all the boxes, click OK, then edit the individual shapes as you would any other object.

➤ Choose View > Hide Edges to see the edits to the flare more easily.

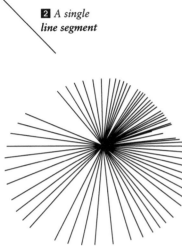

1 *Drawing tool pop-out menu*

2 *A single line segment*

3 *Lines drawn with the **Line Segment** tool with ` (grave accent) held down*

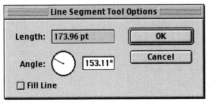

4 *Lines drawn with the **Line Segment** tool with **Shift-`** held down*

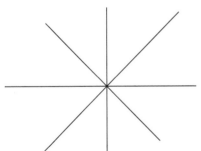

5 *Choose settings for the **Line Segment** tool in its **Options** dialog box.*

The Line Segment, Arc Segment, Spiral, Rectangular Grid, and Polar Grid tools **1**, all on the same tool pop-out menu, create independent objects or groups of objects.

The Line Segment tool (and the Arc Segment tool, which is discussed on the next page), create either one line or multiple, separate lines. After dragging with either tool, the next point you click will be a new, separate path.

To draw using the Line Segment tool: *10.0!*

I. Choose the Line Segment tool.

2. Click to start the line, then drag in any direction to finish it **2**. As you drag, you can do any of the following:

Press Option/Alt to extend the line outward from both sides of the origin point.

Press Shift to constrain the line to the nearest 45° angle.

Press Spacebar to move the line.

Press ` (grave accent) to create multiple lines of varied lengths, from the same center point, at any angle **3**. Move the mouse quickly to spread the lines apart.

Press Shift-~ (tilde) to create multiple lines at 45° angles **4**.

To draw a line segment by entering *10.0!* values:

I. Choose the Line Segment tool.

2. Click where you want the segment to appear.

3. In the Line Segment Tool Options dialog box **5**, enter the desired line Length.

4. Enter an Angle or move the dial.

5. *Optional:* Check Fill Line to have the line be stored with the current Foreground color (see Chapter 9). If the line is subsequently joined to another line or segment, that color will be used as the fill. With this option unchecked, the line's fill will be None, though it can be changed later.

6. Click OK.

➤ The values of the last segment created are displayed in the Line Segment Tool Options dialog box. To restore the default values, Option/Alt click Reset.

Line Segment Tool

The Arc Segment tool creates quick curves.

To draw an arc segment:

1. Choose the Arc Segment tool.

2. Click where you want the arc to begin, then drag to create the arc **1**. As you drag, you can do any of the following:

   Press X to toggle between a concave and convex arc.

   Press C to toggle between an open and closed arc **2**–**3**.

   Press F to flip the arc, keeping the origin point constant.

   Press (or press and hold) the up arrow or down arrow to increase or decrease the angle of the arc.

   Press Option/Alt to extend the arc outward from both sides of the origin point.

   Press Spacebar to move the arc.

   Press ` (grave accent) to create multiple arc segments from the same origin point.

To draw an arc segment by entering values:

1. Choose the Arc Segment tool.

2. Click where you want the arc segment to appear.

3. In the Arc Segment Tool Options dialog box **4**, enter a Length X-Axis value for the width of the arc and a Length Y-Axis value for the height of the arc. Click a corner on the square icon to change the origin point.

4. From the Type pop-up menu, choose whether the arc will be Open or Closed.

5. From the Base Along pop-up menu, choose whether the arc will be measured from the X Axis or the Y Axis.

6. Move the Slope slider or enter a value for the steepness of the curve.

7. *Optional:* Check Fill Arc to have the arc fill with the current Foreground color.

8. Click OK.

➤ To restore the default values to the Arc Segment Tool Options dialog box, Option/Alt click Reset.

Using arc segments

In Chapter 10 you'll learn how to draw curves "from scratch" using the Pen tool. You can use the **Join** command (see pages 129–130) to combine pen and arc segments into a single object or you can **add** segments to an arc using the Pen tool.

1 *We used **Ruler guides** and **smart guides** to position the starting and ending points in an **arc segment**.*

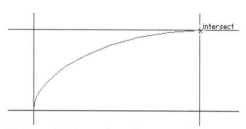

2 *Drawing a closed arc segment*

3 *After releasing the mouse, the arc fills with the current Foreground color (see Chapter 9).*

Arc Segment Tool Options

Length X-Axis: 123 pt OK
Length Y-Axis: 100 pt Cancel
Type: Closed
Base Along: Y Axis
Concave Slope: 54 Convex
☑ Fill Arc

4 *Choose options for the **Arc Segment** tool in its **Options** dialog box.*

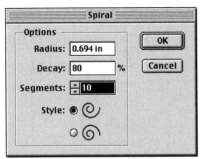

1 *In the Spiral dialog box, enter Radius and Decay values, choose a number of Segments, and click a Style button.*

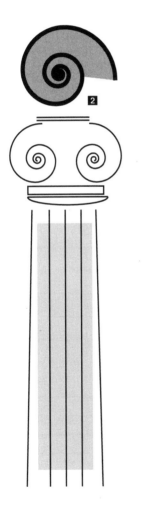

To create a spiral by entering values:

1. Choose the Spiral tool.
2. Click roughly where you want the center of the spiral to be.
3. Enter a Radius value for the distance from the center of the spiral to the outer-most point **1**.
4. Enter a Decay percentage (5–150) to specify how tightly the spiral will wind.
5. Choose a number of Segments (quarter revolutions around the center point) for the spiral by clicking the up or down arrow or by entering a number.
6. Click a Style button for the direction the spiral will wind from the center point.
7. Click OK **2**.
8. Apply a stroke color to the spiral (see pages 148–150).

To create a spiral by dragging:

1. Choose the Spiral tool.
2. Drag in the illustration window, starting from where you want the center of the spiral to be.
3. While dragging, do any of the following:

   Drag away from or towards the center to **resize** the spiral.

   Option-drag/Alt-drag outward to **add segments** from the center of the spiral as you change its size. Option-drag/Alt-drag inward to **delete segments**.

   Keep the mouse button down, then press or hold down the up or down arrow key to **add** to or **delete segments** from the center of the spiral.

   Drag in a circular fashion to **rotate** the spiral.

   Hold down Shift while dragging to **constrain** the rotation of the entire spiral to an increment of 45°.

   Hold down Spacebar while dragging to **move** the spiral.

   Hold down Cmd/Ctrl and drag slowly away from or toward the center to

(Continued on the following page)

Spiral Tool

control how **tightly** the spiral winds (the Decay value).

4. When you release the mouse, the spiral will be selected and it will be colored with the current fill and stroke colors 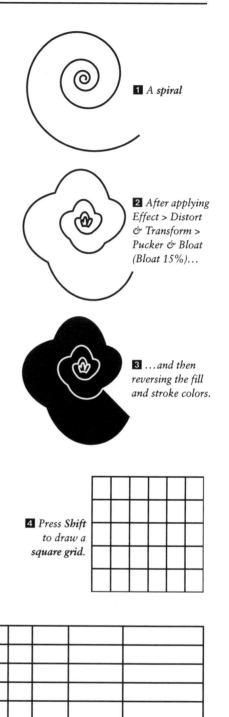–**3**.

10.0! A rectangular grid can be created by dragging (instructions on this page) or by entering values in a dialog box (instructions on the following page). In addition, you can choose default values for the tool by double-clicking it. The grid is composed of a group of separate lines and a rectangle or rectangles. You can't put anything into it, but you can put it on its own layer (lock it to make it uneditable), and then create objects or type on a layer above it (see Chapter 11).

To create a rectangular grid by dragging:

1. Choose the Rectangular Grid tool (it's on the Line Segment tool pop-out menu). ▦

2. Drag diagonally. After you start dragging, you can press any of the following keys:

   Shift to constrain the grid to a square **4**.

   Option/Alt to draw the grid from the center.

   Shift-Option/Shift-Alt to draw a square grid from the center.

   Spacebar to move the grid as you draw.

   To adjust the grid **dividers,** press any of the following key modifiers:

   Up Arrow or **Down Arrow** to add or remove horizontal dividers.

   Right Arrow or **Left Arrow** to add or remove vertical dividers.

   X to change the logarithmic skew value of the horizontal dividers to the left by increments of 10% **5** or **C** to change the logarithmic skew value of the horizontal dividers to the right (the dividers will be progressively closer together).

   F to change the logarithmic skew value of the vertical dividers to the bottom by increments of 10% or **V** to change the logarithmic skew value of the vertical dividers to the top.

1 *A spiral*

2 *After applying Effect > Distort & Transform > Pucker & Bloat (Bloat 15%)...*

3 *...and then reversing the fill and stroke colors.*

4 *Press Shift to draw a square grid.*

5 *Press X to draw a grid with a logarithmic skew.*

74

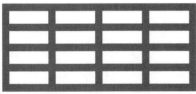

1 *Choose parameters for the* **Rectangular Grid** *tool in its* **Options** *dialog box.*

2 *Use* **Outside Rectangle as Frame** *on. The outer segment is a single rectangle.*

3 *Use* **Outside Rectangle as Frame** *off. Each of the four outer segments is a separate object.*

4 *Polar grids*

To create a rectangular grid by *10.0!* entering values:

1. Choose the Rectangular Grid tool (it's on the Line Segment tool pop-out menu). ▦

2. Click in the illustration window to establish an origin point for the grid.

3. In the Default Size area **1**, enter Width and Height values for the overall grid, and to specify the point the grid will be drawn from, click a corner on the square Origin Point icon.

4. Enter the Number of Horizontal Dividers to be inserted between the top and bottom edges of the grid. *Optional:* Choose a Skew value above or below 0 to weight the dividers toward the bottom or top.

5. Enter the number of Vertical Dividers to be inserted between the left and right edges of the grid. *Optional:* Choose a Skew value above or below 0 to weight the dividers toward the right or left.

6. *Optional:* Check Use Outside Rectangle As Frame to have the top, bottom, left, and right segments be a separate rectangular object instead of a line **2**–**3**.

7. *Optional:* Check Fill Grid to fill the grid with the current fill color.

8. Click OK.

You can draw a polar (elliptical) grid by *10.0!* dragging (instructions on this page) or via a dialog box (instructions on the following page). In addition, you can choose default values for the tool by double-clicking it.

To create a polar grid by dragging:

1. Choose the Polar Grid tool (it's on the Line Segment tool pop-out menu). ◉

2. Choose Fill and Stroke colors (see Chapter 9), then drag diagonally **4**. As you drag, you can do any of the following:

   Press Shift to constrain the grid to a circle.

   Press Option/Alt to resize the grid from all sides of the origin point.

   Press Option-Shift/Alt-Shift to constrain the grid to a circle as it extends from the origin point.

   Press Spacebar to move the grid.

   (Continued on the following page)

Rectangular Grid, Polar Grid Tools

Polar Grid Tool

3. To adjust the grid dividers, do any of the following as you drag:

   Press Up Arrow or Down Arrow to add or remove concentric circles.

   Press Right Arrow or Left Arrow to add or remove radial lines.

   Press X to change, by 10% inward, the concentric dividers' logarithmic skew value.

   Press C to change, by 10% outward, the concentric dividers' logarithmic skew value.

   Press F to change the radial dividers' logarithmic skew value upward by 10% or press V to change it downward.

10.0!

To create a polar grid by entering values:

1. Choose Fill and Stroke colors (see Chapter 9).

2. Choose the Polar Grid tool, 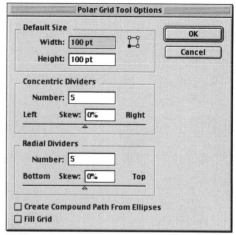 then click to establish the grid's origin point.

3. In the Default Size area **1**, enter Width and Height values for the overall grid, and to specify the point the grid will be drawn from, click a corner on the square Origin Point icon.

4. Enter the Number of curved Concentric Dividers to appear inside the grid **2**. *Optional:* Choose a Skew value above or below 0 to weight the concentric dividers toward the outside or inside of the grid **3**.

5. Enter the number of straight Radial Dividers to appear between the center and the circumference of the grid. *Optional:* Choose a Skew value above or below 0 to weight the straight dividers in a clockwise or counterclockwise direction around the grid **4**. Try moving the slider a short distance.

6. Check Create Compound Path From Ellipses to have each concentric circle be converted into a separate compound path.

7. Click Fill Grid to have the whole grid be filled with the current Fill color. If Create Compound Path From Ellipses is checked, alternating circles will be filled **5**.

8. Click OK.

1 *The Polar Grid Tool Options dialog box. Note: In Windows, the Concentric Dividers Skew slider extremes are marked "In" and "Out."*

2 *Both Skew values at zero*

3 *Concentric Dividers: Skew 120%*

4 *Radial Dividers: Skew -128%*

Bug! In the Mac OS, the Radial and Concentric Skew functions are switched. T'will be fixed, we assume.

5 *Create Compound Path From Ellipses and Fill Grid on: The white rings are see-through. The Fill color is applied to the non-see through rings automatically and the Stroke color (gray, in this case) is applied to the radial and concentric dividers.*

1 *Blue-footed booby, drawn with the Pencil tool*

2 *The booby in Outline view*

Sketching

If you enjoy sketching objects "by hand," you'll gravitate to the Pencil tool, especially if you have a stylus. Pencil paths can be reshaped like any other paths (see Chapter 8). *Note:* If you need to draw straight lines or smooth curves, you'll go mad trying to do it with the Pencil; use the Line Segment, Arc, or Pen tool instead!

The Pencil tool performs three distinctly different functions. If you drag in an empty area of the artboard with the Pencil, you'll create a new, open path. If you drag along the edge of an existing, selected path (open or closed), the Pencil will reshape the path (see page 123). And if you drag from an endpoint on an existing open path, you will add a new segment to the path (see page 121).

To draw using the Pencil tool:

1. Choose the Pencil tool (N).

2. Click the Stroke color box 🔲 on the Color palette, then choose a stroke color. Choose stroke attributes from the Stroke palette (see Chapter 9).

3. Click the Fill Color box ◼ on the Color paletee, then click the None button ⊘ at the bottom of the palette so the curves on the path won't fill in.

4. Draw a line. A dotted line will appear as you draw. When you release the mouse, the line will be colored with the current fill and stroke settings and its anchor points will be selected (Preview view) **1**. In Outline view, you'll see only a wireframe representation of the line **2**.

   Note: To create a closed path with the Pencil tool, hold down Option/Alt before and as you release the mouse.

➤ Read about the Pencil tool preferences on the next page.

➤ To close an existing Pencil line, choose the Selection tool (V), select the line, then choose Object > Path > Join (Cmd-J/ Ctrl-J). The two endpoints will be joined by a straight segment.

The Fidelity and Smoothness settings for the Pencil tool control the number of anchor points and the size of the curve segments the tool produces. If you change these settings, only subsequently drawn lines are affected—not existing lines.

To choose Pencil tool settings:

1. Double-click the Pencil tool (or press "N" to choose the tool, then press Return/Enter).

2. Choose a Fidelity value (0.5–20) **1**–**3**. The lower the Fidelity, the more closely the line will follow the movement of the mouse and the greater the number of anchor points will be created. The higher the Fidelity, the smoother the path.

3. Choose a Smoothness value (0–100). The higher the Smoothness, the smoother the curves; the lower the smoothness, the more bends and twists in the path.

4. *Optional:* Leave the "Keep selected" box checked to keep a Pencil path selected after it's created. This is handy if you like to add to a path after it's drawn.

5. We'll discuss the reshaping function of the Pencil tool on page 123. Checking the "Edit selected paths" box activates this function. In the Within [ ] pixels field, enter the minimum distance the pointer must be from a path in order for the tool to reshape it. Uncheck "Edit selected paths" if you want to be able to draw multiple Pencil lines near each other without reshaping any existing selected paths.

6. Click OK.

➤ Click Reset in the Pencil Tool Preferences dialog box to restore the tool's default preferences.

➤ To smooth an existing path, use the Smooth tool (see page 124).

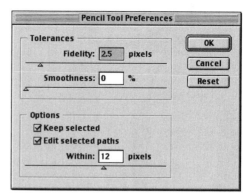

The Pencil tool has its own Preferences dialog box.

2 *A line drawn with a high Fidelity value*

3 *A line drawn with a low Fidelity value*

Diane Margolin

Chapter 5: Objects Basics ◆ Study Guide

Learning Objectives

- Delete objects.
- Draw geometric objects.
- Draw freehand objects with the Pencil tool.

Get Up and Running Exercises

- Draw the side of a bus. Which tools would work best for the body, windows, and wheels?
- Create a flag. For this exercise, any flag that contains rectangular areas and stars will work well. When drawing stars, how do you adjust the star size, the rotation angle, and number of points (as you draw the shape, before you release the mouse)?
- Use the drawing tools to draw a pair of eyeglasses in any style.
- Find an object in the room and use the Pencil tool to sketch it. Can you customize the tool's drawing behavior?

Class Discussion Questions

- How do you:
  - ▲ Delete one object?
  - ▲ Simultaneously delete several objects that are next to each other?
  - ▲ Simultaneously delete several objects some distance away from each other, when there are other objects between them that you want to keep.
- What's the difference between dragging and clicking with a shape tool?
- Why are there two Radius options in the Star tool dialog box?
- How are tools affected by pressing keys, such as pressing the Option key when drawing the Rectangle tool, or the arrow key when drawing with the Star tool?

Review Questions

Multiple choice

1. How do you set the default Corner Radius value?
   A. Choose Effect > Convert to Shape > Rounded Rectangle.
   B. Open the General panel of the Preferences dialog box.
   C. Click the Rectangle tool on the artboard.
   D. Double-click the Rounded Rectangle tool in the toolbox.

2. Which key lets you reposition a shape as you draw it?
   A. Option/Alt
   B. Cmd/Ctrl
   C. Shift
   D. Spacebar

3. Which key lets you constrain the rotation angle when using a tool such as the Polygon tool?
   A. Option/Alt
   B. Shift
   C. Spacebar
   D. Up arrow/down arrow

4. Which key lets you adjust the number of points in a star when drawing with the Star tool?
   A. Up arrow/down arrow
   B. Left arrow/right arrow
   C. Page Up/Page Down
   D. Any number key (type the number of points you want)

5. Which option controls how closely the Pencil tool follows how you dragged the mouse?
   A. Decay
   B. Fidelity
   C. Smoothness
   D. Radius

Fill-in-the-blank

1. When drawing with the Line Segment tool, you can set the angle precisely by _____ and entering a value.

2. As you drag a new shape with the Polar Grid tool, you can add radial lines by pressing the _____ key.

3. To create a closed path with the Pencil tool, press the _____ key before and as you release the mouse.

4. To create multiple copies of a polygon or star as you drag the Polygon or Star tool, press the _____ key.

5. To extend the length of the arms of a star as you drag the Star tool, press the _____ key.

6. To round the corners of an existing object without permanently changing the object, choose the _____ command.

Definitions

1. What does it mean to constrain?

2. What's corner radius?

3. In the Spiral tool dialog box, what is the Decay option?

4. For the Rectangular Grid tool, what is a logarithmic skew?

5. With the Polar Grid tool, what does the Create Compound Path from Ellipses option do?

SELECT/COPY 6

In Chapter 5 you learned basic methods for creating objects. In later chapters you will learn how to reshape, recolor, transform, and distort objects. Objects can't be modified unless they're selected, though, so the first thing you'll learn in this chapter is how to select and deselect objects. You'll also learn how to move objects; use smart guides to align objects; hide/show an object's anchor points and direction lines; hide/show whole objects; lock/unlock objects; copy objects within the same file or between files; and offset a copy of a path.

If you like to move or position objects by entering values or measuring distances, after you learn the fundamental techniques in this chapter, read Chapter 23, Precision Tools.

Selection Tools (side tab)

A few pointers

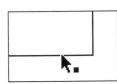

The pointer over an unselected segment

The pointer over a selected segment*

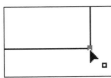

The pointer over a selected point*

Selecting

The six selection tools

Selection tool

The **Selection (V)** tool is used to select or move whole paths and to resize or rotate a path using its bounding box. If you click on the edge (or the fill**) of an object with the Selection tool, all the points on that object will become selected.

Direct-selection tool

The **Direct-selection (A)** tool is used to select one or more individual anchor points or segments of a path. If you click on a curve segment with the Direct-selection tool, that segment's direction lines and anchor points will become visible. (Straight line segments don't have direction lines—they only have anchor points.) If you click on the fill* of an object in Preview view using this tool, all the points on the object will become selected.

(Continued on the following page)

*Bounding box hidden.
**If the Use Area Select option is on in Edit > Preferences > General.

The **Group-selection** tool can be used to select all the anchor points on a single path, but its primary use is to select groups of objects that are nested inside larger groups. Click once to select an object; click twice to select that object's group; click three times to select the next group that was added to the larger group, and so on.

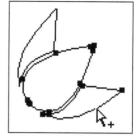

Group-selection tool

➤ The easiest way to access the Group-selection tool is by holding down Option/ Alt when the Direct-selection tool is active (note the plus sign in the pointer).

The **Lasso** tool is used to select whole paths (open or closed) by dragging a freeform marquee around them.

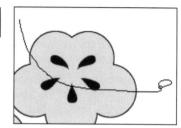

Lasso tool

The **Direct-select Lasso** tool is used to select points or segments on one or more paths by dragging a freeform marquee around those points or segments.

10.0!

The **Magic Wand** tool selects objects of the same or a similar fill color, stroke color, stroke weight, opacity, or blending mode to the object you click on. You can choose options for this tool.

Direct-select Lasso tool

Quick select

To select all the objects on a **layer** or **sublayer** (even in a one-layer document), click the selection area for that layer at the far right side of the **Layers palette** (a colored square will appear). You can also click the selection area for an individual object or group. Read all about layers in Chapter 11.

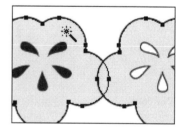

Magic Wand tool

Using area select

If **Use Area Select** is checked in Edit > Preferences > General and you click on an object's fill when your illustration is in Preview view, the entire path will become selected. If you find this feature to be unnecessary or annoying, by all means turn it off. If Use Area Select is unchecked or the path has no fill, you have to click on the edge of the path to select it. (See Chapter 9.)

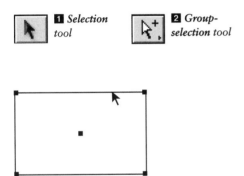

1 *Selection tool*   **2** *Group-selection tool*

3 *The Selection tool is used to select a path and all its anchor points.*

To select an object or objects:

1. Choose the Selection tool (V) **1** or the Group-selection tool **2**.

2. Click on the edge of the path **3**.
   or
   If the path has a color fill, your illustration is in Preview view, and the Use Area Select option is on (see the sidebar), click on the fill.
   or
   Position the pointer outside the path(s) you want to select, then drag a marquee across all or part of it **4**. The whole path will be selected, even if you only marquee a portion of it.
   or
   If the illustration is in Outline view, click on the edge of the path.

➤ Hold down Option/Alt to use the Group-selection tool while the Direct-selection tool is chosen, and vice versa.

Be sure to read more about the Lasso tools on page 84!

To add or subtract objects from a selection:

Choose the Selection tool (V), then Shift-click or Shift-drag (marquee) any selected objects to deselect them or do the same for any unselected objects to add them to the selection.
or
Choose the Lasso tool (it's on the Direct-select Lasso tool pop-out menu), then Shift-drag partially or completely around or across any unselected objects to add them to the selection. Or Option-drag/Alt-drag across or around selected objects to deselect them.

4 *Marqueeing two paths with the Selection tool.*

You will learn how to reshape objects in Chapter 8. But before you can proceed to reshaping, you have to know how to activate individual points and segments. And it's important to be precise about which components you select.

To select anchor points or segments:

1. Choose the Direct-selection tool (A).

2. Click the edge of the path (not the fill!). A **segment** will become selected. If you click a curve segment, the direction lines for that segment will become visible.
   or
   If the path isn't selected, click the edge of the path (not the fill!). Then click on an **anchor point** –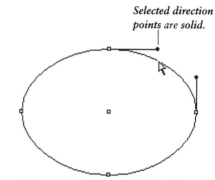.
   or
   Position the pointer outside the object or objects whose **anchor points** you want to select, then drag a marquee across them (a dotted marquee will define the area as you drag over it). Only the points you marquee will be selected –.

3. To select additional anchor points or segments or deselect selected anchor points or segments individually:

   Shift-click or Shift-marquee those points or segments with the Direct-selection tool.
   or
   Choose the Direct-select Lasso tool (Q), then Shift-drag partially or completely around any unselected points or segments to select them or Option-drag/ Alt-drag around any selected points or segments to deselect them.

➤ If you've got a non-selection tool selected and you need to use either the Selection tool or the Direct-selection tool, hold down Cmd/Ctrl instead of switching tools. The pointer will temporarily function like whichever of those two selection tools was last used (note the pointer icon).

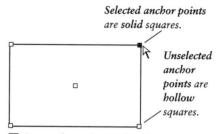

Selected anchor points are solid squares.

Unselected anchor points are hollow squares.

1 *One anchor point is selected with the Direct-selection tool (Outline view).*

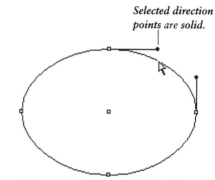

Selected direction points are solid.

2 *A segment is selected with the Direct-selection tool.*

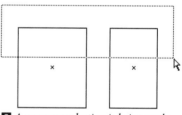

3 *A marquee selection is being made with the Direct-selection tool.*

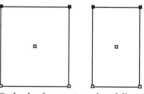

4 *Only the four points that fell within the marquee became selected.*

Reselect

Let's say you just used a Select > Same submenu command and you love it so much you want to choose it again. Just press **Cmd-6/Ctrl-6**. And unlike the Undo command, this command doesn't need to be executed right away; you can perform other operations, and Illustrator will still remember which Select > Same submenu command was last used. Watch out, though. You may get unexpected results, depending on what object is selected.

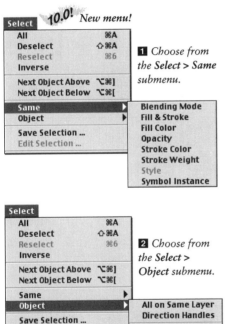

1 *Choose from the Select > Same submenu.*

2 *Choose from the Select > Object submenu.*

3 *Control-click/ Right-click and choose from the Select submenu.*

The Select commands select objects whose characteristics are similar to that of the last selected (or currently selected) object. Each command is aptly named for the attributes it searches for. *10.0!*

To select using a command:

Do any of the following:

Select an object to base the search on or deselect all objects to have the search be based on the last object that was selected, then from the Select > **Same** submenu **1**, choose **Blending Mode, Fill & Stroke, Fill Color, Opacity, Stroke Color, Stroke Weight, Style,** or **Symbol Instance.**
or
Select an object or objects, then from the Select > **Object** submenu **2**, choose **All on Same Layer** to select all the objects on the layer that object resides on (or layers, if objects from more than one layer are selected). Or choose **Direction Handles** to select all the points on the currently selected object or objects (this is equivalent to using the Direct-selection tool).
or
With or without an object selected, from the Select > Object submenu, choose **Brush Strokes** to select objects that have the same brush strokes; **Clipping Masks** to select masking objects (helpful for getting the edges of a masking object to display on screen); **Stray Points** to select lone points that are not part of any path (so they can be deleted easily); or **Text Objects** to select all the text objects in the illustration.
or
Select an object above or below the object you want to select, then Control-click/Right-click and choose Select > **First Object Above, Next Object Above, Next Object Below,** or **Last Object Below 3**. Or choose Select > Next Object Above (Cmd-Option-]/Ctrl-Alt-]) or Next Object Below (Cmd-Option-[/Ctrl-Alt-[).

Let's say you need to select a few points on one path and a couple of points on a nearby path. Until now you would probably grab the Direct-selection tool and click on the points individually (tedious) or marquee them (works only if the points in question fall conveniently within the rectangular marquee). With the Direct-select Lasso tool, you can weave an irregular pathway around just the points you want to select. Or with the Lasso tool, you can select just the whole paths you drag over. Both tools are very handy for selecting paths that are close to or overlapping other paths.

To select using a lasso tool:

1. Deselect (click on a blank area of the artboard).

2. Choose the Lasso tool (it's on the Direct-select Lasso tool pop-out menu) 🔾, then drag around the paths you want to select **1**–**2**. You can drag right through a path or around a path. You don't need to "close" the lasso path.
   or
   Choose the Direct-select Lasso tool (Q) 🔾, then encircle just the points you want to select **3**–**4**.

➤ To move the newly-selected path or points, use a selection tool.

1 *Drag through or around the object you want to select with the Lasso tool.*

2 *The whole object becomes selected.*

3 *Wend your way around parts of objects with the Direct-select Lasso tool.*

4 *Only the points you surround become selected.*

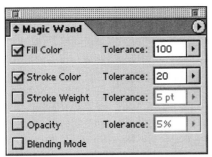

1 *The Magic Wand palette*

The Magic Wand tool selects all objects in a document with the same or similar fill *10.0!* color, stroke color, stroke weight, opacity, or blending mode to the one you click on. First you need to choose options for the tool.

To use the Magic Wand tool, see the instructions on the following page.

To choose options for the Magic Wand tool:

1. To open the Magic Wand palette, double-click the Magic Wand tool or choose Window > Magic Wand. If the three panels aren't visible (as in **1**), choose Show Stroke Options and Show Transparency Options from the palette menu.

2. On the left side of the dialog box, click the attributes you want the tool to select: Fill Color, Stroke Color, Stroke Weight, Opacity, or Blending Mode.

3. For each option you checked in the previous step (except Blending Mode), choose a Tolerance range. Choose a low value to select only colors, weights, or opacities that match or are very similar to the pixel you click or choose a high value to allow the tool to select a broader range of colors, weights, or opacities. For Fill Color or Stroke Color, choose a value (the range will be 0–255 for RGB or 0–100 for CMYK depending on the document color mode); for Stroke Weight, choose a width Tolerance (0–1000 pt); for Opacity, choose a percentage (0 –100).

4. To permit the Magic Wand tool to select objects on all layers, make sure the Use All Layers command on the palette menu has a checkmark. To allow the tool to select objects only on the current layer, leave this option unchecked.

➤ To reset the Magic Wand palette to its default values, choose Reset from the palette menu.

Magic Wand Palette

10.0!

To use the Magic Wand tool:

1. Choose the Magic Wand tool.

2. To create a **new** selection, click a color in the illustration window. Depending on which options are checked on the Magic Wand palette, other objects with the same or a similar fill color, stroke color, stroke weight, opacity, or blending mode will become selected **1**–**2**.

3. To **add** to the selection, Shift-click a color in the illustration window with the Magic Wand tool.

   To **subtract** from the selection, Option-click/Alt-click a color in the illustration window with the Magic Wand tool.

To select all the objects in an illustration:

Choose Select > All (Cmd-A/Ctrl-A). All unlocked objects in your illustration will be selected, whether they are on the artboard or on the scratch area. Hidden objects or objects on hidden layers (eye icon off on the Layers palette) won't become selected.

➤ If the pointer is in a text block when the Select > All command is executed, the entire text story will become selected— not all the objects in the illustration.

To prevent objects from being modified, you must deselect them.

To deselect all objects:

Choose Select > Deselect (Cmd-Shift-A/ Ctrl-Shift-A).
or
Choose a selection tool, then click on a blank area of the artboard.

➤ To deselect an individual object within a multiple object selection, see page 81.

➤ To deselect an object in a group, Shift-click it with the Direct-selection tool. Grouping is discussed on page 185.

To select all the deselected objects, and vice versa:

Choose Select > Inverse.

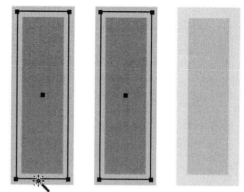

1 *These objects have the same **stroke** color, but the square on the far right has a lower **opacity** (50%). The Opacity option is **on** for the Magic Wand tool, and the tool is clicked on the stroke of the object on the left. Only the objects with the same stroke color **and opacity** become selected.*

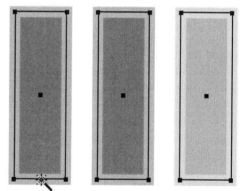

2 *This time the Magic Wand tool is used with the Opacity option off. All three objects become selected, and **opacity** is **ignored** as a factor.*

Give it a nudge

Press any arrow key to move a selected object by the current Keyboard Increment: **Keyboard Increment** value in Edit > Preferences > General. The default increment is 1 pt.

 1 *Selection tool*

2 *You can drag the edge of an object using the Selection tool.*

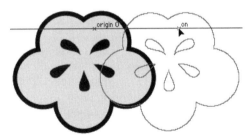

3 *Or if the object has a fill color and the Use Area Select option is on, you can drag an object's fill. Here, Smart Guides are used to move the object along the horizontal axis.*

Moving

There are many ways to move objects: By dragging, nudging (arrow keys), or using a dialog box. Precise methods for positioning objects, such as the Move dialog box, the Transform palette, and Transform Each, are covered in Chapter 23, Precision Tools. We'll start with the most direct approach first.

To move an object by dragging:

1. Choose the Selection tool (V) **1**.

2. Drag the object's **edge** (you can do this in Outline or Preview view) **2**.
   or
   If the Use Area Select option is on in Edit > Preferences > General, the illustration is in Preview view, and the object has a fill color, drag the **fill** **3**. This can also be done with the Direct-selection tool.

➤ Use smart guides to guide you (see the following two pages).

➤ If View > Snap To Point is on (Cmd-Option-"/Ctrl-Alt-") and there are ruler guides on your artboard, the part of an object that is directly underneath the pointer will snap to a guide if it comes within two pixels of it (the pointer becomes hollow when it's over a guide).

➤ Hold down Shift while dragging an object to constrain the movement either to a multiple of 45° or to the current Constrain Angle in Edit > Preferences > General, if the latter is a value other than 0.

Move an Object

Smart guides are temporary guides that appear when you draw, move, duplicate, or transform an object. They are designed to help you align objects with one another or along a particular axis. And smart guides have magnetism: Drag an object near one, and the pointer will snap to it.

To turn smart guides on or off, choose View > Smart Guides (Cmd-U/Ctrl-U). Smart guides settings are chosen in Edit > Preferences > Smart Guides ■. You'll understand smart guides pretty quickly once you start working with them—they're easier done than said.

To start with, try using smart guides to move an object along an axis or align one object with points on another object. Here's how it works.

To use smart guides to align objects:

1. Make sure View > Smart Guides (Cmd-U/Ctrl-U) is on (has a checkmark) and make sure View > Snap to Grid is off.

2. Go to Edit > Preferences > Smart Guides & Slices, and make sure Text Label Hints **2** and Object Highlighting **3** are checked. (Construction Guides, Transform Tools, and other Smart Guides options are discussed on page 439.)

3. Choose the Selection tool (V). ▶

4. To use angle lines to position an object: Start dragging an object. Smart guide angle line guides will appear as you move the object (e.g., 0°, 45°, 90°). Release the mouse any time the word "**on**" appears next to the pointer, to position the object along that angle. You don't need to hold down Shift to constrain the movement— that's the whole point!
   or
   To align one object to another, start dragging an object, position the pointer over the edge of another path, and release the mouse when the word "**anchor**" or

Use them for finding

Smart Guides aren't just used for aligning objects. With **Text Label Hints** checked in Smart Guides & Slices Preferences, you can use Smart Guides to help you locate individual points on any object, whether the object is selected or not. With **Object Highlighting** checked, you can use Smart Guides to locate the edges of objects—irregularly-shaped objects, objects in a group, objects in a mesh, etc. Object Highlighting works even when View > Hide Edges is chosen.

■ *The Snapping Tolerance is the maximum distance the pointer can be from an object for the snap function to work.*

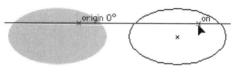

2 *Text label hints display when an object is moved along one of the axes.*

3 *The edge of an object highlights when the pointer is moved over it (with the mouse button up).*

Use Smart Guides

Interesting angle

You can specify the angle for smart guides in Edit > Preferences > Smart Guides & Slices. You can choose a predefined **Angles** set from the pop-up menu or you can enter your own angles. If you switch from Custom Angles to a predefined set and then switch back to Custom Angles at a later time, the last-used custom settings will be restored.

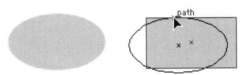

1 *An ellipse is moved over a rectangle. As the mouse is dragged over the rectangle's path, the word "**path**" appears on the unselected object.*

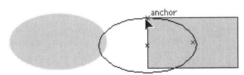

2 *An ellipse is dragged by an anchor point and is aligned with an anchor point on the rectangle (as revealed by the word "**anchor**") on the rectangle.*

"**path**" appears next to the pointer **1**. You can also align an object's **center** point or path to another object's center point or path. The word "center" will appear. *Note:* In order for the center point to show up as a Smart Guide, the object's center point must be visible (see the following page).

or

To align objects by anchor points: Make sure the object you want to move is not selected, then position the pointer over one of its anchor points (the word "**anchor**" will appear). Drag the object over an anchor point on another object, and release the mouse when the word "anchor" appears on the second object **2**.

Note: You could also align a path of one object to an anchor point or the center point on another object or an anchor point of one object to the path of another object.

➤ You can't lock smart guides—they vanish as quickly as they appear. To create guides that stay on screen, drag from the horizontal or vertical ruler into the artboard (see page 410).

➤ Smart guides are the same color as the current Guides color, which is chosen in Edit > Preferences > Guides & Grid.

Use Smart Guides

Hiding and locking

When the Hide Edges feature is on, anchor points and direction lines are invisible, yet objects are still fully editable. Try hiding edges to see how different stroke attributes, effects, flares, etc. look in Preview view or to make distracting points invisible when you're working in Outline view.

Note: The Hide Edges command won't hide the bounding box. To hide the bounding boxes of all objects in a document, choose View > Hide Bounding Box (Cmd-Shift-B/Ctrl-Shift-B). –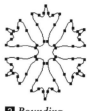. Re-choose the command to redisplay the boxes.

1 *Bounding box on*

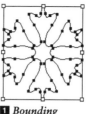
2 *Bounding box off*

To hide the anchor points and direction lines of an object or objects:

1. Select an object or objects.

2. Choose View > Hide Edges (Cmd-H/Ctrl-H). To redisplay the anchor points and direction lines, choose View > Show Edges.

You can use an object's center point like a handle to drag the object. You can also align objects via their center points using smart guides, but the objects' center points must be visible in order to do this.

To hide/show an object's center point:

1. Select the object (or objects) whose center point you want to show or hide. Or to show or hide the center point for all the objects in the illustration, choose Select > All (Cmd-A/Ctrl-A).

2. Show the Attributes palette **3**.

3. If the Show Center point options aren't visible on the palette, choose Show All from the palette menu.

4. Click the Don't Show Center button 🔳 **4**.
   or
   Click the Show Center button 🔳 **5**.

5. Deselect the object(s).

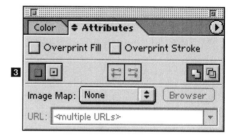
4 *Center point hidden*

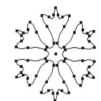
5 *Center point showing*

Use the Layers palette!

Here we go again, singing the praises of the **Layers** palette. It can be used to quickly show/hide or lock/unlock a layer, a group, or an individual object. For show/hide, see page 195. For lock/unlock, see page 194.

If your illustrations tend to be complex, you'll find the Hide Selection command to be useful for isolating the objects you want to work on and for boosting screen redraw. Hidden objects don't print, and are invisible in both Outline and Preview views. When you close and reopen a file, hidden objects remain hidden (a change from version 9). **10.0!**

We generally prefer to use the Layers palette to show/hide (and lock/unlock) objects, but since we can't bear to throw out old pages, here it is, for whatever it's worth.

To hide an object or objects:
1. Select the object or objects to be hidden.
2. Choose Object > Hide > Selection (Cmd-3/Ctrl-3).

Note: There is no command for selectively redisplaying individual hidden objects, but you can use the Layers palette to show them individually (see page 195).

To redisplay all hidden objects:
Choose Object > Show All (Cmd-Option-3/Ctrl-Alt-3).

A locked object cannot be selected or modified. If you close and reopen the file, locked objects remain locked. For other lock commands, see page 194.

To lock an object or objects:
1. Select the object or objects to be locked. You can't lock or hide part of a path.
2. Choose Object > Lock > Selection (Cmd-2/Ctrl-2). **10.0!**

Locked objects can't be unlocked individually using a command, but they can be unlocked individually using the Layers palette.

To unlock all locked objects:
Choose Object > Unlock All (Cmd-Option-2/Ctrl-Alt-2). The newly unlocked objects will be selected and any previously selected, unlocked objects will be deselected.

Hide Objects; Lock Objects

Copying

On this page we discuss two straight-forward methods for copying: dragging and nudging. These are some other methods:

- Copy an object using the Clipboard (page 93).
- Copy an object using a Transform tool (Chapter 7).
- Copy an object to a different layer (page 190).
- Copy a layer and all the objects on it (page 190).
- Copy an object using the Move dialog box (page 415).

To drag-copy an object:

1. Choose the Selection tool (V).

2. Option-drag/Alt-drag the fill or edge of an object (don't drag a bounding box handle) **1**–**2**. You can release the mouse in the same document or in another document window. The pointer will turn into a double arrowhead. Release the mouse before releasing Option-Alt.

or

To constrain the position of the copy to the horizontal or vertical axis (or the Constrain Angle in Edit > Preferences > General), start dragging the object, then hold down Option-Shift/Alt-Shift and continue to drag. You could also use smart guides for positioning.

➤ To create another copy of the object, choose Object > Transform > Transform Again (Cmd-D/Ctrl-D). Repeat for more copies.

To copy an object by nudging:

1. Choose the Selection tool (V).

2. Select an object or objects.

3. Press Option-arrow/Alt-arrow to copy the object and move the copy the Keyboard Increment from Edit > Preferences > General. The default unit is one point.

or

Press Option-Shift-arrow/Alt-Shift-arrow to copy the object and move it ten times the current Keyboard Increment.

Copying grouped objects

If you copy an object in a group by dragging (start dragging with the Direct-selection tool, then continue dragging with Option/Alt held down), the copy will become **part** of that group.

If you use the **Clipboard** to copy and paste an object that was in a group, the object will paste **outside** the group. The Group command is discussed on page 179.

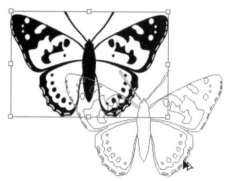

1 *To copy an object, **Option-drag/Alt-drag** it. Note the double arrowhead pointer.*

2 *A copy is made.*

If you select an object or a group and then choose the Cut or Copy command, that object or group will be placed onto the Clipboard, a temporary storage area in memory. The previous contents of the Clipboard are replaced each time you choose Cut or Copy.

The Paste command places the current Clipboard contents in the center of the currently active document window. The Paste in Front and Paste in Back commands paste the object in its original x/y location in front of or behind the current selection. The Paste in Front and Paste in Back commands are handy for positioning the Clipboard contents in a particular stacking position.

Objects are copied to the Clipboard in the PDF and/or AICB format, depending on which of those options is currently chosen in Edit > Preferences > Files & Clipboard (see page 442). The same Clipboard contents can be pasted an unlimited number of times.

To copy or move objects from one document to another using the Clipboard:

1. Open two documents.

2. Select the object or group that you want to copy or move.

3. Choose Edit > Cut (Cmd-X/Ctrl-X). The object or group will be removed from the current document.
   or
   To move a copy of the object or group, choose Edit > Copy (Cmd-C/Ctrl-C).

4. Click in the destination document, and click a layer name on the Layers palette.

5. *Optional:* Select an object whose stacking position you want to paste the copied object in front of or behind.

6. Choose Edit > Paste (Cmd-V/Ctrl-V).
   or
   If you've selected an object in the destination document, choose Edit > Paste in Front (Cmd-F/Ctrl-F) or Paste in Back (Cmd/B/Ctrl-B).

Use the Clipboard

The Offset Path command copies a path and offsets the copy around or inside the original path by a specified distance. The copy is also reshaped automatically so it fits nicely around the original path; its fill and stroke attributes match those of the original.

To offset a copy of a path:

1. Select an object **1**. Try using this command on a path that has a stroke, but no fill.

2. Choose Object > Path > Offset Path.

3. In the Offset field, enter the distance you want the offset path to be from the original path **2**. Be sure your Offset value is larger or smaller than the stroke weight of the original path so the copies will be visible.

4. Choose a Joins (bend) style: Miter (pointed), Round (semicircular), or Bevel (square-cornered).

5. *Optional:* Enter a different Miter Limit for the maximum amount the offset path's line weight (as measured from the inside to the outside of the corner point) can be enlarged before the miter join becomes a bevel join. The Miter limit value times the stroke weight value equals the maximum inner-to-outer corner measurement. What? Here's a simple rule of thumb: Use a high Miter Limit to create long, pointy corners; use a low Miter limit to create bevel joins.

6. Click OK **3**–**4**. The offset path will be a separate path from, and stacked behind, the original path. And regardless of whether the original object was open or closed, the offset path will be closed.

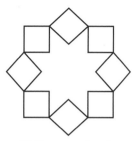

1 *The original path*

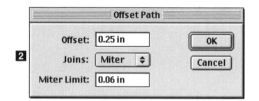

3 *After applying the Offset Path command*

4 *After recoloring the objects*

Offset a Copy of a Path

Chapter 6: Select/Copy ◆ Study Guide

Learning Objectives

- Select and deselect objects.
- Move objects.
- Align objects using smart guides.
- Hide/show objects and object attributes.
- Lock/unlock objects.
- Copy objects.

Get Up and Running Exercises

- Practice selecting objects. Start by drawing several shapes with any of the basic shape tools. Draw between five and ten of them. Keep it simple—the only requirement for this exercise is that the shapes each have a few anchor points and segments. How would you complete the following selection tasks?
  - ▲ Select the entire object by clicking on it once and without pressing any keys.
  - ▲ Select one anchor point.
  - ▲ Select two anchor points that aren't adjacent.
  - ▲ Select a segment.
  - ▲ Select three whole objects that aren't adjacent.
- Draw an ellipse. How can you draw a second ellipse below the first so that the top edge of the second ellipse is aligned exactly with the bottom of the first ellipse?
- Practice selecting multiple objects with like attributes. Choose Window > Stroke, apply a thick stroke weight to three of the objects, then choose Select > Deselect. How would you simultaneously select all three of the objects with the same thick stroke weight, without using the Selection, Direct selection, Lasso, or Direct-select Lasso tools? What do you do if the Magic Wand tool isn't selecting what you expect?
- How would you select everything except two objects—one with a thin stroke and one with a thick stroke?
- How can you quickly create a row of stars? How can you quickly make a grid of stars that's four stars wide and three stars deep?

Class Discussion Questions

- What's the difference between the Selection tool and the Direct-selection tool?

- If you choose Select > All and all the objects in the illustration don't become selected, what might be happening?

- If pressing the Shift key isn't constraining an object to the angles you expect, what should you do?

- What are two ways to tell if the pointer is directly over an anchor point?

- What's a convenient way to create a copy of an ellipse (not a circle) inside the original, with a diameter one pica less than the original ellipse?

Review Questions
Multiple choice

1. Which tool will let you select whole multiple paths by dragging a non-rectangular area?
   A. Direct-select Lasso tool
   B. Direct-selection tool
   C. Lasso tool
   D. Selection tool

2. If you see a hollow dot next to the Direct-selection tool pointer, what does it mean?
   A. The pointer is over an anchor point.
   B. The pointer is over a center point.
   C. The pointer is over a guide.
   D. The pointer is over a path segment.

3. How do you activate the Group-selection tool?
   A. Press Cmd/Ctrl when the Selection tool is active.
   B. Press Cmd/Ctrl when the Direct-selection tool is active.
   C. Press Option/Alt when the Direct-select Lasso tool is active.
   D. Press Option/Alt when the Direct-selection tool is active.

4. Which tool will let you instantly select all objects with the same fill color wherever they are in the document?
   A. Direct-selection tool
   B. Lasso tool
   C. Magic Wand tool
   D. Selection tool

5. Which key do you press to drag-copy objects with the Selection tool?
   A. Cmd/Ctrl
   B. Option/Alt
   C. Shift
   D. Spacebar

Fill-in-the-blank

1. To select a group nested within a larger group, use the _____.

2. To nudge objects by ten times the current preference value for Keyboard Increment, press the _____ key along with an arrow key.

3. The color of Smart Guides is the same as the current _____ color.

4. To locate and select all anchor points that aren't part of any path, choose Select > Object > _____.

5. To make the Smart Guides feature emphasizes object edges as you move the pointer over them, turn on the _____ preference.

Definitions

1. What is the Use Area Select preference?

2. In the Magic Wand palette, what is Stroke Weight Tolerance?

3. What are Smart Guides?

4. What does the Object > Path > Offset Path command do?

5. What is the Snapping Tolerance?

TRANSFORM 7

This chapter covers methods for transforming an object. You'll learn how to use the five individual transformation tools (Rotate, Scale, Reflect, Shear, and Blend), the Free Transform tool, an object's bounding box, the Transform Each command, the Transform Effect command, and the Make Blend command. The Transform palette is discussed on page 416, the Move command on page 415.

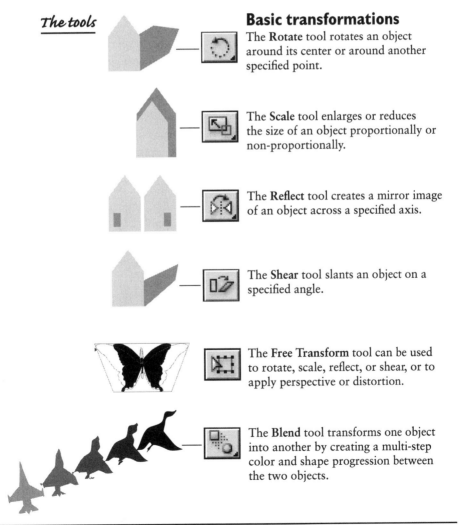

The tools

Basic transformations

The **Rotate** tool rotates an object around its center or around another specified point.

The **Scale** tool enlarges or reduces the size of an object proportionally or non-proportionally.

The **Reflect** tool creates a mirror image of an object across a specified axis.

The **Shear** tool slants an object on a specified angle.

The **Free Transform** tool can be used to rotate, scale, reflect, or shear, or to apply perspective or distortion.

The **Blend** tool transforms one object into another by creating a multi-step color and shape progression between the two objects.

Using the transformation tools

Before we delve into the individual transformation tools in detail, here's a summary of the basic ways they are used.

Dialog box method

Select the whole object, then double-click the Rotate, Scale, Reflect, or Shear tool to open the tool's dialog box or Control-click/Right-click in the document window and choose a command from the Transform submenu on the context menu **1**. The default point of origin at the object's center will now be visible. Check the Preview box in the tool dialog box, enter numbers (press Tab to apply a value and move to the next field), then click OK or click Copy.

To use a point of origin other than the object's center, select the object, choose a transform tool, then Option-click/Alt-click on or near the object to establish a new point of origin. A dialog box will open.

Dragging method

Select the whole object; choose the Rotate, Scale, Reflect, Shear, or Free Transform tool; position the pointer outside the object; then drag.

➤ Once the point of origin is established, for finer control position the pointer (arrowhead) far from the point of origin before dragging. You can use Smart Guides (Cmd-U/Ctrl-U) for positioning.

To use a point of origin other than the object's center **2**, select the object, choose an individual transform tool (not the Free Transform tool), and click to establish a new point of origin **3**, reposition the mouse **4**, then drag to complete the transformation **5**. The point of origin can also be dragged to a different location using the transform tool.

Hold down Option/Alt while dragging with an individual transform tool to transform a copy of the original (release the mouse first).

To transform an object using its bounding box, see page 103.

➤ Watch the rotate angle or other readouts on the Info palette as you transform an object.

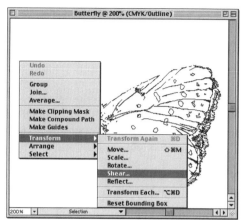

1 *Select an object, and then choose a command from the Transform submenu on the context menu.*

2 *Point of origin indicator*

3 *Click to establish a point of origin.*

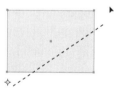

4 *Reposition the mouse.*

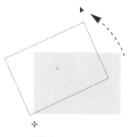

5 *Drag to transform.*

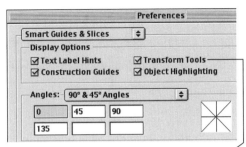

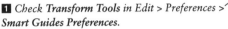

1 *Check **Transform Tools** in Edit > Preferences > Smart Guides Preferences.*

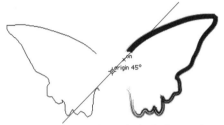

2 *Using Smart Guides with the **Reflect** tool.*

3 *Using Smart Guides with the **Scale** tool.*

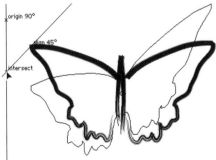

4 *Using Smart Guides with the **Shear** tool.*

Repeating a transformation

Once you have performed a transformation on an object (other than a blend), you can repeat the transformation using the same values by choosing Object > Transform > **Transform Again** (Cmd-D/Ctrl-D). If you make a copy of an object while transforming it and then apply Transform Again, yet another copy will be transformed.

➤ To constrain all transform commands to a custom angle, change the Constrain Angle in Edit > Preferences > General (Cmd-K/Ctrl-K).

Transforming fill patterns

If you transform an object that contains a pattern fill and Patterns is checked in the transformation tool's dialog box or Transform Pattern Tiles is checked in Edit > Preferences > General, the pattern will also transform. Checking or unchecking this option in one dialog box automatically resets it in the other dialog box.

To transform a pattern but not the object that contains it, uncheck Objects and check Patterns in the transformation tool's dialog box. Or choose any individual transformation tool except Free Transform, click to establish the point of origin, then hold down "~" and drag.

To use smart guides as you rotate, scale, or shear an object:

1. Choose Edit > Preferences > Smart Guides & Slices, and make sure Transform Tools is checked **1**. You can also choose a different Angles set or enter custom angles, if you like.

2. Make sure View > Smart Guides is turned on (has a checkmark).

3. Select the object to be transformed using the Selection (V) tool or Lasso tool.

4. Choose any individual transform tool except Free Transform.

5. As you drag the mouse to transform the object, Smart Guides will appear temporarily **2**–**4**. Move the pointer along a Smart Guide to transform along that axis. (More about smart guides on page 439.)

Use Smart Guides as you Transform

To rotate an object using a dialog box:

1. Select an object (or objects) using the Selection tool or the Lasso tool .

2. Double-click the Rotate tool if you want to rotate the object around its center. ⟳

or

Choose the Rotate tool, then Option/Alt click near the object to establish a new point of origin.

3. Check Preview.

4. Enter a positive Angle (then press Tab) to rotate the object counterclockwise or a negative Angle to rotate the object clockwise (-360–360) **2**.

5. *Optional:* If the object contains a pattern fill and you check Patterns, the pattern will rotate with the object. Checking Transform Pattern Tiles in Edit > Preferences > General does the same thing.

6. Click Copy to rotate a copy of the object (not the original object) and close the dialog box.

or

Click OK to rotate the original object **3**–**4**.

To rotate an object by dragging:

1. Select an object (or objects) using the Selection tool or the Lasso tool **1**.

2. Choose the Rotate tool (R). ⟳

3. Drag around the object to use the object's center as the point of origin.

or

Click to establish a new point of origin (the pointer will turn into an arrowhead), reposition the mouse as far from the origin as possible for better control, then drag to rotate the object.

or

To rotate a copy of the object, start dragging, then press Option/Alt (release the mouse before you release Option/Alt).

➤ Hold down Shift while dragging to rotate in 45° increments. Release the mouse before you release Shift.

➤ Press Cmd-D/Ctrl-D to repeat the last transformation on any selected object **5**.

1 *The shadow object is selected.*

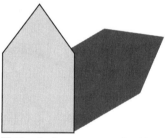

2 *Enter an Angle in the Rotate dialog box.*

3 *The shadow was rotated –60°, and then moved.*

4 *An object is copy-rotated.*

5 *And then the Transform Again command is applied twice (Cmd-D/Ctrl-D).*

Rotate

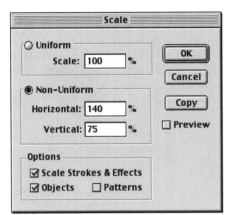

2 *The Scale dialog box*

2 *The original object*

3 *The object scaled **Uniformly**, **Patterns** box **checked***

4 *The original object scaled **Non-uniformly**, Patterns box **checked***

5 *The original object scaled **Non-uniformly**, Patterns box **unchecked***

To scale an object using a dialog box:

1. Select an object (or objects) using the Selection tool or the Lasso tool.

2. To scale the object from its center, double-click the Scale tool.
   or
   Choose the Scale tool, then Option/Alt click near the object to establish a new point of origin.

3. Check Preview.

4. To scale the object proportionally, click Uniform, then enter a Scale percentage (press Tab to apply) **1**.
   or
   To scale the object non-proportionally, click Non-Uniform, then enter in the Horizontal and Vertical percentages (press Tab to apply).

   Note: Enter 100 to leave a dimension unchanged.

5. *Optional:* Check Scale Strokes & Effects to also scale the stroke thickness and any effects from the Effects menu by the same percentage. This option can also be chosen in Edit > Preferences > General.

6. *Optional:* Check Patterns if the object contains a pattern fill and you want the pattern to scale with the object. Uncheck Objects to scale only the pattern and not the object.

7. Click Copy to scale a copy of the original (not the original object) and close the dialog box.
   or
   Click OK to scale the original object **2**–**5**.

➤ Enter a negative percentage in the Scale dialog box to rotate the selected object(s) 180°.

➤ You can enter any number in the Angle field in any Transform tool dialog box. Illustrator will substitute the nearest acceptable value between 360 and -360.

Scale

When you scale an object, the stroke may or may not scale accordingly depending on whether Scale Strokes & Effects is checked either in Edit > Preferences > General or the Scale dialog box. Checking or unchecking this option on in one location automatically resets it in the other location.

To scale an object by dragging:

1. Select an object (or objects) using the Selection tool or the Lasso tool.

2. Choose the Scale tool (S).

3. To scale from the object's center, drag (without clicking first) away from or toward the object.

   or

   Click near the object to establish a point of origin 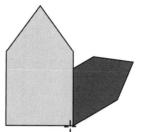 (the pointer will turn into an arrowhead), reposition the mouse 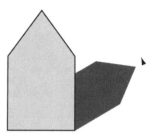, then drag away from the object to enlarge it or drag toward the object to shrink it 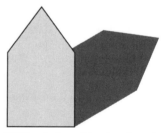.

   or

   To scale a copy of the object, start dragging, then press Option/Alt 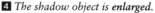 (release Option/Alt first).

   Shift-drag diagonally to scale the object proportionally. Release the mouse before you release Shift.

➤ To flip and scale simultaneously, drag completely across the object with the Scale tool.

1 *Click to establish a point of origin.*

2 *Reposition the mouse…*

3 *…then drag away from the object.*

4 *The shadow object is enlarged.*

Scale

Default angle

The default Horizontal angle is 0°; the default Vertical angle is 90°. The default starting point for measuring the degree of an angle is the horizontal *(x)* axis (the three o'clock position).

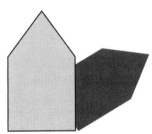

1 *In the Reflect dialog box, click Horizontal or Vertical or enter Angle.*

2 *The original objects*

3 *The shadow reflected across the Vertical Axis (90°).*

To reflect (flip) an object using a dialog box:

1. Select an object (or objects) using the Selection tool or the Lasso tool.

2. To reflect from the object's center, double-click the Reflect tool (O) 🔲 (it's on the Rotate tool pop-out menu).
   or
   Choose the Reflect tool, then Option/Alt click near the object to establish a new point of origin.

3. Check Preview.

4. Click Axis: Horizontal or Vertical (the axis the mirror image will flip across) **1**.
   or
   Enter a number between 360 and –360 in the Angle field (press Tab). Enter a positive number to reflect the object counterclockwise or a negative number to reflect the object clockwise. The angle is measured from the horizontal *(x)* axis.

5. *Optional:* Check the Patterns box if the object contains a pattern fill and you want the pattern to reflect with the object.

6. Click Copy to reflect a copy of the original (not the original object) and close the dialog box.
   or
   Click OK to reflect the object **2**–**3**.

➤ You can enter any Angle. Illustrator will substitute the nearest acceptable value.

To reflect an object by dragging:

1. Select the object (or objects) using the Selection tool or the Lasso tool.

2. Choose the Reflect tool (O). 🔲

3. Click near the object to establish a new point of origin (the pointer will turn into an arrowhead), reposition the mouse, then drag horizontally or vertically toward, across, or around the point of origin. The object will flip across the axis you create by dragging.

   Start dragging, then press Option/Alt to reflect a **copy** of the object.

   Shift-drag to **reflect** the object along a multiple of 45°. Release the mouse first.

To shear (slant) an object using a dialog box:

1. Select an object (or objects) using the Selection tool or the Lasso tool **1**.

2. To shear the object from its center, double-click the Shear tool (it's on the Scale tool pop-out menu). 🗇
   or
   Choose the Shear tool, then Option-click/Alt-click near the object to establish a new point of origin.

3. Check Preview.

4. Enter a number between 360 and −360 in the Shear Angle field (press Tab) **2**.

5. Click Axis: Horizontal or Vertical (the axis along which the object will be sheared) **3**.
   or
   Click Axis: Angle, then enter a number in the Angle field (press Tab). The angle will be calculated clockwise relative to the horizontal *(x)* axis **4**.

6. *Optional:* Check the Patterns box to shear a pattern fill with the object.

7. Click Copy to shear a copy of the original (not the original object) and close the dialog box.
   or
   Click OK to shear the original object.

To shear an object by dragging:

1. Select an object (or objects) using the Selection tool or the Lasso tool.

2. Choose the Shear tool. 🗇

3. To slant from the object's center, without clicking first, position the pointer outside the object, then drag away from the object.
   or
   Click near the object to establish a new point of origin, reposition the mouse, then drag.

   Start dragging, then press Option/Alt to shear a copy of the object. To shear the object to a multiple of 45°, start dragging, then hold down Shift. Release the mouse button first.

Shear (side tab)

Get the numbers

Each transformation dialog box displays the last-used values for that type of transformation (whether a tool or a dialog box was used) until those values are changed or you quit/exit Illustrator.

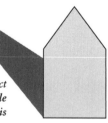

1 *The shadow object is selected.*

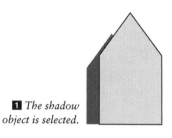

2 *In the Shear dialog box, enter a Shear Angle, then choose an Axis.*

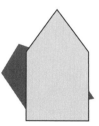

3 *The shadow object sheared at a −35° Angle on the Horizontal Axis*

4 *The shadow object sheared at a −35° Angle on a 35° Axis: Angle*

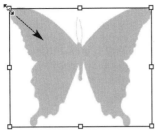

1 *Option-drag/Alt-drag to scale an object from its center.*

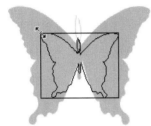

2 *The object is scaled down.*

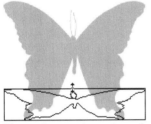

3 *To reflect an object, drag a bounding box handle all the way across it.*

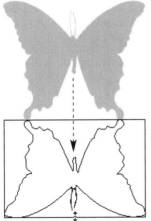

4 *A reflection of the object is made.*

This the fastest way to transform objects.

To transform an object using its bounding box:

1. If bounding boxes are currently hidden, choose View > Show Bounding Box (Command-Shift-B/Ctrl-Shift-B).

2. Select an object (or objects) using the Selection tool or the Lasso tool. A rectangular box with eight handles will surround the object(s). The handles and box will be the color of the object's layer.

3. To **scale** the object along two axes, drag a corner handle; to resize along one axis, drag a side handle. Shift-drag to resize proportionally. Option-drag/Alt-drag to scale the object from its center **1**–**2**. Option-Shift-drag/Alt-Shift-drag to do both. *Note:* You can't choose a point of origin.
   or
   To create a **reflection** (mirror image) of the object, drag a side handle all the way across it **3**–**4**.
   or
   To **rotate** the object, move the pointer slightly to the right of a corner handle, (the pointer will be a *curved* double-arrow), then drag in a circular direction.
   or
   To **rotate** the object 180°, drag a corner handle all the way across the object or Shift-drag a side handle. Option-drag/Alt-drag to do this from the object's center.

➤ If all of an object's anchor points are selected and then the Selection tool is chosen, the bounding box will appear.

After rotating a box using either the Rotate tool or the Free Transform tool, the bounding box will no longer align with the *x/y* axes of the page. The Reset Bounding Box command resets the orientation of the bounding box (but not the orientation of the object).

To square off the bounding box:

With the object selected, choose Object > Transform > Reset Bounding Box or Control-click/Right-click and choose Transform > Reset Bounding Box.

Transform using Bounding Box

The Free Transform tool does everything the transformation tools do, plus distort and perspective. *Note:* The Free Transform tool always works from the center of the object or objects. You can't choose a different point of origin.

To use the Free Transform tool:

1. Select an object(s) or a group. The Free Transform tool won't make a clone, so copy the object now if you want to transform a copy of it.

2. Choose the Free Transform tool (E).

3. To **scale** in two dimensions, drag a corner handle. Shift-drag to scale proportionally; Option-drag/Alt-drag to scale the object from its center; Option-Shift-drag/Alt-Shift-drag to do both. To resize the object in one dimension, drag a side handle.

   To **rotate** the object, position the pointer outside it, then drag in a circular motion. Shift-drag to rotate in 45° increments.

   To **shear**, drag a side handle then hold down Cmd/Ctrl and continue to drag **1**–**2**. To constrain the movement, drag a side handle, then Cmd-Shift-drag/Ctrl-Shift-drag. To shear along the *x* or *y* axis from the object's center, start dragging, then hold down Cmd-Option-Shift/Ctrl-Alt-Shift and continue to drag.

   To **reflect**, drag a side handle all the way across the object. To rotate the object 180°, drag a corner handle all the way across it. To reflect or rotate from the object's center, Option-drag/Alt-drag a side or corner handle. Include the Shift key to reflect or rotate proportionally.

   To **distort**, drag a corner (not a side) handle, then hold down Cmd/Ctrl and continue to drag **3**–**4**. *Note:* This doesn't work on type.

   To apply **perspective**, drag a corner handle, then hold down Cmd-Option-Shift/Ctrl-Alt-Shift and continue to drag **5**–**6**. The perspective will occur along the *x* or *y* axis, depending on which direction you drag. *Note:* You can't apply perspective to type.

4 The *distorted* object

3 *Distort*

1 *Shear*

2 *The sheared* object

5 *Perspective*

6 *The object with applied* **perspective**

Free Transform

The original formation

The formation rotated 15° via the Rotate tool

*The formation rotated 15° via the **Transform Each** command with the **Random** box **unchecked***

1 *The **Transform Each** command vs. the **Rotate** tool*

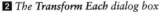

2 *The **Transform Each** dialog box*

Point of origin

*(See also **1** and **2** on the following page.)*

The Transform Each command modifies one or more selected objects relative to their *individual* center points. The transformation tools, by contrast, transform multiple objects relative to a single, *common* center point **1**. To make your illustration look less regular and more hand-drawn, apply the Transform Each command to a bunch of objects with the Random box checked.

To perform multiple transformations via Transform Each:

1. Select one or more objects. Objects in a group can't be transformed individually.

2. Choose Object > Transform > Transform Each (Cmd-Option-Shift-D/Ctrl-Alt-Shift-D).
   or
   Control-click/Right-click and choose Transform > Transform Each.

3. Check Preview, and move the dialog box out of the way, if necessary.

4. Do any of the following **2**:

   Move the Horizontal or Vertical **Scale** slider (or enter a percentage and press Tab) to scale the objects horizontally and/or vertically from their center point.

   Choose a higher Horizontal **Move** value to move the objects to the right or a lower value to move them to the left and/or choose a higher Vertical Move value to move the objects upward, or vice versa.

   Enter a number in the **Rotate** Angle field and press Tab, or rotate the dial.

   Check the **Reflect X** or **Reflect Y** box to create a mirror reflection of the objects.

   Check **Random** to have Illustrator apply random transformations within the range of the values you've chosen for Scale, Move, or Rotate. For example, at a Rotate Angle of 35°, a different angle between 0° and 35° will be used for each selected object. Check Preview on and off to get different random effects.

   Click a different **point of origin** (the point that will remain stationary).

5. Click OK.

Transform Each

1 *The original objects*

2 *After applying* **Transform Each** *(***Horizontal Scale** *120,* **Vertical Scale** *80,* **Horizontal Move** *13,* **Vertical Move** *–13, and* **Rotate** *17°—non-matching Horizontal and Vertical Scale values)*

If you apply transformations via the Transform Effect dialog box, you will be able to edit (not just undo) those transformations long after you've closed the dialog box, and even after you close and reopen the file.

To use the Transform Effect dialog box to apply editable effects:

1. Select one or more objects.

2. Choose Effect > Distort & Transform > Transform.

3. Follow the instructions for the Transform Each dialog box on the previous page. The Transform Effect dialog box looks and behaves just like the Transform Each dialog box, with one exception: In the Transform Effect dialog box, you can specify how many copies you want **3**.

4. To edit the transformation, select the object, then double-click "Transform" on the Appearance palette **4**. That reopens the Transform Effect dialog box. This is a sneak preview of what's to come in Chapter 19, Appearances/Styles.

3 *Apply* **editable** *effects via the* **Transform Effect** *dialog box.*

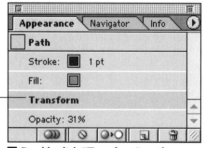

4 *Double-click "***Transform***" on the* **Appearance** *palette to edit a transformation.*

Creating blends
Blends are live!

Both the Blend tool and the Make Blend command create a multi-step color and shape progression between two or more objects. Using the Blend tool, you can control which parts of the objects are calculated for the blend, whereas the Make Blend command controls this function automatically.

If you reshape, recolor, or reposition any of the individual objects in a blend or reshape, reposition, or transform the path that controls the whole blend, the blend will update automatically. You can also alter the appearance of an existing blend by reshaping the straight path (spine) that the Blend tool or command creates using any path editing tool, or by selecting the blend and changing the number of steps or other options in the Blend Options dialog box.

To blend colors between objects without blending their shapes, use a Blend filter (see page 162).

Before you create a blend, keep these guidelines in mind:

- You can blend non-matching shapes and shapes with different fill and stroke attributes (even brush strokes).

- You can blend gradients or other blends, but not mesh objects.

- You can blend two open paths, two closed paths, or a closed path and an open path.

- If you blend two instances of the same symbol, the intermediate steps will be linked instances of the symbol. If you blend instances of different symbols, the intermediate steps won't be linked to the original symbols. In either case, the symbolism tools can be used on the blend.

Process or spot?

- If one of the original blend objects contains a **process** color and another object contains a **spot** color, the intermediate objects will be painted with **process** colors.

- If you blend objects containing more than one **spot** color, the intermediate objects will be painted with **process** colors.

- If you blend **tints** of the **same spot** color, the intermediate objects will be painted with graduated **tints** of that color. To blend between a spot color and white, change the white fill to 0% of the spot color.

To blend between objects using the Make Blend command:

1. Position two or more open paths or two or more closed paths (or even groups), allowing room for the transition shapes that will be created between them, and select all the objects using the Selection tool or the Lasso tool **1**.

2. Choose Object > Blend > Make (Cmd-Option-B/Ctrl-Alt-B) **2**–**3**.

3. To change the appearance of the blend, read the instructions on the following three pages.

➤ If you don't like the blend, use the Undo command or release the blend (instructions below).

➤ To prevent banding, see pages 111 and 451.

To release a blend:

1. Select the blend with the Selection tool (or using the Layers palette).

2. Choose Object > Blend > Release (Cmd-Option-Shift-B/Ctrl-Alt-Shift-B). The original objects and the *path* created by the blend will remain; the transitional blend objects will be deleted.

Recoloring blend objects

To recolor **all** the objects in a blend, use Filter > Colors > **Adjust Colors**.

To recolor one of the **original** blend objects, deselect the blend, choose the **Direct-selection** tool, select one of the **original** objects, then choose a color from the Color or Swatches palette. The transitional objects can't be recolored individually.

To recolor a blend of **symbols**, use the **Symbol Stainer** tool on a selected instance (see Chapter 16).

1 *The original objects: A white butterfly on top of a black butterfly.*

2 *After choosing Object > Blend > Make, with Spacing: Smooth Color chosen in the Blend Options dialog box (see the following page).*

3 *The original objects after choosing Object > Blend > Make, with Spacing: Specified Steps (7) chosen in the Blend Options dialog box (see the following page).*

1 *Choose **Spacing** and **Orientation** options for existing and future blends in the **Blend Options** dialog box.*

2 *Spacing: **Smooth Color***

3 *Spacing: **Specified Steps** (7)*

4 *Orientation: **Align to Page***

5 *Orientation: **Align to Path***

Note: If you change the settings in the Blend Options dialog box, the new settings will be applied automatically to any and all currently selected blends as well as to any subsequently created blends.

To choose or change blend options:

1. *Optional:* To change the blend options for any existing blends, select them now.

2. Double-click the Blend tool (W)(not the Gradient tool!).
   or
   Select an existing blend and choose Object > Blend > Blend Options.

3. Check Preview to preview changes on any currently selected blends.

4. Choose an option from the Spacing pop-up menu **1**:

   Smooth Color to have Illustrator automatically calculate the necessary number of blend steps (transition shapes) to produce smooth, non-banding color transitions **2**. This option may take a moment to preview on existing objects.

   Specified Steps, then enter the desired number of transition steps for the blend (press Tab to preview). Use this option if you want to create distinct, discernible transition shapes **3**.

   Specified Distance, then enter the desired distance between the transition shapes in the blend. The Specified Distance has no effect on the overall length of the blend.

5. Click Orientation: **Align to Page** (the first button) to keep the blend objects perpendicular to the page (on the horizontal axis) **4**.
   or
   Click Orientation: **Align to Path** (the second button) to keep the blend objects perpendicular to the blend path **5**.
   (To place blend objects on a user-drawn spine, see page 113.)

6. Click OK.

Blend Options

Editing blends

- To recolor any of the original objects in a blend, use the Direct-selection tool.

- To recolor all the objects in a blend, use a filter on the Filter > Colors submenu.

- To transform an entire blend, use a transform tool or the Free Transform tool.

- To reshape a blend path, move one of the original objects (Direct-selection tool) or use any of the path-reshaping tools (e.g., Direct-selection, Add-anchor-point, or Convert-anchor-point tool).

- Use the liquify tools to reshape a blend object or blend path.

The original blend

The same blend after recoloring the rightmost snowflake, adding points to the blend path, and reshaping the path

The 39 Steps

To **print** a Smooth Color blend, Illustrator automatically calculates the number of steps needed to produce a smooth blend based on the difference in CMYK color-component percentages between the blend objects (e.g., changes in the percentage of Magenta between each object), and based on the assumption that the blend will be output on a high-resolution device (1200 dpi or higher). To specify the number of steps for a blend, choose Object > Blend > Blend Options, choose Spacing: Specified Steps, then enter the desired number (1–1000) in the field. Banding is more likely to occur in a color blend if it spans a wide distance (wider than seven inches). For better results, use Adobe Photoshop to create a wide color blend, then place it into Illustrator.

Outputting blends to the Web is a whole different story. See pages 482 and 484.

The Reverse Front to Back command changes the stacking order of blend objects—not their *x/y* locations.

To reverse the stacking position of objects in a blend:

1. Select the blend with the Selection tool (or using the Layers palette; more about layers later) **1**.
2. Choose Object > Blend > Reverse Front to Back **2**. The original and transitional objects will now be in their reverse stacking order (e.g., what was originally the backmost object will now be the frontmost object, and vice versa).

The Reverse Spine command swaps the *x/y* location of all the blend objects, but it doesn't change their stacking position.

To reverse the location of objects in a blend:

1. Select the blend with the Selection tool (or using the Layers palette) **1**.
2. Choose Object > Blend > Reverse Spine. The blend objects will swap locations **3**.

1 *The original blend*

2 *After applying the Reverse Front to Back command*

3 *The previous figure after applying the Reverse Spine command*

To blend objects using the Blend tool:

1. Position two or more different-shaped open paths or two or more closed paths, allowing room for the transition shapes that will be created between them. You can apply different colors or gradients to each object.

2. Choose the Blend tool (W).

3. To let Illustrator decide which anchor points to use for the blend, click on the fill of the first object (but not on the center point).

   or

   If you want to control which anchor point will be used, click on an anchor point on the first object **1**. The little square on the Blend tool pointer will change from hollow to filled when it's over an anchor point.

4. Click on the fill or on an anchor point on the next object **2**. If the path is open, click on an endpoint. For the smoothest shape transitions, click on corresponding points on all the objects (e.g., the top left corner point of all the objects; not the top left corner point of one object and the lower right corner point of another object). You can add points in advance so the objects have an equal number of points. The blend will appear **3**–**4**.

   Repeat this step for any other objects you want to include in the blend. The blend will update automatically! See "Blends are live" on page 107.

5. To change the appearance of the blend, (e.g., change Specified Steps to Smooth Color), see page 109.

➤ If you don't like the blend, use Undo or choose Object > Blend > Release.

➤ If the original objects contain different pattern fills, the transition shapes will be filled automatically with the pattern fill from the topmost object.

➤ Apply a stroke color to the blend if you want the transition shapes to be clearly delineated. To do this after the blend is created, use the Selection tool, click the blend, then apply a stroke.

1 *Click on the fill or an anchor point of one object.*

2 *Then click on the fill or an anchor point of another object.*

3 *The blend appears.*

4 *This is what happens if you click on non-corresponding points.*

1 *Select a user-drawn path and a blend.*

2 *After choosing **Replace Spine**, the blend flows along the user-drawn path.*

To apply an existing blend to a path:

1. Create a blend, then draw a separate path along which you want the blend to flow. The path you draw can be closed or open. If it's closed, the blend will wrap around the object as best as it can.

2. Select both the blend and the path using the Selection tool or the Lasso tool **1**.

3. Choose Object > Blend > Replace Spine. The blend will now follow along the user-drawn path **2**.

➤ If you release a blend that has a user-drawn path (Object > Blend > Release), the path will be preserved, but it won't have a stroke. You can locate the path in Outline view or using Smart Guides (Object Highlighting).

➤ To change the orientation of the blend objects, select the blend, choose Object > Blend > Blend Options, then click the Orientation: Align to Page or Align to Path icon, whichever icon isn't currently highlighted (see **5** and **6** on page 109).

➤ Appearances and effects can be applied to blend objects, either before or after the blend is created. To learn more about blends and appearances, see page 329.

Apply Blend to Path

Use a blend to create a 3-D effect:

1. Select an object , and apply a fill color and a stroke of None.

2. Double-click the Scale tool.

3. Click Uniform, enter a number between 60 and 80 in the Scale field, then click Copy.

4. With the copy still selected, choose a lighter or darker variation of the original fill color (or black or white) . (For a process color, you can Shift-drag a process color slider on the Color palette to lighten or darken the color.)

5. Make sure the smaller object is in front of the larger object so you'll be able to see the blend, then select both objects using the Selection tool or the Lasso tool.

6. Choose Object > Blend > Make (Cmd-Option-B/Ctrl-Alt-B) . If the resulting blend doesn't look smooth, select it, double-click the Blend tool, choose Smooth Color from the Spacing pop-up menu, then click OK.

➤ You can modify either blend object at any time. Select the object using the Direct-selection tool, and then reposition or recolor it. You can scale the selected object using the Free Transform tool, the Scale tool, or the object's bounding box. The blend will redraw automatically.

➤ A similar effect can be achieved on a single object using Object > Create Gradient Mesh (choose Appearance: To Center).

1 *The original object*

2 *A reduced-size copy of the object is created, and a white fill is applied.*

3 *The two objects are blended together.*

4 *Here's another variation.*

Chapter 7: Transform ◆ Study Guide

Learning Objectives

- Transform objects using the five transformation tools: Rotate, Scale, Reflect, Shear, and Blend.

- Transform objects using an object bounding box and the Free Transform tool.

- Use the Transform Each command.

- Use the Effect > Distort & Transform > Transform command.

- Create blends using the Blend tool and the Make Blend command.

Get Up and Running Exercises

- Create the markings for a dial, such as a speedometer or volume control knob, as in the example below. (You won't need to add dial numbers in this exercise.) Start by drawing a circle, then draw a line segment from about the seven o'clock position to halfway to the center of the circle. How would you transform the line segment to quickly create the speed marks around the arc of the dial, to about the four o'clock position?

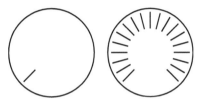

Before transforming (left), and after completing the exercise (right)

- Before starting the following transformation exercises, create an object to transform. Make the shape asymmetrical, so you can easily keep track of the transformation. A type character or word would work well for this (if you're not familiar with the type tools, ignore this suggestion!). If you do use type, select it and choose Type > Create Outlines (some transformation methods only affect path outlines, not text blocks).

(Continued on the following page)

Chapter 7: Transform ◆ Study Guide ◆ Exercises

■ Practice using transformation tools. Using the object you created, try applying each transformation using several different methods. For example, if you're practicing scaling, see if you can do it using:

▲ The Scale tool (by dragging)

▲ The Scale tool dialog box

▲ The Free Transform tool

▲ The object's bounding box

■ How can you apply a perspective effect to an object using a transformation tool?

■ Create a pattern made up of a single object transformed randomly, like an irregular pattern you might find on gift wrapping or wallpaper. An example is shown below. Start by duplicating one object into a grid six objects wide and six objects deep. How can you turn this into a randomized pattern by applying a dialog box command only once? (Don't use the symbol feature for this exercise.)

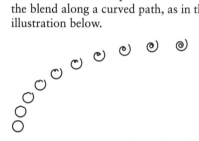

Before transforming (left), and after completing the exercise (right)

■ How can you use a blend to create a radio-wave illustration such as the one below on the left? After you create the blend, how can you create the version below on the right in just two quick steps involving the Weight option on the Stroke palette?

After blending (left), and after editing the blend (right)

■ Blend a circle into a spiral and run the blend along a curved path, as in the illustration below.

■ Create a sphere with 3-D shading, like a billiard ball.

Class Discussion Questions

- How can you scale an object while maintaining its exact proportions, but without using the keyboard?

- Why are there so many ways to transform an object? What are some situations that would require a specific transformation method?

- What's the difference between using the Object > Transform > Transform Each command and a transformation tool?

- How can you apply transformations so that they are completely reversible at any time in the future?

- When blending between colors or shades, how can you make sure the blend prints smoothly on a high-resolution printer?

Review Questions
Multiple choice

1. Which method of transforming doesn't let you move the point of origin?

   A. Free Transform tool

   B. Scale tool

   C. Reflect tool

   D. Shear tool

2. When dragging a transformation tool, which key do you press to transform a pattern but not the object that contains it?

   A. Cmd/Ctrl

   B. Option/Alt

   C. Shift

   D. Tilde (~)

3. What happens when you click a transformation tool instead of dragging it (and without pressing any keys)?

   A. The Free Transform tool is activated.

   B. The most recent transformation values for that tool are applied.

   C. The point of origin is repositioned where you clicked.

   D. The tool's dialog box opens.

4. Which of the following can't be blended?

   A. Meshes

   B. Paths with brush strokes

   C. Polar grids

   D. Stars

5. In a blend, which command reverses the location of the original objects?

   A. Object > Blend > Expand

   B. Object > Blend > Reverse Front to Back

   C. Object > Blend > Replace Spine

   D. Object > Blend > Reverse Spine

Fill-in-the-blank

1. The _____ tool slants an object on a specified angle.

2. To create a copy of an object as you drag to transform it, hold down the _____ key.

3. The path a blend follows is called the _____.

4. To edit one of the original objects in a blend, use the _____ tool.

5. To constrain object rotation to 45 degrees (or the current constrain angle preference), hold down the _____ key while dragging the Rotate tool.

6. If you blend objects containing more than one spot color, the intermediate objects will be painted with _____.

Definitions

1. What is the point of origin?

2. What does the Blend tool do?

3. What does the Reset Bounding Box command do?

4. What does the Free Transform tool do?

5. What does it mean to release a blend?

RESHAPE 8

In Chapter 5 you learned how to draw closed and open paths without thinking about their individual components. In this important chapter, you will learn how to reshape paths using the nuts and bolts that all paths are composed of: direction lines, direction points, anchor points, and segments. Once you learn how to alter the profile of an object by changing the number, position, or type of anchor points on its path, you'll be able to create just about any shape imaginable.

You will learn these techniques: to move anchor points, direction lines, or path segments to reshape a path; to convert a corner anchor point into a smooth anchor point (or vice versa) to reshape the segments that it connects; to add or delete anchor points and segments; and to use the Erase, Pencil, Paintbrush, Smooth, Twist, and Reshape tools to quickly reshape all or part of a path. You will also learn how to average anchor points; join endpoints; combine paths; split a path; cut paths using the Divide Objects Below command; and carve away parts of a path using the Knife tool. Three practice exercises are also included in this chapter.

Path Building Blocks

The path building blocks

Paths are composed of curved and/or straight segments. A curve consists of two anchor points connected by a curve segment, with at least one direction point and one direction line attached to each anchor point. An anchor point that connects a curve and a straight line segment has one direction line. An anchor point that connects two curve segments has a pair of direction lines.

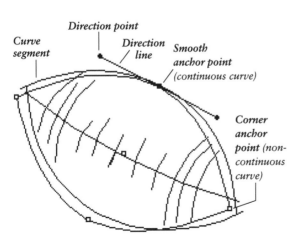

Curve segment
Direction point
Direction line
Smooth anchor point (continuous curve)
Corner anchor point (non-continuous curve)

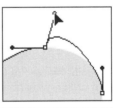

The **angle** of a direction line affects the **slope** of the curve into the anchor point.

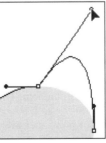

The **length** of a direction line affects the **height** of the curve.

Corners and curves

If you move an anchor point, the segments that are connected to it will reshape. If you move a curve segment, the connecting anchor points will remain stationary. If you move a straight line segment, connecting anchor points will move.

To move an anchor point or a segment:

1. Choose the Direct-selection tool (A).
   Note: You can move more than one point at a time, even points on different paths. To select them, Shift-click them individually or drag a marquee around them.

2. Drag an anchor point **1**, or drag the middle of a segment **2**, or press an arrow key. You can use Smart Guides for precise positioning (Cmd-U/Ctrl-U).

➤ Shift-drag to constrain the movement of an anchor point to a multiple of 45°.

➤ If all the anchor points on a path are selected, you will not be able to move an individual point or segment. Deselect the object, then reselect an individual point.

In the instructions above, you learned that you can drag a curve segment or an anchor point to reshape a curve. A more precise way to reshape a curve is to lengthen, shorten, or change the angle of its direction lines.

To reshape a curve segment:

1. Choose the Direct-selection tool (A).

2. Click an anchor point or a curve segment **3**.

3. Drag a direction point (the end of the direction line) toward or away from the anchor point **4**.
   or
   Rotate the direction point around the anchor point. The anchor point will remain selected when you release the mouse. Use Shift to constrain the angle.

➤ Direction line antennae on a smooth curve always move in tandem. They'll stay in a straight line even if the curve segment or anchor point they are connected to is moved.

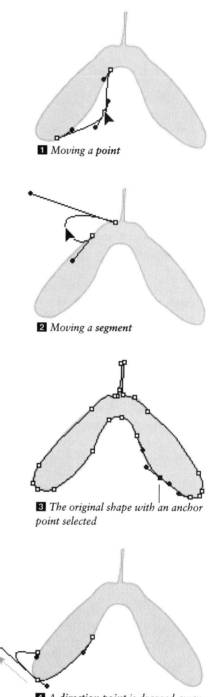

1 *Moving a point*

2 *Moving a segment*

3 *The original shape with an anchor point selected*

4 *A **direction point** is dragged away from its anchor point.*

Move Point or Segment; Reshape Curve

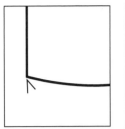

1 To convert a corner point into a smooth point, press with the Convert-anchor-point tool on the anchor point...

2 ...then drag away from the point.

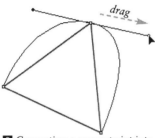

drag

3 Converting a **corner** point into a **smooth** point

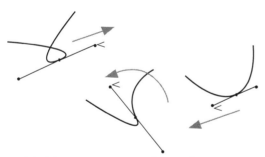

4 If the curve twists around the anchor point, rotate the direction line to un-twist it.

To convert a corner anchor point into a smooth anchor point:

1. Choose the Convert-anchor-point tool. It's on the Pen tool pop-out menu. (Shift-C is the shortcut, but it works better for right-handed mousers than left-handed mousers—grrr...).
   or
   Choose the Pen tool (P).

2. Cmd-click/Ctrl-click the edge of the object to display its anchor points.

3. If you're using the Convert-anchor-point tool, press on an anchor point **1**, then drag away from it **2**. Direction lines will appear as you drag. If you're using the Pen tool, do the same thing with Option/Alt held down.

4. *Optional:* To further modify the curve, choose the Direct-selection tool (A), then drag the anchor point or a direction line **3**.

   Note: If the new curve segment twists around the anchor point as you drag, keep the mouse button down, rotate the direction line back around the anchor point to undo the twist, then continue to drag in the new direction **4**.

➤ To reshape paths using a vector filter, try Filter > Stylize > Round Corners. To reshape paths using an effect, try Effect > Stylize > Round Corners.

Convert Corner Point into Smooth Point

To convert a smooth anchor point into a corner anchor point:

1. Choose the Convert-anchor-point tool (Shift-C). 📐

   or

   Choose the Pen tool (P). ✒

2. Cmd-click/Ctrl-click the edge of the object to display its anchor points.

3. If you're using the Convert-anchor-point-tool, click on a smooth anchor point—don't drag! Its direction lines will be deleted **1**–**2**. If you're using the Pen tool, do the same thing with Option/Alt held down.

The direction lines in a pinched curve rotate independently of each other—they don't stay in a straight line. In these instructions, you'll learn how to pinch an existing curve.

To pinch a curve inward:

1. Choose the Direct-selection tool (A).

2. Click the edge of an object to display its anchor points, then click a point **3**.

3. Choose the Convert-anchor-point tool (Shift-C). 📐

   or

   Choose the Pen tool (P) ✒ and hold down Option/Alt.

4. Drag a direction point at the end of one of the direction lines. The curve segment will reshape as you drag **4**. Release Option/Alt, if it's pressed down.

5. Choose the Direct-selection tool (if it isn't already chosen), click the anchor point, then drag the other direction line for that anchor point **5**.

➤ To revert an independent-rotating direction line pair back to its previous straight-line alignment and produce a smooth, unpinched curve segment, choose the Convert-anchor-point tool, then press on, and drag away from, the anchor point (if you just click on it, you'll create a corner).

1 *Click with the Convert-anchor-point tool on a smooth point...*   **2** *...to convert it into a corner point.*

3 *A point is selected on an object.*

4 *A **direction line** is moved independently using the **Convert-anchor-point** tool.*

5 *The second **direction line** is moved.*

Nice curves

It's hard to get a symmetrical curve if you place points at the high point of a curve.

You'll get a more symmetrical curve if you place points only at the ends.

1 *Click on a segment to add a new point…*

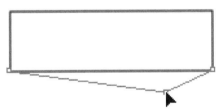

2 *…and then move the new anchor point, if desired.*

Adding points

Another way to reshape a path is to manually add or delete anchor points from it. Adding or deleting points from a closed path won't split or open it.

Note: If you want to use the Pen tool to add points to a path, make sure Disable Auto Add/Delete is unchecked in Edit > Preferences > General. Then all you have to do is click a segment on a selected path to add a point to it.

To add anchor points to a path manually:

1. Choose the Selection tool (V) **⬉** or the Lasso tool, **⬗** then select the object you want to add a point or points to.

2. Choose the Add-anchor-point tool (+). **⬗** It's on the Pen tool pop-out menu.
or
Choose the Pen tool (P). **⬗** See the Note, above.

3. Click the edge of the object. A new, selected anchor point will appear **1**. Repeat, if desired, to add more points.

   Note: An anchor point added to a curve segment will be a smooth point with direction lines. An anchor point added to a straight segment will be a corner point.

4. *Optional:* Use the Direct-selection tool (A) to move the new anchor point (or its direction lines) **2**.

➤ Hold down Shift to disable the Auto Add/Delete function of the Pen tool. Release Shift before releasing the mouse.

➤ If you don't click precisely on a segment with the Add-anchor-point tool, a warning prompt may appear. Click OK, then try again.

➤ Hold down Option/Alt to use the Delete-anchor-point tool when the Add-anchor-point tool is selected, and vice versa.

Add Anchor Points

The Add Anchor Points command inserts one anchor point midway between every two existing anchor points in a selected object.

To add anchor points to a path using a command:

1. Choose the Selection tool (V) or the Lasso tool, then select the object or objects to which you want to add points.

2. Choose Object > Path > Add Anchor Points **1**–**3**. Repeat, if desired.

1 *The original object*

Handy shortcuts

Pen tool	**P**
Add-anchor-point tool	**+**
Delete-anchor-point tool	**-**
Convert-direction-point tool	**Shift-C**
Pencil tool	**N**
Paintbrush tool	**B**
Scissors tool	**C**
Direct-select Lasso tool	**Q**
Access Convert-direction-point tool with Pen tool chosen	**Option/Alt**
Disable Auto Add/Delete function of Pen tool	**Shift**
Access last-used selection tool with Pen tool chosen	**Cmd/Ctrl**
Use Delete-anchor-point tool when Add-anchor-point tool is chosen, and vice versa	**Option/Alt**
Access Smooth tool with Pencil or Paintbrush tool chosen	**Option/Alt**
Average points	**Cmd-Option-J/ Ctrl-Alt-J**
Join points	**Cmd-J/Ctrl-J**
Average and join points	**Cmd-Option- Shift-J/Ctrl-Alt- Shift-J**

2 *After **adding anchor points** to the original object and then applying the Punk and Bloat filter (Punk 70%)*

Diane Margolin

3 *After adding **more anchor points** and then applying the Punk and Bloat filter (Bloat 70%)*

1 *The pointer is positioned over an endpoint.*

2 *The path is added onto.*

3 *The pointer is positioned over an endpoint. Note the slash next to the pen.*

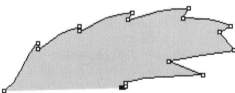

4 *After clicking the endpoint, it becomes solid.*

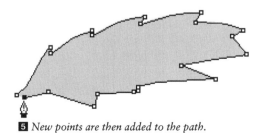

5 *New points are then added to the path.*

You can use the Pencil tool to add to any open path. It doesn't matter which tool was used to draw the path initially, and the path can have a brush stroke.

To add to an open path using the Pencil tool:

1. Choose the Selection tool (V), then select an open path.

2. Choose the Pencil tool (N).

3. Position the pointer directly over an endpoint, then draw an addition to it. When you release the mouse, the path will remain selected.

➤ If you end up with a separate path instead of an addition to an existing path, delete the new path and try again.

To add to a brush stroke path using the Paintbrush tool:

1. Choose the Selection tool (V), then select an open path that has a brush stroke.

2. Choose the Paintbrush tool (B).

3. Position the pointer directly over an endpoint, then draw an addition to it **1**. When you release the mouse, the path will remain selected **2**.

To add a segment to an open path:

1. Choose the Pen tool (P).

2. Position the pointer over the endpoint of one of the paths to which you want to add a segment (the path doesn't have to be selected). A slash will appear next to the Pen pointer when the tool is positioned correctly **3** (use Smart Guides!).

3. Click the endpoint to make it a corner point or drag to make it a smooth point. The point will become solid **4**.

4. Position the pointer where you want the additional anchor point to appear.

5. Again, click to create a corner point or drag to create a smooth point **5**.

6. Continue to add points, if desired. Choose another tool when you're done.

➤ To close a path or join two separate paths using the Pen tool, see page 130.

Deleting points

Note: If you want to use the Pen tool to delete points from a path, make sure the Disable Auto Add/Delete box is unchecked in Edit > Preferences > General. Then all you have to do to delete a point is click on it.

To delete anchor points from a path:

1. Choose the Delete-anchor-point tool (-). It's on the Pen tool pop-out menu.
   or
   Choose the Pen tool (P).

2. Cmd-click/Ctrl-click the edge of the object from which you want to delete anchor points.

3. Click an anchor point (don't press Delete!). The point will be deleted and an adjacent point will become selected **1**–**2**. Repeat to delete other anchor points, if desired.

➤ Hold down Shift to disable the add/ delete function of the Pen tool. Release Shift before releasing the mouse button.

➤ If you don't click precisely on an anchor point with the Delete-anchor-point tool, you'll either hear a beep (if Disable Warnings is checked in General Preferences) or a prompt will appear (if Disable Warnings is unchecked). You can use Smart Guides (Text Label Hints option) to help you find anchor points.

1 *Click an anchor point with the **Delete-anchor-point** tool (or the Pen tool).*

2 *The point is removed.*

1 *The original objects*

2 *Using the Erase tool*

3 *Reshaping a path using the **Pencil** tool. (Caps Lock was pressed to turn the cursor into a crosshair.)*

4 *The path is reshaped.*

Quick reshaping

The Erase tool deletes points, too—but you don't have to click on them individually.

To erase part of a path using the Erase tool:

1. Choose the Erase tool. It's on the Pencil tool pop-out menu.
2. Cmd-click/Ctrl-click an object (not a gradient mesh or a text path).
3. Position the eraser (black) part of the pencil pointer directly over the area from which you want to remove points, then drag once across that area **1**–**2**. If you erase points from a closed path, you'll end up with an open path. If you erase points from an open path (not endpoints), you'll end up with two separate paths.

You already know how to use the Pencil and Paintbrush tools to draw freehand shapes. Now we'll show you how they can be used for quick-'n'-easy reshaping.

To reshape a path using the Pencil or Paintbrush tool:

1. To reshape a non-brush-stroked path, choose the Pencil tool (N) **3**.
   or
   To reshape a brush-stroked path, choose the Pencil tool (N) or the Paintbrush tool (B).
2. Cmd-click/Ctrl-click on a path to select it.
3. Position the pointer directly over the edge of the path, then start dragging **3**. If you want the path to close up or stay closed, finish up over another edge of the path. The path will reshape instantly **4**.

➤ Be sure to position the pointer right on the edge of the path. If you don't, you'll create a new path instead of a reshaped path. Press Caps Lock and nudge the mouse to turn the pointer into a Precise Cursor (crosshair). Press Caps Lock again to restore the default cursors.

➤ To add to an open path using the Pencil or Paintbrush tool, see page 121.

To smooth part of an existing path:

1. Choose the Selection tool (V) or the Lasso tool, select an open or closed path, then choose the Smooth tool  (it's on the Pencil tool pop-out menu).

   or

   If the Pencil or Paintbrush tool is currently chosen, Cmd-click/Ctrl-click an open or closed path to select it, then hold down Option/Alt to access the Smooth tool.

2. Drag along the path. Any bumps on the path will be smoothed out **1**. Some anchor points may be removed. Next, read about the Smooth Tool Preferences, which affects how drastic an effect this tool may have on a path.

To choose settings for the Smooth tool:

1. Double-click the Smooth tool.

2. Choose a Fidelity value (0.5–20) **3**–**4**. The higher the Fidelity, the more anchor points will be removed.

3. Choose a Smoothness value (0–100). The higher the Smoothness value, logically, the greater the amount of smoothing; the lower the smoothness, the less drastic the reshaping.

4. Click OK.

➤ Click Reset to reset the preferences to their defaults.

1 *Using the Smooth tool*

2 *Smooth Tool Preferences*

3 *The Smooth tool used with **high Fidelity** and **Smoothness** settings.*

4 *The Smooth tool used on the original object with **moderate Fidelity** and **Smoothness** settings.*

1 *The* **Zig Zag** *dialog box*

Some of the Illustrator filters and effects can be used to explode a simple shape into a more complex one in one fell swoop. The Zig Zag filter, for example, adds anchor points to a path or line and then moves those points to produce waves or zigzags. The Effect menu version applies the Zig Zag effect without actually altering the path. Effect menu commands are reeditable; Filter menu commands are not. (This is just a preview. Read more about effects and filters in Chapter 22.)

To apply the Zig Zag effect:
1. Select a path.
2. Choose Effect > Distort & Transform (upper part of the menu) > Zig Zag.
3. Check Preview **1**–**5**.
4. Click Points: Smooth (bottom of the dialog box) to make curvy waves or click Corner to create sharp-cornered zigzags.
5. To move the added points by a percentage of the size of the object, click Relative, then choose a Size percentage.
   or
   To move the added points a specified distance, click Absolute, then choose the actual distance via the Size slider or field (the increment is chosen in File > Document Setup: Units).
6. Choose a number of Ridges per segment for the number of anchor points to be added between existing points. If you enter a number, press Tab to preview.
7. Click OK.

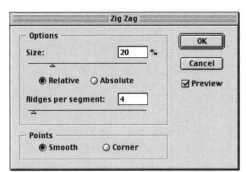

2 *The original star*

3 *After applying the* **Zig Zag** *effect (Size 45, Ridges 4, Smooth)*

4 *The original circle*

3 *After applying the* **Zig Zag** *effect (Size 24, Ridges 20, Corner)*

The Twist tool, just for the sheer pleasure of confusing you, was called the Twirl tool in *10.0!* previous application versions.

To use the Twist tool:
1. Select an object or objects.
2. Choose the Twist tool (it's on the Rotate tool pop-out menu).
3. Drag to twist the object from its center **6**–**7**. Or click to establish a point of origin, then drag; the object will twist around that point.

6 *The original objects*

7 *After using the* **Twist** *tool*

Zig Zag Effect; Twist Tool

125

The Reshape tool is hard to describe in words. It's the best tool for gentle reshaping because it causes the least amount of distortion. Our favorite way to use this tool is to select a handful of points with it, then drag. That portion of the path will keep its overall contour while it elongates or contracts, and the rest of the path will stay put.

To use the Reshape tool:

1. Click on the edge of a path using the Direct-selection tool. Only one point or segment should be selected.

2. Choose the Reshape tool (it's on the Scale tool pop-out menu).

3. Drag any visible point. A square border will display around the point when you release the mouse.
   or
   Drag any segment of the path. A new square border point will be created.
   or
   Try this: Shift-click or marquee multiple points on the path using the Reshape tool (squares will display around these points), then drag. For smooth reshaping, leave at least one point on the path unselected (with no square around it) to act as an anchor for the shape **1**–**2**.

➤ Option-drag/Alt-drag with the Reshape tool to make a copy of the object as it's reshaped.

➤ Choose Edit > Undo to undo the last Reshape.

➤ To reshape multiple paths at the same time, leave at least one point on each path unselected by the Reshape tool (with no square around it) to act as an anchor. For fun, try this on a series of lines. Their endpoints will remain stationary.

➤ A path can also be reshaped using the Warp tool, which is discussed on page 367 (try using a small brush size and low intensity). Also compare the Reshape tool, which adds one new point a time, with the Liquify tools, which add many new points as they perform a more drastic reshaping function.

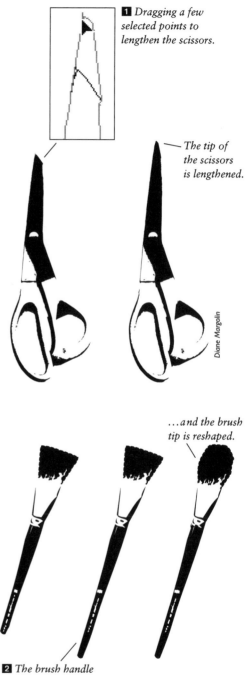

1 *Dragging a few selected points to lengthen the scissors.*

The tip of the scissors is lengthened.

Diane Margolin

...and the brush tip is reshaped.

2 *The brush handle is lengthened...*

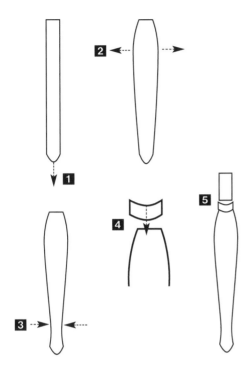

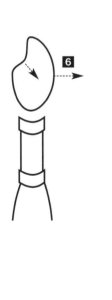

Exercise

Draw a paintbrush using the Reshape tool

1. Using the Rectangle tool, draw a narrow vertical rectangle, white fill, black stroke.

2. Choose the Direct-selection tool (A), deselect the shape, then click on the edge of the path.

3. Choose the Reshape tool, then drag downward from the middle of the bottom segment **1**.

4. Drag the upper middle of the right vertical segment slightly outward and drag the upper middle part of the left vertical segment outward the same distance **2**.

5. Drag each side of the bottom vertical segments inward to pinch the stem **3**.

6. Draw a small horizontal rectangle. Then choose the Direct-selection tool, deselect the rectangle, then click its edge.

7. Choose the Reshape tool again, click the middle of the top segment, Shift-click the middle of the bottom segment, then drag downward **4**.

8. Choose the Selection tool (V), place the rectangle over the top of the brush stem, scale it to fit.

9. Draw a vertical rectangle above the horizontal rectangle in a slightly narrower width. Choose Object > Arrange > Send to Back **5**.

10. Using the Selection tool, Option-Shift/Alt-Shift drag the horizontal rectangle up to the top of the vertical rectangle.

11. Using the Ellipse tool, draw an oval for the brush tip. Choose the Direct-selection tool (A), deselect the oval, then click the edge of the oval path.

12. Choose the Reshape tool, drag the right middle point outward, drag the upper left segment inward **6**, and drag the top point upward to lengthen the tip **7**.

13. With the Selection tool, move the brush tip over the brush stem, then choose Object > Arrange > Send To Back.

Averaging points

The Average command reshapes one or more paths by precisely realigning their endpoints or anchor points along the horizontal and/or vertical axis.

To average points:

1. Choose the Direct-selection tool (A) or Direct-select Lasso tool (Q).

2. Shift-click or marquee two or more anchor points **1**. They can be on different paths.

3. Choose Object > Path > Average (Cmd-Option-J/Ctrl-Alt-J).
   or
   Control-click/Right-click on the artboard and choose Average from the context menu.

4. Click **Horizontal** to align the points along the horizontal *(x)* axis **2**. Points will move vertically.
   or
   Click **Vertical** to align the points along the vertical *(y)* axis. Points will move horizontally.
   or
   Click **Both** to overlap the points along both the horizontal and vertical axes. Choose this option if you're going to join them into one point (instructions on the following page).

5. Click OK **3**.

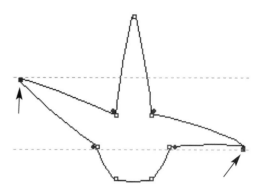

1 *Two anchor points are selected.*

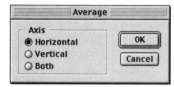

2 *Click an Axis button in the Average dialog box.*

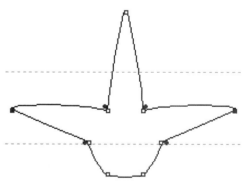

3 *After averaging the selected points, Axis: Horizontal, the points now align horizontally.*

Average Anchor Points

All at once

You can use this keystroke to **average** and **join** two selected endpoints: Cmd-Option-Shift-J/ Ctrl-Alt-Shift-J. Don't apply this to a selected path.

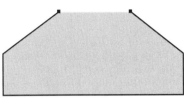

1 *Two endpoints are selected.*

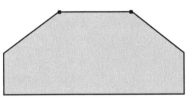

2 *The endpoints are joined, and a segment is added between them automatically.*

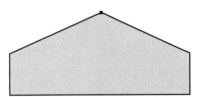

3 *Click Points: Corner or Smooth in the Join dialog box.*

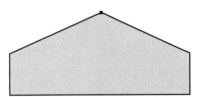

4 *This is Figure* **1** *after the two endpoints were averaged and then joined into* **one** *point.*

Joining

If you align two endpoints on top of each other and then execute the Join command with the endpoints selected, they will combine into one anchor point (that's method 1, below). If the endpoints are not on top of each other when they're joined, a new straight segment will be created between them. The Join command won't add direction lines to the new anchor point.

Note: The endpoints you join can be on separate open paths or on one open path. If you join an open path with a path in a group, the resulting path will be outside the group.

To join two endpoints:

Method 1

1. Choose the Direct-selection tool (A) or Direct-select Lasso tool (Q).

2. *Optional:* If you want to combine two endpoints into one, move one endpoint on top of the other manually and marquee them to select them both, or use the Average command (Axis: Both) to align them (instructions are on the previous page).

3. Marquee two endpoints **1**.

4. Choose Object > Path > Join (Cmd-J/ Ctrl-J) or Control-click/ Right-click on the artboard and choose Join from the context menu. If the endpoints are not on top of each other, the Join command will connect them with a straight line segment **2**.

If the endpoints are right on top of each other, the Join dialog box will open **3**. In the Join dialog box:

Click **Corner** to join corner points into one corner point with no direction lines; or to connect two smooth points into one smooth point with independent-moving direction lines; or to connect a corner point and a smooth point into a smooth point with one direction line. This is the default setting.

or

(Continued on the following page)

Join Endpoints

Click **Smooth** to connect two smooth points into a smooth point with direction lines that move in tandem.

5. Click OK.

Method 2

1. Choose the Pen tool (P).

2. Position the pointer over the endpoint of one of the paths you want to join. A small slash will appear next to the Pen pointer when the tool is positioned correctly ▮1 (and the word "anchor," if you're using Smart Guides with the Text Label Hints option checked).

3. Click the endpoint.

4. Position the pointer over the other end-point of the same path (a small hollow circle will appear next to the Pen pointer) or an endpoint on another path (a small square with a line behind it will appear next to the pointer) ▮2.

5. Click the second endpoint. A new segment will appear between the two points you clicked on ▮3.

➤ If the path has an effect applied to it that makes it hard to locate its actual end-points, use Smart Guides to help you.

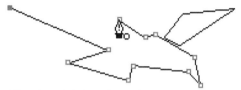

▮1 *To join two endpoints, position the* **Pen** *over one* **endpoint**...

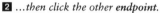

▮2 *...then click the other* **endpoint**.

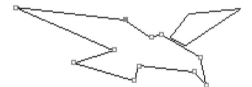

▮3 *The two points are joined by a* **new segment**.

Join Endpoints

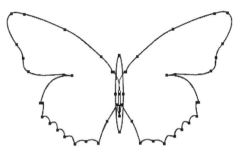

1 *Two or more objects are arranged so they overlap, and then they're selected.*

2 *After clicking the Add to Shape Area button on the Pathfinder palette, the individual shapes are combined into a single shape.*

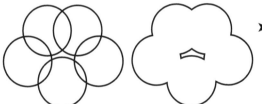

3 *The original objects*　　**4** *After applying the Add to Shape Area command*

5 *The original objects*　　**6** *After applying the Add to Shape Area command*

Using the tools that create shapes, such as the Rectangle, Ellipse, Star, or even the Pencil or Paintbrush, together with the reshaping functions covered in this chapter and occasionally some of the Pathfinder palette commands that are discussed in Chapter 17, you can create complex objects without having to draw with the Pen tool.

Rather than joining individual points, the shape mode commands on the Pathfinder palette combine whole objects. Here's an introduction to one of the most straightforward and useful shape mode commands: Add to Shape Area.

To combine objects using a command:

1. Position two or more objects so they overlap **1**.

2. Choose any selection tool.

3. Marquee at least some portion of all the objects.

4. On the Pathfinder palette, click the Add to Shape Area (first) button. The individual objects will combine into one closed compound shape **2**–**6** and will be colored with the topmost object's paint attributes. To learn more about compound shapes, see Chapter 17.

➤ A stroke color that's applied to the new object will appear only on the perimeter of the overall combined shape, not on the interior segments. The interior segments are editable, but you can't apply a stroke color to them. If at some point you want to delete those interior segments, click Expand on the Pathfinder palette.

➤ You can use the new closed object as a masking object. (You could not have created a single mask with the original objects before they were united.)

Add to Shape Area Command

Slicing and dicing

The Scissors tool can be used either to open a closed path or split an open path into two paths. A path can be split at an anchor point or in the middle of a segment.

To split a path:

1. Choose any selection tool.

2. Click on an object to display its points. *Note:* You can split a closed path with text inside it (area text), but you can't split an open path that has text on it or inside it.

3. Choose the Scissors tool (C). ✂

4. Click on the object's path **1**. If you click once on a **closed** path, it will turn into a single, open path. If you click in **two** different spots on a closed path, the object will be split into two open paths. If you click once on an **open** path, it will split into two paths.

   If you click on a **segment**, two new endpoints will appear, one on top of the other. If you click on an anchor **point**, a new anchor point will appear on top of the existing one, and it will be selected.

To move the two new endpoints apart:

5. Choose the Direct-selection tool (A). ▶

6. Drag the selected point away to reveal the other new endpoint underneath it **2**. (To move the bottom endpoint instead, marquee both endpoints, Shift-click the top one, then press and hold an arrow key.)

This is a quick way to split a path, albeit not nearly as clean as the method described above. If you delete a point from a closed path, the adjacent segments will be deleted; if you delete an endpoint from an open path, the adjacent segment will be deleted; and if you delete a point or segment within an open path, it will split into two shorter paths.

To split a path by deleting a point or a segment:

1. Deselect the object you want to split.

2. Choose the Direct-selection tool (A). ▶

3. Click an anchor point or segment.

4. Press Delete/Backspace.

1 *Click with the Scissors tool on an anchor point or a segment.*

There is no segment, and thus no stroke, between the endpoints.

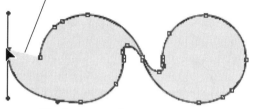

2 *After moving the new endpoint. If you apply a stroke color to an open path, you'll be able to see where the missing segment is. An open path can have a fill.*

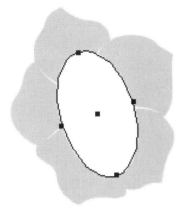

1 *The white oval is the cutting object.*

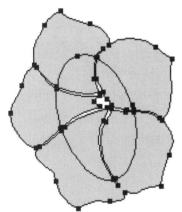

2 *After choosing Divide Objects Below, all the resulting objects become selected.*

3 *After recoloring the five separate paths that originally formed an oval.*

The Divide Objects Below command uses an object like a cookie cutter to cut the objects underneath it, and then deletes the cutting object. *Note:* The Divide Objects Below command was called the Slice command in previous versions of Illustrator.

To cut objects using the Divide Objects Below command:

1. Create or select an object to be used as the cutting shape. The Slice command will cause this object to be deleted, so make a copy of it now if you want to preserve it.

2. Place the cutting object on top of the objects you want to cut **1**.

3. Make sure no other objects are selected except the cutting object.

4. Choose Object > Path > Divide Objects Below. The topmost shape (cutting object) will be deleted automatically and the underlying objects will be cut into separate paths where they meet the edge of the cutting object **2**–**3**.

   The resulting objects will be ungrouped, if they were previously in a group, and will also be selected.

➤ To prevent an object from being affected by the Divide Objects Below command, hide or lock it (see pages 194–195).

Divide or Divide Objects Below?

Compare the **Divide Objects Below** command, discussed on this page, with the **Divide** command on the Pathfinder palette, which is discussed on pages 301–302. With Divide Objects Below, the top cutting object is deleted and the resulting objects aren't grouped. With Divide, the paint attributes of the topmost object are preserved, though the object is divided, and the resulting objects are grouped. You'll usually end up with smaller pieces with Divide than with Divide Objects Below.

The Knife tool reshapes paths like a carving knife, and is a wonderful tool for artists who have a freehand drawing style.

Note: The Knife tool works on a closed path or a filled, open path, but not on an unfilled open path. To carve up type, first convert it to outlines.

To cut an object into separate shapes:

1. *Optional:* If you select an object (or objects) before using the Knife tool, the tool won't cut any of the unselected objects. This is useful if there are many objects close together in the illustration and you don't want them all to be cut. If you don't select any objects first, any object the Knife passes across is fair game.

2. Choose the Knife tool (it's on the Scissors tool pop-out menu). Don't confuse it with the Slice tool!

3. Starting from outside the object(s), drag completely across it to divide it in two or carve off a chunk of it ▮–▮.
   or
   Option-drag/Alt-drag to cut in a straight line. (Press and hold Option/Alt before dragging.) Option-Shift-drag/Alt-Shift-drag to constrain the cutting strokes to a multiple of 45°.

➤ If you make a curved or circular cut completely inside the object (not across its edges) with the Knife, the resulting shape will be a compound and the line you created using the Knife will be like a rip or tear in the object. To open up the tear, use the Direct-selection tool to select it, then pull on its direction lines or segments.

➤ Choose Object > Group to group the newly separated shapes together, and then use the Direct-selection tool if you need to select individual shapes within the group.

▮ *The original mother and child elephants.*

▮ *After carving hills and valleys using the Knife tool to create more realistic elephant shapes.*

▮ *The final image, after applying a black fill.*

Diane Margolin

Knife Tool

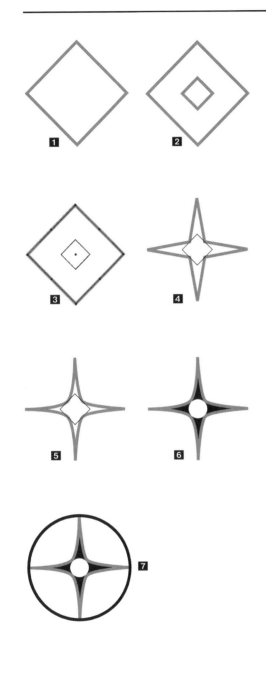

Exercise
Change a square into a star

1. Choose the Rectangle tool (M). Choose a fill of None and a stroke of 2 pt. on the Color palette (see Chapter 9).

2. Click on the artboard.

3. In the Rectangle dialog box, enter 2″ in the Width field, click the word Height, then click OK.

4. Double-click the Rotate tool, enter 45 in the Angle field, then click OK **1**.

5. Double-click the Scale tool, enter 30 in the Uniform Scale field, then click Copy **2**.

6. Choose View > Guides > Make Guides (Cmd-5/Ctrl-5) to turn the small diamond into a guide.

7. Choose the Selection tool, then select the large diamond shape. Choose Object > Path > Add Anchor Points **3**.

8. Choose the Direct-selection tool (A). Deselect, then click on the edge of the diamond.

9. Drag each of the new midpoints inward until it touches the guide shape. Use Smart Guides to drag on a 45° angle **4**.

10. Choose the Convert-anchor-point tool (Shift-C), and drag each of the inner midpoints to create a curve. Drag clockwise and drag along the edge of the guide shape **5**.

11. Choose the Ellipse tool (L), position the pointer over the center point of the star shape, then Option-Shift-drag/Alt-Shift-drag until the circle touches the curves of the star.

12. Fill the circle with white, stroke of None. Apply a black fill and a gray stroke to the star shape **6**.

13. *Optional:* Select the circle. Choose the Scale tool (S). Start dragging, hold down Option-Shift/Alt-Shift, and continue to drag until the copy of the circle touches the outer tips of the star. Fill the large circle with None, and apply a 2-point stroke **7**.

Exercise
Draw a light bulb

1. Draw a **circle** (about 1" dia.) and a **rectangle** (about .5" x .5"). Apply a fill of None and a 4-point black stroke to both objects.

2. Select the bottom point of the circle with the **Direct-selection** tool (A), and drag the point downward. Select **both** objects using the Selection tool.

3. Option-click/Alt-click the **Add to Shape Area** button on the Pathfinder palette. Use the **Add-anchor-point** tool (+) to add a point on the bottom segment (1), then use the **Direct-selection** tool to drag the new point downward.

(1)

4. Click on each point where the curve meets the straight line segment (2). Rotate the direction line upward to 90° vertical. Use Smart Guides for this.

(2)　　　　*(2)*

5. Make sure the bulb has a white fill.

6. Create a rounded rectangle or an oval that's wider than the base of the bulb. Rotate it using the **Rotation** tool (R). Choose the Selection tool, and Option-Shift/Alt–Shift drag two copies downward.

7. Fill the ovals (no stroke), and position them on the bottom area of the bulb.

8. Use the **Star** tool to create a 20-point star (Radius 1: .4", Radius 2: .69"). Apply a light fill color and a stroke of None. Scale the star, if necessary, so it's larger than the bulb.

9. Position the star over the bulb. On the Layers palette, drag the star object below the bulb object.

10. Select the star. Choose Effect > Distort & Transform > Roughen (Size: 2, Detail: 3–6, Relative). On the Transparency palette, set the blend mode to Overlay.

11. Use the **Pencil** tool (N). Choose a fill of None, a black stroke, and a stroke Weight of 1–2 pt. Draw a filament line inside the bulb. It should be the topmost object on the Layers palette.

12. Select the bulb. On the Transparency palette, set the Opacity slider to 60-70%, Normal mode.

13. Select the bulb, star, and filament. Choose Effect > Stylize > Drop Shadow (Opacity 50–60%, Blur 1–3 pt.).

Chapter 8: Reshape ◆ Study Guide

Learning Objectives

- Move anchor points, direction lines, and path segments.
- Convert a smooth point to a corner point (or vice versa).
- Add or delete anchor points and segments.
- Use the following tools to reshape paths:
  - ▲ Erase
  - ▲ Pencil
  - ▲ Paintbrush
  - ▲ Smooth
  - ▲ Twist
  - ▲ Reshape
  - ▲ Knife
- Average and join anchor points.
- Combine and split paths.

Get Up and Running Exercises

Students can do the three exercises at the end of the chapter in addition to the exercises suggested here.

- Find a natural object with an irregular outline, such as a stone or leaf, or find a photo of one. How can you use a shape tool to create an initial sketch of it, and then use other tools to refine the shape?

- Create a silhouette from several objects. For example, draw a silhouette of a skyline by drawing and positioning individual buildings, then combining them into a single silhouette after you finalize the composition. What quick method could be used to combine the shapes?

- Experiment with filters and effects that reshape objects, as in the examples on page 125. Try the commands on the Filter > Distort or Effect > Distort & Transform menus.

  - ▲ Start with simple shapes like a single straight or curved segment, or a rectangle or ellipse. Duplicate an object and apply a different filter or effect to each copy.

  - ▲ Try slightly more complex shapes, such as an object drawn by hand, or a star or other shape to which a filter or effect has already been applied.

  - ▲ Using the shapes you've altered by applying effects, change them further using other methods, such as adding or deleting points or using the Reshape tool.

Class Discussion Questions

- What are the building blocks of a path?
- What are some ways to reshape a curve segment using the Direct-selection tool?
- What are some ways to add points to a path?
- What are some ways to divide shapes?
- What are the differences among the Scissors tool, Erase tool, and Knife tool?

Review Questions

Multiple choice

1. What should you do to adjust the slope of a curve segment without changing the overall path shape?

   A. Adjust the angle of a direction line.

   B. Adjust the length of a direction line.

   C. Adjust the position of an anchor point.

   D. Drag the middle of a curve segment.

2. What happens if you choose the Object > Path > Join command when there's some distance between the two selected points?

   A. The points are joined by a new curved segment that's automatically created to produce a smooth transition between the existing segments.

   B. The points are joined automatically by a new straight segment.

   C. The points are moved to the average position between them and then joined.

   D. The points aren't joined.

3. Which tool can you drag to cut a shape into two pieces?

   A. Erase tool

   B. Knife tool

   C. Scissors tool

   D. Slice tool

4. Which of the following reshaping features works by adding anchor points to a path?

   A. Reshape tool

   B. Averaging points

   C. Smoothing

   D. Zig Zag effect

Fill-in-the-blank

1. To move individual anchor points, use the _____ tool.

2. To change a smooth anchor point to a curved anchor point, use the _____ tool.

3. It's easier to make a symmetrical curve if points are placed only at the _____ of the curves.

4. To extend, push, or pull part of an object while maintaining the object's overall shape, use the _____ tool.

5. To align two selected anchor points along either or both of the *x* and *y* axes, choose the Object > Path > _____ command.

Definitions

1. What is a smooth anchor point?

2. What is a direction line?

3. What does the Scissors tool do?

4. What does the Add to Shape Area button do on the Pathfinder palette?

5. What is the Auto Add/Delete feature of the Pen tool?

FILL & STROKE

In this chapter you will learn to fill the inside or stroke the edge of an object with a solid color or pattern and choose stroke attributes like dashes and joins. You'll learn how to change a document's color mode and choose colors for print or Web output. You'll learn to save, copy, edit, replace, delete, merge, move, and duplicate color swatches. You'll learn to select objects for recoloring; globally replace or edit a color; apply fill and stroke colors simultaneously using the Paint Bucket tool; sample colors using the Eyedropper tool; and blend fill colors between objects. You'll also learn to invert, adjust, convert, and saturate/desaturate colors. Finally, you'll learn how to create and modify fill patterns.

Related topics

Gradients, Chapter 18

Appearance palette, Chapter 19

Chris Spollen

Mixing and applying colors

Fills and strokes

The flat color, pattern, or gradient that's applied to the inside of a closed or open shape is called the **fill**. The color or brush stroke that's applied to the edge of a closed or open path is called the **stroke**. A stroke can be solid or dashed, and it can have an applied brush stroke, but not a gradient.

Colors and patterns can be applied using the **Color** or **Swatches** palette, buttons on the **Toolbox**, or the **Paint Bucket** tool. The **Stroke** palette is also used to apply characteristics such as stroke thickness (weight) and style (dashed or solid). The color attributes of a selected object are displayed on the Toolbox and the Color and Appearance palettes. The current fill and stroke colors are automatically applied to any new object you create. You can store any color, pattern, or gradient on the Swatches palette for later use.

Note: Before you start working with color, you should calibrate your monitor (see pages 471–472). Then, for the instructions in this chapter, open the Color, Stroke, and Swatches palettes. And of course work with your illustration in Preview view so you can see colors on screen as you apply them.

Fills and Strokes

Here's a quick method for applying color, just to get you started. The beauty of this method is that you don't need to choose any particular tool or select anything in your document. Try this method, then keep on reading—there's a lot more to this chapter!

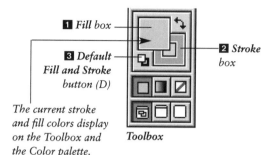

1 *Fill box*

3 *Default Fill and Stroke button (D)*

2 *Stroke box*

The current stroke and fill colors display on the Toolbox and the Color palette.

Toolbox

QuickStart drag-color:
Click the Fill **1** or Stroke **2** box on the Toolbox or the Color palette, click a color on the color bar on the Color palette **4**, then drag from the active box right over an object's fill or stroke—whichever element you want to recolor. The object doesn't have to be selected. If the object is selected, clicking a color swatch or a color on the color bar will automatically change the fill or stroke, depending on which of those boxes is currently active.

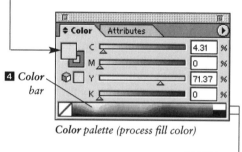

4 *Color bar*

Color palette (process fill color)

5 *White and black selectors*

➤ You can also drag from the Color box on the expanded Gradient palette or drag a swatch from the Swatches palette **6**.

➤ Shift-drag to apply a stroke color if the fill box is active or apply a fill color if the stroke box is active.

To apply a fill or stroke of black or white:
1. Select an object.
2. Click the Fill or Stroke box on the Color palette **1**–**2**, then click the white or black selector at the right end of the color bar on the Color palette **5** or click the white or black swatch on the Swatches palette **6**.
   or
   To apply a white fill *and* a black stroke, click the Default Fill and Stroke button (D) on the Toolbox **3**.

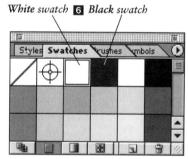

White swatch **6** *Black swatch*

Swatches palette

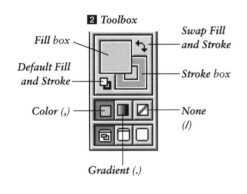

Fill color *Stroke color*

Color models

None *A process color slider* *Color bar* *Black/White selectors*

1 *The Color palette*

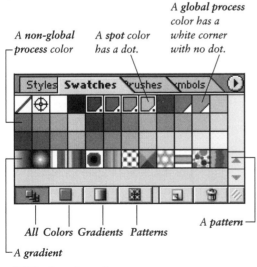

2 *Toolbox*

Fill box *Swap Fill and Stroke*

Default Fill and Stroke *Stroke box*

Color (,) *None (/)*

Gradient (.)

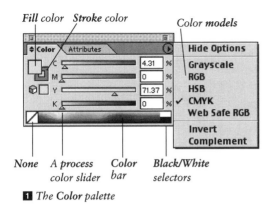

A non-global process color *A spot color has a dot.* *A global process color has a white corner with no dot.*

All *Colors* *Gradients* *Patterns*

A pattern

A gradient

3 *The Swatches palette*

The palettes you'll use for coloring

Color palette

The Color palette is used to mix and choose solid colors. The color boxes on the Color palette display the current fill and stroke colors of the currently or most recently selected object **1**. The palette options change depending on whether the Grayscale, RGB, HSB, CMYK, or Web Safe RGB color model is chosen from the palette menu. You can click a color on the color bar or mix a process color using exact percentages. Choosing a color model for the palette doesn't change the document color mode (see page 144).

Toolbox

The Fill and Stroke boxes on the Toolbox display the attributes of the currently or most recently selected object and any changes made to the current fill or stroke color via the Color or Swatches palette **2**. Click the Color or Gradient button to reapply the most recently chosen solid color or gradient.

Swatches palette

The Swatches palette contains process color (RGB or CMYK, depending on the current document color mode), spot color, pattern, and gradient swatches **3**. You can append additional swatches from other libraries (e.g., PANTONE). If you click a swatch, that color will appear on the current Fill or Stroke box (whichever is currently active) on the Toolbox and on the Color palette, and it will apply immediately to all currently selected objects. If a selected object contains a color or colors from the Swatches palette, those swatches will be highlighted on the palette.

Illustrator supplies default process color, spot color, pattern, and gradient swatches as well as other swatch libraries. You can also create your own swatches, which will save with the file in which they're created.

None

The None button is located on the Color palette, the Swatches palettes, and the Toolbox. Select an object and then click this button to remove any fill or stroke color, depending on which color box is currently active on the Color palette and the Toolbox.

The basic coloring steps

Open the Toolbox and the Color, Swatches, and Stroke palettes.

1. Select the objects whose color attributes you want to change.

2. Make sure the box for the attribute that you want to change (Fill or Stroke) is active on the Color palette or Toolbox.

3. To choose a solid color, choose a color model from the Color palette menu, then click the color bar on the palette or choose or enter specific color percentages.
or
Click a swatch on the Swatches palette to apply that color or pattern to the selected object(s). (You can also drag a swatch over an unselected object.)

4. Adjust the stroke weight and other attributes using the Stroke palette (see pages 148–150).

5. *Optional:* To save the current color, follow the instructions below.

Swatches that are stored on the Swatches palette save only with the current file.

To save the current fill or stroke color as a swatch:

Drag the Fill or Stroke box from the Color palette or the Toolbox to an empty area of the Swatches palette to make it the last swatch **1** or release the mouse between two colors to insert the new color between them.
or
Make sure the Fill or Stroke button is active on the Color palette—whichever you want to save as a swatch—then click the New Swatch button on the Swatches palette **2**.
or
To choose options for the new swatch as you save it, Option-click/Alt-click the New Swatch button, enter a Swatch Name, choose a Color Type (Process Color or Spot Color), check or uncheck the Global box, choose a Color Mode, then click OK. Cmd-click/Ctrl-click the New Swatch button to save the color as a spot color.

➤ Cmd-drag/Ctrl-drag to convert a process color into a spot color as you save it.

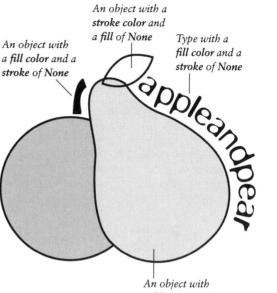

An object with a stroke color and a fill of None

An object with a fill color and a stroke of None

Type with a fill color and a stroke of None

An object with a fill color and a stroke color

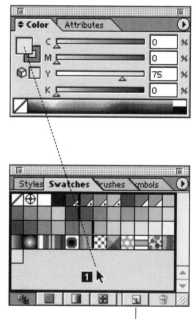

2 *New Swatch button*

Don't be fooled

Illustrator's **Color Settings** command works with the system's color management software to ensure more accurate color matching between the on-screen display of CMYK or RGB colors and the printed version of those colors. This command utilizes monitor and printer device profiles and output intents chosen by the user to better translate color between particular devices. However, the profiles won't produce a perfectly reliable on-screen proof.

For print output, you shouldn't mix or choose process colors or choose spot colors (e.g., PANTONE) based on how they look on the screen, because screen colors won't look like the printed colors. Instead, use **matching system books** to choose spot colors or mix process colors, and be sure to run a color **proof** (or two or three) of your document. Really.

1 *The Registration color appears on every plate when a file is color separated.*

Global process colors have a white triangle with no dot in the lower right corner (see the next page).

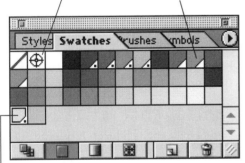

Spot colors have a dot in the lower right corner.

Colors for print

Spot colors are used for offset printing. Each **spot** color appears on its own plate after color separation. On a rare occasion you might mix a spot color yourself, but normally you'll pick a named, numbered, pre-mixed spot color from a matching system book (e.g., PANTONE). You can use spot colors exclusively if your illustration doesn't contain any continuous-tone (raster) images—as many spot colors as your budget permits.

➤ If you mix your own spot color, to ensure that it separates onto its own plate, double-click the swatch for the color on the Swatches palette, choose Color Type: **Spot Color**, then click OK.

➤ You can achieve a pleasing range of tints using a black plate and a single spot color plate by using varying tint percentages of that spot color throughout your illustration.

Process colors are printed from four plates, one each for Cyan (C), Magenta (M), Yellow (Y), and Black (K). You can enter process color percentages yourself or you can choose a pre-mixed process color from a matching system (e.g., TRUMATCH or PANTONE Process). (FOCOLTONE, DIC Color, and Toyo are rarely used in the United States.)

Process printing *must* be used for any document that contains continuous-tone images, because it's the only way to achieve a range of graduated tones. Budget permitting, you can use both: four-color process and a handful of spot color plates.

➤ The Registration color is used for crop marks and the like **1**. To change the Registration color (let's say your illustration is very dark and you need white Registration marks), double-click the swatch and adjust the sliders.

➤ Double-click a spot color swatch to display its process color breakdown.

Note: Normally, Illustrator converts all spot colors into process colors when they're color separated. To make your spot colors separate

(Continued on the following page)

properly to their own plates, uncheck **Convert to Process** in File > Separation Setup.

To define a color as process or spot, double-click the swatch on the Swatches palette, choose Color Type: Process Color or Spot Color, decide whether the process color will be Global or not Global, choose a Color Mode, then click OK **1**.

➤ The Info palette shows the color breakdowns for the currently selected object. The breakdown on the left is the current fill color; the breakdown on the right is the current stroke color **2**. (If the bottom portion of the palette isn't visible, choose Show Options from the palette menu.) If two or more objects with different color values are selected simultaneously, the bottom portion of the palette will be blank.

Global colors

If a process color is **global** (that is, the Global box is checked for that color in the Swatch Options dialog box) and you modify its swatch, it will update on all objects to which it was previously applied. If you modify a **non-global** color (Global box unchecked), that color will update only on any currently selected objects. See page 158.

Colors for the Web

The Mac OS, Windows, and other platforms have 216 colors in common. These colors are called "Web safe," which means they won't shift when viewed in either of the popular Web browsers.

If you mix a color in the RGB model that is not Web safe, the **Out of Web** color warning (cube) button will appear on the palette, and the closest Web safe version of that color will appear in the little swatch next to it **3**. Click the cube or the swatch to convert the color to the closest Web safe version.

When you create illustrations for the Web, you should choose the **Web Safe RGB** color model for the Color palette. Note how the sliders align with the vertical notches **4**.

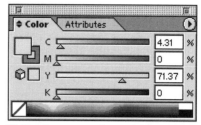

1 Use the **CMYK** color model for print output.

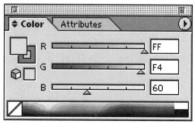

2

Fill info   Stroke info

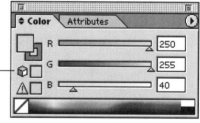

3 The RGB color model showing the Out of Web color warning.

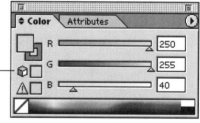

4 Use the **Web Safe RGB** color model for Web design. The sliders have **notches**.

Recoloring type

- To recolor **all** the type in a block, highlight it with the Selection tool.

- To recolor only a **portion** of a type block, select it with a Type tool.

- To recolor a **type object** (not the type), click on the edge of it with the Direct-selection tool. See pages 219–221.

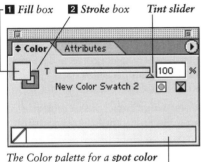

1 *Fill box*   **2** *Stroke box*   *Tint slider*

The Color palette for a spot color

3 *Tint ramp*

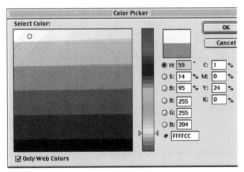

4 *In the Color Picker, you can enter HSB, RGB, or CMYK percentages. Check **Only Web Colors** to choose Web safe colors. This is the Adobe Color Picker in the Mac OS.*

To choose a fill or stroke for a path before or after you create it:

1. Select an existing object (not all the anchor points need to be solid).
or
Choose the tool with which you want to draw a new object.

2. Click the Fill **1** or Stroke **2** box on the Color palette or the Toolbox. To toggle between these two boxes, press "X".

3. Click a color or pattern swatch on the Swatches palette. If you chose a spot color swatch or a global process color swatch, you can move the Tint (T) slider on the Color palette or click or drag inside the Tint ramp to adjust the percentage of that color **3**.
or
Choose a color model from the Color palette menu, then choose color percentages (instructions on the next page).
or
Double-click the Fill or Stroke box on the Color palette, then mix a color using the Color Picker **4**.

To choose a color from a matching system (e.g., PANTONE), see page 147.

4. If you're applying a stroke color, define stroke attributes using the Stroke palette (see pages 148–150).

5. Your color is chosen. If you chose a drawing tool for step 1, now you're ready to use it. The tool will use the current Color and Stroke palette attributes.

➤ You can fill an object with any of the patterns that are supplied with Illustrator or you can create and use your own patterns (see pages 164–166). Just remember not to apply a path pattern as a fill—it won't look right.

➤ A gradient cannot be applied as a stroke. For a workaround, see page 303.

Choose Fill or Stroke Color

Document Color Mode

When you created your new document, you were asked to choose a Color Mode: CMYK or RGB. (The current color mode displays in the document title bar.) Any colors you mix or choose in a document automatically conform to the current document color mode. If you want to create two versions of an illustration, one for Web output (RGB mode) and one for print output (CMYK mode), you can make a copy of the file and then change the color mode for the copy.

Note: Changing the color mode changes all colors in the illustration to the new mode, and color shifts will occur, particularly if you go in the direction of CMYK to RGB. That's why we suggest you copy your file first, and leave the original file unchanged. To reverse a document mode change, *don't* re-choose the prior color mode. Instead, to restore the original colors, use Edit > Undo.

To change a document's color mode:

1. Use File > Save As to create a copy of your illustration.

2. Choose File > Document Color Mode > CMYK Color or RGB Color.

In the mode

➤ Any process or spot colors you create for a document will be in the document color mode—regardless of which mode is currently chosen on the Color Mode pop-up menu in the Swatch Options dialog box (see page 163). You can create colors in your illustration in either CMYK or RGB—but not both.

➤ When a spot color is displayed on the Color palette, a current document mode icon will also display on the palette **1**.

➤ The Swatches palette uses the default palette for the current document color mode (CMYK or RGB).

➤ Blend and gradient colors conform automatically to the current document color mode: all CMYK or all RGB.

➤ Placed and pasted images, linked or embedded, are converted to the current document color mode.

➤ The color mode options in the Rasterize dialog box will change depending on the current document color mode.

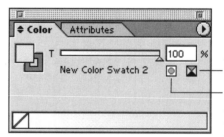

Document color mode indicator

*Color type indicator: A **circle** for a **spot** color, a **solid gray square** for a **global process** color*

1 *Click either indicator to convert a spot or global process color in a selected object to the current document mode. Both buttons produce the same result. To convert the colors on selected objects, choose Filter > Colors > Convert to Grayscale or Convert to CMYK or Convert to RGB (depending on the document's current color mode).*

What's the gamut?

If your document is in CMYK color mode and an exclamation point appears below the Color boxes on the Color palette **3**, it means the current RGB or HSB color has no **CMYK** equivalent, and thus will **not** be **printable** on a four-color press. If you click the exclamation point, Illustrator will substitute the closest CMYK (printable) equivalent.

If you're outputting **online**, your document color mode is **RGB**, and the exclamation point appears, it means the current color is outside the Web-safe gamut.

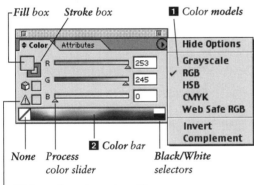

Fill box   Stroke box   **1** Color models

2 Color bar

None   Process   Black/White
        color slider   selectors

3 An exclamation point will appear
if you mix a color that's out of **gamut**.

If the fill or stroke colors differ among currently selected objects, a question mark will appear in the corresponding Fill or Stroke box on the Color palette and the Toolbox, but you can go ahead and apply a new fill and/or stroke color to all the selected objects.

Follow these instructions to mix your own process color. (To apply a color from a color matching system, like TRUMATCH or FOCOLTONE, see page 147.)

To mix a process color:

1. *Optional:* To recolor an existing object or objects, select them now, and click the Fill or Stroke box on the Color palette (X). To choose a color for an object you're about to draw, make sure no objects are selected.

2. Choose a color model from the Color palette menu **1**:

   Choose **Grayscale** to convert colors in any selected objects to grayscale or to choose a gray shade.

   Choose **RGB** to mix colors for video output.

   Choose **HSB** to individually adjust a color's hue (location on the color wheel), saturation (purity), or brightness.

   Choose **CMYK** to create process colors for output on a four-color press. Use a matching system book for this.

   Choose **Web Safe RGB** to choose colors for Web output.

3. Click a color on the color bar at the bottom of the Color palette **2**.
   and/or
   Move the sliders to adjust the individual color values (0–255 for RGB; 0–100 for CMYK; 0, 33, 66, CC, or FF for Web).

4. *Optional:* To save the newly mixed color as a swatch, drag from the Fill or Stroke box (whichever is active) on the Color palette to the Swatches palette.

➤ Premixed swatches and colors that are applied to objects remain associated with their color model. If you click a swatch or an object to which a color is applied, the Color palette will reset to reflect that color's model.

Color Shortcuts

Color editing shortcuts

➤ Shift-click the color bar on the Color palette to cycle through the color **models**. You can also convert the current color by choosing a different color model from the palette menu. If a color has been saved as a swatch, the swatch won't change.

➤ Press "X" to toggle between the **Fill** and **Stroke** boxes on the Toolbox and the Color palette.

➤ To make the fill color the **same** as the stroke color, or vice versa, drag one box over the other on the Toolbox or the Color palette.

➤ If you've chosen a fill or stroke of None for a path and then want to restore the last-applied colors to the path, click the **Last Color** button on the Color palette **1**.

➤ Choose **Invert** or **Complement** from the Color palette menu to invert the current color or convert it into its complement within the same color model.

➤ Shift-drag any RGB or CMYK slider on the Color palette to change that color's **strength**—the other sliders will readjust automatically.

➤ To select objects with the same paint attributes via a command, see page 157.

The Color, Gradient, and None buttons

Click the Color, Gradient, or None button on the Toolbox to change the current fill color (if the Fill box is active) to a solid color, a gradient, or a fill of none, respectively, or to change the current stroke to a solid color or none. The Color button displays the last solid color that was chosen; the Gradient button displays the last gradient that was chosen. If an object is selected, it will be recolored or its color will be removed when you click a different button.

➤ Clicking the Color button on the Toolbox causes the Color palette and any other palettes that are grouped with or docked to the Color palette to display.

No mousing around!

These are the shortcuts for activating the Color, Gradient, and None buttons:

Color   , (comma)

Gradient   . (period)

None   / (slash)

The comma, period, and slash keys appear next to each other on the keyboard, which makes them easy to remember. Let's say the Fill box on the Toolbox happens to be selected and you want to remove a stroke from a selected object. Press "X", then "/".

➤ **Option-drag/Alt-drag** in the **color bar** to modify the stroke while the Fill box is active, or vice versa.

➤ Press "**X**" to toggle between the Fill and Stroke boxes on the Toolbox and Color palette.

➤ Press **Shift-X** to swap the Fill and Stroke colors.

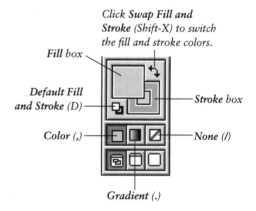

Click Swap Fill and Stroke (Shift-X) to switch the fill and stroke colors.

Fill box

Default Fill and Stroke (D)

Stroke box

Color (,)

None (/)

Gradient (.)

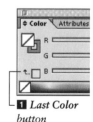

1 *Last Color button*

Quick-append

If you apply a color to a path directly from some library palettes, the color will be added to the current document's Swatches palette automatically. This doesn't work for some libraries (e.g., Pastels, Web). If you want to keep a color that you've applied to a path that didn't copy to the Swatches palette automatically, but you've already closed the library palette, select the object, then drag the Fill or Stroke box from the Color palette to the Swatches palette.

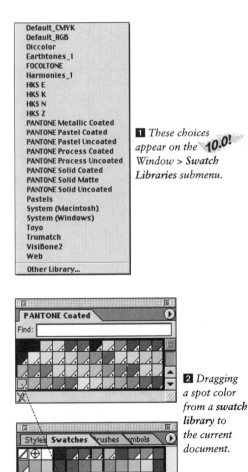

1 *These choices appear on the Window > Swatch Libraries submenu.*

2 *Dragging a spot color from a swatch library to the current document.*

In order to apply a color from a matching system, like the PANTONE or TRUMATCH, or from the Web palette, you must open that swatch library and then drag a swatch from the library palette onto your document's Swatches palette. The swatch will convert to the current document color mode. The Web palette contains the 216 Web safe RGB colors commonly used by Web browsers.

To add matching system or Web colors to the Swatches palette:

1. Display the Swatches palette.
2. Choose a color matching system name from the Window > Swatch Libraries submenu **1**.
3. Click a swatch (or swatches) on the swatch library palette. The new color will be added to your document's Swatches palette automatically.
   or
   To add multiple swatches at a time, Cmd-click/Ctrl-click them individually or click, then Shift-click a contiguous series of them, then choose Add to Swatches from the swatch library palette menu.
   or
   Locate the desired color on the newly opened swatch library palette (scroll downward or expand the palette, if necessary), then drag it onto your document's Swatches palette **2**.

➤ To locate a color, if the Find field isn't visible, choose Show Find Field from the Swatches or library palette menu, then start typing the color number (or name) in the field. The swatch will become highlighted on the palette.

➤ If two or more swatch libraries are grouped in the same palette and you want to close one library in a group, drag its tab out of the palette, then click that palette's close box.

➤ You can't modify swatches on a swatch library palette (note the non-edit icon in lower left corner of palette)—the Swatch Options dialog box won't be available. You *can* edit any swatch once it's saved to your document's Swatches palette.

Changing stroke attributes

You can change a stroke's color, weight (thickness), and style (dashed or solid, rounded or sharp corners, flat or rounded ends). First, the width.

To change the width of a stroke:

1. Select an object or objects.

2. On the Stroke palette:

   Click the up or down arrow on the palette to change the current stroke weight one unit at a time. Or click in the Weight field, then press the up or down arrow on the keyboard.
   or
   Choose a preset weight from the Weight pop-up menu.
   or
   Enter a width in the Weight field (.01–1000 pt) **1**. *Note:* A stroke narrower than .25 pt. may not print. A weight of 0 produces a stroke of None. The stroke will be balanced on the path: Half the stroke width on one side of the path, the other half on the other side of the path **2**–**3**.

➤ Don't apply a wide stroke to small type—it will distort the letterforms.

➤ You can enter a number in inches (in), millimeters (mm), centimeters (cm), picas (p), or pixels (px) in the stroke Weight field. When you click Return/Enter or Tab, the value you enter will be converted automatically to the Stroke unit currently chosen in Edit > Preferences > Units & Undo.

1 *To change a stroke's thickness, enter a value in the stroke **Weight** field, or click the up or down arrow, or choose from the pop-up menu.*

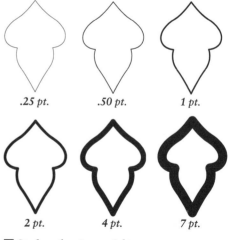

The path

2 *The stroke is centered on the path.*

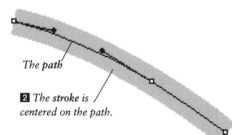

.25 pt.   .50 pt.   1 pt.

2 pt.   4 pt.   7 pt.

3 *Strokes of various weights*

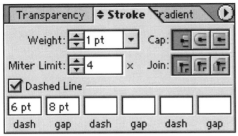

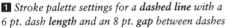

1 *Stroke palette settings for a **dashed line** with a 6 pt. dash **length** and an 8 pt. **gap** between dashes*

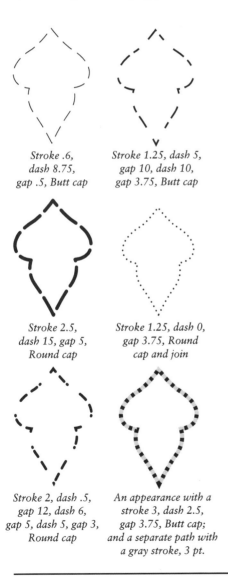

Stroke .6, dash 8.75, gap .5, Butt cap

Stroke 1.25, dash 5, gap 10, dash 10, gap 3.75, Butt cap

Stroke 2.5, dash 15, gap 5, Round cap

Stroke 1.25, dash 0, gap 3.75, Round cap and join

Stroke 2, dash .5, gap 12, dash 6, gap 5, dash 5, gap 3, Round cap

An appearance with a stroke 3, dash 2.5, gap 3.75, Butt cap; and a separate path with a gray stroke, 3 pt.

Using Illustrator's Dashed Line feature, you can easily edit a line for any individual path.

To create a dashed stroke:

1. Select an object. Make sure it has a stroke color and its stroke is wider than zero.

2. If the Stroke palette options aren't fully displayed, choose Show Options from the palette menu.

3. Click a Cap button for the dash shape **1**.

4. Check the Dashed Line box.

5. Enter a number in the first dash field (the length of the first dash, in points), then press Tab to proceed to the next field. If you don't enter values in any of the other dash fields, the first dash value will be used for all the dashes. The default first dash unit is 12 pt.

6. *Optional:* Enter an amount in the first gap field (the length of the first gap after the first dash), then press Tab to proceed to the next field or press Return/Enter to exit the palette. If you don't enter a gap value, the dash value will also be used as the gap value.

7. *Optional:* To create dashes of varying lengths, enter values in the other dash fields. The more different values you enter, the more irregular the dashes will look.

8. *Optional:* Enter different amounts in the other gap fields to create gaps of varying lengths. If you enter an amount only in the first gap field, that amount will be used for all the gaps.

➤ To create a dotted line, click the second Cap button, enter 0 for the Dash value, and enter a Gap value that is greater than or equal to the stroke Weight.

➤ You can enter a value in inches (in), millimeters (mm), centimeters (cm), picas (p), or pixels (px) in the dash or gap fields. That number will be translated automatically into the Stroke unit currently chosen in Edit > Preferences > Units & Undo.

➤ User-defined values will remain in effect until you change them or quit/exit Illustrator.

Dashed Stroke

149

To modify stroke caps and/or joins:

1. Select an object. Make sure it has a stroke color and its stroke is wider than zero.

2. If the Stroke palette options aren't fully displayed, choose Show Options from the palette menu.

3. To modify the endpoints of a solid line or all the dashes in a dashed line:

   Click the **Butt** (left) **Cap** button ◼ to create square-cornered ends in which the stroke stops at the endpoints, or to create thin rectangular dashes. Use this option if you need to align your paths very precisely.

   Click the **Round** (middle) **Cap** button to create semicircular ends or dashes that end in a semicircle.

   Click the **Projecting** (right) **Cap** button to create square-cornered ends in which the stroke extends beyond the endpoints or to create rectangular dashes.

4. To modify the bends on corner points (not curve points) of the path:

   Click the **Miter** (left) **Join** button to produce pointed bends (miter joins) ◼.

   Click the **Round** (middle) **Join** button to produce semicircular bends (round joins).

   Click the **Bevel** (right) **Join** button to produce square-cornered bends (bevel joins). The sharper the angle, the wider the bevel.

5. *Optional:* Change the Miter Limit (1–500) value for the point at which a miter (pointed) corner becomes a bevel corner. When the measurement from the inside to the outside of the corner point becomes greater than the miter limit value times the stroke weight, the miter corner is replaced with a bevel corner. Incomprehensible? Don't worry about how it works, just use a high Miter Limit to create long, pointy corners or a low Miter limit to create bevel join corners.

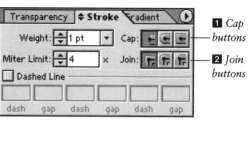

◼ *Cap buttons*

◼ *Join buttons*

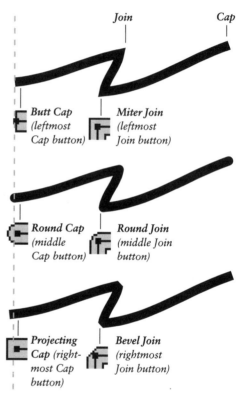

Butt Cap (leftmost Cap button)

Miter Join (leftmost Join button)

Round Cap (middle Cap button)

Round Join (middle Join button)

Projecting Cap (rightmost Cap button)

Bevel Join (rightmost Join button)

Stroke Caps and Joins

A global process color has a white corner with no dot.

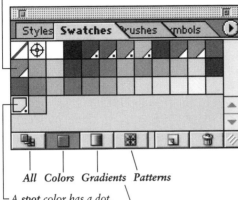

All   Colors   Gradients   Patterns

A spot color has a dot.

1 *Use the Swatches palette **display** buttons to control which categories of swatches are displayed on the palette (in this figure only color swatches are displayed).*

RGB document color mode

Non-global process   Spot   Global process

2 *The swatches in List View*

Using the Swatches palette

You can control whether the Swatches palette displays all types of swatches or only certain categories of swatches, and whether the swatches are large or small.

To choose swatch display options:

1. Click a display button at the bottom of the Swatches palette to control which category of swatches is displayed **1**: Show All, for all types (colors, gradients, and patterns); Show Color, for solid colors only; Show Gradient, for gradients only; or Show Pattern, for patterns only.

2. Choose a view for the currently chosen category of swatches from the palette menu: Small Thumbnail View, Large Thumbnail View, or List View. In List View **2**, the palette also displays an icon for the color's color model.

   ➤ Choose Large Thumbnail View for gradients and patterns.

3. Choose Sort by Name to sort the swatches alphabetically by name.
   or
   From the palette menu, choose Sort by Kind to sort swatches into color, then gradient, then pattern groups (use when all the categories of swatches are displayed).

   ➤ To choose a swatch by typing, choose Show Find Field from the palette menu, click in the field, then start typing. A swatch, if found, will become selected. This may not work perfectly in Windows.

   ➤ If you've chosen different views for the different categories of swatches (colors, gradients, and patterns) and you want to force all the categories of swatches to display in the same view, hold down Cmd-Option/Ctrl-Alt as you choose Small Thumbnail View, Large Thumbnail View, or List View from the palette menu.

10.0!

Whatever swatches are on the Swatches palette will save with the current file. (To load matching system colors, see page 147.)

To load swatches from one Illustrator file to another:

1. With the file that you want to load swatches into open, choose Window > Swatch Libraries > Other Library.

2. Locate the Illustrator file you want to copy swatches from (that file should not be open), then click Open.

3. Drag a swatch from the newly opened (secondary) swatch palette into the current document's Swatches palette **1**. To load multiple swatches at a time, first Cmd/Ctrl click them individually or click, then Shift-click, a contiguous series of them, then drag.
   or
   Click the swatch you want to load, then choose Add to Swatches from the secondary swatch palette's option menu. The selected color will appear on the current document's Swatches palette.

➤ Pattern library files are stored in the Adobe Illustrator 10 > Presets > Patterns folder. Gradients are stored in the Gradients folder. **10.0!**

Auto copy

If you **drag-and-drop** an object from one file to another, any swatches that are applied to that object will also appear in the destination file.

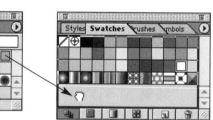

1 *Open a swatch library from another file, then* **drag** *a swatch or swatches from one swatch palette to another.*

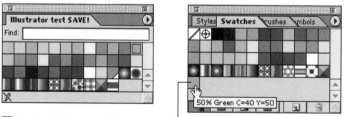

2 *A* **copy** *of the swatch shows up on the* **Swatches** *palette.*

Swatches at launchtime

If you want to control which colors appear on the Swatches palette when the application is launched, add those colors to the **Startup** file (see page 433).

If you enable the **Persistent** command on a swatch library palette menu, that swatch library palette will reopen automatically when you re-launch Illustrator, with the same tab in front.

There's no simple way to restore the Swatches palette to its default state. You have to manually drag swatches from either of the two Default palettes.

To restore default swatches to the Swatches palette:

1. *Optional:* To clear your document's Swatches palette before restoring the default palette, click the first swatch after None and Registration, Shift-click the last swatch, click the Delete button, then click Yes.

2. Choose Window > Swatch Libraries > Default_CMYK or Default_RGB (depending on the current document color mode).

3. On the Default_CMYK or Default_RGB palette that you just opened, select the swatches you want to restore to your document (Click, then Shift-click to select multiple, contiguous swatches).

4. Choose Add to Swatches from the Default_CMYK or Default_RGB palette menu **1**–**2**.
   or
   Drag the selected swatches to your document's Swatches palette.

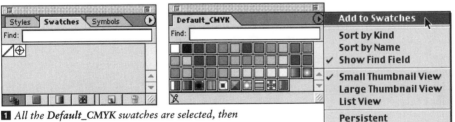

1 *All the **Default_CMYK** swatches are selected, then* **Add to Swatches** *is chosen from the palette menu.*

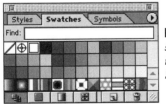

2 *The **Default_CMYK** swatches appear on the current document's Swatches palette.*

To delete swatches:

1. Click the swatch you want to delete. Or click, then Shift-click a series of contiguous swatches or Cmd-click/Ctrl-click individual swatches.

   or

   To select only the swatches that aren't currently applied to objects in your document, choose Select All Unused from the palette menu. To limit the selection to a particular category (e.g., patterns or gradients), make sure only those swatches are displayed on the palette before choosing Select All Unused.

2. Click the Delete button at the bottom of the Swatches palette, then click Yes **1**.

   or

   Choose Delete Swatch from the palette menu, then click Yes.

   or

   Option-click/Alt-click the Delete button to bypass the alert dialog box.

   or

   Drag the swatch(es) you want to delete over the Delete button (you won't get a prompt with this method, either).

➤ If you delete a global process color or a spot color that is currently applied to an object or objects, those objects will be recolored with the non-global process color equivalent to the deleted colors.

➤ To restore a deleted swatch or swatches, choose Undo right away. To restore swatches from a default library or any other library, see the instructions on the previous page.

Quick fix

If you delete a color, gradient, or pattern swatch that was applied to an object in the current file, you can retrieve it by selecting the object and then dragging the Fill box from the Toolbox or the Color palette onto the Swatches palette.

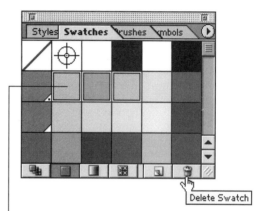

1 *Select the swatch or swatches that you want to delete from the Swatches palette, then click or Option-click/Alt-click the **Delete Swatch** button.*

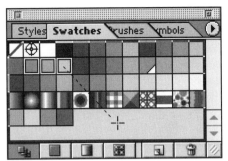

1 *Three swatches are **selected**, then they're **moved** to a new location on the palette.*

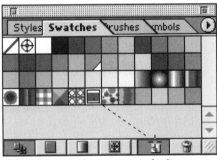

2 *Drag the swatch you want to **duplicate** over the New Swatch button.*

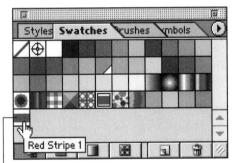

3 *The **duplicate** appears on the palette.*

To move a swatch or swatches:

Drag a swatch to a new location on the palette **1**. A dark vertical line will show the swatch location as you drag it. (To select multiple swatches, click a swatch, then Shift-click the last swatch in a series of contiguous swatches, or Cmd-click/Ctrl-click to select individual swatches.)

To duplicate a swatch:

Select the swatch you want to duplicate, then choose Duplicate Swatch from the palette menu or click the New Swatch button. The duplicate swatch will appear next to the last swatch on the palette.

or

Drag the swatch to be duplicated over the New Swatch button **2–3**.

➤ If no swatch is selected when you click the New Swatch button, a new swatch will be created for the current fill or stroke color.

➤ Option-drag/Alt-drag one swatch over another to replace the existing swatch with the one you're dragging.

Move Swatch; Duplicate Swatch

Resolving swatch conflicts

If you copy and paste or drag-and-drop an object from one document window to another, that object's colors will appear as swatches on the target document's Swatches palette. If a global process or spot color on the copied object contains the same name, but different color percentages, as an existing global process or spot color swatch in the target document, the Swatch Conflict dialog box will open **1**. Choose from these options:

Click **Merge swatches** to apply the swatch of the same name in the target document to the copied objects. Or click **Add swatches** to add the new swatch to the Swatches palette in the target document (choosing this option will prevent colors in the copied objects from changing).

Check the **Apply to all** box to have the current Options setting apply to any other name conflicts that crop up for other objects being copied. This will prevent the alert dialog from opening repeatedly if more than one name conflict crops up.

Normally, if there are two spot colors that have the same color breakdown, but different names, Illustrator will color separate each of those colors to a separate sheet of film. You can use the Merge Swatches command to selectively merge colors into the same swatch so it will print from one plate.

To merge spot color swatches:

I. The first swatch you select will replace all the other selected swatches, regardless of its location on the palette, so take a minute to strategize. On the Swatches palette, select the swatches to be merged. Click, then Shift-click to select contiguous swatches or Cmd-click/Ctrl-click to select non-contiguous swatches **2**.

2. Choose Merge Swatches from the Swatches palette menu **3**. If any of the merged swatches were applied to objects in the file, the first swatch that was selected for merging will be applied to all those objects.

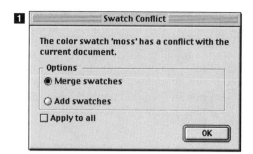

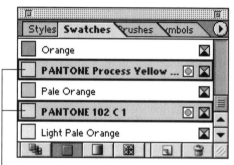

2 Select the spot colors you want to merge.

3 After choosing **Merge Swatches** from the palette menu, the swatches are merged into the first swatch that was selected.

Select same tint percentage

When **Select Same Tint Percentage** is checked in Edit > Preferences > General, the Select > Same > Fill Color and Stroke Color commands will select only colors that have the same tint percentage (spot color percentage) as the selected object.

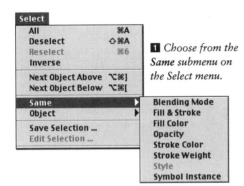

1 *Choose from the Same submenu on the Select menu.*

2 *The original group of objects*

3 *All the colors **inverted***

Changing colors

To select objects with the same paint attributes:

1. Select an object whose paint or other attributes you want to change.
   or
   With no object selected, choose the attributes that you want to search for from the Swatches palette, the Color palette, or the Stroke palette.

2. Choose Select > Same > Fill & Stroke, Fill Color, Opacity, Stroke Color, or Stroke Weight to select objects with the same paint attributes as you chose in the previous step **1**. All objects with those paint attributes will now be selected. A spot color in different tint percentages is treated as the same color.

3. With the objects still selected, mix a new color using the Color palette.
   or
   Click a new swatch on the Swatches palette.
   or
   Choose a new Weight or other attributes from the Stroke palette.

➤ To globally change a spot color or a global process color by replacing its swatch, see the next page.

The Invert command converts each color in an object into its color negative.

To invert colors:

1. Select the object or objects whose colors you want to invert.

2. Choose Filter > Colors > Invert Colors **2**–**3**. This filter converts only **non-global process colors**. It will not convert spot colors, global process colors, gradients, or patterns.
   or
   To invert only the object's **fill** or **stroke** color, click either box on the Color palette, then choose Invert from the Color palette menu. This command will convert any kind of solid color—spot, global process, or non-global process.

This is what happens when colors are replaced:

➤ If you replace a spot or global process color swatch with a different swatch, that color (or a tint of that color) will automatically update in *all* the objects to which it is currently applied—whether or not those objects are selected. The object's original tint percentage will be preserved.

➤ If you re-mix a non-global process color swatch, only the currently *selected* object or objects containing that color will be recolored.

To replace a swatch globally:

On the Color palette, mix a brand-new color (not merely a tint variation of the global process or spot color that you want to replace). Then Option-drag/Alt-drag the Fill or Stroke box from the Color palette over the swatch on the Swatches palette that you want to replace.

or

Option-drag/Alt-drag one swatch over another swatch.

or

To edit a gradient swatch, use the Gradient palette (see pages 310–311). To edit a pattern swatch, follow the instructions on page 165.

The new color will replace the old color in all objects to which the original swatch is currently applied (the objects don't have to be selected).

Follow these instructions to edit a process color globally. To change spot colors in multiple objects, use the method described in the sidebar instead (select the objects, then choose a new swatch).

To edit a color globally:

1. Double-click a global process swatch on the Swatches palette.

2. Modify the color using the Color Type menu, the Color Mode menu, or by moving the sliders, and then click OK. The color will update in all objects to which it is currently applied. Individual tint variations will be preserved.

Change without changing

If you want to globally change a color without changing the swatch from which it originated, use a command on the Select > Same submenu command to select all the objects that contain that color (see the previous page), then choose a new swatch or mix a new color for the selected objects. Use this method to assign a different spot color to existing objects.

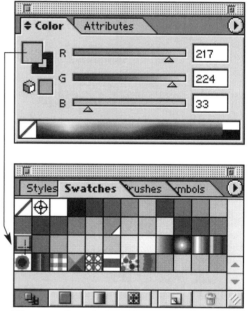

1 *Option-drag/Alt-drag the current color from the* **Fill** *or* **Stroke** *box over the* **spot** *or* **global process** *swatch you want to replace. Objects to which that color is currently applied will update.*

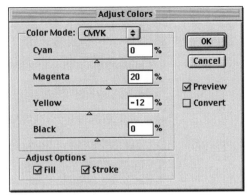

1 Use the **Adjust Colors** filter to adjust solid colors in any kind of object.

Use the Adjust Colors filter to adjust color percentages or convert color modes in one or more selected path objects; text objects; or an opened or placed Photoshop TIFF, EPS, or flattened .psd image—but not gradients or patterns. To adjust individual .psd layers, convert them into separate Illustrator objects first (see pages 252–253).

To adjust or convert colors:

1. Select the object or objects whose colors you want to adjust or convert.

2. Choose Filter > Colors > Adjust Colors.

3. Check Preview to preview color adjustments in your illustration while the dialog box is open **1**.

4. Check Adjust Options: Fill and/or Stroke to adjust one or both of those attributes.

5. If the selected objects contain colors from more than one mode, the sliders will represent the first mode that's present, in the following order: Global mode, then either CMYK mode or RGB mode, then Grayscale mode. Make sure Convert is unchecked, then move the sliders or enter new percentages in the fields. Only object colors in that mode will be adjusted. After you adjust colors in one mode, you can choose another mode and continue adjusting colors. Only the color modes that are present in the selected objects will be available on the pop-up menu.
   or
   To convert all the currently selected objects to the same color mode, regardless of their original mode, check Convert, choose a Color Mode from the pop-up menu, then move the sliders.

6. Click OK.

To convert an object's colors to a different mode:

1. Select the object or objects whose colors you want to convert.

2. Choose Filter > Colors > Convert to Grayscale, or either Convert to CMYK or Convert to RGB. Spot colors will be converted into process colors.

If you click with the Paint Bucket tool on an object, that object will be filled *and* stroked using the current Color and Stroke palette settings. Neither palette needs to be displayed for you to use the Paint Bucket.

To use the Paint Bucket tool:

1. With no objects selected, choose the Paint Bucket tool (K).

2. Choose fill and stroke colors from the Color or Swatches palette.
   or
   Option-click/Alt-click on a color anywhere in any open Illustrator window (this is a temporary Eyedropper).

3. Choose a stroke weight, and choose other stroke options, if desired.

4. Click an object (the object does not have to be selected). The object will become colored with the current Color and Stroke palette attributes –**2**. If the object you click doesn't have a fill color or if the illustration is in Outline view, position the black spill of the Paint Bucket pointer on the path outline before clicking.

Use the Eyedropper/Paint Bucket Options dialog box to change the default attributes for either or both tools.

To choose paint attributes the Eyedropper picks up or the Paint Bucket applies:

1. Double-click the Eyedropper or Paint Bucket tool.

2. Click check box options on or off **3**. Click the arrowhead for Appearance, Character, or Paragraph, if necessary, to expand those lists.

3. Click OK.

1 *The original illustration*

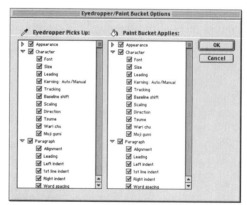

Diane Margolin

2 *After using the Paint Bucket to apply a white fill and a dashed stroke to the leaves on the left side*

3 *Eyedropper/Paint Bucket Options*

Paint Bucket Tool

Grab a color from another application

Open the application that you want to sample colors from. Move the window or palette that you want to sample from over to one side of the screen and move the Illustrator document window so you can see the other application window behind it. Choose the Eyedropper tool (I), drag from the Illustrator document window over to a color in another application window, then release the mouse (the color will appear on Illustrator's Toolbox and Color palette). Save the color as a swatch. Repeat for other colors.

If you click a path or a placed image with the Eyedropper tool, it will sample the object's paint attributes and style (if any), display them on the Toolbox and the Color and Stroke palettes, and apply them to any currently selected objects—all in one step.

To use the Eyedropper tool:

1. *Optional:* Select an object or objects if you want them to be recolored immediately with the attributes you pick up with the Eyedropper.

2. Choose the Eyedropper tool (I).

3. Click an object in any open Illustrator window that contains the color, gradient, or pattern you want to sample. The object doesn't have to be selected.

   Note: If the object you're sampling from has a style applied to it, the Eyedropper will pick up the style. If you want the tool to pick up only the color it clicks on—not the style—Shift-click the color. The color will be copied to the fill or stroke of any selected objects, depending on whether the Fill or Stroke box is currently active on the Color palette.
   or
   Drag from the Illustrator document window into any location on your screen—in another application or on the Desktop.

   If you selected any objects before using the Eyedropper tool, the paint attributes of the object you click on with the tool will be applied to the selected objects automatically.

   ➤ Hold down Option/Alt to use the Paint Bucket tool while the Eyedropper is selected, or vice versa.

   ➤ To preserve the sampled color to use again, drag the Fill or Stroke box from the Toolbox or the Color palette onto the Swatches palette.

The Saturate filter deepens or fades colors in selected objects by a relative percentage.

To saturate or desaturate colors:

1. Select the object(s) whose solid colors you want to saturate or desaturate.

2. Choose Filter > Colors > Saturate.

3. Check Preview to preview color changes in your illustration.

4. Move the Intensity slider or enter a percentage for the amount you want to intensify or fade the color or colors 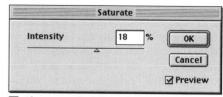. A 100% tint cannot be further saturated.

5. Click OK.

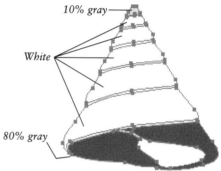

1 *Change a color's* **Intensity** *in the* **Saturate** *dialog box.*

To blend fill colors between objects:

1. Select three or more objects that contain a fill color. Objects with a fill of None won't be recolored. The more objects you use, the more gradual the blend will be.

   Note: The two objects that are farthest apart (or frontmost and backmost) cannot contain gradients, patterns, global colors, or different spot colors. The frontmost and backmost objects can contain different tints of the same spot color. Objects will stay on their respective layers.

2. From the Colors submenu under the Filter menu, choose:

   Blend Front to Back to create a color blend using the fill colors of the frontmost and backmost objects as the starting and ending colors.

   Blend Horizontally to create a color blend using the fill colors of the leftmost and rightmost objects as the starting and ending colors.

   Blend Vertically to create a color blend using the fill colors of the topmost and bottommost objects as the starting and ending colors **2**–**3**.

   Any selected objects that are stacked between the frontmost and backmost objects (or between the leftmost and rightmost or topmost and bottommost objects) will be assigned intermediate blend colors. Stroke colors won't change.

2 *Seven objects are selected.*

3 *After applying the* **Blend Vertically** *filter*

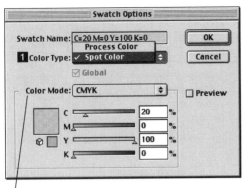

*Regardless of whether **CMYK** or **RGB** is chosen from the **Color Mode** pop-up menu, only the option that matches the document's color mode will be applied when you click OK.*

Quick conversion

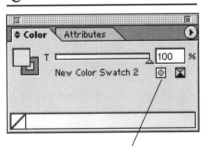

*Click this button to convert the spot color on the currently selected object to the current **document color mode** (CMYK or RGB). This won't change the original spot swatch.*

To convert a process color into a spot color, or vice versa:

1. Mix a color on the Color palette.
   or
   Select the object that contains the color you want to convert.

2. If the color isn't already on the Swatches palette, drag the Fill or Stroke box from the Color palette or the Toolbox onto the Swatches palette.

3. Double-click the swatch to open the Swatch Options dialog box.

4. Choose Color Type: Process Color or Spot Color **1**, and rename the color, if desired.

5. For a process color, check or uncheck Global. If you edit a global process color that has been applied to objects in a file, the color will update on those objects. Not so for a non-global color.

6. Choose Color Mode: Grayscale, RGB, HSB, CMYK, or Web Safe RGB.

7. Click OK.

➤ By default, spot colors are converted to process colors during color separation. To prevent this conversion from occurring, uncheck Convert to Process in File > Separation Setup.

A 1-bit TIFF or 1-bit Photoshop (.psd) image that is opened or placed in Illustrator (not drag-and-dropped) can be colorized via the Color palette. Black areas in the TIFF will be recolored; transparent areas won't change.

To colorize a 1-bit TIFF image:

1. Use File > Open or Place to open a 1-bit TIFF image in Illustrator (1-bit images have only black and transparent areas). Link or embed a 1-bit TIFF image or embed a 1-bit .psd image.

2. Click the <Image> listing on the Layers palette.

3. Apply a fill color (not a stroke).

➤ To make transparent areas in a 1-bit TIFF look as if they're colorized, create an object with the desired background color and send it behind the TIFF.

Creating fill patterns

To create a fill pattern:

1. Draw an object or objects to be used as the pattern . They may not contain a gradient, mask, blend, mesh, pattern, or bitmap image. Simple shapes are least likely to cause a printing error. The objects can contain brush strokes.

2. *Strictly optional:* Apply Filter > Distort > Roughen or Effect > Distort & Transform > Roughen at a low setting to make the pattern shapes look more hand drawn.

3. Marquee all the objects with the Selection tool (V).

4. Choose Edit > Define Pattern.
   or
   Drag the selection onto the Swatches palette, deselect the objects, then double-click the new swatch.

5. Type a name in the Swatch Name field.

6. Click OK 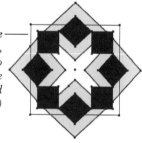–.

You can use a rectangle to control the amount of white space around a pattern or to crop parts of the objects that you want to eliminate from a pattern.

To use a rectangle to define a fill pattern:

1. Draw objects to be used as the pattern.

2. Choose the Rectangle tool (M or Shift-M).

3. Drag a rectangle or Shift-drag a half-inch to one-inch square around the objects (use the Info palette to check the dimensions). Fit the rectangle closely around the objects if you don't want any blank space to be part of the pattern (use Smart Guides to assist you) . If the pattern is complex, make the rectangle small to crop the objects to facilitate printing.

4. Choose Object > Arrange > Send to Back. The rectangle must be behind the pattern objects.

5. Apply a fill and stroke of None to the rectangle if you don't want it to become

1 *Select one or more objects. You can use anything from geometric objects to freehand lines. The simpler, the better.*

2 *After dragging the selected objects onto the Swatches palette.*

3 *An object is **filled** with the pattern from figure **1**.*

4 *Draw a rectangle around the objects, and send it to the back. (All the objects are selected in this figure.)*

5 *An object is **filled** with the pattern from figure **4**.*

Create Fill Pattern

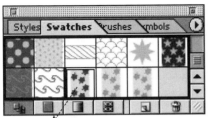

Drag the pattern you want to modify out of the Swatches palette.

2 *The original pattern swatch*

3 *The pattern is modified, selected, and then dragged back over the original swatch.*

The modified pattern is used as a fill.

part of the pattern. Apply a fill color to the rectangle if you want it to become the background color in the pattern.

6. Follow steps 3–6 in the previous set of instructions (**5**, previous page).

You can modify any pattern, including any pattern that's supplied with Illustrator. To change an existing pattern, first you have to drag its swatch back into a document.

Note: Patterns are fun, patterns are beautiful, patterns choke printers. Try to keep it simple.

To modify a fill pattern:

1. Display a blank area in your document window, then drag the pattern swatch out of the Swatches palette **1**. it will consist of a group with a bounding rectangle (with a fill and stroke of None) behind it **2**.

2. Modify the pattern objects. Use the Direct-selection tool (A) to select individual components **3**. The pattern will be listed as nested groups on the Layers palette.

3. Choose the Selection tool (V).

4. Click on any of the pattern objects to select the whole group.

5. Option-drag/Alt-drag the selected pattern shapes over the original pattern swatch. Objects already filled with the pattern in the file will update automatically.

Note: If you don't want to save over the original pattern, drag the selection onto the Swatches palette without holding down Option/Alt, then double-click the new swatch to rename it. The original swatch won't change and the pattern won't update in any objects.

➤ Read about transforming patterns on page 97.

Modify Fill Pattern

Note: To create a pattern that repeats seamlessly, see the Illustrator User Guide.

To create a geometric fill pattern:

1. Create a symmetrical arrangement of geometric objects – using the Rectangle, Ellipse, Polygon, Spiral, Star, or any other tool.

   To copy an object, Option-drag/Alt-drag it using a selection tool. Add Shift to constrain the movement horizontally or vertically. Position objects so they abut each other. To help you align the objects, use the grid or Smart Guides (see pages 88–89).

2. *Optional:* Apply assorted fill colors to add variety to the pattern.

3. Choose the Rectangle tool (M).

4. Choose a fill and stroke of None, then carefully draw a rectangle around the objects, preserving the symmetry so the pattern will repeat properly **3**.

5. With the rectangle still selected, choose Object > Arrange > Send to Back.

6. Marquee all the objects with the Selection tool (V), drag the selection onto the Swatches palette, and use it as a fill in any object **4**.

To expand a pattern fill into individual objects:

1. Select an object that contains a pattern fill **5**–**6**.

2. Choose Object > Expand.

3. Check Fill, then click OK **7**. The pattern fill will be divided into the original shapes that made up the pattern tile. Any stroke will become a compound path, and the expanded shapes will now be a group inside a clipping mask. You can release the mask (select the topmost group first), change the mask shape, or delete it.

shifting patterns

To reposition the pattern fill in an object without moving the object itself, hold down "~" and drag inside it with the Selection tool.

1 *Draw geometric objects.*

2 *Copy the object(s) and arrange the copies symmetrically.*

3 *Draw a rectangle and position it so it will create symmetry in the pattern tile.*

4 *The **geometric** pattern fill.*

5 *The original pattern*

6 *A detail of the pattern expanded (Outline view)*

Diane Margolin

7 *After applying the **Expand** command, releasing the mask, and applying Effect > Distort & Transform > Roughen (low settings)*

Chapter 9: Fill & Stroke ◆ Study Guide

Learning Objectives

- Fill the inside or stroke the edge of an object.
- Change the document color mode.
- Work with color swatches.
- Use color to manipulate objects.
- Manipulate colors applied to objects.

Get Up and Running Exercises

- You have a client that wants you to create a warm color palette, featuring yellows and reds, for a fall season print media ad campaign. The client's production staff prefers to work with an uncluttered palette, so only the colors used for the campaign should be available in the ad documents. How would you approach this project?

- Work with strokes. Start by drawing a shape; it can be a star, a polygon, or a freeform shape (don't make the shape too complicated). Assign the default fill and stroke to the shape, and then make several copies of it. How can you make each of the copies look very different from the others by changing only the stroke attributes?

- Draw a simple map of a real or fictional place, using fills to mark areas. Consider going beyond the simple use of color by using pattern fills. For example, you might use a pattern of blue waves to mark water, green triangles to mark wooded areas, and a tan-colored dot pattern to mark sand. Build the patterns yourself, draw the areas, and fill the areas with your patterns.

  Your map probably contains important linear features such as streets, highways, railroads, and rivers. How would you use stroke attributes creatively to distinguish these features from one another?

- Create or open an illustration that uses color extensively. Can you select specific colors across the entire document and change them?

Class Discussion Questions

- What tools does Illustrator provide for applying color?

- How do you apply a color to an object's fill? An object's stroke?

- What's the difference between White and None?

- What are some ways to sample an object's color and apply it to other objects?

- What's the difference between spot and process colors?

- How do you create a pattern?

- How do you crop or add extra area around a pattern tile?

- How do you take apart a pattern?

Review Questions

Multiple choice

1. What does it mean when you see a question mark in the Fill or Stroke box?

   A. The color hasn't been saved as a swatch.

   B. The color is out of gamut.

   C. The currently selected objects have different colors applied to them.

   D. No color is applied to the selection.

2. Which toolbox button swaps an object's fill and stroke color?

3. If you want a stroke to stop squarely at the endpoints of a path, which cap option would you choose?

   A. Bevel

   B. Butt

   C. Projecting

   D. Round

4. In which Swatches palette view will you see an icon representing each swatch's color model?

   A. List

   B. Sort by Name

   C. Large Thumbnail

   D. Sort by Kind

5. What does it mean when you see a dot in the lower-right corner of a swatch on the Swatches palette?

   A. It's a global process color.

   B. It's a process color.

   C. It's a registration color.

   D. It's a spot color.

6. In Illustrator, how does the stroke width extend from a path?

   A. Stroke width grows outward in the direction you specify.

   B. Stroke width grows outward from the center of a path.

   C. Stroke width grows outward from the left side of a path, relative to the path direction.

   D. Stroke width grows outward from the right side of a path, relative to the path direction.

Fill-in-the-blank

1. To sample an object's fill and stroke attributes and make them the current defaults, use the _____ tool.

2. To make sure a certain swatch library palette always opens when you start Illustrator, turn on the _____ option from the swatch library palette menu.

3. If an icon with an exclamation point inside a triangle appears next to a swatch, it means that _____.

4. Instead of clicking the Default Fill and Stroke button, you can press the _____ key.

5. To help ensure that you specify the correct spot color, refer to a _____.

6. If a cube icon appears next to a swatch, it means that _____.

7. If a path contains a tight angle that causes an extremely long point at a miter join, you might want to reduce the _____ value.

8. To load swatches from another Illustrator file, choose the _____ command.

Definitions

1. What is the default fill and stroke?
2. What is a spot color?
3. What is a process color?
4. What is a global color swatch?
5. What is a cap?
6. What is a join?
7. What is HSB and what does this abbreviation stand for?

PEN 10

Mastering the Pen tool—Illustrator's most difficult tool—requires patience and practice. Once you become comfortable creating Pen tool paths, read Chapter 8 to learn how to reshape them. If you find the Pen tool too difficult to use, remember that you can always transform or combine simple shapes into a complex shape or draw a freehand shape using the Pencil or Paintbrush tool and then reshape it. Simpler methods for creating shapes are covered in Chapter 5.

Daniel Pelavin

1 *This **corner** point joins two **straight** segments. It has **no** direction lines.*

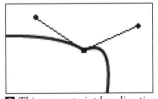

2 *A smooth point always has a pair of direction lines that move in tandem. This is a continuous curve.*

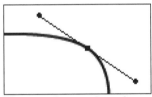

3 *This **corner** point has direction lines that move **independently**. This is a non-continuous curve.*

Drawing with the Pen tool
What the Pen tool does

The Pen tool creates precise curved and straight line segments connected by anchor points. If you click with the Pen tool, you will create corner points and straight line segments with *no* direction lines **1**. If you drag with the Pen tool, you will create smooth points and curve segments *with* direction lines **2**–**3**. The distance and direction in which you drag the mouse determine the shape of the curve segment.

In the instructions on the following pages, you'll learn how to draw straight sides, continuous curves, and non-continuous curves using the Pen tool. Once you master these three types of path shapes and start using the Pen tool as an illustrator, you'll naturally combine all three techniques without really thinking about it. Drag-drag-click, drag, click-click-drag...

Pen Tool

167

Click with the Pen tool to create an open or closed straight-sided polygon.

To draw a straight-sided object using the Pen tool:

1. If a color (not None) is selected for the Fill box on the Color palette, the Pen path will be filled as soon as three points are created (you'll see this only in Preview view, of course). To create segments that appear as lines only, choose a stroke color and a fill of None now (or at any time while you're drawing the path).

2. Choose the Pen tool (P).

3. Click to create an anchor point.

4. Click to create a second anchor point. A straight line segment will now connect the two points.

5. Click to create additional anchor points. They will be also connected by straight line segments.

6. To complete the shape as an **open** path:

   Click the Pen tool or any other tool on the Toolbox.
   or
   Hold down Cmd/Ctrl and click outside the new shape to deselect it.
   or
   Choose Edit > Deselect All (Cmd-Shift-A/ Ctrl-Shift-A).

   To complete the shape as a **closed** path, position the Pen pointer over the starting point (a small circle will appear next to the pointer), and click on it 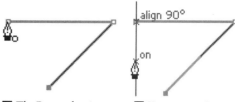.

➤ Hold down Shift while clicking with the Pen tool to constrain a segment to a multiple of 45°.

➤ Use Smart Guides to help you align points and segments (see pages 88–89) 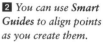.

➤ If the artboard starts to get filled with extraneous points, use the Object > Path > Clean Up command with only the Stray Points box checked.

1 *The Pen tool pointer is positioned over the starting point to close the new shape.*

2 *You can use Smart Guides to align points as you create them.*

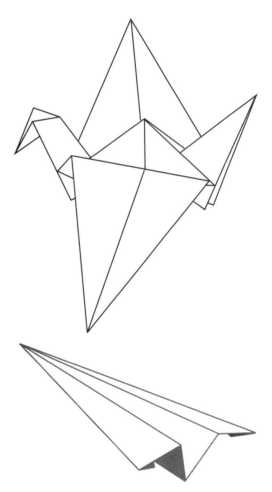

1 *Drag to create the first anchor point.*

2 *Release and reposition the mouse, then drag in the direction you want the curve to follow.*

3 *Continue to reposition and drag the mouse.*

4 *Continue to reposition and drag.*

Follow these instructions to create continuous curves, which consist of smooth anchor points connected by smooth curve segments, each with a pair of direction lines that move in tandem. The longer the direction lines, the steeper or wider the curve. You can practice drawing curves by tracing over a placed image that contains curve shapes or by converting curved objects into guides and then tracing over the guide lines (see pages 411 and 203).

To draw continuous curves using the Pen tool:

1. Choose the Pen tool (P). ✎ *Optional:* Turn on Smart Guides (Cmd-U/Ctrl-U toggle).

2. Drag to create the first anchor point **1**. The angle of the pair of direction lines that you create will be determined by the direction you drag.

3. **Release** the mouse, **move** it away from the last anchor point, then drag a short distance in the direction you want the curve to follow to create a second anchor point **2**. A curve segment will connect the first and second anchor points, and a second pair of direction lines will be created. The shape of the curve segment will be defined by the length and direction you drag the mouse.

   Remember, you can always reshape the curves later (see Chapter 8). When you drag a direction line after it's drawn, only one of the curves that the smooth point connects will reshape.

4. Drag to create additional anchor points and direction lines **3**–**4**. The points will be connected by curve segments.

(Continued on the following page)

Draw Continuous Curves

169

5. To complete the object as an **open** path:

Choose a different tool.

or

Click a selection tool (or hold down Cmd/Ctrl), then click away from the new object to deselect it.

or

Choose Edit > Deselect All (Cmd-Shift-A/Ctrl-Shift-A).

To complete the object as a **closed** path, position the Pen pointer over the starting point (a small loop will appear next to the pointer; if Text Label Hints is on in Edit > Preferences > Smart Guides & Slices, the word "anchor" will appear), drag, then release the mouse.

➤ The fewer the anchor points, the smoother the shape. Too many anchor points will produce bumpy curves, and also could cause printing errors. Also, don't make your direction lines too long. You can always lengthen them later.

Adjust as you go

■ If the last created anchor point was a **smooth** point and you want to convert it into a **corner** point, click on it with the Pen tool, move the mouse, and continue to draw. One direction line from that point will disappear.

■ If the last-created point was a **corner** point and you want to convert it into a **smooth** point, position the Pen tool pointer over it, then drag. One direction line will appear. Continue to draw.

■ To move a point as it's being created, keep the mouse button down, hold down **Spacebar**, and drag the point.

Favorite toggles (Pen tool selected)

Convert-direction-point tool	Option/Alt
Last-used selection tool	Cmd/Ctrl

Be smart with your pen

Smart Guide angle lines will appear for existing points as you click or drag with the Pen tool to produce new points **1**. Make sure **Construction Guides** is checked in Edit > Preferences > Smart Guides.

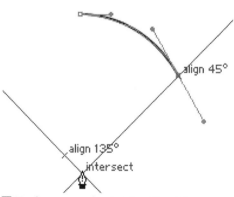

1 *To align new anchor points with existing, unselected anchor points, use Smart Guides.*

Draw Continuous Curves

1 *Drag to create the first anchor point.*

2 *Release the mouse, reposition it, then drag to create a second anchor point.*

3 *Option-drag/Alt-drag from the last anchor point in the direction you want the new curve to follow. The direction lines are on the same side of the curve segment.*

4 *Drag to create another anchor point, and so on.*

You can use the Pen tool to create corner points that join non-continuous curves, which are segments that curve on the same side of an anchor point. (Segments curve on both sides of a smooth anchor point.) If you move one direction line from a corner point, only the curve on that side of the point will reshape. Smooth points and corner points can be combined in the same path, of course. You can convert smooth points into corner points (or vice versa) as you draw them (instructions on this page) or after you draw them (instructions on the next page).

To convert smooth points into corner points as you draw them:

1. Choose the Pen tool (P).

2. Drag to create the first anchor point **1**.

3. **Release** the mouse, **move** it away from the last anchor point, then drag to create a second anchor point **2**. A curve segment will connect the first and second anchor points, and a second pair of direction lines will be created. The shape of the curve segment will be determined by the length and direction you drag.

4. Position the pointer over the last anchor point, then Option-drag/Alt-drag from that point to create a new independent-moving direction line. Drag in the direction you want the curve to follow **3**.
   or
   Click the last anchor point to remove one of the direction lines from that point.

5. Repeat the previous two steps to draw a series of anchor points and curves **4**.

6. To close the shape:
   Drag on the starting point to keep it as a smooth point.
   or
   To convert the starting point to a corner, click on it.

This is a recap of the various ways to use the Convert-anchor-point tool. These techniques were covered in three separate sets of instructions in Chapter 8.

To convert points in an existing object:

1. Choose the Direct-selection tool (A).

2. Click on the path.

3. Choose the Convert-anchor-point tool (Shift-C).
   or
   Choose the Pen tool (P), then hold down Option/Alt.

4. Position the pointer over the anchor point that you want to convert.

5. Drag new direction lines from a corner point to convert it into a smooth point **1**.
   or
   To convert a smooth point into a corner point with a non-continuous curve, rotate a direction line from the anchor point so it forms a "V" shape with the other direction line **2**.
   or
   Click on a smooth point to convert it into a corner point with no direction lines **3**–**4**.

6. Repeat the previous step to convert other anchor points.

1 *Converting a **corner** point into a **smooth** point*

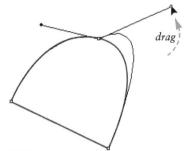

2 *Converting a **smooth** point into a **corner** point (**non-continuous** curve)*

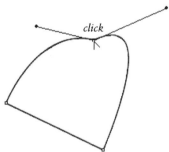

3 *Converting a **non-continuous** curve into a **corner** point with **no** direction lines*

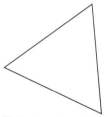

4 *Back to the original triangle*

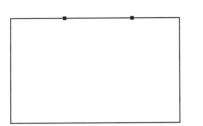

1 *Click to add two anchor points at the ⅓ points along the rectangle's top segment.*

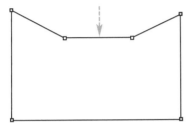

2 *Drag the segment between the new points downward.*

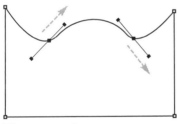

3 *Convert each new point into a smooth point.*

Exercise
Convert a rectangle into a costume mask

The outer part of the face mask

1. Draw a rectangle with a fill of None and a 1 pt. black stroke, and select it using the Direct-selection tool.

2. Choose the Pen tool (P), 🖋 and make sure Disable Auto Add/Delete is unchecked in Edit > Preferences > General.

3. Click to add two anchor points at the ⅓ points along the rectangle's top segment **1**.

4. Cmd-drag/Ctrl-drag the segment between the new points downward **2**.

5. Option-drag/Alt-drag the new point on the left upward and to the right to convert it into a smooth point, and Option-drag/Alt-drag the new point on the right downward and to the right **3**.

6. Option-drag/Alt-drag the bottom left corner point upward and to the left and the bottom right corner point downward and to the left **4**.

7. Release Option/Alt, then click to add a point in the middle of the bottommost segment.

8. Hold down Cmd/Ctrl, click on the new center point, then drag it slightly upward **5**.

(Continued on the following page)

Exercise: Rectangle into Costume Mask

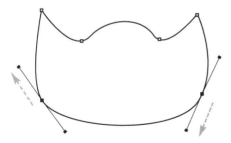

4 *Convert the rectangle's bottom corner points into smooth points.*

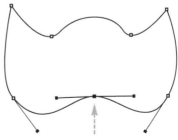

5 *Add a point in the center of the rectangle's bottom segment, then drag the new center point upward.*

The eye holes

1. Choose the Ellipse tool (L), then draw a small ellipse for an eye hole **1**.

2. Choose the Direct-selection tool (A). Deselect, click on the leftmost anchor point of the ellipse, then drag it upward to form an eye shape **2**.

3. Click the bottommost anchor point of the ellipse, then drag the left handle of that point to the left to widen the bottom segment **3**.

4. Click the top middle point of the ellipse, then drag the right handle of that point upward and to the right to widen the top right segment **4**.

5. Choose the Selection tool (V), then move the ellipse to the left side of the mask shape.

6. Choose the Reflect tool (O).

7. Option-click/Alt-click the center of the face mask. In the dialog box, check Preview, click Vertical, enter 90° in the Angle field, press Tab to force a preview, if desired, then click Copy **5**.

8. Use the Selection tool to marquee all three shapes, and fill the shapes with a color. Leave them selected.

9. Choose Object > Compound Path > Make (Cmd-8/Ctrl-8) or click the Subtract from Shape Area button  on the Pathfinder palette to create a compound shape. The eye holes, which now cut through the face mask **6**, can be modified using the Direct-selection tool.

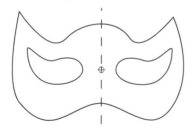

5 *To create the second eye hole, Option-click/ Alt-click in the center of the mask shape with the Reflect tool. Check Preview, click Vertical, enter 90° in the Angle field, then click Copy.*

1 *Create a small ellipse for the eye holes.*

2 *Drag the leftmost anchor point upward with the Direct-selection tool.*

3 *Drag the left direction handle of the bottommost anchor point to the left.*

4 *Drag the right handle of the top middle anchor point point upward and to the right.*

6 *All the shapes are selected and made into a compound. A fill color is applied to the compound shape. (The gray rectangle behind reveals the transparency in the compound.)*

10.0!

Chapter 10: Pen ◆ Study Guide

Learning Objectives

- Understand how the Pen tool works.
- Draw corner points and smooth points.
- Draw curved segments connected by corners.
- Edit existing objects.

Get Up and Running Exercises

Students can use the exercise at the end of the chapter in addition to the Pen tool exercise suggested here.

- Draw the shapes below, using only the Pen tool. You might want to start by roughing out the path, and then go back to adjust or convert points. Once you get the hang of it, try drawing each shape with the Pen tool in a single pass, without going back to adjust anything.

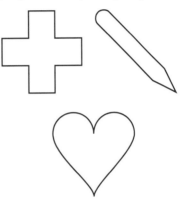

Class Discussion Questions

- What three types of combinations are possible when segments are joined by an anchor point?

- What are some ways to end a path as an open path?

- When drawing with the Pen tool, what are your options for adjusting the next segment as you draw it?

Review Questions

Multiple choice

1. If a point has no direction lines, what kind of a point is it?

    A. A corner point connecting a straight segment to a curved segment

    B. A corner point connecting straight segments

    C. A smooth point connecting curved segments

    D. A smooth point connecting straight segments

2. If you need to move a point while you're adding it with the Pen tool, which key do you press?

    A. Spacebar

    B. Option/Alt

    C. Cmd/Ctrl

    D. Shift

3. Which of the following would result in smoother curves that are also easier to edit and output?

    A. More anchor points

    B. Shorter direction lines

    C. Fewer anchor points

    D. Shallower direction line angles

4. If you want to create an anchor point with direction lines at different angles, which key do you press as you create the point?

    A. Spacebar

    B. Option/Alt

    C. Cmd/Ctrl

    D. Shift

Fill-in-the-blank

1. While the Pen tool is selected, you can temporarily switch to the Convert-anchor-point tool by pressing the _____ key.

2. While the Pen tool is selected, you can temporarily switch to the last-used selection tool by pressing the _____ key.

3. On a smooth point, direction lines move _____.

4. You can tell that you're about to close a path when a _____ appears next to the pointer.

Definitions

1. What is a direction line?

2. What defines a continuous curve?

3. What does the Convert-anchor-point tool do?

LAYERS ‖ 11

In this chapter you will learn how to create top-level layers
and sublayers; activate layers; select objects using the Layers
palette; create and edit groups; restack, duplicate, and delete
layers and objects; choose layer options such as hide/show,
lock/unlock, view, and print; merge and flatten layers;
and trace objects manually and using the Auto Trace tool.

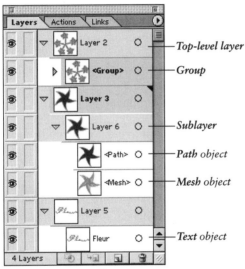

— *Top-level layer*
— *Group*

— *Sublayer*

— *Path object*

— *Mesh object*

— *Text object*

1 The objects in an illustration
(paths, texts, images, meshes, etc.)
are contained by top-level layers and
sublayers at various stacking levels.

2 The Layers palette for
this illustration is shown
in the previous figure.

Layer upon layer

Until now (unless you snuck ahead to this
chapter), you've been creating objects on a
single, default layer that was created automatically when you created your document.
Each new path you drew was added above the
next path in the document's stacking order.

Now it's time to get acquainted with the feature that displays the stacking order—the
Layers palette. With a document open, click
the Layer 1 arrowhead on the Layers palette
to reveal the list of objects on that layer.
Layer 1 is called a **top-level layer** (meaning
it's not nested within another layer) **1**–**2**.

You can add as many layers as you like to
an illustration (memory permitting). You
can also create **sublayers** (indented layers)
within any top-level layer. The actual objects
that make up the illustration—paths, text,
images, etc.—are nested within one or more
top-level layers (or on sublayers within
top-level layers). You can activate, select,
restack, show/hide, or lock/unlock any
layer, sublayer, group, or individual object.

Unless it's moved to a different layer, each
object in an illustration is nested within
whichever layer was active when that object
was created. Up to 29 indent levels can
be created.

(Continued on the following page)

By default, each new vector object you create is assigned the name **<path>**; each placed raster image or rasterized object is assigned the name **<image>**; each new mesh object is assigned the name **<mesh>**; each new symbol is assigned the name of that symbol (e.g., "Button"); and each new **text** object is assigned the first few characters in that object (e.g., "The planting season has started" might be shortened to "The plan").

➤ Double-click an object or layer to assign a custom name to it. Leave the word "group" or "path" in the name to help you identify it later.

You may say "Whoa!" when you first see the long list of names on the Layers palette. Once you get used to working with it, though, you may become enamoured with its clean, logical design, and you'll enjoy how easy it makes even simple tasks like selecting and restacking objects.

➤ Layers and sublayers are numbered in the order in which they are created, regardless of their position in the stacking order or whether they are at the top level or indented.

You can choose different Layers palette options for each document.

To choose Layers palette options:

1. Choose Palette Options from the bottom of the Layers palette menu.

2. Do any of the following **1**–**2**:

   Check Show Layers Only to list only top-level layers and sublayers—not individual objects.

   For the layer and object thumbnail size, click a Row Size (Small, Medium, or Large) or click Other and enter a custom size (12–100 pixels).

   Check which Thumbnails are to be displayed: Layers, Groups, or Objects. For the Layers option, check Top Level Only to have thumbnails display for top-level layers, but not for sublayers.

3. Click OK.

One catchall name

In this book, we refer to paths, images, mesh objects, and text objects collectively as **objects**. If we need to refer to one of these categories individually for some reason, we will.

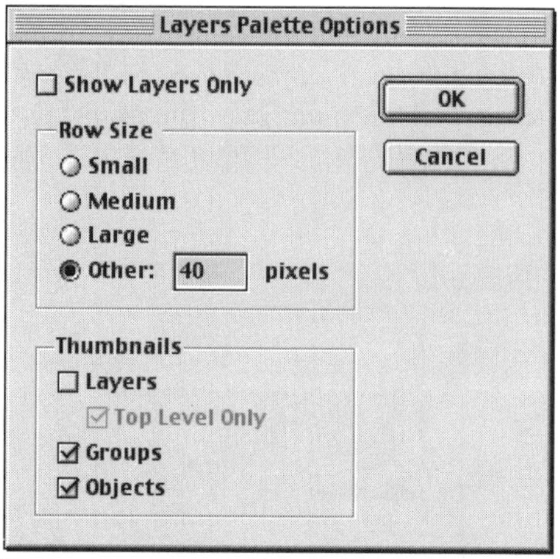

1 *You can* ***customize the Layers palette*** *for each file.*

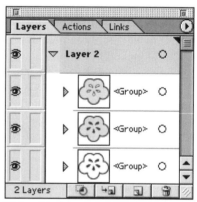

2 *For this document, we chose a large, custom Row Size (Other: 40 pixels), with Thumbnails for Layers off.*

Quick layer

To insert a new top-level layer in the topmost layer palette position, **Cmd-click/Ctrl-click** the New Layer button.

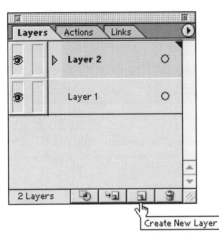

1 *Option-click/Alt-click the Create New Layer button on the Layers palette to choose options for or rename a new layer as you create it.*

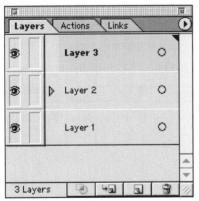

2 *The new Layer 3 appears above Layer 2.*

Creating layers

In these instructions, you'll learn how to create the granddaddy of layers—top-level layers.

To create a new top-level layer:

Method 1 (quick, no options)

1. On the Layers palette, click the top-level layer name that you want the new layer to appear above.

2. To create a layer without choosing options for it, click the Create New Layer button **1**–**2**. Illustrator will assign to the new layer the next number in order and the next available color from the Color pop-up menu in the Layer Options dialog box.

Method 2 (choose options)

1. On the Layers palette, click the top-level layer name that you want the new layer to appear above.

2. Option-click/Alt-click the Create New Layer button.
   or
   Choose New Layer from the Layers palette menu.

3. Do any of the following:
   Change the layer **Name**.

   Choose a different selection border color for objects on the layer via the **Color** pop-up menu. The various selection colors are there to help you identify which layer or sublayer a selected object is on. Colors are assigned to new layers in the order in which they appear on this pop-up menu. If the fill or stroke colors are similar to the selection border colors, it may be difficult to distinguish among them. In that case, choosing a different selection color helps.

   Choose other layer options (see page 192).

4. Click OK.

➤ A group or an object will always be nested within a top-level layer or sublayer—it can't float around by itself.

Once you're accustomed to adding and using top-level layers, you're ready for the next level of intricacy: sublayers. Each sublayer is nested within (indented under) a top-level layer or another sublayer, and layer options can be chosen separately for each individual sublayer. If you create a new object or group of objects while a sublayer is selected, the new object or group will be nested within that sublayer.

Note: By default, every sublayer has the same shading and the same name ("Layer") as its top-level layer, which can be very confusing. To make it easier to distinguish between layers and sublayers, you can rename them (e.g., "poem" or "order form" or "tyrannosaurus").

To create a sublayer:

Method 1 (quick, no options)

1. On the Layers palette, click the top-level layer (or sublayer) name within which you want the new sublayer to appear.

2. To create a new layer without choosing options for it, click the Create New Sublayer button **1**–**2**. ⊞

Method 2 (choose options)

1. On the Layers palette, click the top-level (or sublayer) layer within which you want the new sublayer to appear.

2. To create a new sublayer and choose options for it, Option-click/Alt-click the Create New Sublayer button ⊞ or choose New Sublayer from the Layers palette menu.

3. Enter a Name for the new sublayer.

4. *Optional:* Change the selection Color for the sublayer, and check or uncheck any of the Template, Show, Preview, Lock, Print, or "Dim Images to" options (see pages 192–193).

5. Click OK.

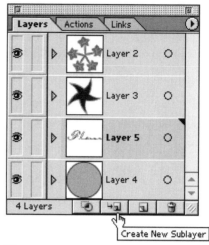

1 *Activate a layer name, then click the Create New Sublayer button.*

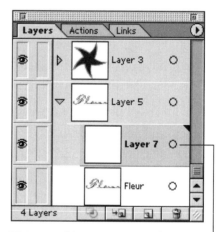

2 *A new sublayer name (in this case Layer 7) appears within Layer 5.*

Create a Sublayer

1 *First, select the objects to be grouped. You can draw a marquee around them...*

If you group objects together, you can easily select, cut, copy, paste, transform, recolor, or move them as a unit. When objects are grouped, they are automatically placed on the same top-level layer (the top-level layer of the frontmost object in the group) and are assigned the same selection color. You can group any types of objects together (e.g., text objects with placed images) and you can select and edit individual objects in a group without having to ungroup them.

To create a group:

1. Choose the Selection tool (V). ▶ Then, in the illustration window, Shift-click or marquee all the objects to be grouped **1**.
   or
   Shift-click the selection area or the target circle (○) at the far right side of the Layers palette for each object you want to be part of the group. A selection square will appear for each of those objects **2**. (You'll learn more about the selection area later in this chapter.)

2. Choose Object > Group (Cmd-G/ Ctrl-G) **3**.
   or
   Control-click/Right-click the artboard and choose Group from the context menu.

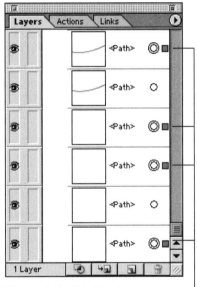

2 *...or Shift-click the selection area on the Layers palette for each object.*

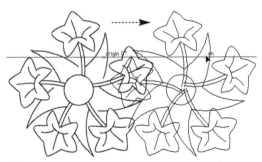

3 *If you move a group using the selection tool, all the objects in the group will move in unison.*

Activate Layers and Objects

Activating layers

If you want to control where a newly created (or pasted) path will be positioned within the overall stacking order of an illustration, you need to activate (highlight) a top-level layer, sublayer, group, or object on the Layers palette before pasting or drawing the object.

Note: Activating a top-level layer or sublayer will not cause objects on those layers to become selected. To learn how to select objects using the Layers palette, see pages 182–183.

➤ If a top-level layer is active when a new object is created but no sublayer is active, the new object (e.g., "<Path>" or "<Mesh>") will be listed just below that top-level layer name.

➤ If a sublayer or group is active when a new object is created or placed but no objects in the sublayer or group are selected, the new object will be listed either directly above or inside that sublayer or group.

➤ If an object is active when a new object is created or placed, the new object will appear directly above that active object within that object's sublayer or group, if any.

To activate a layer, sublayer, group, or object:

Click a top-level layer, sublayer, group, or object name. Click the name—not the selection area at the far right side of the palette. The current layer indicator will appear at the far right side of the palette **1**.

To activate more than one layer, group, or object at a time, follow the instructions on the next page.

Quick activate

Cmd-Option-click/Ctrl-Alt-click anywhere on the Layers palette list, then start typing a layer, group, or object name. You can type a layer number without typing the word "Layer." Caveat: Illustrator won't find a sublayer, group, or object unless its name is visible on the palette (in other words, its layer list has to be expanded).

Current layer indicator

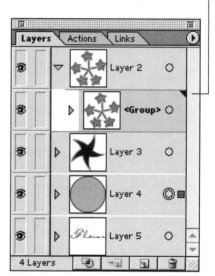

1 *Click to the right of the name of the layer, sublayer, group, or object you want to activate.*

Circles and squares 10.0!

The column of little circles on the far side of the Layers palette are used to **target** an object, group, or layer for applying appearance attributes (read about appearances in Chapter 19).

The target circle has a slightly different function in version 10, due to user feedback. Clicking the **target circle** or the **selection area** for a group or object serves the same function: The object or group becomes **selected** and becomes active on the Appearance palette (read more about selection methods on the next page).

For a top-level layer or sublayer, the situation is a little different. To select all the objects on a top-level layer or sublayer, use the selection area. To target a top-level layer or sublayer and make it active on the Appearance palette, click the target circle. In other words, you can't target a top-level layer or sublayer using its selection area.

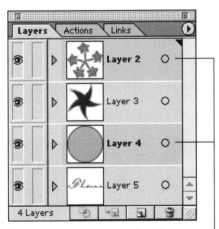

1 Two **non-contiguous** top-level layers are activated (note the darker highlight color).

When more than one layer, sublayer, or object is active, they can be restacked on the palette en masse and the same layer options can be applied to them. *Note:* Selecting an object won't cause its layer to become active, and vice versa. Activating and selecting are two different functions.

First, some rules.

➤ You can activate more than one sublayer within the same top-level layer, but you can't activate sublayers from different top-level layers.

➤ You can activate more than one item of the same category (e.g., all top-level layers), but you can't activate items from different nesting levels at the same time (e.g., not top-level layers with sublayers).

➤ You can activate multiple objects (e.g., paths) in the same top-level layer, but you can't activate objects from different top-level layers.

To activate multiple items:

1. On the Layers palette, click a top-level layer, sublayer, or object name.

2. Shift-click another layer, sublayer, or object name. The items you clicked on and all items in between them of a similar kind will become active (highlighted).
   or
   Cmd-click/Ctrl-click non-contiguous layer, sublayer, or object names **1**. Only the names you click on will become active.

➤ Cmd-click/Ctrl-click to deactivate one item (name) when more than one item is active.

To deactivate all layers:

Click in a blank area below all the listings on the Layers palette (you may need to scroll downward to make the blank area visible).

Activate, Deactivate Multiple Items

Selecting objects

We like to use the Layers palette to select paths or groups. Here we're talking about selecting for editing or reshaping—selection handles and all—not just activating, which we discussed on the previous two pages.

To select all the objects in a layer:

Click the selection area for a top-level layer or sublayer at the far right side of the Layers palette. A selection square will appear for every sublayer, group, and object on that layer; every object on the layer, regardless of its indent level, will become selected in the illustration window; and the target circle will also become selected for each item (it will become a double ring) **1**–**2**.

➤ To deselect any selected object individually, expand the object's top-level layer or sublayer list, then Shift-click its selection square.

To deselect all the objects in a layer:

Shift-click the selection square or target circle for the layer. All the objects in the layer will be deselected, including any objects contained in any of its sublayers or groups.

To select one object:

1. Make sure the object name is visible on the palette. Expand any top-level layer, sublayer, or group list, if necessary.

2. At the far right side of the Layers palette, click the selection area or target circle for the object you want to select **3**.

   To select multiple objects on different layers, see the instructions on the following page.

➤ If you click the selection area for a top-level layer or sublayer but there is no object on that layer or sublayer (its thumbnail is blank), no selection square will appear.

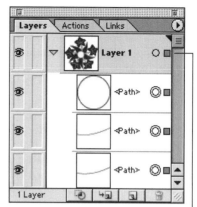

1 *Click the **selection area** for a layer to select all the paths and groups on that layer.*

2 *All the paths and path groups on our "flowers" layer became selected in the illustration window.*

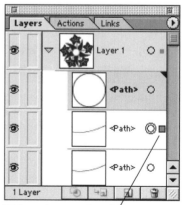

3 *One object is **selected.***

Seelect Objects

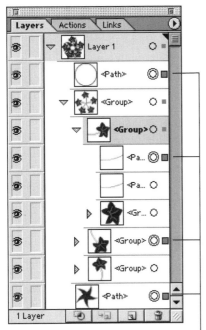

1 *Objects from non-consecutive stacking levels are selected (note the selection squares).*

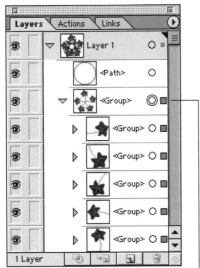

2 *If you click the selection area for a group, all the objects in the group will become selected.*

You can select multiple groups or objects on different—even non-consecutive—top-level layers or sublayers.

Note: Selecting an object won't cause it to become active, and vice versa. Activating and selecting are two different functions.

To select multiple objects on different layers:

Method 1

Expand any layer or group lists so the names of all the nested objects you want to select are visible. Click the **selection area** or **target circle** for any object, then Shift-click any other individual groups or objects you want to add to the selection **1**. The groups or objects don't have to be listed consecutively.

Method 2

Option-drag/Alt-drag upward or downward through a series of consecutive top-level or sublayer **names** (not the selection areas) to select all the objects on those layers.
or
Or expand a sublayer or group list, then Option-drag/Alt-drag upward or downward through a series of consecutive object **names**.

➤ To deselect any selected object individually, Shift-click its selection square or target circle.

Working with groups
To select all the objects in a group:
Method 1 (Layers palette)

1. Expand a top-level layer on the palette that contains a nested group.

2. To select all the objects in a group, (including any objects in groups that may be nested inside it), click the group's selection area or target circle at the far right side of the Layers palette **2**.
or
To select all the objects in a group that's nested inside another group, expand the list for the larger group, then click selection area only for the nested group.

(For Method 2, see the following page.)

Select Multiple Objects

Method 2 (illustration window)

To select an entire group, click any item in the group with the Selection tool (V). ⬆

or

To select an object in a group—or individual anchor points or segments on an object in a group—click the object, point, or segment with the Direct-selection tool (A). ⬆

or

To select a group that's nested within a larger, parent group, use the Direct-selection tool while holding down Option/Alt or use the Group-selection tool ⬆⁺ (it's on the Direct-selection tool pop-out menu). Click once to select an object in a group **1**; click again on the same object to select the whole group that object is part of **2**; click a third time on the object to select the next larger group that the newly selected group is a part of **3**, and so on.

➤ To display a selection's bounding box, make sure Show Bounding Box is chosen from the View menu, keep the object(s) selected, and choose the Selection tool.

1 *Click once to select an object in a group.*

2 *Click again to select the remaining objects within the same group.*

3 *Keep clicking to select other groups that may be nested inside the larger group.*

1 To *select multiple objects in a group,* expand the group list, then Shift-click the *selection area* for each object. A *selection square* will appear for each object.

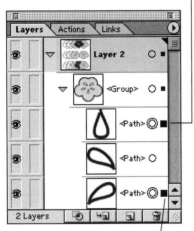

2 To *deselect an object in a group,* Shift-click its selection square.

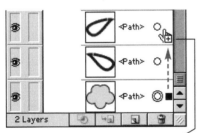

3 To *copy an object in a group,* Option-drag/Alt-drag its selection square upward or downward (note the plus sign).

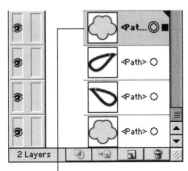

4 *The duplicate appears.*

To select some objects in a group:

Expand the group's list on the Layers palette, then Shift-click the selection area or target circle at the far right side of the palette for each object in the group you want to select **1**.
or
Choose the Group-selection tool (it's on the Direct-selection tool pop-out menu), then Shift-click objects in a group (or nested groups) in the illustration window.
or
Choose the Direct-selection tool (A), then Cmd-Shift-click/Ctrl-Shift-click multiple items (or nested groups) in the illustration window.

To deselect an object in a group:

On the Layers palette, expand the group list, then Shift-click the selection square or target circle for an object in the group **2**.
or
Choose the Direct-Selection tool, then Shift-click the object in the illustration window.

To copy an object in a group:

Method 1 (Layers palette)

1. Expand the group list.
2. Click the selection area for the object you want to copy.
3. Option-drag/Alt-drag the selection square upward or downward, then release the mouse when the little outline square is at the desired stacking position either inside the same group or in another sublayer or top-level layer **3**–**4**. (To restack the copy after it's created, see page 188.)

Method 2 (illustration window)

1. Choose the Direct-selection tool, then select the object you want to copy.
2. To keep the copy inside the group, Option-drag/Alt-drag the object.
   or
   To have the copy appear outside the group, copy the object (Cmd-C/Ctrl-C), deselect, then paste (Cmd-V/Ctrl-V).

Follow these instructions to add an existing object to a group. The object will stay in its original *x/y* position.

To move an existing object (or group) into a group:

Method 1 (the easier way)

1. Make sure the name of the object you want to add to the group is visible on the Layers palette.

2. Drag the object name upward or downward in the palette. Release the mouse when the large, black arrowhead points to the name of the group you want to move the object to **1**. The group list will expand, if it isn't already expanded **2**.

Method 2 (the old way)

1. Choose the Selection tool (V).

2. Select the object (or group) to be added to the group.

3. Choose Edit > Cut (Cmd-X/Ctrl-X).

4. Select the object in the group that you want the additional object to appear in front of or behind.

5. Choose Edit > Paste in Front (Cmd-F/Ctrl-F) or Paste in Back (Cmd-B/Ctrl-B).

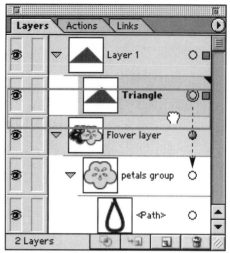

1 *The "Triangle" object is dragged downward to the "petals group."*

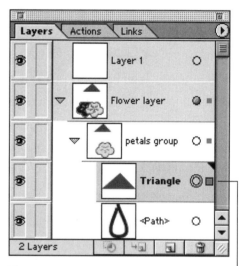

2 *The petals group list expands, and the Triangle object is on the list.*

Move Object into a Group

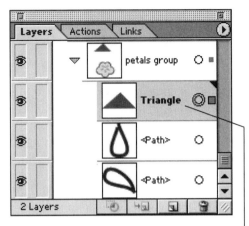

1 *The name of an object in a group is clicked on.*

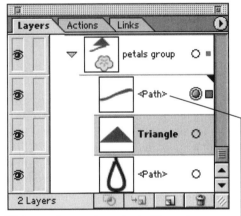

2 *A new object is drawn in the illustration window. The word "<path>" appears within the petals group list.*

You can choose a group for an object before it's created. *Note:* This works only for path objects drawn in Illustrator—not placed images.

To add a new object to a group:

1. Deselect all objects (Cmd-Shift-A/ Ctrl-Shift-A).

2. On the Layers palette, expand the list for the group you want to add a new object to.

3. Click the object name (not the selection area) above which you want the new object to appear **1**.

4. Draw a new object. The new object will be listed directly above the object you chose in the previous step, within the same group **2**.

There comes a time when a group has to be disbanded.

To ungroup a group:

1. If the group isn't already selected:

   Choose the Selection tool (V), ▶ then click the group in the illustration window.
   or
   Click the selection area or target circle for the group on the Layers palette.

2. Choose Object > Ungroup (Cmd-Shift-G/ Ctrl-Shift-G).
   or
   Control-click/Right-click on the artboard and choose Ungroup from the context menu. If the command isn't available, it means no group is selected.

➤ Keep choosing the same command again to ungroup nested groups.

Restacking

The order of objects (and layers) on the Layers palette matches the front-to-back order of objects (and layers) in the illustration. You can move a group or object to a different stacking position within the same layer, move a group or object to a different top-level layer or sublayer, or even move a whole top-level layer or sublayer upward or downward on the list.

On this page you'll use the Layers palette for restacking. On the next page, you'll use commands. Shop and compare.

To restack a layer, group, or object:

Drag a top-level layer, sublayer, group, or object name upward or downward on the Layers palette (the pointer will turn into a hand icon). Release the mouse between layers or objects to keep the object on the same level of indent (e.g., keep a path within a group) **1**–**2**. Or release the mouse when the large black arrowhead points to a different group or layer **3**–**4**. The illustration will redraw with the objects in their new stacking position.

Beware! If you move an object that's part of a group or clipping mask to a different top-level layer, the object will be released from the group or mask.

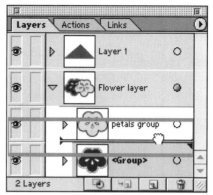

1 *Drag a layer, sublayer, group, or object name upward or downward on the list. Here the mouse is released at the **same indent level**.*

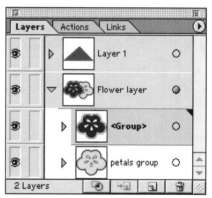

2 *The dark flower group is restacked.*

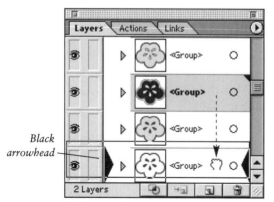

Black arrowhead

3 *The dark flower group is moved into a different group.*

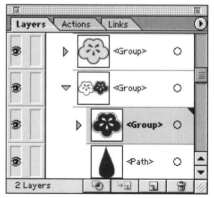

4 *The dark flower group is in a new stacking position and indent level.*

Restack

Upside down

To reverse the order of sublayers, groups, and objects within a layer, make all the elements you want to reverse active (active—not selected). To activate non-contiguous items, Cmd-click/Ctrl-click them; to activate contiguous items, Shift, then Shift-click. Then choose **Reverse Order** from the Layers palette menu.

1 *Select the object you want to restack, then choose Edit > Cut.*

2 *Select the object that you want to paste directly in front of or directly behind.*

3 *Choose Edit > Paste In Front or Paste in Back. (In this case, Paste in Back was chosen.)*

The Paste In Front and Paste In Back commands paste the Clipboard contents directly in front of or directly behind the currently selected object within the selected object's layer in the same horizontal and vertical *(x/y)* position from which it was cut.

To restack an object in front of or behind another object:

1. Choose the Selection tool (V), ↖ then select an object **1**.

2. Choose Edit > Cut (Cmd-X/Ctrl-X).

3. Select the object (in the same document or a different document) that you want to paste directly in front of or directly behind **2**. If you don't select an object, the Clipboard contents will be pasted to the top or bottom of the currently active top-level layer.

4. Choose Edit > Paste In Front (Cmd-F/Ctrl-F).
   or
   Choose Edit > Paste In Back (Cmd-B/Ctrl-B) **3**.

This is the old-fashioned way to restack. We like the method on the previous page better.

To restack using a command:

1. Choose the Selection tool (V), ↖ then select the object or group you want to restack.

2. To move the object to the bottom or top of the same layer, choose Object > Arrange > Send To Back or Bring To Front or Control-click/Right-click and choose either command from the Arrange submenu.
   or
   To shift the object one level at a time within the same layer, choose Object > Arrange > Bring Forward or Send Backward or Control-click/Right-click and choose either command from the Arrange submenu.

➤ If you restack an object in a group, it will stay in the group.

Restack

189

Duplicating

If you duplicate an entire top-level layer, all the sublayers and objects from that layer will appear in the duplicate. The duplicate layer will be stacked directly above the original from which it is made.

To duplicate a layer, sublayer, or object:

Activate the layer, sublayer, or object you want to duplicate, then choose Duplicate "[name]" from the Layers palette menu.
or
Drag a layer, sublayer, or object name over the Create New Layer button **1**–**2**. **↴** If you duplicate a top-level layer or sublayer, the word "copy" will appear in the duplicate name.

Follow these instructions to copy all the objects from a top-level layer and any sublayers or groups contained within it to an existing layer or sublayer of your choice. (In the previous set of instructions, the duplicate objects appeared in a brand new layer.)

To copy objects between layers:

1. Click the selection area for a top-level layer, sublayer, group, or object.

2. Option-drag/Alt-drag the selection square for the layer, sublayer, group, or object upward or downward on the list. Release the mouse when the selection square is in the desired location **3**. The duplicate objects will appear in the same *x/y* location as the original objects.

➤ If you Option-drag/Alt-drag a <clipping path> (a mask) into a different top-level layer, the mask copy won't clip any objects below it. It will be a basic path with a Fill and Stroke of None.

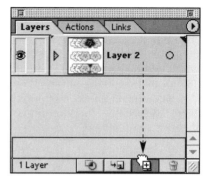

1 To *duplicate* a layer, sublayer, group, or object, drag it over the **Create New Layer** button (note the plus sign).

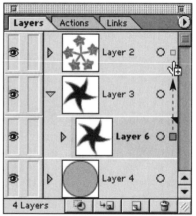

2 A *copy* of Layer 2 is made.

3 To *copy* an object to another layer, Option-drag/Alt-drag its **selection square** upward or downward to the desired location.

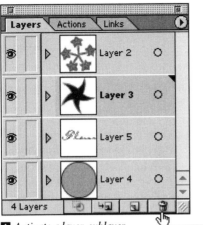

1 *Activate a layer, sublayer, group, or object, then click the* **Delete Selection (trash) button.**

Deleting

You know how to make 'em. Now you need to learn how to get rid of 'em.

Beware! If you delete a top-level layer or a sublayer, any and all objects on that layer will be removed from the file.

To delete a layer, sublayer, group, or object:

1. Activate all the layers, sublayers, groups, and objects you want to delete. To activate more than one, Cmd-click/Ctrl-click their names. Remember, you can activate more than one layer of the same category (e.g., all top-level layers), but not different kinds of layers (e.g., not a top-level layer and objects from a different top-level layer).

2. Choose Delete "[layer or object name]" from the Layers palette menu or click the Delete Selection (trash) button at the bottom of the palette **1**. If there are any objects on a layer or sublayer you're deleting, an alert dialog box will appear. Click Yes.
   or
   Drag the activated layers or objects over the Delete Selection (trash) button. No alert dialog box will appear.

➤ To retrieve a deleted layer and the objects it contained, choose Edit > Undo Deletion (Cmd-Z/Ctrl-Z) immediately.

Delete Layer or Object

Choosing layer options

To choose multiple options (e.g., color, lock, show/hide, and print) for a layer or object from one central dialog box, use the Layer Options dialog box, which is discussed on this page and the next page (one-stop shopping). To choose individual options for a layer or an object (e.g., hide a layer or change its view mode), read through pages 194–196.

If you choose Layer Options for a top-level layer, those options will apply to all the sublayers, groups, and objects within that layer. You can also choose options for a sublayer, group, or individual object.

To choose layer or object options:

1. Double-click a layer, sublayer, group, or object on the Layers palette.
   or
   Click a layer, sublayer, group, or object on the Layers palette, then choose Options for "[ ]" from the palette menu.
   or
   Activate more than one layer, sublayer, group, or object, then choose Options for Selection from the palette menu.

2. For the active layer, sublayer, group, or object, do any of the following **1**–**2**:

   Type a different **Name** for the layer, sublayer, group, or object.

   Check **Show** to display that object or all the objects on the layer or sublayer; uncheck to hide the object or objects. Hidden layers won't print.

   Check **Lock** to prevent that object or all the objects on that layer or sublayer from being edited; uncheck to allow the objects to be edited.

   ➤ You can also lock/unlock a layer or sublayer by clicking in the second column on the Layers palette. It's faster! (See page 194.)

   ➤ You can unlock a whole illustration via the Lock submenu on the Object menu, but not individual objects. Using the Layers palette, however, you can unlock one object at a time.

Making layers non-printable

There are three ways to make a layer non-printable, and there are significant differences among them:

➤ If you **hide** a layer, the layer can't be printed, exported, or edited.

➤ If you turn a layer into a **template**, it can't be printed, exported, or edited, but it will be visible (images on the layer can be dimmed).

➤ If you turn off the **Print** option in the Layer Options dialog box, the layer won't print, but it can be exported and edited, and it will be visible.

1 *The Layer Options dialog box for a layer*

2 *The Options dialog box for a path*

For a layer or sublayer, do any of the following:

Choose a different **Color** for the object's selection border in the illustration and its selection square on the Layers palette. This is handy if the current selection color is very similar to the artwork color, and thus is hard to distinguish. You can choose a color from the pop-up menu or double-click the color swatch and mix a color yourself using the color picker.

Choose **Template** to convert a layer or sublayer into a tracing layer, which will be uneditable and non-printable. Any images and raster objects on the layer will be dimmed (more about templates on page 197). Template layer names are listed in italics.

Check **Preview** to display the layer in Preview view; uncheck to display the layer in Outline view.

➤ To switch views for a layer without opening the Layer Options dialog box, see "To change the view for a top-level layer" on page 196.

Check **Print** to make the layer printable; uncheck to prevent all the objects on that layer from printing. The names of non-printable layers appear in italics.

➤ Another way to make a layer non-printable is to hide it (click the eye icon on the Layers palette).

To dim any placed images or rasterized objects on that layer, check **Dim Images to** and specify a percentage by which you want those images dimmed (use this for tracing); uncheck this option to display placed images normally. Unlike template layers, dimmed images are editable and print normally.

Choose Layer/Object Options

A locked object can't be selected or edited. If a whole layer is locked, none of the objects on that layer will be editable. Locked layers stay locked even if you close and reopen the file.

To lock/unlock layers or objects:

Click in the edit column for a layer, sublayer, group, or object to make the padlock icon 🔒 appear **1**. Click the padlock icon to unlock.

or

To lock multiple layers, sublayers, groups, or objects, drag upward or downward in the edit column. Drag back over the padlock icons to unlock.

or

Option-click/Alt-click in the edit column for a top-level layer to lock or unlock all the other top-level layers except the one you're clicking on.

or

Activate the layer(s) you want to remain unlocked—then to lock all the non-active layers, choose Lock Others from the Layers palette menu.

or

Select the layer you want to remain unlocked (or a nested object on that layer), then choose Object > Lock > Other Layers. **10.0!**

Note: You can't unlock an object individually if the top-level layer in which the object is nested is locked; you have to unlock the top-level layer before you can unlock the object.

➤ To lock a selected object via a command, choose Object > Lock > Selection (Cmd-2/Ctrl-2). There is no Object menu command for unlocking an individual object. **10.0!**

➤ To Unlock All objects: Cmd-Option-2/ Ctrl-Alt-2.

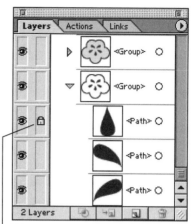

1 *Click in the edit column to lock a layer, group, or object (the padlock icon will appear).*

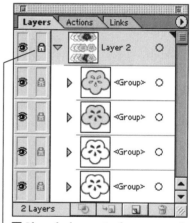

2 *If you lock an entire layer, none of the objects on that layer will be editable.*

New commands 10.0!

Hide artwork above the selected object(s)	Select object, then Object > Hide > **All Artwork Above***
Lock artwork above the selected object(s)	Select object, then Object > Lock > **All Artwork Above***

*Minor detail: These commands sound good on paper, but as of version 10.0, they don't work!

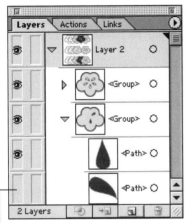

1 *You can hide individual **objects** or **groups**...*

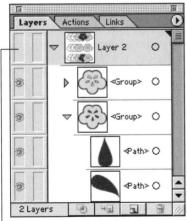

2 *...or you can hide whole **layers**.*

What have you got to hide? Well, for one thing, if your illustration is crowded with objects, hiding the objects you're not working on will make your screen redraw faster. For another, it will make it easier to locate and focus on the parts of your illustration that you are working on. You can hide a top-level layer and all its nested layers; hide a group; or just hide an individual object. If it's hidden, it won't print.

To hide/show layers or objects:

Note: If you want to show an object, but its top-level layer is hidden, you must show the top-level layer first.

Click the eye icon 👁 (in the first column) for a top-level layer, a sublayer, a group, or an object **1**–**2**. If you hide a top-level layer or a sublayer, any objects nested within that layer or sublayer will be hidden, whether or not they are selected. To redisplay what was hidden, click where the eye icon was.
or
Drag upward or downward in the eye column to hide multiple, consecutive top-level layers, sublayers, groups, or objects. To redisplay what was hidden, drag again.
or
Option-click/Alt-click the eye column 👁 to hide/show all the top-level layers except the one you're clicking on.
or
Make sure all the layers are visible (choose Show All Layers from the Layers palette menu if they aren't), make the top-level layer or layers you want to remain visible active, then choose Hide Others from the Layers palette menu or select the layer and choose Object > Hide > Other Layers. 10.0!

➤ To hide a selected object via a command, choose Object > Hide > Selection (Cmd-3/Ctrl-3). There is no command for showing an individual object.

➤ To make a visible layer non-printable, uncheck Print in the Layer Options dialog box. You can also show or hide an entire layer via that dialog box.

Hide Layer or Object

If you change the view for a top-level layer, all of its nested layers and objects will be displayed in that view.

To change the view for a top-level layer:

To display a top-level layer in Outline view, regardless of the current view for the illustration, Cmd-click/Ctrl-click the eye icon 👁 for that layer. The eye will become hollow ◼. To redisplay the layer in Preview view, Cmd-click/Ctrl-click the eye icon again.

or

Double-click the layer name, then check or uncheck the Preview box.

To display all top-level layers in Outline view except one:

Cmd-Option-click/Ctrl-Alt-click a top-level layer eye icon 👁 to display all layers in Outline view except the one you're clicking on.

or

Click the top-level layer that you want to display in Preview view, then choose Outline Others from the Layers palette menu.

➤ To display all layers in Preview view, choose Preview All Layers from the Layers palette menu.

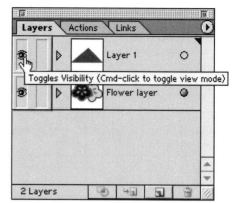

◼ *Cmd/Ctrl click the eye icon to toggle between **Outline** and **Preview** views for that top-level layer.*

Show or hide 'em

To **show/hide** all **template layers**, use this shortcut: **Cmd-Shift-W/Ctrl-Shift-W**.

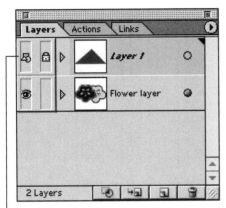

1 *The* **template** *layer icon. The template layer name is in italics.*

Objects on template layers are locked, non-printable, and non-exportable, and any images on template layers are dimmed. You can use a template layer either to trace an object or a placed image using the Auto Trace tool or as a guide to help you draw new objects. Read about tracing on pages 203–206.

To create a template layer:

Method 1 (choose options)

1. Double-click an existing top-level layer name.
   or
   To create a new top-level layer to become the template layer, Option-click/Alt-click the Create New Layer button ▣ at the bottom of the Layers palette.

2. Check Template.

3. *Optional:* Change the "Dim Images to" percentage for any placed images or rasterized objects on the template layer.

4. Click OK. A template icon ▧ will appear in place of the eye icon for the layer and any nested layers or objects in that layer will be locked **1**.

Method 2 (quick)

1. Click an existing layer name.

2. Choose Template from the Layers palette menu.

Method 3 (for placed images)

To create a template layer as you place an image into Illustrator, check Template in the File > Place dialog box.

Create Template

Layer management

With the abundance of information on the Layers palette comes one minor drawback: Sometimes it's hard to find things. Luckily, Adobe built in a locator command. Now, how about a locator command for the contents of Elaine's handbag?

To locate an object on the Layers palette:

1. Choose the Selection tool (V).

2. Select the object in the illustration window that you want to locate on the Layers palette. You can select more than one object; they will all be found. (To select an object in a group, use the Direct-selection or Group-selection tool.)

3. Choose Locate Object from the Layers palette menu. The selected object's top-level layer list will expand, if it isn't already expanded, and a selection square will appear for the object.

➤ If "Locate Layer" appears on the palette menu instead of "Locate Object," choose Palette Options from the palette menu and uncheck the Show Layers Only option. The Locate Object command will then become available.

The Collect in New Layer command moves all the currently highlighted top-level layers, sublayers, groups, or objects into a brand new layer.

To move layers, sublayers, groups, or objects to a new layer:

1. Cmd-click/Ctrl-click the layer, group, or object names you want to gather together ■. They all have to be at the same indent level (e.g., all objects from the same sublayer or a series of consecutive sublayers). Don't select the layers!

2. Choose Collect in New Layer from the Layers palette menu. The sublayers, groups, or objects you chose will be nested inside a new sublayer within the same top-level layer ■. Active top-level layers will be nested as sublayers within a new top-level layer.

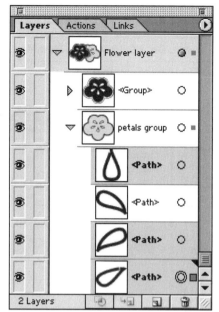

■ *Three paths are made **active**.*

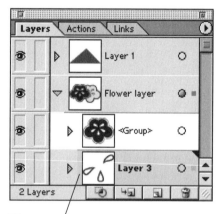

■ *After choosing **Collect in New Layer**, the three active paths are gathered into a new top-level layer (Layer 3, in this case).*

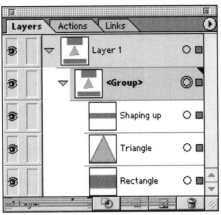

1 *A group is activated on the Layers palette.*

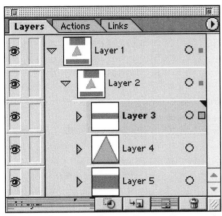

2 *After choosing Release to Layers (Sequence)*

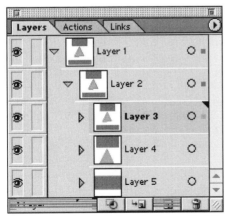

3 *After choosing the Release to Layers (Build)*

The Release to Layers command moves all the objects or groups that are nested within the currently active layer onto separate layers within that active layer.

If you're planning to export your Illustrator file to Adobe LiveMotion or Macromedia Flash to use as the contents of an object or frame animation, first release any groups and expand any appearances or blends, and then release those objects to individual layers (nested within a top-level layer) via a Release to Layers command. Flash or LiveMotion will then be able to convert the layers from the placed file into separate objects or into a sequence. See pages 459–460 and 463–464.

Read step 2 carefully before choosing either of the two Release to Layers commands.

To move objects to new, separate layers:

1. On the Layers palette, click a top-level layer, sublayer, or group name (not an object) **1**.

2. From the Layers palette menu, choose:

   Release to Layers (Sequence) **2**. Each object in the active layer or group will be nested in its own new layer within the original layer. The object's original stacking order will be preserved. If the objects were originally in a group, that group name ("<group>") will be removed from the palette.
   or
   If you want to build a cumulative animation sequence, choose Release to Layers (Build) **3**. The bottommost layer will contain only the bottommost object; the next layer above that will contain the bottommost object plus the next object above it; the next layer above that will contain the two previous objects plus the next object above, and so on. If you're going to use another application to create a frame animation of objects that are added in succession, choose this option.

(Continued on the following page)

Release to Layers

➤ If you release a layer or a sublayer that contains a clipping mask that was created using the Layers palette, the mask will still clip the objects within the same layer or sublayer.

➤ If you release a layer or group that contains a scatter brush, the brush object will remain as a single <Path>. If, on the other hand, you activate only the brush object and release to layers, each object in the scatter brush will be moved to a separate layer; the original scatter brush path will be preserved. If the brush object was originally in a group, the new layer will be outside the group.

Remembering layers

If you want to paste an object to the top of its own layer or sublayer rather than to a different layer, turn on the **Paste Remembers Layers** option via the Layers palette menu. If this option is on and the original layer is deleted after the object is copied, but before the Paste command is used, the object(s) will paste onto a brand-new layer.

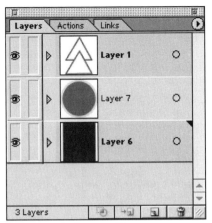

1 *Activate the layers, sublayers, groups, or objects you want to merge.*

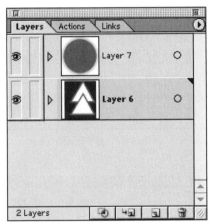

2 *After choosing* **Merge Selected**, *the two active layers are merged into the topmost of the currently active layers (or groups).*

Merging and flattening

Dire warning! If there's a chance you're going to want to work with the individual layers in your file again, save a copy of the file using File > Save As before applying the Merge Selected or Flatten Artwork command.

If you have more layers and sublayers on the Layers palette than you can comfortably handle, you can consolidate the list by merging some of them together. You can also merge two or more groups or merge a group with individual non-grouped objects. In the latter case, the objects will become part of the group and will appear at the top or bottom of the group.

Note: A non-grouped object can be merged with a sublayer or a group, but not with another object.

To merge layers, sublayers, groups, and objects:

1. Activate two or more layers, sublayers, or groups. To merge non-contiguous top-level layers or sublayers, Cmd-click/ Ctrl-click to activate them. Locked and/or hidden layers can be merged.

2. Choose Merge Selected from the Layers palette menu **1**–**2**.

➤ If you merge two groups and one of the groups contains a clipping path, that clipping path may be released, depending on the original stacking order of the groups.

Merge

Flatten

Warning! The Flatten Artwork command **discards** hidden top-level layers (read that again) and flattens **all** layers in the file into **one top-level layer**, with any sublayers and groups nested within it. Actually, you'll get an alert dialog box which will give you the option to keep the hidden artwork when layers are flattened, but you still need to think ahead.

Warning! Flatten Artwork also **removes** transparency, effects, paint attributes, and any layer clipping sets from top-level layers. Otherwise, the appearance of the artwork in the illustration window won't change. The objects will be fully editable after the command is chosen. If you flatten the artwork into an active layer that has appearances attached to it, those appearances will be applied to all the objects.

To flatten artwork:

1. Make sure there are no hidden top-level layers that you want to keep **1**.

2. By default, if no layers are active, the Flatten Artwork command merges all the currently visible layers into the bottom-most top-level layer. To flatten into a layer of your choice, activate it now.

3. Choose Flatten Artwork from the Layers palette menu. If there are any hidden layers that contain artwork, an alert dialog box will appear **2**–**3**. Click Yes to discard the hidden artwork or click No to preserve the artwork in the flattened document. You can choose Undo right away, if need be.

Note: If you try to flatten artwork into a hidden, locked, or template layer, Illustrator will flatten all the layers into the next higher top-level layer that isn't hidden, locked, or a template instead.

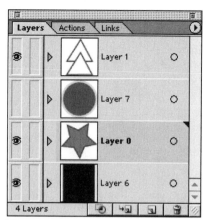

1 *The original four-layer illustration. Since at least one layer is hidden and contains artwork (Layer 7, in this case), an alert dialog box will appear when the **Flatten Artwork** command is chosen.*

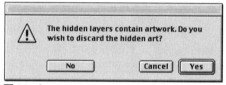

2 *It's always nice to get a second chance.*

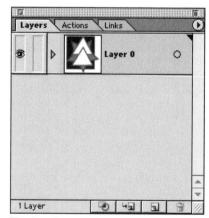

3 *After choosing the **Flatten Artwork** command, all the layers are flattened into the layer that was active when the command was chosen (Layer 0, in this case).*

1 *The placed artwork in the document window*

➤ *When placing an EPS for tracing, do not link the file, as this will produce either an inferior screen image or no screen image at all. A template layer isn't required for auto tracing a placed image.*

2 *After tracing the outer path*

3 *The outer and inner paths traced*

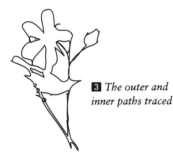

4 *The final objects after applying black and white fills*

Tracing

You can use the **Auto Trace** tool to trace any image that's opened via File > **Place**, such as a scanned photo or drawing. This tool tends to create extraneous anchor points and also places points in inappropriate locations, so you'll need to do some cleanup afterwards. If your artwork is simple (high contrast) or if you're deliberately looking for a rough, hand-drawn look, this is the tool to use. For photographs, you'll be better off tracing with the **Pen** or **Pencil** tool (see page 206). P.S. Adobe **Streamline** traces more accurately and offers many more options than Illustrator's Auto Trace tool.

Note: To control how exactly the Auto Trace tool traces a path, go to Edit > Preferences > Type & Auto Tracing. The higher the **Auto Trace Tolerance** (0–10 pt), the less precisely an object will be traced, and the fewer anchor points will be created. The **Tracing Gap** (0–2 pt) is the minimum width a gap in linework must be in order to be traced. With a high Tracing Gap setting, you'll probably get a lot of extraneous points.

To use the Auto Trace tool:

1. Open a file, then choose File > Place.

2. Locate and highlight an EPS, PDF, TIFF, or PSD file of a silhouetted image, then click Place **1**. (For a PSD file, click the "Flatten..." option, then click OK.) Lock the image using the Layers palette.

3. Above the image, create a layer or click an existing layer.

4. For now, choose a fill of None and a black stroke.

5. Choose the Auto Trace tool ▨ (it's on the Blend tool pop-out menu).

6. To trace, click on or drag over the interior or edges of the image. The shapes will be traced automatically **2**–**3**. Apply a fill of None to prevent the new tracing shapes from obscuring the placed image.

7. Fill the traced shapes, as desired **4**. To check your progress, hide the image by clicking its eye icon ▧ on the Layers palette.

Auto Trace

203

To trace letters manually:

The Auto Trace tool traces quickly and is useful if the feel of the relatively coarse rendering it produces is appropriate for your particular project. If you need to create smoother shapes, you can either refine the Auto Trace tool paths or trace the template manually **1**. What follows is a description of how you can use Illustrator to produce your own letterforms using the Pen tool.

I. *Scan the artwork*

To make sure the baseline of your letterwork squares with the horizontal guides in Illustrator, trim the edge of your drawing parallel to the baseline, then slide it against the glass frame of the scanner. Scan your artwork at a resolution between 72 and 150 ppi. Save it as a PICT, TIFF, EPS, or PSD. Even at 300% view, you will see only a minor difference in crispness between a placed 72-ppi PICT and a placed, non-linked, 250-ppi EPS.

2. *Trace manually*

Place an image in an Illustrator file via File > Place, Template checked **2**.

Use the Pen tool ![pen] to trace the upright letters. In the illustration at right, anchor points were placed on the topmost, bottommost, leftmost, and rightmost parts of the curve **3**. Most rounded shapes can be created using as few as four anchor points. Hold down Shift to draw out the direction lines horizontally or vertically.

To create the inclined letter shown in **3**, choose the Measure tool, click the base of a letter (e.g., the lowercase "t"), then click the top of the letter. The Info palette will show that angle. Choose Edit > Preferences > General, enter that angle in the Constrain Angle field, then click OK. Choose View > Show Grid. The grid lines will now follow the slope of the letters. Extend the direction lines of the leftmost and rightmost points of the letter to align with the grid.

Here's an alternate method: Choose File > Preferences > Smart Guides, and enter that angle into the first blank field in the Angles

1 *A closeup of an **Auto Trace** of a letter: Note the non-systematic distribution of anchor points and direction lines.*

Peter Fahrni

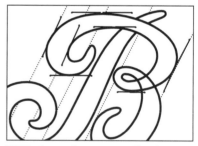

2 *A closeup of the placed artwork*

3 *The letters drawn **manually** (the artwork is hidden): All the direction lines are horizontal or on the same diagonal.*

Manual Trace

1 *The hand-drawn "B"*

2 *The final "B" after clicking the Add to Shape Area button on the Pathfinder palette*

area. Smart Guides will display on that angle as you drag with the Pen tool.

3. *Fine-tune the flow of curves*
Click an anchor point, then move it by pressing the arrow keys. The length and the angle of the direction lines won't change. Select a curve segment, and press the arrow keys to adjust its shape. The length, but not the angle, of the direction lines will change.

The manually traced "B" consisted of two closed, crisscrossing paths **1**. The Add to Shape Area command was used to combine the two paths into one **2**.

Comparing an Auto Traced character and an Adobe font character

Placed artwork in Illustrator

*The character **Auto Traced***

*A character in the Goudy 100 **Adobe PostScript** font, created as type in Illustrator*

Using the Pen or Pencil tool, you can manually trace over any placed image. When you manually trace an image, you can organize and simplify path shapes as well as control their stacking order. If you create separate paths on separate layers, you'll be able to restack and edit them more easily later on.

To manually trace over a placed image:

1. Create or open an Illustrator document, then choose File > Place .

2. Locate and highlight the image you want to trace, check Template if desired, then click Place. If you checked Template, the image will appear dimmed on its own uneditable layer. The layer options can be changed at any time by double-clicking the top-level layer name.

   ➤ If you decide to place the image without checking the Template option, you can lower the opacity of the image object at any time to make your tracing lines stand out better.

3. Create a new layer above the placed image layer.

4. Choose the Pen (P) tool 🖋 or the Pencil (N) tool. ✏️

5. Trace the placed image . You can periodically hide the image or the template to check your progress. To hide the template, click the template icon 🖻 on the Layers palette; or choose View > Hide Template; or press Cmd-Shift-W/ Ctrl-Shift-W. Redisplay it when you're ready to resume tracing.

   ➤ If you're using the Pencil tool, double-click the tool to change its Tolerances: Smoothness and/or Fidelity settings.

   ➤ You can transform a placed image before you trace it.

1 *A placed image*

2 *After **tracing** the image using the **Pen** tool, filling and stroking the paths with various shades of black, applying the Roughen effect with low Size and Detail settings to give the path strokes a more handmade appearance, and adding a radial gradient*

Chapter 11: Layers ◆ Study Guide

Learning Objectives

- Organize objects in an illustration on layers and sublayers using the Layers palette.
- Use groups to organize objects.
- Trace objects manually or automatically.

Get Up and Running Exercises

- Create a template for a store advertisement. The client wants the advertisement to be filled in by each store, but some of the background elements will stay the same. In the example shown below, the price, date, and product picture will change, but not the "Super Saver" text and the dark background rectangles. Design a template to meet these requirements. You don't have to duplicate the ad exactly, but your solution should meet the functional requirements. How would using layers make the job easier?

- Practice using the Layers palette. Create a document that uses ten layers and a few sublayers, and make sure there are visible objects on each layer. You might want to do this by re-creating a layered design you found in a magazine or book. Now do each of the following exercises:

  ▲ Hide all the layers except one, with one click.

  ▲ Make any two layers display in Outline mode.

  ▲ Change the color of the selection handles for a layer.

  ▲ In two quick steps, create a new layer that contains several selected objects.

  ▲ Flatten a document's layers.

  (Continued on the following page)

- For the next two exercises, have a layered document ready. It can be a document you created in previous exercises, a document from the Illustrator product CD, or one that your instructor provides.
- Using only the Layers palette, select (with one click):
  - ▲ One object.
  - ▲ All the objects on a layer or sublayer.
  - ▲ All the objects in a group.
  - ▲ One object in a group.
  - ▲ Three objects that aren't next to each other on the Layers palette or on the artboard.

Class Discussion Questions

- Why use layers instead of groups?
- Is there any difference between the current layer and the active layer?
- What's the difference between activating a layer and selecting objects on a layer?
- What happens to a layer when you turn on its Template option?
- What's the difference between restacking objects via the commands on the Object > Arrange submenu and restacking them using the Layers palette?

Review Questions

Multiple choice

1. What's the maximum number of layers allowed in an Illustrator document?

   A. 100.

   B. 999.

   C. As many as your computer's memory can handle.

   D. There is no limit.

2. What happens when you group objects that reside on different layers?

   A. The group is created on the layer that contains a selected object, and the objects are moved to that layer.

   B. The group is created on the lowest layer that contains a selected object, and the objects are moved to that layer.

   C. The group is created on the highest layer that contains a selected object, and the objects are moved to that layer.

   D. The group is created on the highest layer containing a selected object. If you later ungroup the group, the objects will go back to their original layers.

3. What happens when a selected object exists at the top of the middle layer in a three-layer document and you choose Object > Arrange > Send to Back?

   A. The object remains in its current position in the stack because it's not on the back layer.

   B. The object moves behind the next object back in the stacking order on the same layer.

   C. The object moves to the back of its current layer.

   D. The object moves to the back of the document's backmost layer.

4. What happens when a selected object is in a group and you choose Object > Arrange > Send to Back?

   A. The object moves to the back of the group.

   B. The object moves out of and behind the group on the same layer.

   C. The object moves to the back of the layer that currently contains it.

   D. The object moves to the back of the document's backmost layer.

5. Let's say three layers are active in a seven-layer document. Which Layers palette menu command would, in a single step, move all the objects from the active layers to the uppermost of the three active layers?

   A. Collect in New Layer

   B. Flatten Artwork

   C. Merge Selected

   D. New Layer

Fill-in-the-blank

1. You can create up to _____ levels of nested layer indents.

2. On the Layers palette, you can differentiate between layers and objects because object names _____.

3. To activate a layer on the Layers palette, _____.

4. To set up a layer as a tracing layer that won't print or export, use the _____ option.

5. When you select an object on the artboard but you don't know where it is on the Layers palette, find it by choosing the _____ command on the Layers palette menu.

6. To convert multiple objects or a group to separate layers for a frame animation, choose the _____ command from the Layers palette.

7. To ensure that objects pasted from the Clipboard paste to their original layers instead of the current layer, check the _____ command on the Layers palette menu.

8. To have Illustrator draw paths that follow the contours of an image automatically, use the _____ tool.

Definitions

1. What is a top-level layer?

2. What does the Color option in the Layer Options dialog box do?

3. What is flattening?

4. What is merging?

5. What is nesting?

6. What is the selection area in the Layers palette?

CREATE TYPE 12

This chapter is an introduction to Illustrator's type tools. First you'll learn how to create freestanding type, type inside an object, and type along a path. Then you'll learn how to import type from another application, link type, copy type or a type object, and convert type into graphic outlines. Typographic attributes are modified using the Character, Paragraph, and MM (Multiple Master) Design palettes, which are covered in the next chapter, along with methods for selecting type.

The Type tool creates freestanding type or type in a rectangle.

1 *Type tool*

The Area Type tool enters type into a path of any shape. Area Type looks best when it's Justified. We gave this ellipse a stroke so you can see how the type fits inside the

2 *Area Type tool*

The Path Type tool enters type along a path

3 *Path Type tool*

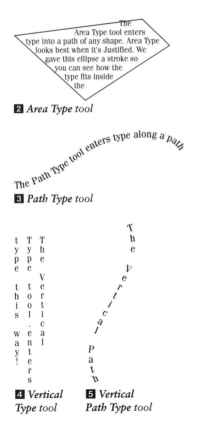

4 *Vertical Type tool*   **5** *Vertical Path Type tool*

Creating type
The type tools

There are three horizontal type tools: The Type tool, the Area Type tool, and the Path Type tool. Each of these tools has a counterpart for creating vertical type: the Vertical Type tool, the Vertical Area Type tool, and the Vertical Path Type tool. Some of these tools' functions overlap, but each of them has unique characteristics for producing a particular kind of type object.

The **Type** tool creates a freestanding block of type that is not associated with a path **1**. You can also draw a rectangle with it and enter type inside the rectangle; you can use it to enter type along the edge of an open path; or you can use it to enter type inside a closed path. It's the most versatile of the type tools.

The **Area Type** tool creates type *inside* an open or closed path. Lines of type created with the Area Type tool automatically wrap inside the path **2**.

The **Path Type** tool creates a line of type along the outer *edge* of an open or closed path **3**.

The **Vertical Type** tool has the same function as the Type tool, except it creates vertical type **4**.

The **Vertical Area Type** tool creates vertical type *inside* an open or closed path.

The **Vertical Path Type** tool creates vertical type along the outer *edge* of an open or closed path **5**.

The Type Tools

A few things to know about fonts

Some fonts, such as Helvetica, Courier, Arial, and Times, are automatically installed, in the Mac OS, in System Folder > Application Support > Adobe > Fonts > Reqrd > Base; in Windows, in Program Files > Common Files > Adobe > Fonts > Reqrd > Base. Only Adobe products can access and utilize this folder. Type rasterization and font management are performed internally within Illustrator (not by Adobe Type Manager). You must have the printer fonts for a typeface in a location that Illustrator can find in order to print that typeface from Illustrator.

If you open a file that uses a font that is unavailable to the System, an alert dialog box will appear **1**. You can Open the document as is, Cancel, or Obtain Fonts. If the missing font subsequently becomes available to the System, it will reappear on Illustrator's font list and the type should display correctly. Illustrator 10 supports the activation and deactivation of fonts of ATM 4 Deluxe and later.

Freestanding type stands by itself—it's neither inside an object nor along a path. Use it to create a picture caption, pull quote, or other independent body of text.

To create freestanding type:

1. Choose the Type tool **T** or Vertical Type tool. **|T**

2. Click on a blank area of the artboard where you want the type to start (not on an object). A flashing insertion marker will appear.

3. Enter type. Press Return/Enter each time you want to start a new line **2**.

4. Choose a selection tool on the Toolbox (don't use a keyboard shortcut to select the tool), then click outside the type block to deselect it.
   or
   Click the Type tool again to complete the type block and start a new one.

➤ To align separate blocks of freestanding type, use the Align palette (see page 418.)

Choose type attributes first?

If you like to choose character and paragraph attributes before you create type, use the Character and Paragraph palettes. They're discussed in depth in the next chapter.

Recolor after?

When type is entered inside an object or on a path, the object becomes filled and stroked with None. After the type is entered, if you want to apply fill and/or stroke colors to the type object, deselect it, then click the edge of the object with the Direct-selection tool. To recolor the type itself, first select it using a type tool or a selection tool (methods for selecting type are discussed in the next chapter).

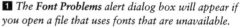

1 *The* **Font Problems** *alert dialog box will appear if you open a file that uses fonts that are unavailable.*

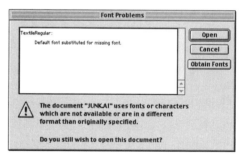

2 *Freestanding type created using the Type tool*

No going back

Once you place type inside or along a graphic object, it becomes a type object, and it can only be converted back into a graphic object via the Undo command. To preserve the original graphic object, Option-drag/Alt-drag it to copy it, then convert the copy into a type path. You can't enter type into a compound path, a mask object, a gradient mesh object, or a blend, and you can't make a compound path from a type object. If you create type on a path that has a brush stroke, the brush stroke will be removed.

'It spoils people's clothes to squeeze under a gate; the proper way to get in, is to climb down a pear tree.'

1 *Drag with the* **Type** *tool to create a rectangle, then enter type. To see the edges of the rectangle, go to Outline view or use Smart Guides with Object Highlighting.*

2 *Drag with the* **Vertical Type** *tool, then enter type. Type flows from top to bottom and from right to left.*

C
l
a   i
     m
p   B
e
a   d
R   o
          w
T   N
r
e
e
E
.
.
.

'It spoils people's clothes to squeeze under a gate; the proper way to get in, is to climb down a pear tree.'

3 *After reshaping the type rectangle using the Direct-selection tool*

Use this method if you want to define the shape of the type container before creating the type. To enter type in a non-rectangular object, see the instructions on the next page.

To create a type rectangle:

1. Choose the Type tool **T** or the Vertical Type tool. **T**

2. Drag to create a rectangle. When you release the mouse, a flashing insertion marker will appear.

   ➤ To draw a square, start dragging, then hold down Shift and continue to drag. To create vertical type using the Type tool or horizontal type using the Vertical Type tool, hold down Shift before and while dragging.

3. Enter type. Press Return/Enter only when you need to create a new paragraph. The type will wrap automatically to fit into the rectangle **1**–**2**.

4. Choose a selection tool on the Toolbox (don't use a keyboard shortcut to select the tool), then click outside the type block to deselect it.
   or
   To keep the type tool selected so as to create another, separate type rectangle, press Cmd/Ctrl to temporarily access the last-used selection tool, then click outside the type block to deselect it. Release Cmd/Ctrl, then click again to start the new type block. (You could also click the type tool again to complete the type object.)

   Note: If the overflow symbol appears on the edge of the rectangle (tiny cross in a tiny square) and you want to reveal the hidden type, deselect the rectangle, then reshape it using the Direct-selection tool. You can use Smart Guides (with Object Highlighting) or go to Outline view to locate the rectangle. The type will reflow to fit the new shape **3**. Another option is to spill the overflow type into another object via linking (see page 213).

   ➤ To turn a path created with the Rectangle tool into a type rectangle, click the edge of the path with the horizontal or vertical Type or Area Type tool, then enter type.

Type Rectangle

Use the Area Type or Vertical Area Type tool to place type inside a rectangle or an irregularly shaped path, or onto an open path. The object will turn into a type path.

To enter type inside an object:

1. If the object is a closed path, choose the Area Type tool 􀀀, Vertical Area Type tool 􀀀, or either of the Type tools (T or T). For an open path, choose either Area Type tool.

2. Click precisely on the edge of the path. A flashing insertion marker will appear, and any fill or stroke on the object will be removed. The object will now be listed as <Type> (not <Path>) on the Layers palette.

3. Enter type in the path, or copy and paste text from a text editing application into the path. The text will stay inside the object and conform to its shape ▮–▮. Vertical area type flows from top to bottom and from right to left.

   ➤ The smaller the type, the more snugly it will fit inside the shape. Justify it to make it hug both sides of the object, and turn on hyphenation.

4. Choose a selection tool, then click outside the type object to deselect it.
   or
   To keep the type tool selected so as to enter type in another object, press Cmd/Ctrl to temporarily access the last-used selection tool, click away from the type block to deselect it, release Cmd/Ctrl, then click the next type object. You could also click again on the type tool you used to create the type object.

   ➤ With any type tool selected, you can press Shift to toggle between the vertical or horizontal equivalent of that tool (once type is entered, you can't switch).

To make a whole horizontal type block vertical, or vice versa:

1. Choose the Selection tool.
2. Click on a type block.
3. Choose Type > Type Orientation > Vertical or Horizontal.

Switcheroo

To rotate vertical area type characters, highlight just the characters you want to convert, then choose **Direction: Rotate** on the Character palette (choose Window > Type > Character to open the palette, and if the Direction pop-up menu isn't visible, choose Show Multilingual from the palette menu).

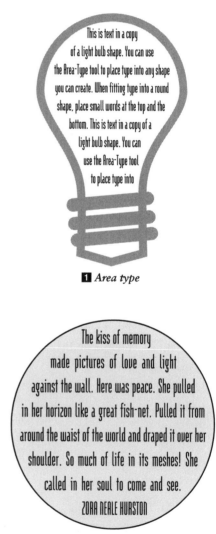

▮ *Area type*

▮ *Type in a circle*

Area Type; Type Orientation

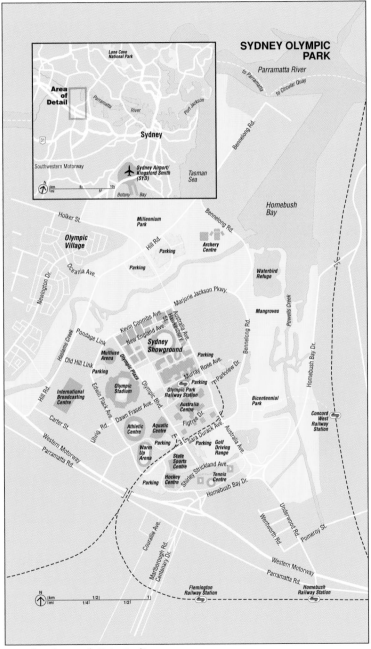

SYDNEY OLYMPIC PARK

©Mark Stein, Mark Stein Studios

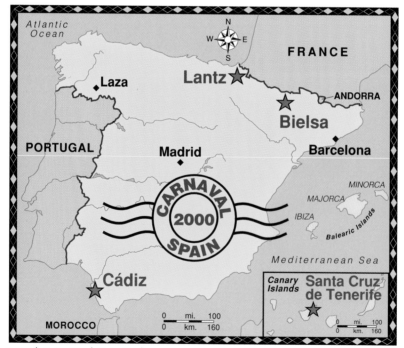

©Mark Stein, Mark Stein Studios

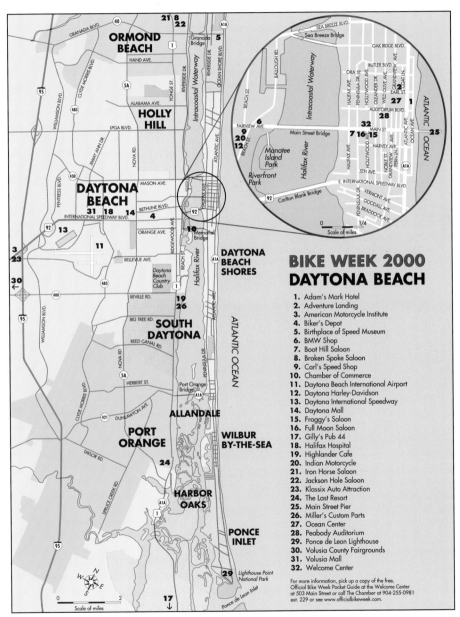

BIKE WEEK 2000 DAYTONA BEACH

1. Adam's Mark Hotel
2. Adventure Landing
3. American Motorcycle Institute
4. Biker's Depot
5. Birthplace of Speed Museum
6. BMW Shop
7. Boot Hill Saloon
8. Broken Spoke Saloon
9. Carl's Speed Shop
10. Chamber of Commerce
11. Daytona Beach International Airport
12. Daytona Harley-Davidson
13. Daytona International Speedway
14. Daytona Mall
15. Froggy's Saloon
16. Full Moon Saloon
17. Gilly's Pub 44
18. Halifax Hospital
19. Highlander Cafe
20. Indian Motorcycle
21. Iron Horse Saloon
22. Jackson Hole Saloon
23. Klassix Auto Attraction
24. The Last Resort
25. Main Street Pier
26. Miller's Custom Parts
27. Ocean Center
28. Peabody Auditorium
29. Ponce de Leon Lighthouse
30. Volusia County Fairgrounds
31. Volusia Mall
32. Welcome Center

For more information, pick up a copy of the free, Official Bike Week Pocket Guide at the Welcome Center at 503 Main Street or call The Chamber at 904-255-0981 ext. 229 or see www.officialbikeweek.com.

©Mark Stein, Mark Stein Studios

Mark Stein

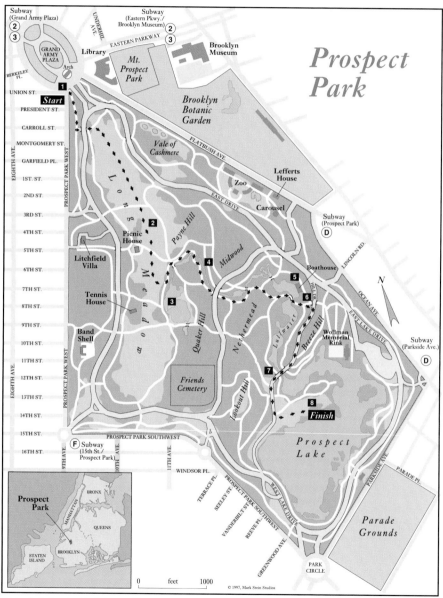

Subway
(Grand Army Plaza)
② ③

Subway
(Eastern Pkwy./
Brooklyn Museum)
② ③

UNDERHILL AVE.

EASTERN PARKWAY

Brooklyn
Museum

Library

GRAND
ARMY
PLAZA

Arch

BERKELEY
PL.

UNION ST.

Start ①

PRESIDENT ST.

CARROLL ST.

MONTGOMERY ST.

GARFIELD PL.

1ST. ST.

2ND ST.

3RD ST.

4TH ST.

5TH ST.

6TH ST.

7TH ST.

8TH ST.

9TH ST.

10TH ST.

11TH ST.

12TH ST.

13TH ST.

14TH ST.

15TH ST.

16TH ST.

EIGHTH AVE.

PROSPECT PARK WEST

EIGHTH AVE.

PROSPECT PARK WEST

*Mt.
Prospect
Park*

*Brooklyn
Botanic
Garden*

*Prospect
Park*

*Vale of
Cashmere*

FLATBUSH AVE.

**Lefferts
House**

Zoo

EAST DRIVE

Carousel

② **Picnic
House**

**Litchfield
Villa**

**Tennis
House**

**Band
Shell**

Long

Meadow

Payne Hill

Midwood

③

④

⑤

Boathouse

⑥

HILL DR.

LINCOLN RD.

OCEAN AVE.

EAST LAKE DRIVE

Quaker Hill

Nethermead

Lullwater

Breeze Hill

**Wollman
Memorial
Rink**

*Friends
Cemetery*

Lookout Hill

⑦

⑧ *Finish*

*Prospect
Lake*

Subway
(Prospect Park)
Ⓓ

Subway
(Parkside Ave.)
Ⓓ

Ⓕ Subway
(15th St./
Prospect Park)

PROSPECT PARK SOUTHWEST

9TH AVE.

10TH AVE.

11TH AVE.

WINDSOR PL.

TERRACE PL.

SEELEY ST.

VANDERBILT ST.

REEVE PL.

PROSPECT PARK SOUTHWEST

EAST LAKE DRIVE

GREENWOOD AVE.

PARK
CIRCLE

PARKSIDE AVE.

PARADE PL.

*Parade
Grounds*

N

**Prospect
Park**

BRONX

MANHATTAN

QUEENS

BROOKLYN

STATEN
ISLAND

0   feet   1000

© 1997, Mark Stein Studios

©Mark Stein, Mark Stein studios

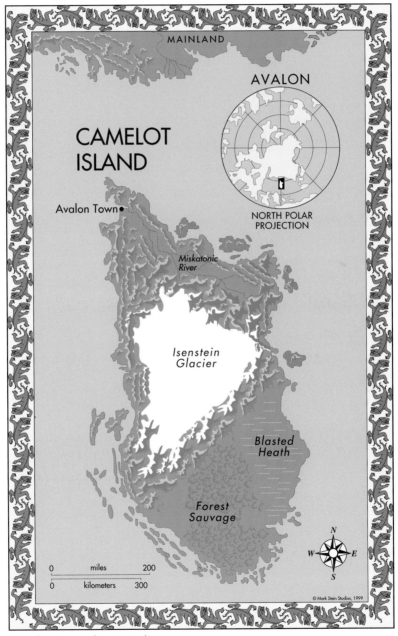

MAINLAND

AVALON

CAMELOT
ISLAND

Avalon Town•

NORTH POLAR
PROJECTION

*Miskatonic
River*

*Isenstein
Glacier*

*Blasted
Heath*

*Forest
Sauvage*

N
W   E
S

| 0 | miles | 200 |
| 0 | kilometers | 300 |

© Mark Stein Studios, 1999

©*Mark Stein, Mark Stein Studios*

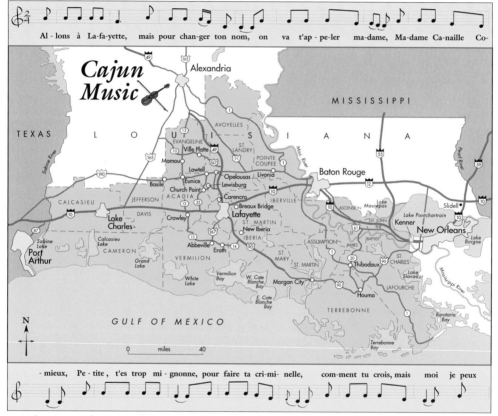

Jim Spiece

©*Jim Spiece*

©*Jim Spiece*

Chris Spollen

©Chris Spollen

©Nancy Stahl, Big Dot

Nancy Stahl

©Nancy Stahl, Liner

Barbara Friedman

©Daniel Pelavin, magazine cover for Publishers Weekly

Daniel Pelavin

Daniel Pelavin

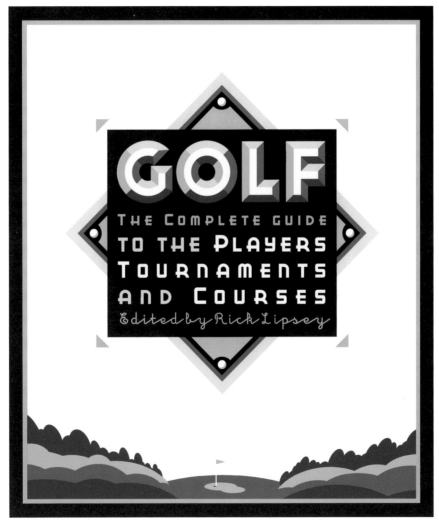

Marti Shohet

©Marti Shohet, illustration for CIO magazine

©*Marti Shohet, self-promotion*

Led Pants

Led Pants

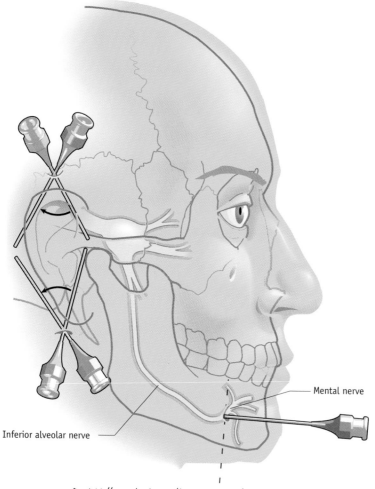

Mental nerve

Inferior alveolar nerve

Bart Vallecoccia (©Medic Art Research Inc.)

Yoshinori Kaizu

©Yoshinori Kaizu, Fish

©Yoshinori Kaizu, Cockatoo

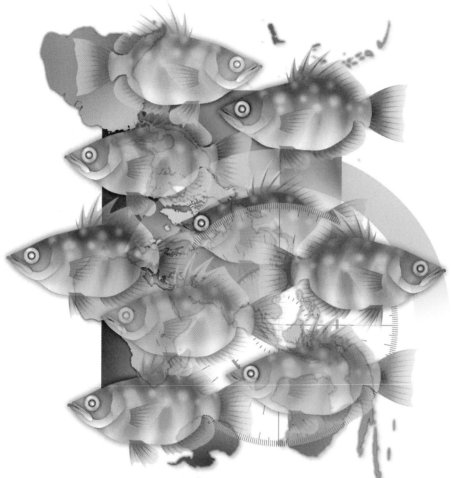

©Yoshinori Kaizu, Gradient Fish

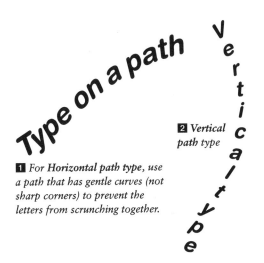

2 *Vertical path type*

1 *For Horizontal path type, use a path that has gentle curves (not sharp corners) to prevent the letters from scrunching together.*

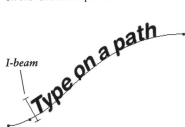

3 *The baseline shift field on the Character palette*

I-beam

4 *Path type, normal baseline position*

5 *Path type, Baseline shifted downward*

Use the Path Type tool to place type on the inner or outer edge of a path. Type cannot be placed on both sides of the same path, but it can be moved from one side to the other after it's created. Only one line of type can be created per path.

To place type along an object's path:

1. Choose the Path Type, or Vertical Path Type tool, then click the top or bottom edge of a closed path. Or choose the Type, T or Vertical Type IT tool, then click an open path. The path can be selected, but it doesn't have to be.

2. When the flashing insertion marker appears, enter type. Don't press Return/Enter. The type will appear along the edge of the object, and the object will now have a fill and stroke of None **1**–**2**.

3. Choose a selection tool, then click outside the type object to deselect it.
   or
   If you want to enter type into a new type block, click the type tool again.

To adjust the position of type on a path:

1. Choose the Selection tool (V) or Direct-selection tool (A).

2. Click on the type.

3. Drag the I-beam to the left or the right along the edge of the path.
   or
   To flip the type to the other side of the path, move the I-beam inside the path or double-click the I-beam.
   or
   To shift *all* the characters slightly toward or away from the center of the path, but keep their orientation, click or marquee the path with the Selection tool; to shift some but not all of the characters, double-click the type with the Selection or Direct-selection tool, and highlight the desired characters. Then change the baseline shift value on the Character palette **3**–**5** (Window > Type > Character to open the palette; choose Show Options from the palette menu if the baseline shift field isn't visible).

Path Type

Importing type

You can import Microsoft Word, NotePad (Win), SimpleText (Mac OS), or ASCII text into an Illustrator document. The text will appear in a new rectangle.

Note: To place text onto a custom path, first place it by following the instructions on this page, then copy and paste it into or onto the custom path (see "To move type from one object to another" on page 215).

To import type:

1. Choose File > Place.

2. Highlight the name of the text file you want to import.

3. Click Place. If the text file was saved in the Text Only format, the Text import Options dialog box will open **1**. Choose options, then click OK.

   The text file will appear in a rectangle, with its original font, size, and paragraph breaks, but not necessarily its original line breaks **2**.

4. *Optional:* Reshape the rectangle either of two ways. Choose the Selection tool, then drag a handle on the bounding box (choose Window > Show bounding box if the box isn't visible). Or choose the Direct-selection tool, then drag or Shift-drag a segment on the rectangle.

➤ Type styling will be lost if you open or place a Text Only format file (as used in SimpleText or NotePad). Both the Word Document and the Rich Text Format, on the other hand, preserve most type styling.

➤ To export text from Illustrator, see pages 215 and 457.

➤ To create columns and rows of type, see page 238.

➤ If you create type in a layout program, save the file in EPS format, and then open the EPS file using Illustrator's Open command, you'll be able to manipulate it as you would any type in Illustrator. Beware, though: a new freestanding type block will be created for each word in the imported text, and the blocks will be grouped.

Don't space out!

If you press Spacebar to access the Hand tool while a Text tool is chosen, you'll end up adding spaces to your text instead of moving the illustration. Instead, press Cmd-Spacebar/Ctrl-Spacebar, then very quickly release Cmd/Ctrl, and you'll have your Hand tool.

And watch where your pointer is. If it's in a palette field, you won't be able to edit text in your illustration window!

1 *For text in the* **Text Only** *format, choose* **Text Import Options.**

2 *Placed type appears in a rectangle.*

Paul Gauguin

Import Type

Overflow path type

To reveal hidden overflow path type text, you can do one of three things: Make the type smaller (Select All first); make the path longer (to extend a path, see page 121); or delete some words (the old standby!).

Here was peace. She pulled in her horizon like a great fish-net. Pulled it from around the waist of the world and draped it over

*The **overflow** symbol*

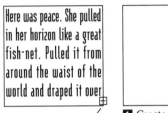

1 *Create a **new** rectangle with the Rectangle tool.*

Here was peace. She pulled in her horizon like a great fish-net. Pulled it from around the waist of the world and draped it over

her shoulder. So much of life in its meshes! She called in her soul to come and see.

Zora Neale Hurston

2 *The objects are **linked**, and the overflow type spills from the first object into the second object.*

Linking type

If your type overfloweth

If a type rectangle is almost, but not quite, large enough to display all the type inside it, you can enlarge it to reveal the hidden type.

➤ Click the type block with the **Selection** tool, then drag a handle on its **bounding box** (choose Window > Show bounding box if the box isn't visible).

➤ Or select only the rectangle—not the type—with the **Direct-selection** tool (turn on Smart Guides with Object Highlighting or go to Outline view to locate the rectangle), then **Shift-drag** a **segment**.

Another way to deal with overflow type that was created using a horizontal or vertical Type or Area Type tool is to spill it into a different object (instructions on this page) or into a copy of the same object (instructions on the next page).

To link overflow type to another object:

1. If you don't want to link to an existing object, create a new object now. For example, you could draw a rectangle using the Rectangle tool (M) **1**.

2. Choose any selection tool.

3. Shift-click or marquee the original type rectangle and the second rectangle.

4. Choose Type > Blocks > Link. Overflow type from the first rectangle will flow into the second rectangle **2**.

Linking causes text blocks to be stacked consecutively behind the frontmost text block. A chain of linked text blocks will occupy the same layer on the Layers palette.

To change the order in which type flows from one object to another:

1. Choose the Direct-selection tool (A), then click the type object whose stacking position you want to change.

2. Choose Object > Arrange > Bring to Front, Send to Back, Bring Forward, or Send Backward.

Link Type; Reflow Type

213

To link overflow type to a copy of an existing object:

1. Turn on Smart Guides (check Object Highlighting in Edit > Preferences > Smart Guides & Slices) or put your illustration into Outline view.

2. Choose the Direct-selection tool (A). ▶

3. Click away from the type object to deselect it.

4. Click on the edge of the type object. The type should not be underlined after you click. Don't move the mouse yet!

5. Option-drag/Alt-drag a copy of the type object away from the original object. Option-Shift-drag/Alt-Shift-drag to constrain the movement to a multiple of 45°. Release the mouse, then release Option/Alt (and Shift, if used). The overflow type will appear inside the new object ■.

6. *Optional:* Choose Object > Transform > Transform Again (Cmd-D/Ctrl-D) to create additional linked copies.

➤ If both the type and the type object are selected when you drag, a copy of the object and type will be created, but the original and copy won't be linked.

To unlink two or more type objects:

1. Choose the Selection tool (V), then click one of the linked type objects. All the linked objects in that chain will become selected.

2. Choose Type > Blocks > Unlink. All the objects will unlink; the type in each object will be separate and unlinked.

➤ To rejoin the type, use a type tool to cut and paste it back into the original object.

To remove one type object from a chain and keep the text stream intact:

1. Choose the Direct-selection tool (A). ▶

2. Click the edge of the type object to be removed.

3. Press Delete/Backspace twice. The type will reflow into the remaining objects.

The kiss of memory made pictures of love and light against the wall. Here was peace.

She pulled in her horizon like a great fish-net. Pulled it from around the waist of the world and

■ *Overflow type from the first object appears in a **linked copy** of that object. (A paragraph indent was applied to the type to pull it away from the edge of the objects.)*

Italics into Photoshop

If you copy or drag-and-drop italic type characters from Illustrator into Photoshop, part of the rightmost character in some fonts may be cropped. To prevent this from happening, convert the characters into outlines before copying them.

To test whether an italic character will copy properly, select the character with any Type tool. Any portion of the character that extends beyond the highlight will be cropped.

1 *Freestanding type is **highlighted**, put on the Clipboard via Edit > **Cut**...*

2 *...and then **pasted** into a rectangle.*

Copying type

To copy or move type with or without its object, you can use the Clipboard, a temporary storage area in memory. The Clipboard commands are Cut, Copy, and Paste. You could also use the drag-and-drop method to move a type object (see pages 259–260).

To copy type and its object between Illustrator documents or between Illustrator and Photoshop:

1. Choose the Selection tool (V).
2. Click on the edge of the object, on the type, or on the baseline of the type you want to copy.
3. Choose Edit > Copy (Cmd-C/Ctrl-C).
4. Click in another Illustrator document window, then choose Edit > Paste (Cmd-V/Ctrl-V). The type and its object will appear.
   or
   Click in a Photoshop document window, choose Edit > Paste, click Pixels, then click OK. The type and its object will appear as imagery on a new layer.

To move type from one object to another:

1. Choose the Type tool T or Vertical Type tool.
2. Highlight the type (or a portion of the type) you want to move **1**.
3. Choose Edit > Cut (Cmd-X/Ctrl-X). The object you cut the type from will remain a type object.
4. Hold down Cmd/Ctrl, click another object, then release Cmd/Ctrl.
5. Click inside or on the edge of the second object. A flashing insertion marker will appear.
   or
   Drag to create a type rectangle.
6. Choose Edit > Paste (Cmd-V/Ctrl-V) **2**.

Creating outlines

The Create Outlines command converts each character in a type object into a separate graphic object. As outlines, the paths can then be reshaped, used in a compound or as a mask, or filled with a gradient or gradient mesh, like any non-type object. *Beware!* Once type is converted into outlines, unless you Undo immediately, you won't be able to change the font or other typographic attributes or convert the outlines back into type.

To create type outlines:

1. Create type using any type tool. *All* the characters in the type object or on the path are going to be converted.

2. Choose the Selection tool (V).

3. If the type isn't already selected, click a character or the baseline.

4. Choose Type > Create Outlines (Cmd-Shift-O/Ctrl-Shift-O) –**3**.
   or
   Control-click/Right-click and choose Create Outlines from the context menu.

   The characters' original fill and stroke attributes will be preserved, but the path object, if any, will be deleted.

➤ Make sure the Type 1 font (screen font and printer outlines) or the TrueType font for the typeface you are using is installed in your system or in the Adobe Font folder (see page 208). Otherwise, Illustrator will use a substitute font to recreate the missing font and font outlines.

➤ If the original character had an interior counter—as in an "A" or a "P"—the outside and inside shapes will form a compound path as a result of a conversion to outlines. To release the compound into separate objects, choose Object > Compound Path > Release, then Object > Ungroup; to reassemble the parts, select them both, then choose Object > Compound Path > Make.

Converter beware

The Create Outlines command is most suitable for creating logos or other large characters that require reshaping. Printer fonts are not required in order to print type outlines properly from another application. *Note:* Small type (e.g., body type) shouldn't be made into outlines, because the Create Outlines command removes the hinting information that is designed to preserve character shapes during printing. Outline "characters" are also slightly heavier than their pre-outline counterparts, and thus less legible, particularly if a stroke is applied to them. Also, outlines occupy more file storage space.

1 *The original type*

2 *The type converted into* **outlines**

3 *The outlines are reshaped and filled with a gradient. The arrows point to sections that were reshaped.*

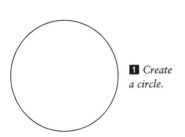

1 *Create a circle.*

2 *Create path type on the top of the circle. The circle will have a stroke of None. (This is Outline view.)*

3 *Option-drag/ Alt-drag the type I-beam to the bottom of the circle.*

4 *Select the type on the bottom of the circle, and type the words that you want to appear on the bottom.*

5 *Baseline shift the path type on the bottom of the circle copy downward, and center it on the circle.*

Exercise

Putting type on both sides of a circle, and having all of it read vertically, requires creating two circles.

Type on a circle

Type on the top

1. Open the Character and Color palettes (Window menu).

2. Choose Edit > Preferences > Units & Undo, choose General: Inches, then click OK.

3. Choose the Ellipse tool (L), then click on the artboard (don't drag).

4. Enter "3" in the Width field, click the word "Height," then click OK **1**.

5. On the Character palette, enter 24 in the Size field and choose a font.

6. Choose the Path Type tool.

7. Click the top of the circle, then type the text that you want to appear on the top of the circle (*"type on the top,"* in our example) **2**.

8. Choose the Selection tool, then drag the I–beam to the left, if necessary, to reposition the type.

Type on the bottom

1. Option-drag/Alt-drag the I-beam downward into the circle (the type and its path will be duplicated) **3**. Center the bottom type.

2. Triple-click the bottom type with the Selection tool (the Type tool will be chosen automatically), type the words that you want to appear there **4**, then choose the Selection tool.

3. With the type still selected, on the Character palette, click the down arrow for baseline shift to move the type downward (the appropriate amount will depend on the typeface and type size) **5**. Then deselect the type.

(Continued on the following page)

Exercise: Type on a Circle

4. Reposition the bottom type as necessary, but don't drag it outside the circle.

5. Marquee both circles.

6. *Optional:* To recolor the type, apply a fill color and a stroke of None to each string of characters.

➤ You can use the Layers palette to select individual type objects. If you prefer to select the type manually in the document window, check Type Area Select in Edit > Preferences > Type & Auto Tracing to make the selection easier.

7. Choose Object > Group (Cmd-G/ Ctrl-G) **1**. To recolor either circle, use the Direct-selection tool.

➤ Set the baseline shift field back to zero (with no type selected) to prevent the negative baseline shift value from being applied to any subsequently created type.

➤ To select either type block separately, click on it with the Direct-selection tool or click its selection area on the Layers palette.

1 *This is the final type. The circles still have a stroke of None.*

Chapter 12: Create Type ◆ Study Guide

Learning Objectives

- Create freestanding type.
- Type inside an object.
- Type along a path.
- Import type from another application.
- Manage type objects.
- Convert type into graphic outlines.

Get Up and Running Exercises

- Practice the different ways to create type objects.

  ▲ Reproduce a classified ad found in a newspaper. It should contain at least one paragraph of text. Use the Type tool to recreate the classified ad. The font and type size don't have to match exactly. Concentrate on entering the text and reproducing the line breaks as efficiently as you can; that is, with the least amount of effort. Which Type tool features are most appropriate for this exercise?

  ▲ Reproduce the placement of text on a compact disc cover. You don't need to use the exact font. Concentrate on reproducing the position of each short block of text. Which Type tool features are most appropriate for this exercise?

  ▲ Draw a non-rectangular path object, then type some text inside it, as in the examples on page 210.

  ▲ Create type that hangs vertically as in the hotel sign example in the figure below, without using any transformation tools.

(Continued on the following page)

- Find a real-world example of a single-page layout that contains multiple type objects. For example, use Illustrator to reproduce an existing poster or brochure. To mimic how such a project might actually happen, prepare the text in a word processor or e-mail program (as if your client had sent it to you that way) and import the text into Illustrator. If the text ends up flowing from one area to another, link the type objects.

- Create a type-based logo. Suppose that your city has hired you to create a new logotype for the city's name. They want the type to have a perspective distortion, as covered in Chapter 7 of this book. How would you use a feature covered in this chapter to complete the project?

Class Discussion Questions

- What's the difference between area (rectangle) type and freestanding type?
- When would you use linked type?
- When is it useful to create outlines from type? What are the disadvantages of using type converted to outlines?
- Why do you have to be careful when using keyboard shortcuts as you work with text?

Review Questions

Multiple choice

1. Which tool can create freestanding type?

   A. Area Type tool

   B. Path Type tool

   C. Type tool

   D. Vertical Path Type tool

2. How do you change the order in which type flows between linked type objects?

   A. Change the order in which the type objects appear so that the type objects you want to flow first are closer to the top left corner of the page.

   B. Change the stacking order of the type objects.

   C. Use the commands on the Type > Blocks submenu to unlink and relink type objects in the desired order.

   D. Choose the Direct-selection tool and click linked type objects in the desired order.

3. Which of the following statements about type converted to outlines is not true?

   A. The font used to create the type is no longer required to export that type object.

   B. You won't be able to edit the type with the type tools.

   C. You can flow text inside the converted outlines.

   D. Fewer options are available for filling the type.

4. Which of the following text file formats can't be imported directly into Illustrator?

   A. ASCII text

   B. Microsoft Word

   C. WordPerfect

   D. NotePad

Fill-in-the-blank

1. To adjust the position of type on a selected path, _____.

2. To create a line of type that runs horizontally along the outer edge of a path, use the Type tool or the _____ tool.

3. To create type that runs vertically inside a path, use the Vertical Type tool or the _____ tool.

4. To make path type straddle a path instead of resting solely on one side or the other, change its _____ value.

5. The Text Import Options dialog box appears only when you import a document saved in the _____ format.

Definitions

1. What is overflow text?

2. What is linked type?

3. What is path type?

4. What does the Type > Create Outlines command do?

5. What is freestanding type?

STYLE & EDIT TYPE

In this chapter, first you will learn how to select type. Then you will learn how to use the Character palette to apply character-based typographic attributes (font, size, leading, kerning, tracking, baseline shift, horizontal scaling, and vertical scaling) and the Paragraph palette to apply para-graph-wide attributes (alignment, indentation, inter-paragraph spacing, hanging punctuation, word spacing, and letter spacing).

You'll also learn how to use Illustrator's word processing features to check spelling, export text, and find and replace fonts or text; create text rows and columns; apply professional typesetter's marks; turn on hyphenation; and apply tabs. And finally, you'll learn a few nifty tricks, such as how to sample and apply type attributes using the Eyedropper and Paint Bucket tools, wrap text around an object, create type with a shadow, and create slanted type.

To apply styles or appearances to type, see Chapter 19. To change type opacity, see Chapter 20.

Selecting type

Before you can modify type, you must select it. If you use the **Selection** tool, both the type and its object will be selected **1**. If you use the **Direct-selection** tool, you can select the type object alone or the type object *and* the type **2**. If you use a **type** tool to select type, only the type itself will be selected, not the type object **3**.

If we
shadows
have
offended,
Think but
this—
and all is
mended—

1 *Type and type object selected with the Selection tool*

If we
shadows
have
offended,
Think but
this —
and all is
mended—

2 *Type object selected with the Direct-selection tool*

If we
shadows
have
offended,
Think but
this —
and all is
mended—

William Shakespeare

3 *Type (but not its object) selected with the Type tool*

Note: Use this selection method if you want to move, transform, restyle, or recolor a *whole type block*. To reshape or recolor a type *object*, use the first selection method on the next page. To edit type or to restyle or recolor *part* of a type *block*, use the second selection method on the next page.

To select type and its object:

1. Choose the Selection tool (V).

2. Turn on Smart Guides (Cmd-U/Ctrl-U), with Object Highlighting (Edit > Preferences > Smart Guides & Slices).

3. If Type Area Select is checked in Edit > Preferences > Type & Auto Tracing, click on the type. Or click inside the type object if the object has a fill **1**.
   or
   In Outline view, click the edge of the type object. In Preview view, click the Smart Guide (Object Highlighting).
   or
   Click the baseline of any character **2**.

If you select freestanding type (type that's created by clicking, then entering text with the Type or Vertical Type tool), the type will have a solid anchor point before the first character and each line will be underlined. The bounding box will also display, if that option is on (View menu).

If you select a linked type object, all the objects that are linked to it will also become selected.

➤ To modify the paint attributes of type, use the Color palette (see the sidebar on page 208).

➤ To move, scale, rotate, shear, or reflect type, use a command on the Object > Transform submenu or use a transform tool.

➤ If type and its object are selected, but you only want the object to be selected, Shift-click the type with the Direct-selection tool.

Hot tip

If you double-click a type character in an existing type object with any selection tool, the **type** and the **Type tool** will become selected automatically.

Appearances and type

The relationship between type color and appearances is confusing, to say the least. If you select a type object with the Selection tool, "Type" will be listed at the top of the Appearance palette, with "Characters" listed among the attributes. *10.0!*

If you highlight text characters using a type tool, "Characters" will be listed at the top of the Appearance palette, followed by the "Stroke" and "Fill" attributes. To learn more about the Appearance palette, see Chapter 19. To work with type color and appearances, see steps 1–3 on page 324, and see also page 350.

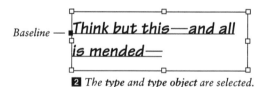

x Think but this—and all
is mended—

1 *To select* freestanding *type in* Outline *view, click the "x." Or if the Type Area Select option is on, click the type itself.*

Baseline — Think but this—and all
is mended—

2 *The* type *and* type object *are selected.*

Inserting and deleting

To **add** more type to an existing block, choose a Type tool, click to create an insertion point, then start typing.

To **delete** one character at a time, choose a Type tool, click to the right of the character you want to delete, then press Delete/Backspace. To delete a text string, select it with a Type tool, then press Delete/Backspace.

1 *The type object is selected; the type is not.*

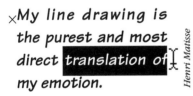

2 *The type object is reshaped.*

My line drawing is the purest and most direct **translation of** my emotion.

Henri Matisse

3 *Two words are selected.*

Use this selection method if you want to reshape a type object (and thus reflow the type) or recolor a type object.

To select a type object but not the type:

1. Choose the Direct-selection tool (A).

2. Click on the edge of the type object **1**–**2**. Use Smart Guides (Object Highlighting) to assist you, or go to Outline view. Now, modifications you make will affect only the type object—not the type.

Use this selection method to select only the type—not the object—so you can edit the text or change its character, paragraph, or paint attributes.

To select type but not its object:

1. Choose any type tool.

2. For horizontal type, drag horizontally with the I-beam pointer to select and highlight a word or a line of type **3**. For vertical type, drag vertically.
   or
   For horizontal type, drag vertically to select whole lines of type. For vertical type, drag horizontally to select lines.
   or
   Double-click to select a word.
   or
   Triple-click to select a paragraph.
   or
   Click in the text block, then choose Select > All (Cmd-A/Ctrl-A) to select all the type in the block or on the path and any type it's linked to.
   or
   Click to start a selection, then Shift-click where you want the selection to end. (Shift-click again to extend the selection.)

3. After modifying the type, click anywhere in the type block to deselect it and keep the flashing insertion marker in the type block for further editing.
   or
   Choose a selection tool, then click away from the type object to deselect it.

➤ If Smart Guides are on and text characters are highlighted, choose a selection tool after choosing a color to see the color change.

Select Type Object; Select Type

Applying type attributes
The type palettes

➤ Press **Tab** to apply a value in a field and highlight the next field.

➤ Press **Shift-Tab** to apply a value in a field and highlight the previous field.

➤ Press **Return/Enter** to apply a value and exit the palette.

Character palette

Use the Character palette (Cmd-T/Ctrl-T or Window > Type > Character) to modify font, type size, leading, kerning, and tracking values in one or more highlighted text characters **1**. Choose Show Options from the palette menu to expand the palette for baseline shift, horizontal scale, and vertical scale adjustments.

If you want to know what a feature is, use **tool tips** *(hold the mouse over the icon).*

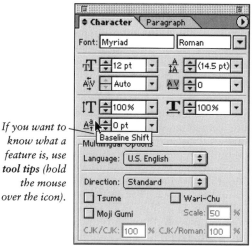

1 *The Character palette*

Paragraph palette

Use the Paragraph palette (Cmd-M/Ctrl-M) to modify paragraph-wide attributes, such as alignment and indentation **2**. Choose Show Options from the palette menu to expand the palette for word spacing, letter spacing, auto hyphenation, hanging punctuation, and East Asian font options.

To change the paragraph attributes of *all* the text in a type object or on a path, select the object or path with the Selection tool. To isolate a paragraph or series of paragraphs, select just those paragraphs with a type tool.

Note: A paragraph is created when the Return/Enter key is pressed within a type block. Choose Type > Show Hidden Characters to reveal the symbols for line breaks and spaces.

2 *The Paragraph palette*

MM Design palette

Use the **Multiple Master** Palette to modify the Weight, Width, and Design Values of characters in a multiple master (MM) font **3**. Choose Window > Type > MM Design when text in a MM font is highlighted. The axes that can be adjusted vary depending on the MM font. Use a Multiple Master font if you require a type style that's slightly slimmer or heavier than an existing style. The palette will combine two existing weights to produce the desired weight.

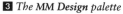

3 *The MM Design palette*

The Type Palettes

10.0!

10.0!

Fast info

The size, font, and tracking info for selected type are listed on the **Info** palette **1**.

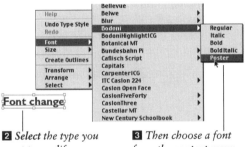

1 *The Info palette when the Type tool is selected*

2 *Select the type you want to modify.*

3 *Then choose a font from the context menu.*

.Font change

4 *The font is changed from Gill Sans Bold to Bodoni Poster.*

You can, of course, choose a font before entering your text—just skip the type selection step.

To choose a font:

1. Choose any type tool, then select the type you want to modify **2**.

   or

   Choose the Selection tool, then click on the type object.

2. Control-click/Right-click on the type and choose a font from the Font submenu on the context menu **3**–**4**.

   or

   On the Character palette in the Mac OS, Choose a font from the Font drop-down menu (and from a submenu if the font name has an arrowhead next to it). In Windows, choose from the Font and style drop-down menus.

   or

   In the Mac OS, double-click the Font field on the Character palette or in Windows just click the Font field, then start typing the first few characters of the desired font name. When the name appears, press Tab. In addition, for a style other than Roman (or Regular), start typing the style name in the next field, then press Return/Enter. You need only enter the first few letters of the font name or style—the name or style with the closest spelling match will appear in the field **5**–**6**.

➤ You can also choose from the Type > Font submenu.

➤ Press Cmd-Option-Shift-M/Ctrl-Alt-Shift-M to quickly highlight the Font field on the Character palette. The palette will open, if it isn't open already.

Enter a font name and style.

Or choose from the Font drop-down menu.

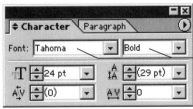

5 *The Character palette in the Mac OS*

6 *The Character palette in Windows*

Enter or choose a font and style.

Choose a Font

To resize type:

1. Choose any type tool, then highlight the type you want to modify.

   or

   Choose the Selection tool (V), then click the type object.

2. *On the Character palette (Cmd-T/Ctrl-T):*

   Enter a point size in the Font Size field (.1–1296), then press Return/Enter to apply and exit the palette or press Tab to apply the value and highlight the next field **2**–**3**. You don't need to reenter the unit of measure.

   Note: If the selected type is in more than one point size, the Font Size field will be blank. Entering a size now will change all selected type to the new size.

   or

   Choose a preset size from the Font Size drop-down menu or click the up or down arrow. Or click in the Font Size field, then press the up or down arrow on the keyboard.

   or

   To use the keyboard, hold down Cmd-Shift/Ctrl-Shift and press ">" to enlarge or "<" to reduce. The increment by which the type resizes each time you use this shortcut is specified in the Size/ Leading field in Edit > Preferences > Type & Auto Tracing. Two points is the default increment. Cmd-Option-Shift/ Ctrl-Alt-Shift increases/decreases the point size by five times the current Size/ Leading increment.

   To choose a size via the context menu:
   Control-click/Right-click on the type and choose a preset size from the context menu. Choosing Other from the context menu highlights the size field on the Character palette.

➤ If you use the Undo command while entering a value on the Character palette, that field will stay highlighted.

➤ You can also choose a preset type size from the Type > Size submenu. That's the slowest method.

Resize by dragging

Select freestanding type or path type using the Selection tool, then drag a handle on its **bounding box 1** (choose View > Show Bounding Box if the box isn't visible). Or scale type and its object using the **Scale** tool. To scale uniformly using either method, hold down Shift.

1 *Shift-drag a handle on the type object's bounding box to scale the type **uniformly.***

2 *On the **Character** palette, enter a number in the **Font Size** field, or click the up or down arrow, or choose a preset size from the drop-down menu.*

3 *Type enlarged*

Resize Type

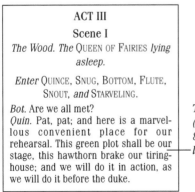

1 On the **Character** palette, enter the desired leading in points in the **Leading** field or choose Auto or a preset leading amount from the pop-up menu.

ACT III

Scene I

The Wood. The QUEEN OF FAIRIES *lying asleep.*

Enter QUINCE, SNUG, BOTTOM, FLUTE, SNOUT, *and* STARVELING.

Bot. Are we all met?

Quin. Pat, pat; and here is a marvellous convenient place for our rehearsal. This green plot shall be our stage, this hawthorn brake our tiring-house; and we will do it in action, as we will do it before the duke.

2

—*Loose leading (8-point type; 12 point leading)*

ACT III

Scene I

The Wood. The QUEEN OF FAIRIES *lying asleep.*

Enter QUINCE, SNUG, BOTTOM, FLUTE, SNOUT, *and* STARVELING.

Bot. Are we all met?
Quin. Pat, pat; and here is a marvellous convenient place for our rehearsal. This green plot shall be our stage, this hawthorn brake our tiring-house; and we will do it in action, as we will do it before the duke.

3

Tight leading (8-point type; 8.75 point leading)

Leading is the distance from baseline to baseline between lines of type, and it is traditionally measured in points. Each line of type in a block can have a different leading value. (To adjust the spacing between whole paragraphs, follow the instructions on page 232.)

Note: To change the vertical spacing in vertical type, change the horizontal tracking (see the next page). Changing the leading for vertical type changes the horizontal spacing between vertical columns.

To change leading using the Character palette:

1. *Select the type you want to modify:*

Click anywhere in a type block with the Selection tool to change the leading of the entire block.

or

Highlight an entire paragraph with a type tool (triple-click anywhere in the paragraph) to change the leading of all the lines in that paragraph.

or

Highlight an entire line with a type tool (including any space at the end) to change the leading of only that line.

2. *On the Character palette (Cmd-T/Ctrl-T):*

Enter a number in the Leading field, then press Return/Enter or Tab to apply **1**–**3**.

or

Choose a preset leading amount from the Leading drop-down menu or click the up or down arrow.

or

Choose Auto from the drop-down menu to set the leading to 120% of the largest type size on each line.

or

To make the leading value match the point size of the type, make sure all the type in the block is the same point size, then double-click the leading button. This is called "solid" leading.

To change leading using the keyboard:

1. Select the type you want to modify (see step 1 on the previous page).

2. Option-press/Alt-press the up arrow on the keyboard to decrease the leading or the down arrow to increase the leading. The increment by which leading changes each time you use this shortcut is specified in the Size/Leading field in Edit > Preferences > Type & Auto Tracing.

   Hold down Cmd-Option/Ctrl-Alt as you press an arrow to change leading in five times the Size/Leading increment.

Kerning is the addition or removal of space between a *pair* of adjacent characters. Kerning values for specific character pairs (e.g., the uppercase "T" and the lowercase "a") are built into all fonts. The built-in kerning values are adequate for small text (e.g., body type), but not for large type (e.g., headlines and logos). This awkward spacing can be remedied by careful manual kerning. To kern a pair of characters, the cursor must be inserted between them.

Note: Built-in kerning can be turned on or off for individual groups of characters. Before kerning text manually, turn built-in kerning off by choosing Auto from the Kerning pop-up menu on the Character palette (**1**, next page), then choosing or entering 0.

Tracking is the simultaneous adjustment of the space between each of *three or more* characters. It's normally applied to a range of type—a paragraph or a line. To track type, first highlight the type you want to track using a type tool or select an entire type block with a selection tool.

To kern or track type:

1. Zoom in on the type you want to kern or track. Choose a type tool, then click to create an insertion point between the two characters you want to kern or highlight the range of text you want to track.
   or

Spacing out

➤ To adjust the **overall** word or letter spacing in a text block, use the Word Spacing and Letter Spacing fields on the Paragraph palette (see page 232).

➤ Tracking/kerning changes the vertical spacing of characters in **vertical** type.

1 *Kerning field and pop-up menu*

Tracking field and pop-up menu

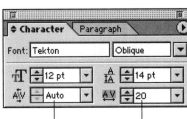

2 *Normal type*

3 *After adding space between the first two characters (kerning)*

4 *After removing space between the last five characters (kerning or tracking)*

5 *Click one of the three options in the Change Case dialog box.*

To track all the type in an object, choose the Selection tool, then click the object.

2. In the Kerning or Tracking field on the Character palette (Cmd-Option-K/Ctrl-Alt-K), enter a positive number to add space between characters or a negative number to remove space, then press Return/Enter or Tab to apply **1**–**4**.
or
Choose a preset kerning or tracking amount from the drop-down menu or click the up or down arrow.
or
Hold down Option/Alt and press the right arrow on the keyboard to add space between letters or the left arrow to remove space. The amount of space that is added or removed each time you press an arrow is specified in the Tracking field in Edit > Preferences > Type & Auto Tracing. Hold down Cmd-Option/Ctrl-Alt to track in larger increments.
or
Use this shortcut: Cmd-Shift-[or]/Ctrl-Shift-[or].

The Change Case command changes selected text to all UPPER CASE, all lower case, or Mixed Case (only initial capitals).

To change case:

1. Highlight the text you want to modify with a type tool.

2. Choose Type > Change Case.

3. Click Upper Case (ABC); Lower Case (abc); or Mixed Case (Abc; the first character in each word is uppercase, the other characters lowercase) **5**.

4. Click OK.

➤ Some fonts, such as Lithos and Castellar, do not have lowercase characters.

The Fit Headline uses tracking to fit a one-line paragraph of horizontal or vertical area type to the edges of its container.

To fit type to its container:

1. Choose any type tool.

2. Highlight a one-line paragraph (not a line in a larger paragraph; we're talking about a stand-alone line).

3. Choose Type > Fit Headline **1**–**2**. When applied to a Multiple Master font, Fit Headline adjusts both the weight and the tracking **3**–**4**.

The Horizontal Scale feature extends (widens) or condenses (narrows) type. The Vertical Scale feature makes type taller or shorter. The default scale is 100%.

Note: In the Multiple Master typefaces and the typefaces that are narrow or wide by design (e.g., Univers Extended or Helvetica Narrow), the weight, proportions, and counters (interior spaces) are adjusted along with the width. For this reason, they look better than Regular characters that are extended or narrowed via Illustrator's Horizontal or Vertical Scale command. That being said…

To scale type horizontally and/or vertically:

Select the type you want to modify, change the percentage in the Horizontal or Vertical Scale field on the Character palette, then press Return/Enter or Tab to apply **5**–**6**. Or choose a preset value from the drop-down menu or click the up or down arrow.
or
To scale point or path type manually, select it using the Selection tool, then drag a side handle of the bounding box without holding down Shift.
or
To scale a selected type block by a percentage, double-click the Scale tool, then change the Non-Uniform: Horizontal or Vertical value.

To restore normal scaling:

Select the type, then choose 100% from both Scale fields on the Character palette (Cmd-Shift-X/Ctrl-Shift-X).

1 *The original, selected characters*

2 *In non-Multiple Master type, the **Fit Headline** command only adds space **between** characters.*

3 *The original, selected Multiple Master characters*

4 *The **Fit Headline** command adds **space** between, and changes the **weight** of, Multiple Master characters.*

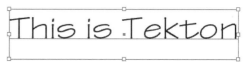

Vertical Scale field   **5** *Horizontal Scale field*

6 DANIELLE
Normal type (no scaling)

DANIELLE
75% horizontal scale

DANIELLE
125% horizontal scale

1 *Baseline Shift field*

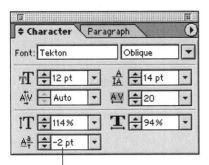

2 *Characters on a path, baseline shifted downward*

Alicia

3 *The "A" is baseline shifted 9 points downward.*

*Hanging
punctuation*

'Lo! all these trophies of affections hot,
Of pensiv'd and subdued desires the tender,
Nature hath charg'd me that I hoard them not,
But yield them up where I myself must render,
That is, to you, my origin and ender:
For these, of force, must your oblations be,
Since I their altar, you enpatron me.

— *William Shakespeare*

4 *Let it hang out.*

The Baseline Shift command repositions characters above or below the baseline. You can use this command to offset curved path type from its path or to create superscript or subscript characters. (There is no superscript or subscript type style in Illustrator—or any button for applying an italic or underline style, for that matter. You have to choose a font with the desired attributes.)

To baseline shift type:

1. Highlight the type you want to modify.

2. In the Baseline Shift field on the Character palette (choose Show Options from the palette menu if the field isn't visible), enter a positive number to baseline shift characters upward or a negative number to baseline shift characters downward, then press Return/Enter to apply **1**–**3**. Or choose a preset amount from the drop-down menu or click the up or down arrow.
   or
   Option-Shift-press/Alt-Shift-press the up arrow to shift highlighted characters upward or the down arrow to shift characters downward. The amount type shifts each time you press an arrow is specified in the Baseline Shift field in Edit > Preferences > Type & Auto Tracing. (Cmd-Option-Shift-press/Ctrl-Alt-Shift-press to shift in larger increments.)

Use hanging punctuation to make the edges of your paragraphs look more uniform. This option works only with area type. The period, comma, quotation mark, apostrophe, hyphen, dash, colon, and semicolon are affected.

To hang punctuation:

1. Select a paragraph with a type tool.
   or
   Select a type object with a selection tool.

2. Check the Hang Punctuation box in the Options area at the bottom of the Paragraph palette **4**. If this option isn't visible, choose Show Options from the palette menu.

Alignment and indent values affect whole paragraphs.

➤ To create a new paragraph (hard return) in a text block, press **Return/Enter**. Type preceding a return is part of one paragraph; type following a return is part of the next paragraph. Type that wraps automatically is part of the same paragraph.

➤ To create a line break (soft return) within a paragraph in non-tabular text, press **Shift-Return** or press **Enter** (on the keypad).

To change paragraph alignment:

1. Choose a type tool, then click in a paragraph or drag through a series of paragraphs.
or
Choose a selection tool and select a type object.

2. At the top of the Paragraph palette, click the Align Left, Align Center, Align Right, Justify Full Lines, or Justify All Lines alignment button **1**–**2**.
or
Use one of the keyboard shortcuts listed in the sidebar on this page.

➤ Don't apply Justify Full Lines or Justify All Lines alignment to path type or to freestanding type (type that's not in an object or in a block). Those type objects don't have edges, thus nothing to justify the type to.

Paragraph alignment shortcuts

Left	Cmd-Shift-L/Ctrl-Shift-L
Center	Cmd-Shift-C/Ctrl-Shift-C
Right	Cmd-Shift-R/Ctrl-Shift-R
Justify	
Justify Full Lines	Cmd-Shift-J/Ctrl-Shift-J
Justify All Lines	Cmd-Shift-F/Ctrl-Shift-F

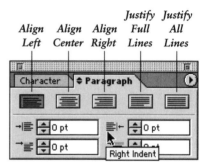

1 *The five Alignment buttons on the Paragraph palette*

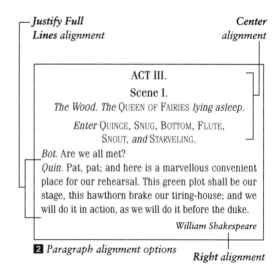

2 *Paragraph alignment options*

Selecting paragraphs for modification

If you want to change paragraph attributes for *all* the text in a type object or on a path, select the object or path with the Selection tool. To isolate a paragraph or series of paragraphs, select just those paragraphs with a type tool.

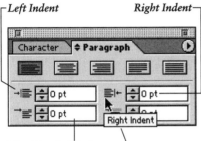

Left Indent　　　　*Right Indent*

First Line Left Indent

1 *If you forget which Indent field on the Paragraph palette is which, rest the mouse over an icon—the tool tip will remind you.*

You can apply Left and/or Right Indent values to area type; use only a Left Indent value for freestanding type.

To change paragraph indentation:

1. Choose a type tool, then select the paragraph(s) you want to modify or click to create an insertion point in a single paragraph.
   or
   Choose a selection tool, then select a type object.

2. *On the Paragraph palette:*
   Change the Left and/or Right Indent value, then press Return/Enter or Tab to apply **1**–**2**.
   or
   Click the up or down arrow.
   or
   To indent only the first line of each paragraph, enter a positive First Line Left Indent value.

➤ You can enter a negative value in the Left Indent, First Line Left Indent, or Right Indent field to expand the measure of each line. The type will be pushed outside its object, but it will still display and print **3**.

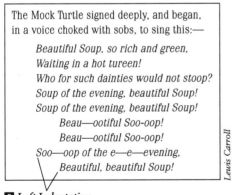

The Mock Turtle signed deeply, and began, in a voice choked with sobs, to sing this:—

Beautiful Soup, so rich and green,
Waiting in a hot tureen!
Who for such dainties would not stoop?
Soup of the evening, beautiful Soup!
Soup of the evening, beautiful Soup!
Beau—ootiful Soo-oop!
Beau—ootiful Soo-oop!
Soo—oop of the e—e—evening,
Beautiful, beautiful Soup!

Lewis Carroll

2 *Left Indentation*

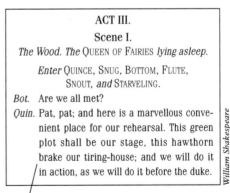

ACT III.

Scene I.

The Wood. The QUEEN OF FAIRIES *lying asleep.*

Enter QUINCE, SNUG, BOTTOM, FLUTE, SNOUT, *and* STARVELING.

Bot. Are we all met?

Quin. Pat, pat; and here is a marvellous convenient place for our rehearsal. This green plot shall be our stage, this hawthorn brake our tiring-house; and we will do it in action, as we will do it before the duke.

William Shakespeare

3 *To create a hanging indent, as in the last paragraph in this illustration, enter a number in the Left Indent field and the same number with a minus sign in front of it in the First Line Left Indent field.*

Paragraph Indents

Use the Space Before Paragraph field on the Paragraph palette to add or subtract space *between* paragraphs in area type. Point type isn't modified by this feature. (To adjust the spacing between lines of type *within* a paragraph (leading), see pages 225–226.)

To adjust inter-paragraph spacing:

1. Select the type you want to modify. To modify the space before only one paragraph in a type block, select the paragraph with a type tool. To change all the type in an object, select the object with the Selection tool.

2. In the Space Before Paragraph field on the Paragraph palette **1**, enter a positive value to move paragraphs apart or a negative value to move them closer together, then press Return/Enter or Tab to apply **2**.
   or
   Click the up or down arrow.

➤ To create a new paragraph (hard return), press Return/Enter. To create a line break within a paragraph (soft return), press Shift-Return/Shift-Enter.

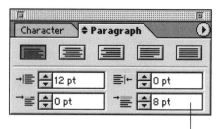

1 *The Space Before Paragraph field on the Paragraph palette*

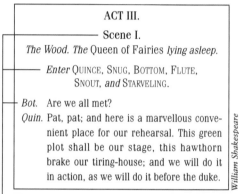

William Shakespeare

ACT III.

Scene I.

The Wood. The Queen of Fairies *lying asleep.*

Enter QUINCE, SNUG, BOTTOM, FLUTE, SNOUT, *and* STARVELING.

Bot. Are we all met?

Quin. Pat, pat; and here is a marvellous convenient place for our rehearsal. This green plot shall be our stage, this hawthorn brake our tiring-house; and we will do it in action, as we will do it before the duke.

2 *Higher Space Before Paragraph values were applied to these paragraphs to add space above them.*

Word and letter spacing

To change the horizontal word or letter spacing for justified paragraphs, change the percentage in the **Minimum, Desired,** or **Maximum Word Spacing** or **Letter Spacing** fields on the Paragraph palette **3**–**5** (choose Show Options from the Paragraph palette menu if those options aren't visible). Non-justified type is affected only by the Desired value. Headlines are usually improved by reduced word spacing.

Ocean

Body more immaculate than a wave,
salt washing away its own line,
and the brilliant bird
flying without ground roots.

Pablo Neruda

3 *Normal word and letter spacing*

Ocean

Body more immaculate than a wave,
salt washing away its own line,
and the brilliant bird
flying without ground roots.

4 *Loose letter spacing*

Ocean

Body more immaculate than a wave,
salt washing away its own line,
and the brilliant bird
flying without ground roots.

5 *Tight word spacing*

Word processing

Use the Find/Change command to search for and replace characters.

To find and replace text:

1. *Optional:* Click with a type tool to create an insertion point from which to start the search. If you don't do this, the search will begin from the most recently created object.

2. Choose Type > Find/Change.

3. Enter a word or phrase to search for in the "Find what" field **1**.

4. Enter a replacement word or phrase in the "Change to" field **2**. Leave the "Change to" field blank to delete instances of the "Find what" text altogether.

5. *Do any of these optional steps:*

   Check **Whole Word** to find the "Find what" letters only if they appear as a complete word—not as part of a larger word (e.g., "go" but not "going").

   Check **Case Sensitive** to find only those instances that match the exact uppercase/lowercase configuration of the "Find what" text. With this box unchecked, case will be ignored as a criteria.

   Check **Wrap Around** to search the whole file from the current cursor position to the end of the text object or string of linked objects and then continue the search from the most recently created object. With Wrap Around unchecked, the search will proceed only from the current cursor position forward to the end of that text object; you'll have to click Find Next to resume the search.

   Check **Search Backward** to search backward from the current cursor position.

6. Click **Find Next** to search for the first instance of the "Find what" word or phrase or to skip over a word **3**.

7. Click **Change** to replace only the currently found instance of the "Find what" text.
   or
   Click **Change All** to replace all the instances at once **4**.
   or
   Click **Change/Find** to replace the current instance and search for the next instance.

8. Click Done (Return/Enter or Esc).

   Beware: The corrected word will take on the styling of the text preceding it and will lose its original styling.

1 *Enter the text you want to search for in the "Find what" field.*

2 *Enter the text you want to change the found text to in the "Change to" field.*

3 *Click Find Next.*

4 *Click Change, Change All, or Change/Find.*

Find/Change

Find what:
`popup`

Change to:
`pop-up`

☑ Whole Word   ☐ Case Sensitive
☑ Search Backward   ☑ Wrap Around

[Done]
[Find Next]
[Change]
[Change All]
[Change/Find]

The Find/Change dialog box

The Check Spelling command checks spelling in an entire document using a built-in dictionary. You can also create and edit your own word list for the Check Spelling feature to use.

To check spelling:

1. Choose Type > Check Spelling. Any words not found in the application or user dictionary will appear on the Misspelled Words list ■.

2. Leave the currently highlighted Misspelled Word selected or click a different word on the list. The selected misspelled word will be highlighted in your illustration.

3. *Optional:* Check Case Sensitive to display the Misspelled Word both ways if it appears in both upper and lower case (such as *Spelle* and *spelle*). With this option off, only the first instance of the word will be listed.

4. If the correctly spelled word appears on the **Suggested Corrections** list, double-click it ■. Or to change all instances of the misspelled word instead, click the correctly spelled word, then click **Change All**. The next misspelled word will now become highlighted.
   or
   If the correct word doesn't appear on the list, or no words appear at all (because there are no similar words in the Illustrator dictionary), type the correctly spelled word in the field at the bottom of the dialog box. Then click **Change** to change only the first instance of the highlighted Misspelled Word to the currently highlighted Suggested Correction, or click **Change All** to change all instances of the Misspelled Word.

   For any word, you can click **Skip** to leave the current instance of the Misspelled Word as is, or click **Skip All** to leave all instances of the Misspelled Word as is.

5. *Optional:* Click Add to List to add the currently highlighted Misspelled Word or Words to the Learned Words list. To add more than one word at a time, Cmd-click/Ctrl-click them first.

Check spelling in Dutch?

Click Language in the Check Spelling dialog box, locate and highlight the dictionary you want to use in Adobe Illustrator 10 folder > Plug-ins > Text Filters, then click Open.

Note: The Check Spelling command can only be used with Roman fonts—not with Chinese, Japanese, or Korean fonts.

■ *Misspelled words*

■ *Correctly spelled potential replacement words*

Check Spelling

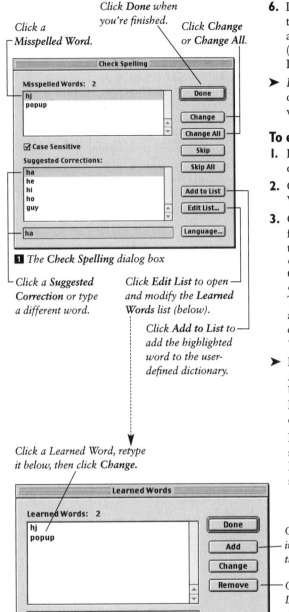

Click *Done when you're finished.*

Click *a Misspelled Word.*

Click *Change or Change All.*

❶ *The Check Spelling dialog box*

Click *a Suggested Correction or type a different word.*

Click *Edit List to open and modify the Learned Words list (below).*

Click *Add to List to add the highlighted word to the user-defined dictionary.*

Click *a Learned Word, retype it below, then click Change.*

❷ *Create your own word list using the Learned Words dialog box.*

Or *type a new word in the bottom field, then click Add.*

Or *highlight a Learned Word, then click Remove.*

6. If you finish going through all the words that Illustrator finds, a prompt will appear. Click OK, then click Done (Return/Enter or Esc). You can also click Done at any time to stop spell-checking.

➤ *Beware!* The replacement word will take on the styling of the text preceding it and will lose its original styling.

To edit the user-defined dictionary:

1. If the Check Spelling dialog box isn't open, choose Type > Check Spelling **❶**.

2. Click Edit List to open the Learned Words list dialog box **❷**.

3. Click a word in the list, correct it in the field at the bottom of the dialog box, then click **Change**.
or
Click a word, then click **Remove**.
or
Type a completely new word in the field at the bottom of the dialog box, then click **Add**. Hyphenated words—like "pop-up"—are permitted.

➤ In the Mac OS, the default dictionary for American users of Illustrator is saved as USEnglish 10.0 in Adobe Illustrator 10.0 > Plug-Ins > Text Filters. The user-defined dictionary is saved as AI User Dictionary.

In Windows, the default dictionary is saved as usEnglsh.dct in Plug-ins > Text Filters. The user-defined dictionary is saved as AIUser.dct.

Use the Export command to prepare Illustrator text so it can be imported into, and used as text in, another application. Path information isn't included.

To export text:

1. Select the text you want to export with a type tool or a selection tool.

2. Choose File > Export.

3. Choose a location in which to save the text file **1**.

4. Enter a Name for the new file.

5. Choose Text Format (TXT) from the Format pop-up menu (Mac OS)/Save as Type drop-down menu (Windows). Text Format is a text-only format.

6. Click Export.

The Find Font command can be used to generate a list of the fonts currently being used in an illustration or it can be used to actually replace fonts. When fonts are replaced, the type color, kerning, tracking, and other attributes are retained.

To find and replace a font:

1. Choose Type > Find Font.

2. In the Include in List area at the bottom of the dialog box, check Type 1, Standard, Roman, TrueType, CID, Multiple Master, or OTF, if desired, to have only fonts of those types appear on the scroll lists. For Multiple Master fonts, you must check Type 1.

3. To have the replacement font list display only fonts of the types checked in step 2 that are currently being used in your document, leave the Replace Font From menu option on Document.

or

Choose System from the Replace Font From pop-up menu to display on the replacement font list all the fonts currently available in your system. If you need to choose this option, be patient while the list updates.

1 *Choose* **Text Format** *(TXT) for your selected text from the* **Format** *pop-up menu.*

4. Click a font to search for on the Fonts in Document scroll list **1**. The first instance of that font will be highlighted in your document.

5. Click a replacement font on the replacement font list.

6. Click **Change** to change only the current instance of the currently highlighted font.
or
Click **Change All** to change all instances of the currently highlighted font. Once all the instances of a font are replaced, that font will be removed from the Fonts in Document list.
or
Click **Find Next** to search for the next instance of the currently highlighted font or click the font name on the Fonts in Document list again.
or
Click **Skip** to leave the current instance of the font unchanged and proceed to the next instance of the font.

7. *Optional:* To save a list of the fonts currently being used in the illustration as a text document, click Save List, enter a name, choose a location in which to save the file, then click Save. The text document can later be opened directly from the Desktop or it can be imported into a text editing or layout application.

8. Click Done.

➤ Use Undo to undo font changes made using Find Font.

*Choose **System** from the **Replace Font From** pop-up menu to display on the replacement font list all available fonts in the System of the types checked or choose **Document** to list only the fonts currently being used in your illustration.*

1 Click a font to search for on the Fonts in Document scroll list.

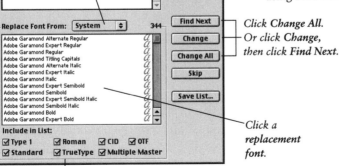

*Click **Change All**.
Or click **Change**, then click **Find Next**.*

Click a replacement font.

Uncheck any font types to narrow the selection of replacement fonts.

To arrange text in linked rows and columns:

1. Choose the Selection tool (not a type tool).

2. Select one type object or a series of linked type objects. No freestanding type!

   ➤ Make a copy of the type object(s) before proceeding.

3. Choose Type > Rows & Columns.

4. Check Preview to apply changes immediately 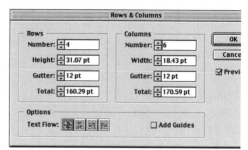. Uncheck Preview if the redraw is tediously slow.

5. Click the up or down arrow or enter values in the fields to choose:

   The total Number of Rows and Columns to be produced.
   and
   The Height of each Row and the Width of each Column.
   and
   The Gutter (space) between each Row and each Column.
   and
   The Total width and Total height of the entire block of Rows and Columns. If you change the Total values, the height or width of the boxes will change, but the gutter values will remain constant.

6. Click a different Text Flow button to control the direction of the text flow.

7. *Optional:* Check Add Guides to make guides appear around the text blocks. Make sure the ruler origin is in the correct location if you do this.

8. Click OK **2**–**3**.

   ➤ If you select the entire block of rows and columns with the Selection tool and then reopen the Rows & Columns dialog box, the current settings for that block will be displayed.

1 *The Rows & Columns dialog box*

Hey! diddle, diddle,
The cat and the Fiddle,
The cow jumped over the moon;
The little dog laugh'd
To see such sport,
And the dish ran away with the spoon.

2 *One text object...*

Hey! diddle, diddle,
The cat and the
Fiddle,

The cow jumped
over the moon;
The little dog

laugh'd
To see such sport,
And the dish ran

away with the
spoon.

3 *...is converted into two rows and two columns.*

Dialog box option	Keyboard	Smart punctuation
ff, fi, ffi Ligatures	ff, fi, ffi	ff, fi, ffi
ff, fl, ffl Ligatures	ff, fi, ffl	ff, fi, ffl
Smart Quotes	' "	' " ' '
Smart Spaces (one space after a period)	. T	. T
En [dashes]	--	–
Em Dashes	---	—
Ellipses	...	...
Expert Fractions	1/2	½

The Smart Punctuation command converts keyboard punctuation into professional typesetter's marks.

Note: With the exception of the "fi" ligature, which is available in most serif fonts in the Mac OS, to apply Ligatures and Expert Fractions, the Adobe Expert font set for the font you are using must be available in your system. The Expert set is required for all ligatures in Windows.

To create smart punctuation:

1. *Optional:* Select text with the Type tool to smart-punctuate that text only. Otherwise, the command will affect the entire document.

2. Choose Type > Smart Punctuation.

3. Check any of the Replace Punctuation boxes **1** (and see the sidebar).

4. Click Replace In: Selected Text Only if you selected text for step 1, otherwise click Entire Document.

5. *Optional:* Check Report Results to display a list of your changes.

6. Click OK **2**–**3**.

➤ Windows users, press Num Lock and one of these keystrokes to produce a fraction: ¼ = Alt-0188; ½ = Alt-0189; ¾ = Alt-0190.

1 *Check Replace Punctuation options in the Smart Punctuation dialog box.*

He supposed Miss Petiigrew might have leaned over the sugar bowl and said, "Mayor," which Daddy said was all she ever called him anymore, "I'd be pleased to have a chimpanzee." And Daddy supposed the mayor frumped himself up a little and muddied his expression and said, "Sister darling, your chimpanzee is just around the corner."

"Louis!" Momma said. Daddy was hardly ever a very big hit with Momma.

2 *Dumb punctuation: Straight quotes and two spaces after each period*

He supposed Miss Petiigrew might have leaned over the sugar bowl and said, "Mayor," which Daddy said was all she ever called him anymore, "I'd be pleased to have a chimpanzee." And Daddy supposed the mayor frumped himself up a little and muddied his expression and said, "Sister darling, your chimpanzee is just around the corner."

"Louis!" Momma said. Daddy was hardly ever a very big hit with Momma.

T.R.Pearson

3 *Smart punctuation: Curly quotes and one space after each period*

Smart Punctuation

To turn on auto hyphenation:

1. Auto hyphenation affects only currently selected or subsequently created text. If you want to hyphenate existing text, select it with a type tool or selection tool now.

2. On the Paragraph palette, check Options: Auto Hyphenate **1**. (If this option isn't visible, choose Show Options from the palette menu.)

3. To choose hyphenation options, choose Hyphenation from the Paragraph palette menu.

4. In the "Hyphenate [ ] letters from beginning" field, enter the minimum number of characters to precede any hyphen **2**. Fewer than three letters before or after a hyphen can impair readability.

5. In the "Hyphenate [ ] letters from end" field, enter the minimum number of characters to carry over onto the next line following a hyphen **3**.

6. In the "Limit consecutive hyphens to" field, enter the maximum allowable number of hyphens in a row **4**. More than two hyphens in a row impairs readability and looks unsightly.

7. Click OK. Look over the newly hyphenated text, and correct any undesirable breaks.

➤ To hyphenate using rules of a different language for selected text in the current document only, choose Show Multilingual from the Character palette menu, then choose from the Language pop-up menu. You can change the default hyphenation language for the application in Edit > Preferences > Hyphenation. You can also enter hyphenation exceptions or specify how particular words are to be hyphenated in that dialog box. Turn Auto Hyphenate off and then on again to apply Preferences changes. See page 440.

➤ To hyphenate a word manually: Cmd-Shift--(hyphen)/Ctrl-Shift--.

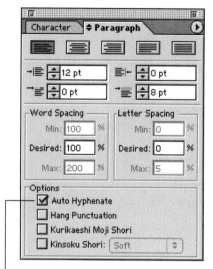

1 *Check* **Auto Hyphenate** *on the Paragraph palette.*

AN OVER-ABUN-DANCE OF HY-PHENS MAKES FOR TIR-ING READ-ING.

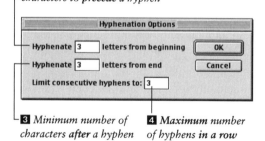

2 *Minimum number of characters to* **precede** *a hyphen*

3 *Minimum number of characters* **after** *a hyphen*

4 *Maximum number of hyphens* **in a row**

Out of hiding

To show the tab characters that are hidden in your text, along with other non-printing characters, such as paragraph returns, soft returns, and spaces, choose Type > **Show Hidden Characters**. Tab characters display as right-pointing arrows **1**. Choose the command again to turn it off.

→	**Front.9.→**	**Back.9.→**	**Total**¶
Tiger.→	*34.→*	*34.→*	*68*¶
Jack.→	*38.→*	*44.→*	*82*¶
David.→	*34.→*	*38.→*	*72*¶
Phil.→	*35.→*	*38.→*	*73*∞

1 *Text aligned using custom tab stops*

To align columns of text correctly, you must use tabs—not spaces. The Tab Ruler palette is used to set custom left-, center-, right-, and decimal-justified tabs in horizontal type, and top-, center-, bottom-, and decimal-justified tabs in vertical type. The default tab stops are half an inch apart.

To insert tabs into text:

Press Tab **once** as you input copy before typing each new column. The cursor will jump to the next tab stop.

or

To add a tab to already inputted text, click just to the left of the text that is to start a new column, then press Tab. The text will move to the next default tab stop.

To set custom tab stops, see the next page.

Insert Tabs

Custom Tabs

To set or modify custom tab stops:

1. Choose the Selection tool, then click a text object.
   or
   Choose a type tool and select some text.

2. Choose Window > Type > Tab Ruler (Cmd-Shift-T/Ctrl-Shift-T).

3. *Optional:* Check Snap to have a tab marker snap to the nearest ruler tick mark as you insert or move it. Or to turn on/off the Snap feature temporarily (the opposite of the current Snap state), Cmd-drag/Ctrl-drag a marker.

4. Click just above the Tab Ruler to insert a new stop (the selected text will align to that stop) **1**, then click a tab alignment button in the top left corner of the palette. Or Option-click/Alt-click a tab stop to cycle through the alignment types for it. Repeat to insert more stops.

5. *Optional:* To delete a tab stop, drag the tab marker upward and out of the ruler. As you drag it, the word *delete* will display on the palette. Shift-drag to delete a marker and all markers to its right.

6. *Optional:* To move a tab stop, drag the marker to the left or the right. Its location will display next to the "X." Shift-drag a marker to move all the markers to the right of it along with it.

➤ Tab Ruler measurements display in the currently chosen Artboard: Units from File > Document Setup.

What's the question?

The tab stops from the first line of selected text are shown on the ruler. If a **question mark** appears in the ruler instead of a stop, it means that stop isn't present in one or more lines of the selected text. Click the question mark to apply that stop to all the selected text.

*Click the **Left-**, **Center-**, **Right-**, or **Decimal-Justified** tab button (or **Top-** or **Bottom-Justified** button for vertical type).*

*Click the **Alignment** box to realign the tab ruler with the left and right margins of the selected text for horizontal type or the top and bottom margins for vertical type.*

Snap option

Location of the currently selected tab marker

Default stop

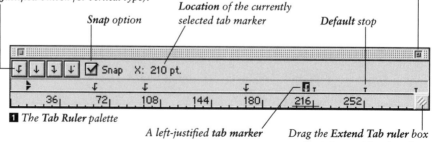

1 *The Tab Ruler palette*

*A left-justified **tab marker***

*Drag the **Extend Tab ruler** box to the right to widen the ruler.*

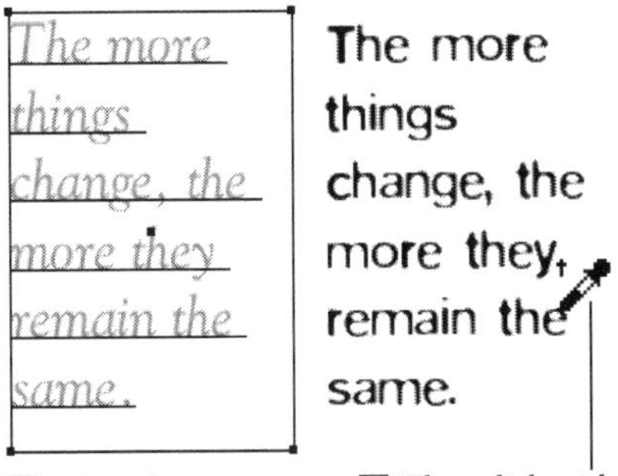

1 *Select the type object whose attributes you want to change.*

2 *Then click with the Eyedropper on the attributes you want to copy.*

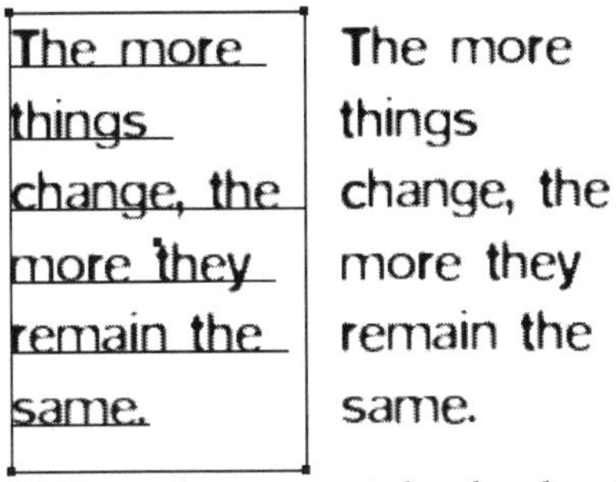

3 *The attributes are copied to the selected type.*

Copy type attributes

When you click a type object with the Eyedropper tool, the tool samples the type's character, paragraph, fill, stroke, and appearance attributes, copies them to the Character, Paragraph, Color, Stroke, and Appearance palettes, and applies them to any currently selected text—a temporary "style sheet" on the fly.

Note: To choose which attributes the Eyedropper picks up or the Paint Bucket applies, see the following page.

To copy type attributes using the Eyedropper or Paint Bucket:

1. Choose the Selection tool, then select the type object or objects whose attributes you want to change **1**.

2. Choose the Eyedropper tool.

3. Click on any unselected type in any open document window that has the desired attributes **2** (a tiny "t" will appear next to the pointer). The type attributes will be copied to the Character, Paragraph, Color, and Stroke palettes and to the selected type **3**.
   or
   To apply only fill or stroke attributes (depending on which box is active on the Toolbox and Color palette), Shift-click unselected text that has the desired attributes.

4. *Optional:* To apply the newly sampled effects and type attributes to yet another type object, Option-click/Alt-click any other type object (this is a temporary Paint Bucket tool).

To choose which attributes the Eyedropper picks up or the Paint Bucket applies:

1. Double-click the Eyedropper or Paint Bucket tool.

2. Click a triangle to expand the Appearance, Character, or Paragraph list, then check any individual attributes on or off 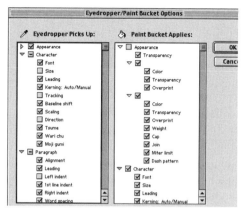. By default, all the attributes are checked.
   or
   Check or uncheck Appearance, Fill, Stroke, Character, or Paragraph to turn all the attributes in that category on or off.

3. Click OK.

1 *Choose which attributes the Paint Bucket Applies or the Eyedropper Picks Up.*

Special effects with type

To wrap type around an object:

1. Create area type inside an object.

2. Choose the Selection tool.

3. Select the object the type is to wrap around **2**. It can be a placed image with a clipping path from Photoshop.

4. Choose Object > Arrange > Bring To Front or use the Layers palette to bring the object forward (drag it upward).

5. Drag a marquee around both objects.

6. Choose Type > Wrap > Make **3**. The text block and the object are now listed as a group on the Layers palette.

➤ Use the Direct-selection tool to move the object the type is wrapping around. For multiple objects, Shift-click them first.

➤ To adjust the space between the type and the wrap object, change the Left or Right Indentation value on the Paragraph palette for the type.

➤ To wrap type around part of a placed image or vector object, create a separate object with the desired shape for the wrap with a stroke and fill of None, select the type and that object, choose Type > Wrap > Make, then bring the separate placed image to the front. To adjust the wrap, move or adjust the anchor points on the blank object with the Direct-selection tool.

Unwrap

To undo a type wrap, select both objects using the Selection tool, then choose Type > Wrap > **Release**.

2 *Select a type object (not point or path type) and the object the type is going to wrap around.*

Just picture a large sparrow cage made of bamboo grillwork and having a coconut-thatch roof, divided off two parts by the curtains from my old studio. One of the two parts makes a bedroom, with very little light, so as to keep it cool. The other part, with a large window up high, is my studio. On the floor, some mats and my old Persian rug; and I've decorated the rest with fabrics, trinkets, and drawings. *Paul Gauguin*

3 *The type **wraps** around the palm tree.*

Working with the shadow

➤ Use the **Layers palette** to select the type object or its shadow object.

➤ Use the **Free Transform** tool to vertically **scale** or **shear** a type block (move the top center handle for both)(see page 104).

➤ Use the **Free Transform** tool to **reflect** the shadow block. Drag the top center handle all the way across the object.

1 *The shadow is created and sent to the back.*

2 *The shadow is shortened using the Scale tool.*

3 *The shadow is slanted using the Shear tool.*

4 *The type is reflected using the Reflect tool.*

An advantage of using the following method instead of Effect > Drop Shadow is that here the shadow is an independent vector object.

To create type with a shadow:

1. Create freestanding type (see page 208).

2. *Optional:* Select the type with the Type tool, then track the characters out (Option/Alt right arrow).

3. Choose the Selection tool, then click the type block.

4. Apply a dark fill color, stroke of None.

5. Option-drag/Alt-drag the type block slightly to the right and downward. Release the mouse, then Option/Alt.

6. With the copy of the type block still selected, lighten its shade.

7. On the Layers palette, drag the copy of the type below the original **1**.

8. Choose Effect > Stylize (on the upper part of the menu) > Feather, check Preview, choose a Radius value, click OK, then lower the transparency of this shadow.

9. Reposition either type block—press any arrow key to move it in small increments.

*To **slant** the shadow:*

1. Select the shadow object using the Layers palette.

2. Double-click the Scale tool, click Non-uniform, enter 100 in the Horizontal field, enter 60 in the Vertical field, then click OK **2**.

3. With the shadow type still selected, double-click the Shear tool.

4. Enter 45 in the Shear Angle field, click Axis: Horizontal, then click OK **3**.

5. Use the arrow keys to move the baseline of the shadow text so it aligns with the baseline of the original text.

*To **reflect** the shadow:*

1. Select the shadow type.

2. Double-click the Reflect tool, click Axis: Horizontal, then click OK.

3. Move the two blocks of type together so their baselines meet **4**.

Shadow Type

To slant a type block:

1. Choose the Rectangle tool (M), ▢ then draw a rectangle.

2. Choose the Area Type tool. ⊤

3. Click the edge of the rectangle, then enter type **2**.

4. With the rectangle still selected, double-click the Rotation tool. ⟳

5. Enter 30 in the Angle field, then click OK **3**.

6. Make sure Smart Guides is on (Cmd-U/ Ctrl-U) with Object Highlighting (Edit > Preferences > Smart Guides & Slices). Deselect the object.

7. Choose the Direct-selection tool (A), ▸ then Shift-drag the top segment diagonally to the right until the side segments are vertical **4**–**5**.

8. *Optional:* Drag the right segment of the rectangle a little to the right to enlarge the object and reflow the type.

Use the shears

You can use the Shear tool ▱ to slant a block of type (it's on the Scale tool pop-out menu) **1**.

1 *Select the type, click with the **Shear** tool on the center of the type, then drag upward or downward from the edge of the type block. (Hold down Shift to constrain vertically or horizontally.)*

2 *The original type object*

3 *The type rotated 30°*

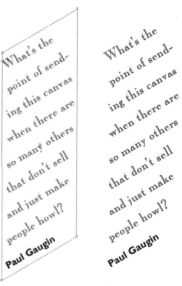

4 *The top segment dragged diagonally to the right*

5 *The final type object in Preview view*

Slanted Type

Chapter 13: Style & Edit Type ◆ Study Guide

Learning Objectives

- Select type.
- Apply character-level typographic attributes.
- Apply paragraph-wide attributes.
- Perform word-processing tasks such as finding and replacing text and fonts, and checking spelling.
- Apply text wrap and drop shadows.

Get Up and Running Exercises

- Open or create an Illustrator file that contains type objects. Now do the following:
  - ▲ Change the size of a single word, or of two words that aren't next to each other.
  - ▲ Change the font of all of the type in the type object, but without using any type tools or the Find Font command.
  - ▲ Apply a red 2-point stroke to the type object.
  - ▲ Change the type size without using a type tool.
- Find a published example of good typography. It can be a page out of a book (such as this one), a brochure, or a direct-mail piece from your mailbox. Use the techniques in this chapter to reproduce the typography of the pieces in Illustrator. If you don't have the exact fonts used in the piece, use similar ones, and concentrate on reproducing the overall look of the type.
- Find a Web page that contains large paragraphs of text. Import the text into Illustrator via copy and paste. Add an object to the page, and set up the object so that text automatically wraps around the object (doesn't run on top of it). Look for places where keyboard punctuation can be converted to professional punctuation (e.g., curly quotation marks).
- Create a transportation timetable, such as one published by your city's bus system. If a local timetable is not available, use the Web to find a timetable (from anywhere, such as New York or Paris). Create a version of it for print. What Illustrator feature can make this a relatively quick and easy job?

Class Discussion Questions

- What are three ways to select type objects and their contents?
- What are some ways to resize type?
- What's the difference between kerning and tracking?
- When would you use leading instead of inter-paragraph spacing?
- What are some ways to create tables in Illustrator?

Review Questions

Multiple choice

1. Which feature lets you move individual characters above or below the rest of the characters in the same sentence?
   A. Vertical Scale
   B. Baseline Shift
   C. Leading
   D. Space Before Paragraph

2. Which tool do you use to select a path that contains type without selecting the type?
   A. Direct-selection tool
   B. Selection tool
   C. Group-selection tool
   D. Type tool

3. Which tool copies type attributes without copying the type?
   A. Direct-selection tool
   B. Eyedropper tool
   C. Type tool
   D. Selection tool

4. How do you create a hanging indent in the Paragraph palette?
   A. Enter a positive First Line Left Indent value, and enter zero in the Left Indent value field.
   B. Enter a positive First Line Left Indent value, and enter the same number as a positive value in the Left Indent value field.
   C. Enter a negative First Line Left Indent value, and enter the same number as a positive value in the Left Indent value field.
   D. Enter the same value in the Left Indent and First Line Left Indent fields.

5. How do you delete a tab stop?
   A. Drag it off the Tab Ruler.
   B. Select it and press Delete/Backspace.
   C. Option/Alt-click it.
   D. Select it and click the trash icon.

Fill-in-the-blank

1. You can view the type size of selected type on the Character or _____ palettes.

2. To apply most ligatures and Expert Fractions, you need to have the appropriate _____ installed on your computer.

3. If you want to know exactly where tabs, soft returns, and other nonprinting characters are inserted in text, turn on the _____.

4. To hyphenate a word manually, press _____.

5. Illustrator instantly switches to the type tool when you _____.

6. To use the options on the MM Design palette, the font must be _____.

7. In the Character palette, you can instantly set leading to the same size as the type by _____.

Definitions

1. What is solid leading?

2. What is hanging punctuation?

3. What is a hanging indent?

4. What is a decimal-justified tab?

5. What is type wrap?

In this chapter you will learn how to get images into Illustrator via the Open command, the Place command, and drag-and-drop. You will also learn how to work with the Links palette to edit, locate, update, replace, and convert linked images.

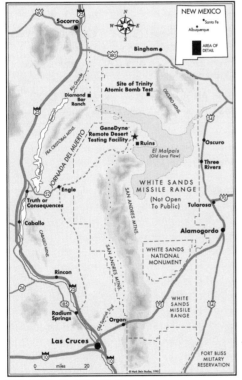

©Mark Stein, Mark Stein Studios

Opening and placing images
How images are acquired

You can use Illustrator to open or import objects or images in a variety of file formats, which means you can work with imagery that was originally created in other applications. Methods for acquiring images from other applications include the Open command, the Place command, and drag-and-drop. The method you choose to use depends on which file formats are available for saving the file in its original application and how you intend to use the imagery in Illustrator.

If you open a document from another drawing (vector) application using the **Open** command, a new Illustrator file will be created, and the acquired objects can then be manipulated using any Illustrator tool, command, filter, or effect. If you open a document from a bitmap program other than Photoshop using the Open command, the image won't be converted into separate objects; it will stay as one object in its outlined box.

The **Place** command inserts imagery or text into an existing Illustrator document. For print output, the best formats to use for saving an image for placement into Illustrator are EPS and TIFF. Both formats preserve the color, detail, and resolution of the original image.

(Continued on the following page)

For Web output, an image saved as .psd (Photoshop) format works fine. If you place a layered .psd image in Illustrator, you can have it appear either as a single flattened object or as separate objects on separate layers. If you want to put the image on a template layer for tracing, check Template in the Place dialog box. The Template option can be turned on or off at any time.

A bitmap image that is acquired in Illustrator via the Open, Place, or drag-and-drop method can be moved, placed on a different layer, masked, modified using any transformation tool, or modified using any color or raster (bitmap) filter.

➤ If you reduce the scale of an opened or placed TIFF or EPS image, the resolution of that image will increase accordingly. Conversely, if you enlarge such an image, its resolution will decrease.

Both the Open and Place commands preserve the resolution of the original image, regardless of whether the image is linked or embedded when it's imported.

File formats

File formats you can **Open** in Illustrator:

Native formats: Illustrator versions 1.0 through 10.0 (.ai).

File formats you can **Open** or **Place** in Illustrator:

Native formats: EPS, Adobe PDF.

Raster (bitmap) formats: BMP, FLM, GIF89a, JPEG, Kodak PhotoCD, PCX, PIXAR, PNG, Photoshop, TGA, and TIFF.

Vector formats: CorelDRAW versions 5 through 8 in the Mac OS and versions 5 through 10 in Windows.

Graphics (vector) formats: CGM, DXF, DWG, FreeHand up to version 9, Macintosh PICT (from DeltaGraph or a CAD program), SVG, and WMF/EMF.

Text file formats: Plain text (ASCII), DOC, MS RTF, and MS Word (up to 2000).

Easy reopen

From the File > **Open Recent Files** submenu, you can choose from a list of up to ten of the most recently opened files.

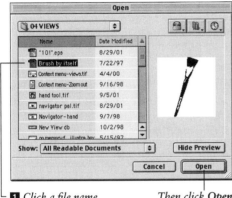

1 *Click a file name.*   *Then click* **Open.**

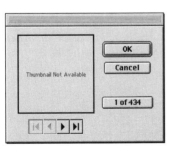

2 *This* **Discard Profile** *prompt will appear if your Edit > Color Settings are set to* **Emulate Adobe Illustrator 6** *(Color Management off).*

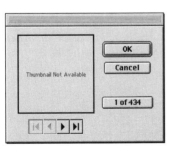

3 *For a* **multi-page** *PDF, choose the page you want to open.*

A list of file formats that can be opened in Illustrator appears on the previous page.

To open a file from within Illustrator:

1. Choose File > Open (Cmd-O/Ctrl-O).

2. *Mac OS:* Click Show Preview to display a thumbnail of the illustration, if it contains a preview that Illustrator can display. (If the button says "Hide Preview," the preview is already showing.) QuickTime must be loaded for the preview to display.

3. *Mac OS:* Choose Show: All Documents to list files in all formats or choose All Readable Documents to list only files in the formats Illustrator can read.

   Windows: Filter out files by choosing from the Files of Type drop-down menu, or choose All Formats (the default setting) to display files of all formats.

4. Locate and highlight a file name, then click Open (Return/Enter) **1**.
   or
   Double-click a file name.

   Note: If you get a warning prompt about a linked file, see page 251. If you get the Discard Profile prompt **2**, see page 473.

5. If you're opening a multi-page PDF, another dialog box will open **3**. Click an arrow to locate the desired page (or click the "1 of [ ]" button, enter the desired page), then click OK.

➤ If you Open an EPS that contains a clipping path, the image will be nested inside a <Group> on the Layers palette (the words "<Clipping Path>" will appear directly above the <Image> listing). If the clipping path is composed of several paths, it will be listed as "<Compound Clipping Group>" instead. To select the clipping path, use the Layers palette; to move or reshape it, use the Direct-selection tool.

To open a file from the Mac OS Finder or Windows Explorer:

Double-click an Illustrator file icon. Illustrator will launch if it hasn't already been launched **1**.

A placed image can be moved to a different *x/y* location; restacked within the same layer or to a different layer; masked; transformed; or modified using any raster filter. You can also change its opacity and blending mode. For a list of file formats that can be placed into Illustrator, see page 248.

To place an image from another application into an Illustrator document:

1. Open an Illustrator file. If your file contains more than one layer, activate a top-level layer.

2. Choose File > Place.

3. Locate and click the name of the file that you want to place **2**.

4. Check Link to place only a screen version of an image into Illustrator (the image must reside on your hard disk). The actual, original image will remain separate from the Illustrator file at its original resolution. If you modify and resave a linked image in its original application, it will automatically update in the Illustrator document (see pages 254–255).
   or
   Uncheck Link to embed (parse) the actual image into the Illustrator file. This increases a file's storage size.

   Read more about linking on pages 254–258.

5. *Optional:* Check Template to place a dimmed version of the image on a template layer for tracing.

6. Click Place (Return/Enter). (You could also double-click a file name instead of clicking Place).

Replace one placed image with another

To replace one placed image with another, select the image you want to replace, choose File > Place, click a replacement image, check **Replace**, check or uncheck Link, then click Place. Any transformations that were made to the original placed image will be applied automatically to the newly placed one.

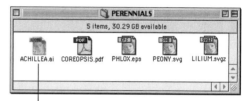

1 *Double-clicking an existing Illustrator file icon will cause the application to launch, if it hasn't already been launched.*

2 *Locate and click a bitmap or vector file name in the Place dialog box.*

Open a File; Place an Image

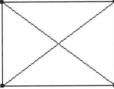

1 *Check Show Images in Outline in the Document Setup dialog box.*

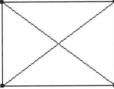

2 *Placed image, Outline view*

3 *Placed image, Outline view, Show Images in Outline checked*

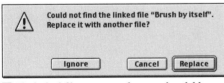

4 *Linked, placed image selected, Preview view: The "X" across the outline box designates this image as linked.*

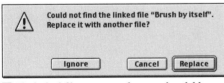

5 *If a linked file was **moved** to another folder or is otherwise **missing**, Illustrator will alert you with this dialog box when you open the illustration. To reestablish the link, click **Replace**, then locate the file.*

If a placed image was saved in its original application with a preview that Illustrator recognizes, it will render fully in Preview view, whether or not "Show Images In Outline" is checked in Document Setup. If you place an image that *doesn't* contain a preview that Illustrator recognizes, when selected the image will display as an empty outlined box with an "x" through it in either view. Follow these instructions to have images display in black-and-white in their outlined box in Outline view.

To display a placed image in Outline view:

1. Choose File > Document Setup.
2. Choose Artboard from the topmost pop-up menu.
3. Check View: Show Images In Outline **1**–**4**.
4. Click OK.

Reopening a file that contains linked images

If the actual linked image is moved from its original location after the file into which it was placed was last saved, you will be prompted to re-link the image when you reopen the Illustrator file. Click **Replace** **5**, relocate the same file or a different file, then click Replace again.

If you click **Ignore**, the linked image will not display, but a question mark icon will display for the file on the Links palette and its bounding box will still be visible in the Illustrator file in Outline view or if Smart Guides is turned on. To completely break the link and prevent any alert prompts from appearing in the future, delete the bounding box and resave the file.

Read about the Links palette on pages 254–258.

Photoshop to Illustrator

If you **drag-and-drop** a Photoshop selection or layer into Illustrator, the image and a clipping path will be nested within a new <Group> layer within the currently active layer. The opacity of the selection or layer will become 100%. Layer masks will be applied to the image; blending modes will be ignored. A generic clipping path will be created, and it will be sized to fit either the object or the width and height of the Photoshop file. Any clipping paths in the Photoshop file will be ignored, and the background of the image will be opaque white. All the effects filters can be applied to the image (the commands that are listed below the horizontal black dividing line on the Effect menu).

➤ A white background in an imported image can be removed using a blending mode in Illustrator. Change the Transparency percentage or apply Multiply, Color Burn, or Darken mode.

➤ You can use the Add-anchor-point tool to add points to a generic clipping path that was created for an imported image. The added points can be repositioned with the Direct-selection tool to follow the contour of the image more closely.

If you **place** a Photoshop image with **Link** checked in the Place dialog box, it will appear on the Layers palette as one image nested inside the currently active layer—not a group—and no clipping path will be generated by Illustrator. Any Photoshop clipping path will remain in effect.

If you embed a Photoshop image as you place it (Link unchecked), the Photoshop Import dialog box will open **1**. (The Photoshop Import dialog box will also open if you open a Photoshop image in Illustrator.) In this dialog box, you can choose from two options for how the Photoshop layers will be treated: layers can either be converted into separate objects or flattened into one.

If you opt to **convert** Photoshop layers into objects, each object will be nested within an

Photoshop to Illustrator

Photoshop text into Illustrator

When a Photoshop text layer is imported into Illustrator, the text becomes rasterized. To import a text layer as vector outlines instead, in Photoshop, use Layer > Type > **Convert to Shape**, save the file, then Open or Place the Photoshop file in Illustrator.

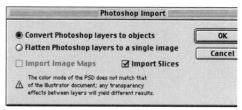

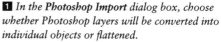

1 *In the Photoshop Import dialog box, choose whether Photoshop layers will be converted into individual objects or flattened.*

When layers don't become objects

In Photoshop, the placement of a shape or adjustment layer in the layer stack affects how these layers are converted into objects in Illustrator. Any layers above a shape or adjustment layer will be converted into separate objects. Any layers below a shape or adjustment layer will be flattened with the shape or adjustment layer into one object.

image group within the currently active layer. All transparency levels, blending modes, and layer masks will be preserved. They will be listed as editable appearances (see page 325), and will be targeted to the appropriate converted object in Illustrator. Any clipping path saved with the Photoshop file will remain in effect, and it will be placed at the top of the stack of objects in the group.

If you opt to flatten Photoshop layers into one image by clicking **Flatten Photoshop layers to a single image,** that image will be nested within the currently active layer. All transparency levels, blending modes, and layer mask effects will be preserved in the flattened image, but those attributes won't be listed as editable appearances in Illustrator. Any clipping path saved with the Photoshop file will remain in effect and will be stacked above the nested image within a group.

If a Photoshop image containing multiple layers is opened or placed into Illustrator with the Link option unchecked and the **Convert Photoshop layers to objects** button is clicked in the Photoshop Import dialog box, the Background layer from the Photoshop file will become one of the nested objects within Illustrator, and it will be opaque (you can change its opacity). If you don't want the background object, you can either delete it in Photoshop before opening or placing the image in Illustrator or delete it afterwards using the Layers palette in Illustrator.

Also, in the Photoshop Import dialog box, check **Import Image Maps** and/or **Import Slices** to bring in any image maps or slices that were saved with the Photoshop file.

➤ Each converted layer from a Photoshop image will be listed as a separate item on the Links palette.

Photoshop to Illustrator

10.0!

Linking images

To reduce a file's size, you can link any imported EPS, GIF, JPEG, PICT, or TIFF images to the file instead of embedding them into the file. A copy of the image will act as a placeholder in your Illustrator document, but the actual image will remain separate from the Illustrator file. If you revise a linked image via the Edit Original button, the image will update in the Illustrator document (this can't be done with embedded images).

To link a file, use the File > Place command, and check the **Link** option. Instructions for placing and linking images are on page 250. Illustrator's Links palette helps you and your service bureau or print shop keep track of linked files. It lists all the linked and embedded files in your Illustrator document and puts a number of useful controls at your fingertips **1**.

Raster filters can be applied to an embedded image, but not to a linked image. Effect menu filters can be applied to either type of image, and those effects will be editable. To embed a linked image, see page 258. The Object > Rasterize command automatically embeds a linked image; the Effect > Rasterize command does not. A linked image can be transformed (moved, rotated, sheared, or reflected).

To edit a linked image in its original application:

1. Show the Links palette (Window > Show Links), then click the image name on the palette.

2. Click the Edit Original button at the bottom of the palette ▭ or choose Edit Original from the Links palette menu. The application in which the linked image was created will launch if it isn't already open, and the image will open. *Note:* Edit Original may not work in Windows, depending on where the linked file is located.

3. Make your edits, resave the file, and then return to Illustrator. If a warning prompt appears, click Yes (see the sidebar) **2**. The linked image will update.

Edit Linked Image

Update options

To specify how linked images are updated when the original files are modifed, choose from the **Update Links** pop-up menu in Edit > Preferences > Files & Clipboard:

Automatically: Illustrator will update linked images automatically whenever their original files are modified.

Manually: Linked images remain unchanged when the original files are modified. You can always use the Links palette to update links.

Ask When Modified: A dialog box will appear if the original files are modified and you return to Illustrator or reopen the file (click Yes or No).

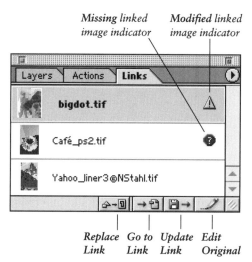

Missing linked image indicator   *Modified linked image indicator*

Replace Link   Go to Link   Update Link   Edit Original

1 *The Links palette lets you keep track of linked images, link to new files, and convert linked images into embedded ones.*

2 *This prompt will appear if you edit a link in its original application via the Edit Original button.*

Linked and embedded files

To a linked or embedded EPS file, you can apply opacity and blending modes, the Feather command, and filters on the Effect menu. These attributes will become appearances on the image object. Color filters on the Filter menu can also be applied to an embedded EPS. A linked EPS image will be listed on the Layers palette as a placed object within the currently active layer. Any clipping path in the file will be applied, but it won't be listed separately.

An embedded image in a non-EPS format will be listed on the Layers palette as a nested image object within a group sublayer within the currently active layer. If a clipping path is included, it will be active and will be listed on the Layers palette as a clipping path within the group sublayer, stacked above the image object.

1 Click the linked image you want to replace, then click the **Replace Link** (first) button.

2 The linked image is **replaced**.

If you replace one linked image with another, any transformations that were applied to the original image, such as scaling or rotating, will be applied to the new image.

To replace one linked image with another:

1. On the Links palette, click the name of the file that you want to replace **1**.

2. Click the Replace Link button at the bottom of the Links palette.
   or
   Choose Replace from the Links palette menu.

3. Locate the replacement file, then click Place **2**.

➤ To replace a linked image another way, click the existing image in the document window, choose File > Place, check Replace, locate the replacement image, then click Place.

When a linked image is located using the Go To Link command, it becomes selected in the document window.

To locate a linked image in an Illustrator file:

1. Open the illustration that contains the linked image.

2. Click the name of the linked image on the Links palette list.

3. Click the Go To Link (second) button at the bottom of the palette.
   or
   Choose Go To Link from the Links palette menu.

To view file information for a linked image:

1. Double-click an image thumbnail on the Links palette.

   or

   Click a file name on the Links palette, then choose Information from the palette menu.

   A dialog box with the image's file format, location, size, modifications, and transform information will appear **1**.

2. Click OK.

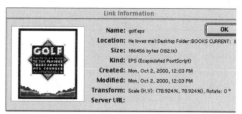

1 *The Link Information dialog shows the linked image's file format, location, size, and modifications.*

To choose Links palette display options:

To change the size of the **thumbnail** images that are displayed in the Links palette, choose **Palette Options** from the Links palette menu, click the preferred size, then click OK. To display just the file icons without the thumbnails, click None.

To change the **order** of links on the palette, from the Links palette menu choose **Sort by Name** (alphabetical order), **Sort by Kind** (file format) or **Sort by Status** (missing, then modified, then embedded, then fully linked) **2**–**3**. To sort only selected links, first click, then Shift-click consecutive names or Cmd-click/Ctrl-click non-consecutive names.

To control which **type** of links display on the palette, choose **Show All, Show Missing, Show Modified,** or **Show Embedded** from the Links palette menu.

2
> Go To Link
> Update Link
> Edit Original
> Replace...
> Placement Options...
>
> Verify Workgroup Link
> Save Workgroup Link...
>
> Embed Image
>
> Information...
>
> ✓ Show All
> Show Missing
> Show Modified
> Show Embedded
>
> Sort by Name
> Sort by Kind
> Sort by Status
>
> Palette Options...

With the exception of TIFFs, the names of embedded images aren't listed on the palette.

Embedded images are identified by this icon.

Linked images don't have an icon.

3 *The Links palette with the Show All and Sort by Status display options chosen.*

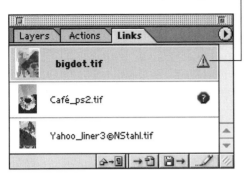

1 *Modified image icon*

An exclamation mark icon appearing to the right of a link on the Links palette list indicates that the original file has been modified and the link is outdated. You can use the Update Link button to update it.

Note: If you edit a linked image via the Edit Original button, you will need to update it this way only if Manually is chosen from the Update Links pop-up menu in Edit > Preferences > Files & Clipboard. If Automatically is chosen as the setting, the image will be updated automatically. Or if Ask When Modified is chosen, you'll get a warning prompt.

You can't update a missing linked image (missing linked images have a question mark). You can either physically move it back to its original location or you can replace it (see page 255).

To update a modified linked image:

1. Click the name of the modified image on the Links palette list **1**.

2. Click the Update Link (third) button at the bottom of the palette.
   or
   Choose Update Link from the Links palette menu.

The Embed Image command will cause a file that's separate from, but linked to, your Illustrator document to become embedded into (part of) your Illustrator document. *Beware!* Embedding an image will cause the Illustrator file size to increase.

To convert a linked image to an embedded image:

1. On the Links palette list, click the name of the image that you want to embed ▇.

2. Choose Embed Image from the Links palette menu ▇.

   Note: There is no command to turn an embedded image into a linked image, but you can either Undo immediately or use the Replace command on the Links palette menu to replace the embedded image with a linked image.

3. *Optional:* If the linked image is a multi-layer Photoshop file, then the Photoshop Import dialog box will open. Follow the instructions on pages 252–253.

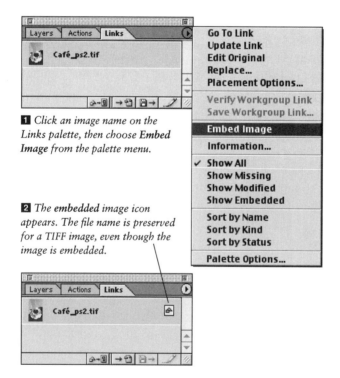

▇ *Click an image name on the Links palette, then choose* **Embed Image** *from the palette menu.*

▇ *The* embedded *image icon appears. The file name is preserved for a TIFF image, even though the image is embedded.*

Drag-and-drop

A few pointers before you begin:

➤ Drag-and-drop does not use the Clipboard; whatever is currently on the Clipboard is preserved.

➤ If you drag-and-drop an image from Photoshop to Illustrator via Photoshop's Move tool, the image will be embedded as an RGB at the resolution of the original image. Any opacity or blending modes for the Photoshop selection or layer will be removed in Illustrator. The dropped object will have an opaque white background. If you're going to print the image, use the following method instead: In Photoshop, convert the file to CMYK Color mode and save it as a TIFF or EPS, then acquire it in Illustrator using Place or Open.

➤ You can drag-and-drop objects between Illustrator documents or between Illustrator and Adobe GoLive, Adobe InDesign, Adobe Acrobat, or any other drag-aware application. In the Mac OS, you can drag-and-drop a path from Photoshop to Illustrator; the path copy will be dropped as a compound shape. **10.0!** In Windows, select a path in Photoshop, then Ctrl-Alt drag the path into an Illustrator document window. On either platform, you could also copy a path from Photoshop, paste it into Illustrator, then edit the pasted path in Illustrator.

➤ Currently, Windows supports drag-and-drop only between OLE-compliant applications. The dropped vector object will be rasterized in the receiving application.

To drag-and-drop an object:

1. Select the object you want to drag-and-drop in an Illustrator or Photoshop document. It can be any kind of object, even text. You can drag-and-drop a whole layer from the document window using the Move tool in Photoshop.

(Continued on the following page)

2. Open the Illustrator or Photoshop file to which you want to copy the object.

3. Drag the object into the destination document window, and presto, the destination window will become active and a copy of the object will appear inside it. In Photoshop, the object will become a new layer of pixels in the color mode and resolution of the Photoshop image.
or
Hold down Cmd/Ctrl while dragging a path object from Illustrator to Photoshop to preserve the object as a path in Photoshop.

➤ Hold down Shift after you start dragging into Photoshop to position the "dropped" pixels in the center of the Photoshop document window.

➤ If you drag an Illustrator object to the Desktop in the Mac OS, a Picture Clipping file will be created in PICT format. This intermediate file can then be dragged into any drag-aware application.

➤ You don't have to rasterize an Illustrator object before you drag-and-drop it into Photoshop, but if you do, check Create Clipping Mask in the Rasterize dialog box to make the object's background transparent in Photoshop.

Drag-and-Drop

Chapter 14: Acquire ◆ Study Guide

Learning Objectives

- Open non-Illustrator files.
- Place files of various formats.
- Import Photoshop files.
- Manage links to imported images.
- Drag-and-drop files into Illustrator.
- Know when to use each method for acquiring images.

Get Up and Running Exercises

- Create a document that uses multiple images and text prepared in other programs. For example, create a page of personal ads and descriptions, an ad insert for a newspaper, or a real-estate flyer. Can you prepare all of the images and text files in formats that Illustrator can read?

- Practice importing different types of Photoshop files. Can you successfully import Photoshop files that use the following features?
  - ▲ Multiple layers
  - ▲ Image maps
  - ▲ Slices
  - ▲ Layers with transparency and blending modes applied
  - ▲ Layer masks
  - ▲ A clipping path

  If the Photoshop image doesn't import successfully, review the chapter to determine which import method or setting(s) needs to be changed.

- Link and embed multiple imported images in an Illustrator document. If you created the advertisement exercise in Chapter 11, you can use it for this exercise; otherwise, simply import several linked images into a document. How would you use Illustrator's linking and embedding features to accomplish the following tasks?
  - ▲ Find out if an image was rotated in Illustrator.
  - ▲ Open an image in the application that was used to save it (if it's installed).
  - ▲ Convert a linked image into an embedded image.

Class Discussion Questions

- How many ways are there to acquire images in Illustrator?

- What are the differences between opening and placing images?

- What are the differences between linking and embedding images? How can you convert one into the other?

- What happens to editable Photoshop type when it's imported into Illustrator?

- Why is it important to check and update the status of all linked images before final printed output? How would you do it?

Review Questions

Multiple choice

1. Which acquisition method usually works best if you want to edit individual objects in a vector graphics file?

   A. Drag-and-drop

   B. Opening

   C. Placing

   D. Cutting and pasting

2. When creating an Illustrator file for a high-resolution commercial print job, which format would be the best choice for saving the images you'll place in Illustrator?

   A. PCX

   B. PICT

   C. TIFF

   D. WMF

3. When you want each layer of a Photoshop file to become a separate object in Illustrator, which of the following conditions is required?

   A. The Photoshop file must be pre-rasterized.

   B. The Photoshop file must be embedded in the Illustrator file.

   C. The Photoshop file can't contain image maps or slices.

   D. The Photoshop file must be flattened before placing it.

4. If you apply transformations to a linked image, and then decide to use the Links palette to replace the image with a different one, what happens to the transformations?

   A. The image can't be replaced until the Illustrator transformations are removed.

   B. Transformations applied in Illustrator are added to transformations applied in the program that created the replacement image.

   C. Transformations are lost and must be re-applied to the replacement image.

   D. Transformations are preserved and applied to the replacement image.

5. What happens when you click the Go To Link button →🖼 in the Layers palette?

   A. The linked image for the item highlighted on the Layers palette is selected and centered in the document window.

   B. The Links palette highlights the item that corresponds to the graphic you selected in the document window.

   C. The linked image's source file is revealed in Explorer (Windows) or the Finder (Mac OS).

   D. The location of the linked image's source file is verified, and the link is updated.

6. How can you change an embedded image so that it's linked instead?

   A. Select the image on the artboard, and then uncheck Embed Image on the Links palette menu.

   B. Select the image on the artboard, and then choose Update Link from the Links palette menu.

   C. Select the image on the artboard, choose Replace from the Links palette menu, select the original version of the embedded image, check Link, then click Place.

   D. There is no way to change an embedded image into a linked image.

Fill-in-the-blank

1. To dim and lock an image for use as a tracing image, check the _____ option when placing the image.

2. When you reduce the scale of an opened or placed TIFF or EPS image, the image's resolution _____.

3. You can move or reshape the clipping path of an imported Photoshop file's using the _____ tool.

4. You can't apply a raster filter to an imported image if the image is _____.

5. If you double-click a link in the Links palette, the _____ dialog box will appear.

6. If the name of an imported image is blank on the Links palette, it means the image is _____.

7. In Windows, you can drag-and-drop between applications only if both applications support _____.

8. When dragging and dropping an object into Illustrator, you can center the object inside the Illustrator document window by holding down _____ as you drag.

Definitions

1. What is linking?

2. What is embedding?

3. What does the Edit Original command or button do?

4. What is a modified link?

5. What does it mean to replace a link?

BRUSHES 15

In this chapter you will learn how to embellish paths with shapes and textures using Illustrator's four types of brushes: calligraphic, scatter, art, and pattern. You will learn how to create and edit custom brushes; add, modify, and remove brush strokes from existing paths; open and create brush libraries; and duplicate, move, and delete brushes from the Brushes palette.

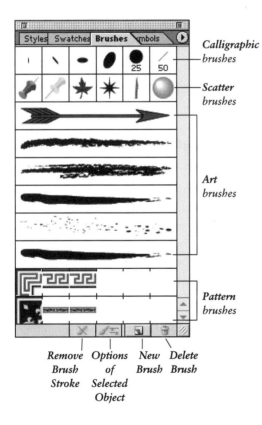

Calligraphic brushes

Scatter brushes

Art brushes

Pattern brushes

Remove Brush Stroke Options of Selected Object New Brush Delete Brush

Using brushes

Illustrator's brushes are an illustrator's dream. They combine the ability to draw variable, freehand brush strokes or apply a pattern or objects to a path with all the advantages of vector graphics—small file sizes, resizability, and crisp output.

There are two ways to work with brushes. You can either choose the Paintbrush tool and a brush and draw a shape right off the bat with a brush stroke built into it or you can apply a brush stroke to an existing path.

To change the contour of a brush stroke, you can use any tool or command you'd normally use to reshape a path, such as the Reshape, Pencil, Smooth, Erase, Add-anchor-point, or Convert-anchor-point tool.

The brushes come in four flavors: **scatter, calligraphic, art,** and **pattern,** and they are stored on and accessed from the Brushes palette. The brushes that are currently on the Brushes palette save with the document. If you modify a brush that was applied to any existing paths in a document, you'll be given the option via an alert box to update those paths with the revised brush. You can also create your own brushes.

As an introduction to the brushes, grab the Paintbrush tool, click one of the brushes on the Brushes palette, and draw (see the instructions on the following page).

Note: If you use a stylus and a pressure-sensitive tablet, the Paintbrush tool will respond to pressure. The harder you press on the tablet, the wider will be the shape.

To draw with the Paintbrush tool:

1. Choose the Paintbrush tool (B), and choose a fill of None.

2. Show the Brushes palette (Window > Show Brushes), then click any brush—calligraphic, scatter, art, or pattern.

3. Draw with the Paintbrush tool to create an open path shape **1**–**2**. Drag, then Option-drag/Alt-drag to draw a closed path (release Option/Alt last).

   For quick reshaping, use the Pencil or Paintbrush tool (see page 123). For precise reshaping, use the Direct-selection tool.

Preferences you choose for the Paintbrush affect only future (not existing) brush strokes. You'll learn how to choose options for individual brushes later on in this chapter.

To choose preferences for the Paintbrush:

1. Double-click the Paintbrush tool (or choose the tool, then press Return/Enter).

2. Choose a Fidelity value (0.5–20) **3**. A low Fidelity setting produces a path very close to the way you drag the tool. A high setting produces a smoother path with fewer anchor points that only approximates the path you drag.

3. Choose a Smoothness value (0–100). The higher the Smoothness, the fewer the irregularities in the path.

4. *Do any of the following:*

   Check "Fill new brush strokes" to have new paths be filled with the current Foreground color.

   Check Keep Selected to keep the newly drawn path selected.

   Check Edit Selected Paths and choose a distance range (2–20 pixels) within which selected paths will be affected by the Paintbrush tool.

5. Click OK.

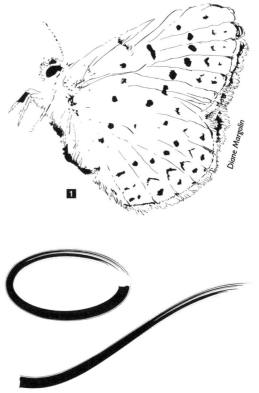

1

Diane Margolin

2 *Strokes drawn with an art brush*

3 *Choose settings for the **Paintbrush** in its Preferences dialog box.*

What's the difference?

On the surface, the pattern and scatter brushes may look similar, but they have different reasons for being. For a scatter brush, you can make the size, spacing, scatter, and rotation variables more or less random via the Brush Options dialog box. You can't do this with a pattern brush. They are not called scatter brushes for nothing. Pattern brushes, on the other hand, are made of up to five tiles: Side, Outer Corner, Inner Corner, Start, and End. Pattern brushes fit more tightly on a path than scatter brushes.

1 *Select a path.*

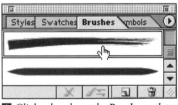

2 *Click a brush on the Brushes palette.*

3 *A **calligraphic** brush stroke is applied.*

To apply a brush stroke to an existing path:

1. Choose Window > Brushes, if the palette is not already displayed.

2. Click a brush on the brushes palette, then drag the selected brush onto an existing path (the path need not be selected first; it can be a type path). Release the mouse when the hand pointer is directly over the edge of the object.
   or
   Select a path of any kind **1**, then click a brush on the Brushes palette **2**–**7**.

➤ To create or modify a brush, see the instructions for the individual brush types starting on page 266.

➤ If you scale an object that has a brush stroke, the stroke will resize along with the object if Scale Strokes & Effects is checked in the Scale dialog box or in Edit > Preferences > General.

➤ Choose Select > Object > Brush Strokes to select all the brush-stroked paths in an illustration.

Diane Margolin

4 *An **art** brush stroke*

6 *Another **scatter** brush stroke (made from five birds)*

5 *A **scatter** brush stroke*

7 *A **pattern** brush stroke*

Apply Brush Stroke to Existing Path

After opening another brush library, you can apply a brush from that library directly to a path or you can move select brushes to the current document's Brushes palette. You can modify any brush from any library.

To add brushes from other libraries:

I. Choose a library name from the Window > Brush Libraries submenu.
or
To open a library that is not in the Brush Libraries folder, choose Window > Other Library, locate and highlight a custom library, then click Open.

2. Deselect all the objects in your illustration (Cmd-Shift-A/Ctrl-Shift-A).

3. Drag a brush from the library palette onto an object in the illustration window (you don't have to select the object). The brush stroke will appear on the object and the brush will appear on the Brushes palette.
or
Click a brush on the library palette. It will appear on the Brushes palette. To drag multiple brushes, Shift-click or Cmd-click/Ctrl-click them first **1**–**2**.
or
Select one or more brushes, then choose Add To Brushes from the library palette menu.

Note: You can drag a library palette tab into another palette group, but it will only stay there until you relaunch Illustrator. To make a whole library palette open automatically when you re-launch Illustrator, choose Persistent from the library palette's menu. To save individual brushes with a document, add them to the brushes palette using any method in step 3, above.

➤ To delete brushes from the Brushes palette, see page 271.

➤ To close a library palette that's not in a palette group, click its close box. To close a palette in a group, drag its tab out of the palette group, then click its close box.

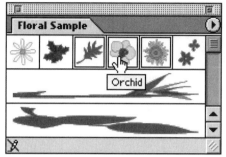

1 *To append multiple brushes, Shift-click or Cmd-click/Ctrl-click them.*

3 *The brushes appear on the current document's Brushes palette.*

1 *The original object with a **brush stroke***

2 Remove Brush Stroke

path

3 *The brush stroke is **removed** from the object.*

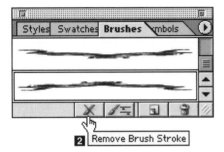

4 *The original **brush stroke** on an object*

5 *The brush stroke is now an object, **separate** from the original path (they were ungrouped and moved away from each other for this illustration).*

When a brush stroke is removed from a path, you're left with a plain path.

To remove a brush stroke from an object:

1. Select the object or objects from which you want to remove the brush stroke **1**.

2. Click the Remove Brush Stroke button at the bottom of the Brushes palette **2**–**3**.
   or
   Click the Stroke box on the Toolbox, then click the None button. ⬛

If you expand a brush stroke, it will be converted into editable outlined paths that are no longer associated with the original brush. In other words, if you edit the original brush that was applied to the object, you won't be able to update the brush stroke on the object—it no longer functions like a brush stroke.

To convert a brush stroke into outlined paths:

1. Select the brush-stroked object **4**.

2. Choose Object > Expand Appearance. The brush stroke is now a separate object or objects **5**. The outlined paths will be nested (or double- or triple-nested) in a group sublayer on the Layers palette.

To choose brush display options:

With **List View** checked on the Brushes palette menu, for each brush there will be a small thumbnail, the brush name, and an icon for the brush type (calligraphic, scatter, art, pattern) **1**. With **Thumbnail View** checked, a large thumbnail for each brush will display without a name or icon **2**.

To control which **brush types** (categories) display on the palette, choose a brush type from the palette menu (Show...) to check or uncheck that option.

You can **drag** a brush to a different spot on the Brushes palette within its category. To move multiple brushes, select them first (click, then Shift-click a consecutive string or Cmd-click/Ctrl-click them individually).

Creating and modifying brushes

Scatter objects are placed evenly or randomly along the contour of a path. You can create a scatter brush from an open or closed path, text object, text outline, blend, or compound path, but not from a gradient, bitmap image (placed or rasterized), mesh, or clipping mask.

To create or modify a scatter brush:

1. To create a new brush, select an object(s) **3** or a blend, click the New Brush button on the Brushes palette **⬛**, click New Scatter Brush, then click OK.
   or
   To modify an existing brush, deselect, then double-click the brush on the Brushes palette. Or click a brush, then choose Brush Options from the palette menu.

2. Enter a new name or modify the existing name (**1**, next page).

3. For an existing brush, check Preview to preview changes on any selected paths to which the brush is currently applied.

4. Each of the four brush properties (Size, Spacing, Scatter, and Rotation) can be set to the Fixed, Random, or Pressure variation via the pop-up menu next to each option. Choose **Fixed** to use a single, fixed value.

Dupe it

To create a **variation** of an existing brush of any type, either **drag** the brush over the **New Brush** button on the Brushes palette or click the brush and choose **Duplicate Brush** from the palette menu. Then modify the duplicate.

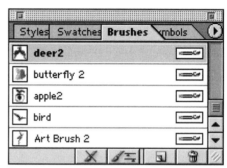

1 *With the **List View** option **checked** on the Brushes palette menu*

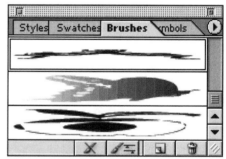

2 *With the **Thumbnail** option **checked** on the Brushes palette menu*

3 *The original objects*

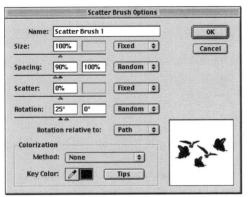

1 *The Scatter Brush Options dialog box*

2 *The new scatter brush applied to a path*

3 *The same scatter brush after moving the Size sliders apart (Random setting)*

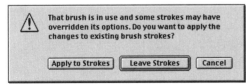

4 *This prompt will appear if you modify a brush that is currently applied to objects in the file.*

Choose **Random**, then move the sliders (or enter different values in the left and right fields) to define a range within which that property value can vary.

Choose **Pressure** and move the sliders (or enter different values in the left and right fields) to define a range within which that property can respond to stylus pressure. A light pressure will produce a brush property based on the minimum property value (left field); a heavy pressure will produce a brush property based on the maximum property value (right field). Pressure will be available only if you're using a graphics tablet.

Size controls the size of the scatter objects.

Spacing controls the spacing between the scatter objects.

Scatter controls the distance the objects are from either side of the path. When Scatter is set to Fixed, a positive value places all the objects on one side of the path, a negative value places all the objects on the opposite side of the path. The further the Scatter value is from 0%, the greater will be the distance from the path, and the less prominent will be the path shape.

Rotation adjusts the amount objects rotate relative to the page or the path. Choose **Page** or **Path** from the **Rotation relative to** pop-up menu for the axis the rotation will be based on.

5. For the Colorization options, see the sidebar on page 271.

6. Click OK **2**–**3**. If the brush was already applied to existing objects in the document, an alert box will appear. Click Apply to Strokes to update those objects with the revised brush or click Leave Strokes to leave the existing objects unchanged **4**.

➤ You'll find scatter brushes in the Animal Sample, Arrow Sample, Floral Sample, and Object Sample libraries.

(Continued on the following page)

Create/Modify Scatter Brush

➤ Shift-drag a slider to move its counterpart gradually along with it. Option-drag/ Alt-drag a slider to move its counterpart apart or together the same distance from the center.

➤ To make the scatter objects' orientation along a path uniform, set Scatter and Rotation to Fixed, set Scatter to 0°, and choose Rotation relative to: Path **1**–**2**.

The calligraphic brushes create strokes that vary in thickness as you draw, like traditional calligraphy media.

To create or modify a calligraphic brush:

1. To create a new calligraphic brush, click the New Brush button on the Brushes palette ▣, click New Calligraphic Brush, then click OK.
   or
   To modify an existing brush **3**, double-click the brush on the Brushes palette **4**.

2. Enter a new name or modify the existing name **5**.

3. For an existing brush, check Preview to preview changes on any selected paths to which the brush is currently applied. The brush shape will also preview in the dialog box.

4. The Angle, Roundness, and Diameter can be set to the Fixed, or Random, or Pressure variation via the pop-up menu next to each option.

   Choose **Fixed** to keep the value constant.

   Choose **Random** and move the Variation slider to define a range within which the specific brush attribute value can vary. A stroke can range between the set value for angle, roundness, or diameter plus or minus the Variation value. For example, a 50° angle with a Random Variation value of 10 could have an angle anywhere between 40° and 60°.

   Choose **Pressure** and move the Variation slider to define a range within which the specific brush attribute value can respond

1 *Illustrator's default "Fish"* **scatter** *brush applied to a path*

2 *After choosing the Fixed option for Scatter and Rotation and setting Scatter to 0%*

3 *After applying a* **calligraphic** *brush to a plain object*

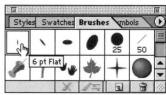

4 **Double-click** *a brush on the Brushes palette.*

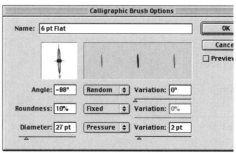

5 *Modify the brush via the* **Calligraphic Brush Options** *dialog box.*

That brush is in use and some strokes may have overridden its options. Do you want to apply the changes to existing brush strokes?

| Apply to Strokes | Leave Strokes | Cancel |

1 *If you* **modify** *a brush that has been* **applied** *to objects in the file, this alert prompt will appear.*

2 *The Angle and Diameter were set to Random in the Calligraphic Brush Options dialog and Apply to Strokes was clicked when the prompt appeared. The brush strokes* **update** *on the object.*

to pressure from a stylus (this option is available only for a graphics tablet). Light pressure will produce a brush attribute based on the set value for angle, roundness, or diameter minus the Variation value. Heavy pressure will produce a brush attribute based on the set value plus the Variation value.

5. Enter an **Angle** value or drag the gray arrowhead in the preview box. The angle controls the thickness of the horizontals and verticals in the stroke. A 0° angle will produce a thin horizontal stroke and a thick vertical stroke; a 90° angle will produce the opposite effect. Other angles will produce different effects.

6. Enter a **Roundness** value or reshape the tip by dragging either black dot inward or outward on the ellipse.

7. For the brush size, enter a **Diameter** value or drag the slider.

8. Click OK. If the brush was already applied to existing paths in the document, an alert box will appear **1**. Click Apply to Strokes to update the existing strokes with the revised brush or click Leave Strokes to leave existing strokes unchanged **2**.

Create/Modify Calligraphic Brush

269

An art brush can be made from one or more objects, including a compound path, but not a gradient, mask, or mesh. When it's applied to a path, an art brush stroke follows the shape of the path. If you reshape the path, the art brush stroke will stretch or bend to conform to the new path contour.

To create or modify an art brush:

1. To create a new brush, select one or more objects **1**, then drag the object(s) onto the Brushes palette. The New Brush dialog box will open automatically. Click New Art Brush **2**, then click OK.
   or
   To modify an existing brush, double-click that brush on the Brushes palette. Or choose an art brush, then choose Brush Options from the palette menu.

2. For a new brush, enter a Name **3**.

3. For an existing brush, check Preview to preview changes on any selected paths to which the brush is currently applied.

4. Click a Direction button to control the orientation of the object on the path. The object will be drawn in the direction the arrow is pointing. The Direction will be more obvious for objects with a distinct directional orientation, such as text outlines, or a recognizable object, such as a vase or leaf.

5. Enter a Size: Width to scale the brush. Check Proportional to preserve the proportions of the original object as its size is changed.

6. *Optional:* Check Flip Along to reverse the object on the path (left to right) and/or Check Flip Across to reverse the object across the path (up and down).

7. Choose a Colorization option (see the sidebar on the following page).

8. Click OK **4**.

➤ You'll find art brushes in Illustrator's Animal Sample, Arrow Sample, Artistic Sample, Floral Sample, and Object Sample libraries.

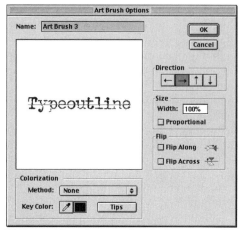

1 *To create a new art brush, select an object or objects. These objects are text outlines.*

2 *Click New Art Brush.*

3 *Enter a Name for a new brush; change any of the settings to modify an existing brush.*

4 *The new art brush is applied to a path.*

Create/Modify Art Brush

The Colorization options

From the Colorization pop-up menu (available for all brush types except calligraphic), choose:

None to leave the colors unchanged.

Tints to change black areas in the brush stroke to the current stroke color at 100% and non-black areas to tints of the current stroke color. White areas stay white. Use for grayscale or spot color.

Tints and Shades to change non-black or non-white colors in the brush stroke to tints of the current stroke color. Black and white areas don't change.

Hue Shift to apply the current stroke color to areas containing the most frequently used color on the object (called the "Key Color") and to change other colors in the brush stroke to related hues. Use for multicolored brushes.

If you're editing the brush itself (not a brush stroke), you can click the **Key Color** eyedropper and then click a color in the preview area of the dialog box to change the Key Color.

Click **Tips** in the Colorization Tips dialog box to learn more **1**.

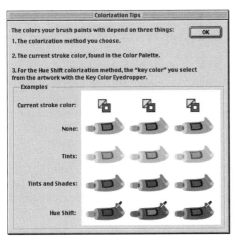

1 *Click* **Tips** *in the Stroke Options dialog box to read these* **Colorization Tips.**

Beware! If you delete a brush from the Brushes palette that is currently applied to any objects in your illustration, you will be given a choice via a prompt: the brush strokes can be expanded or they can be removed from those objects.

To delete a brush from the Brushes palette:

1. Deselect all objects in your illustration.

2. Click the brush you want to delete.

3. Choose Delete Brush from the palette menu or click the Delete Brush button on the palette, then click Yes **2**.
   or
   Drag the selected brush over the Delete Brush button.

   Note: If the brush is currently applied to any objects in the current document, an alert dialog will appear **3**. Click Expand Strokes to expand the brush strokes (they will look the same, but they won't function as brush strokes) or click Remove Strokes to remove them from the objects.

➤ To restore the deleted brush to the palette, choose Undo immediately. Or if the brush is from a library, you can add it again (see page 264).

➤ To delete all the brushes that are not being used in a file, choose Select All Unused from the Brushes palette menu, then use any method in step 3, above, to delete the selected brushes.

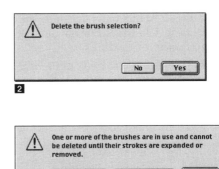

Delete a Brush

The pattern brush renders patterns along the edge of a closed or open path, and can be used to create custom frames, borders, or other decorative elements. You can use up to five different-shaped tile pieces when you create a path pattern: a Side tile, an Outer Corner tile, an Inner Corner tile, a Start tile, and an End tile. Each type of tile adapts to fit its assigned location on the path. Here's how to design your own tiles.

To create tiles for a pattern brush:

1. Draw closed path shapes for the side pattern tile. Try to limit the tile to about an inch wide, two inches at the most. You can resize it later via the Pattern Brush Options dialog box.

2. Since a pattern brush places side tiles perpendicular to the path, you should rotate any design that is taller than it is wide. To do this, choose the Selection tool, select the shapes for the side tile, double-click the Rotate tool, enter 90° for the Angle, then click OK.

3. Draw separate shapes for the corner, start, and end tiles **1**, if necessary, to complete the design. Corner tiles should be square, and they should be exactly the same height as the rotated side tile.

4. Choose the Selection tool, then select one of the tile shapes.

5. Drag the selection onto the Swatches palette **2**, then deselect the tile shape.

6. Double-click the new swatch, then enter a Swatch Name. Type words like "side," "outer," "start," and "end" after the tile name to help you remember the tile's placement. Click OK **3**.

7. Repeat steps 4 through 6 for the other tile shapes.

8. Follow the steps on the next page to make the new tiles that are now on the Swatches palette into a pattern brush **4**.

➤ You don't have to use a bounding rectangle behind the shapes when you create a pattern brush tile, but you can do so if it helps you fit the tiles together. Apply

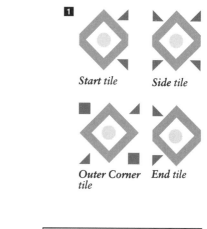

1

Start tile   *Side tile*

Outer Corner tile   *End tile*

2 *Drag the tile shape onto the Swatches palette.*

3 *Swatch Options dialog box*

4 *The pattern tiles made into a pattern brush and then applied to a path*

Tiles for a Pattern Brush

Side tile *Outer corner tile* *Inner corner tile* *Start tile* *End tile*

Pattern Brush Options

Name: Pattern Brush1

OK

Cancel

Size

Scale: 100%

Spacing: 0%

None
Original
*10 dpi-50%
*10 lpi-20%
*10 lpi-50%
*6 lpi-70%
*6 lpi-90%
Bird feet
Blossoms

Flip

☐ Flip Along

☐ Flip Across

Colorization

Method: None

Key Color:

Tips

Fit

● Stretch to fit
○ Add space to fit
○ Approximate path

1 *The Pattern Brush Options dialog box*

a fill and stroke of None to the rectangle, and make sure none of the pattern shapes extend beyond it. The rectangle won't act as a cropping device as it would in a pattern fill.

➤ When they're applied to a path, corner tiles will be rotated 90° for each corner of the path, starting from the upper left corner.

➤ Apply global process fill and stroke colors to the tile shapes, and name the colors appropriately so they can be readily associated with the tile. The tiles can then be recolored easily by changing the global process colors.

➤ To make geometric shapes look more hand drawn, before making shapes into a pattern brush, apply Effect > Distort & Transform > Roughen at a low setting.

To create a pattern brush:

1. Create tiles for the pattern brush (instructions start on the previous page).

2. Click the New Brush button on the Brushes palette ⬛, click New Pattern Brush, then click OK.

3. Enter a Name.

4. Click a tile button (along the top) to assign the pattern to that part of a path, then click a pattern name on the scroll list **1**. (The scroll list displays pattern tiles that are currently on the Swatches palette.) Repeat for the other tile buttons, if desired. The icons under the buttons are there to help you distinguish one type of tile from another. To assign no pattern for a position on the path, choose None. For a round object, you'll need to assign only a Side tile.

5. Click OK. Now you can apply the brush to a path. To modify a pattern brush, see the instructions on the following page.

➤ If you reshape a path that has a pattern brush stroke, the pattern will reshape along with the path. Corner and side tiles will be added or removed as needed.

(Continued on the following page)

Create a Pattern Brush

➤ Effect menu commands can be applied to objects to be used in a pattern tile or to an object to which a pattern brush stroke is applied.

➤ Illustrator's Border Sample library contains pattern brushes, and additional pattern brushes can be found in the Illustrator Extras > Brush Libraries folder on the Adobe Illustrator 10 CD-ROM.

10.0!

To edit a pattern brush via its options dialog box:

1. On the Brushes palette, double-click the pattern brush you want to modify.
   or
   Click a pattern brush, then choose Brush Options from the palette menu.

2. Check Preview to preview changes on any selected paths to which the pattern brush is currently applied.

3. To change tile patterns, click a **tile** button, then click a different name on the scroll list **1**. Repeat for the other tile buttons, if desired. Use the icons under the buttons to distinguish one type of tile from another. To assign no pattern for a tile position, choose None. For a round object, you need to assign only one tile.

   Note: To restore the settings to the currently selected tile button (from when the dialog box was opened), click Original on the scroll list.

4. Do any of the following:

   Change the Size: **Scale** percentage for the pattern tiles (1–10000%).

   To adjust the blank spacing between pattern tiles, change the Size: **Spacing** percentage (0–10000%).

   To alter the pattern tile's orientation on the path, check **Flip Along** and/or **Flip Across**. Be sure to preview this—you may not like the results.

   In the Fit area, click **Stretch to fit** to have Illustrator shorten or lengthen the tiles, where necessary, to fit on the path. Or click **Add space to fit** to have Illustrator add blank space between tiles, where

*A **pattern** brush stroke*

1 *Reassign different tiles and choose other options in the* **Pattern Brush Options** *dialog box.*

Edit Pattern Brush via Options

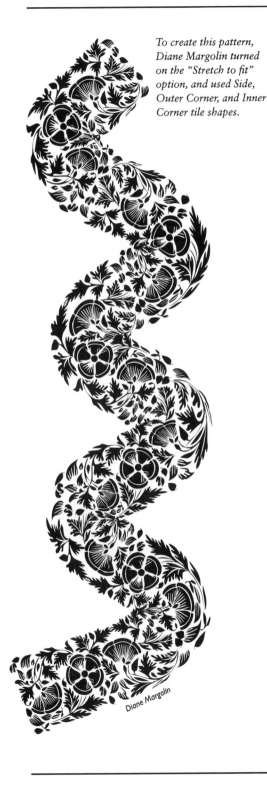

To create this pattern, Diane Margolin turned on the "Stretch to fit" option, and used Side, Outer Corner, and Inner Corner tile shapes.

Diane Margolin

necessary, to fit the pattern along the path, factoring in the Spacing amount, if one was entered.

For a rectangular path, if you click **Approximate path**, the pattern tiles will be applied slightly inside or outside the path, rather than centered on the path, in order to produce even tiling.

5. For the **Colorization** option, see the sidebar on page 271.

6. Click OK. If the pattern brush is currently applied to a path or paths in the file, an alert dialog box will appear. Click Apply to Strokes to update the existing strokes with the revised brush or click Leave Strokes to leave them unchanged.

In addition to editing a brush via its Options dialog box, you can also edit a brush by reshaping or recoloring it manually.

To edit a scatter, art, or pattern brush manually:

1. Drag the brush from the Brushes palette onto a blank area of the artboard (**1**–**2**, next page).

2. To recolor or transform the entire brush, select it using the Selection tool (**3**, next page). To recolor or transform individual objects within the brush or individual pattern brush tiles, select them using the Direct-selection tool or the Layers palette.

3. For a **scatter** or **art** brush:

   Choose the Selection tool (V), and select the modified brush object or objects. Start dragging the objects onto the Brushes palette, hold down Option/Alt when you pass over the Brushes palette, then release the mouse when the pointer is over the original brush icon and the icon is highlighted, then click OK.

   ➤ To make the revised object(s) into a new brush, separate from the original, drag it (or them) into the palette without holding down Option/Alt.

(Continued on the following page)

Edit Brush Manually

For a **pattern** brush:

Drag each revised tile individually onto the Swatches palette, then deselect all the tiles on the artboard.
then
Double-click each new swatch on the Swatches palette, enter an appropriate name for each, then click OK.

Then do either of the following:
Double-click the original pattern brush on the Brushes palette, reassign the new tiles to the appropriate tile buttons (see page 273), then click OK. If the brush is currently applied to paths in the document, an alert dialog box will appear. Click **Apply to Strokes** to update those paths with the revised brush or click **Leave Strokes** to leave the existing brush strokes unchanged **4**–**5**.
or
Start dragging the new pattern tile shape, hold down Option/Alt as you pass over the Brushes palette, and release the mouse when the new tile is over a specific tile slot to replace only that highlighted tile. The Pattern Brush Options dialog box will open with the new tile in the chosen tile position. Click OK.

➤ On the Brushes palette, the tiles for a pattern brush are arranged from left to right in the following order: Outer Corner, Side, Inner Corner, Start, and End.

By organizing brushes into a library, you will be able to locate them easily and use them in other files.

To create a new brush library:

1. Create brushes in a document or move them to the current document's Brushes palette from other libraries.

2. Choose File > Save, and save the file in the Adobe Illustrator 10 > Presets > Brushes folder. Use a descriptive name.

3. Re-launch Illustrator. The new library will appear on the Window > Brush Libraries submenu.

➤ For step 2, above, you could also drag the saved file's icon into the Adobe Illustrator 10 > Presets > Brushes folder.

1 *The original pattern brush stroke*

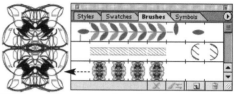

2 *Drag the brush onto the artboard.*

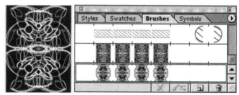

3 *The pat-   **4** ...and then the brush is updated
tern is edited   on the **Brushes** palette.
manually...*

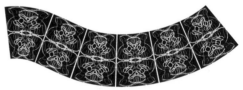

5 *The **edited** pattern brush stroke*

1 *Select an object or objects to which a brush has been applied.*

2 *Choose* **Stroke** *Options for the brush.*

3 *The* **brush stroke** *is altered on the* **object.**

If you edit a brush, every object to which that brush has been applied will update to reflect the changes. If you want to modify a brush stroke on a selected object or objects without editing the brush itself, follow these instructions instead. The Colorization option is fun to play with.

To change the stroke options for an individual object:

1. Select one or more objects to which the *same* brush is currently applied **1**.

2. If you want to recolor the brush stroke, choose a stroke color now.

3. Click the Options of Selected Object button on the Brushes palette ⟨🖊⟩.

4. Check Preview **2** (and **1**–**2**, next page).

5. For a scatter brush stroke, follow step 4 starting on page 266.

   For a calligraphic brush stroke, follow steps 4–7 starting on pages 268–269.

   For an art brush stroke, follow steps 5–6 on page 270.

   For a pattern brush stroke, follow step 4 starting on page 272.

6. From the **Colorization** pop-up menu (this is *not* available for calligraphic brushes), choose:

   None to leave the colors unchanged.

   Tints to change black areas in the brush stroke to the stroke color at 100% and non-black areas to tints of the current stroke color. White areas stay white.

   Tints and Shades to change non-black or non-white colors in the brush stroke to tints of the current stroke color. Black and white areas stay as they are.

   Hue Shift to apply the current stroke color to areas containing the most frequently used color on the object (the Key Color) and to change other colors in the brush stroke to related hues.

   Note: If you're editing the brush itself (not a brush stroke), you can click the

   (Continued on the following page)

Key Color eyedropper and then click on a color in the brush or pattern tile preview area of the dialog box to change the Key Color.

7. *Optional:* Click Tips to see an illustration of the Colorization options.

8. Click OK (**3**, previous page). Only the selected object or objects will change; the brush itself on the Brushes palette will not.

➤ To restore the original brush stroke to the object, select the object, click a different brush on the Brushes palette, then click back on the original brush.

➤ If you've used the Options of Selected Object button to customize a brush stroke on a selected object, you can apply a different art brush using those same settings by Option/Alt clicking a different brush. This is a nifty trick!

Here's a way to create a variation on an existing brush—a slimmer or fatter version, for example.

To duplicate a brush:

I. Click the brush you want to duplicate.

2. Choose Duplicate Brush from the palette menu.
or
Drag the selected brush over the New Brush button 🔲 **3**–**4**.

The word "copy" will be appended to the brush name. To modify the brush, see the individual instructions for that brush type earlier in this chapter.

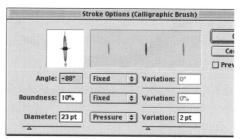

1 *Stroke Options for a calligraphic brush*

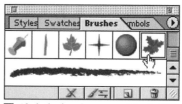

2 *Stroke Options for a scatter brush*

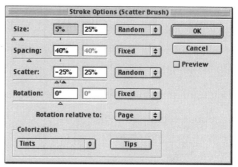

3 *Click the brush you want to duplicate.*

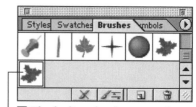

4 *The duplicate brush appears after the last brush icon in that category.*

Chapter 15: Brushes ◆ Study Guide

Learning Objectives

- Distinguish between and draw with the four types of brushes in Illustrator.
- Create and edit custom brushes.
- Work with the Brushes palette.
- Work with brush libraries.

Get Up and Running Exercises

- Create an illustration using only the Paintbrush tool and each of the four types of brushes in the Brushes palette.
- Practice editing brush options:
  - ▲ Edit the brush strokes applied to the selected object, but not to other existing strokes that were created using that brush.
  - ▲ Edit all current and future strokes of a brush.
- Use a brush to create a coupon border or a picture frame with distinctive corners.
- Design a brush whose stroke looks like a leaky ink pen leaving a trail of spots, as in the figure below. (Your version doesn't have to look exactly like ours.) Which brush types can you use to create a brush like this? How does the choice of brush type affect the attributes of the brush?

Class Discussion Questions

- How are each of the brush types different from the other brush types?
- How can a graphics tablet enhance the use of brushes?
- How are Paintbrush Tool Preferences different from Brush Options?
- How do you create a pattern brush?
- What determines the color a brush applies?

Review Questions

Multiple choice

1. When you create a new brush, where does Illustrator save it?

   A. In a brush library file.

   B. In the Illustrator document that was open when the brush was created.

   C. In the Illustrator startup file.

   D. In the Illustrator Preferences file.

2. In addition to clicking the Remove Brush Stroke button in the Brushes palette, what's another way to remove a brush stroke from an object?

   A. Select the object, then click the trash icon in the Brushes palette.

   B. Select the object, then press Delete/Backspace.

   C. Drag the Stroke entry on the Appearance palette to the Delete Selected Item button.

   D. Set the object's stroke to Black.

3. Which scatter brush option controls how far objects can stray from the path?

   A. Diameter

   B. Scatter

   C. Spacing

   D. Size

4. Which colorization method affects all the colors in a brush except black and white?

   A. None

   B. Tints

   C. Tints and Shades

   D. Hue Shift

5. Which brush type would you use to create a border that automatically applies a specific brush design component at the corners of a path?

   A. Art

   B. Calligraphic

   C. Pattern

   D. Scatter

Fill-in-the-blank

1. To convert a brush stroke to outlined paths, choose the _____ command.

2. To instantly see and edit brush options, _____.

3. Scaling an object will also scale a brush stroke if the _____ option is on in the Scale or Preferences dialog boxes.

4. For shapes to be available for use in a pattern brush, they must first be stored in the _____.

5. After you create a brush library, the new library won't be available in Illustrator until you _____.

6. To enable the Pressure brush option, you need to use a _____.

Definitions

1. What does the Tints colorization method do?

2. What is an art brush?

3. What is a side tile?

4. For a pattern brush, what does the Approximate Path option do?

5. What is the purpose of the pair of sliders that can be split apart for some Scatter Brush options?

Size:	128%	177%	Pressure

SYMBOLS 16

New chapter! 10.0!

In this chapter you will learn how to work with symbols, which are objects that are stored on the Symbols palette. You will learn how to place symbol instances into a document either by dragging or by using the Symbol Sprayer tool and how to edit those instances using the Symbol Shifter, Scruncher, Sizer, Spinner, Stainer, Screener, and Styler tools. You will also learn how to create, rename, duplicate, edit, and delete symbols.

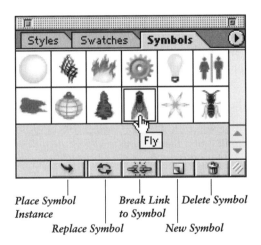

Place Symbol Instance — Break Link to Symbol — Delete Symbol

Replace Symbol — New Symbol

1 *The Symbols palette is used to save and delete symbols and place and replace symbols instances.*

Symbol Sprayer — Symbol Scruncher — Symbol Spinner — Symbol Screener

Symbol Shifter — Symbol Sizer — Symbol Stainer — Symbol Styler

2 *The symbolism tools*

Using the Symbols palette

Any object that you can create in Illustrator can be stored on the Symbols palette **1** for potential reuse in any document. To place one symbol onto the artboard, all you have to do is drag it out of the Symbols palette. A placed symbol is called an **instance** to distinguish it from the original symbol.

To place multiple instances of a symbol, drag or hold the mouse down with the **Symbol Sprayer** tool **2**. A collection of instances in its own bounding box, called a **symbol set**, will be created. Using symbols lets you create complex art quickly and easily. Spray a tree symbol, spray a grass symbol, then spray with a flower symbol to create a flowering forest meadow with just a few mouse clicks.

Using any of the other symbolism tools (**Symbol Shifter, Scruncher, Sizer, Spinner, Stainer,** or **Screener**), you can change the closeness (density), position, stacking order, size, rotation, transparency, color tint, or style of multiple symbol instances in a selected symbol set, while still maintaining the link to the original symbol. Because of this link, if you edit the original symbol, any instances of that symbol in the document will update to reflect the change automatically. Also, you can apply styles, effects, or tranformations to a single instance or a whole set.

(Continued on the following page)

Symbols

Another advantage of using symbols is that each time you create an instance, Illustrator uses the original symbol instead of creating individual objects multiple times. For example, say you draw a boat, save it as a symbol in the Symbols palette, and then drag with the Symbol Sprayer to create multiple instances in a symbol set. Even though fifty instances of the boat appeared in the symbol set, Illustrator defines the object in the document code only once. This not only saves you time, it also keeps the illustration file size down. When outputting files to the Web in SVG (Scalable Vector Graphics) or SWF (Flash) format, file size is critical. Because each symbol is defined only once in the exported SVG image or Flash animation, the size of the export file is kept small, significantly reducing download time.

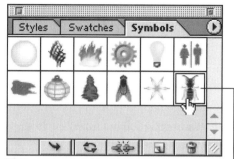

1 *Drag a symbol from the Symbols palette...*

When you drag a symbol out of the Symbols palette, a copy of the symbol (called an "instance") is made automatically; the original symbol remains on the palette. To begin with, you can use the default symbols on the Symbols palette. On page 282, you'll learn how to create your own symbols.

To place symbol instances into a document one at a time:

Drag a symbol from the Symbols palette onto the artboard **1**–**2**.
or
Click a symbol on the Symbols palette, then click the Place Symbol Instance button ⎣↘⎦ on the palette. The instance will appear in the center of the document window.

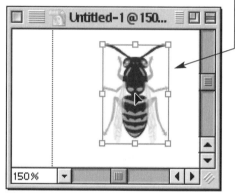

2 *...onto the artboard.*

Repeat to add more instances. Each instance is automatically linked to its original symbol. To demonstrate this point, select an instance on the artboard, then look at the Symbols palette; its original symbol will be selected automatically. You'll learn how to preserve or break this link later in this chapter.

➤ To duplicate an instance, Option-drag/Alt-drag the instance on the artboard. To place many instances of a symbol quickly, it's much more efficient (and fun) to use the Symbol Sprayer tool (see page 286).

Place Symbol in Artwork

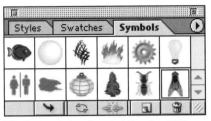

1 *The Symbols palette in Thumbnail View*

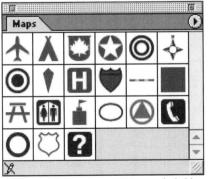

2 *The Symbols palette in Small List View*

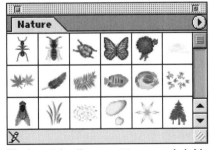

To change the Symbols palette display:

From the palette menu, choose:

Thumbnail View **1** to display symbols as swatches. Use Tool Tips to learn the names.
or
Small List View **2** to display symbols as small swatches with their names listed.
or
Large List View **3** to display symbols as large swatches with their names listed.

➤ Choose Sort by Name from the palette menu to sort the symbols alphabetically by name.

Already bored with the default selection on the Symbols palette? Take a peek at some of the Adobe symbol libraries.

To use symbols from other libraries:

1. Choose Window > Symbol Libraries > Charts, Default CMYK, Default RGB, Maps (map symbols), Nature, or Objects. A library palette will open **4**–**5**.

2. Click a symbol on the library palette to add it to the Symbols palette. Or to add multiple symbols, click the first symbol in a series of consecutive symbols, then Shift-click the last symbol in the series (or Cmd-click/Ctrl-click non-consecutive symbols), then drag them to the Symbols palette.

➤ If you drag a symbol from a library into your document, the symbol will appear on the Symbols palette automatically.

➤ Once you create your own symbols files, you can use Window > Symbol Libraries > Other Library to open them.

3 *The Symbols palette in Large List View*

4 *The Adobe Illustrator **Maps** symbols library*

5 *The Adobe Illustrator **Nature** symbols library*

When you apply a different symbol to an existing instance in a document, any transformations, transparency, or effects that were applied to the instance will also appear in the replacement.

To apply a different symbol to an existing instance:

1. Choose the Selection tool, then click an instance in your document **1**.

2. On the Symbols palette, click a symbol.

3. Click the Replace Symbol button ⟳ on the palette **2**.
   or
   Choose Replace Symbol from the palette menu.

Now that you're acquainted with the Symbols palette, it's time to get personal and start creating your own symbols. Any Illustrator object—path, compound path, gradient mesh, embedded raster image, text, group of objects, or even another symbol—can be made into a new symbol. Within reason, that is. If you're going to use the Symbol Sprayer to spray a gazillion instances of a symbol, it's probably wise to create the symbol out of an object that's not overly complex.

Note: If the object (to become a symbol) contains a brush stroke, blend, effect, style, or other symbols, those attributes will become fixed parts of the new symbol, which means they can't be reedited in a linked instance of that symbol (see page 284).

To create a symbol from an object in your artwork:

1. Create an object, scale it to the desired size, and leave it selected. Or select an existing object in your document **3**.

2. Choose the Selection tool, then drag the object onto the Symbols palette **4**.
   or
   Click the New Symbol button 🔲 at the bottom of the palette.
   or
   Choose New Symbol from the palette menu, type a name, then click OK.

To rename the new symbol, follow the instructions on the next page.

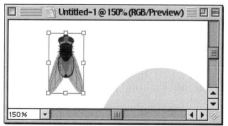

1 *Click an instance in your document...*

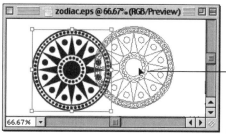

2 *...click a different symbol on the Symbols palette, then click the Replace Symbol button on the palette. The fly is replaced with crayons.*

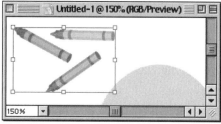

3 *Drag an object or group from the document...*

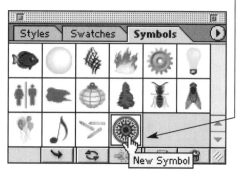

4 *...onto the Symbols palette. The object (New Symbol) appears on the palette.*

Symbol Options

Name: Zodiac

OK

Cancel

1 *Change or edit a symbol **name** in the **Symbol** Options dialog box.*

Symbol names are visible when the Small List View or List View is chosen as the display option for the Symbols palette. You'll also see a name (Tool Tip) if you move the pointer over a symbol icon.

To name or rename a symbol:

1. Double-click a symbol on the Symbols palette.
or
Click a symbol on the palette, then choose Symbol Options from the palette menu.

2. Type a new Name or change the existing Name **1**, then click OK.

If you delete a symbol that is linked to instances on the artboard, an alert box will appear. At that point you can choose to expand the instances, delete the instances, or cancel the deletion.

To delete a symbol:

1. Drag the symbol you want to delete over the Delete Symbol button [🗑] at the bottom of the palette.
or
Click a symbol on the Symbols palette, then click the Delete Symbol button [🗑] at the bottom of the palette or choose Delete Symbol from the palette menu.

2. An alert box will display if the document contains any linked instances of the symbol being deleted **2**. Click Expand Instances to expand the linked instances into standard, non-linked objects or click Delete Instances to delete the linked instances (or click Cancel to cancel the whole operation).

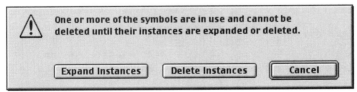

⚠ One or more of the symbols are in use and cannot be deleted until their instances are expanded or deleted.

Expand Instances   Delete Instances   Cancel

2 *This prompt will appear if you try to **delete** a symbol that is **linked** to instances on the artboard.*

To modify instances:

Modifications that are made to an instance or set have no effect on the symbol or the link to the symbol the instance originated from. You can modify an instance or set in the following ways : move it; transform it (using the Transform palette, by dragging its selection handles, or using an Object menu > Transform command); change its opacity; change its blending mode; or apply styles or effects to it. You can't recolor it directly.

1 The original **instance** of a symbol

To modify any live effects that were applied to an instance or set after it was placed into the artwork, on the Appearance palette double-click the effect, then change the settings.

You can also use the Symbol Shifter, Symbol Scruncher, Symbol Sizer, Symbol Spinner, Symbol Stainer, Symbol Screener, or Symbol Styler tool to modify instances or sets. You'll learn about these tools later in this chapter.

➤ Expanding an instance breaks the link between the instance and the original symbol (see page 298).

➤ We got confusing results when we applied Effect > Pathfinder submenu commands to instances. Skip them for now.

2 After **enlarging** the instance, lowering its **opacity**, and applying the Drop Shadow **effect** to it

On the next page you'll learn how to edit a symbol (we're talking there about editing the original symbol—not an instance). When you do this, you may want to work on a duplicate of the symbol rather than the original.

To duplicate a symbol:

On the Symbols palette, drag the symbol you want to duplicate over the New Symbol button [icon] at the bottom of the palette **3**–**4**.

or

Click the symbol you want to duplicate, then choose Duplicate Symbol from the palette menu.

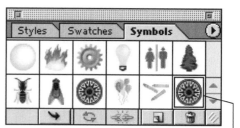

3 Drag a symbol over the **New Symbol** button.

The duplicate symbol will appear after the last symbol.

➤ You can drag a symbol icon to a different position on the palette.

➤ Option/Alt-drag one symbol over another symbol to copy the first symbol and remove the second symbol.

4 A **duplicate** of the symbol appears on the palette.

1 *The original* **instance**

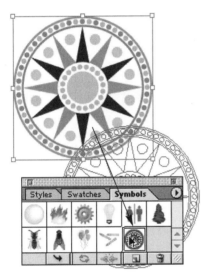

2 *After* **breaking** *the* **link** *between the instance and the original symbol, the former instance is* **edited** *(recolored, in this case), and then* **Option/ Alt** *dragged over the original symbol.*

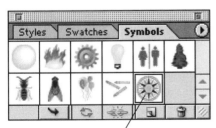

3 *The redefined symbol*

To edit a symbol, the first step is to break the link between the symbol and one of its instances. Next, you'll modify the former instance. And finally, you'll use that object to redefine the original symbol.

Beware! Every instance is linked to its original symbol. If you redefine a symbol, those changes are automatically reflected in any and all instances in the document that originated from that symbol. This makes for efficient document editing, of course, but it can also wreak havoc if you don't keep it in mind.

To redefine a symbol:

1. Create an instance of a symbol (or a duplicate of a symbol) in the artwork **1**. To duplicate a symbol, see the previous set of instructions.

2. Click the Break Link button [icon] at the bottom of the Symbols palette.

3. Modify the resulting object (former instance) to your liking as you would any object.

4. With the object still selected:

   Option-drag/Alt-drag the object over the symbol you want to redefine on the Symbols palette **2**–**3**.
   or
   Click a symbol icon on the palette, then choose Redefine Symbol from the palette menu.

   All instances that are currently linked to the now redefined symbol will automatically update to reflect the changes that were made to the symbol. And any transformations, effects, opacity values, brush strokes, etc. that were applied to those instances before the symbol was redefined will be preserved.

➤ To create a new symbol instead of redefining an existing symbol, drag the object onto a blank area of the Symbols palette.

Redefine Symbol

Using the symbolism tools

There are eight symbolism tools . If the Adobe gang couldn't think of a name for a tool that began with the letter "S," the tool got scrapped (just kidding; no e-mails on this, please).

The Symbol Sprayer tool is used to quickly spray multiple instances of the same symbol onto the artboard. Each time you use this tool, the objects that result are grouped together into what is called a "symbol set." The Symbol Sprayer can also be used to delete instances from a set.

The other symbolism tools (Symbol Shifter, Symbol Scruncher, Symbol Sizer, Symbol Spinner, Symbol Stainer, Symbol Screener, and Symbol Styler), which are discussed individually on the following pages, are used to modify the position, size, orientation, color, transparency, or style of a symbol instance or symbol set while preserving the link to the original symbol.

First, the Sprayer. You can choose from a slew of options for this tool, but before you get into that, do some spraying.

To use the Symbol Sprayer tool:

1. Choose the Symbol Sprayer tool (Shift-S).

2. Click a symbol on the Symbols palette.

3. Use the mouse in any of the following ways: Click once; or click and hold the mouse in the same spot **2**; or drag across the artboard (see **2**, next page) . As you drag, a wireframe representation of the instances will display on the artboard. When you release the mouse, the fully drawn instances will appear in a set with a bounding box around it.
   or
   To remove instances, Option-click/ Alt-click or Option-drag/Alt-drag inside a symbol set.

➤ To move a whole symbol set on the artboard, drag one of the objects in the set with the Selection tool. To transform all the instances in a symbol set, drag any of the handles on its bounding box (see page 103).

Symbol Sprayer   *Symbol Scruncher*   *Symbol Spinner*   *Symbol Screener*

Symbol Shifter   *Symbol Sizer*   *Symbol Stainer*   *Symbol Styler*

1 *The symbolism tools, shown on a tear-off toolbar*

2 *Instances placed on an artboard by **holding down** the **Symbol Sprayer** tool in one spot. When we created the original symbol, we gave it an opacity of 50%. You can also drag with the tool.*

1 *Choose global and individual properties for the symbolism tools in the* **Symbolism Tool Options** *dialog box.*

2 *The Symbol Sprayer tool used with* **high** *Intensity and Symbol Set Density values*

3 *The Symbol Sprayer tool used with* **low** *Intensity and Symbol Set Density values*

4 *High Intensity cursor*

5 *Low Intensity cursor*

The Symbolism Tool Options dialog box contains global settings that apply to all the symbolism tools, as well as settings that apply only to individual tools. Individual tool settings are covered in the instructions for each tool on the following pages.

To choose global properties for the symbolism tools:

1. If you're going to adjust the Density for the Symbol Sprayer, you may want to select a symbol set in your document now. That way, you will be able to preview the Density changes while the dialog box is open.

2. To open the Symbolism Tool Options dialog box, double-click any symbolism tool.

3. To choose a default brush size for all the symbolism tools, enter a value in the Diameter field or press the arrowhead and drag the Diameter slider **1**.

4. To adjust the rate at which the tools apply their effect, choose an Intensity value (the higher the Intensity, the more quickly an effect is applied). Or to have a stylus control this option instead, check Use Pressure Pen.

5. To specify how close instances will be to each other when applied with the Symbol Sprayer tool, choose a Symbol Set Density value **2**–**3**. The higher the Symbol Set Density, the more tightly the instances will be packed within each set. This option will preview in any sets that are currently selected in your document.

6. Check "Show Brush Size and Intensity" to have the current Diameter and Intensity settings display on screen in the cursor when a symbolism tool is used. The Intensity setting is expressed as a shade in the brush cursor: black for high intensity **4**, gray for middle intensity, and light gray for low intensity **5**.

7. Click OK.

Symbolism Tool Options

To choose options for the Symbol Sprayer tool:

1. Double-click the Symbol Sprayer tool.

or

Double-click a Symbolism tool, then click the Symbol Sprayer (first) button in the Symbolism Tool Options dialog box.

2. Choose Diameter, Intensity, and Symbol Set Density settings **1** (see the previous page for definitions). The higher the Intensity value, the more instances will be sprayed.

3. The Scrunch, Size, Spin, Screen, Stain, and Style pop-up menus define the parameters for instances that are placed by the Symbol Sprayer.

Choose Average from a property's pop-up menu to add instances based on an average sampling from neighboring instances in the set within the diameter of the brush cursor in its current location.

or

Choose User Defined from a property pop-up menu to add instances based on a predetermined value (see the sidebar).

Note: The setting chosen for each of the six individual tool pop-up menus has no relationship to the Method setting, which applies to the other symbolism tools.

4. Click OK.

➤ For more information, read about the peculiarities of each tool on the following pages.

➤ When you use a symbolism tool (such as the Symbol Shifter, Scruncher, or Sizer) to modify instances in a symbol set, keep these two seemingly conflicting tendencies in mind: Instances try to stay as close as possible to their original position in the set in order to maintain their original set density, but at the same time they also try to stay apart.

User Defined defined

For the Symbol Sprayer tool, you can choose either Average or User Defined for each property. If you choose User Defined, this is the variable each property is based on:

Scrunch (density) and **Size** are based on the original symbol size.

Spin is based on the mouse direction.

Screen is based on 100% opacity.

Stain is based on the current Fill color at a 100% tint.

Style is based on the the style currently selected on the Styles palette.

1 *The pop-up menus in the lower portion of the Symbolism Tool Options dialog box appear when the Symbol Sprayer tool is chosen.*

For all the symbolism tools

When you use a symbolism tool, you can maximize your control by interactively readjusting the brush size and intensity (e.g., a small brush will affect a handful of instances; a large brush will affect a larger number of instances).

To **increase** a brush's **intensity** interactively as you use a symbolism tool, press **Shift-]**. To **decrease** brush's intensity, press **Shift-[**.

To **enlarge** a brush interactively as you use a symbolism tool, press **]**. To **shrink** it, press **[**.

The effect of the symbolism tools is strongest in the **center** of the brush cursor and fades toward the edge of the cursor. The longer the mouse button is **held down**, the stronger the effect.

You can't add symbols to an existing set using the Place Symbol command, but you can do so using the Symbol Sprayer tool. Similarly, you can't select or delete instances in a set using the Selection tool, but as we showed you on page 286, you can delete instances by Option/Alt clicking or dragging with the Symbol Sprayer tool.

To add instances to a symbol set:

1. Choose the Selection tool, then click a symbol set in your document.

2. Choose the Symbol Sprayer tool.

3. The icon for the symbol that was last sprayed in a symbol set will become selected on the Symbols palette when the set is reselected. You can either continue to spray with that symbol or you can click a different symbol icon on the palette. Drag inside the selected set **1**.

➤ If a selected set contains instances that originated from two or more different symbols and you click one of those symbols in the Symbols palette, modifications will be limited to only those instances. If you want to modify all the instances in a set, first make sure no symbols are selected by clicking an empty area of the Symbols palette.

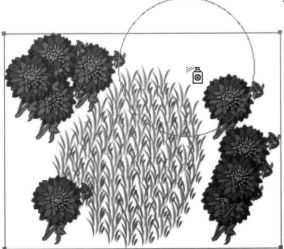

1 *To add to a set, select it, click a different symbol on the Symbols palette, then drag inside the set.*

With the exception of the Symbol Sprayer, all of the symbolism tools—Shifter, Scruncher, Sizer, Spinner, Stainer, Screener, and Styler—are used to modify the position, size, orientation, color, transparency, or style of individual symbol instances or all the instances in a set.

The Symbol Shifter tool shifts instances in a symbol set sideways based on the direction you drag the cursor. The tool can also change the stacking order (front-to-back position) of instances within a set, bringing an instance forward or sending it back behind other instances. For example, if a symbol set contains trees and figures where the trees obscure the figures, you could use the Symbol Shifter tool to move the trees closer together to create a forest, then bring the figures forward in front of the trees.

To use the Symbol Shifter tool:

1. Select a symbol set in your document.
2. Choose the Symbol Shifter tool. ▨
3. Drag inward where you want to pull instances together or drag outward to move instances apart. The tool will try to preserve the current density and arrangement of instances as it does its job.

   or

   Shift-click an instance to bring it in front of adjacent instances **1**–**2**.

   or

   Option-Shift/Alt-Shift click an instance to send it behind adjacent instances.

To choose Symbol Shifter tool options:

1. Double-click the Symbol Shifter tool. ▨
2. Choose a brush Diameter **3**.
3. Choose an Intensity value for the rate of shifting and the amount of space the tool will create between shifted instances. The higher the Intensity, the greater the space and shifting.
4. Choose a Symbol Set Density value to specify how much the tool will try to keep the instances together.
5. Click OK.

1 *The Symbol Shifter tool is used (with Shift held down) on this symbol set...*

2 *...to* **shift the plovers into a more naturalistic** *front-to-back order.*

3 *Options for the Symbol Shifter tool*

Symbol Shifter

One method for all

The current choice on the **Method** pop-up menu applies to all the symbolism tools except the Symbol Sprayer and Symbol Shifter.

1 *Option/Alt dragging across a symbol set with the Symbol Scruncher tool*

2 *The plovers are moved apart.*

3 *Options for the Symbol Scruncher tool*

The Symbol Scruncher tool pulls symbol instances closer together or pushes them apart. A symbol set of birds, for example, could be contracted (scrunched) to move the birds closer together or expanded to create more space between the birds. You can either drag the mouse with the tool or hold the mouse button down in one spot.

To use the Symbol Scruncher:

1. Select a symbol set in your document.

2. Choose the Symbol Scruncher tool.

3. To move instances closer together, either click and hold in one spot or drag inside the set.
or
To push symbol instances away from each other, Option-click/Alt-click or Option-drag/Alt-drag **1**–**2**.

To choose Symbol Scruncher options:

1. Double-click the Symbol Scruncher tool.
or
To change the density in an existing set, click the set, then double-click the Scruncher tool.

2. Choose a brush Diameter and choose a Symbol Set Density value to specify how much the tool will try to keep the instances together **3**.

3. Choose an Intensity value to control how quickly, and how much of, a density change the tool produces.

4. For the Method:

Choose User Defined to gradually increase or decrease the amount of space between symbol instances based on the way you click or drag.
or
Choose Average to even out and make more uniform the amount of space between instances based on an average of the existing density of instances. This Method will produce a minor effect if the spacing is already averaged.
or
Choose Random to randomize the amount of space between instances.

5. Click OK.

Symbol Scruncher

The Symbol Sizer tool's job is to reduce or enlarge instances within a symbol set. The Symbol Sprayer tool only creates instances of a uniform size, so this tool comes in handy for resizing individual instances within a set.

To use the Symbol Sizer:

1. Click a symbol set in your document.
2. Choose the Symbol Sizer tool.
3. Click on or drag over instances to increase their size .
   or
   Option-click/Alt-click or Option-drag/Alt-drag over instances to reduce their size.

   Note: If very little happens when you use this tool, change the Method to User Defined or Random (see step 5, below).

➤ Use a small brush diameter to select instances with more precision.

To choose Symbol Sizer options:

1. Double-click the Symbol Sizer tool.
2. Choose brush Diameter and Symbol Set Density values **2**.
3. Choose an Intensity value for the rate and amount of resizing. The higher the Intensity, the wider the range of scale changes.
4. *Optional:* Check Proportional Resizing to resize instances without distortion.
5. *Optional:* Check Resizing Affects Density to force instances to move away from each other when they're scaled up or move closer together when they're scaled down, while maintaining the current set density. With this option unchecked, more overlapping of instances can occur.
6. For Method,
   Choose User Defined to gradually increase or decrease the size of instances based on the way you click or drag.
   or
   Choose Average to make the instances more uniform in size. If the sizes are already near uniform, this Method will produce little effect.
   or

1 *Instances* ***scaled*** *using the* ***Symbol Sizer*** *tool*

2 *Options for the* ***Symbol Sizer*** *tool*

Symbol Sizer

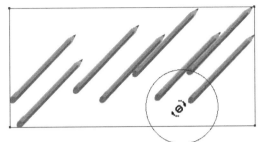

1 *Dragging across a symbol set with the Symbol Spinner tool with Method: Random chosen*

2 *The pencils are **rotated** randomly.*

3 *Options for the Symbol Spinner tool*

Choose Random to randomize scale changes within the brush diameter.

7. Click OK.

➤ With Average or Random chosen as the brush Method, Shift-click or Shift-drag to scale instances while maintaining maintain (if possible) the current density.

The Symbol Spinner tool changes the orientation of instances within a symbol set.

To use the Symbol Spinner tool:

I. Click a symbol set in your document.

2. Choose the Symbol Spinner tool.

3. Drag a symbol instance or instances in the direction you want them to rotate, using the arrows as an orientation guide **1**–**2**. Clicking and holding has no effect.

➤ If the arrows are hard to see, change the selection color for the layer the set is on.

➤ The smaller the brush's diameter, the easier it will be to isolate individual symbol instances for rotating.

To choose Symbol Spinner tool options:

I. Double-click the Symbol Spinner tool.

2. Choose brush Diameter and Symbol Set Density values **3**.

3. Choose an Intensity value for the rate and the amount the instances can be rotated. The higher the Intensity, the sharper the angles of rotation using the least amount of mouse movement.

4. For Method,

Choose User Defined to rotate the symbol instances in the direction of the cursor.
or
Choose Average to gradually even out and make uniform the orientation of all instances within the brush's diameter.
or
Choose Random to randomize the orientation of instances.

5. Click OK.

Symbol Spinner

Like the Colorization: Tints and Shades option for brushes, the Symbol Stainer tool colorizes symbol instances with varied tints of the current fill color. It changes solid fills, but not patterns or gradients. Use it to vary the shades of green in foliage, the shades of brown in buildings, and so on.

Note: The Symbol Stainer tool increases file size and decreases performance, so don't use it if you're going to export your file in the Flash SVG format or if memory is a concern.

To use the Symbol Stainer tool:

1. Select a symbol set in your document.
2. Choose the Symbol Stainer tool. 🖌️
3. Choose a fill color to be used for the staining.
4. Click on an instance to apply a tint of the current fill color to the current object color. Continue clicking to increase the amount of colorization, up to the maximum amount.

   or

   Drag across the symbol set to colorize any instances within the brush's diameter **1**–**2**. Drag again to intensify the effect.

➤ Option-click/Alt-click or Option-drag/ Alt-drag to decrease the amount of colorization and reveal more of the original symbol color.

➤ Shift-click or Shift-drag to tint only instances that have already been stained, while leaving instances that haven't been stained unchanged.

To choose Symbol Stainer tool options:

1. Double-click the Symbol Stainer tool.
2. Choose brush Diameter and Symbol Set Density values **3**.
3. Choose an Intensity value for the rate and amount of the tint the Stainer applies.
4. For Method:

   Choose User Defined to gradually tint symbol instances with the fill color.

   or

1 *Dragging across a symbol set with the Symbol Stainer tool*

2 *The fireworks are **tinted** gradually.*

3 *Options for the Symbol Stainer tool*

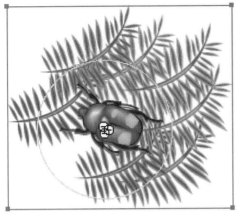

1 *Holding the mouse down on an instance (the beetle) with the Symbol Screener tool*

2 *The beetle is screened.*

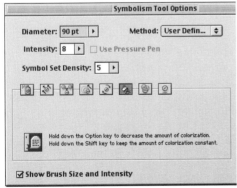

3 *Options for the Symbol Screener tool*

Choose Average to even out the amount of existing colorization among selected instances without applying new tints.
or
Choose Random to randomize the colorization for a more naturalistic effect.

5. Click OK.

The Symbol Screener tool increases or decreases the opacity of instances within the brush's diameter. Use this tool to fade instances and make them more transparent.

To use the Symbol Screener tool:

1. Select a symbol set in your document.

2. Choose the Symbol Screener tool.

3. Click and hold on or drag across instances to make them more transparent **1**–**2**.
or
Option-click/Alt-click on or Option-drag/Alt-drag across instances to make them more opaque.

Note: If nothing happens when you use this tool, change the Method to User Defined or Random (see step 4, below).

To choose Symbol Screener tool options:

1. Double-click the Symbol Screener tool.

2. Choose brush Diameter and Symbol Set Density values **3**.

3. Choose an Intensity value for the rate and amount of transparency that is applied. The higher the Intensity, the more quickly and intensely instances will fade out.

4. For Method:

Choose User Defined to have transparency increase or decrease gradually.
or
Choose Average to even out and make more uniform the amount of transparency among instances within the brush's diameter.
or
Choose Random to gradually add transparency in a random fashion.

5. Click OK.

Symbol Screener

295

The Symbol Styler tool applies the currently selected style to instances in a set. By selecting a different style in the Styles palette, you can apply one or more styles to a symbol set. The tool can also be used to remove styling.

To use the Symbol Styler tool:

1. Select a symbol set in your document.

2. Choose the Symbol Styler tool. 🔘

3. Click a style on the Styles palette **1**.
   Note: Be sure to choose the symbolism tool first. If you choose a style while a non-symbolism tool is selected, the style will be applied to the entire symbol set.

4. Click and hold on, or drag across, an instance or instances to apply the selected style within the brush's diameter **2** (and **3**, next page). The longer you hold the mouse down, the more intensely the style will be applied. Pause for the screen to redraw. This can take some time even on a fast machine.
   or
   Option-click/Alt-click or Option-drag/Alt-click to undo the styling.

➤ Shift-click or Shift-drag to gradually apply the currently selected style to instances that have already been styled, while keeping unstyled instances unchanged.

To choose Symbol Styler tool options:

1. Double-click the Symbol Styler tool.

2. Choose brush Diameter and Symbol Set Density values.

3. Choose an Intensity value for the rate and amount a style is applied. The higher the Intensity, the more intensely and quickly the styling will be applied.

4. For Method:
   Choose User Defined to gradually increase or decrease the amount of applied styling.
   or
   Choose Average to even out the amount of applied styling among instances within the brush diameter without applying new styling.
   or

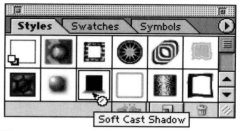

1 *Choose the Symbol Styler tool, then click a style on the Styles palette.*

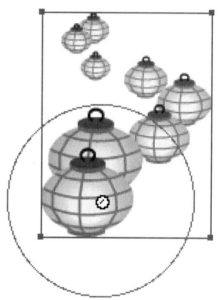

2 *Clicking an instance with the Symbol Styler tool*

When saving

When saving a file containing symbols, consider unchecking **Create PDF Compatible File** in the Illustrator Native Format Option dialog box. Doing so will significantly reduce the file size and speed up the save and open operations.

Saving a file containing symbols as an EPS will result in a large file size. Consider taking the resulting EPS file and distilling it using Acrobat to produce a smaller **PDF** file.

Choose Random to apply styling gradudally and randomly.

5. Click OK.

Note: To view the attributes used in an applied style, click the symbol set, choose Object > Expand, check Fill and Stroke, then click OK. On the Layers palette, click the target circle for one of the expanded instances, then look at its appearance attributes on the Appearance palette.

3 *To produce this illustration, various* *styles* *were applied to* *different* *instances.* *Compare with* **2** *on the previous page.*

The Expand command can be used for two different purposes. If it's applied to a symbol set, it breaks the set apart without changing the instances themselves or their link to the original symbol. The instances will be nested inside a group on the Layers palette.

If the Expand command is applied to an individual instance (an instance that wasn't placed using the Symbol Sprayer tool), it does break the link to the original symbol. The individual paths from the former instance will be nested inside a group on the Layers palette.

To expand an instance or a symbol set:

1. Select a symbol set, an instance, or multiple individual instances in your document.

2. Choose Object > Expand (or Object > Expand Appearance if the instance has an effect applied to it).

3. Check Object and Fill **1**, then click OK.

4. If you expanded a symbol set, you can now use the Direct-selection tool or Group-selection tool to move the individual instances apart, if desired. They are still linked to the original symbol.

   ➤ To transform one path in an expanded set, using the Layers palette, locate and select the path to be modified inside the nested groups, then use its bounding box for the modifications. You can also use the Expand command on any instance in an expanded set.

   If you expanded an individual instance, it will now be a group of paths. Select any path using the Layers palette to modify it.

➤ If the original symbol artwork contained any live appearances or effects, they will be editable once an individual instance from that symbol (not from a set) is expanded. Select the group, show the Appearance palette, then double-click Contents until the word "Path" displays. The applied effects will be listed on the palette, and are editable. You can also use the Layers palette to select any individual path. To use the edited object to redefine a symbol, see page 285.

Select all instances

To select all the individual instances of a particular symbol in your document (not in a set), click the symbol on the Symbols palette, then choose **Select All Instances** from the palette menu.

1 Check *Object* and *Fill* in the *Expand* dialog box.

Expand Instances

Chapter 16: Symbols ◆ Study Guide

Learning Objectives

- Use the Symbols palette.
- Use the Symbol Sprayer tool.
- Use the Symbolism tools.
- Work with symbol sets.

Get Up and Running Exercises

- Reproduce a map that uses icon-based graphics, such as a map for a national park or shopping mall. Draw the basic map and then use Illustrator's symbols for things such as telephones and restrooms.

- Create a swarm of ants that moves along a specific course, as in the figure below. How can you "steer" the ant swarm in the direction you want?

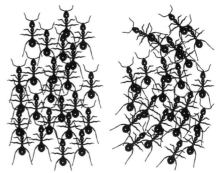

Ants drawn with the default Symbol Sprayer settings (left) and after changing the direction of ants in the swarm (right).

(Continued on the following page)

- Create an illustration in which a trail has been blown through a thick pile of autumn leaves, as if by a leaf blower. Everything you need to complete this exercise is included in Illustrator, so you shouldn't even have to draw the leaves. Try to complete this exercise using only two tools.

- Use the Symbol Sprayer to create an illustration of bubbles, similar to the figure below. While the Symbols palette contains a bubble symbol, the bubbles need to be different sizes for this exercise, from small to large. Find the fastest way to vary the size of the bubbles.

Class Discussion Questions

- Why use symbols to create multiples of objects instead of using Illustrator's powerful object duplication features?

- What are some examples of uses for symbols?

- What's the difference between dragging a symbol from the Symbols palette to the artboard, and using the Symbol Sprayer tool?

- How do you edit a symbol?

Review Questions

Multiple choice

1. Which Symbolism tool option controls the rate at which tools apply their effect?

   A. Intensity

   B. Screen

   C. Style

   D. Symbol Set Density

2. Which Symbolism tool option controls the distance between symbol instances as they're drawn?

   A. Diameter

   B. Screen

   C. Size

   D. Symbol Set Density

3. Which Symbolism tool moves symbol instances in the direction you drag the tool?

   A. Symbol Scruncher

   B. Symbol Sizer

   C. Symbol Shifter

   D. Symbol Sprayer

4. Which Symbolism tool controls the opacity of symbol instances?

   A. Symbol Screener

   B. Symbol Shifter

   C. Symbol Stainer

   D. Symbol Styler

5. Which Symbolism tool applies the current fill color to symbol instances?

   A. Symbol Screener

   B. Symbol Sprayer

   C. Symbol Stainer

   D. Symbol Styler

Fill-in-the-blank

1. To stop a symbol instance from updating when the symbol is redefined, select the instance, then click the _____ button on the Symbols palette.

2. To reverse the effect of a Symbolism tool as you use it, press the _____ key.

3. For some Symbolism tool options, choosing _____ as the Method setting lets you use the tool to make the symbols in a set more uniform.

4. For some Symbolism tool options, setting the Method to _____ lets the tool's effect be controlled by how it's clicked and dragged.

5. To break apart a symbol set, select the set, then choose Object > _____.

6. When you break apart an individual symbol instance, the resulting paths are contained within a _____.

Definitions

1. What is a symbol?

2. What is a symbol instance?

3. What is a symbol set?

4. In the Method option in the Symbolism Tool Options dialog box, what is the function of the Average setting?

5. What does the Symbol Screener tool do?

In this chapter, first you will learn about the shape mode commands, which create editable compound shapes. Second, you will learn about the pathfinder commands, which form a new, flattened, closed object or compound path by dividing, merging, cropping, outlining, etc. Then finally you will learn how to join two or more objects into a compound path; add objects to a compound path; reverse an object's fill in a compound path; and release a compound path.

shop and compare

For a comparison of compound shapes and compound paths, see page 304.

Subtract from *shape area*   *Exclude* overlap-*ping shape areas*
Add to *shape area*   *Intersect* *shape areas*

1 *The shape mode buttons on the **Pathfinder** palette*

Shape modes 10.0!

The shape mode buttons **1** on the Pathfinder palette produce a compound shape from selected, overlapping objects. And like appearances and effects, compound shapes are editable and reversible. The original objects are nested as individual objects within a <Compound Shape> layer on the Layers palette, making it easy to select them for editing. Individual objects within a compound shape can be moved, restacked, or reshaped, and the overall compound shape adjusts accordingly. And finally, if a compound shape is released, the objects are restored to their original appearances.

A few rules to keep in mind:

■ Shape modes can be applied to multiple paths, compound paths, groups (nesting is preserved), blends, envelopes, editable text, or even other compound shapes.

■ Shape modes can't be applied to a group alone, but they can be applied to a group that's selected along with an individual object.

■ With the exception of the "Subtract from shape area" command, the color attributes of the topmost selected object (or the topmost object in a selected group) are applied to the entire compound shape.

■ Effects in the original objects are preserved, but only distort and warp effects will be visible in the compound shape. The

(Continued on the following page)

Shape Modes

presence of a raster effect (from the bottom portion of the Effect menu) in any of the original objects will cause that object to become hidden in the compound shape.

10.0! The shape mode buttons

Add to shape area 1: Joins the outer edges of selected objects into one compound shape, hiding interior object edges (see also page 131). Open paths are closed.

Subtract from shape area 2: Subtracts the objects in front from the backmost object. Only the paint attributes from the backmost object are preserved.

Intersect shape areas 3: Preserves areas that overlap; hides areas that don't overlap. Works best when used on two objects that partially overlap.

Exclude overlapping shape areas 4: Areas where objects overlap become transparent.

➤ You can apply a shape mode to an object that's already in a compound shape. Select the object with the Direct-selection tool, then click a shape mode button. Try clicking, say, "Subtract from shape area" to make an object disappear.

➤ If you copy a compound shape in Illustrator and then paste it into Photoshop, in Photoshop it will become a shape layer containing multiple paths. If you copy and paste a Photoshop shape layer containing two or more paths into Illustrator, it will be a compound shape.

10.0!

When a compound shape is expanded, the result is a single path, unless the compound shape had cutouts, in which case the end result is a compound path. Compare this with the Release Compound Shape command, which is discussed on the next page.

To expand a compound shape:

1. Select the compound shape with the Selection tool.

2. Click the Expand button on the Pathfinder palette.
   or
   Choose Expand Compound Shape from the palette menu.

1 *The original objects: The leaf is the topmost object.*

Add to shape area

2 *The frontmost object will be cut out of the black square.*

Subtract from shape area turns it into a compound shape.

3 *The original objects*

Intersect shape areas: Only areas that originally overlapped other objects remain.

4 *The original objects*

Exclude overlapping shape areas: Where the objects overlap turns into a cutout.

Shape Mode Buttons; Expand

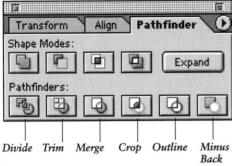

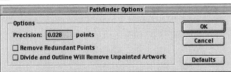

Divide   Trim   Merge   Crop   Outline   Minus Back

1 *The pathfinder buttons on the Pathfinder palette*

Pathfinder options, in brief

To open the Pathfinder Options dialog box **2**, choose Pathfinder Options from the Pathfinder palette menu.

The higher the **Precision** value, the more precisely a command is applied—but the longer it takes to process.

With **Remove Redundant Points** checked, any anchor points with a duplicate in the same location are deleted when the pathfinder command is applied.

For "Divide and Outline Will Remove...," see the Note at right.

3 *The original objects*

Divide (We recolored the resulting shapes.)

Releasing a compound shape restores the original objects used within the compound shape, with their original appearances.

To release a compound shape:

1. Select the compound shape with the Selection tool.

2. Choose Release Compound Shape from the Pathfinder palette menu.

Pathfinders 10.0!

The pathfinder commands determine where selected paths overlap and then divide, trim, merge, crop, outline, or subtract from them to produce non-overlapping (flattened) closed paths or lines. Object colors and appearances are preserved, and the resulting paths are put into a group. The pathfinder commands, like the shape modes, are applied using the Pathfinder palette **1**.

Here are a few guidelines:

➤ Unfortunately, the original objects can't be restored after applying a pathfinder command, except using Undo. Make a copy of your objects first!

➤ We like to apply the pathfinders to closed paths. If applied to an open path, Illustrator may close the path for you before performing the command. To control how a path is closed, see page 303.

➤ Pathfinders can be applied to an object that has a gradient mesh fill, pattern fill, brush stroke, or applied effect.

➤ To apply pathfinders to type, first convert the type into outlines.

(To apply pathfinders via Effects menu commands, see page 383. For the Trap command on the palette menu, see page 518.)

Note: If "Divide and Outline will remove unpainted artwork" is checked in the Pathfinder Options dialog box (choose Pathfinder Options from the palette menu), the Divide and Outline commands will delete any non-overlapping areas of selected paths that have a fill of None.

Divide: Each overlapping area becomes a separate, non-overlapping object **3**.

(Continued on the following page)

➤ After applying the Divide command, click away from all objects to deselect them, choose the Direct-selection tool, click any of the objects, and apply new fill colors or effects; or apply a fill of None or transparency to make an object see-through; or remove an object to create a cutout.

Trim 1: The frontmost object shape is preserved; parts of objects that are behind it and overlap it are deleted. Adjacent or over-lapping objects of the same color or shade remain separate (unlike the Merge command). Stroke colors are deleted (except if effects were applied to the original objects).

Merge 2: Adjacent or overlapping objects with the same fill attributes are united. Stroke colors are deleted (except if effects were applied to the original objects).

Crop 3: Areas of selected objects that extend beyond the edge of the frontmost object are cropped away, and the frontmost object loses its fill and stroke. Stroke colors are removed (except if effects were applied to the original objects). Crop works like a clipping mask, except in this case the original objects can't be restored except by using Undo.

Outline 4: All the selected objects turn into stroked line segments, with the fill colors of the original objects becoming the stroke colors. Transparency settings are preserved; fill colors are removed. The resulting strokes can be scaled and recolored individually.

Minus Back 5: Objects in back are sub-tracted from the frontmost object, leaving only portions of the frontmost object. The paint attributes and appearances of the frontmost object are applied to the new path. The objects must at least partially overlap for this command to produce an effect.

Shortcuts to remember

To repeat the last-used Pathfinder palette command: **Cmd-4/Ctrl-4**.

To turn a shape mode command into a pathfinder command: **Option-click/Alt-click** the button.

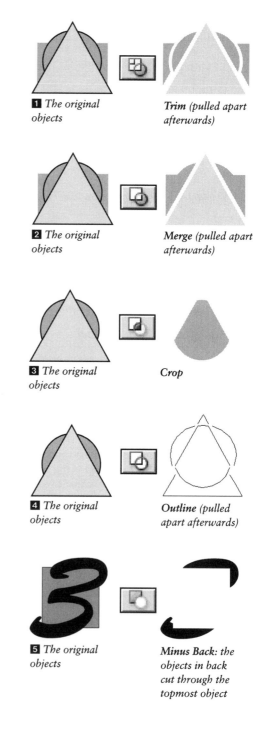

1 *The original objects*   **Trim** *(pulled apart afterwards)*

2 *The original objects*   **Merge** *(pulled apart afterwards)*

3 *The original objects*   **Crop**

4 *The original objects*   **Outline** *(pulled apart afterwards)*

5 *The original objects*   **Minus Back:** *the objects in back cut through the topmost object*

Trim, Merge, Crop, Outline, Minus Back

1 *Select an object that has a stroke. To produce the button shown below, a gradient fill and a stroke were applied to the object before applying the* **Outline Stroke** *command.*

2 *The* **Outline Stroke** *command converted the stroke into a compound path. We selected the outer ring with the Selection tool, applied a gradient fill to it, then dragged the Gradient tool downward across it to make it contrast with the gradient fill in the inner circle. Finally, we selected the gradient in the inner circle using the Layers palette, then modified that gradient.*

3 *Place smaller objects on top of a larger object and make sure all the objects are selected...*

4 *...then Control-click/ Right-click and choose* **Make Compound Path** *from the context menu.*

If you're going to apply a pathfinder command to an open path, you can use the Outline Stroke command first to turn the stroke into a filled object instead of letting the pathfinder command close it for you. Another reason to use this command is to convert a line or a stroke into a closed path so it can be filled with a gradient or prepared more easily for trapping.

To turn a stroke or an open path into a filled object:

1. Select an object that has a stroke color **1**.

2. Choose Object > Path > Outline Stroke. The new filled object **2** will have the same width as the original stroke. Any fill from the original object will be preserved as a separate object.

Compound paths

The compound path command joins two or more objects into one object—that is, until or unless the compound path is released. Where the original objects overlapped, a transparent hole is created, through which shapes or patterns behind the object are revealed. Regardless of their original paint attributes, all the objects in a compound path are painted with the attributes of the backmost object, and they form one unit.

To create a compound path:

1. Arrange the objects you want to see through in front of a larger shape **3**. Closed paths work best. The paths can have brush strokes.

2. Select all the objects using the Selection tool (V) or Lasso tool.

3. Choose Object > Compound Path > Make (Cmd-8/Ctrl-8).
   or
   If the objects aren't grouped, you can Control-click/Right-click on the artboard and choose Make Compound Path from the context menu **4**.

(Continued on the following page)

Outline Stroke; Create Compound Path

The frontmost objects will cut through the backmost object like a cookie cutter **1**–**2**. The words "<Compound Path>" will appear on the Layers palette, but the original objects will no longer be listed as separate objects; the original objects will be part and parcel of the compound path object. (Compound shapes, in contrast, are preserved as individual objects and are listed as such on the Layers palette.)

The fill and stroke attributes of the backmost object will be applied to areas of objects in front of it that overlap it or that extend beyond the edge of it.

If the holes don't result, see page 305.

➤ Regardless of which layers the objects were on originally, the compound path will be placed on the layer of the frontmost object.

➤ Don't overdo it. To avoid a printing error, don't make your compound paths from very complex shapes or create too many compound paths in the same illustration.

1 *The objects are converted into a compound path.*

2 *We placed a background object behind the compound path and applied a white stroke to the black circle.*

Compound shapes	*Compound paths*	*How they're the same*
Subpaths are listed as **separate** objects on the Layers palette.	Subpaths are part of a **<Compound Path>** layer.	Use the **Selection** tool to select or move a whole compound shape or compound path.
Click with the **Direct-selection** tool to select a whole subpath within a compound shape.	**Option-click/Alt-click** with the Direct-selection tool to select a whole subpath within a compound path.	**Reshape** any subpath within a compound shape or compound path by the usual methods (e.g., add points, delete points, move points).
There are **four** shape mode buttons to choose from. And after a compound shape is created, additional shape modes can be applied to individual objects within it.	There is only **one** kind of compound path: Overlapping areas are subtracted from the backmost object, period.	Only one **fill color** can be applied to a compound shape or compound path at a time.
When released, the objects' **original** appearances (e.g., effects, opacity, blending modes) are restored.	When released, the objects take on the appearances of the **compound path**, not their original appearances.	

1 *Click an object in a compound path.*

Use Even-Odd Fill Rule

Use Non-Zero Winding Fill Rule

2 *Reverse Path Direction Off*   **3** *Reverse Path Direction On*

4 *The color of two of the buttonholes is reversed.*

To add an object to a compound path:

1. Using the Selection tool or the Lasso tool, select both the compound path and the object you want to add to it.

2. Choose Object > Compound Paths > Make (Cmd-8/Ctrl-8).

You can remove the fill color of any shape in a compound, making the object transparent, or vice versa, by flicking the Reverse Path Direction switch on the Attributes palette.

To reverse an object's fill in a compound path:

1. Deselect the compound path (Cmd-Shift-A/Ctrl-Shift-A).

2. Choose the Direct-selection tool (A).

3. Click the object in the compound path whose color you want to reverse **1**.

4. Show the Attributes palette (Window > Show Attributes).

5. Click the Reverse Path Direction Off button or the Reverse Path Direction On button—whichever button isn't currently highlighted **2**–**4**.

➤ If the Reverse Path Direction buttons have no effect, it means you have selected the whole compound path. Select only one path in the compound and try again.

The fill rules *10.0!*

In case you're wondering what those buttons are on the right side of the Attributes palette, here's a brief explanation:

Non-Zero Winding Fill Rule is Illustrator's default rule for combined paths. The Reverse Path Direction buttons (discussed above) are only available when this button is clicked.

The Use Even-Odd Fill Rule makes every other overlapping shape within a compound transparent. It produces more cutouts than the Non-Zero Winding Fill Rule.

Add To, Reverse Object Fill In, Compound Path

You can release a compound path back into its individual objects at any time.

To release a compound path:

1. Choose the Selection tool, then click on the compound path **1**.

2. Choose Object > Compound Path > Release (Cmd-Option-8/Ctrl-Alt-8).
   or
   Control-click/Right-click the artboard and choose Release Compound Path from the context menu.

   All the objects will be selected, and they will be painted with the attributes, effects, and appearances from the compound path—not their original, pre-compound appearances **2**. Use Smart Guides (Object Highlighting) to figure out which shape is what.

➤ The released objects will all be nested within the same top-level layer that originally contained the compound path.

➤ A compound path is created automatically when the Create Outlines command is used on a type character that has a counter (interior shape). If you release this type of compound path, the counter will become a separate shape with the same paint attributes and appearances as the outer part of the letterform **3**–**4**.

1 *Click on the compound path.*

2 *The compound path is released. The buttonholes are no longer transparent.*

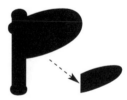

3 *Type outlines (a compound path)*

4 *The compound path is released into separate objects. (We moved the counter of the "P.")*

Chapter 17: Combine Paths ◆ Study Guide

Learning Objectives

- Understand shape modes.
- Understand pathfinder commands.
- Work with compound paths.

Get Up and Running Exercises

- Compare compound shapes and compound paths. Draw two objects with different fill colors and overlap them. Duplicate them. You should end up with two copies, such as those in the figure below.

  - ▲ Apply the Intersect shape mode to one pair of objects and the Crop pathfinder to the other. How are the results similar and different?
  - ▲ What happens when you release each example?

- Using the Ellipse tool, draw a filled circle and duplicate it until you have four circles in a row, as in the object in the left side of the figure below. Convert the four circles into one compound path. Without changing the fill color or editing any subpaths, how can you make all overlapping areas unfilled, as in the object in the right side of the figure below, in a single step?

Class Discussion Questions

- What's the difference between shape modes and pathfinder commands?
- What's the difference between a compound shape and a compound path?
- Why are there rules for how a fill is applied to compound paths?

Review Questions

Multiple choice

1. Which shape mode preserves only the areas of selected objects that overlap?

   A. Add to shape area

   B. Exclude overlapping shape areas

   C. Intersect shape areas

   D. Subtract from shape area

2. Which pathfinder works like a clipping mask, except that the original objects can't be restored by any method other than Undo?

   A. Crop

   B. Merge

   C. Minus Back

   D. Trim

3. Which shape mode deletes areas shared by all selected shapes?

   A. Add to shape area

   B. Exclude overlapping shape areas

   C. Intersect shape areas

   D. Subtract from shape area

4. Which pathfinder preserves the frontmost object and unites adjacent or overlapping objects that have the same fill attributes?

   A. Crop

   B. Merge

   C. Outline

   D. Trim

Fill-in-the-blank

1. When a shape mode is applied to objects of differing colors, the color attributes of the _____ selected object are applied to the resulting compound shape.

2. To convert a compound shape into a single path, _____ it.

3. To restore the original objects that were selected to create a compound shape, choose the _____ command from the Pathfinder palette menu.

4. If stroke colors aren't deleted when the Trim or Merge pathfinder is applied, it's because _____.

5. When you apply a shape mode, the resulting object is labeled on the Layers palette with the name _____.

6. You can switch the filled and unfilled states in any object in a compound path by selecting it with the _____ tool, then clicking either the _____ button or the _____ button.

Definitions

1. What is a shape mode?

2. What is a pathfinder?

3. What is a compound shape?

4. What is a compound path?

GRADIENTS 18

A gradient fill is a gradual blend between two or more colors.
In this chapter you will learn how to fill an object or objects
with a gradient; create and save gradients; edit a gradient using
the Gradient palette; and change the way a gradient fills an
object or objects using the Gradient tool.

You will also learn how to use the Mesh tool, the Gradient
Mesh command, and the Expand command to create painterly
gradient mesh objects, and how to modify mesh objects by
adding, moving, deleting, or recoloring mesh points and lines.

Chris Spollen, New York Retro

Gradient basics

Gradients are used to create volume in realistic objects or to soften abstract shapes. The simplest gradient fill consists of a starting color and an ending color, with the point where the colors are equally mixed together located midway between them. A gradient can be **linear** (side-to-side) or **radial** (outward-from-center). You can apply a gradient fill to one object or across several objects. A set of predefined gradients is supplied with Illustrator, but you can also create your own gradients using the **Gradient palette**.

Once an object is filled with a gradient, you can use the **Gradient tool** to modify how the fill is distributed within the object. You can change the direction of the gradient, or change how quickly one color blends into another. You can also change the location of the center of a radial gradient fill.

You'll be using the Color, Gradient, and Swatches palettes for the instructions in this chapter.

Follow these instructions to apply an existing gradient to an object. You can use a gradient that's supplied with Illustrator, but you're more than likely going to want or need to create your own. To create your own gradient, follow the instructions that begin on the next page.

To fill an object with a gradient:

1. Select an object, then click a gradient swatch on the Swatches palette 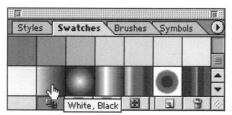–**2**.
   or
   Drag a gradient swatch from the Swatches palette or the Gradient Fill box from the Gradient palette over a selected or unselected object.

2. *Optional:* If the object contains a Linear gradient, you can select it and then change the Angle on the Gradient palette.

➤ If a selected object has a solid color or pattern fill, but it previously had a gradient fill, you can reapply the gradient by clicking the Gradient Fill box on the Gradient palette **3**, or clicking the Gradient button on the Toolbox, or pressing "." (period).

➤ You can't apply a gradient to a stroke, but here's a workaround: Make the stroke the desired width, apply Object > Path > Outline Stroke to convert the stroke into a closed object (see page 303), then apply the gradient.

➤ To fill type with a gradient, first convert it into outlines (Type > Create Outlines). Or select the type, choose Add New Fill from the Appearance palette menu, then click a gradient swatch.

1 *A gradient is selected on the Swatches palette.*

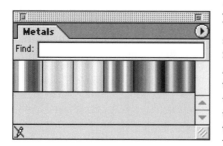

2 *An object filled with a radial gradient*

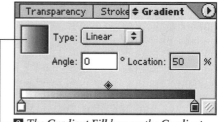

3 *The Gradient Fill box on the Gradient palette*

More gradients

To access the other gradient libraries that are supplied with Illustrator, choose Window > Swatch Libraries > Other Library, open the Adobe Illustrator 10 > Presets > Gradients folder, highlight the library you want to open, then click Open. If you click any swatch on the library palette, it will appear on your file's Swatches palette.

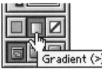

1 *First click the **Gradient Fill** box on the Gradient palette…*

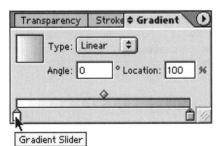

2 *…or on the Toolbox.*

3 *Choose a color for the **left gradient square** and the **right gradient square**.*

4 *Move the **midpoint diamond** to adjust the amount of each color.*

A gradient can be composed of all CMYK colors, all RGB process colors, tints of the same spot color, or multiple spot colors.

To create and save a two-color gradient:

1. Display the full Gradient palette, with its options panel.
2. Click the Gradient Fill box on the Gradient palette **1**.
   or
   Click the Gradient (middle) button on the Toolbox or press "." **2**.
3. Drag a solid color swatch from the Swatches palette over the left gradient square on the Gradient palette **3**.
   or
   Click the left gradient square on the Gradient palette. Then use the Color palette to mix a solid color; or Option-click/Alt-click a solid color swatch on the Swatches palette; or Shift-click a color anywhere in the document window using the Eyedropper tool.
4. Repeat the previous step to choose a solid color for the right gradient square.
5. From the Type pop-up menu on the Gradient palette, choose Linear or Radial.
6. *Optional:* Move the midpoint diamond to the right to produce more of the starting color than the ending color, or to the left to produce more of the ending color than the starting color **4**. Or click the diamond, then change the Location value.
7. *Optional:* For a Linear gradient, you can change the Angle.
8. If you select another object or swatch now, the new gradient will be lost—unless you save it. To save the gradient:
   Drag the Gradient Fill box from the Gradient palette onto the Swatches palette.
   or
   Click the Gradient Fill box on the Gradient palette, then click the New Swatch button at the bottom of the Swatches palette. **5**
   or

(Continued on the following page)

Create Two-Color Gradient

309

To name the gradient as you save it, click the Gradient Fill box on the Gradient palette, Option-click/Alt-click the New Swatch button on the Swatches palette, enter a name, then click OK.

➤ To swap the starting and ending colors or any other two colors in a radial or linear gradient, Option-drag/Alt-drag one square over the other.

➤ To delete a gradient swatch from the Swatches palette, drag it over the Delete Swatch (trash) button.

It's hard to tell whether a gradient is going to look good until it's been applied to an object. Luckily, gradients are easy to edit. You can either recolor a gradient in an object and leave the swatch alone or you can assign new colors to a gradient swatch, with or without recoloring any objects that the gradient is currently applied to.

To assign new colors to a gradient:

1. Choose the Selection tool, then click an object that contains the gradient you want to edit. For type, click the type, then click the Fill attribute on the Appearance palette that has a gradient icon, if it isn't already active.
   or
   Click the gradient swatch on the Swatches palette that you want to edit. In addition, you may also select any objects that contain that gradient.

2. On the Gradient palette, click the gradient square you want to change. Then choose a color from the Color palette or Option-click/Alt-click a solid color on the Swatches palette.
   or
   Drag a solid color swatch from the Swatches palette over a gradient square.

3. To resave the edited swatch, Option-drag/Alt-drag from the Gradient Fill box over the swatch.

Start from something

To use an existing gradient as a starting point for a new gradient, click a gradient swatch on the Swatches palette, choose **Duplicate Swatch** from the palette menu, then edit the gradient (see the instructions on this page).

Color-separating gradients

■ To color-separate a gradient that changes from a spot color to white on one piece of film (one plate), create a gradient with the spot color as the starting color and **0%** tint of the **same** color as the ending color.

■ If you're going to color-separate a gradient that contains more than one spot color, get some advice from your prepress specialist. He or she may tell you to assign a different screen angle to each color using File > Separation Setup (uncheck Convert to Process). See page 512. If you need to convert each spot color to a process color, click the spot color square, then choose a process color model from the Color palette menu.

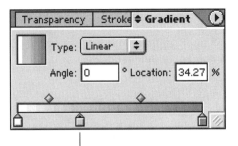

1 *Click below the gradient bar to add a new square, then choose a color.*

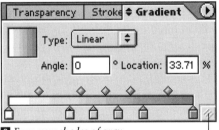

2 *Four new shades of gray were added to this gradient.*

You can drag the resize box to widen the palette if your gradient contains a lot of colors.

3 *Multicolored gradients*

A gradient can contain over 100 colors. The colors can be changed and color squares can be added or removed at any time.

To add colors to a gradient:

1. Follow the steps starting on page 309 to produce a two-color gradient.
   or
   On the Swatches palette, click an existing gradient swatch.

2. On the Gradient palette, click below the gradient bar to add a gradient square **1**. Then use the Color palette to mix a color or Option-click/Alt-click a swatch on the Swatches palette.
   or
   Drag a solid color swatch from the Swatches palette over to the gradient bar on the Gradient palette. A new square will be created automatically.

3. *Do any of the following optional steps:*

   Move a square to the left or to the right to change how abruptly that color spreads into its adjacent colors.

   Move the midpoint diamond located above the gradient bar to the left or right of the new color to adjust the amount of that color.

   ➤ To remove a square, drag it downward out of the Gradient palette.

   Repeat step 2 to add more colors **2**–**3**.

4. If you edited an existing swatch, Option-drag/Alt-drag from the Gradient Fill box on the Gradient palette over the swatch.
   or
   If you created a multicolored gradient from scratch, or if you want to save your modified gradient as a new swatch instead of saving over the original, drag it to the Swatches palette without holding down Option/Alt. Also remember to save your document!

   ➤ To make a gradient appear in every new Illustrator document, save it in either or both of the two Illustrator Startup files (see page 433).

   ➤ Option-drag/Alt-drag a square to copy it.

Multicolor Gradients

You've already learned how to edit a gradient swatch. Now you'll learn how to adjust the angle and location of a gradient in an object using the Gradient tool. You can change how abruptly colors blend, change the angle of a linear fill, or change the center location of a radial gradient fill. On the next page, you'll learn how to apply a gradient across a series of objects.

To use the Gradient tool:

1. Apply a gradient fill to an object, and keep the object selected.

2. Choose the Gradient tool (G).

3. Drag across the object in any direction (e.g., right-to-left or diagonally):

   To blend the colors abruptly, drag a short distance **1**–**3**. To blend the colors more gradually across a wider span, drag a longer distance.

   To reverse the order of the colors in a linear gradient, drag in the opposite direction.

   For a radial gradient, position the pointer where you want the center of the fill to be, then click or drag **4**–**5**.

   ➤ You can start to drag or finish dragging with the pointer outside the object. In this case, the colors at the beginning or end of the gradient fill won't show up in the object.

4. If you don't like the results, drag in a different direction. Keep trying until you're satisfied with the results.

➤ If you use the Gradient tool on an object and then apply a different gradient to the same object, the Gradient tool effect will be applied to the new gradient.

➤ To restore the original gradient to the object, make sure the object is selected, then click the swatch on the Swatches palette once. If you edited the gradient, you may need to click the swatch more than once.

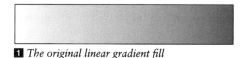

1 *The original linear gradient fill*

2 *Dragging a short distance with the **Gradient tool***

3 *After using the Gradient tool, as shown in the previous figure*

4 *The original radial gradient fill*

5 *After dragging outward from the center of the rose with the Gradient tool: The center of the gradient is in a new location.*

To spread a gradient across multiple objects:

1. Select several objects, and fill them all with the same gradient **1**.
2. Choose the Gradient tool (G). █
3. Drag across all the objects **2**. Shift-drag to constrain the angle to a multiple of 45° (actually, to a multiple of the current Constrain Angle in Edit > Preferences > General).

➤ Once multiple objects are filled with the same gradient, don't combine them into a compound path. Doing so may change how the gradient looks, and the resulting object may also be too complex to print.

1 This is the original gradient fill. The gradient starts *anew in each type outline*.

2 After dragging across all the objects using the **Gradient tool** in the direction shown by the arrow. The gradient starts in the **first** type outline and ends in the **last** type outline.

Gradient meshes

What is a gradient mesh?

A gradient mesh is an object that contains multiple gradients in various directions and locations with seamless transitions between them **1**. Using the gradient mesh features, you'll be able to easily render and modify photorealistic or painterly objects and complex modeled surfaces, such as skin tones, objects of nature, or machinery.

Both the **Mesh tool** and the **Create Gradient Mesh command** convert a standard object into a mesh object with lines and intersecting points. A gradient mesh can be produced from any path object or bitmapped image, even a radial or linear blend. To produce a mesh from a compound path, text object, or linked image, it must be rasterized first.

After you create a mesh object, you'll assign colors to mesh points or mesh patches. Then you can add or delete gradient colors or sharpen or soften color transitions by manipulating the points and lines. It's like a watercolor or airbrush drawing with a flexible armature above it. Reconfigure the armature, and the colors beneath the armature will shift right along with it.

Mesh building blocks

A mesh object consists of anchor points, mesh points, mesh lines, and mesh patches **2**. A gradient mesh can be reshaped by manipulating its anchor or mesh points or mesh lines.

- **Anchor points** on the bounding box appear as square points in the mesh. They are the standard Illustrator anchor points that can be added, deleted, or moved in order to reshape the overall object.

- **Mesh points** are diamond-shaped (called "anchor points" by Smart Guides). They are used for assigning colors to gradients, and they can be added, deleted, or moved.

- **Mesh lines** crisscross the object to connect the mesh points. They act as guides for placing and moving points.

- A **mesh patch** is an area that is defined by four mesh points.

Mesh another way

The Object > Envelope Distort > **Make with Mesh** command can also be used to produce a mesh. It will have the same components, and can be edited using the same techniques, as a mesh created using the Mesh tool or Gradient Mesh command (see pages 315–316).

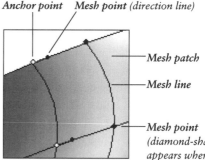

1 Illustrator's **gradient mesh** features are ideal for rendering naturalistic forms.

Anchor point   Mesh point (direction line)

Mesh patch

Mesh line

Mesh point (diamond-shaped; appears where two mesh lines intersect)

2 Gradient mesh objects have anchor points, mesh points, mesh lines, and mesh patches. This is a closeup.

Gradient Mesh Building Blocks

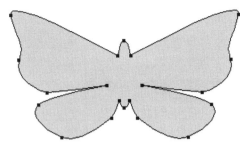

1 *Select an object that has a fill.*

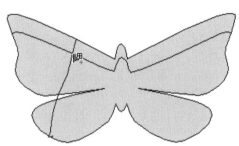

2 *Click the object—it will convert immediately into a **gradient mesh** object.*

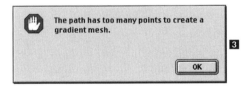

The path has too many points to create a gradient mesh.

OK

3

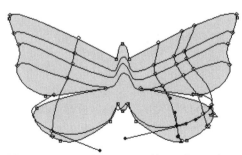

4 *Continue to click to create additional sets of mesh lines.*

Note: If you're converting a complex object into a gradient mesh, your best bet is to use the Create Gradient Mesh command. If you're converting simple objects, on the other hand, you can use either the Create Gradient Mesh command or the Mesh tool, whichever you prefer. The Gradient Mesh command creates more regularly spaced mesh points and lines than the Mesh tool.

Beware! A mesh object cannot be converted back to a path object except by choosing Undo.

To convert an object into a gradient mesh using the Mesh tool:

1. Select an object (not a text object, compound path, or linked image) and apply a solid color fill to the object if it doesn't already have one **1**. The object can have an applied brush stroke, but the brush stroke will be removed. You can use a bitmap image. Copy the object before you convert it if you want to preserve a non-gradient mesh version of it.

2. Choose the Mesh tool (U).

3. Click on the object to place a mesh point. The object will be converted immediately into a mesh object with the minimum number of mesh lines **2**.

   If you get an alert box **3**, it means you must remove points from the path before you can convert it into a gradient mesh. You can do this using the Delete-anchor-point tool or the Smooth tool.

4. Click to create additional sets of mesh lines **4**.

5. Proceed to page 317 to learn how to apply colors to the mesh.

Create Gradient Mesh

Note: Complex gradient meshes increase file size and require a significant amount of computation, so try to keep them as simple as is reasonably possible. To avoid printing errors, build your drawing from a few mesh objects instead of one large, complex mesh.

To convert an object into a gradient mesh using a command:

1. Choose the Selection tool (V), select an object (not a text object, compound path, or linked image), and apply a solid color fill to the object if it doesn't already have one. The object can have an applied brush stroke, but the brush stroke will be removed. You can use a bitmap image. Copy the object if you want to preserve a non-gradient mesh version of it.

2. Choose Object > Create Gradient Mesh.

3. Click Preview **1**.

4. Enter the number of horizontal Rows and vertical Columns for the mesh grid.

5. From the Appearance pop-up menu, choose Flat for a uniform surface with no highlight; To Center for a highlight at the center of the object; or To Edge for a highlight at the edges of the object.

6. If you chose the To Center or To Edge Appearance option, enter an intensity percentage (0–100%) for the white Highlight.

7. Click OK **2**–**4**. Now recolor the gradient mesh (instructions on the next page).

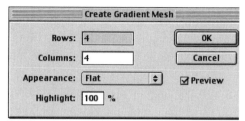

1 *The Create Gradient Mesh dialog box*

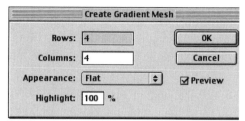

2 *Create Gradient Mesh command, Appearance: Flat*

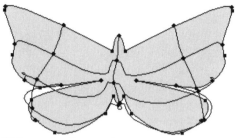

3 *Create Gradient Mesh command, Appearance: To Center*

4 *Create Gradient Mesh command, Appearance: To Edge (shown here on a dark background so you can see the highlight on the edge)*

Create Gradient Mesh

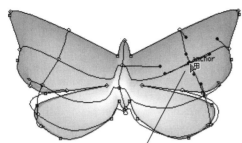

1 *Click an existing mesh point.*

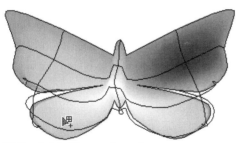

2 *The point is recolored.*

3 *Or click inside a mesh patch.*

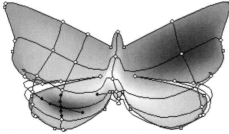

4 *A new mesh point is created.*

Each mesh point or mesh patch can be assigned a different color, and each color will blend into its surrounding colors. Click a mesh point to assign a color to a small area, or click a mesh patch to assign a color to a wider area.

To recolor a gradient mesh:

1. Zoom in on a mesh object (you should still see the entire object in the document window, though) and deselect it.

2. Choose the Direct-selection tool (A), then click the mesh object.

3. Do any of the following:

   Click a mesh point **1** or marquee several points, then choose a fill color from the Color or Swatches palette **2**. You can also recolor mesh points using the Mesh tool (U), but select the object first using the Direct-selection tool, otherwise you won't be able to see where the points are, except by using Smart Guides (check Text Label Hints in Edit > Preferences > Smart Guides & Slices).

   Drag a color from the Swatches palette over a mesh point or mesh patch.

   Choose a fill color from the Swatches palette, choose the Mesh tool (U), then click inside a mesh patch **3**–**4**. A new point with connecting mesh lines will be created in the fill color you chose.

   Click a mesh patch, then choose a fill color from the Color or Swatches palette. The four mesh points that surround the patch will be recolored.

➤ Read about other ways to recolor a mesh object on the next page.

Recolor Gradient Mesh

To add mesh points or lines:

1. If the mesh object isn't already selected, choose the Direct-selection tool (A), then click the mesh object.

2. Choose the Mesh tool (U).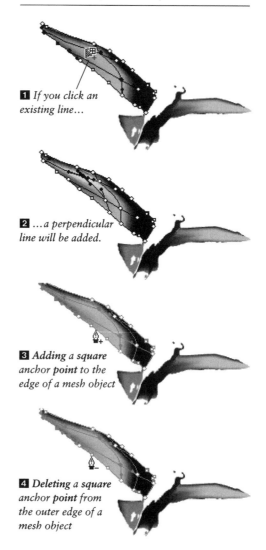

3. Choose a color from the Swatches or Color palette or using the Eyedropper tool (I), then click inside a mesh patch. A new point and connecting mesh lines will appear, and the current fill color will be applied to that point.

   or

   Choose a fill color, then click an existing mesh line to add a new line perpendicular to it **1**–**2**.

   or

   Shift-click a mesh line to add a mesh point using the existing color from that line.

4. *Optional:* To recolor the new mesh point with a color from another part of the same object, keep the point selected, choose the Eyedropper tool (I), then Shift-click a color in the object.

➤ You can also recolor a gradient mesh using Filter > Colors > Adjust Colors, Convert to CMYK (or Convert to RGB), Invert Colors, or Saturate.

Follow these instructions to add or remove square-shaped (not diamond-shaped) anchor points from a mesh object. These points are used to reshape the edge of the overall mesh object—not to push colors around on the mesh. To add diamond-shaped mesh points with their connecting mesh lines, follow the previous set of instructions instead.

To add or remove square points:

1. Select a mesh object and zoom in on it, if necessary.

2. To add an anchor point, choose the Add-anchor-point tool (+), then click the outer edge of the mesh object or click a mesh line inside the object **3**.

   or

   To delete a user-created anchor point, choose the Delete-anchor-point tool (-), then click the point **4**.

Recoloring tips

To select and recolor multiple instances of the same color, choose the Direct-selection tool, click a mesh point that contains the color you want to change, choose Select > Same > **Fill Color**, then choose a new color from the Color palette or the Swatches palette.

To make a color area **smaller**, add more mesh lines around it in a different color. To **spread** a color, delete mesh points around it or assign the same color to adjacent mesh points.

1 *If you click an existing line...*

2 *...a perpendicular line will be added.*

3 *Adding a square anchor point to the edge of a mesh object*

4 *Deleting a square anchor point from the outer edge of a mesh object*

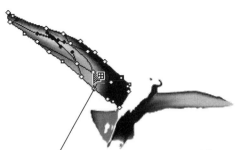

1 *Option-click/Alt-click a mesh point to delete it.*

2 *The point is deleted.*

3 *Drag a direction line.*

4 *Drag a mesh point.*

When a mesh point is deleted, the mesh lines that cross through that point are also deleted.

To delete a mesh point:

1. Choose the Direct-selection tool (A), then click the gradient mesh object to select it.

2. Click the mesh point you want to delete, then press Delete/Backspace.
   or
   Choose the Mesh tool (U), then Option-click/Alt-click the point you want to delete (a minus sign will appear next to the pointer) **1**–**2**.

To reshape mesh lines:

1. Choose the Direct-selection tool (A), then click the gradient mesh object to select it.

2. Click a mesh point or an anchor point.

3. Do any of the following:

   Lengthen or rotate either of the point's direction lines to reshape its adjacent mesh lines **3**. To constrain the line angle to a multiple of 45° (or the current Constrain Angle in Edit > Preferences > General), start dragging the line, then Shift-drag.

   Drag a mesh point **4**. You can drag a point outside the object. This is an easy, fun way to push mesh colors around.

   Drag a mesh patch **5**. This is like electronic sculpting. You can drag a patch outside the object.

   Shift-drag a mesh point to drag it along an existing mesh line.

   To convert a mesh point into a corner point with direction lines that move independently of each other, choose the Convert-direction-point tool (Shift-C), click the point, then drag one of its direction lines.

5 *Drag a mesh patch.*

Delete Mesh Points; Reshape Mesh Lines

To expand a standard gradient into separate objects:

1. Select the object that contains a gradient (not a gradient mesh) 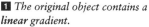.

2. Choose Object > Expand.

3. Click Expand Gradient To: Specify, then enter the desired number of objects to be created **2**. To print a gradient successfully, you'll need to enter a number that's high enough to produce smooth color transitions.

4. Click OK **3**. *Note:* The resulting number of objects may not match the specified number of objects if there were minimal color changes in the original gradient.

➤ You could also use the Expand command to simplify a gradient fill that won't print.

➤ To expand a gradient using the last-used "Specify [ ] Objects" setting, hold down Option/Alt and choose Object > Expand.

Here is another, albeit less-useful, method for creating a mesh object.

To expand a radial or linear gradient into a gradient mesh:

1. Select an object that contains a radial or linear gradient **1**.

2. Choose Object > Expand.

3. Click Expand Gradient To: Gradient Mesh.

4. Click OK **4**. The resulting expanded objects can be a little confusing. You'll have a clipping path object that limits the gradient color area, with the mesh object below it. Use the Layers palette to view the nested groups, clipping path, and mesh.

Bird by Diane Margolin

1 *The original object contains a linear gradient.*

2 *In the Expand dialog box, Specify the number of Objects the Gradient will be expanded into.*

3 *After applying the Expand command, the gradient is converted into a series of separate rectangles, grouped with a clipping mask. Each rectangle is a different shade.*

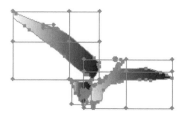

4 *This is the original object after expanding it into a gradient mesh.*

Chapter 18: Gradients ◆ Study Guide

Learning Objectives

■ Fill an object with a gradient.

■ Create and save gradients.

■ Edit a gradient using the Gradient palette and the Gradient tool.

■ Apply a gradient mesh to an object.

Get Up and Running Exercises

■ Draw a shape, and apply a black-to-white linear gradient to it. How might you use a linear gradient to shade an object?

▲ Can you draw a pen, and then apply a linear gradient to shade the pen's cyndrilical shape?

▲ Can you draw a circle and then apply a radial gradient to shade the circle to make it look like a sphere?

■ Create a multicolor gradient and save it with the current document so that it can be reused.

■ Apply a gradient to type. What extra step must be performed in order to do this? Then, how do you make a single gradient extend across the entire word or paragraph, instead of individual gradients in each letter?

■ Use a gradient mesh to model a real-world object. Find an object with uneven shading, such as drapery, clothing, landforms, a human face, a car, or the body of an airplane, and try to model the surface using a gradient mesh.

Class Discussion Questions

- What are the similarities and differences between gradients, gradient meshes, and blends?
- How do you edit a gradient once it's applied to an object?
- What are some issues to be concerned with when color-separating gradients?
- How do you control gradient meshes?

Review Questions

Multiple choice

1. Which of the following types of objects can be converted to a mesh object?
   - A. A compound path
   - B. A linked image
   - C. A shape drawn with the Star tool
   - D. A type object

2. Which feature stores a gradient in the current document?
   - A. A gradient library
   - B. The Gradient palette
   - C. The Gradient tool
   - D. The Swatches palette

3. Which feature lets you shape gradients in a freeform manner, as if sculpting surfaces?
   - A. Gradient tool
   - B. Gradient palette
   - C. Mesh tool
   - D. Radial gradient

4. In a gradient mesh, where would you drop a color in order to change multiple mesh points at once with one click?
   - A. Mesh lines
   - B. Mesh patch
   - C. Mesh point
   - D. Anchor point

Fill-in-the-blank

1. To make a gradient appear in every new Illustrator document, save it in _____.

2. You can change the angle of a linear gradient by using the Gradient palette or the _____.

3. In Illustrator, the only way to apply a gradient to a stroke is _____.

4. To add a new color to a gradient, _____.

5. You can make a gradient mesh by using the Gradient tool or _____.

Definitions

1. What is a gradient?

2. What is a linear gradient?

3. What is a radial gradient?

4. What is a gradient mesh?

APPEARANCES/STYLES

In this chapter you will learn how to create, apply, copy, modify, and remove appearance attributes, which are editable strokes, fills, effects, transparency settings, etc. You will also learn how to use the Styles palette to save appearance attributes as styles; apply styles to an object, group, or layer; and copy, edit, merge, and delete styles.

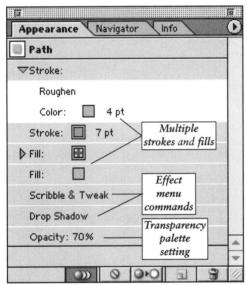

1 *The Appearance palette is used to apply, restack, and remove **appearance attributes** from layers, sublayers, groups, objects, and styles. This screenshot illustrates the appearance attributes for an **object**.*

Using appearances

Appearances provide a whole new approach to object editing. Before appearances, you could apply only one stroke and fill to an object. With appearances, you can now apply multiple fills and strokes to the same object, and to each stroke or fill you can apply a different opacity level, blending mode, or Effect menu command. Furthermore, appearance attributes change how an object looks, but they don't actually alter the path's underlying shape. Appearances add flexibility—and complexity—to object editing.

Since appearance attributes only change an object's appearance, not its actual underlying path, you can save, close, and reopen an illustration, and you'll still be able to re-edit or remove the appearance attributes in the saved file. When an object is selected, its appearance attributes are listed on the Appearance palette. This palette is also used to re-edit, restack, and remove appearance attributes.

➤ Copy an object, then experiment with different appearance attributes for each copy. No commitment, no obligation. Create a handful of variations on a basic shape, and then gradually hone in until you achieve a combination or combinations of appearance attributes that you're satisfied with.

➤ Once you learn about the Appearance palette, read the Effects & Filters chapter to learn how to apply editable effects.

Appearances and layers

If attributes other than just the basic stroke and fill have been applied to an object, those additional attributes are called **appearance attributes**, and a gray **target circle** will appear for that object on the Layers palette **1**.

Instead of applying appearance attributes to individual objects one by one, you can also target a whole top-level layer or group for appearances. In this case, the appearance attributes that you choose will apply to all the objects nested within the targeted layer or group. For example, if you target a layer and then modify its opacity or blending mode, all objects nested within that layer will have the same opacity or blending mode, and that attribute can be re-edited quickly by retargeting the layer.

These are the basic techniques:

➤ To **select** an object or group, click the **selection area** or the **target circle** on the Layers palette. To select (not target) a layer, click the selection area (see the sidebar on this page).

➤ To **target** an object, group, or layer for **appearance attributes**, click the **target** circle on the Layers palette.

➤ To **view** and **modify** the existing **appearance attributes** for an object, group, or layer, click the **gray** target circle; Shift-click the gray circle to deselect that object, group, or layer.

To target appearances to a group or layer:

To target appearance attributes to a whole group or top-level layer, click its target circle on the Layers palette. A ring will appear around the circle, indicating an active target, and all the objects in that group or on that layer will become selected in the illustration. (Shift-click the ring to un-target.)

Layers and appearances

Even though selecting and targeting both cause objects to become selected in your illustration, they are not interchangeable operations when you're working with whole layers. If you **target** a layer by clicking its target circle and then apply appearance attributes (e.g., fill color, Effect menu command, Transparency palette values), those attributes will be applied to, and will be listed on the Appearance palette for, the layer as a **whole**.

If you click the **selection** area for a layer instead of the target circle and then apply appearances, those attributes will be applied separately to each object or group in that layer, not to the layer as a whole. In this case, you won't see an itemized list of appearance attributes on the Appearance palette—you'll just see the generic words "mixed appearances" at the top of the palette. Nor will they be listed if you subsequently target the layer.

This layer is active, but not targeted, and it doesn't contain appearances.

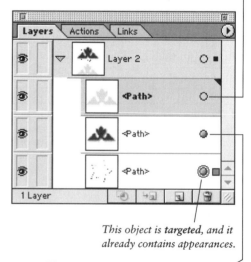

This object is targeted, and it already contains appearances.

1 *This path object contains appearances, but it's not currently targeted.*

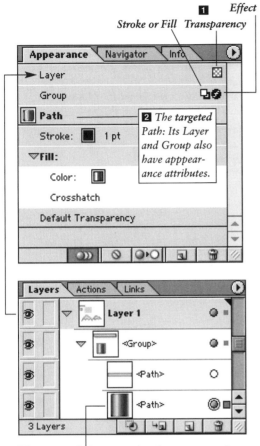

Effect

Stroke or Fill Transparency

1

2 *The targeted Path: Its Layer and Group also have appearance attributes.*

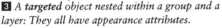

3 *A targeted object nested within a group and a layer: They all have appearance attributes.*

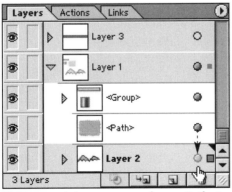

4 *Moving existing appearances from a <Path> to a layer (Layer 2)*

Understanding the icons

One of three icons may display in the upper portion of the Appearance palette to the right of the word "Layer" or "Group" **1**:

➤ 🖵 means a stroke or fill is applied to a layer or group.

➤ 🖊 means an effect is applied to a layer or group.

➤ ▨ means transparency is applied to a layer or group.

The generic name for the currently targeted item—"Layer," "Group," "Path," etc.— is listed in boldface at the top of the Appearance palette. If an object is targeted, and that object is nested within a layer and/or group to which appearance attributes have been applied, the words "Layer" and/or "Group" will also appear above the word "Path" at the top of the palette **2**–**3**.

10.0!

Note! If the selected object is a mesh, the word "Mesh" will appear instead of the word "Path." The same holds true for type ("Type"), an image ("Image"), a symbol ("Symbol"), an envelope ("Envelope"), a compound shape ("Compound Shape")— you get the idea. Whatever name appears on the Layers palette will also appear on the Appearance palette.

To copy or move appearance attributes via the Layers palette:

To copy appearance attributes, Option-drag/ Alt-drag the target circle for the item from which you want to copy onto the target circle for another layer, group, or object. Pause for the appearances to copy.

or

To move appearance attributes from one item to another, drag a target circle from one layer, group, or object to another without holding down any keys **4**. The appearance attributes will be removed from the original layer, group, or object.

Palette Icons: Copy, Move Appearances

When you apply appearance attributes, your object will have a totally new look that can be modified or removed at any time, even after the file is saved, closed, and reopened.

To apply appearance attributes:

1. In the document window, select the object whose appearance attributes you want to modify.
   or
   On the Layers palette, click the gray circle for a layer, group, or object to target that item for appearance changes.

2. Display the Appearance palette (Window > Appearance).

3. On the Appearance palette, do any of the following **1**:

   Click Stroke to select the Stroke square on the Color palette, then modify the stroke color and/or stroke width via the Stroke palette.

   Click Fill to select the Fill square on the Color palette, then modify the fill color.

   Double-click Default Transparency (or the current transparency appearance attribute) to show the Transparency palette, then modify the Opacity value and/or change the blending mode.

   Choose a command from a submenu on the Effect menu (for starters, try an effect from the Distort & Transform or Stylize submenu), modify the dialog box settings, then click OK. The Effect command will be listed at the top of the attributes area of the palette. (Read more about effects on pages 379–382.)

   Note: Remember to choose appearance commands from the Effect menu, not the Filter menu. Filter menu commands will permanently rasterize an object. Effect menu commands, on the other hand, since they are vector effects, can be re-edited or removed at any time without permanently changing the object. Some of the vector filters, for which there are Effect menu equivalents, are illustrated on pages 396–403.

Working with attributes

If a layer or group is targeted, the word **Contents** will appear on the attributes list on the Appearance palette. If an individual text object is targeted, you'll see the word **Type**. If an object with gradient mesh fill is targeted, you'll see the words **Mesh Points**.

Moving any attribute up or down on the palette changes the order and appearance of that attribute on the actual item.

The item that the appearance attributes are being targeted to is listed at the top of the palette: **Layer, Group,** *or* **Object.**

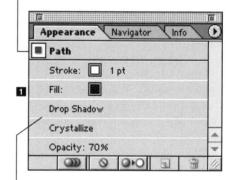

The actual **appearance attributes** *are listed in this part of the palette.*

Apply Appearances

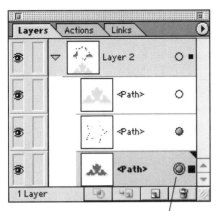

1 *A path is* **targeted** *on the Layers palette.*

2 *The* **Fill** *appearance attribute is clicked on the* **Appearance** *palette.*

3 *Various attributes are applied, and then the* **Fill** *list is expanded.*

Aside from merely listing appearance attributes, the Appearance palette can also be used to open palettes and other dialog boxes (e.g., Effect menu, Stroke) for previously applied appearance attributes in order to edit them.

To edit or restack appearance attributes:

1. In the document window, select the object whose appearance attributes you want to modify.
   or
   On the Layers palette, click the gray circle for a layer, group, or object to target that item for appearance changes.

2. On the Appearance palette, double-click any appearance attribute to open its dialog box or show its palette, and make modifications.
   and/or
   Drag any appearance attribute (except Object Opacity) upward or downward on the list. Not only will its location change on the list, but its appearance on the actual object will change because of its new stacking position. For example, if you drag a stroke below a fill attribute and then lower the opacity of the fill attribute, the stroke will then show through the fill.

To edit a stroke or fill appearance attribute:

1. Target an object **1**. (To apply a stroke or fill to a layer or group, see next page.)

2. On the Appearance palette, click Stroke or Fill **2**.

3. Change the opacity or blending mode using the Transparency palette and/or apply an Effect menu command. These attributes will apply only to the selected Stroke or Fill—not to the whole object.

   Click the triangle for the Stroke or Fill list to see its nested attributes **3**; click the triangle again to collapse the list.

   A brush can be applied to a stroke. The brush name will appear next to the Stroke attribute on the Appearance palette. Double-click the brush name to open the Stroke Options dialog box.

Edit, Restack Appearances

To remove a brush stroke from a stroke attribute:

1. Target a layer, group, or object.

2. Show the Brushes palette, then click the Remove Brush Stroke button [X] at the bottom of the palette.
   or
   Click the Stroke attribute on the Appearance palette, then click the Delete Selected Item (trash) button at the bottom of the palette. The stroke becomes None.

To apply multiple stroke or fill attributes:

1. Target a layer, group, or object **1**.

2. Choose Add New Fill or Add New Stroke from the Appearance palette menu. *Mac OS:* Cmd-/ or Cmd-Option-/; *Windows:* Ctrl-/ or Ctrl-Alt-/.
   or
   Click an existing Stroke or Fill on the Appearance palette, then click the Duplicate Selected Item button [ ] at the bottom of the palette **2**.
   or
   Drag Stroke or Fill over the Duplicate Selected Item button [ ] at the bottom of the Appearance palette.

3. A new Stroke or Fill attribute will appear on the palette **3**–**4**. Now modify its attributes.

➤ Make sure narrower strokes are stacked above wider strokes on the palette list. If the narrower strokes are on the bottom, you won't see them. Similarly, apply opacity and blending modes to upper fill attributes, not the lower ones.

➤ If a layer, group, or object has multiple Fills or Strokes, be careful about clicking the specific attribute you want to modify.

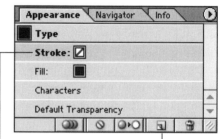

1 *Select the original text object using the Selection tool. This text has a stroke and fill of None.*

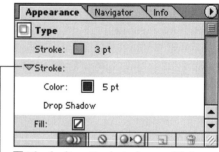

2 *Click the attribute you want to duplicate, then click the **Duplicate Selected Item** button.*

3 *The duplicate Stroke is then modified.*

4 *After duplicating the Stroke, widening the duplicate, and applying the Drop Shadow effect to the duplicate*

Remove Brush Stroke; Apply Multiple Appearances

To duplicate an appearance attribute:

I. Target a layer, group, or object.

2. Choose Duplicate Item from the Appearance palette menu.
   or
   Click an attribute, then click the Duplicate Selected Item button at the bottom of the palette. Or drag an attribute over that button.

To remove an appearance attribute:

I. Target a layer, group, or object.

2. On the Appearance palette, click the attribute you want to remove.

3. Choose Remove Item from the palette menu.
   or
   Click the Delete Selected Item (trash) button at the bottom of the palette or drag the attribute over that button.

➤ The last remaining Fill and Stroke appearance attributes can't be removed. Clicking the Delete Selected Item (trash) button for either of these appearance attributes will produce a fill or stroke of None.

To remove all appearance attributes from an item:

1. Target an object, layer, sublayer, or group.

2. Click the Clear Appearance button ⌐☉⌐ at the bottom of the Appearance palette to remove all the appearance attributes and apply a stroke and fill of None.
or
Click the Reduce to Basic Appearance button ⌐☉▸☉⌐ at the bottom of the Appearance palette to remove all the appearance attributes and apply the bottommost stroke and fill **1**–**2**.

➤ If you target a layer or group, any appearances that were applied directly to nested paths within that layer or group won't be removed using the above commands. To remove appearances from a nested path, you need to target the path itself, not the path's layer or group.

To choose appearance options for new objects:

If the **New Art Has Basic Appearance** command on the Appearance palette menu has a checkmark or you click the **New Art Has Basic Appearance** button ⌐☉☉⌐ at the bottom of the palette, newly created objects will have only one fill and one stroke. With this option unchecked in either location, the currently displayed appearance attributes will apply automatically to new objects.

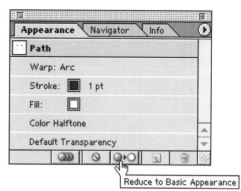

1 *Target a layer, group, or object, then click the **Reduce to Basic Appearance** button at the bottom of the Appearance palette.*

2 *All appearance attributes are removed from the targeted entity.*

10.0!

1 *The Drop Shadow effect was applied to the bottom horse, but not to the top one. The drop shadow gradually fades upward.*

Blends and appearances

If you blend objects that contain different appearance attributes (e.g., effects, fills, or strokes), those appearance attributes will be in full force in the original objects and have sequentially less intensity in the intermediate blend steps **1**. The blend command automatically nests the blend objects on a blend sublayer.

If you blend objects containing different blending modes, the blending mode for the topmost object will be applied to all the intermediate blend steps. The <Blend> sublayer on the Layers palette will have a gray target circle, indicating that an appearance attribute is applied to the objects. Also, the Knockout Group option will be checked on the Transparency palette by default. This prevents the blend steps from blending with or showing through each other. Uncheck Knockout Group if you want the blend steps to show through or blend with each other. Regardless of whether Knockout Group is on or off, though, objects behind the blend will always be visible if the blend objects are less than 100% opaque or have a blending mode other than Normal.

To attach appearance attributes to, and view the Transparency palette options for, an entire blend, first click the target circle for the <Blend> sublayer on the Layers palette, or select the blend with the Selection tool.

Blends and Appearances

Using styles

Styles are used to apply sets of attributes. Any kind of appearance attribute can be saved in a style, such as color, gradient, or pattern (stroke and fill); stroke attributes (weight, dash pattern, etc.); blending mode; transparency; or live effect. Even Attribute palette overprint options can be saved to a style. In short, any appearance attribute that can be applied to an object can also be saved as a style.

Styles are created, saved, and applied via the Styles palette **1**–**2**. Each style's individual attributes, however, are listed on the Appearance palette, and the Appearance palette is also used to create or modify those attributes.

There are three main advantages to working with styles:

■ By applying a style, you can apply many attributes at once with the click of a button. This saves you time and your employer or client money.

■ Like an appearance attribute, a style changes the way an object looks, but it doesn't actually change the underlying object. This means a style can be turned on or off easily, and a different style can be applied at any time.

■ If you edit a style, the style will update on any objects to which that style is already linked. This streamlines object editing and ensures consistency from object to object.

Illustrator styles differ in one significant way from styles in a layout or word processing program. If you modify an attribute directly on an object to which an Illustrator style is already applied, that modification breaks the link between the selected object and the style. The object's style attributes won't be removed, but if you subsequently edit the style, that object's appearance won't change because it is no longer associated with that style. This "local styling" has no effect on the original style, nor on any other objects that may be linked to that style.

1 Illustrator's **Default RGB** styles palette

The original object   Blue Goo

Flames   Pastel Pinstripes

Multicolored Dots   Soft Cast Shadow

2 We applied a few Illustrator **styles** to a star, just to give you an idea about what styles can do.

1 *The Styles palette in **Thumbnail View***

2 *The Styles palette in **Small List View***

3 *The Styles palette in **Large List View***

As always, we'd like you to learn a few ground rules first:

- A style can be applied to a layer, sublayer, group, or object. A style will be associated with all the objects in a layer or group, as well as any new objects that are added to a layer or group after the style is applied.

- Only one style can be associated with a layer, sublayer, group, or object at a time.

- If you close and reopen a file that contains styles, those styles will remain associated with the objects to which they were applied.

➤ To produce more dramatic results on a placed image or rasterized object, apply a style that contains raster effects (from the lower portion of the Effect menu). These effects can also be applied to vector objects.

To warm up, start by getting acquainted with the Styles palette.

To choose a view for the Styles palette:

1. Show the Styles palette (Window > Styles).

2. From the palette menu, choose one of the following:

   Thumbnail View to display styles as thumbnails only **1**.

   Small List View to display style names with small thumbnails **2**.

   Large List View to display style names with large thumbnails **3**.

Styles Palette Views

To apply a style to an object:

1. Choose the Selection tool (V), then select an object or objects in the document window.
   or
   On the Layers palette, click the target circle for an object –**2**.

   Remember, for a top-level layer, selecting and targeting have different functions! See page 181.

2. Click a style name or thumbnail on the Styles palette **3**–**4**.
   or
   Drag a style name or thumbnail from the Styles palette over a group or object in the illustration window. The object doesn't have to be selected.

➤ To access other Illustrator style libraries, choose from the Window > Style Libraries submenu (see page 338).

➤ The name of the currently applied style will be listed at the top of the Appearance palette.

If you apply a style to a layer or a group, that style will be applied to all the current and subsequently created objects on that smooth point, subsmooth point, or group.

To apply a style to a layer, sublayer, or group:

1. On the Layers palette, click the target circle for a layer, sublayer, or group.

2. Click a style name or thumbnail on the Styles palette **5**.

1 *The original text object*

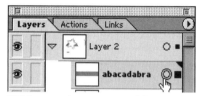

2 *The text object is **targeted** for an appearance change on the Layers palette.*

3 *Our custom Powder puff **swatch** is clicked.*

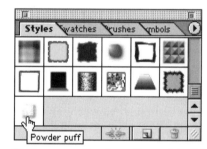

4 *The style appears on the **object**.*

5 *Here, the same style is also applied to a **group**.*

Apply Style

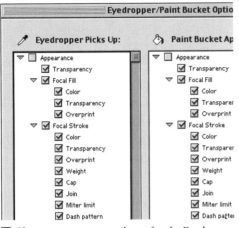

1 *Choose appearance attributes for the Eyedropper tool in* **Eyedropper/Paint Bucket Options.**

2 *An object is clicked on with the* **Eyedropper** *tool.*

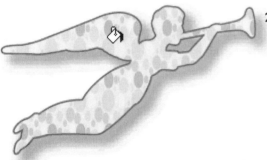

3 *An object is clicked on with the* **Paint Bucket** *tool. The style from the text object is applied to the angel.*

4 *Or drag this* **icon** *from the* **Appearance** *palette over an object.*

To copy a style or an appearance attribute from one object to another:
(Method 1)

1. Double-click the Eyedropper tool (I).

2. Check the Appearance box to activate all appearance options.
   or
   Click the triangle for Appearance, if that list isn't already expanded, then uncheck any attributes you don't want the Eyedropper to pick up.

3. Click OK **1**.

4. Click with the Eyedropper on the object whose style or appearance attributes you want to copy **2**.

5. Choose the Paint Bucket tool (K) or hold down Option/Alt to toggle to the Paint Bucket tool **3**.

6. Click the object or objects to which you want to apply the copied style.

➤ Don't try to copy a style from a group or layer using the Eyedropper.

(Method 2)

1. Choose the Selection tool (V), then click an object whose style or appearance attributes you want to copy.

2. Drag the square icon from the top left corner of the Appearance palette over an unselected object **4**.

To break the link between a style and a layer, sublayer, group, or object:

I. Choose the Selection tool (V), then select an object or objects in the illustration window, or click the target circle for an object on the Layers palette.

or

If the style was applied to a group or layer, click the target circle for a layer, sublayer, or group on the Layers palette.

2. Click the Break Link to Style button at the bottom of the Styles palette **1**.

or

Change any appearance attribute for the selected item (e.g., apply a different fill color, stroke color, pattern, gradient, or effect).

The style name will no longer be listed on the Appearance palette for the selected item.

Next, we offer two methods for creating a new style. In the first set of instructions, you will create a style based on an object. This method will probably feel the most natural and intuitive, especially if you're going to experiment with various settings for the new style. If you already have a good idea of what attributes you want the new style to have, follow the instructions on the next page instead.

To create a new style using an object:

I. Target an object that has the attributes you want to save as a style, then use the Appearance palette to create attributes you want the style to have **2**.

2. From the Styles palette menu, choose New Style, enter a name for the style, then click OK **3**. The new style will appear at the bottom of the list or below the existing swatches on the Styles palette **4**.

or

Drag the icon next to the item name from the top of the Appearance palette onto the Styles palette. Double-click the new style swatch, type a name for the style, then click OK.

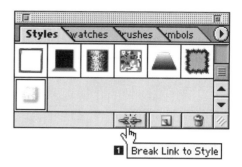

1 Break Link to Style

2 *Click the object whose attributes you want to* **save** *as a style.*

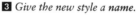

3 *Give the new style a* **name***.*

4 *The new style swatch appears at the bottom of the* **Styles** *palette.*

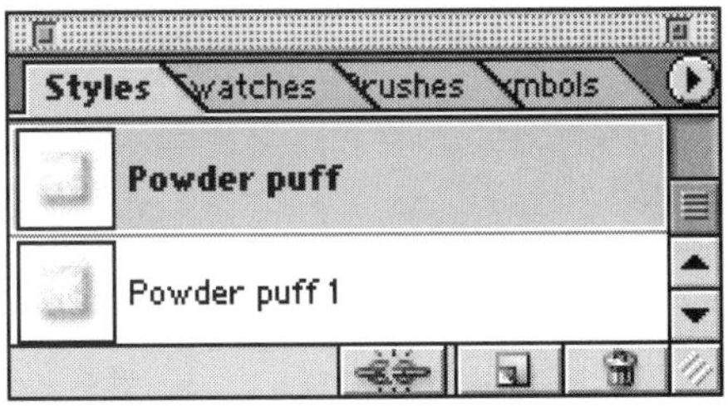

1 *Our Powder puff style is duplicated.*

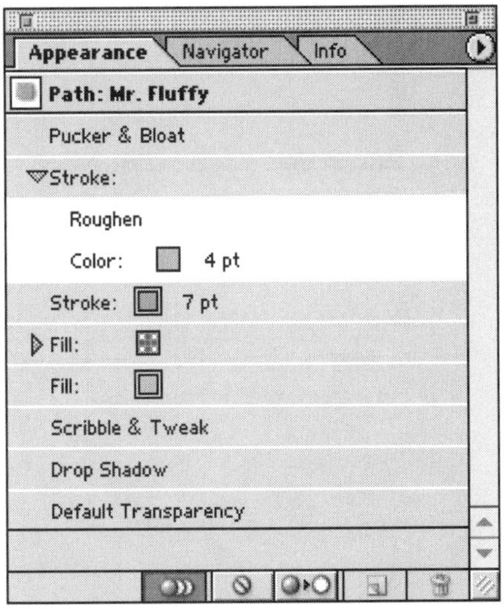

2 *The duplicate style is renamed, and then its attributes are edited via the Appearance palette. The style name is listed at the top of the palette.*

To duplicate a style:

1. On the Styles palette, click the style you want to copy.

2. Click the New Style button ⬚ or drag the swatch over the New Style button. The number "1" will be added to the existing style name **1**.

   or

   Choose Duplicate Style from the Styles palette menu, double-click the duplicate, type a name for the style, then click OK.

3. Click the duplicate style swatch or name, then use the Appearance palette to edit the style so that it contains the desired attributes **2**.

Duplicate a Style

Beware! If you edit a style, that style will update on any objects it was applied to prior to its being modified. If you don't want this to happen, duplicate the style instead (see the previous page) and then edit the duplicate.

To edit a style:

1. In order to "preview" your changes, apply the style you want to edit to an object **1**.

2. Via the Appearance palette, edit or restack the existing appearance attributes or add new attributes **2**.

3. Choose Redefine Style "[style name]" from the Appearance palette menu.
   or
   Option-drag/Alt-drag the object icon from the top left corner of the Appearance palette over the original style swatch on the Styles palette.

   With either method, the style swatch will update to reflect the modifications **3** and any objects to which the style is currently applied will update automatically **4**.

➤ While editing a style, don't click on other styled objects or style swatches, or you'll lose your current appearance attributes settings.

1 *Start by* **applying** *the style you want to edit to an object.*

2 *The style is edited on the object via the* **Appearance** *palette.*

3 *The style is replaced on the* **Styles** *palette.*

4 *The style also* **updates** *automatically on other objects to which it was previously applied.*

What stays; what goes

Attributes are listed on the Appearance palette in the order in which they are applied. The order of fills in the list of attributes on the Appearance palette is controlled by the order of swatches that were originally selected on the Styles palette. The fill of the selected style listed closest to the top of the Styles palette (in list view or swatch view) will be listed above any and all other fills in the merged style. If you merge styles that contain solid fills, only the topmost fill will be visible.

To achieve different results using the same fills, edit their opacity and/or blending modes or restack them on the Appearance palette list (and thus change the order in which they are applied).

If you have two styles whose attributes you want to combine into one style, you can merge them into one new, additional style. The original swatches won't be altered. Please read the sidebar at left.

To merge styles:

1. Cmd-click/Ctrl-click two or more style swatches or names on the Styles palette.

2. Choose Merge Styles from the Styles palette menu **1**.

3. Enter a name for the new merged style, then click OK **2**. A new style swatch will appear at the bottom of the list of names or below the existing swatches, depending on the current palette view **3**.

If you delete a style that's associated with any objects in your document, the object's appearances will remain. However, the objects will no longer be associated with the style, since the style no longer exists.

To delete a style from the Styles palette:

1. On the Styles palette, click the style you want to remove.

2. Click the Delete Style (trash) button on the palette.
   or
   Choose Delete Style from the Styles palette menu.

3. Click Yes.

➤ You can Undo a style deletion.

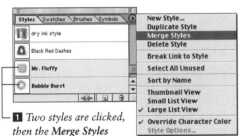

1 *Two styles are clicked, then the **Merge Styles** command is chosen.*

2 *The merged style is given a new **name**.*

3 *The **merged** style appears on the Styles palette.*

Styles from Illustrator's predefined style files or any other Illustrator 10 files can be imported into the current document's Styles palette using the Style Libraries command. Style libraries are stored in the Adobe Illustrator 10.0 > Presets > Styles folder. The styles in a Style library can't be deleted or edited. A library style that is copied into the current document can be edited.

To add a style from a library or another document to the Styles palette:

1. Open the Styles palette.

2. If the style library you want to add is already in the Adobe Illustrator 10 > Presets > Styles folder (such as a predefined style library), choose Window > Style Libraries > [style library name], then open the library ■–■.
   or
   If the style library is in a location other than the Adobe Illustrator 10 > Presets > Styles folder, choose Window > Style Libraries > Other Library, then locate and open the library. You can use this command to open any Illustrator 10 file, and then use that file's Styles palette as a library.

3. To add a style, select an object, then click a style swatch in the library. Or drag a style swatch from the library over a selected or unselected object. The new style will appear on the Styles palette.
   or
   To add a style to the Styles palette without using an object, click a library style swatch.
   or
   Shift-click consecutive styles or Cmd-click/Ctrl-click individual styles on the library palette, then drag the selected styles onto the Styles palette or choose Add to Style from the library palette menu.

➤ To make an Illustrator file appear as a library choice on the Style Libraries submenu, drag the file from the Desktop into the Adobe Illustrator 10 > Presets > Styles folder, then relaunch Illustrator.

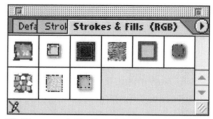

■ *Illustrator's* ***Strokes & Fills (RGB)*** *style library*

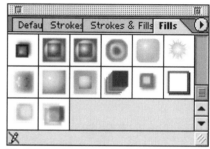

■ *Illustrator's* ***Fills*** *style library*

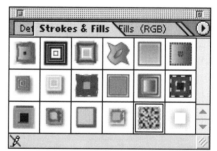

■ *Illustrator's* ***Strokes & Fills*** *style library*

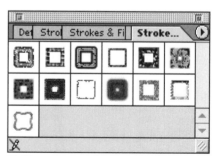

■ *Illustrator's* ***Strokes (RGB)*** *style library*

To create a style library:

1. In a new Illustrator document, create objects with the desired appearance attributes, and save those appearances as styles on the Styles palette.

2. *Optional:* To remove all styles from the Styles palette that are not currently applied to objects in the document, choose Select All Unused from the Styles palette menu, click the Delete Style button on the palette, then click Yes.

3. Choose File > Save, enter a name for the library file, and choose the Adobe Illustrator format.

4. Locate and open the Styles folder inside the Adobe Illustrator 10.0 > Presets > folder, then click Save.

5. Quit/Exit Illustrator, then relaunch. The new style library will be listed on the Window > Style Libraries submenu.

➤ Any brush shape that is used in a style in the style library but that isn't present on the document's Brushes palette will be added to the document's Brushes palette if the library style is applied to an object in the document.

➤ To restore the default style swatches to the Styles palette, choose Window > Style Libraries > Default_RGB or Default_CMYK, then add the needed swatches (follow the instructions on the previous page).

To expand an object's appearance attributes:

1. Select an object that has the appearances (or style) you want to expand **1**–**2**.

2. Choose Object > Expand Appearance **3**. On the Layers palette, you'll see a <Group> (or a nested series of groups) containing the original object and the effects and appearance attributes listed either as paths or images.

1 *An object to which a style is applied is selected.*

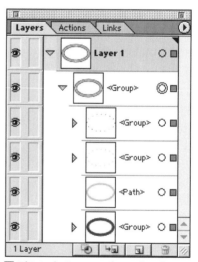

2 *The Layers palette* **before** *choosing the* **Expand Appearance** *command: The* <Path> *object is targeted.*

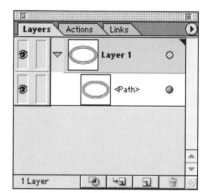

3 *This is the Layers palette* **after** *choosing the* **Expand Appearance** *command.*

Expand Appearance

Chapter 19: Appearances/Styles ◆ Study Guide

Learning Objectives

- Understand the differences between appearances and basic object attributes such as fill and stroke.
- Use appearances to work with object attributes.
- Learn how stacking order and object levels affect appearances.
- Work with object attributes using styles.
- Understand the relationship between appearances, styles, and effects.

Get Up and Running Exercises

- Reproduce the type outlines in the figure below. Use only one layer, don't make any copies of the type, and don't apply any commands from the Filter or Effect menus. It isn't necessary to match the font.

- In the same document you used for the first exercise, add a few more type objects, and apply the same outline treatment. Suppose this is a professional assignment where you know the client is likely to change the outline weights or colors later. How can you make it easy to edit these attributes later, in all of the type objects in which they're used?

- In a new, empty document, create two layers. On one layer, draw two objects, then apply a different appearance to each object, including stroke attributes. Leave the other layer empty, but apply a 5-point blue stroke to the layer's appearance. What happens when you move an object from the first layer to the second, and why?

Class Discussion Questions

- When are appearances useful?
- When are styles useful?
- What are the differences between appearances and styles?
- Why is it important to understand how to target objects for appearances?
- What's the difference between applying an appearance to a targeted layer and applying an appearance to a selected layer?
- If an appearance doesn't produce the desired results, what are some things you can try to fix it?

Review Questions

Multiple choice

1. Which of the following is never affected by an appearance?
   - A. The object's color
   - B. The object's opacity
   - C. The object's path
   - D. The object's stroke weight

2. Suppose you designed a visual treatment that combines a specific fill color, transparency, and drop shadow. Which feature would make it easy to apply your treatment to several different objects?
   - A. An appearance
   - B. An attribute
   - C. A symbol
   - D. A style

3. What is it called when you specify the part of the document that will be affected by the next change you make to appearances?
   - A. Activating
   - B. Selecting
   - C. Targeting
   - D. Viewing

4. Which button on the Appearance palette resets an object to a white fill with a black stroke in one step?
   - A. Reduce to Basic Appearance button
   - B. New Art Has Basic Appearance button
   - C. Clear Appearance button
   - D. Delete Selected Item button

5. Which of the following Layers palette icon combinations indicates that an object is targeted and has no appearance applied to it?

   A. ○

   B. ◎□

   C. ◉

   D. ◎□

6. Which of the following Appearance palette illustrations indicates that an appearance includes an effect and transparency, but not a stroke/fill?

   A. Layer   ⊠

   B. Layer   ▣ ⊠

   C. Layer   ◉ ⊠

   D. Layer   ▣◉ ⊠

Fill-in-the-blank

1. If you don't want the current appearance to affect new objects, click the _____ button on the Appearance palette.

2. To confirm which objects or layers will be affected by applying an appearance or style, look for the _____ on the Layers palette.

3. If you see this symbol ◉ on the Appearance palette, it means that _____ is applied.

4. To use the Layers palette to copy appearance attributes from one object to another, _____.

5. To add another stroke to an object, _____.

6. One way to copy a style from one object to another is by using the _____ tool.

Definitions

1. What is an appearance?

2. What is targeting?

3. What is a style?

4. What is the Break Link to Style button?

5. What is a style library?

MASKS/TRANSPARENCY 20

In this chapter you will learn how to create a clipping mask, which works like a picture frame, and then you'll learn how to restack, select, copy, lock, edit, or add objects to the clipping group.

You will also learn how to use the Transparency palette to apply opacity levels and blending modes to a layer, group, or object; restrict those effects to specific objects; use the Transparency Grid; create, reshape, and use opacity masks; and apply the Feather and Drop Shadow commands.

Daniel Pelavin (icon appears courtesy DFS Group, Ltd.)

The **masking** object   A **masked** object

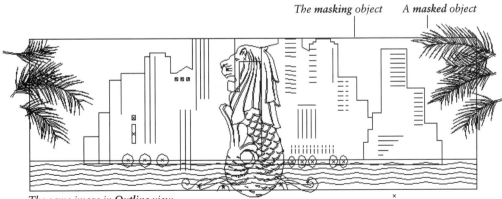

*The same image in **Outline** view*

Clipping masks

In Illustrator, a clipping mask works like a picture frame or mat. While it is in effect, it hides (clips) parts of an illustration that fall outside its borders; only parts of objects within the confines of the masking object will be visible. Masked objects can be moved, restacked, reshaped, or repainted.

To create a clipping mask:

1. Arrange the object or objects to be masked **1**. They can be grouped or ungrouped. To avoid a printing error, don't use very intricate objects.

2. Put the masking object, which we call the "clipping path," in front of the objects it will be masking. If you need to restack it, on the Layers palette, drag its name upward on the list. The clipping path can be an open path or closed path. It can have a brush stroke, but remember, the path itself—not the brush stroke—will be used as the clipping path. You can use type as a clipping path without having to convert it to outlines, and you can use a compound path as a clipping path.

3. Choose the Selection tool (V).

4. Select the clipping path and the object or objects behind it to be masked.

5. Choose Object > Clipping Mask > Make (Cmd-7/Ctrl-7) **2**. The clipping path will now have a stroke and fill of None, and all the objects will remain selected. The words "<Clipping Path>" (underlined) will appear on the Layers palette (unless text was used as the clipping path, in which case the text character[s] will be underlined instead). Also, the clipping path and masked objects will be moved into a <Group> in the top-level layer of the original clipping path.

   Note: To recolor the stroke or fill of a clipping path, see page 345.

➤ Don't let the inconsistency between the command name ("Clipping Mask > Make") and the listing on the Layers palette ("Clipping Path") confuse you. They refer to the same thing.

Clipping masks and sets

The **Make/Release Clipping Mask** button at the bottom of the Layers palette clips objects, groups, and even other clipping masks that are nested within the currently active **top-level layer**, and any selected objects in layers below it. What results is called a "clipping set." We recommend putting all the objects to be masked on one top-level layer before clicking this button.

The instructions on pages 343–346 in this chapter also apply to clipping sets that are made with objects nested within one layer (instead of working with a clipping group, you'll be working with a clipping set). To release a clipping set, activate the top-level layer containing the set, then click the Make/Release Clipping Mask button again.

A clipping set will export to Photoshop as a layer with a layer clipping path, whereas a clipping mask will export to Photoshop as a layer with no clipping path.

1 *The original objects: A standard type character on top of a placed bitmap image.*

2 *After selecting both objects and applying Object > Clipping Mask > Make*

1 *The object to be added (the star) is moved over the clipping group (the banner shape) to the desired x/y location.*

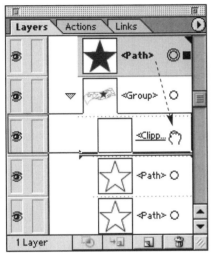

2 *A path is moved downward into the clipping group.*

3 *The object is has been **added** to the clipping group.*

We'll refer to a clipping mask and the objects it's masking as a "clipping group."

To select a whole clipping group:

On the Layers palette, click the selection area for the clipping group.
or
Choose the Selection tool (V), then click the clipping path or one of the masked objects in the document window.

To select an individual clipping path or masked object:

On the Layers palette, click the selection area for the clipping path or a masked object.
or
Choose the Direct-selection tool (A), then click the clipping path or a masked object in the document window. You can use Smart Guides to help you locate the objects (check Object Highlighting in Edit > Preferences > Smart Guides & Slices).

To select all the clipping masks in your illustration:

Deselect all objects, then choose Select > Object > Clipping Masks. (With the *10.0!* Selection tool, Shift-click the edge of any masking object you don't want selected.)

To add an object to a clipping group:

1. Choose the Selection tool (V).

2. In the document window, move the object to be added over the clipping group **1**.

3. On the Layers palette, expand the list for the clipping <Group>.

4. Drag the object to be added to the group upward or downward into the <Group> **2**, and release when the object name is in the desired position **3**.

➤ To change the stacking order of an object in a clipping group, drag it upward or downward on the Layers palette.

➤ Using Object > Expand (check Fill) on an object that contains a gradient or pattern fill creates a clipping mask automatically.

Select Objects in, Add Object to, Clipping Group

Basic stacking techniques are explained on pages 185–189.

To restack a masked object within its clipping group:

On the Layers palette, drag the object name upward or downward to a new position within the group **1**–**4**.

To copy a masked object:

1. On the Layers palette, click the selection area for the object you want to copy.

2. Option-drag/Alt-drag the selection square upward or downward, and release it somewhere within the same clipping <Group>.

3. It will be in the same *x/y* location as the original object, so you'll probably want to reposition it. You can use the Direct-selection tool to do this. Or select the masked object via the Layers palette, then move it using the Selection tool.

➤ If you drag the object's selection square outside its clipping group or layer, the copy won't be in the clipping group.

Using the Layers palette, you can lock any object within a clipping group or lock an entire group to prevent it from being moved.

To lock a clipping group or an object within it:

To lock the whole clipping group, click the blank box in the second column for the <Group>.

or

To lock one object in the group, expand the clipping <Group> list on the Layers palette, then click the blank box in the second column for the clipping path or a masked object.

➤ To unlock a clipping group or object, click its padlock icon (the padlock will disappear).

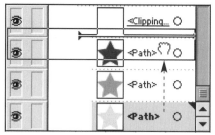

1 *The original **clipping group**, masked by a rectangle*

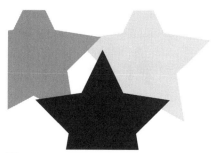

2 *The lightest star <Path> is dragged **upward**...*

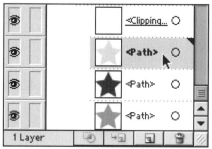

3 *...to the **top** of its clipping group.*

4 *The lightest star is now in **front** of the other masked objects.*

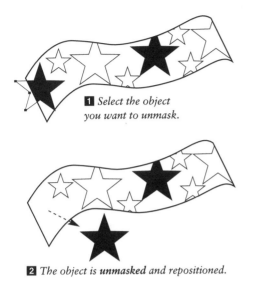

1 *Select the object you want to unmask.*

2 *The object is **unmasked** and repositioned.*

3 *The original clipping mask*

4 *After applying a black **fill** to the clipping mask object and recoloring the masked objects*

It's easy to unmask an object. All you gotta do is drag it outside the clipping group or top-level layer on the Layers palette.

To unmask one object:

1. Expand the clipping group list on the Layers palette.

2. *Optional:* For the object you want to unmask, click the object name on the Layers palette. Or choose the Direct-selection tool, then click the object in the illustration window **1**.

3. On the Layers palette, drag the nested object upward or downward out of the group **2**.

➤ To simultaneously unmask an object and delete it from the illustration, select it, then press Delete/Backspace.

To recolor a clipping path:

1. Select the clipping path by clicking in its selection area on the Layers palette.

2. Apply color as you would to any object **3**–**6**. The fill will appear behind the masked objects; the stroke will appear in front of the masked objects.

5 *The original clipping mask object (the zebra) and masked objects (the stripes)*

6 *The recolored clipping mask object and masked objects*

If you release a clipping group, the complete, original objects will redisplay. The former clipping path will be listed as a standard path on the Layers palette and the clipping group name will disappear from the Layers palette.

To release a clipping group:

1. Choose the Selection tool (V).

2. In the illustration window, click any part of the clipping group .
   or
   On the Layers palette, click the selection area for the clipping group you want to release.

3. Choose Object > Clipping Mask > Release (Cmd-Option-7/Ctrl-Alt-7) 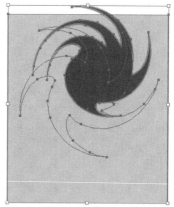.

➤ If no fill or stroke was applied to the clipping path, that object won't display in Preview view. To find it, use Smart Guides with Object Highlighting checked in Edit > Preferences > Smart Guides & Slices.

To release a clipping set:

1. On the Layers palette, click the name of the top-level layer that contains the clipping set or click the selection area for that layer.

2. Click the Make/Release Clipping Mask button ⟨icon⟩ at the bottom of the Layers palette. *Note:* A clipping set cannot be selected using the Selection tool; you have to use the Layers palette.

Learn from the masters

Once you've mastered the basics, we highly recommend Sharon Steuer's four-color **The Illustrator 10 Wow! Book** (Peachpit Press), which features advanced tips and techniques from Illustrator pros.

1 *The original clipping group*

2 *After choosing Object > Clipping Mask > Release*

Exporting transparency

Exporting a file that contains transparency to another application involves choosing options in the File menu > Export dialog boxes and the Document Setup dialog box. Read about these options in Chapter 26.

1 *Various opacities and blending modes were applied to some of these objects.*

Transparency

Using Illustrator's transparency controls **1**, artists can add a touch of realism to their drawings. Study a real object on your desk for a minute, such as a lamp, or your keyboard if it's in one of the jelly colors. When a lamp is on, the shade looks semi-transparent rather than solid. You might say "The shade is white" when you describe it, but in reality it's not a dense, solid white, especially when a light bulb is projecting light through it. Objects in real life have different densities, depending on what material they're made of. If you have the capacity to render light filtering through various materials, you can create a sense of realism.

If you draw a window, for example, you can then draw a tinted, semi-sheer, diaphanous curtain on top of it. If you draw a vase on a table, you can create a realistic shadow for the vase that feathers softly into the table color.

In Illustrator, the opacity of any kind of object can be changed at any time, even the opacity of editable type. You can also choose a blending mode for any object (the standard lineup of blending modes from Photoshop) to control how it blends with objects below it.

And finally, you can turn any object into an opacity mask. Light and dark values in the object's fill will control the transparency of the objects it masks. We'll show you how to do all of the above on the following pages.

Transparency

The Opacity slider on the Transparency palette controls the transparency of each object. The blending modes control how an object's color is affected by the colors in underlying objects. When a group or layer is targeted, the transparency settings affect all the objects in that group or layer. Objects that are added to a group or layer take that group or layer's transparency settings.

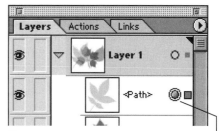

1 *Click the* **target** *button for an object, group, or layer.*

To change the opacity or blending mode of an object, group, or layer:

1. Show the Layers palette, then select, or click the target circle for **1**, an object whose opacity or blending mode you want to change. For an image that was pasted, or dragged and dropped, target the <Image>. To edit the appearance of all the objects on a group or layer, you must click that group or layer's target circle.
   or
   Select some type characters with a type tool, or select a whole type object using the Selection tool.

2. Show the Transparency palette (Window > Transparency). The thumbnail for the selected layer, group, or object will display on the palette.

3. Move the Opacity slider (0–100%) **2**–**3**.
   and/or
   Choose a different blending mode from the pop-up menu (see "The blending modes" beginning on the next page).

To change the opacity or blending mode of only an object's fill or stroke:

1. Click the target circle for an object on the Layers palette. To change a type object's stroke or fill separately, see the sidebar on page 350.

2. On the Appearance palette, click Fill or Stroke.

3. On the Transparency palette, move the Opacity slider **4** and/or choose a different blending mode. Attribute changes will be nested under the targeted object's Fill or Stroke attribute on the Appearance palette.

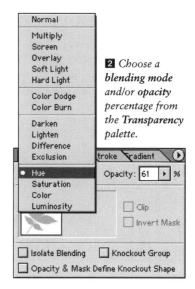

2 *Choose a* **blending mode** *and/or* **opacity** *percentage from the* **Transparency** *palette.*

3 *The* **opacity** *of the* **entire** *type character is lowered to 29%*

4 *The type* **Fill opacity** *is lowered to 29%; the Stroke opacity is left at 100%.*

10.0!

Applying blending modes

To change the blending mode for any individual object, first **target** that **object**, then choose a blending mode from the Transparency palette.

Or to ensure consistency, **target** a **group** or **layer** before choosing a blending mode. That mode will apply to all existing and future objects that are nested within that group or layer.

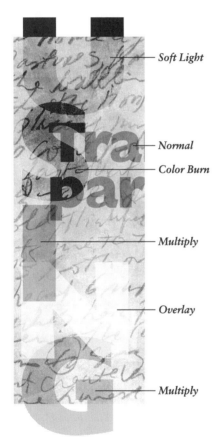

— Soft Light

— Normal
— Color Burn

— Multiply

— Overlay

— Multiply

Text objects in front of an image object

The blending modes

You can choose from 16 blending modes on the Transparency palette—the very same modes that you may already be familiar with if you use Photoshop. The blending mode you choose for an object affects how that object modifies underlying colors (the "base color").

NORMAL
All base colors are modified equally. At 100% opacity, the object color will be opaque.

MULTIPLY
A dark object color removes the lighter parts of the base color to produce a darker base color. A light object color darkens the base color less. Good for creating semi-transparent shadows.

SCREEN
A light object color removes the darker parts of the base color to produce a lighter, bleached base color. A dark object color lightens the base color less.

OVERLAY
Multiplies (darkens) dark areas and screens (lightens) light base colors. Preserves luminosity (light and dark) values. Black and white areas aren't changed, so details are preserved.

SOFT LIGHT
Lightens the base color if the object color is light, darkens the base color if the object color is dark. Preserves luminosity values in the base color. Creates a soft, subtle lighting effect.

HARD LIGHT
Screens (lightens) the base color if the object color is light, multiplies (darkens) the base color if the object color is dark. Greater contrast is created in the blended color areas. Good for creating glowing highlights and composite effects.

COLOR DODGE
Lightens the base color if the object color is light. A dark object color tints the base color slightly.

(Continued on the following page)

COLOR BURN

A dark object color darkens the base color. A light object color tints the base color slightly.

DARKEN

Base colors that are lighter than the object color are modified; base colors that are darker than the object color are not. Use with an object color that is darker than the base colors you want to modify.

LIGHTEN

Base colors that are darker than the object color are modified; base colors that are lighter than the object color are not. Use with an object color that is lighter than the base colors you want to modify.

DIFFERENCE

Creates a color negative effect on the base color. When the object color is light, the negative (or inverse) effect is more pronounced. Produces marked color changes.

EXCLUSION

Grays out the base color where the object color is dark. Inverts the base color where the object color is light.

HUE

The object color's hue is applied. Saturation and luminosity values aren't changed in the base color.

SATURATION

The object color's saturation is applied. Hue and luminosity values aren't changed in the base color.

COLOR

The object color's saturation and hue are applied. The base color's light and dark (luminosity) values aren't changed, so detail is maintained. Good for tinting.

LUMINOSITY

The base color's luminosity values are replaced by tonal (luminosity) values from the object color. Hue and saturation are not modified in the base color.

Blending Modes

Changing a type object's stroke or fill

Before you can change the opacity of a type object's stroke separately from its fill, or vice versa, you have two options. One option is to convert the type to outlines. A second option, which keeps the type editable, is to follow these instructions:

I. Select the type object using the Selection tool.

2. Choose **Add New Fill** or **Add New Stroke** from the Appearance palette menu, then choose fill and stroke colors and a stroke weight.

3. Double-click the type object (a type tool will become selected automatically).

4. Select all the characters, then choose a fill and stroke of None for them.

5. Choose the Selection tool, then click Fill or Stroke on the Appearance palette.

6. Modify the fill or stroke attribute by moving the Opacity slider and/or choosing a different blending mode on the Transparency palette.

1 *The original objects (an image and a group of squares): Each square's blending mode and opacity interact with all the underlying layers.*

2 *With **Isolate Blending** on for the group of nested squares, the blending modes only affect objects within the group (where the objects in the group don't overlap each other, though, you can still see through to the globe below the group).*

If you apply a blending mode to multiple selected objects, that mode will become an appearance for each of those objects. In other words, the objects will blend with one another, and with underlying objects below them. Checking the Isolate Blending option, discussed on this page, "seals" a collection of objects so the blending modes will only affect those objects—not underlying objects below them.

Note: The Isolate Blending option has no effect on opacity settings, which means underlying objects will still show through any object that isn't fully opaque.

To restrict a blending mode effect to specific objects:

1. On the Layers palette, click the target circle for a group or layer that contains nested objects to which a blending mode or modes are applied **1**.

2. Check Isolate Blending on the Transparency palette **2**. Nested objects within the group or layer will blend with each other, but those objects won't blend with any underlying objects outside the layer or group.

   Note: To reverse the effect, re-target the group or layer, then uncheck Isolate Blending.

➤ Isolate Blending can also be used on individual objects that have overlapping strokes and/or fills. Each stroke or fill can have a different blending mode.

➤ With Isolate Blending checked for objects nested within a group or layer, the group will be preserved as a separate layer when the file is exported to Photoshop.

Isolate Blending

The Knockout Group option on the Transparency palette controls whether or not objects nested in a group or layer will show through each other (knock out) where they overlap. This option only affects objects within the currently targeted group or layer.

To knock out objects:

1. Nest objects in the same group or layer and arrange them so they partially overlap each other. In order to see how the Knockout Group option works, apply an opacity value or values below 100% and/or a blending mode or modes other than Normal to some or all of the nested objects.

2. On the Layers palette, target the group or layer the objects are nested within **1**.

3. On the Transparency palette, keep clicking the Knockout Group box until a checkmark displays **2**. With this option checked, objects won't show through each other, and if their opacities are below 100%, you will still be able to see through them to objects below them.

➤ If both Knockout Group and Isolate Blending are checked, nested objects will look as if they have a blending mode of Normal, regardless of their actual blending mode.

➤ To apply the Knockout Group option to an object or outline type that only has transparency applied to its stroke, click Default Transparency on the Appearance palette to target the whole object, then check Knockout Group. The object's stroke will no longer be transparent to its fill **3**–**4**.

To turn off the Knockout Group option:

1. Target the group or layer to which the option is applied.

2. On the Transparency palette, keep clicking the Knockout Group box until the checkmark disappears.

When to put it in neutral

Objects whose opacity is below 100% will show through each other whether the Knockout Group icon is blank (unchecked) or **neutral**. Neutral is a dash in the Mac OS, a gray checkmark in Windows. Choose the neutral setting for a group of objects nested within a larger group if you want to make the nested group independent of the Knockout Group setting for the larger group.

1 *The original group of nested objects on top of an image, with Knockout Group off*

2 *With Knockout Group on, objects are no longer transparent to each other and no longer blend with each other.*

3 *Knockout Group off: Half the stroke is transparent to the object's fill.*

4 *Knockout Group on: The stroke knocks out the object's fill.*

Knockout Group

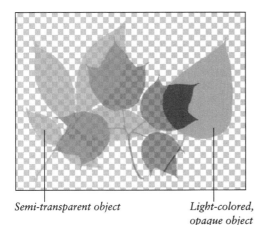

Semi-transparent object　　　*Light-colored, opaque object*

1 *With the **transparency grid** showing, you can easily see which objects are opaque and which are not.*

2 *Choose preferences for the transparency grid in the **Transparency** pane of the **Document Setup** dialog box.*

Once you start working with semi-transparent objects, it may be hard to distinguish between objects that have a light but solid tint and those that are semi-transparent. With the transparency grid turned on, you'll be able to see the gray and white checkerboard behind any object whose opacity is below 100%.

To show/hide the transparency grid:

Choose View > Show Transparency Grid (Cmd-Shift-D/Ctrl-Shift-D) **1**. To turn this feature off, choose View > Hide Transparency Grid or use the shortcut again.

You can change the transparency grid colors or size to make the grid contrast better with colors in your artwork.

To choose preferences for the transparency grid:

1. Choose File > Document Setup (Cmd-Option-P/Ctrl-Alt-P) **2**.

2. Choose Transparency from the first pop-up menu.

3. Choose the desired Grid Size: Small, Medium, or Large.

4. To choose Grid Colors:

From the pop-up menu, choose the Light, Medium, or Dark grayscale grid or choose one of the preset colors.
or
To choose custom colors, click the top color swatch (this color will also be the Artboard color when no transparency grid is showing), choose a color from the color picker, then click OK. Then click the second swatch, click a second color, and click OK again.

5. *Optional:* Check Simulate Paper if you want objects and placed images in the illustration to look as if they're printed on colored paper. The object color will blend with the "colored paper" (the paper color being the color chosen for the top color swatch). To see this effect, the transparency grid must be hidden.

6. Click OK.

Transparency Grid

10.0! The Flatten Transparency command converts areas where selected paths overlap into separate, non-overlapping objects. Strokes are converted into thin, non-overlapping objects; fills will look the same, but their transparency will no longer be editable. (Read about printing and exporting transparency on pages 465–468.)

To flatten objects and preserve the look of transparency:

1. *Optional:* The results from Flatten Transparency will be permanent as soon as you save your file, so we recommend you do a Save As before you proceed.

2. Choose the Selection tool (V).

3. Select the objects to be flattened **1**. This should include both the transparent objects and the objects that are visible beneath them.

4. Choose Object > Flatten Transparency.

5. Check Preview.

6. Move the Raster/Vector Balance slider **2**, and as you do so, watch the preview in the illustration window so you can see how the selected objects are affected. You may have to move the slider quite a ways to see any change on screen.

7. Choose a Rasterization Resolution. For Web output, choose 72 dpi. For print output, choose between 150 and 300 dpi. Usually, the print resolution is 1.5 to 2 times the screen resolution of the final printing device (see page 466).

8. Click OK **3**. If you change your mind, Undo right away.

➤ Flatten Transparency has other uses. You can use it to manually control the flattening of transparent appearances before saving a file to an older version of Illustrator or for export to programs that don't support transparency (at this time, that includes most programs except Photoshop, Acrobat 5, and InDesign 2).

Get in balance

The **Raster/Vector Balance** slider controls which selected objects will stay as vectors when flattened and which will become rasterized to preserve the look of transparency. The farther to the left the slider is, the more likely the selected objects will be rasterized. To learn more about flattening transparency, see pages 465–468.

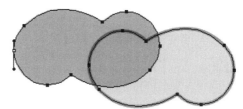

1 *Two objects are selected. The object with the stroke is transparent; the object behind it doesn't have a stroke.*

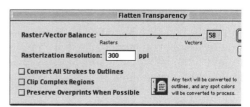

2 *The Raster/Vector Balance slider is moved in the Flatten Transparency dialog box.*

3 *After applying the Flatten Transparency command, the paths now total five instead of two. (We pulled the paths apart to show you.)*

Flatten Transparency

1 *Two objects are selected: a normal type object containing a radial fill and a placed bitmap image.*

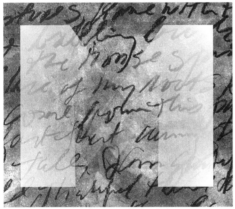

2 *After applying the Make Opacity Mask command*

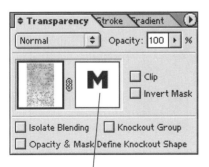

3 *The Mask thumbnail*

Opacity masks

An opacity mask is an object whose shape and fill controls the opacity (transparency) of the objects it masks. The topmost object in a selection of objects works as the opacity mask. The masking is controlled by the value level (grayscale equivalent) of the top object's fill. In the mask, black or dark values will make the underlying masked object(s) totally transparent (seethrough); white or very light values will make the underlying masked object(s) opaque; and shades of gray (mid-range color values) will make the underlying masked object(s) partially transparent.

To create an opacity mask:

1. Arrange the object to be used as the mask and the object or objects to be masked, then select them all **1**. As the mask, you may use editable text, a placed (linked or embedded) image, an object containing a pattern or gradient, or a mesh.

2. Choose Make Opacity Mask from the Transparency palette menu **2**. The Make Opacity Mask command links the object(s) and the mask. On the Transparency palette, a thumbnail of the object(s) being masked will appear on the left and a thumbnail for the mask will appear on the right, with the link icon between them **3**. (If the thumbnails aren't visible, choose Show Thumbnails from the Transparency palette menu.)

   (See also figures **1** and **2** on the following page.)

   If you used only two objects in step 1, those objects will be combined into one; if you used more than two objects, they will be nested within a <Group>. The new object or <Group> name will have a dashed underline, indicating the presence of an opacity mask.

➤ The object-mask combination can be transformed, recolored, or assigned transparency attributes, effects, or styles—like any object.

Make Opacity Mask

You can choose whether or not an opacity mask will clip parts of an object(s) that extend beyond its edges, in addition to changing the transparency of those objects.

To choose a Clip setting for an opacity mask:

1. Choose a selection tool, then select an opacity mask object using the Layers palette **3**.

2. Check or uncheck Clip on the Transparency palette **4**–**5**.

➤ To have future opacity masks be clipped by default, make sure the New Opacity Masks Are Clipping command on the Transparency palette menu has a checkmark.

The Invert Mask option reverses the value levels in the masking object.

To invert an opacity mask:

1. Choose a selection tool, then select the opacity mask object using the Layers palette.

2. Check Invert Mask on the Transparency palette. (Uncheck the box to un-invert the mask.)

➤ To have future opacity masks be inverted by default, make sure the New Opacity Masks Are Inverted command on the Transparency palette menu has a checkmark.

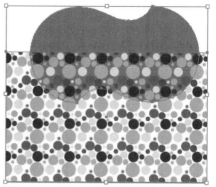

1 *A rectangle with a **pattern** fill on top of an irregular shape containing a **solid gray** fill: The pattern works as the opacity mask.*

2 *After choosing the **Make Opacity Mask** command, the value levels in the pattern fill mask out areas in the underlying object. We put a black rectangle behind the other objects to demonstrate how the whites are transparent.*

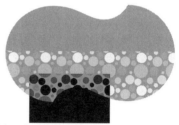

3 *The original objects*

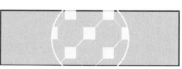

4 *After choosing **Make Opacity Mask** with the **Clip** option on...*

5 *...and with the **Clip** option off.*

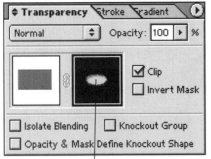

1 *Opacity mask thumbnail*

2 *Enter a Feather Radius value for the masking object.*

3 *After applying the Feather effect to a masking object (the "M" is the opacity mask)*

Follow these instructions to edit a masking object separately from the masked objects.

To reshape or edit an opacity masking object:

1. Select the opacity masking object using the Layers palette.

2. Click the mask thumbnail (right thumbnail) on the Transparency palette **1**.

3. Do any of the following: Use any path reshaping tool to change the contour of the mask; transform the object; change its color, pattern, or gradient fill; change its opacity; or apply an effect or style to it.

4. When you're done, be sure to click the object thumbnail on the Transparency palette.

➤ Option-click/Alt-click the opacity mask thumbnail on the Transparency palette to toggle between viewing just the masking object and the full illustration in the document window.

➤ When the opacity mask thumbnail is active, all you'll see on the Layers palette is an <Opacity Mask> layer containing a nested object or objects. You can target the layer or individual objects for appearance changes. To go back to the normal Layers palette display, click the object thumbnail on the Transparency palette.

Stylize > Feather is only one of the many Effect menu commands that can be applied to a masking object.

To feather the edge of a masking object:

1. Target an opacity mask object using the Layers palette.

2. Click the mask thumbnail on the Transparency palette.

3. Choose Effect > Stylize > Feather.

4. Check Preview, then choose a Feather Radius value for the width of the feathered area **2**.

5. Adjust the Feather Radius, if desired, then click OK **3**.

If you want to reposition the masking object relative to the masked object(s), you first have to unlink the mask.

To move mask objects independently:

1. Choose a selection tool, then select the opacity mask object.

2. On the Transparency palette, click the link icon between the object thumbnail and the mask thumbnail **1**.
   or
   Choose Unlink Opacity Mask from the Transparency palette menu.

3. Click the object or mask thumbnail, then reposition either object in the document window **2**–**3**.

4. Make sure the object thumbnail is selected, then click again between the thumbnails to relink the mask. The link icon is accessible only when the object thumbnail is selected.

To temporarily disable a mask:

1. Select the opacity mask object using the Layers palette.

2. Shift-click the mask thumbnail on the Transparency palette.
   or
   Choose Disable Opacity Mask from the Transparency palette menu.

   A red "X" will appear over the thumbnail and the mask effect will disappear from view.

3. To reinstate the mask, Shift-click the mask thumbnail again or choose Enable Opacity Mask from the palette menu.

1 *Click the* **link** *icon to unlink (not unmask!) the masking and masked objects.*

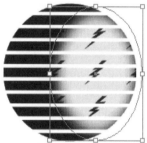

2 *The masking object is selected...*

3 *...and then it's moved.*

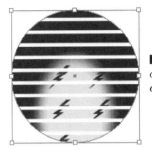

1 *The original object, with an opacity mask*

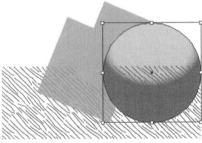

2 *After releasing the mask*

3 *With Knockout Group on, the opacity mask covers shapes that are nested in the same layer.*

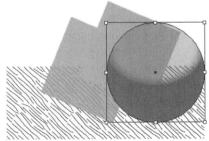

4 *After checking Opacity & Mask Define Knockout Shape, shapes nested in the same layer are revealed through the opacity mask.*

If an opacity mask is released, the masked object(s) and the masking object will become separate objects. Any modifications that were made to the mask will be preserved, along with the objects' original appearances.

To release an opacity mask:

1. Select the opacity mask object using the Layers palette **1**.

2. From the Transparency palette menu, choose Release Opacity Mask **2**. The opacity mask thumbnail will disappear from the Transparency palette.

If the Knockout Group option is on for a group or layer and that group or layer contains an opacity mask, Knockout Group will prevent any nested group or objects from displaying through any transparency in the mask. To reveal nested objects below the opacity mask, do as follows.

To use an opacity mask within a knockout group or layer:

1. On the Layers palette, target a group or sublayer that contains an opacity mask as well as other nested objects below the mask. Make sure the Knockout Group option is checked for the group or sublayer.

2. Target the opacity mask object.

3. On the Transparency palette, check Opacity & Mask Define Knockout Shape **3**–**4**. Any objects in the same nested group that are below the opacity mask object will now show through areas of transparency in the opacity mask.

➤ Regardless of whether Opacity & Mask Define Knockout Shape is on or off, objects on lower layers will always show through transparent or semi-transparent areas in the opacity mask.

Release Opacity Mask; Mask in Knockout

359

The Drop Shadow dialog box creates soft, naturalistic shadows, and it can be applied either as a filter or as an effect. The Drop Shadow filter creates a new shadow object, separate from the original object. The filter dialog box also offers a Create Separate Shadows option that nests the object and the shadow into a new <Group> on the Layers palette.

Unlike the filter, the Drop Shadow effect becomes an appearance on the original object. One advantage of applying a shadow as an effect is that you can then double-click the Drop Shadow effect attribute on the Appearance palette to reopen its dialog box and edit any of the settings, including the color. Also, the shadow appearance can be removed at any time.

1 *Sometimes we're satisfied with the default settings in the* **Drop Shadow** *dialog box; other times we might change the* **Opacity** *or* **Blur** *value.*

To create a drop shadow:

1. Select one or more objects. The Drop Shadow filter can be applied to editable type—it doesn't have to be converted into outlines.

2. Choose Filter > Stylize > Drop Shadow or Effect > Stylize > Drop Shadow. If you chose the command from the Effect menu, check Preview.

3. Choose a blending Mode **1**.

4. Choose an Opacity value for the shadow.

5. Enter an X Offset for the horizontal distance between the object and the shadow and a Y Offset for the vertical distance between the object and the shadow.

6. Enter a Blur value for the width of the shadow.

7. *Optional:* Click Color, click the color square, then choose a different shadow color from the Color Picker. Or click Darkness, then enter a percentage of black to be added to the shadow.

8. *Optional:* If you're using the Drop Shadow filter, check Create Separate Shadows to have the object grouped with its shadow. With this option checked, each shadow will be nested directly below its matching object in a new group. With

1 *After applying the Drop Shadow effect, using the default settings*

2 *After applying the Drop Shadow filter. Looks the same*

this option unchecked, the whole shadow object will be placed below all the nested objects in the same group or layer. We like to check this option.

9. Click OK **1**–**3**.

If you applied the Drop Shadow effect and now choose Object > Expand Appearance, the result will be a group containing the original object and the effect transformed into an image object.

For the filter or an expanded effect, the shadow object can then be transformed, reshaped, repositioned by dragging, or recolored via the Adjust Colors filter— separately from the object. Also, the shadow object can be deleted at any time without affecting the original object.

➤ Highlight the current Opacity or Blur value, then press the up or down arrow on the keyboard to increase or decrease it.

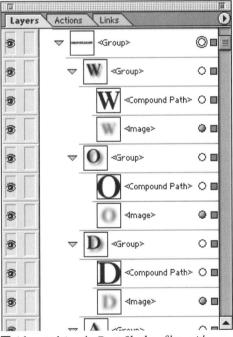

3 *After applying the Drop Shadow filter with Create Separate Shadows checked: Each shadow is stacked directly below its matching object.*

Drop Shadow

10.0! The Hard Mix effect simulates overprinting; the Soft Mix effect creates an illusion of semi-transparency. Both effects can only be applied to a targeted group, layer, or type.

Note: We prefer to use the Transparency palette to produce transparency because it offers superior opacity and blending mode controls.

To apply the Hard Mix and Soft Mix commands:

1. Target a group that contains two or more objects that at least partially overlap.

2. To simulate overprinting, choose Effect > Pathfinder > Hard Mix. The highest C, M, Y, and K, or R, G, and B values from each of the original objects will be mixed in areas where they overlap. The greater the difference between the original colors, the more marked the resulting effect will be. Stroke colors are removed.

or

To create an illusion of semi-transparency, choose Effect > Pathfinder > Soft Mix, choose a Mixing Rate, then click OK. The higher the Mixing Rate, the more transparent and changed the color of the frontmost object will become. Stroke colors are removed **1**–**5**.

➤ Double-click the Mix listing on the Appearance palette to open the Pathfinder Options dialog box. Use Expand Appearance to convert areas where objects overlap into separate objects. Their fill colors will be changed to a mixture of their formerly overlapping colors.

➤ If either Mix effect is applied to a mixture of global or non-global process colors and spot colors, and then the effect is expanded, all the colors will be converted to non-global process colors in the current document color mode.

➤ You can choose a different Pathfinder effect from the Operation pop-up menu in the Pathfinder Options dialog box (check Preview).

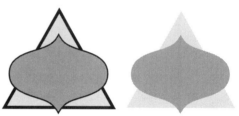

1 Choose a **Mixing Rate** for the **Soft Mix** command in the **Pathfinder Options** dialog box.

2 *The original objects*   **3** *Hard Mix*

4 *The original objects*   **5** *Soft Mix (50%)*

Soft Mix, Hard Mix

Learning Objectives

- Create a clipping mask.
- Work with transparency attributes, including opacity levels, blending modes, and opacity masks.
- Use Feather and Drop Shadow commands.

Get Up and Running Exercises

- In a blank Illustrator document, place a photo. Now create a vignette, so that the outer edge of the photo gradually fades out to the white artboard. What are one or two ways to do this using the methods described in this chapter? How would you change the method if you wanted to use a custom shape for the vignette?

- Position an object, such as type, over a texture or a low-contrast photograph, such as a brick wall. What feature can you quickly use to make the object stand out without creating additional objects?

- Opacity values and blending modes apply transparency uniformly—that is, the transparency method is applied the same way across the entire object. What if you wanted to change the opacity at different places within an object? Which techniques would you try in order to achieve such an effect?

Class Discussion Questions

- How is a clipping mask different from an opacity mask?

- How is opacity different from an opacity mask?

- How do you create a clipping mask?

- How do you create an opacity mask?

- What's the difference between opacity and blending modes?

- When you manually flatten objects, how should you decide on the settings for Resolution and Raster/Vector Balance?

Chapter 20: Masks/Transparency ◆ Study Guide ◆ Exercises & Discussion Questions

Review Questions

Multiple choice

1. Which method would you use if you only want to define the shape of a mask using a path?

  A. Blending mode

  B. Clipping mask

  C. Opacity mask

  D. Opacity value

2. How do you add an object to a clipping group?

  A. Release the compound path.

  B. Paste the new object into the clipping mask.

  C. Ungroup the clipping group and add the object.

  D. Use the Layers palette to drag the object into the clipping group.

3. Which of the following blending modes never changes the hue of an object?

  A. Difference

  B. Luminosity

  C. Multiply

  D. Soft Light

4. Which feature would you use to let an image show through only the lightest colors/shades of a second image?

  A. Use the second image as an opacity mask

  B. Change the opacity value of the second image

  C. Apply the Difference blending mode to the second image

  D. Use the second image as a clipping mask

5. When an opacity mask is selected, how would you go about editing just the opacity mask?

  A. Click the link icon on the Transparency palette.

  B. Click the mask thumbnail on the Transparency palette.

  C. Shift-click the mask thumbnail on the Transparency palette.

  D. Simply select the mask using the Direct-selection tool.

Fill-in-the-blank

1. To make sure a blending mode only applies to objects within a layer or group, check the _____ option on the Transparency palette.

2. To apply transparency to objects in a layer or group as a unit instead of each object individually, check the _____ option on the Transparency palette.

3. To distinguish between the white areas and true transparent areas in an illustration, turn on the _____.

4. To edit an opacity masking object without releasing it, click the _____ on the Transparency palette.

5. To soften a mask edge, apply _____.

6. To select a clipping path without selecting the clipped objects, use the _____ tool.

Definitions

1. What is a clipping mask?

2. What is a blending mode?

3. What is flattening?

4. What is an opacity mask?

5. What are the Hard Mix and Soft Mix effects?

6. What is the Multiply blending mode?

New chapter! 10.0!

In this chapter, first you will learn about the tools that do strange things: Warp, Pucker, Bloat, Twirl, Scallop, Crystallize, and Wrinkle. If that's not enough distortion for you, keep reading to learn about envelopes, which are used to sculpt whole objects.

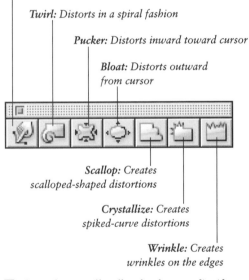

Warp: Distorts by pushing or pulling an edge

Twirl: Distorts in a spiral fashion

Pucker: Distorts inward toward cursor

Bloat: Distorts outward from cursor

Scallop: Creates scalloped-shaped distortions

Crystallize: Creates spiked-curve distortions

Wrinkle: Creates wrinkles on the edges

1 *This is the tear-off toolbar for the seven* **liquify** *tools. The keyboard shortcut for the Warp tool is* **Shift-R**. *None of the other liquify tools have default shortcuts.*

Liquify tools

The seven liquify tools **1**—Warp, Twirl, Pucker, Bloat, Scallop, Crystallize, and Wrinkle—let you create brushes that are used to distort the edges of individual objects or groups of objects. You push and pull on an object's edges with the brush's circular cursor, much as you would sculpt a piece of clay by pushing and pulling the clay. Each tool offers different sculpting controls.

To use one of the liquify tools, you first specify option settings for the particular tool, then drag the mouse over an object. You don't have to select the object or group of objects, but it's helpful to select an object first to prevent other nearby objects from becoming distorted, too.

The distortions produced by the liquify tools depend on three factors:

- The size and angle of the tool cursor.
- The tool's Intensity setting.
- The length of time the cursor is clicked and held over an object and/or the distance the cursor is dragged.

As with any feature that offers a lot of options, you'll need to spend some time working with the liquify tools in order to discover how they can be of service to you or how you can achieve the desired effect—or degree of effect. Experiment with different global brush dimensions and individual tool options settings.

(Continued on the following page)

Liquify Tools

As usual, first we'll give you a few ground rules so you can get your bearings:

- The liquify tools can be used on an individual object, a multi-object selection, a group, or any combination thereof.
- The liquify tools can be used on an object that contains appearances, effects, brush strokes, or styles.
- To use a liquify tool on a pattern fill, the fill must be expanded first (Object > Expand).
- To use a liquify tool on text, the text must be converted to outlines first (Type > Create Outlines).
- To use a liquify tool on a symbol instance or set, the instance or set must first be unlinked from the original symbol (click the Break Link to Symbol button on the Symbols palette).

For every liquify tool there is an options dialog box in which you can choose Global Brush Dimensions settings 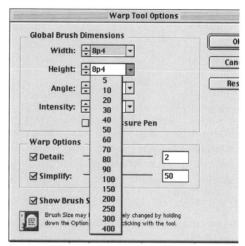, among other options. The global settings—the dimensions and angle of the cursor as well as the intensity of the liquify effect—apply to all the liquify tools and remain in effect until they're changed in any of the tool option dialog boxes. To choose non-global settings for an individual liquify tool, see page 366.

To choose global brush dimensions:

1. Double-click any liquify tool to open that tool's options dialog box. To choose a value for the cursor, enter a value in the appropriate field; or choose a value from the pop-up menu; or click the up or down arrowhead to the left of a field to increase/decrease (nudge) the current value **2**. For Angle and Intensity, each click of an arrow nudges the existing value up or down by 1.

   ➤ Shift-click a nudging (up/down) arrowhead to change the value by increments of 10.*

   ➤ Click a keyboard arrow, alone or in combination with Shift, to nudge the value in the currently active entry field upward or downward.

1 The Global Brush Dimensions and Show Brush Size options, shown here in the Warp Tool Options dialog box, are present in the options dialog box for all the Liquify tools.

	Click	Shift-Click*
Points	±1 pt	±6 pt
Picas	±p3	±1p
Inches	±1/8"	±1"
Millimeters	±1 mm	±10 mm
Centimeters	±0.1 cm	±1 cm
Pixels	±1 px	±10 px

2 Nudge value changes for a cursor's Width and Height.

*The first click rounds off the value in the current meaurement units, then the next Shift-click raises or lowers the value by the quantity shown in the table.

1 *Two liquify tool **cursors**: The cursor on the left is ½" x ½"; the cursor on the right is 1" x ½" at a -30° angle.*

2. Enter Width and/or Height values in any unit of measure.

3. Choose the Angle for the cursor **1**. The Angle is measured in a counterclockwise direction from the vertical axis.

4. Choose an Intensity (1%–100%) for the rate of change and amount of pull or push the tool exerts on the edges of an object(s). At 5%, edges will hardly be distorted. At 100%, the edges will follow the cursor exactly as it's dragged **2**.

5. To have a pen or graphics tablet control the Intensity, check Use Pressure Pen.

6. Click OK. To choose individual liquify tool options, see the instructions on the following page.

➤ Click Reset to restore the options settings for the current tool and all global dimensions to their default values.

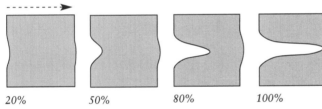

20%   50%   80%   100%

2 *The **Warp** tool is used with increasing **Intensity** on a square. In each case, the cursor was dragged from the left edge of the square to the right edge. At 20% Intensity, distortion was minimal. At 100%, the distortion followed the cursor almost all the way to the right edge.*

In contrast to the Global Brush Dimensions discussed on the previous page, the options in the lower portion of a liquify tool's options dialog box affect only that tool. In other words, you could choose different Detail and Simplify settings for the Warp tool than for the Bloat tool.

The options that are present in all or most of the options dialog boxes (Detail, Simplify, and Show Brush Size) are discussed below. Some tools also have additional options, such as the Complexity setting for the Scallop tool. These options are mentioned in the instructions for the applicable tool(s).

To choose options for an individual liquify tool:

1. Double-click a liquify tool to open that tool's options dialog box.

2. All the liquify tools have a Detail option **1**–**2** which controls the spacing of points that are added to produce distortion. To use this option, check the box, then enter a value (1–10) or drag the slider. The higher the Detail value, the closer the added points will be to one another. With Detail unchecked, distortion will be produced using only the existing points on the path, and no new anchor points will be added.

3. The Simplify option **3**–**4**, which is only available for the Warp, Twirl, Pucker, and Bloat tools, smoothes the distorted path by reducing extraneous points. Enter a value (0.2–100) or drag the slider. The higher the Simplify value, the smoother the curve. With Simplify unchecked, the resulting distortion will have many more anchor points than are necessary or desirable.

4. Check Show Brush Size to have the cursor display as an ellipse using the current Global Brush Dimensions (width, height, and angle) so you can see the cursor dimensions relative to the object(s) you're distorting. If unchecked, the familiar crosshairs cursor will be used instead.

5. Click OK.

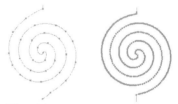

1 Use the **Detail** and **Simplify** options in any liquify tool option dialog box to control the spacing of added points and the smoothness of the distortion.

2 At left, the **Detail** for the **Twirl** tool was set to 1; at right, to 10 (with Simplify unchecked for both). Note how many points were added and how close together they are.

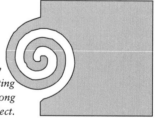

3 Here the **Twirl** tool is used at the minimum **Simplify** setting (0.2), resulting in rough bumps along the edge of the object.

4 Here the **Twirl** tool is used at the maximum **Simplify** setting (100). The edges look smoother.

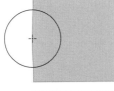

Distortion produced by the Warp tool

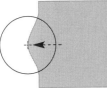

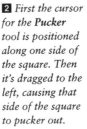

*First the cursor for the **Pucker** tool is positioned along one side of the square. Then it's dragged to the left, causing that side of the square to pucker out.*

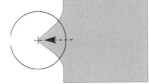

The original object

*After dragging toward the middle of the screw with the **Pucker** tool*

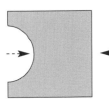

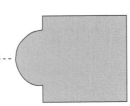

*After dragging into a square with the **Bloat** tool*

*After dragging away from the square with the **Bloat** tool*

In the instructions that follow, we'll discuss the Warp, Pucker, and Bloat tools. The Warp tool produces distortion by pushing a portion of an object's edge in the direction the cursor is dragged. It works like the Bloat tool, except the results are softer.

The Pucker tool acts like a magnet to squeeze an object's contour. As the tool nears the edge of an object, a point on the path moves toward the center of the brush cursor.

The Bloat tool expands the edge of an object outward from the center of the cursor, filling the cursor's circumference. If you drag the tool into an object, it will look as if the cursor cut a chunk out of it. If you drag the tool away from an object, it will bulge out and look as if the cursor shape was added to it.

To use the Warp, Pucker, or Bloat tool:

1. Double-click the Warp (Shift-R), Pucker, or Bloat tool.

2. Choose Detail and/or Simplify options (see page 366). *Note:* The Detail setting seems to make little difference for the Pucker or Bloat tool.

3. Click OK.

4. *Optional:* Select an object or group to prevent the tool from editing other nearby objects.

5. Click and hold, or drag, the tool over an object or objects.

➤ A bulge or indentation produced by the Bloat tool can't extend outside the circumference of the tool cursor.

Resize/reshape cursor interactively

To **resize and reshape** the cursor interactively, check the Show Brush Size option, then Option-drag/Alt-drag drag away from or toward the center of the cursor. To **resize** the cursor **proportionately**, Option-Shift-drag/Alt-Shift-drag away from or toward the center of the cursor. *Beware!* Both shortcuts establish a new global cursor size for all the liquify tools.

Warp, Pucker, Bloat Tools

The Twirl tool twirls a whole object from its center—if used with a large brush cursor. If the Twirl tool is used with a small brush cursor, each edge of an object will be twirled separately.

To use the Twirl tool:

1. Double-click the Twirl tool.

2. Under Twirl Options, choose or enter a Twirl Rate (-180°–180°). A positive value will produce a counterclockwise twirl; a negative value will produce a clockwise twirl. The Twirl Rate controls the speed at which the spiral is created and the amount of twirl. The higher the value (the further the slider is moved from 0°), the greater the distortion.

   ➤ To decelerate the rate of distortion, lower the Intensity setting.

3. Choose Detail and/or Simplify options (see page 366).

4. Click OK.

5. *Optional:* Select an object, group, or combination thereof.

6. Click and hold, or drag, the Twirl tool over an object **1**–**2**.

   ➤ Hold down Option/Alt after you start dragging to reverse the direction of the twirl.

Next, we'll discuss the Scallop, Crystallize, and Wrinkle tools. The Scallop tool produces curves or spikes that move toward the center of the cursor. Try using it to produce soft folds or gathers **3**. For a sharper-edged distortion, try using the Crystallize tool. It produces spiked curves that move away from the center of the cursor **4**. And finally, for a more random, wrinkled-edge distortion, try using the Wrinkle tool (**1**, next page). As with the Twirl tool, the longer the Wrinkle tool is clicked and held over an edge, the stronger the effect.

To use the Scallop, Crystallize, or Wrinkle tool:

1. Double-click the Scallop ▢, Crystallize ▢, or Wrinkle ▢ tool.

1 *The original object*

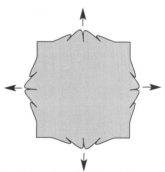

2 *After using the Twirl tool: Intensity 50%, Twirl Rate -59°, Detail 5, Simplify 60*

3 *To produce this shape, the Scallop tool was moved away from each edge of a square in the direction shown by the arrows.*

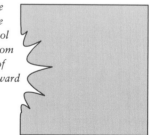

4 *To produce this shape, the Crystallize tool was moved from the left edge of the square toward the center of the square.*

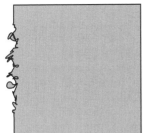

1 *Distortion produced using the **Wrinkle** tool: The cursor was placed at the middle of the left edge, then moved to the left, away from the object.*

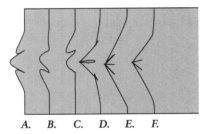

2 *The Scallop Tool Options dialog box*

A.   B.   C.   D.   E.   F.

3 *How the different "Brush Affects" checkboxes affect the distortion produced by the **Scallop** tool:*

A: Brush Affects In Tangent Handles and Brush Affects Out Tangent Handles checked.

B: Brush Affects In Tangent Handles checked.

C: Brush Affects Out Tangent Handles checked. Note the reflected direction of distortion between B and C.

D: Brush Affects Anchor Points checked.

E: Brush Affects Anchor Points and Brush Affects In Tangent Handles checked.

F: Brush Affects Anchor Points and Brush Affects Out Tangent Handles checked.

2. Choose a Complexity value (0–15) **2**. The higher the Complexity, the more curves or spikes will be generated. At a Complexity setting of 0, only existing anchor points will be modified; no new points will be created.

3. Choose a Detail setting. In addition to the spacing between points, this option also controls the number of curves or spikes generated by the tool.

4. For the Scallop or Crystallize tool, check one or two of the available "Brush Affects" boxes. For the Wrinkle tool, you can check one, two, or all three of the Brush Affects options. Brush Affects Anchor Points repositions anchor points; Brush Affects In Tangent Handles and Brush Affects Out Tangent Handles change the control handles of added points **3**.

   Note: To preserve the current position of the anchor points, don't check Brush Affects Anchor Points.

   ➤ When using the Scallop tool, if only one Brush Affects Tangent Handles option is checked and Brush Affects Anchor Points is unchecked, distortion won't be pulled to the center of the cursor, and the effect will be more subtle (finger-like).

5. Click OK.

6. *Optional:* Select an object, group, or combination thereof.

7. Click and hold, or drag, the tool over an object or objects.

Scallop, Wrinkle, Crystallize Tools

Envelopes

With version 10, Illustrator has added a powerful envelope distortion feature. First you create a container, called an "envelope," for one or more objects. Then you distort the envelope shape, and the object within the envelope conforms to that distortion. Envelopes can be created using one of three different commands on the Object > Envelope Distort submenu:

■ By creating a mesh first and then manipulating it (**Make with Mesh** command).

■ Using a preset, but editable, warp (**Make with Warp** command).

■ Or by converting a user-drawn path into an envelope (**Make with Top Object** command).

Regardless of which method is used to create the envelope, both the envelope and the object will remain fully editable, both while the object is contained in the envelope and after it's expanded. If you're familiar with using gradient meshes, you'll be way ahead of the game here because envelopes are really meshes, and they work the same way. The only difference is that envelope meshes are used to distort shapes, whereas gradient meshes are used to apply color areas.

Envelopes can be applied to just about any Illustrator object, including paths (simple and compound), placed (embedded) images, images rasterized in Illustrator, text, clipping masks, objects with applied effects, styles, or brush strokes, and symbol instances.

When you're done using an envelope to distort an object, you have two choices: You can either expand the result, leaving the distorted object but deleting the envelope, or you can release the result, thus creating two separate objects—the envelope shape on top of the original, undistorted object.

➤ Editable text can be contained within an envelope, and it will remain editable. However, if the envelope is expanded, the text will convert automatically to outline paths.

Another way to warp

You can also create envelopes using the commands on the **Effect > Warp** submenu, but with one notable disadvantage. When an envelope is applied via an effect, the only way to edit the envelope is via the Warp Options dialog box, which is reopened by double-clicking the Warp effect listed on the Appearance palette. You won't be able to manipulate the points or segments on the warp shape itself.

If you use the **Envelope Distort** commands, on the other hand (discussed at left), you will have the option to readjust the mesh points and segments at any time.

1 *The original object*

2 *A **warp** envelope distortion using a horizontal arc with a 50% bend and a -50% horizontal distortion*

3 *A **mesh** using a 3x3 grid that was then distorted manually*

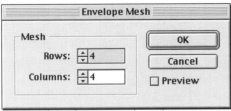

1 *Choose Rows and Columns values for the envelope mesh in the Envelope Mesh dialog box.*

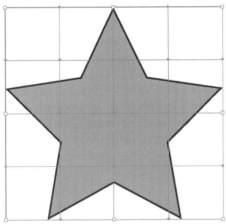

2 *A 4x4 mesh envelope on a five-pointed star*

➤ When enveloping a placed image, if the Envelope Distort commands are grayed out, it means the image must be embedded in the file prior to being enveloped (to embed images, see page 258). A linked TIFF image can be enveloped, and if the envelope is expanded or released, the TIFF will remain linked to the file.

➤ An envelope for a clipping path will be scaled automatically in order to cover both the visible and clipped parts of the objects.

In the following instructions you will create an envelope as a mesh. Since all envelopes essentially are meshes, we think working with a mesh first will help you get a handle, in visual terms, on how the distortion process works.

To create a mesh envelope:

1. Select an object or group.

2. Choose Object > Envelope Distort > Make with Mesh (Cmd-Option-M/ Ctrl-Alt-M).

3. Check Preview **1**.

4. Enter the desired number of Rows and Columns or click an up or down arrowhead.

5. Click OK. An envelope will be created in a grid, using your specifications, overlaying the object **2**. To edit the envelope mesh, see page 374.

➤ The arrowheads change existing values by ±1. Using Shift-click, the arrowheads change existing values by ±10.

Another way to create an envelope is to use a preset shape to produce the distortion, such as an arc, arch, shell, fish, or fisheye. You're not limited to the preset shape, though. With the Warp Options dialog box open, you can apply distortion to the envelope, and then you can further customize it after closing the dialog box.

To create a warp envelope:

1. Select an object or group.

2. Choose Object > Envelope Distort > Make with Warp (Cmd-Option-W/ Ctrl-Alt-W).

3. Check Preview **1**.

4. Choose one of the 15 preset Styles.

5. Click Horizontal or Vertical for the warp orientation.

6. Enter a Bend value (-100–100) or move the slider to the desired value to control the extent of the Warp style **2**.

7. Enter or choose Horizontal and Vertical Distortion values (-100–100) to specify how much additional horizontal and vertical distortion the chosen warp style will contain.

8. Click OK. A warp grid will now overlay the object(s) using the specifications from the Warp Options dialog box **3**. To edit the envelope path, see page 374.

➤ To change the current warp style used for the envelope, select the envelope, then choose Object > Envelope Distort > Reset with Warp again.

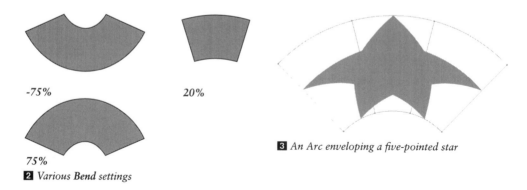

1 In the **Warp Options** dialog box, the first step is to choose a preset **Style**. Then, if you like, you can customize the distortion either by using the dialog box or by manipulating the mesh after closing the dialog box.

-75%

20%

75%

2 Various **Bend** settings

3 An Arc enveloping a five-pointed star

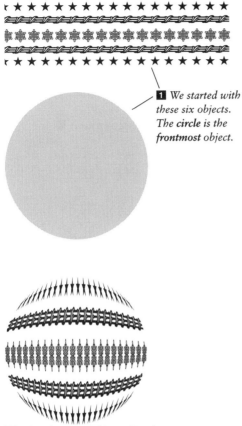

 1 *We started with these six objects. The* **circle** *is the* **frontmost** *object.*

2 *After choosing Object > Envelope Distort >* **Make with Top Object**

3 *After adding* **mesh points** *and moving them around*

And finally, a third way to create an envelope is to produce it from your own path. Be creative!

To create an envelope from a user-created path:

1. Create a path to use for the envelope. The path can be open or closed. Don't worry about whether it has a fill or stroke; both will be removed automatically.

2. Make sure the path to be used as the envelope is on top of the objects to be put into the envelope. Either choose Object > Arrange > Bring to Front (Cmd-Shift-]/ Ctrl-Shift-]) or restack the object on the Layers palette. This really matters.

3. Select the path and the object(s) to be enveloped. They can overlap each other, but they don't have to. When you choose the Make with Top Object command (the next step), the objects will be sucked into the envelope like a vacuum cleaner. Watch.

4. Choose Object > Envelope Distort > Make with Top Object (Cmd-Option-C/ Ctrl-Alt-C). The objects will be moved into, and will be scaled automatically to fit, the envelope **1**–**3**. To edit the envelope, see the next page.

➤ If you use an open path for the envelope, it won't stay that way. When you choose Make with Top Object, the path will be closed automatically.

➤ To use a text character for an envelope, first it has to be converted to outlines, released from its compound path, and ungrouped. You can only use one character at a time.

Envelope from Path

As we said before, envelope meshes work like gradient meshes (a mesh is a mesh is a mesh). If you're not familiar with meshes yet, no big deal; they're easy to work with. The techniques for editing meshes are summarized in the following instructions. For more detailed instructions on editing meshes, see pages 318–319.

To edit an envelope:

1. Make sure Smart Guides are showing so you will be able see the envelope and anchor points without selecting the envelope (View > Smart Guides or Cmd-U/ Ctrl-U).

2. The envelope will be listed as <Envelope> on the Layers palette **1**. To select it, click its target circle.

3. Do any of the following (try to have fun):

   Use the Add Anchor Point tool (+) to add mesh points to existing mesh lines. Option/Alt-click with the Add Anchor Point tool to delete mesh points that don't have lines crisscrossing through them.

   Use the Mesh tool (U) to add mesh points with mesh lines that crisscross through them. Option-click/Alt-click with the Mesh tool to delete mesh lines or points. Or drag with the Mesh tool to move mesh points.

   Use the Direct-selection tool (A) to move mesh points or mesh patches.

   Modify the mesh points or lines using a transform tool, such as Scale, Rotate, or Move, or push them around using a liquify tool, such as Warp, Bloat, or Wrinkle.

➤ To edit the contents of an envelope but not the envelope itself, follow the instructions on the next page.

Back to square one

Choose Object > Envelope Distort > **Reset with Warp** (Cmd-Option-W/Ctrl-Alt-W) or **Reset with Mesh** (Cmd-Option/M/Ctrl-Alt-M) to reset the envelope to its state prior to any manual mesh point or line additions or changes.

If you choose the Reset with Mesh command, check **Maintain Envelope Shape** **2** to reset the inner mesh points while preserving the envelope's outer shape. Or uncheck this option to reset the entire envelope to a rectangular mesh.

1 *An Envelope listing*

2 *The Reset Envelope Mesh dialog box*

Keeping up with appearances

The Appearance palette lists different attributes depending on which part of an envelope is currently being edited. When you edit the envelope itself, attributes or applied effects for the envelope, if any, will be listed. When you edit the contents, attributes for the object will be listed. Merely toggling between the Edit Contents and Edit Envelope commands doesn't target the correct object. To avoid confusion, before adding or editing appearances, be sure to **target the correct object**!

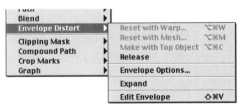

1 *With the envelope selected, you can switch to editing the object's **contents**...*

2 *...or with an object selected, you can switch back to **editing the envelope**.*

In these instructions, you will learn how to edit objects within an envelope without changing the envelope itself. You can toggle back and forth between editing objects and the envelope whenever you need to.

To edit objects in an envelope:

1. With an envelope selected, choose Object > Envelope Distort > Edit Contents (Cmd-Shift-V/Ctrl-Shift-V) **1**.

2. An expand arrowhead will appear next to the <Envelope> listing on the Layers palette. Click the arrowhead to expand the list, then click the circle for an individual path to target it for editing. You can edit the object contents as you would any non-enveloped object. The Appearance palette will update.

3. When you're done editing the objects, choose Object > Envelope Distort > Edit Envelope (Cmd-Shift-V/Ctrl-Shift-V) **2**. The envelope will recenter itself on the edited object automatically. If you click the target circle for the "Envelope," any appearances you apply now will affect the envelope—not its contents.

Once you're done editing the object and envelope, you can use either the Release or the Expand command.

The Release command is useful if you have an envelope that you like, and you think you might want to use it again. If you've taken a preset warp style and fiddled with it, for example, you can release the envelope and preserve it as a separate object so it can be used to envelope other objects (use the Make with Top Object command).

To release an envelope:

1. Select an envelope.

2. Choose Object > Envelope Distort > Release. This command will leave the original object(s) unaltered, with the former envelope on top . On the Layers palette, you will see a <Mesh> listing for the envelope and one or more <Path> listings for the objects .

Use Expand as a final step once you're satisfied with the distortion. To choose expand options for both raster images and vector objects, see the following page.

To expand an envelope:

1. Select an envelope. The Expand command will delete the envelope, so make a copy of it for safekeeping, if desired.

2. Choose Object > Envelope Distort > Expand. The distortion will be applied to the object 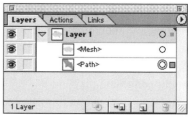. The envelope will be discarded and can't be retrieved, except by choosing Undo. A <Group> containing the distorted object(s) will be created 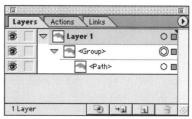. To learn how Illustrator expands different kinds of attributes, such as live effects, appearances, and styles, see the following page.

➤ If an envelope containing a gradient mesh is expanded, it will remain a mesh.

➤ If an envelope containing a symbol or brush stroke is expanded, the symbol or brush stroke will be converted to standard paths.

➤ Text that is expanded will be converted automatically to outline paths.

1 *After choosing Object > Envelope Distort > **Release**, the envelope is placed on top of the object; the object is unchanged. (We applied an Opacity of 75% to the envelope.)*

2 *The Layers palette after choosing the **Release** command*

3 *After choosing the **Expand** command, the envelope distortion is applied to the star, and the envelope itself is discarded.*

4 *The Layers palette after applying the **Expand** command*

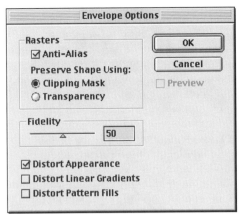

1 *Envelope Options*

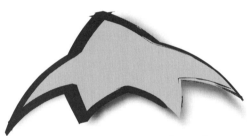

2 *A five-pointed star with effects is distorted using a 70% Bend, Horizontal Arc Warp. Then* **Distort Appearance** *is checked in* **Envelope Options.**

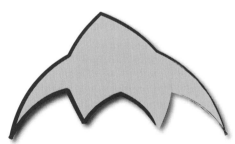

3 *The same five-pointed star with* **Distort Appearance** *unchecked in* **Envelope Options**

Envelope Options control how content (appearances, gradients, and patterns) is distorted, as well as what happens to that content when the envelope is expanded.

To choose envelope options:

1. To change the settings for an existing envelope, select it now (or select multiple envelopes).
   or
   To choose settings for subsequently created envelopes, deselect all.

2. Choose Object > Envelope Distort > Envelope Options.

3. Check Preview.

4. For raster images (placed images or images rasterized in Illustrator), check Anti-Alias **1** to smooth the edges. This operation can increase the distortion time.

5. For Preserve Shape Using:

   Click Clipping Mask to place a raster image in a clipping mask if it's expanded.
   or
   Click Transparency to make the background of the expanded raster image transparent by use of an alpha channel.

6. Enter a Fidelity value (0–100) for the number of new anchor points to be added to a path to make it fit the envelope shape. The higher the Fidelity value, the more points will be added.

7. Check Distort Appearance **2** to have an object's appearances (live effects, brushes, styles, etc.) be distorted by the envelope. If the envelope is expanded, each appearance will also be expanded into a plain path or group, which will be listed separately on the Layers palette. For example, if an appearance consisting of two strokes was applied to the object, when the envelope is expanded each stroke will be listed separately on the Layers palette.

   Uncheck Distort Appearance to distort the object, but not any appearances. Any appearances will be applied after distortion **3**. If you then expand the envelope,

(Continued on the following page)

the appearances will remain applied to the object and the resulting group will contain only one object.

Note: If appearances are applied to an envelope, those appearances won't be applied to the objects within the envelope. However, if the envelope is expanded, the appearances will be applied to the resulting group.

8. When Distort Appearance is checked, these two additional options become available:

    Check Distort Linear Gradients to have a linear gradient fill be affected by an envelope distortion. If the envelope is then expanded, the gradient will become a mesh nested within a sequence of nested groups. If Distort Linear Gradients is off and the envelope is expanded, the linear gradient will be part of the resulting <Path>.
    and/or
    Check Distort Pattern Fills **1**–**2** to have pattern fills be affected by an envelope distortion. If the envelope is then expanded, the pattern will become a sequence of nested groups containing components of the pattern. If Distort Pattern Fills is off and the envelope is expanded, pattern fills will remain undistorted and will be a part of the resulting <Path>.

9. Click OK.

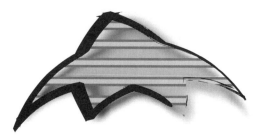

1 *Distort Pattern Fills off:* The pattern does *not* conform to the envelope distortion.

2 *Distort Pattern Fills on:* The pattern *conforms* to the envelope distortion.

Chapter 21: Distort ◆ Study Guide

Learning Objectives

- Use liquify tools to distort objects.
- Use envelopes to distort objects.

Get Up and Running Exercises

- Experiment with the liquify tools.
  - ▲ Try the same liquify tool on a variety of paths, including straight, curved, horizontal, and vertical segments.
  - ▲ Practice controlling intensity and direction. Can you control intensity and brush size as you draw?
  - ▲ Do the liquify tools behave differently depending on where and in which direction they're dragged?
- How would you reproduce the following type distortion in a single step? (Hint: None of the Object > Envelope Distort commands were used.)

(Continued on the following page)

- Draw a face and apply the Object > Envelope Distort > Make with Mesh command. Explore how you can create facial expressions simply by editing the mesh grid. The figure below shows one example.

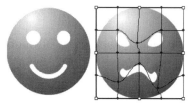

- In the following figure, a symbol set was created using the Fish1 symbol from the Nature symbols library. How can you use a distortion feature to quickly reproduce the school of fish below?

Class Discussion Questions

- What's the difference between using a liquify tool and a distortion envelope? For example, why would you decide to use the Twirl tool instead of the Twist envelope, or vice versa?

- How do you control the strength of the distortions applied by a liquify tool?

- What are the different ways to create an envelope, and when would you want to use each one?

- How do you switch between editing a distortion envelope and editing the objects inside the envelope?

- What's the difference between releasing and expanding a distortion envelope?

Review Questions

Multiple choice

1. What would be the most efficient way to apply a simple distortion centered across an entire object?

    A. Choose Effect > Warp > Fisheye

    B. Choose Object > Envelope Distort > Make with Warp, and choose the Fisheye warp.

    C. Use the Bloat tool

    D. Use the Pucker tool

2. Which liquify tool pulls object points in the direction of the center of the cursor?

    A. Bloat tool

    B. Pucker tool

    C. Scallop tool

    D. Warp tool

3. Which method would be a good starting point for creating a distortion that's a slight variation on an arc?

    A. Choose Effect > Warp > Arc.

    B. Choose Object > Envelope Distort > Make with Mesh.

    C. Choose Object > Envelope Distort > Make with Warp, then choose Style: Arc.

    D. Manually draw an arc, select the arc and the object to distort, then choose Object > Envelope Distort > Make with Top Object.

4. Which distortion method lets you make a distortion envelope from any shape you can draw?

    A. Object > Envelope Distort > Edit Envelope

    B. Object > Envelope Distort > Make with Top Object

    C. Object > Envelope Distort > Make with Warp

    D. Effect > Warp submenu

5. Which liquify tool option can help prevent unwanted bumps on paths distorted by the liquify tool?

    A. Detail

    B. Fidelity

    C. Intensity

    D. Simplify

Fill-in-the-blank

1. To use a liquify tool on a pattern fill, the fill must be _____ first.

2. To see options for a liquify tool, _____ the tool.

3. The tool intensity, cursor angle, and cursor dimensions are controlled for all liquify tools in the _____ settings group.

4. To push the edge of an object outward as far as the size of the tool cursor, use the _____ tool.

5. To distort a selected object using a rectangular distortion grid as a starting point, choose the _____ command.

6. If you applied a brush to an object and you want it to be distorted according to the object's distortion envelope, check _____ in Envelope Options.

Definitions

1. What is a liquify tool?

2. What is an envelope?

3. What is the Detail option for liquify tools?

4. What is a warp envelope?

5. What is a mesh envelope?

This chapter begins with a comparison between effects and filters, and a how-to section for applying them. We also provide specific instructions for applying some of the effects and filters (including Hatch Effects and Photo Crosshatch), and for reference, a complete illustrated compendium of all the raster filters.

Apply Fisheye	⇧⌘E
Fisheye...	⌥⇧⌘E
Document Raster Effects Settings...	
Convert to Shape	▶
Distort & Transform	▶
Path	▶
Pathfinder	▶
Rasterize...	
Stylize	▶
SVG Filters	▶
Warp	▶
Artistic	▶
Blur	▶
Brush Strokes	▶
Distort	▶
Pixelate	▶
Sharpen	▶
Sketch	▶
Stylize	▶
Texture	▶
Video	▶

Stylize submenu:
- Add Arrowheads...
- Drop Shadow...
- Feather...
- Inner Glow...
- Outer Glow...
- Round Corners...

1 *The Effect menu is divided into two sections, with mostly vector effects (and a few raster effects) in the top portion and only raster effects on the bottom.*

Effects and filters

Illustrator's effects and filters are used to apply distortion, texture, color adjustments, and various other artistic and stylistic "special effects" to objects and images. Many of the filters on the Filter menu have a matching counterpart under the Effect menu **1**. In fact, the Filter and Effect menus are so interdependent, settings used for a command on one menu become the settings for its counterpart on the other menu.

However, there are significant differences between effects and filters, both in terms of what kind of objects they can be applied to and whether the result is editable after the command is applied. We'll discuss some of those differences next.

Using effects

Unlike filters, effects change only the appearance of an object, not its underlying path. Filter menu commands change the underlying object and are not reeditable, whereas Effect menu commands don't change the object and are reeditable. Effects lend themselves to experimentation because an effect can be reedited or deleted at any time without affecting the object or any other effects or appearance attributes currently applied to that object. What's more, the underlying object's path can be reshaped at any time, and the effects will adjust accordingly. In other words, they're live!

(Continued on the following page)

Using Effects

On the top portion of the Effect menu you'll find vector commands that have counterparts on the Filter menu, such as Drop Shadow and Roughen, as well as some commands that are not found on the Filter menu, such as Feather, Inner Glow, Outer Glow, and Convert to Shape (see pages 385–388). All the raster effects on the lower part of the Effect menu have counterparts on the Filter menu. These effects can be applied to any kind of object, not just images!

➤ Raster effects become rasterized (do not remain vector) when exported to a vector format such as SVG. But remember, this increases the file size.

Effects can be applied to **any** kind of object, even editable text (it doesn't have to be converted into outlines first), and the text will remain editable. In fact, if you use the Outline Object effect to convert text into outlines, the underlying text will remain editable, as long as its font is available in your system.

Like object attributes, applied effects are listed on the Appearance palette for each selected object **1**. If an effect is applied to a targeted layer, sublayer, or group, that effect will be applied to all existing and future objects on that layer, sublayer, or group. Furthermore, since effects display on the Appearance palette along with other attributes, they can also be saved in a style, and you can re-edit any effect that is contained in a style at any time.

Using filters

Unlike effects, commands on the Filter menu **2** change the "**actual**" objects. Some filters are designed primarily for use on vector (path) objects, and they are grouped in submenu categories in the upper portion of the menu. Some of these filters are discussed individually in this chapter **3**.

Filters that are designed for use on bitmap images and rasterized objects are grouped in ten submenu categories at the bottom of the Filter menu: Artistic, Blur, Brush Strokes, Distort, Pixelate, Sharpen, Sketch, Stylize, Texture, and Video. If you're a Photoshop

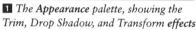

1 The **Appearance** palette, showing the Trim, Drop Shadow, and Transform **effects**

The **vector** filters, which are applied to path objects (except Photo Crosshatch and Object Mosaic, which are raster filters)

The **raster** filters, which are applied to placed images or RGB color mode bitmap objects

2 The **Filter** menu

3 Hatch lines created using Illustrator's Pen & Ink > **Hatch Effects** filter

Diane Margolin

Quickly reapply

Reapply last-used effect	**Cmd-Shift-E/ Ctrl-Shift-E**
Open last-used effects dialog box	**Cmd-Option-Shift-E/ Ctrl-Alt-Shift-E**
Reapply last-used filter using the same settings	**Cmd-E/Ctrl-E**
Open last-used filter dialog to choose new settings	**Cmd-Option-E/ Ctrl-Alt-E**

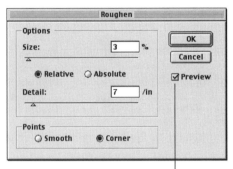

1 *Check the* **Preview** *box in any effect or filter dialog box that offers this option to see a preview in the illustration window.*

2 *Other effect and filter dialogs have a* **preview window** *inside the dialog box.*

user, you may already be familiar with them. The raster filters are discussed and illustrated in the latter part of this chapter.

➤ Some raster filters work on RGB or Grayscale images, but not on CMYK or 1-bit bitmap images.

You can also apply Photoshop-compatible filters to placed images and to objects that are rasterized in Illustrator. To make them accessible in Illustrator, copy the filters (or aliases of the filters) into the Photoshop Filters folder inside Illustrator's Plug-ins folder, then relaunch the application.

Applying effects and filters

Some effects and filters are applied simply by choosing the command from a submenu while others are applied via a dialog box in which special options are chosen. To make things easier, we recommend memorizing the shortcuts listed in the sidebar at left.

➤ Some filters are memory-intensive, but using lower or different settings in a filter dialog box can help speed things up.

Many vector effect and filter dialog boxes have a Preview box **1**. Check this box to preview a filter in your illustration while the dialog box is open. After entering a new value in a field, press Tab to update the preview.

Raster effect and filter dialog boxes have a preview window inside the dialog box **2**. In most dialog boxes, you can drag inside the preview window to move the image inside it. Click the + button to zoom in on the image in the preview window, or click the – button to zoom out. A flashing line below the preview percentage indicates the preview is rendering.

➤ In a raster effect or filter dialog box, you can hold down Option/Alt and click Reset to reset the slider settings to what they were when the dialog box was opened.

Note: Some Illustrator filters are covered in other chapters: for example, the Drop Shadow filter on page 360. For other page locations, look up the filter name under "Filters" in the index.

In these instructions, you will apply an effect directly to a layer, sublayer, group, or object. In the instructions on the following page, you will add to, or edit an effect in, a style.

To apply an effect:

1. On the Layers palette, target a layer, sublayer, group, or object **1**.

Note: To limit an effect to only an object's stroke or fill, select the object, then click the Stroke or Fill attribute on the Appearance palette.

2. Choose an effect from a submenu on the Effect menu.

3. Check the Preview box, if there is one, to preview the effect as you choose options, then choose options **2**.

4. Click OK **3**. If you applied the effect to only a stroke or fill, the effect name will be nested below the Stroke or Fill attribute on the Appearance palette. Expand the attribute list, if necessary, to see the effect list.

To edit an effect:

1. On the Layers palette, target the layer, sublayer, group, or object to which the effect you want to edit is applied. If the effect was applied to only an object's stroke or fill, select the object, then expand the Stroke or Fill attribute on the Appearance palette.

2. Double-click the effect name on the Appearance palette **4**.

3. Make the desired adjustments, then click OK.

1 The original **targeted** object

2 A value is chosen in the effect dialog box.

3 The Feather effect is applied.

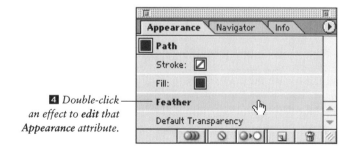

4 Double-click an effect to **edit** that Appearance attribute.

Apply Effect; Edit Effect

Effect	
Apply Exclude	⇧⌘E
Exclude	⌥⇧⌘E
Document Raster Effects Settings...	
Convert to Shape	▶
Distort & Transform	▶
Path	▶
Pathfinder	▶
Rasterize...	
Stylize	▶
SVG Filters	▶
Warp	▶
Artistic	▶
Blur	▶
Brush Strokes	▶
Distort	▶
Pixelate	▶
Sharpen	▶
Sketch	▶
Stylize	▶
Texture	▶
Video	▶

Pathfinder submenu:

Add
Intersect
Exclude
Subtract
Minus Back
Divide
Trim
Merge
Crop
Outline
Hard Mix...
Soft Mix...
Trap...

1 *The Pathfinder commands can be applied as effects via the Effect menu.*

Pathfinder effects 10.0!

The Pathfinder commands that are available on the Pathfinder palette are also available as effects on the **Effect > Pathfinder** submenu **1**. However, the Pathfinder effects don't affect the actual objects, only their appearance. In other words, you can delete a Pathfinder appearance attribute at any time without affecting the actual objects.

A few other differences worth noting. First, the Pathfinder effects do not create compound shapes. Second, the Divide, Trim, and Merge effects don't break up objects' overlapping areas into separate objects for recoloring or repositioning, as their counterparts on the Pathfinder palette do.

Here are a few guidelines for applying Pathfinder effects:

■ Before applying a Pathfinder effect, you must collect the objects that you want to apply the effect to into a sublayer or group, then target that sublayer or group (that's target—not select).

■ Pathfinder effects can be included in a style.

■ Objects remain moveable within, into, and out of a group or sublayer after the effect is applied.

■ A Pathfinder effect can be removed at any time. To remove an effect, drag the effect name onto the Delete Selected Item (trash) icon on the Appearance palette.

■ Double-clicking the effect name opens the Pathfinder Options dialog box, where you can preview other Pathfinder effects and change which Pathfinder effect is applied to the group.

■ If a Pathfinder effect is expanded (Object > Expand Appearance), the result will be neither a compound shape nor a compound path—but just a plain path.

If a group containing a Pathfinder effect is copied and pasted into Photoshop as a shape layer, the shape will be broken apart into separate paths. If a compound shape is pasted as a shape layer, the paths won't be broken apart.

Pathfinder Effects

To add to, or edit an effect in, a style:

1. Click the style name or swatch on the Styles palette **1**. The style name will appear at the top of the Appearance palette.

2. To add an effect, choose an effect from a submenu on the Effect menu, check the Preview box, if there is one, to preview the effect as you choose options, then choose options.
   or
   To edit an existing effect, double-click the effect name on the Appearance palette **2**.

3. Click OK.

4. Choose Redefine Style "[style name]" from the Appearance palette menu to update the style.

Easy come, easy go.

To remove an effect from a layer, object, or style:

1. On the Layers palette, target the layer, sublayer, group, or object that contains the effect to be removed.
   or
   On the Styles palette, click the style name or swatch that contains the effect to be removed.

2. On the Appearance palette, click the effect name.

3. Click on, or drag the effect name to, the Delete Selected Item (trash) button on the Appearance palette.

4. If you're removing an effect from a style, choose Redefine Style "[style name]" from the Appearance palette menu to update the style.

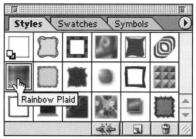

1 *A style is clicked on the Styles palette.*

2 *To edit an effect, double-click the effect name on the Appearance palette.*

1 *The original object*

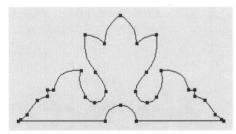

2 *Shape and scale options are chosen in the Shape effect dialog box.*

In these instructions, you'll use the Convert to Shape effects, which are found only on the Effect menu. Like all effects, they change an object's shape without changing the actual underlying path.

To apply a Convert to Shape effect:

1. Select/target an object or objects in the document window or via the Layers palette **1**.

2. Choose Effect > Convert to Shape > Rectangle, Rounded Rectangle, or Ellipse. *Note:* Any of these three options can also be chosen from the Shape pop-up menu once the dialog box is open **2**.

3. Check Preview.

4. Click Absolute, then enter the total desired Width and Height values for the shape appearance.
   or
   Click Relative, then enter the Extra Width or Extra Height that you want added to or subtracted from the object's current shape. Enter a positive value to expand the shape or a negative value to contract the shape.

5. *Optional:* For the Rounded Rectangle shape, you can change the Corner Radius value.

6. Click OK **3**–**4**.

➤ Try also using Effect > Stylize > Round Corners to change the appearance of an object's shape.

3 *A **rectangular shape appearance attribute** is added to the object; the underlying path is unchanged.*

4 *The word "Rectangle" shows up on the Appearance palette.*

Next we'll show you how to use the "live" aspect of effects.

To use live shapes with text:

1. Select a type block .

2. Choose Add New Fill from the Appearance palette menu. *Note:* The original fill or stroke color will be listed on the palette if the type is selected using a type tool, but not (at least not initially) if the Selection tool is used.

3. Click Fill on the Appearance palette, then choose a color from the Color palette.

4. Click the Duplicate Selected Item button at the bottom of the Appearance palette.

5. Click the lower Fill attribute on the Appearance palette, then choose a different color for it .

6. Apply an Effect > Convert to Shape effect to the new Fill attribute, using the Relative option (see steps 2–3 on the previous page) .

7. To see how the live effect works, add or delete some type characters or resize the type. The new fill shape will resize accordingly 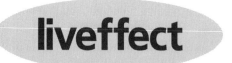.

Outline Object for text

If you open an Illustrator file containing a font that is not currently active in the system, the Font Problem alert box will open (click Open to have Illustrator substitute a font). If Effect > Path > Outline Object was applied to any of the type using a now inactive font, that type will display and print properly—but it can't be edited. If the font used in the Outline Object text *is* active in the system when the document is reopened, the text will be editable in Illustrator and in any other program that reads Illustrator objects.

Unlike the Create Outlines command on the Type menu, Outline Object creates outlined text that remains fully editable as text. You can't reshape a text character's paths using this effect, however, as you can using Type > Create Outlines. The Outline Object effect is better suited for large text than for small text.

effect

1 *The original text*

2 *A new Fill attribute is created and duplicated, and a different color is chosen for it.*

3 *After applying the* **Convert to Shape** *effect to the new Fill (Shape: Ellipse; Relative: Extra Width 13 pt, Extra Height 3 pt)*

4 *When more characters are* **added** *to the text, the* **shape enlarges** *to accommodate it.*

1 *The original group of objects*

2 *Options in the Inner Glow effect dialog box are chosen.*

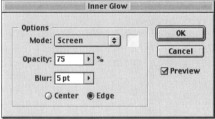

3 *After applying the Inner Glow effect*

4 *After applying the Outer Glow effect*

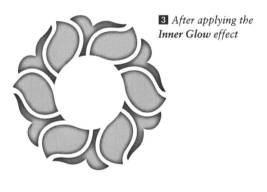

5 *Both Glow effects applied*

The Inner Glow effect applies a color glow that spreads from the edge of an object toward its center. The Outer Glow effect applies a color glow that spreads from the edge of an object outward.

To apply the Feather effect, see page 382. To apply the Drop Shadow effect, see page 360.

To apply the Inner Glow or Outer Glow effect:

1. Select/target a layer, sublayer, group, or object **1**.

2. Choose Effect > Stylize > Inner Glow or Outer Glow.

3. Check Preview **2**.

4. Do any of the following:

   Click the Color square, then choose a different glow color.

   Choose a blending mode for the glow color from the pop-up menu.

   Change the Opacity for the glow color.

   Move the Blur slider to adjust how far the glow extends inward or outward from the edge of the object. The higher the Blur value, the wider the glow.

   For Inner Glow, click Center to have the glow spread outward from the object's center or click Edge to have the glow spread inward from the object's edge to its center.

5. Click OK **3**–**5**.

Inner Glow; Outer Glow

An advantage to using the Effect menu version of Add Arrowheads over the Filter menu version is that it has a preview option.

To apply the Add Arrowheads effect:

1. Select an open path.

2. From the Effect menu or Filter menu, choose Stylize > Add Arrowheads.

3. Check Preview, if you chose the effect command.

4. Click the left or right Start arrow to choose from the various head designs 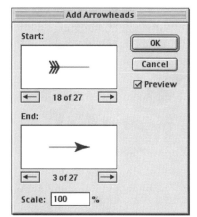. Click until no style appears if you don't want an arrowhead or tail at the start of the path.

5. Click the left or right End arrow to choose from the various head designs. Click until no style appears if you don't want an arrow head or tail at the end of the path.

6. *Optional:* Choose a Scale percentage for the Start and End styles (hard to do without a preview, huh?). To choose a different Scale percentage for the Start and End styles, apply the effect or filter in two separate passes.

7. Click OK. If you used the Filter command, the arrowhead can now be reshaped or moved like any other path (use the Direct-selection tool) **2**–**4**.

➤ If a Filter menu arrowhead or tail winds up on the wrong end of the path, undo it or delete it (use the Direct-selection tool), then redo it. Cmd-E/Ctrl-E reopens the last-used filter dialog box.

➤ To redo an Effect menu arrowhead or tail, double-click the Add Arrowheads appearance attribute on the Appearance palette to reopen the Add Arrowheads dialog box.

1 *In the Add Arrowheads dialog box, click the arrows until you find a style you like (or no style) for the Start and/or End of the path, and enter a Scale percentage (this figure shows the Effect menu version).*

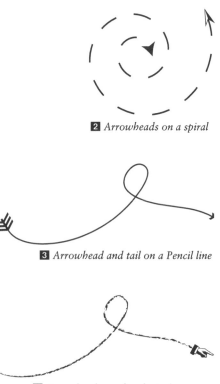

2 *Arrowheads on a spiral*

3 *Arrowhead and tail on a Pencil line*

4 *Arrowhead on a brush stroke*

Add Arrowheads

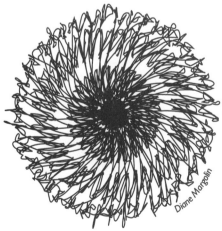

1 *The Scribble and Tweak dialog box*

2 *The original object*

3 *After applying the Scribble & Tweak filter (Horizontal 14.5, Vertical 19.5, "In" and "Out" boxes checked)*

A few vector effects and filters
To scribble or tweak:

1. Select a path object or objects.

2. Choose Effect > Distort & Transform > Scribble & Tweak or Filter > Distort > Scribble & Tweak (it's on the top portion of the menu).

3. Check Preview and move the dialog box out of the way, if necessary **1**.

4. Choose Horizontal and Vertical percentages to control how much anchor points can be moved in either direction.

5. Click Relative to move points by percentages of the size of the object or click Absolute to move points by a specific amount.

6. *Optional:* Check Anchor Points if you want anchor points to move; check "In" Control Points to change the segments that extend to anchor points; check "Out" Control Points to change the segments that extend from anchor points. Or leave Anchor Points unchecked to preserve more of the object's original shape.

7. Click OK **2**–**3**. Corner points will automatically be converted into points with direction lines. How direction lines are moved depends on whether you chose either or both of the "In" or "Out" options.

➤ The greater the number of anchor points on the path, the stronger the Scribble or Tweak. To intensify the result, apply Object > Path > Add Anchor Points one or more times before applying the filter or effect.

Scribble & Tweak

389

The Roughen filter makes an object look more hand-drawn by adding anchor points and then moving them.

To rough up a shape:

1. Select a path object or objects, and choose View > Hide Edges (Cmd-H/Ctrl-H), if you like, to make previewing easier.

2. Choose Effect > Distort & Transform > Roughen or Filter > Distort > Roughen (it's on the top portion of the menu).

3. Check Preview **1**.

4. Choose a Size percentage to specify how far points can be moved. Use a very low Size percentage to preserve the object's basic shape.

5. Click Relative to move points by a percentage of the object's size or click Absolute to move points by a specific amount.

6. Choose a Detail amount for the number of points to be added to each inch of the path segments.

7. Click Smooth to produce soft edges or click Corner to produce pointy edges.

8. Click OK **2**–**3**.

To twist path points around an object's center:

1. Select a path object or objects **4**. If two or more objects are selected, they will be twirled together.

2. Choose Effect > Distort & Transform > Twist or Filter > Distort > Twist (it's on the upper part of the menu).

3. Enter a positive Angle to twirl the path(s) clockwise or a negative number to twirl it/them counterclockwise (-3600–3600).

4. Click OK **5**–**6**. Only an object's outer shape will be twisted, not a pattern or gradient fill.

➤ For comparison, try using the Twist tool (see page 125).

➤ To heighten the Twist, before applying the filter or effect, add points to the path using Object > Path > Add Anchor Points.

1 *The Roughen dialog box*

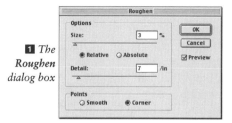

2 *The original object*

3 *After applying the Roughen filter (or eyeing a dog)*

4 *The original objects*

5 *The objects twirled together, Angle 1000°*

6 *The Twist filter applied to **5**, Angle 3000°*

gothic horror

1 *The original type outlines*

gothic horror

2 *After applying the **Pucker** part of the filter/ effect*

3 *The original object*

4 *After applying the **Bloat** filter/effect*

To pucker or bloat an object:

1. Select an object or objects **1** and **2**. Effect > Pucker & Bloat can be applied to editable text.

2. Choose Effect > Distort & Transform > Pucker & Bloat or Filter > Distort > Pucker & Bloat. (This was called Punk & Bloat in previous application versions.)

3. Check Preview.

4. Move the slider to the left toward Pucker (anchor points move outward and curve segments move inward) **3** or move the slider to the right toward Bloat (anchor points move inward and curve segments move outward) **4**.

5. Click OK.

➤ To add points to the path and intensify the Pucker or Bloat, choose Object > Path > Add Anchor Points one or more times before applying the filter or effect. See also Figures 1–3 on page 120.

Raster effects and filters

These are the important rules to remember:

■ All the raster filters are available for a rasterized object or a placed bitmap image in RGB or Grayscale color mode, provided the Illustrator document itself is also in RGB Color mode.

■ Raster effects are available for vector objects and for embedded or linked bitmap images.

■ Only the Blur, Sharpen, and Pixelate filters and effects are available for an embedded, rasterized object or image in CMYK color mode.

■ No raster effects or filters are available for an object or image in Bitmap color mode.

■ Raster filters are available for embedded images, but not for linked images.

Some raster effects and filters introduce an element of randomness or distortion that would be difficult to achieve by hand. Others, like the Artistic, Brush Strokes, Sketch, and

(Continued on the following page)

Texture filters, are designed to make an image look a little less machine-made, more hand-rendered. When a raster filter or effect is applied to a large, high-resolution bitmap image, a progress bar may display while the filter is processing. To cancel a filter or effect in progress, click Stop or press Return/Enter.

In some effect or filter dialog boxes, such as Rough Pastels or Grain, you can choose a texture type from the Texture or Grain Type pop-up menu **1**–**2**. Move the Scaling slider to enlarge or reduce the size of the texture pattern and move the Relief slider, if there is one, to adjust the depth and prominence of the texture on the image's surface. In some dialog boxes, you can load in a bitmap image saved in Photoshop format (files with the ".psd" extension) to use instead of a preset texture. To do this, choose Load Texture from the Texture pop-up menu, click the bitmap file you want to use, then click Open.

In addition to the raster filters, other filters that you can apply to a raster image include Colors submenu > Adjust Colors, Convert to Grayscale, Convert to CMYK or Convert to RGB (depending on the current document color mode), Invert Colors, and Saturate, and also the Photo Crosshatch filter, which is found on the Pen & Ink submenu. There are no effects equivalents for these filters.

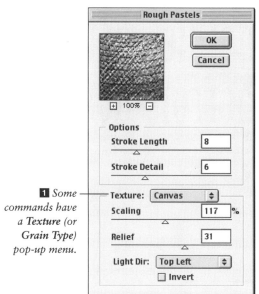

1 *Some commands have a **Texture** (or **Grain Type**) pop-up menu.*

2 *Rough Pastels filter/effect, Burlap **Texture***

Raster Effects and Filters

1 *Choose a* **Color Model** *in the* **Rasterize** *dialog box.*

Before experimenting with the raster filters, you should learn about Illustrator's Rasterize command, which converts a vector (path) object into a bitmap image. You can apply any raster filter to an object once it's rasterized using the proper settings.

Note: All the effects work on vector objects.

To rasterize a path object:

1. Select a path object or objects or target them on the Layers palette.

2. Choose Object > Rasterize or Effect > Rasterize. The Effect is reversible and editable; the Object menu command is permanent.

3. Choose a **Color Model** **1** for the image: CMYK for print output (only the Blur, Sharpen, and Pixelate raster filters and effects will be available) or RGB for video or onscreen display (all raster filters and effects available), depending on the current document color mode; Grayscale for shades of black and white (all raster filters and effects will be available); or Bitmap for only black-and-white or black-and-transparent (no raster effects or filters will be available).

4. Click a **Resolution** setting—choose Screen for Web output; or choose High for imagesetter output; or enter a resolution in the Other field; or click Use Document Raster Effects Resolution to use the global resolution settings as specified in Effect > Document Raster Effects Settings.

5. Click **Background**: White to make the transparent areas in the object opaque white or click Transparent to make the background transparent (see the sidebar).

6. Under Options:

   For a type object, choose **Type Quality**: Streamline to have the type remain at its present width or choose Outline to have the rasterized type be thickened slightly.

   Choose **Anti-Aliasing**: Art Optimized (Supersampling) to have Illustrator soften the edges of the rasterized shape. This

(Continued on the following page)

Rasterize an Object

393

option may make text or thin lines look blurry. Choose Type Optimized (Hinted) for a type object. Edges will be jagged if you choose None.

Check **Create Clipping Mask** if you want Illustrator to generate a clipping mask for the shape so its background will be transparent (see the sidebar).

To have Illustrator add pixels around the object for padding (the bounding box will become larger), enter a value in the **Add [ ] Around Object** field.

7. Click OK. A bounding box will surround the path object.

➤ Once a solid color object is rasterized, its color can be changed using Filter > Colors > Adjust Colors.

➤ If Art Optimized is chosen as the Anti-aliasing option, and you rasterize an object that contains a pattern fill, the pattern color and line weight will be preserved. If you click Background: Transparent, and the object originally had a pattern fill with a transparent background, the transparent background will be preserved.

Transparent versus clipping mask

The **Background: Transparent** and **Create Clipping Mask** options in Object > Rasterize remove an object's background. Unlike Create Clipping Mask, the Transparent option creates an alpha channel in order to remove the background and the resulting image stays as an individual listing on the Layers palette. Any blending mode or opacity settings are removed, but the object keeps any transparency appearances. Blending modes and opacity can be applied to the targeted image at any time. The alpha channel effect will be preserved if the file is exported to Photoshop.

Create Clipping Mask, on the other hand, produces a nested group composed of a clipping path and the image, and the clipping path preserves any transparency appearances. Blending modes and opacity for the object can be adjusted for the targeted <Image>, but not for the <Clipping Path>.

If you choose the Transparent option, you don't need to create a clipping mask. Effect > Rasterize preserves blending and transparency. The SVG format also preserves the appearance of blending and transparency. The SWF format only preserves the appearance of transparency, not blending.

1 *The original image*

*The **Object Mosaic** dialog box*

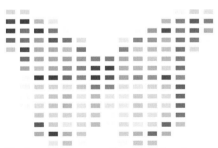

3 *The **Object Mosaic** filter applied*

The Object Mosaic filter breaks up a raster image into a grid of little squares. Each of the squares is a separate object that can be moved or recolored individually. There is no equivalent effect for this filter.

To apply the Object Mosaic filter:

1. Click on a rasterized object or an embedded bitmap image **1**.

2. Choose Filter > Create > Object Mosaic.

3. *Optional:*

   Change the New Size: Width and/or Height values **2**. (The Current Size field displays the width and height of the image in points.) To enter the dimensions in percentages relative to the original, first check Resize using Percentages at the bottom of the dialog box.
   or
   Enter a New Size: Width (or Height), click Constrain Ratio: Width (or Height) under Options to lock in that dimension, then click Use Ratio to have Illustrator automatically calculate the opposite dimension proportionate to the object's original dimensions.

4. Enter the Number of Tiles to fill the width and height dimensions. If you clicked Use Ratio, the Number of Tiles will be calculated automatically.

5. *Optional:* To add space between each tile, enter Tile Spacing: Width and Height values.

6. *Optional:* When it's applied to a bitmap image, the Object Mosaic filter affects a copy of the image that's made automatically, and the original is left unchanged. Check Delete Raster if you want the original image to be deleted.

7. Click Result: Color or Gray.

8. Click OK **3**–**4**.

➤ The mosaic object is listed as a group on the Layers palette.

4 *The **Object Mosaic** filter applied to the original image (**1**) with spacing between the tiles*

Object Mosaic Filter

395

The raster filters illustrated
Artistic filters

Original image

Colored Pencil

Cutout

Dry Brush

Film Grain

Fresco

Neon Glow

Paint Daubs

Palette Knife

Artistic filters

Original image

Plastic Wrap

Poster Edges

Rough Pastels

Smudge Stick

Sponge

Underpainting

Watercolor

Artistic Filters

Blur filters

Original image

Radial Blur

Gaussian Blur

Brush Strokes filters

Original image

Accented Edges

Angled Strokes

Crosshatch

Dark Strokes

Ink Outlines

Brush Strokes filters

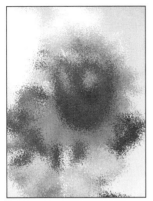

Spatter

Sprayed Strokes

Sumi-e

Distort filters

Original image

Diffuse Glow

Glass (Blocks)

Ocean Ripple

Pixelate filters

Original image

Color Halftone

Crystallize

Mezzotint (Short Strokes)

Mezzotint (Medium Dots)

Pointillize

For the Unsharp Mask filter, see our Visual QuickStart Guide on Photoshop!

Stylize filter

Original image

Glowing Edges

Sketch filters

Original image

Bas Relief

Chalk & Charcoal

Charcoal

Chrome

Conté Crayon

Graphic Pen

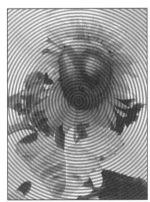

Halftone Pattern (Circle)

Halftone Pattern (Dot)

Sketch filters

Original image

Note Paper

Photocopy

Plaster

Reticulation

Stamp

Torn Edges

Water Paper

Texture filters

Original image

Craquelure

Grain (Enlarged)

Grain (Horizontal)

Mosaic Tiles

Patchwork

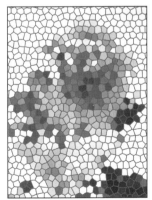

Stained Glass

Texturizer

Texture Filters

The Pen and Ink filters

In this section, we discuss the Hatch Effects filter and the Photo Crosshatch filter. The Hatch Effects filter creates an amazing assortment of linework patterns by turning a path object into a mask and then creating a fill of linework shapes behind the mask. You can choose from 26 preset pen patterns, called hatch styles, that you can use as is or further modify using a wide variety of options. You can also create a new hatch from scratch from an Illustrator object.

To apply the Pen and Ink filter:

1. Select a path object.

2. Choose Filter > Pen and Ink > Hatch Effects.

3. Check Preview to preview the effect in the preview window in the dialog box (not in the document window). Uncheck Preview to speed processing.

4. Choose a predefined effect from the Hatch Effect pop-up menu 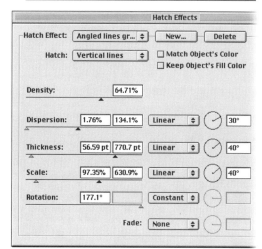. If you're satisfied with the pattern, click OK. To further modify it, follow any of the remaining steps.

5. Choose another predefined hatch from the Hatch pop-up menu to add to the current effect.

6. Move the **Density** slider to adjust the number of hatch shapes in the fill. Or to adjust the density a different way, click a different gray on the vertical grayscale bar next to the preview window 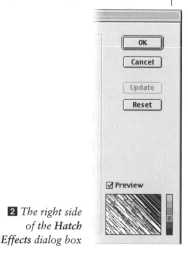.

7. For any of the following options, choose a setting other than None from the corresponding pop-up menu (read the sidebar on the next page), and move one or both of the sliders.

   Dispersion controls the spacing between hatch shapes.

   Thickness controls the line thickness of the hatch shapes. This property is available only for hatch styles that are composed of lines (Cross, Crosshatch 1, Vertical lines, and Worm).

   Scale controls the size of the hatch shapes.

Big hairy monster?

Pen and Ink fills can be quite complex, and their direction lines and line endpoints may extend way beyond the edge of the original object. To prevent inadvertent selection of a Pen and Ink fill, put the Pen and Ink object on its own layer and then lock that layer.

If your Pen and Ink fill doesn't print, try reducing the file's Output resolution (see page 452). Also, don't apply the Pen and Ink filter to an object that already contains a Pen and Ink fill—it will demand too much from your output device.

1 *The left side of the Hatch Effects dialog box*

2 *The right side of the Hatch Effects dialog box*

Pen and Ink Filter

Hatch Effect pop-up menu options

None: No effect.

Constant: Effect repeats without changing across the entire shape.

Linear: Effect intensifies in a progression from one side of the shape to the other.

Reflect: Effect varies from the center of the shape outward.

Symmetric: Like Linear, but more proportionate and even. Hatch shading looks like shading on a cylindrical object.

Random: Effect changes in a random, haphazard fashion across the shape.

The Linear, Reflect, Symmetric, and Random options have two sliders each, and their position controls the range of choices for that option. The greater the distance between a pair of sliders, the wider the range of possibilities for that option. Enter an Angle value or drag the angle dial to specify an axis for the change.

New Hatch

Name: Hatchy-Hatchy   [OK]

[Cancel]

1 *Enter a name for the new hatch. (In Windows, this dialog box is called "New Settings" if you click New in the Hatch Effects dialog box.)*

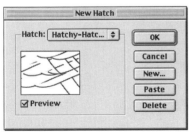

2 *The new hatch previews.*

Rotation controls the angle of the hatch shapes.

8. Check **Match Object's Color** to have the hatch match the object's fill color or check **Keep Object's Fill Color** to make the hatch black and leave the object color unchanged.

9. From the **Fade** pop-up menu, choose whether the hatch style will fade To White or To Black across the shape. If the object's fill was a gradient, choose Use Gradient to color the hatch shapes with the gradient. You can enter an angle for the axis along which the fade will occur.

10. Click OK.

➤ To **save** the current property settings to a custom Hatch Effect variation, click New at the top of the dialog box, enter a Name, then click OK.

➤ To **delete** the current Hatch Effect variation, click Delete, then click Yes. *Warning:* This can't be undone by clicking Cancel or Reset in the Hatch Effects dialog box or by using Undo.

➤ Click **Update** to save the current property settings to the current Hatch Effect variant. *Warning:* Update overwrites the existing Hatch Effect variant.

➤ Click **Reset** to remove any property variations from the current Hatch Effect.

The hatch is the underlying pattern tile that is used by the Pen and Ink filter.

To create a new hatch pattern:

1. Create a small object or objects to use as the hatch pattern (no brush stroke, pattern, gradient, or mesh).

2. Select the object or objects.

3. Choose Filter > Pen and Ink > New Hatch.

4. Click New, type a Name for the hatch **1**.

5. Check Preview to display the new pattern in the preview window **2**. Click OK to close the New Hatch dialog box. The hatch will be saved in the currently open hatch library.

New Hatch Pattern

To edit a hatch pattern:

1. Scroll to a blank area of the artboard, and deselect all objects.

2. Choose Filter > Pen and Ink > New Hatch.

3. Choose the pattern you want to edit from the Hatch pop-up menu.

4. Click Paste.

5. Click OK. The hatch pattern objects will be selected.

6. Zoom in, and modify the hatch pattern.

7. Reselect the hatch pattern object(s).

8. Follow steps 3–5 in the previous set of instructions.

➤ Click Delete to remove the currently chosen style from the Hatch pop-up menu. This can't be undone, even by cancelling out of the dialog box.

To save a hatch library:

1. Create your own custom Hatch Effect variations using Filter > Pen and Ink > New Hatch (see the instructions on the previous page).

2. Choose Filter > Pen and Ink > Library Save As.

3. Type a name for the library, make sure the Adobe Illustrator 10 > Plug-ins > Illustrator Filters > Pen and Ink folder is open (where the default Hatch Sets library is located), then click Save.

   Note: If you don't change the file name from the default name "Hatch Sets," and you then click Save, you will be asked to cancel or replace the existing file. Click Replace only if you want to overwrite the default library!

To open a hatch library:

1. Choose Filter > Pen and Ink > Library Open.

2. Open the Adobe Illustrator 10 > Plug-ins > Illustrator Filters > Pen and Ink folder, click a library name, then click Open.

Fanya, Diane Margolin

Taj Mahal, Diane Margolin

1 *The original grayscale photo*

2 *The **Photo Crosshatch** filter was applied using these settings: Two Layers, Density 3.5 pt., Dispersion Noise 0, Thickness .4 pt., Max. Line Length 24 pt., Rotation Noise 2°, Rotation Variance 100%, and Top angle 40°. The image below is a closeup.*

The Photo Crosshatch filter translates a bitmap image into a crosshatch pattern. When applied at the appropriate density, the crosshatches look like hand-drawn shading—as in an artist's pen drawing.

To convert a continuous-tone image into a crosshatch image:

1. Click a photographic image that you placed into an Illustrator document without a saved clipping path **1**. The filter won't be available for a linked bitmap image or any kind of EPS image. To use a PSD image, flatten it down to a single image as you place it. You can use a rasterized object, with less interesting results.
   or
   Select an image in your illustration, then choose Embed Image from the Links palette menu.

2. Choose Filter > Pen and Ink > Photo Crosshatch.

3. Choose the number of Hatch Layers (1–8). This is similar to choosing levels of posterization. The greater the number of hatch layers, the more levels of shading will be produced in the image. (Don't get confused here. Hatch layers aren't listed on the Layers palette.)

4. *Optional:* Move the sliders under the histogram to determine how different lightness levels in the original image will be rendered by line patterns. Move the rightmost slider to the right to create more line patterning in the image highlights and lessen areas of absolute white, or move the rightmost slider to the left to decrease line patterning in the highlights and increase areas of absolute white. Move the middle slider to increase or decrease line patterning in the midtones. Move the leftmost slider to the right to decrease line patterning in the shadows.

5. Working without the advantage of a preview, move the sliders on the left side of the dialog box to control the hatch lines (**1**, next page):

   The **Density** slider controls the number of hatch lines used. A low Density setting

   (Continued on the following page)

will produce a very dense collection of hatch lines.

The **Dispersion Noise** slider controls the spacing between hatch line segments. 0% Dispersion Noise produces line segments that align perfectly end-to-end to form a long, straight-line texture. A value greater than 0% produces line segments that don't align end-to-end, and thus there are no long straight lines. A low Dispersion Noise creates a hand-drawn look; a high Dispersion Noise produces more obvious patterning and less obvious shading.

The **Thickness** slider controls the stroke weight of the line segments.

The **Max. Line Length** slider controls the length of the line segments.

The **Rotation Noise** slider controls the amount of arbitrary rotation given to individual line segments on each hatch layer. The higher the Rotation Noise setting, the more obvious the patterning and the less obvious the shading.

The **Rotation Variance** slider controls how much each hatch layer is rotated relative to the previous layer. The higher the Rotation Variance, the more distinct the layers and the less smooth the shading.

The **Top Angle** is the angle along which hatch lines are drawn on the topmost hatch layer.

6. Click OK (**2**, previous page, and **2**, this page). To produce shading, some hatch lines are drawn from the edges of the highlights to the midtones in an image or all the way into the shadows; some hatch lines start in the midtones and continue into the shadows; and some hatch lines are drawn only in the shadows.

➤ The Photo Crosshatch filter converts the original image. Copy it before using the filter in order to preserve the original.

➤ To darken selected areas in the resulting crosshatch, lasso some line segments using the Direct-select Lasso tool, then increase their stroke weight.

1 *The Photo Crosshatch dialog box*

2 *This is the image on the previous page after applying the Photo Crosshatch filter using these settings: Two Layers, Density 3.5, Dispersion Noise 15%, Thickness .5, Max. Line Length 24, Rotation Noise 18°, Rotation Variance 90%, Top angle 40°. In this image, the higher Dispersion Noise, Rotation Noise, and Rotation Variance values create a more hand-drawn look, as compared with the image on the previous page. The image below is a closeup.*

Chapter 22: Effects & Filters ◆ Study Guide

Learning Objectives

- Understand the difference between effects and filters.
- Learn about the options and techniques that are common to all filters and effects.
- Be aware of how the Pathfinder effects are different from the Pathfinder palette buttons.

Get Up and Running Exercises

- Use the drawing tools to create an object, and give it a stroke color and a fill color. Duplicate the object so that you have two copies of it. Apply a raster filter to one object and the effect of the same name to the other object. For example, apply Filter > Sketch > Conté Crayon to one object and Effect > Sketch > Conté Crayon to the other object. If you're unable to complete the exercise because commands are dimmed, what do you need to do to make those filters or effect commands available?

- Select a vector object and apply an effect that requires rasterization, or select the vector object from the previous exercise to which you applied a command from the Effect menu. Without using the Edit > Undo command, how would you remove the rasterization effect and restore the vector object?

- Reproduce the Web page menu bar in the following figure. How can you do it using only three freestanding text (not area text) objects?

Class Discussion Questions

- What's the difference between effects and filters?

- What are some features that you can use with most effects and filters?

- Why do some effects and filters rasterize the selected object?

- What's the main difference between applying Pathfinder effects from the menu as opposed to using the Pathfinder palette?

- Why are the Convert to Shape effects useful? When would you want to convert a path into a simple rectangle or ellipse instead of just drawing a rectangular or elliptical shape?

Review Questions

Multiple choice

1. In most raster effect or filter dialog boxes, which key do you hold down to change the Cancel button into a Reset button?

   A. Cmd/Ctrl

   B. Esc

   C. Option/Alt

   D. Shift

2. Which keyboard shortcut will reapply the last-used filter using the same settings?

   A. Cmd-Shift-E/Ctrl-Shift-E

   B. Cmd-Option-Shift-E/Ctrl-Alt-Shift-E

   C. Cmd/Ctrl-E

   D. Cmd-Option-E/Ctrl-Alt-E

3. Which kind of effect requires targeting a layer, group, or type object?

   A. Convert to Shape

   B. Pathfinder

   C. Pen and Ink

   D. Vector effects

4. If you see a flashing line under the preview percentage in a filter preview window, what does it mean?

   A. Applying the filter will rasterize the object.

   B. The preview isn't done rendering.

   C. The filter is ready to be applied.

   D. The zoom percentage is not providing a precise preview.

5. Which of the following filter/effect categories isn't available for an image in CMYK color mode?

   A. Stylize

   B. Blur

   C. Sharpen

   D. Pixelate

Fill-in-the-blank

1. When rasterizing an object, you can convert empty areas of an object's background into a Photoshop-compatible alpha channel if you choose the _____ option.

2. To help text remain editable in its original font even if its font is missing, apply the _____ effect.

3. To use Photoshop-compatible filters that aren't included with Illustrator, _____.

4. You can apply vector-based crosshatch effects using the _____ filters.

5. Any effect you apply from the Effect menu can be edited or deleted using the _____ palette.

6. To apply a preset of your favorite effects and settings or use them as part of a set of appearance attributes, include the effect in a _____.

Definitions

1. What is an effect?

2. What is a filter?

3. What is rasterization?

4. What is a Pathfinder effect?

5. What is a Convert to Shape effect?

6. What is a raster effect or filter?

PRECISION TOOLS 23

There are many tools you can use to position or move objects
with exact precision. In this chapter you will learn how to use
rulers, guides, and grids to align and position objects; move
an object a specified distance via the Move dialog box; use
the Measure tool to calculate distances between objects; use
the Transform palette to move, scale, rotate, or shear objects;
and use the Align palette to align or distribute objects.

Smart Guides are precision tools, too, but they're so helpful
and so easy to use, we discussed them early in the book (see
pages 88–89, 97, and 170). The Transform Each command
is discussed on page 105, Transform Effect on page 106.

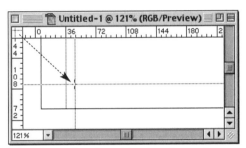

1 To change the **ruler origin**, drag diagonally away
from the intersection of the rulers.

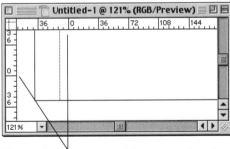

2 Note the new position of the zeros on the rulers.

Ruler and object guides

The rulers are located at the top and left
edges of the document window. Location
measurements (e.g., the X and Y readouts
on the Transform and Info palettes) are read
from the ruler origin, which is the point
where the zeros of both rulers meet. By
default, the **ruler origin** is positioned at the
lower left corner of the page, but it can be
moved to a different location in any individual document to help you measure or position objects. The current pointer location is
indicated by a mark on each ruler.

To move the ruler origin:

1. If the rulers aren't displayed, choose
   View > Show Rulers (Cmd-R/Ctrl-R); or
   deselect all objects, then Control-click/
   Right-click the artboard and choose
   Show Rulers from the context menu.

2. Drag the square (where the two rulers
   intersect) to a new position **1**–**2**. The
   ruler origin will stay in the new location
   even if you close and reopen the file.

➤ If you move the ruler origin, pattern fills
   in any existing objects may shift position.

To restore the ruler origin to its default location:

Double-click where the two rulers intersect at the upper left corner of the document window.

➤ Control-click/Right-click either ruler to open a context menu from which you can choose a different unit of measure for the document. This setting will supercede the units setting in Edit > Preferences > Units & Undo.

For most purposes, Smart Guides work adequately for arranging objects (see pages 88–89). If you need guides that stay on the screen, however, you'll need to create them using either method described on this page. Ruler guides don't print.

If View > **Snap to Point** is on, as you drag an object near a guide, the black pointer will turn white and the part of the object that's under the pointer will snap to the guide. The **Snapping Tolerance** (the distance within which an object will snap to a guide) can be changed in Edit > Preferences > Smart Guides & Slices.

To show/hide guides:

Choose View > Guides > Hide Guides or Show Guides (Cmd-;/Ctrl-;).

To create a ruler guide:

1. *Optional:* Create a new top-level layer expressly for the guides.

2. If the rulers are not displayed, choose View > Show Rulers (Cmd-R/Ctrl-R).

3. Drag a guide from the horizontal or vertical ruler onto your page ■. The guide will be locked and will be listed on the Layers palette as <Guide> in the currently active layer. If View > **Snap to Grid** is on, as you create or move the guide, it will snap to the nearest ruler tick mark. (*Note:* If Pixel Preview is on, Snap to Grid won't be available.)

➤ Option-drag/Alt-drag from the horizontal ruler to create a vertical guide, and vice versa.

Snap to pixel

If View > **Pixel Preview** is on, View > Snap to Grid becomes View > **Snap to Pixel** (and Snap to Pixel is automatically turned on). With Snap to Pixel on, any new objects you create or any existing objects you drag will snap to the pixel grid and anti-aliasing will be removed from any horizontal or vertical edges on those objects.

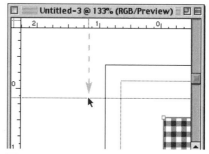

■ *Drag a guide from the horizontal or vertical ruler.*

1 *An object is selected, and then View > Guides > Make Guides is chosen.*

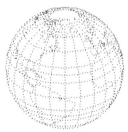

2 *The object is now a guide. The former "path" object will now be listed as "guide" on the Layers palette.*

So far we've shown you how to work with two kinds of guides: ruler guides and smart guides. Now you'll learn how to create guides from standard Illustrator paths. Best of all, the conversion is reversible; an object guide can be converted back into a standard object at any time.

Note: If the object you turn into a guide is part of a group, the guide will also be part of that group.

To turn an object into a guide:

1. Select an object, a group of objects, or an object within a group (not a symbol or an object in a blend) **1**. Copy the object and work off the copy, if desired.

2. Choose View > Guides > Make Guides (Cmd-5/Ctrl-5) **2**.
   or
   Control-click/Right-click and choose Make Guides from the context menu.

➤ You can transform or reshape a guide object, as long as guides aren't locked. Object guides can be selected using the Layers palette (look for <Guide>). Relock guides when you're done editing them.

Back we go.

To turn all object guides back into objects:

1. If guides are locked, Control-click/Right-click and choose Lock Guides from the context menu to uncheck that option.

2. Choose the Selection tool (V).

3. Select one guide or marquee or Shift-click multiple guides.

4. Choose View > Guides > Release Guides (Cmd-Option-5/Ctrl-Alt-5).
   or
   Control-click/Right-click and choose Release Guides from the context menu.

   The guide will revert to an object, with its former fill and stroke.

To turn one guide back into an object:

Cmd-Shift-double-click/Ctrl-Shift-double-click the edge of the guide.

Object Guides

To select or move guides, standard or object, they must first be unlocked. By default, the Lock Guides command is turned on.

To lock or unlock all guides:

Choose View > Guides > Lock Guides (Cmd-Option-;/Ctrl-Alt-;) to check or uncheck the command.
or
Make sure no objects are selected, then Control-click/Right-click the artboard and choose Lock Guides from the context menu.

To lock/unlock one guide:

1. Make sure View > Guides > Lock Guides doesn't have a checkmark. You can also access this command by deselecting all objects and then Right-clicking/Control-clicking on the artboard.

2. On the Layers palette, click in the lock column for any guide you want to unlock.

   Note: Make sure the selection color for a <Guide> (Layers palette) is different from the guide color, otherwise you won't be able to tell whether the guide is selected.

➤ To lock one guide another way, unlock all guides (see the previous set of instructions), click the guide you want to lock, then choose Object > Lock > Selection (Cmd-2/Ctrl-2). It's faster to use the Layers palette.

To remove one guide:

1. Make sure either all guides are unlocked or the guide you want to remove is unlocked.

2. Choose the Selection tool (V), then click the guide.

3. In the Mac OS: Press Delete. In Windows: Press Backspace or Del.

4. Re-lock all the remaining guides, if desired, by choosing View > Guides > Lock Guides.

To remove all guides:

Choose View > Guides > Clear Guides.

Guide control

Since each guide is listed as a separate item on the Layers palette (<Guide>), you can hide/show or lock/unlock each individual guide.

➤ After guides are created, drag all of them into one layer or sublayer. Then if you hide/show or lock/unlock that layer, all those guides will be affected simultaneously. And you will still be able to lock and unlock individual guides.

Lock Guides; Remove Guides

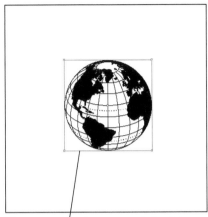

1 *A rectangle is drawn around the globe to define the guide area.*

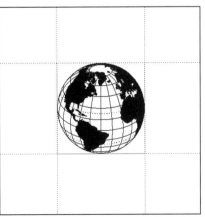

2 *Options are chosen in the Rows & Columns dialog box.*

To place guides around an object or create evenly spaced guides:

1. Choose the Selection tool (V), then select an existing rectangle. Make sure the rectangle is on the printable page. *Warning!* If you use a non-rectangular shape, the shape will revert to a rectangle!
   or
   Choose the Rectangle tool, then drag a rectangle to define the guide area **1**.

2. Make sure the ruler origin is in the default location.

3. Choose Type > Rows & Columns.

4. Check Add Guides and check Preview **2**.

5. To encircle the object with guides without dividing the object, leave the Columns and Rows values as is.
   or
   To divide the object and create guides, enter Number, Height, and Gutter width values for Rows and Columns. Leave the Total as is.

6. Click OK **3**.

7. On the Layers palette, Shift-click the rectangular path object(s) to deselect it, then, with only the lines selected, choose View > Guides > Make Guides (Cmd-5/Ctrl-5) **4**. The guides will be listed as a group on the Layers palette. If you like, you can delete the rectangle that was used to create the guides.

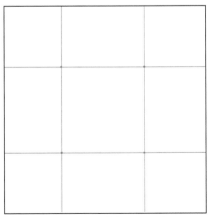

3 *Lines appear around the rectangle.*

4 *The lines are **converted** into **guides**.*

Using the Grid

The grid is like non-printing graph paper. You can use it as a framework to help you arrange objects, either by eye or using Snap to Grid.

You can change the grid style (lines or dots), color, or spacing in Edit > Preferences > **Guides & Grid** (see page 438). Check Grids In Back in Guides & Grid Preferences to have the grid appear in back of all objects instead of in front.

Start by showing the grid.

To show/hide the grid:

Choose View > Show Grid (or Hide Grid) (Cmd-"/Ctrl-") **1**.
or
Deselect, then Control-click/Right-click and choose Show Grid (or Hide Grid) from the context menu.

To use snap to grid:

Choose View > Snap to Grid (Cmd-Shift-"/Ctrl-Shift-"). Now if you move an object near a gridline, the edge of the object will snap to the gridline. This works whether the grid is displayed or not.

The default Constrain Angle is 0°—the horizontal/vertical *(x/y)* axes. When you change the Constrain Angle, any new object that you draw will rest on the new axes and any new object that you move or transform with Shift held down will snap to the new axes. This setting affects the whole application, both future documents and existing documents—whether those documents are open or closed when the Constrain Angle is changed.

To change the Constrain Angle:

Choose Edit > Preferences > General (Cmd-K/Ctrl-K), change the Constrain Angle, then click OK **2**. Enter 0 to restore the default Constrain Angle.

➤ To establish a Constrain Angle based on an object rotated using the Rotate tool, select the object, then enter the Angle readout ⌂ from the Info palette as the Constrain Angle.

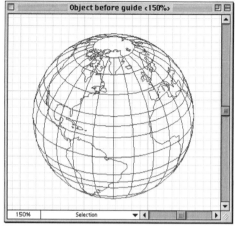

1 *The Grid displayed*

What the Constrain Angle affects

- Text objects
- Rectangle, Ellipse, and Graph tools
- Transformation tools (Scale, Reflect, and Shear, but not Rotate or Blend)
- Gradient tool and Pen tool when used with Shift held down
- Moving objects with Shift held down or using the arrow keys
- Grid
- Smart Guides
- Info palette readouts

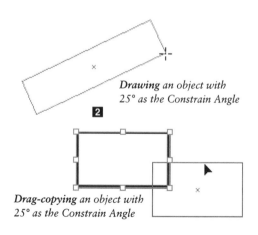

Drawing an object with 25° as the Constrain Angle

2

Drag-copying an object with 25° as the Constrain Angle

shifting patterns

If you move an object that contains a pattern fill manually or using the Move dialog box, and Patterns is unchecked in the Move dialog box, the object will move but not the pattern. If Patterns is checked but Objects is not, and you use the Move command, the pattern position will shift but not the object.

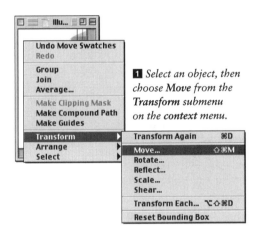

1 *Select an object, then choose* **Move** *from the* **Transform** *submenu on the* **context** *menu.*

2 *In the* **Move** *dialog box enter* **Horizontal** *and* **Vertical** *values or enter the* **Distance** *and* **Angle** *you want the object to move.*

Transforming using numbers

You can precisely reposition an object by entering values in the Move dialog box. Move dialog box settings remain the same until you change them, move an object using the mouse, or use the Measure tool, so you can repeat the same move as many times as you like using the Transform Again shortcut (Cmd-D/Ctrl-D), even on another object.

To move an object a specified distance:

1. *Optional:* Choose a lower view percentage for your illustration so the object won't disappear from view when it's moved.

2. Choose the Selection tool (V).

3. Select the object you want to move.

4. Double-click the Selection tool.
    or
    Control-click/Right-click and choose Transform > Move from the context menu **1**.
    or
    Choose Object > Transform > Move (Cmd-Shift-M/Ctrl-Shift-M).

5. Check Preview.

6. Press Tab to preview these changes:

    Enter positive Horizontal and Vertical values to move the object to the right and upward, respectively; enter negative values to move the object to the left or downward; or enter a combination of positive and negative values **2**. Enter 0 in either field to prevent the object from moving along that axis. You can use any of these units of measure: "p," "pt," "in," "mm," "q," or "cm."
    or
    Enter a positive Distance and a positive Angle between 0 and 180 to move the object upward; enter a positive Distance and a negative Angle between 0 and –180 to move the object downward. The other fields will change automatically.

7. *Optional:* Click Copy to close the dialog box and move a copy of the object (not the object itself).

8. Click OK.

Use the Transform palette to move, scale, rotate, or shear an object or objects based on exact values or percentages. To apply a transformation as an editable and removable effect, see page 106.

To move, scale, rotate, or shear an object using the Transform palette:

1. If the Transform palette isn't open, choose Window > Transform.

2. Select an object or objects.

3. Choose the reference point from which you want the transformation to be measured by clicking one of the nine square Reference Point handles on the left side of the palette ▮.

4. From the Transform palette menu, choose Transform Object Only, Transform Pattern Only, or Transform Both (to transform objects and patterns).

5. If you're going to scale the object(s), decide whether you want the Scale Strokes & Effects option to be on or off (palette menu). With it on, the object's stroke and appearances will scale proportionately. This option can also be turned on or off in Edit > Preferences > General.

6. To apply any of the following values, use one of the shortcuts from the sidebar on this page:

   To **move** the object horizontally, enter a new X position. Enter a higher value to move the object to the right, and a lower value to move it to the left.

   To **move** the object vertically, enter a new Y position. Enter a higher value to move the object upward, a lower value to move it downward.

   To scale the object, enter new **width** and/or **height** values. You can enter a percentage instead of an absolute value. To force the other field (W or H) to change proportionately, press Cmd-Return/Enter Ctrl-Enter.

   Enter a positive Rotate value to **rotate** the object counterclockwise or a negative

Applying Transform palette values

Exit the palette	**Return/Enter** (main keypad in Windows)
Apply a value entered in a field and highlight the next field	**Tab**
Apply a value and re-highlight the same field	**Shift-Return/ Shift-Enter**
Clone the object and exit the palette	**Option-Return/ Alt-Enter**
Clone the object and highlight the next field	**Option-Tab** (Mac only)
Repeat last transformation	**Cmd-D/ Ctrl-D**

*The **x** and **y** axes* location of the currently selected reference point: Enter new values to position the object's reference point at that value on the x or y axis.

The selected object's **Height**

The selected object's **Width**

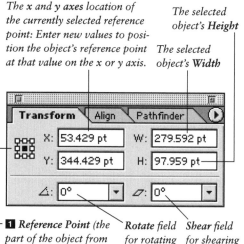

▮ *Reference Point (the part of the object from which Transform palette values are calculated)*

Rotate field for rotating the object

Shear field for shearing the object

Let the palette do the math

In the W or H field on the Transform palette, you can perform simple math to scale an object. Try using any of the following methods:

- After the current number, type an asterisk ***** and then a **percentage** value. For example, to reduce an object's scale by half, click to the right of the current value, then type "*50%" (e.g., 4p would become 2p).

- Replace the entire field with a **percentage**. Enter "75%," for example, to reduce the W or H to three-quarters of its current value (e.g., 4p becomes 3p).

- Enter a **positive** or **negative** value to the right of the current number, as in "+2" or "-2," to increase or decrease, respectively, the current value by that amount.

Press **Tab** to apply the math and advance to the next field or press **Return/Enter** to exit the palette.

value to rotate it clockwise. Or choose a preset angle from the pop-up menu.

To **shear** the object to the right, enter or choose a positive Shear value. To shear an object to the left, enter or choose a negative Shear value.

7. From the palette menu, you can also choose Flip Horizontal or Flip Vertical.

➤ If Use Preview Bounds is checked in Edit > Preferences > General, the full dimensions of an object, including its stroke and any effects, will display on the Width and Height fields on the Transform and Info palettes.

Transform Palette

Align and Distribute

Aligning and distributing

Buttons, type blocks—anything that's lined up in a row or column will require aligning and distributing in order to look neat and tidy. With the Align palette 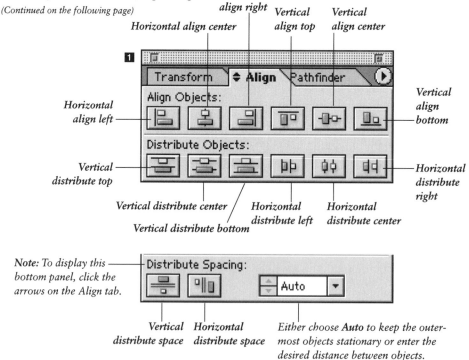, it's easy to do.

To align or distribute objects:

1. To align, select two or more objects or groups. To distribute, select three or more objects. Choose Window > Align.

2. Turn **Use Preview Bounds** on from the Align palette menu or in Edit > Preferences > General to have Illustrator factor in an object's stroke weight and any effects when calculating alignment or distribution. Turn this option off to have Illustrator ignore the stroke weight. The stroke straddles the edge of the path, halfway inside and halfway outside.

3. *For occasional use:* Choose **Align To Artboard** from the palette menu to align the objects along the top, right, bottom, or left edge of the artboard, depending

(Continued on the following page)

Horizontal align right

Horizontal align center

Vertical align top

Vertical align center

Horizontal align left

Vertical align bottom

Vertical distribute top

Horizontal distribute right

Vertical distribute center

Vertical distribute bottom

Horizontal distribute left

Horizontal distribute center

Note: To display this bottom panel, click the arrows on the Align tab.

Vertical distribute space

Horizontal distribute space

*Either choose **Auto** to keep the outermost objects stationary or enter the desired distance between objects.*

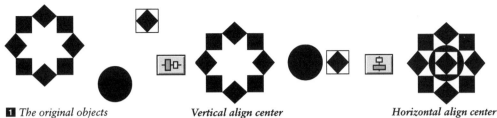

1 *The original objects*   **Vertical align center**   **Horizontal align center**

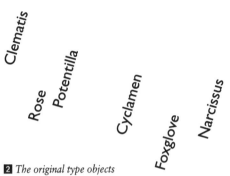

2 *The original type objects*

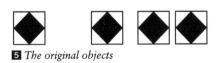

3 *After clicking* **Vertical align bottom…**

4 *…and then clicking* **Horizontal distribute center.** *The paragraph alignment doesn't change.*

5 *The original objects*

Horizontal distribute space

on which Align Objects button is clicked. If Align to Artboard is on and objects are distributed vertically, the topmost object will move to the top edge of the artboard, the bottommost object will move to the bottom edge of the artboard, and the remaining objects will be distributed between them. If objects are distributed horizontally with this option on, objects will be aligned between the leftmost and rightmost edges of the artboard.

4. *Optional:* By default (with Align To Artboard turned off), the topmost, bottommost, leftmost, or rightmost object will remain stationary, depending on which Align Objects button you click. To choose a non-default object to remain stationary, Cmd-click/Ctrl-click that selected object now (that is, after all the objects are selected and before you click an align button). To go back to the default object, choose **Cancel Key Object** from the palette menu (that command will become dimmed).

5. Click an **Align Objects** button on the Align palette **1**.
   and/or
   Click a **Distribute Objects** button **2**–**4**.

   Or for **Distribute Spacing 5**, choose Auto from the pop-up menu to keep the two objects that are farthest apart stationary (topmost and bottommost or leftmost and rightmost) and redistribute the remaining objects evenly between them, or enter an exact distance you want between objects (the outermost objects will probably move); then click either of the two Distribute Spacing buttons.

➤ To apply a different align or distribute option, first Undo the last one.

Align and Distribute

You can use the Measure tool to calculate the distance and angle between two points in an illustration. When you use the Measure tool, the amounts it calculates are displayed on the Info palette, which opens automatically when the tool is used.

The distance and angle calculated using the Measure tool also become the current values in the Move dialog box, which means you can use the Measure tool as a guide to mark a distance and direction, then use the Transform Again shortcut to move any selected object.

To measure a distance using the Measure tool:

1. Choose the Measure tool ![measure] (it's on the Eyedropper tool pop-out menu).

2. Click the starting and ending points that span the distance and angle you want to measure **1**–**2**.
   or
   Drag from the first point to the second point.

   Distance (D) and angle readouts will now display on the Info palette **3**.

3. *Optional:* To move any object the distance and angle you just measured (until those values are changed), select the object, then press Cmd-D/Ctrl-D.

➤ Shift-click or Shift-drag with the Measure tool to constrain the tool to a multiple of 45° or the current Constrain Angle.

1 *Click a starting point. The **Info** palette will open.*

2 *Click an **ending** point. The distance between clicks will display on the **Info** palette.*

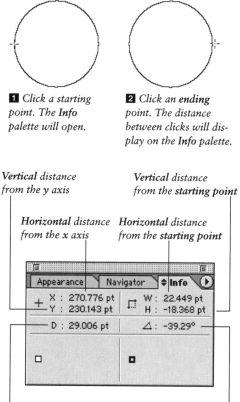

Vertical distance from the y axis

*Vertical distance from the **starting point***

Horizontal distance from the x axis

*Horizontal distance from the **starting point***

*Total distance from the **starting point***

*Angle from the **starting point***

3 *After clicking a starting and ending point with the **Measure** tool, **distance** and **angle** values display on the **Info** palette. The X and Y positions are measured from the ruler origin.*

Chapter 23: Precision Tools ◆ Study Guide

Learning Objectives

- Align objects precisely by using rulers, grids, guides, and the Align palette.
- Move objects a precise distance by using the Move dialog box.
- Apply precise transformations, such as scaling or rotation, by using the Transform palette.
- Determine an exact distance or angle by using the Measure tool.

Get Up and Running Exercises

- Can you recreate the following design in an efficient way? Which precision tools would be most helpful?

- Use only the Transform palette (no object dragging) to perform each of the following actions in a single step:

  ▲ Position an object anywhere on the page. Then move it 37 points down.

  ▲ Position an object anywhere on the page. Then create a duplicate object 2 inches to the right of it.

  ▲ Select an object and double its size without actually figuring out what the new size will be in advance. Try doubling its size proportionally.

- Arrange four objects of different sizes, as in the figures below. Duplicate the entire set until you have a total of three sets. Select the objects, then click an Align palette button to make the first set look like figure **2**. Then, clicking as few Align palette buttons as possible, make the second set align as in figure **3**, and the third set align as in figure **4**. Since most solutions require only one click on the Align palette, undo immediately if you don't get the right result, and try again. Use the tool tips to note which buttons you clicked.

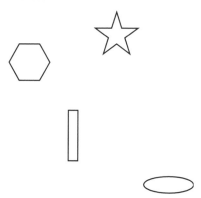

1 *Your original set should look like this. Try to match the position and proportions of the shapes.*

Chapter 23: Precision Tools ◆ Study Guide ◆ Exercises

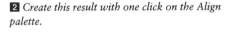

2 *Create this result with one click on the Align palette.*

3 *Start over with the next duplicate set, and create this result with one click.*

4 *Start over with the last duplicate set, and create this result with two clicks.*

Class Discussion Questions

- What are some ways to make sure objects are aligned?
- What are two ways to move an object a precise distance?
- What's an easy way move an object 16.5 points to the left, without having to figure out what its new position value would be? What do you do if the current unit isn't points?
- How does the Constrain Angle work? When might it be useful?
- How is aligning different from distributing?
- How is distributing different from distributing spacing?

Review Questions

Multiple choice

1. After you select the objects you want to align or distribute, how do you specify which object all other selected objects should align to?

   A. Click the object.

   B. Lock the object.

   C. Shift-click the object.

   D. Target the object.

2. Where on the page is the default ruler origin located?

   A. Upper-left corner

   B. Upper-right corner

   C. Lower-left corner

   D. Lower-right corner

3. When you press Enter to apply a value on the Transform palette, which key or keys do you also press to keep the value highlighted on the palette (to make it easy to experiment with different values)?

   A. Cmd/Ctrl

   B. Shift

   C. Option/Alt

   D. Option/Alt-Shift

4. When you press Enter to apply a W or H value on the Transform palette, which key or keys do you also press to scale the object proportionally (also change the other dimension proportionally)?

   A. Cmd/Ctrl

   B. Cmd/Ctrl-Option/Alt

   C. Shift

   D. Option/Alt

5. Which type of alignment sets an equal amount of space between the left edges of each selected object, without moving the outermost selected objects?

   A. Horizontal align left

   B. Horizontal distribute left

   C. Horizontal distribute center

   D. Horizontal distribute space, specified distance

Fill-in-the-blank

1. You can move the ruler origin by _____.

2. To reset the ruler origin to its default location, _____.

3. If, when dragging an object, the pointer is within the Snapping Tolerance of a guide, yet the object won't snap to the guide, make sure the _____ command is checked.

4. To turn any guide into an object, _____.

5. The most convenient place to lock or unlock individual guides is _____.

6. To align objects to the page edge instead of to each other, check the _____ option on the Align palette menu.

7. You can find out the distance between two points by using the _____ tool.

Definitions

1. What is the ruler origin?

2. What is the Constrain Angle?

3. What is the Reference Point?

4. What is alignment?

5. What is distribution?

ACTIONS 24

In this chapter you will learn how to record a sequence of edits and commands in an action. You will also learn how to edit an action using various methods and replay an action on one document or a batch of documents.

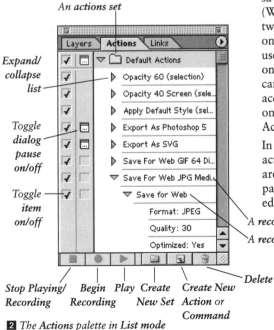

■ *The Actions palette in Button mode*

An actions set

Expand/
collapse
list

Toggle
dialog
pause
on/off

Toggle
item
on/off

A recorded action

A recorded command

Stop Playing/   Begin   Play   Create   Create New   Delete
Recording   Recording   New Set   Action or
                                        Command

■ *The Actions palette in List mode*

Actions and the Actions palette

An action is a recorded sequence of tool and menu events. When an action is replayed, the same series of commands is executed in exactly the same sequence in which it was recorded. Actions can be simple (as short as a single command) or complex—whatever your work demands. And they can be replayed on any document. What's more, actions can be edited, reorganized, included in other actions, and traded around among Illustrator users.

Actions are recorded, played back, edited, saved, and deleted using the Actions palette (Window > Actions). The Actions palette has two modes: Button and List (choose either one from the palette menu). **Button mode** is used only for playback, since in this mode only the action name is listed **■**. Actions can be assigned keyboard shortcuts for fast access in Button mode. To turn Button mode on or off, choose Button Mode from the Actions palette menu.

In **List mode** (Button mode turned off), the actual commands that the action contains are displayed in sequential order on the palette **■**. This mode is used to record, play, edit, save, and load actions.

Note: For the instructions in this chapter, put your Actions palette into List mode.

Actions are organized in sets, which are represented as folder icons on the Actions palette.

To create a new actions set:

1. Click the Create New Set button  at the bottom of the Actions palette.
   or
   Choose New Set from the Actions palette menu **1**.
2. Enter a Name for the set **2**.
3. Click OK. A new folder icon and set name will appear on the palette **3**. (To save the set, see page 429.)

Note: Until you become familiar with using actions, you should practice recording on a duplicate file. Figure out beforehand what the action is supposed to accomplish, and run through the command sequence a few times before you actually record it.

To record an action:

1. Open an existing file or create a new one.
2. On the Actions palette, click the name of the action set you want the new action to belong to. (To create a new set, follow the previous set of instructions on this page).
3. Click the Create New Action button at the bottom of the Actions palette.
4. Enter a name for the action **4**.
5. *Optional:* Choose a keyboard shortcut for the action from the Function Key pop-up menu, and click the Shift and/or Command/Control box. Choose a color for the action name in Button mode from the Color pop-up menu.
6. Click Record.
7. Create and edit objects as you normally would. Any tool and menu commands that are recordable will appear on the action command list.
8. Click the Stop button to end recording.
➤ You can combine smaller actions or parts of actions into one action (see page 428).

1 *Choose New Set from the Actions palette menu (or click the Create New Set button at the bottom of the Actions palette).*

New Action...
New Set...
Duplicate
Delete
Play

Start Recording
Record Again...
Insert Menu Item...
Insert Stop...
Insert Select Path
Select Object...

Action Options...
Playback Options...

Clear Actions
Reset Actions
Load Actions...
Replace Actions...
Save Actions...

Button Mode

Batch...

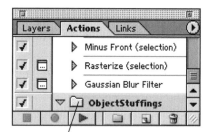

2 *Enter a Name for the new set.*

3 *A new set folder appears on the Actions palette.*

4 *Use the New Action dialog box to change an action's name or keyboard shortcut, or to change its button display color for Button mode.*

(sidebar) **New Actions Set; Record Action**

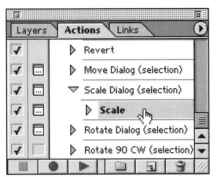

1 *Click the command that you want the new command to follow.*

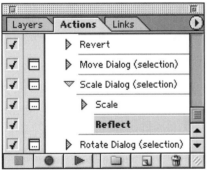

2 *This dialog box opened after we chose Object > Transform > Reflect.*

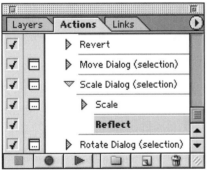

3 *After clicking OK, the new menu item appears on the Actions palette.*

You may find that an action needs to be enhanced or modified from its original recorded version. There are several techniques you can use to edit actions.

To insert a menu item into an action's command list:

1. Put the Actions palette in List mode (turn off the Button Mode option).

2. If the list for the action into which you want to insert the menu item isn't expanded, click the right-pointing triangle.

3. To add a menu command to an action, click the command on the action list that you want the new command to follow **1**.

4. Choose Insert Menu Item from the Actions palette menu.

5. Choose the desired menu command from the menu bar (the command name will appear in the Find field automatically) **2**.
   or
   Type the command name into the Find Field, then click the Find button.

6. Click OK **3**.

➤ Object > Transform commands can be recorded for a selected object. Or use the Selection tool on the handles of the object's bounding box to reshape the object.

Insert Menu Item

If you insert a stop into an action, the action will pause during playback to allow you to perform a manual operation, such as entering type or selecting an object. When you're finished with the manual operation, you can resume the action playback.

To insert a stop in an existing action:

1. Put the Actions palette in List mode, and expand the action into which you want to insert a stop.

2. Click the command after which you want the stop to be inserted **1**.

3. Choose Insert Stop from the Actions palette menu.

4. Type an instructional message in the Record Stop dialog box to tell the user which operations to perform during the stop. At the end of the message, tell the user to click the Play button on the Actions palette when they're ready to resume playback (e.g., "Click the Play button to resume") **2**.

5. *Optional:* Check Allow Continue to permit the user to bypass the pause.

6. Click OK **3**.

➤ To insert a pause while you're recording an action, choose Insert Stop from the Actions palette menu, follow steps 4–6 on this page, then click the Play button to continue recording.

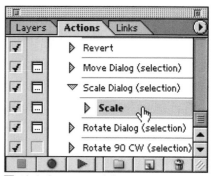

1 *Click the command that you want the stop to appear after.*

2 *Type an instructional message.*

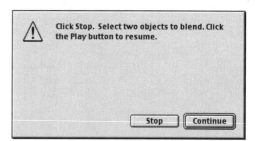

3 *In this example of a **pause** dialog box, the user is instructed to press **Stop**, select two objects for blending, and then click the Play button on the Actions palette to resume the action playback. If the two objects are already selected, the user can click **Continue** instead of Stop.*

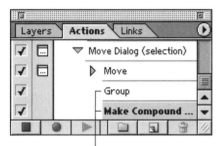

1 *Click the command you want new commands to appear after.*

2 *Two new commands are added.*

In much the same manner as you would insert a menu command, you can record additional commands into an existing action.

To record commands into an existing action:

1. Put the Actions palette in List mode, and expand the action into which you want to insert a command or commands.

2. Choose the command you want the new command(s) to follow **1**.

3. Click the Record (round) button. ●

4. Make modifications to the file as you would normally, using the commands you want inserted in the action. Any recordable tool or menu command that you use now will be added to the action (see the sidebar on page 430).

5. Click the square Stop button ■ to stop recording. The command(s) you just recorded will be listed below the chosen insertion point on the Actions palette **2**.

Note: The first time you play back an action, do it on a duplicate file or on a file that you don't care about preserving.

To replay an action on an image:

1. Open the Illustrator file on which you want to play the action, and select any objects, if necessary.

2. If the Actions palette is in List mode, make sure the checkmark is present for the action you want to play back. Click the name of the action you want to play back, then click the Play button ▶ (triangular) at the bottom of the palette.
   or
   If the palette is in Button mode, just click an action name. *Note:* If the action name is dark (unavailable), go back to List mode and click in the leftmost column for that action to make a checkmark appear.

If you find that you've got the right action for the job, but it contains more commands than you need, you can temporarily exclude the ones you don't need from playing back.

To exclude or include a command from a playback:

1. Put the Actions palette into List mode.

2. Click the right-pointing triangle to expand the command list of the action you want to play back.

3. Click the checkmark ✔ in the leftmost column to disable that command **1** or click in the blank spot to restore the checkmark and enable that command.

For any command or tool that uses a dialog box that requires pressing Return/Enter (also known as a "modal control"), you can insert a pause to enable the user to change any of the dialog settings during playback. To insert this type of pause, you simply click a button on the Actions palette.

To turn on a command's dialog pause:

If a recorded command has a dialog box associated with it, it will have either a pause icon 🔲 or a blank space in the same spot for toggling that icon on and off. Click the icon to disable the dialog pause and use the pre-recorded input instead or click the blank space to enable the command's dialog pause and allow user input.

To re-record a dialog:

1. Put the Actions palette into List mode.

2. Click the right-pointing triangle to expand the action's command list.

3. Select an object in your illustration, then double-click the command you want to re-record **2**. It must have a dialog box icon (or a blank box for the icon).

4. Change any of the dialog settings, then click OK. The next time this action is played back, the new parameters will be used.

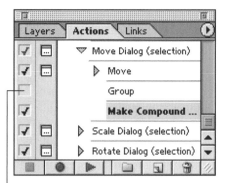

1 *Click in the first column to* **exclude/include** *a command from playback. A* **red checkmark** *next to an action name signifies that at least one of the commands in that action is turned off.*

2 *Double-click the command you want to re-record.*

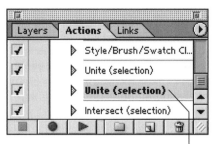

1 *The duplicate command appears on the palette.*

Note: Before you go ahead and wreck all the good work you've done so far, save the actions set you're working on! (See page 429.)

To move a command:

In List mode, click the action command you want to move, then drag it upward or downward to a new location in the same action or into another action (it will appear at the bottom of that list).

To copy a command:

1. In List mode, click the action command you want to copy.

2. Option-drag/Alt-drag the command upward or downward in the same action or into another action list. If you move it to a new list, it will appear at the bottom of that list.
   or
   Drag the command name over the Create New Action button at the bottom of the Actions palette, 🔲 **1** then drag the duplicate command to another location.

Here is a way to include an action in more than one set.

To copy an action from one set to another:

1. In List mode, click the action you want to duplicate.

2. Drag the action over the New Action button.
   or
   Choose Duplicate from the Actions palette menu.

3. Drag the duplicate action into another set.

4. *Optional:* To rename the new action, double-click it.

To delete an action or a command:

Click the action or command you want to delete, click the Delete button 🗑 at the bottom of the Actions palette, then click Yes.
or
To bypass the prompt, drag the action or command over the Delete button.

One way to combine actions is to prompt an action from one set to play back from within another set. You can build a complex action from simpler, smaller actions this way, without having to actually duplicate and move them.

To include one action in another action:

1. If you want to insert a Play Action command as you record an action, skip ahead to step 3.
   or
   If you want to insert a Play Action command into an existing, completed action, click the command after which you want the Play Action to occur, then click the Record button. ●

2. Click the action you want to include.

3. Click the Play button. ▶ The secondary action will play through. When it has completed, it will be listed on the action's command action list as "Play Action." **1**

4. If you're in the middle of recording an action, continue recording.
   or
   If you're inserting the Play Action into an existing action, click Stop to finish.

   Note: If you expand the Play Action command list, you'll see the name of the secondary action to be played and the name of the set that that action belongs to **2**.

➤ If the action or set that the Play Action is calling for has been deleted or renamed, an alert dialog box will appear during playback **3**.

➤ Watch out for any commands in a Play Action that could potentially conflict with the main action. For example, a Deselect command in the Play Action could have an adverse effect on the main action playback.

Actions storeroom

Instead of starting from scratch each time you create a new action, create a set of simple utility actions that you can include in larger actions. Save them in a utility set that you can draw from (see the next page). Remember to supply the utility set along with the main action.

1 *Play action appears on the palette*

2 *The Play action list expanded*

3 *This alert dialog box will appear if the action or set the Play Action is calling for has been **deleted** or **renamed**.*

One Action in Another Action

1 *Enter a* ***Name*** *in the* ***Save Set To*** *dialog box.* ***Note:*** *In* ***Windows****, the actions set file name must have the ".aia" extension.*

2 ***Set Work Path*** *appears on the Actions palette.*

One of the handiest things about actions is that you can share them with other Illustrator users. To do this, you must save them as sets. Try to keep your actions and sets well organized—and back up frequently!

To save an actions set:

1. Click the actions set you want to save.
2. Choose Save Actions from the Actions palette menu.
3. Type a name in the Name field **1**, and choose a location in which to save the set. You can save it in the Action Sets folder inside the Illustrator 10 folder.
4. Click Save.

To load an actions set:

1. Choose Load Actions from the Actions palette menu.
2. Locate and click the actions set you want to load, then click Open. The action will appear on the palette.

If you want a path shape to be part of an action, it has to be inserted as a pre-drawn path.

To record paths for insertion:

1. Have the path(s) you want to insert into the action ready to be selected.
2. Start recording an action.
   or
   To insert the path(s) into an existing action, choose the command after which you want it to appear.
3. Select the paths you want to insert. You can use up to ten paths at a time. You can't use a path that's masked or that's part of a group, blend, compound, or clipping mask. *Note:* To apply stroke and fill attributes to an inserted path, those steps must be recorded separately.
4. Choose Insert Select Path from the Actions palette menu. "Set Work Path" will appear on the action's command list **2**. It cannot be renamed.
5. Click the Stop button, if you're recording.

Save, Load Actions Set; Insert Select Path

Workaround for non-recordable tools

Many tools and commands can't be recorded, such as painting tools, tool options, effects, view menu commands, and preferences. However, for some tools that aren't recordable, their menu equivalents can be recorded as commands in an action.

For example, to make a blend part of an action, use Blend submenu commands instead of the Blend tool. Start recording an action, select the two objects you want to blend, choose Object > Blend > Blend Options, choose a Spacing value, and click OK. Then choose Object > Blend > Make. The two separate blend steps will appear under the same name on the action's command list, but if you expand the command lists, you'll see the differences between the two steps **1**. Continue recording the action or stop recording.

Important note: Back up all your actions sets using the Save Actions command before performing any of the remaining instructions.

To reset actions to the default set:

1. Choose Reset Actions from the Actions palette menu.

2. If you want the default set to **replace all** the actions on the palette, click OK.
   or
   If you want to **append** the original default set to the current actions set list, click Append **2**, then rename the appended set.

To clear all actions sets from the palette:

Choose Clear Actions from the Actions palette menu, then click Yes.

To replace all current actions sets:

1. Choose Replace Actions from the Actions palette menu.

2. Locate and highlight the replacement actions set.

3. Click Open.

What's recordable?

Operations performed by these tools are **recordable**: Ellipse, Rectangle, Rounded Rectangle, Rotate, Scale, Reflect, Slice, Copy, Cut, and Paste. Fill and stroke commands are also recordable, as are opacities and blending modes.

Operations performed by these tools are **not recordable**: Selection, Direct-selection, Lasso, Direct-select lasso, Pen, Add-anchor-point, Delete-anchor-point, Convert-anchor-point, Type, Paintbrush, Pencil, Free Transform, Blend, Graph, Mesh, Gradient, Eyedropper, Scissors, Hand, Zoom, all the Warp tools, as well as the commands on the Effects menu.

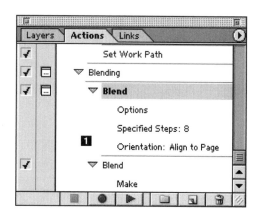

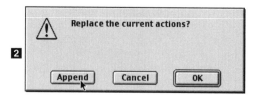

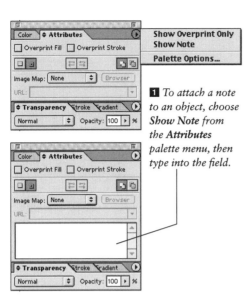

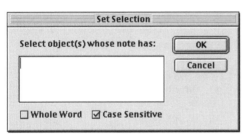

1 *To attach a note to an object, choose **Show Note** from the **Attributes** palette menu, then type into the field.*

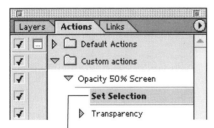

2 *In the Set Selection dialog box, enter the note text you want the action to search for.*

3 *The **Set Selection** command appears in the action.*

Suppose you want to perform an action on some, but not all, objects in a document. One option is to select those objects and then run the action. A second option is to attach notes to the objects you want an action to work on. Then, while playing the action, Illustrator can search for objects with notes that match the search text. Notes can be attached to most items, including groups, clipping paths, and paths containing brush strokes, but not to text, unless it's first converted to outlines.

To attach a note to an object: 10.0!

1. Select the object you want to attach a note to.

2. Show the Attributes palette (Window > Attributes). If the note field isn't visible on the Attributes palette, choose Show Note from the palette menu **1**.

3. Type text into the note field. Don't press Return/Enter, though, as this character will appear in the note field.

4. Deselect the object.

To select notated objects in an action: 10.0!

1. While recording a new action, or with an existing action selected on the Actions palette, choose Select Object from the Actions palette menu.

2. Type the notes that you want the action to search for **2**.

3. Optional: Check Whole Word to limit the criteria to only characters that appear as a complete word—not as part of a larger word (e.g., "go" but not "going").

4. *Optional:* Check Case Sensitive to limit the criteria to only the exact upper/lower case configuration you typed in the field. With this box unchecked, case will not be considered as a criteria.

5. Click OK. Set Selection will appear within the selected action **3**. That action will only work on files that contain objects that fit within the Set Selection criteria.

➤ To edit the selection criteria, double-click Set Selection in the expanded action.

Notate Objects

Actions are a great way to optimize workflow, and being able to perform an action on a designated folder full of files gives you even more power.

Note: Batch processing will end if it encounters a stop command in an action. You should remove any inserted stops from the action that you're going to use for batch processing.

To process multiple files or folders:

1. Make sure all the files for batch processing are located in one folder. The folder can contain subfolders, but only one main folder can be chosen at a time.

2. From the Actions palette menu, choose Batch.

3. Choose a set from the Set pop-up menu **1** and an action from the Action pop-up menu.

4. Choose Source: Folder, click Choose, then locate the folder that contains the files you want to process.

   Check Override Action "Open" Commands to open files from the chosen folder, thus ignoring any Open commands in the recorded action.

   Check Include All Subdirectories if you want to process folders within the folder you've chosen.

Note: For information about working with data sets as the source, refer to the Illustrator User Guide.

5. Choose Destination: None to have the files remain open after processing; or Save and Close to have the edited files be saved over and closed; or Folder to have the files save to a new folder (click Choose to specify the destination folder).

6. *Optional:* If you chose Folder for Destination, check Override Action "Save" Commands to have the files save to the folder designated in step 5, should a Save command occur in the action.

7. Check Override Action "Export" Commands to override any Export command destination used in the action (click Choose to specify the new destination folder).

8. *Optional:* By default, Illustrator will stop the batch process if it encounters an error. If you choose Error: Log Errors to File, the batch process will continue and error messages will be sent to a text file. Click Save As, then give the error log file a name and destination. If this option is chosen, an alert message will inform you of any errors.

Batch Process

10.0!

1 *The Batch dialog box*

Chapter 24: Actions ◆ Study Guide

Learning Objectives

- Play, edit, and record actions.
- Use actions on batches of documents.
- Understand the advantages of using actions in their workflows.

Get Up and Running Exercises

- Draw overlapping filled objects and run the Opacity 40 Screen (selection) action on the top object.

- Make another version of the default action Rasterize that always applies preset values instead of displaying the dialog box. What's the most efficient way to create the new version while preserving the original Rasterize action?

- Record a completely new action that adds a light blue triangle to the document. To make sure it works, change the default fill color before running the action.

- Run the Save for Web 64 Dithered action on ten files. Each file should contain at least one object. For this exercise, make nine copies of the original document and then put all ten in the same folder for processing. Next, create a new, empty folder that you'll use as a destination folder for the batch-processed files. Finally, set up the batch action to process the original files and save the processed copies to the destination folder.

Class Discussion Questions

- What are some examples of when actions are useful?

- How do you run an action on multiple documents?

- What are some guidelines for developing and testing actions?

- Can you make an action that works with a specific shape, such as a logo?

Review Questions

Multiple choice

1. Which Actions palette option or menu command suspends action playback so that messages can be displayed, allowing a user to perform a manual operation?

    A. A checkmark on the far left column

    B. Dialog box pause icon

    C. Insert Menu Item command

    D. Insert Stop command

2. Which Actions palette option or menu command lets you use a drawn shape as part of an action?

    A. Action Options command

    B. Insert Menu Item command

    C. Insert Select Path command

    D. Select Object command

3. Which Actions palette option or menu command excludes or includes a command from a playback?

    A. A checkmark in the far left column

    B. Dialog box pause icon

    C. Insert Stop command

    D. Trash can icon

4. If the Save Actions command is dimmed on the Actions palette menu, which of the following is a likely cause?

    A. The action is locked.

    B. An action, not the overall actions set, is selected.

    C. The checkmark next to the action name is not checked.

    D. The document hasn't been saved.

5. Which Actions palette option or menu command applies an action to objects that have been notated in the document?

    A. Insert Select Path command

    B. Load Actions command

    C. Playback Options command

    D. Select Object command

Fill-in-the-blank

1. To play back one action from another action, _____.

2. To include commands that aren't record-able, use _____.

3. To run actions with one click, _____.

4. To share actions with others, _____.

5. To edit dialog box settings that are part of an existing action, _____.

Definitions

1. What is an action?
2. What is an actions set?
3. What is a stop?
4. What is Button mode?
5. What is batch processing?

PREFERENCES 25

The first skill you will learn in this chapter is how to customize your startup file. Then, using the various panes in the Preferences dialog boxes, you will learn how to choose dozens of default command, tool, and palette settings for current and future documents—Constrain Angle, Use Area Select, Type Options, Units, Undos, Guides, Grid, Smart Guides, Slices, Scratch Disks, Hyphenation, Clipboard, etc.

The startup files

The startup files are stored in the Plug-ins folder in the Adobe Illustrator 10.0 application folder. In the Mac OS, they're called Adobe Illustrator Startup_CMYK and Adobe Illustrator Startup_RGB; in Windows, Adobe Illustrator Startup_CMYK.ai and Adobe Illustrator Startup_RGB.ai.

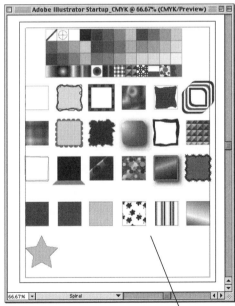

1 *An Adobe Illustrator **Startup** file*

Custom colors, patterns, a gradient, and a brush shape in the bottom two rows

You can create a custom CMYK and/or RGB startup file containing the colors, patterns, gradients, and document settings that you work with regularly so those elements will automatically be part of every new document.

To create a custom startup file:

1. For safekeeping, duplicate the existing startup file, and move the copy to a different folder (see the sidebar).

2. Double-click either of the two Adobe Illustrator Startup file icons (see sidebar).

3. Do any of the following **1**:

   Create new colors, patterns, or gradients, and add these new items to the Swatches palette. For a visual reminder, apply swatches to separate objects in the file.

   Drag-copy swatches from any open swatch libraries to the Swatches palette.

   Create custom brushes or new styles, and apply them to objects as a visual reminder.

   Choose Document Setup, Page Setup, or Print Setup options.

   Choose ruler and page origins.

   Choose a document window size and scroll positions or create new view settings.

4. To help Illustrator launch quickly, delete whatever you don't need in the startup file (e.g., brushes from the Brushes palette).

5. Save the file in the Plug-ins folder using the same name (as listed in the sidebar).

General Preferences

Note! *In Mac OSX, the Preferences submenu is on the **Illustrator** menu.*

Choose Edit > Preferences > General (Cmd-K/Ctrl-K)

Keyboard Increment

This value is the distance (0–1296 pt.) a selected object moves when an arrow is pressed on the keyboard.

Constrain Angle

This is the angle for the *x* and *y* axes. The default setting is 0° (parallel to the edges of the document window). Tool operations, dialog box measurements, and the grid are calculated relative to the current Constrain Angle (see page 414).

Corner Radius

This controls the amount of curvature in the corners of objects drawn with the Rounded Rectangle tool. 0 produces a right angle. Changing this value updates the same field in the Rounded Rectangle dialog box, and vice versa.

Use Area Select

When this option is checked, clicking with a selection tool on an object's fill in Preview view selects the whole object.

Use Precise Cursors

The drawing and editing tool pointers display as a crosshair icon. To turn this option on temporarily when the preference is turned off, press Caps Lock.

Disable Warnings

Check this box to prevent Illustrator from displaying an alert dialog box when a tool is used incorrectly.

Show Tool Tips

Check this box to see an on-screen display of the name of the tool or button currently under the pointer (mouse button up).

Anti-aliased Artwork

When this option is checked, edges of existing and future vector objects (not placed images) look smoother on screen. It has no effect on print output.

Select Same Tint Percentage

When this option is checked, the Select > Same > Fill Color and Stroke Color commands only select other objects with the same spot (not process) color *and* tint percentage as the selected object.

Disable Auto Add/Delete

Checking this option disables the Pen tool's ability to change to the Add-anchor-point tool when the pointer passes over a path segment, or to the Delete-anchor-point tool when the pointer passes over an anchor point.

(Continued on the following page)

Fast track to the Preferences

Use the shortcut that opens the General Preferences dialog box (**Cmd-K/Ctrl-K**), then choose a preferences dialog box from the pop-up menu.

Japanese Crop Marks

Check this box to use Japanese-style crop marks when printing separations. Preview this style in the Separation Setup dialog box.

Transform Pattern Tiles

If this option is checked, and you use a transformation tool on an object that contains a pattern fill, the pattern will also transform. You can also turn this option on or off for any individual transformation tool in its own dialog box, in the Move dialog box, or on the Transform palette.

Scale Strokes & Effects

Check this box to scale an object's stroke weight and appearances when you use the bounding box, the Scale tool, the Free Transform tool, or the Effect > Distort & Transform > Transform command to scale an object. This option can also be turned on or off in the Scale dialog box.

Use Preview Bounds

If this option is checked, an object's stroke weight and any effects are factored in when an object's height and width dimensions are calculated or the Align palette is used. This option changes the dimensions of the bounding box.

Click **Reset All Warning Dialogs** to allow any warning in which you checked "Don't show again" to redisplay if an editing operation causes it to appear.

For the Pencil tool preferences, see page 78.

General Preferences

Type & Auto Tracing Preferences

Choose Edit > Preferences > Type & Auto Tracing

Type Options

Size/Leading; Baseline Shift; Tracking
Selected text is modified by this increment each time a keyboard shortcut is executed for the respective command.

Greeking
This value is the point size at or below which type displays on the screen as gray bars (greeked) rather than as readable characters. Greeking speeds up screen redraw. It has no effect on how a document prints.

Type Area Select
When this option is checked, you can select type by clicking with a selection tool anywhere within a type character's bounding box. When this option is unchecked, you'll have to click right on the type outline to select it.

Show Font Names in English
When this option is checked, two-byte font names display in English on the font pop-up menu. When this option is unchecked, these font names display in a two-byte script.

Auto Trace Options

Auto Trace Tolerance
This value (0–10) controls how closely the Auto Trace tool follows the original path. Enter a low value to have the tool follow the path closely; enter a high Auto Trace Tolerance to have the tool ignore minor irregularities on the path's contour.

Tracing Gap
When tracing the contour of a bitmap image, the Auto Trace tool will ignore gaps that are equal to or less than the number of pixels specified in this field (0–2). The smaller the gap, the more closely an image will be traced, and the more anchor points will be created.

Resetting preferences

To restore all the default Illustrator preferences, trash the Adobe Illustrator 10.0 preferences file. In the Mac OS, it's stored in System Folder > Preferences > Adobe Illustrator 10 > Adobe Illustrator 10.0 Prefs. In Windows, it's stored in Windows > Application Data/ Adobe/Adobe Illustrator 10 > AIPrefs. Whatever you do, don't delete the whole Preferences folder! You need everything else that's in there to run other applications and utilities.

Units & Undo Preferences

Choose Edit > Preferences > Units & Undo

Units

General

This unit of measure is used for the rulers and all dialog boxes for the current document and all new documents.

➤ The Units chosen in File menu > Document Setup (under Artboard: Setup) override the Units chosen here in Units & Undo Preferences (Units: General), but only for the current document (see page 27).

Stroke

This unit of measure is used on the Stroke palette.

Type

This unit of measure is used on the Character and Paragraph palettes. We use Points.

Numbers Without Units Are Points

If this option is checked with Picas chosen as the Units: General, and then you enter a points value in a field, the value won't be converted into picas. For example, if you enter "99," instead of being converted into "8p3," it will stay as "99."

Undo

Minimum Undo Levels

Normally, you can undo/redo up to 200 operations in a row, depending on available memory. If additional RAM is required to perform illustration edits, the number of undos will be reduced to the Minimum [number of] Undo Levels.

Names

Identify Objects By 10.0!

When creating dynamic objects associated with variables, you can specify whether variables are assigned the object's current name or an XML ID number. Consult with your Web developer regarding this option.

Units & Undo Preferences

Guides & Grid Preferences

Choose Edit > Preferences > Guides & Grid

Guides

Color

For Guides, choose a color from the Color pop-up menu. Or choose Other or double-click the color square to open the System color picker and mix your own color.

Style

You can choose a different Style for the guides.

➤ To help differentiate between guides and gridlines, choose the Dots style for guides.

Grid

Color

For the Grid, choose a color from the Color pop-up menu. Or choose Other or double-click the color square to open the System color picker and mix your own color.

Style

You can choose a different Style for the Grid. Subdivision lines won't display if the Dots Style is chosen.

Gridline every

This is the distance between gridlines.

Subdivisions

This is the number of Subdivision lines to be drawn between the gridlines when the Lines Style is chosen for the grid.

Grids In Back

Check Grids In Back to have the grid display behind all objects. With the grid in back, you can easily tell which objects have a fill of None because the grid will be visible underneath them.

➤ Guides will snap to the gridlines as you create or move them if View > Snap to Grid is on.

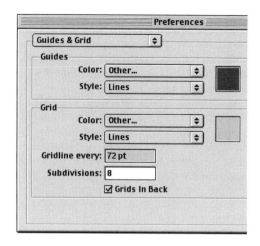

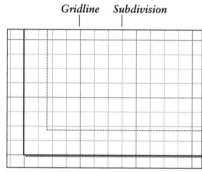

*Gridlines with **four** subdivisions*

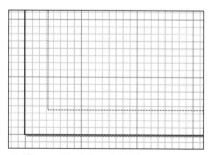

*Gridlines with **eight** subdivisions*

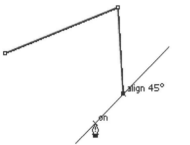

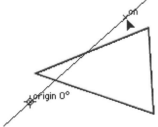

Smart Guides & Slices Preferences
Choose Edit > Preferences > Smart Guides & Slices. To turn on Smart Guides, choose View > Smart Guides (Cmd-U/Ctrl-U).

Display Options
Text Label Hints
These labels display as you pass the pointer over an object, an anchor point, etc.

Construction Guides
Check this option to have angle lines display as you draw or drag an object **1**. Choose or create an angles set in the Angles area (see below).

Transform Tools
Check this option to have angle lines display as you transform an object using a transformation tool or the object's bounding box **2**. Choose or create an angles set in the Angles area (see below).

Object Highlighting
Check this option to have an object's path display as you pass the pointer over it **3**. This is helpful for locating unpainted paths (e.g., clipping masks) or paths behind other paths. Hidden paths won't highlight.

Angles
With Smart Guides on, angle lines display temporarily relative to other objects in the illustration as you drag an object or move the pointer. Choose a preset angles set from the Angles pop-up menu or enter custom angles in any or all of the fields. If you enter custom angles, "Custom Angles" will appear on the pop-up menu. If you switch from Custom Angles to a predefined set and then later switch back to Custom Angles, the last-used custom settings will reappear in the fields.

Snapping Tolerance
This is the distance within which the pointer must be from an object for Smart Guides to display. 4 pt. is the default.

Slicing
Show Slice Numbers *10.0!*
Check this option to have slice numbers display on screen. From the **Line Color** pop-up menu, choose a color for those numbers and for the lines that surround each slice.

1 *Construction guide*

2 *Transform tool guide*

3 *Object Highlight guide*

439

Hyphenation Preferences

Choose Edit > Preferences > Hyphenation

Default Language

Choose the language dictionary Illustrator will use when inserting hyphen breaks. You can choose a different hyphenation language dictionary for the current document from the Multilingual Options: Language pop-up menu on the Character palette.

Exceptions

Enter words that you want hyphenated in a particular way. Type the word in the New Entry field, inserting hyphens where you would want them to appear, or enter a word with no hyphens to prevent Illustrator from hyphenating it; then click Add. To remove a word from the list, click it, then click Delete.

Plug-ins & Scratch Disks Preferences

Choose Edit > Preferences > Plug-ins &
Scratch Disks

Plug-ins folder

Note: For changes made in this dialog box
to take effect, you must quit/exit and then
relaunch Illustrator.

Folder

Illustrator comes with core and add-on plug-in files that provide additional functionality
to the main application. These and other
plug-in files are placed in the Plug-ins folder
in the Adobe Illustrator 10 folder. If for some
reason you need to move the Plug-ins folder,
you must use this Preferences dialog box to
tell Illustrator the new location of the folder.

The current Plug-ins folder location is listed
after the word "Folder." To change the
plug-ins location, click Choose, locate and
click the desired folder name, then click
Open. The new location will now be listed.

➤ Plug-ins use a lotta RAM, so you should
store only the ones you use regularly in
the Adobe Illustrator 10 > Plug-ins folder,
and stash the rest elsewhere.

Scratch Disks

Primary

The Primary (and optional Secondary)
Scratch Disk is used as virtual memory when
available RAM is insufficient for image
processing. Choose an available hard drive—
preferably your largest and fastest—from the
Primary pop-up menu. Startup is the default.

Secondary

As an optional step, choose an alternate
Secondary hard drive to be used as extra
workspace when needed. If you have only
one hard drive, of course you can have only
one scratch disk.

➤ To see how much of Illustrator's memory
allotment is currently available, choose
Free Memory from the status line pop-up
menu at the bottom of the document/
application window, then read the readout.

Plug-ins & Scratch Disks Preferences

Files & Clipboard Preferences

Choose Edit > Preferences > Files & Clipboard

Files

Mac OS only: Choose **Append Extension:** Always or Ask When Saving to have Illustrator append a file's extension when the file is saved for the first time. Check Lower Case to have the extension appear in lower-case characters instead of uppercase. When exporting files, extensions are a must.

To specify how linked images are updated when the original files are modifed, from the **Update Links** pop-up menu, choose:

Automatically to have Illustrator update linked images automatically whenever the original files are modified.

Manually to leave linked images unchanged when the original files are modified. You can use the Links palette at any time to update links.

Ask When Modified to display a dialog box when the original files are modified. (In the dialog box, click Yes to update the linked image or click No to leave it unchanged.)

10.0! If you're working with a lot of linked files, you can enhance performance by checking **Use Low Resolution Proxy for Linked EPS**; placed images will display as bitmap proxies. With this option unchecked, placed images will display at full resolution and vectors will display in full color.

Clipboard

The Clipboard can be used to transfer selections between Illustrator and other Adobe programs, such as Photoshop, GoLive, LiveMotion, and Premiere. When a selection is copied to the Clipboard, it is copied as a PDF and/or AICB, depending on which of those options you choose here. In most programs in Mac OSX, copied artwork pastes as PICT.

Choose either or both of these Copy As formats for copying files to other applications:

PDF to preserve transparency information in the selection. PDF is designed for use with Adobe Photoshop 6, InDesign, and future Adobe applications.

AICB, a PostScript format, to have Illustrator break objects into smaller opaque objects, preserving the appearance of transparency through flattening. Check **Preserve Paths** to copy a selection as a set of detailed paths or check **Preserve Appearance** to preserve the appearance of the selection, producing a simpler outline path.

Note: If you check both PDF and AICB, the receiving application will choose its preferred format. Fills and effects will copy and paste more accurately, but the copying time will be longer and the memory requirements higher.

➤ If you're unable to paste a file format into Illustrator, try using the drag-and-drop feature instead (and vice versa).

➤ If you paste into Photoshop, the Paste dialog box will open, presenting you with various options for pasting data.

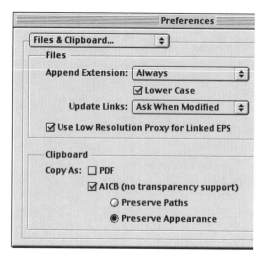

Chapter 25: Preferences ◆ Study Guide

Learning Objectives

- Customize the Illustrator startup files.
- Understand preferences categories and functions.
- Manage preferences.

Get Up and Running Exercises

- Customize the startup files.

  - ▲ Suppose you're helping a magazine implement print and Web design standards. Design CMYK and RGB startup files that can be used for all Illustrator users at the company. The startup files must contain swatches for the three official company colors and a linear gradient swatch that goes from one of the company colors to white. They don't want any other default swatches on the Swatch palette.

    The magazine's official colors are all from the PANTONE Process Coated swatch library: PANTONE DS1-6C, PANTONE DS207-7C, and PANTONE DS270-9C. You can decide which one to use in the gradient.

  - ▲ Optimize the startup files you created so that they load even more quickly.

  - ▲ To test your changes, create new CMYK and RGB files and see if they use the changes you made. If they don't, determine why and try again.

- Set filename handling for a cross-platform workflow. How can you set preferences to comply with a production environment where lower-case filename extensions are required?

- You're preparing to draw in isometric perspective, which requires that various sides of an object be drawn at 30 and 60-degree angles. Which preference should you change to make it easier?

Class Discussion Questions

- Which preferences affect the behavior of selection tools and commands?

- Which preferences affect transformations?

- Which preferences affect performance, and why?

- Which preferences can help you maintain precision and accuracy when you draw?

- Which preferences affect the transfer of documents or objects to and from Illustrator?

Chapter 25: Preferences ◆ Study Guide ◆ Exercises & Discussion Questions

Review Questions

Multiple choice

1. Which preference displays drawing and editing pointers as a crosshair icon?

   A. Construction Guides

   B. Use Area Select

   C. Use Preview Bounds

   D. Use Precise Cursors

2. Which preference accounts for the size of appearance attributes when calculating an object's dimensions?

   A. Constrain Angle

   B. Use Area Select

   C. Use Precise Cursors

   D. Use Preview Bounds

3. Which preference marks the outline of a path as you move the pointer over it, even if the path has no stroke or fill (but is visible—not hidden)?

   A. Object Highlighting

   B. Text Label Hints

   C. Construction Guides

   D. Type Area Select

4. How do you reset Illustrator preferences to their defaults?

   A. Delete the Adobe Illustrator Startup_CMYK and Adobe Illustrator Startup_RGB files.

   B. Open the Adobe Illustrator Startup_CMYK and Adobe Illustrator Startup_RGB files, and in each file, choose File > Revert.

   C. Delete the Adobe Illustrator 10.0 Prefs file.

   D. Delete the Adobe Illustrator folder in the Preferences folder.

5. What's the purpose of the Scratch Disks preference?

   A. It assigns the default disk location where the Save As dialog box will open.

   B. It designates where undo steps will be stored.

   C. It sets aside memory on disk that Illustrator can use when it runs low on memory in RAM.

   D. It determines where Illustrator is allowed to store documents so that large files don't fill up small disks.

Fill-in-the-blank

1. To customize the distance an object moves when you press an arrow key, enter a value in the _____ preference.

2. To adjust how close the pointer needs to be to an object before Smart Guides display, change the _____ preference.

3. To control when Illustrator synchronizes placed images with their original files, set the _____ preference.

4. To have Smart Guides display when an object is rotated, make sure the _____ preference is on.

5. If subdivision lines don't display on the grid, it means the Grid: Style preference is set to _____.

6. To have appearance attributes (such as line weights) resize accordingly when objects are resized, turn on the _____ preference.

Definitions

1. What is an Illustrator startup file?

2. What is the Numbers Without Units Are Points preference?

3. What is the Type Area Select preference?

4. What are the Primary and Secondary Scratch Disks?

5. What is a low-resolution proxy?

OUTPUT/EXPORT **26**

Illustrator objects are described and stored as mathematical commands. But when they are printed, they are rendered as dots. The higher the resolution of the output device, the more smoothly and sharply lines, curves, gradients, and continuous-tone images are rendered. In this chapter you will learn to print an illustration on a PostScript black-and-white or composite color printer, to create crop and trim marks, to print an oversized illustration, and to optimize print performance. You'll also learn how to save a file in a variety of formats for export to other applications, how to output transparency, and how to manage color using the Color Settings dialog box. To produce color separations, see Chapter 28. For Web output, see Chapter 27.

Charles, Nancy Stahl

Norah, Nancy Stahl

Outputting files

To print on a black-and-white or color PostScript printer:

1. Choose File > Document Color Mode > CMYK, if necessary, before outputting to a color printer.

2. *Mac OS:* Open the Chooser (Apple menu), click the desired printer driver, then close the Chooser.

3. *Mac OS:* Choose File > Page Setup (Cmd-Shift-P) **1**.

Win: Choose File > Print Setup (Ctrl-Shift-P), then select a printer.

4. Choose a size from the Paper/Size pop-up menu, make sure the correct Orientation icon is selected (to print vertically or horizontally on the paper), then click OK.

5. Choose File > Print (Cmd-P/Ctrl-P).

6. *Mac OS:* Choose Adobe Illustrator 10 from the pop-up menu **2**.

Mac OS and Win: Choose PostScript®: Level 2 or 3 (depending on your printer and printer driver) **3**.

If you don't know about profiles and Color Settings, read pages 470–478 first.

7. Choose a Print Space profile from the Profile pop-up menu **4**:

Use Same As Source only when a profile has already been set for the document (via Edit > Assign Profile). This profile name will display in the source space area.
or
Choose an appropriate profile for your type of output printer.

➤ The profile you chose in Color Settings for Working Spaces: CMYK is probably a good print profile choice.

8. Leave the Intent: menu option on the default Relative Colorimetric option unless you or your output specialist have a reason to change it. To learn more about intents, see pages 476–477.

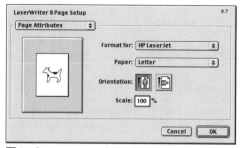

1 *In the **Page Setup** dialog box for a **black-and-white** printer, choose a paper size from the **Paper** pop-up menu.*

2 *In the Mac OS, choose **Adobe Illustrator 10**.*

3 *Choose PostScript®: **Level 2** or **Level 3**.*

4 *Choose a **Print Space** profile from the **Profile** pop-up menu.*

1 *In the* **Print** *dialog box, enter a number of* **Copies** *and which* **Pages** *you want to print.*

9. *Mac OS:* Choose Color Matching from the pop-up menu used in step 6. Choose Print Color: Color/Grayscale. For a color printer, choose the appropriate color options.

Win: Accept the default setting for your printer. If necessary, click the Properties button, click the Page Setup tab, then choose a Color Appearance. For a color printer, choose the appropriate color options.

10. *Mac OS:* Choose General from the pop-up menu. *Mac OS and Win:* Enter the desired number of Copies **1**.

11. To print a single full-page document or a Tile imageable areas document in the Mac OS, leave the Pages: All button selected; in Windows, leave the Print Range: All button selected.
    or
    To print select tiled pages, enter starting and ending page numbers in the From and To fields.

12. *Mac OS:* Click Print. *Win:* Click OK.

Print

Crop marks are short perpendicular lines around the edge of a page that a print shop uses as guides to trim the paper. Illustrator's Crop Marks command creates crop marks around a rectangle that you draw, and they become part of your illustration.

To create crop marks:

1. Choose the Rectangle tool (M).

2. Carefully draw a rectangle to encompass some or all of the objects in the illustration .

3. With the rectangle still selected, choose Object > Crop Marks > Make **2**. The rectangle will disappear, and crop marks will appear where the corners of the rectangle were.

➤ If you don't create a rectangle before choosing Object > Crop Marks > Make, crop marks will be placed around the artboard.

➤ Only one set of crops can be created per illustration using the Crop Marks command. If you apply Object > Crop Marks > Make a second time, new marks will replace the existing ones. To create more than one set of crop marks in an illustration, use the Trim Marks filter (see the next page).

1 *A rectangle is drawn.*

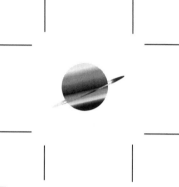

2 *After choosing the **Make Crop Marks** command*

Create Crop Marks

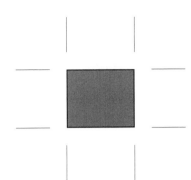

1 *After applying the Trim Marks filter*

To remove crop marks created with the Crop Marks command:

Choose Object > Crop Marks > Release. The selected rectangle will reappear, with a fill and stroke of None. Toggle to Outline view or use Smart Guides (with Object Highlighting option checked in Edit > Preferences > Smart Guides & Slices) to locate it. You can recolor it or delete it.

➤ If crop marks were created for the entire page, the released rectangle will have the same dimensions as the artboard.

➤ To quickly set crop marks for the entire page, make the artboard the same size as the printable page.

The Trim Marks filter places eight trim marks around a selected object or objects. You can create more than one set of Trim Marks in an illustration.

To create trim marks:

1. Select the object or objects to be trimmed.

2. Choose Filter > Create > Trim Marks. Trim marks will surround the smallest rectangle that could be drawn around the selection **1**.

➤ Group the trim marks with the objects they surround so you can move them in unison. On the Layers palette, trim marks are listed as nested objects within a group.

➤ To move or delete trim marks, select them first with the Selection tool or using the Layers palette.

Remove Crop Marks; Create Trim Marks

To print (tile) an illustration that is larger than the paper size:

1. Choose File > Document Setup (Option-Shift-P/Alt-Shift-P) 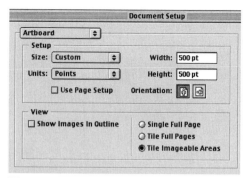.

2. For the illustration's artboard dimensions, make sure Artboard is chosen from the topmost pop-up menu. Then choose a preset size from the Size drop-down menu, or choose a unit of measure from the Units pop-up menu and enter custom Width and Height dimensions.

3. Click Tile Imageable Areas.

4. *Optional:* To change the tile orientation, click Page Setup/Print Setup, then click whichever Orientation button isn't selected.

5. Click OK.

6. Double-click the Hand tool 🖐 to display the entire artboard.

7. *Optional:* Choose the Page tool, 📄 then drag the tile grid so it divides the illustration into better tiling breaks. The grid will redraw **2**.

8. Follow steps 5–12 on pages 444–445. to print.

➤ On a document that's set to Tile Imageable Areas, only tile pages with objects on them will print. If a direction line from a curved anchor point extends onto a blank tile, that page will also print.

1 *In File > Document Setup, choose or enter the appropriate Artboard dimensions and click Tile Imageable Areas.*

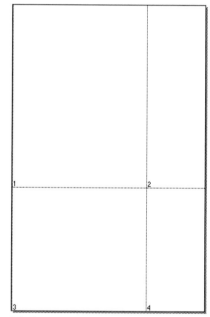

2 *The tile grid*

Oversized Documents

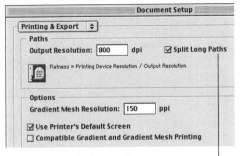

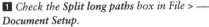

1 *Check the Split long paths box in File >* *Document Setup.*

Solving printing problems

If things don't go as smoothly as you'd like...

Patterns

➤ By default, patterns preview and print. If a document containing patterns doesn't print, place the objects that contain patterns on a new layer, uncheck the Print option for that layer, then try printing again. If the document prints, the patterns were the likely culprit.

➤ Try to limit the number of pattern fills in an illustration.

➤ Make the original bounding rectangle for a pattern tile no larger than one-inch square (see pages 164–165).

➤ Use a PostScript Level 2 or Level 3 printer when printing elaborate patterns.

➤ Don't use a blend, a gradient fill, or type as a pattern fill on a compound path.

Complex paths

Sometimes a file that contains an excessive number of complex paths with many anchor points will cause a printing error (a limit-check or virtual memory error message may appear in the print progress window). If you do get such a message, delete any excess anchor points from long paths using the Delete-anchor-point tool, then try printing again.

If that doesn't work, check Split Long Paths in File > Document Setup > Printing & Export **1** and try printing yet again. Complex closed paths will be split into two or more separate paths, but their overall path shapes won't change. The Split Long Paths option does not affect stroked paths, compound paths, or clipping masks. You can also split a stroked path manually using the Scissors tool. (To preserve a copy of a document with its non-split paths, before checking Split Long Paths, save the document under a new name using File > Save As.) To rejoin split closed paths, select them, click the "Add to shape area" button on the Pathfinder palette, then click Expand. (To rejoin open split paths, select the endpoints of both paths, then choose Object > Path > Join; see pages 129–130.)

(Continued on the following page)

Solving Printing Problems

449

More troubleshooting tips

➤ Clipping masks may cause printing problems, particularly if they're produced from compound paths. In fact, a file containing multiple masks may not print at all. For a complex mask, consider using the Knife tool to cut all the shapes in half—including the mask object itself—before creating the mask. Select and mask each half separately, then move them together.

➤ Choose Object > Path > Clean Up to delete any Stray Points (inadvertent clicks on the artboard with the Pen tool), Unpainted Objects, or Empty Text Paths **1**.

➤ If you get a VM error, try reducing the number of fonts used in the file or convert large type into outlines (Type > Create Outlines) so fewer fonts will need to be downloaded.

➤ Instead of creating compound paths, use the shape modes buttons on the Pathfinder palette to create compound shapes.

➤ To improve gradient fill printing on an older PostScript imagesetter or on a PostScript clone printer, check the Compatible Gradient and Gradient Mesh Printing box in File > Document Setup > Printing & Export, then resave the file. A mesh object will be converted to JPEG format. Don't check this option if your gradients are printing well, as it may slow printing.

➤ If you're using complex elements like compounds, masks, or patterns in a document, and the whole document doesn't print, place a complex object on its own layer, uncheck the print option for that layer, and try printing again. And by the same token, if an object doesn't print, double-click the name of the layer the object is on and make sure the Print box is checked.

➤ If a pattern doesn't print, simplify it.

➤ As a last resort you can lower the output resolution of a file to facilitate printing (see page 452).

Troubleshooting Printing Problems

1

Clean Up

Delete
☑ Stray Points
☑ Unpainted Objects
☑ Empty Text Paths

OK
Cancel

Smoother halftones

If your printer has halftone enhancing software,

Mac OS: Choose File > Print, choose Imaging Options from the second pop-up menu, choose PhotoGrade and/or FinePrint or whatever your particular printer imaging options are, then click OK.

Windows: Choose File > Print Setup, choose Properties, turn on the enhancement option under the Graphics tab or the Device Options tab (on NT, click the Advanced tab), then click OK.

Next, make sure Use Printer's Default Screen is checked in File > Document Setup > Printing & Export (this is the default setting) to enable the printer's halftone method and disable Illustrator's built-in halftone method.

Blur the distinctions

Here's another way to help prevent banding: Convert a gradient to a **raster** image (Object > Rasterize), then apply Filter > Blur > **Gaussian Blur**. This will disperse the gradient colors.

Smoother blends

When printing gradients and blends, consider the relationship between the printer's lines per inch setting and the number of gray levels the printer is capable of producing. The higher the lines per inch (also known as screen frequency), the fewer the printable levels of gray. For the smoothest printing of gradients and blends, use a printer that's capable of outputting 256 levels of gray.

If you—and not the print shop—are supervising the color separation process, first ask your print shop what screen frequency (lpi) you will need to specify when imagesetting your file and what resolution (dpi) to use for imagesetting. Some imagesetters can achieve resolutions above 3000 dpi.

The blend or gradient length

To ensure that a gradient fill or a blend does not band into visible color strips:

➤ Use the correct lines per inch setting for the printer to output 256 levels of gray.

➤ Make sure at least one color component (R, G, or B, or C, M, Y, or K) in the starting color of the gradient or blend differs by at least 50% from the same component in the ending color.

➤ Keep the blend or gradient length to a maximum of 7½ inches. If you need a longer blend or gradient, create it in Photoshop, then place it in Illustrator, or rasterize the blend or gradient object in Illustrator.

Illustrator chooses the number of steps in a gradient or a blend based on the largest difference in percentage between gradient color components. The greater the percentage difference, the greater the potential number of steps, and thus the longer the blend can be. At 256 steps, for example, the blend can be up to 7½ inches long. Here's the formula for calculating the optimal number of blend steps:

Number of steps = Number of gray levels from the printer x The largest color percentage difference

Use the chart on page 365 of the Adobe Illustrator 10.0 User Guide to calculate the maximum blend length based on the number of blend steps.

10.0! The precision with which objects are printed from Illustrator is determined by the Output Resolution setting in Document Setup; this setting affects every object in the current document. If your document doesn't print, try lowering its Output Resolution, then send it to print again.

To lower a document's output resolution to facilitate printing:

1. Open the file that refuses to print, choose File > Document Setup, then choose Printing & Export from the topmost pop-up menu.

2. Enter a lower Output Resolution value (100-9600 dpi), click OK, then try printing the document again. If it prints, but with noticeable jaggedness on the curve segments, you lowered the output resolution too much. Raise the Output value, and try printing again. 800 dpi is the default output resolution.

Flatness versus flattening

Don't confuse Illustrator's process of **flattening** overlapping shapes in order to preserve the look of transparency with **flatness**, which is the printing device resolution divided by the output resolution. The output resolution controls the degree of flatness in path curve segments. For any given printer, lowering the output resolution raises the flatness value. The lower the output resolution (or the higher the flatness value), the less precisely curve segments will print.

Potential gray levels at various output resolutions and screen frequencies

	Output Resolution (DPI)	Screen Frequency (LPI)					
		60	85	100	133	150	180
Laser printers	300	26	13				
	600	101	51	37	21		
Imagesetters	1270	256	224	162	92	72	
	2540		256	256	256	256	
	3000			256	256	256	256

1 *This is the Document Info palette with Document information displayed. This information is always available—whether the Selection Only option is on or off.*

2 *The Document Info palette with the Objects and Selection Only options checked on the palette menu*

To display information about an object or an entire document:

1. *Optional:* Select the object (or objects) about which you want to read info.

2. Choose Window > Document Info to show the Document Info palette **1**.

3. To display information about a selected object (step 1, above), make sure Selection Only on the palette menu has a checkmark **2**.

   or

   To display information pertaining to all the objects in the illustration, uncheck Selection Only.

4. Choose Objects from the palette menu to make the palette list the number of paths, clipping masks, compounds, opacity masks, transparent groups, transparent objects, styled objects, gradient meshes, brushed objects, and color, font and linking info in the selection.

   or

   Choose another category from the palette menu to see a listing of styles, brushes, spot color objects, pattern objects, gradient objects, fonts, linked images, embedded images, or font details (PostScript name, font file name, language, etc.) in a selection or in the entire document.

5. *Optional:* If the Selection Only option is checked on the palette menu, you can click any other object in the document to see info for that object in the currently chosen category.

6. *Optional:* Choose Save from the palette menu to save the currently displayed information as a text document. Choose a location in which to save the text file, rename the file, if desired, then click Save. Use the system's default text editor to open the text document. You can print this file and refer to it when you prepare your document for imagesetting.

Document Info palette

Exporting files

Choose File > Save As to save another version of your file with a location, name, or file format. Or choose File > Save a Copy to save a copy of your file with the word "Copy" after the file name; your original file will remain as the open, active file on screen. Both commands also let you specify a new name, location, or file type: Illustrator 10, PDF, EPS, SVG, or SVG Compressed.

In order to open an Illustrator file in other graphics programs that won't recognize the Illustrator 10.0 file format, you may need to save it in an earlier Illustrator format. While you won't be able to preserve features that are new to Illustrator 10.0, in some situations this might be your only option.

To save as an earlier version of Illustrator:

1. Choose File > Save As or Save a Copy.

2. Mac OS: Choose Adobe Illustrator Document from the Format pop-up menu, then click Save.

   Windows: Choose Illustrator (*.ai) from the Save as Type drop-down menu, then click Save.

3. In the Illustrator Native Format Options dialog box, choose an earlier version of Illustrator **1**.

4. Click "Preserve Paths (discard transparency)" to preserve your objects' paths and eliminate any transparency effects altogether.
   or
   Click "Preserve Appearance (flatten transparency)" to preserve the appearance of transparency.

5. Click OK.

What about AI, EPS, and PDF?

To learn how to save a file in the **Illustrator** format, see pages 44–46. For the **Adobe PDF** format, see pages 50–52; for the **Illustrator EPS** format, see pages 47–49; and for the **SVG** format, see page 504.

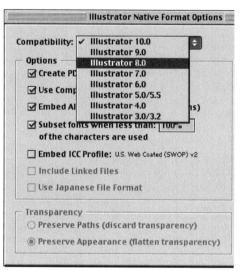

1 *Choose an earlier version of Illustrator from the* **Compatibility** *pop-up menu in the* **Illustrator Native Format Options** *dialog box.*

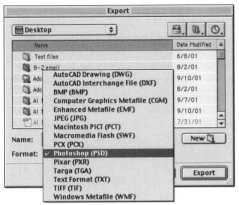

1 *Mac OS: Choose from the* **Format** *pop-up menu.*

2 *Windows: Choose from the* **Save as type** *drop-down menu.*

It doesn't all end in Illustrator. An Illustrator file can be saved in a variety of file formats for export into other applications. Some of these formats are discussed on the following ten pages.

To export a file:

1. With the file open, choose File > Export.

2. If you don't want to use the original file name, enter a new name in the Name field *(Mac)* or File Name field *(Windows).*

   Windows: When saving a file, Illustrator automatically appends the proper file extension to the name (e.g., .ai, .eps, .tif) based on the chosen file format.

   Mac OS: Extensions will be appended if Always is chosen from the Append Extension pop-up menu in Edit > Preferences > Files & Clipboard.

3. Choose from the Format pop-up menu *(Mac OS)* **1** or Save as type drop-down menu *(Win)* **2**.

4. Choose a location in which to save the new version.

   Optional: To create a new folder for the file in the *Mac OS,* click the New folder button, enter a name, then click Create. In *Windows,* click Create New Folder, then enter a name.

5. Click Export/Save (Return/Enter). Choose the desired settings from any secondary dialog box, then click OK. Some of these dialogs are discussed on pages 456–461.

➤ *Mac OS:* If Append Extensions is set to Never in Edit > Preferences > Files & Clipboard, and you don't change the file name in the Export dialog box, when you click Export an alert prompt will appear. Click Replace to save over the original file or click Cancel to return to the Export dialog box.

Export

Secondary export dialog boxes

Raster

If you choose a raster (bitmap) file format, such as BMP, PCX, Pixar, or Targa, the Rasterize dialog box will open **1**. Choose a Color Model for the resulting file color. For file Resolution, choose Screen (72 dpi), Medium (150 dpi), or High (300 dpi), or enter a custom resolution (Other). Check Anti-Alias to smooth the edges of objects (pixels will be added along object edges).

Bitmap (BMP) format

BMP is the standard bitmap image format on Windows and DOS computers. If you choose this format, you will also need to choose the Windows or OS/2 format for use with those operating systems, specify a bit depth, and choose whether you want to include RLE compression.

PCX format

The PCX format was created by Z-Soft for use with its PC Paintbrush program.

PIXAR format (PXR)

The PIXAR format is used for exchanging files with high-end PIXAR workstations, which are used for three-dimensional animation applications.

Photoshop

Exporting to Photoshop is a good idea if you want to preserve transparency effects. If you choose the Photoshop file format, the Photoshop Options dialog box will open **2**. Choose a Color Model, a Resolution (preset or custom), and turn the Anti-Alias option on or off. To export Illustrator layers to Photoshop, check Write Layers. If this option is unchecked, Illustrator will flatten layers and the illustration will appear as one layer in Photoshop. The Write Layers option preserves the stacking appearance of objects and groups nested within a layer, but only the top-level layers will become layers in Photoshop. You also have the option to Write Nested Layers to export layers and sublayers ("nested layers") as separate layers to Photoshop. The sublayers may be stacked below the top-level layer on Photoshop's Layers palette, but you can rearrange them.

Layer upon layer

If you keep layers intact when you export files to Photoshop, you'll then have the opportunity to apply Photoshop filters to those individual layers. You can also drop a native Photoshop PSD file containing Illustrator layers into ImageReady, where you can convert the layers to animations. ImageReady is designed specifically for creating and optimizing raster graphics, rollovers, and animations for the Web.

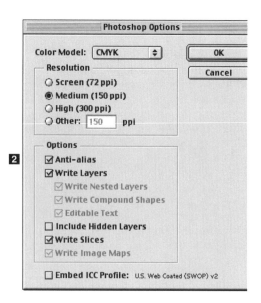

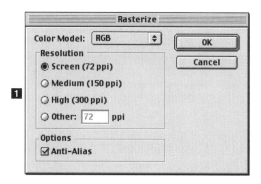

Raster, BMP, PCX, PXR, Photoshop

Photoshop and Illustrator

If you open a Photoshop file in Illustrator, the file's blending modes, transparency, and clipping masks will be preserved, and layers can be converted to separate Illustrator objects 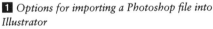.

If you export an Illustrator file to the Photoshop format, opacity masks, layers, and editable type will be preserved. The appearance of blending modes and transparency will be preserved in Photoshop, though on the Layers palette the blending mode of the imported layers will be listed as Normal, Opacity 100%.

Layer masks from Photoshop will be converted to opacity masks in Illustrator, whereas opacity masks from Illustrator will be converted to layer masks in Photoshop. And finally, compound shapes can be traded back and forth between Illustrator and Photoshop. To learn more about Photoshop and Illustrator, see pages 252–253.

10.0!

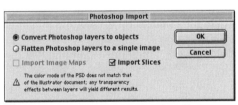

1 *Options for importing a Photoshop file into Illustrator*

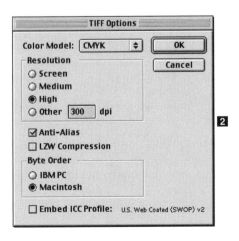

If the Illustrator file contains text, you can check Editable Text to keep the text editable in Photoshop. Text must be stacked as individual objects within a top-level layer.

If the Illustrator file contains compound shapes, you can check Write Compound Shapes to preserve them in Photoshop. The compound shape must be in a top-level layer.

And finally, if the Illustrator file contains hidden layers that you want to include, check Include Hidden Layers. You can also choose to embed an ICC profile in the Photoshop document, if you have assigned one to your Illustrator file.

Tagged-Image File Format (TIFF)

TIFF is a bitmap image format that is supported by virtually all paint, image-editing, and page-layout applications. It supports RGB, CMYK, and grayscale color schemes, and it supports the lossless LZW compression model. You can specify a color space and resolution when you create TIFF files.

If you choose the TIFF file format, the TIFF Options dialog box will open **2**. Choose a Color Model. Choose a Resolution: Screen (72 dpi), Medium (150 dpi), or High (300 dpi), or type in a custom resolution. And turn the Anti-Alias option on or off. Check LZW Compression to compress the file. This type of compression is lossless, which means it doesn't cause loss or degradation of image data. Choose your target operating platform in the Byte Order area. And check Embed ICC Profile if you have assigned such a profile to your file.

JPEG

JPEG format is a good choice if you want to compress files that contain placed, continuous-tone bitmap images, or objects with gradient fills. JPEG is also used for viewing 24-bit images via the Web. (The JPEG format for Web output is discussed on pages 482 and 497).

When you choose an Image Quality, keep in mind that there's a tradeoff between image quality and the amount of compression. The greater the compression, the greater the

(Continued on the following page)

TIFF; JPEG

loss of image data and the lower the image quality. To experiment, export multiple copies of a file and use a different compression setting for each copy, and then view the results in the target application. Or use Illustrator's Save for Web command to preview different compression settings (see pages 497–498).

If you choose the JPEG file format, the JPEG Options dialog box will open 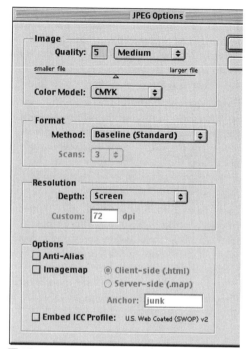:

1. Choose an Image Quality. Enter a numerical value (0–10); or move the slider; or choose Low, Medium, High, or Maximum from the pop-up menu.

2. Choose a Color model: RGB, CMYK or Grayscale.

3. Choose a Format Method: Baseline ("Standard"); Baseline Optimized, which lets you adjust the color quality of the image; or Progressive. A Progressive JPEG displays at increasingly higher resolutions as the file downloads from the Web. Choose the number of scans (iterations) you want displayed before the final image appears. This type of JPEG is not supported by all Web browsers and requires more RAM to view.

4. Choose a Resolution Depth: Screen, Medium, or High. Or choose Custom and enter a Custom resolution (dpi).

5. In the Options section:

   Check Anti-Alias if you want your image to have smooth edges.

   If you have linked objects in your file to URLs, check Imagemap and choose Client-side or Server-side. For Client-side, Illustrator saves the JPEG file with an accompanying HTML file that holds the link information; both files are required by your Web-creation application in order to interpret the links correctly. For Server-side, Illustrator saves the file for use on a Web server.

   Check Embed ICC Profile to embed the file's Color Settings profile.

1 *The **JPEG Options** export dialog box lets you tailor your image for a number of uses, whether it's optimizing it for fast downloading on the Web or preserving enough resolution to output a crisp print.*

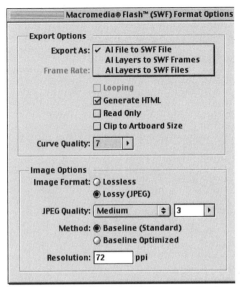

1 *The Macromedia Flash (SWF) Format Options dialog box for Flash export*

The Macromedia Flash (SWF) format is another vector graphics format for the Web. This format is commonly used for animations, as it is compact and scales very well. Adobe LiveMotion imports (using the Load Movie Behavior) and exports SWF format files. Using Illustrator, you can create frames for an animation on separate layers and then export the layers to an animated Flash file.

Keep in mind that the Flash format does not support such transparency appearances as blending modes and opacity masks. Also, gradients that encompass a wide range of color will appear as rasterized shapes. Patterns will also be rasterized.

And finally, Flash supports only some kinds of joins. For example, beveled or square joins and caps will be converted to rounded joins.

To export a Flash file:

1. Choose File > Export.

2. Choose a location and type a name for your file.

3. In the Export dialog box, choose Format/File Type: Macromedia Flash (SWF), then click Export.

4. From the Export Options, Export As pop-up menu **1**, choose AI file to SWF File to export your entire Illustrator file as one Flash frame; AI Layers to SWF Frames to export each layer in your Illustrator file to a separate Flash frame within a Flash document; or AI Layers to SWF Files to export each Illustrator layer to a separate Flash file composed of one frame.

5. Choose a Frame Rate (in frames per second) for your Flash file if you chose AI Layers to SWF Frames in the previous step.

   Then check any of the following options:

   Looping if you want the animation to loop, or leave it unchecked if you want the animation to play once and then stop.

   Generate HTML if you want an HTML file to be created for the exported SWF

(Continued on the following page)

Flash

file. The HTML file will be put in the same location as the exported SWF file.

Read Only to prevent users from modifying the Flash file.

Clip to Artboard Size to export only the artwork that is inside the artboard.

6. Choose a Curve Quality value (0–10) to control how accurate the Bézier curves will be in your Flash file. The higher the Curve Quality value, the more accurate the curves (and the larger the file size).

7. Under Image Options, click an Image Format. Lossless is useful for images with large areas of solid color or for images that are to be edited later, whereas Lossy (JPEG) is useful for bitmapped images, but it decreases the image quality.

If you clicked Lossy (JPEG), choose a JPEG Quality to determine the amount of compression in your placed bitmaps. As quality increases, so does file size. And also click a compression Method. Click Baseline (Standard) for standard compression or click Baseline Optimized for standard plus additional compression.

8. Enter a Resolution value (72–2400 ppi) for your bitmap images. As the resolution increases, so does the file size. If you plan to export rasterized images and scale them up in Flash, choose a resolution above 72 ppi so the scaled images won't appear pixelated.

➤ Choose Release to Layers from the Layers palette menu to put nested objects onto their own layers before exporting them to Flash format.

Flash

Targa (TGA)

The TGA format is designed for use on systems with the Truevision video board. You can specify a resolution and color depth for this format. If you choose the Targa file format and then click OK in the Rasterize dialog box, the Targa Options dialog box will open **1**. Choose a Resolution (bit depth) for the amount of color/shade information each pixel is capable of storing.

Text (TXT)

You can export any text in your Illustrator file to a text file. Choose File > Export, choose Text as your file format, enter a file name, then click Save. Only editable text objects will be saved to the resulting file.

Other file formats

AutoCAD Drawing (DWG) and AutoCAD Interchange File (DXF)

DWG is AutoCAD's standard file format. DXF is a tagged data representation of the information contained in an AutoCAD drawing file. If you export either of these files, you will also need to choose an AutoCAD version, the number of colors you wish to include, and a raster file format.

Metafile formats

A metafile describes a file that functions as a list of commands to draw a graphic. Typically, a metafile is made up of commands to draw objects such as lines, polygons, and text, and commands to control the style of these objects.

Computer Graphics Metafile (CGM)

CGM, a vector-based metafile format, is used mostly for the exchange of graphical images—in particular, complex engineering or architectural images. This format does not work well for artwork that contains text. However, it is considered a platform-independent format.

Windows Metafile (WMF)

WMF is a 16-bit metafile format used on Windows platforms.

Targa; Text; Metafiles

Enhanced metafile (EMF)

EMF is a 32-bit metafile format used on Windows platforms. It can contain a broader variety of commands than a WMF file.

PostScript file format (PS)

PostScript is a language that describes images for output to printers and other printing systems. PostScript Level 1, which is available for Illustrator 8 and earlier versions, represents grayscale vector graphics and grayscale bitmap images. Level 2 adds support for RGB, CMYK, and CIE color, and supports compression techniques for bitmap images. Level 3 adds the ability to print gradient mesh objects to a PostScript 3 printer. You can't save files as PS files directly in Illustrator 10, but you can use the Save as File or print to File option in the Print dialog box to create a PS file if you are using a PostScript printer .

Pasting out of Illustrator

You can use the Clipboard (Copy and Paste commands) to paste an Illustrator object into a document in another Adobe application. In Edit > Preferences > Files & Clipboard Preferences, you have two choices for how objects are copied **2**.

If you copy and paste an object from Illustrator into Photoshop with Clipboard Copy As: AICB (**no transparency support**) checked, the **Paste** dialog box will open **3**. Click Paste As: Pixels to paste the object as a rasterized pixel layer; or click Path to paste the object as an outline path; or click Shape Layer to paste the object as a layer with an editable layer clipping path in the shape of the object with an editable fill of the current Foreground color.

To preserve blending modes and opacity settings for an object pasted into InDesign or Photoshop 6, check Copy As: PDF. With both PDF and AICB checked, the Paste dialog box opens and blending modes and transparency are preserved (see also page 442).

➤ If you drag-and-drop a path object from Illustrator into Photoshop, it will appear as pixels on its own layer. Hold down Cmd/Ctrl while dragging to keep the path object as a path in Photoshop 5.5 or later.

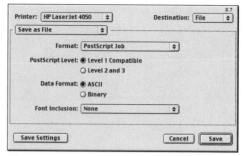

1 *To print to a PostScript file in the Mac OS, choose a PostScript **Printer**, make sure the Destination is **File**, choose **Save as File**, then choose **PostScript Level**, **Data Format**, and **Font Inclusion** options. In Windows, just click **Print to File**.*

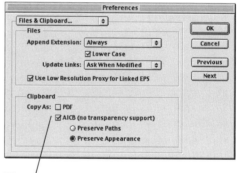

2 *Choose **Clipboard, Copy As** options in the Files & Clipboard Preferences dialog box.*

3

PostScript Format; Paste from Illustrator

To export an Illustrator file to Adobe LiveMotion 1.0:

1. Before placing a file into LiveMotion, ungroup all groups, then, for each top-level layer, choose Release to Layers (Sequence) from the Layers palette menu. *Note:* When the Illustrator file is placed, all objects will initially be one composite object. Use LiveMotion's Convert Layers Into command to convert the object into separate objects or a sequence.

   If the Illustrator file contains effects and/or appearances, use Object > Expand Appearance, ungroup, then release to layers. This seems to work best when there is more than one top-level layer in the Illustrator file. Now do the first technique in step 2 (save, then Place).

2. Save a copy of the file in Adobe Illustrator version 8 format, then place the file using File > Place in LiveMotion. Yes, you read that correctly. Illustrator version 10 files cannot yet be placed into LiveMotion 1.0.
   or
   Mac OS: Select an object or objects in an Illustrator 10 document window, then drag-and-drop them into a LiveMotion document window (arrange and resize the Illustrator and LiveMotion windows so they overlap slightly). You can also drag-and-drop an Illustrator file icon from the Desktop into a LiveMotion window.

   Mac OS and Windows: Copy and paste the objects from an Illustrator file into a LiveMotion document window.

➤ Whenever possible, bring Photoshop images directly into LiveMotion from Photoshop (not through Illustrator), and use LiveMotion's commands, such as its Photoshop filters, to modify the image. You can apply opacity, color changes (Color, Brightness, Contrast, Saturation, etc.), edge softness, 3D effects such as Emboss and Shadow, and other effects within LiveMotion.

(Continued on the following page)

Export to LiveMotion

➤ Any opacity and blending mode appearances in the Illustrator file will be removed by LiveMotion. To preserve the look of opacity or blending mode appearances between two or more objects or images, you can either copy those objects together as one selection into LiveMotion or copy the objects separately and then apply opacity levels to the objects in LiveMotion.

➤ Illustrator's scatter brushes contain groups. To place a path that has a scatter brush stroke, apply Object > Expand Appearance; Ungroup; then release to layers so you'll be able to place the scatter brush path; then, in LiveMotion, convert it into separate objects. Some scatter brush objects contain a lot of separate paths that are grouped together. If this is the case, it will be easier to just copy the grouped object used in the scatter brush, paste it into LiveMotion, and then duplicate, transform, and reposition it in LiveMotion.

➤ LiveMotion's Edit Original command will open a copy of the imported Illustrator object's file in Illustrator without changing the original Illustrator file. You can edit the Illustrator object (say, its shape), save the file, return to LiveMotion, and the imported object will update to reflect the change. Just make sure you don't change the name of the copy of the file that Illustrator generates. Using the Edit Original command, Illustrator can really be used as LiveMotion's "drawing" tool.

Animation

To animate a transition from one shape into another, use Illustrator's Blend tool to create intermediate steps between two objects. In the Blend Options dialog box, use a specified number of steps (say around 10 or 15) to limit the number of layers that will be created in LiveMotion. Expand the blend, ungroup, then release to layers. Finally, place the file into LiveMotion, and use Convert Layers Into and choose Sequence to have LiveMotion automatically create a sequence of frames or Objects to let you manually sequence the objects in the LiveMotion Timeline window.

Don't stop here 10.0!

For a detailed explanation of flattening and the Flattening Preview palette (an Illustrator plug-in), you have several resources at your disposal: The **Flattening Guide.pdf**, which is found in the Adobe Technical Info > White Papers folder on the Illustrator 10 CD; the Flattening_Preview.pdf, which is found in the Adobe Illustrator 10 > Utilities > Flattening Preview folder; and the printed (yes, printed) *Flattening Guide* that ships with Illustrator 10.

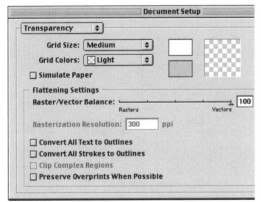

1 *The Document Setup (Transparency) dialog box*

Printing and exporting transparency

Transparency settings (non-default blending modes and opacity levels) in objects, groups or layers are preserved when a document is saved in either of the native Illustrator formats: Adobe Illustrator (version 10) or Adobe PDF 1.4 (Acrobat 5). When a file that contains Transparency palette settings is printed, or saved and exported, in a non-native format, Illustrator uses the settings in the Document Setup dialog box to determine how objects will be flattened and rasterized in order to preserve the look of those transparency settings.

In the process of flattening, Illustrator breaks up overlapping objects that contain transparency. Each overlapping and non-overlapping area becomes a separate, non-overlapping, opaque shape.

Illustrator tries to keep these flattened shapes as vector objects. However, if the look of transparency settings cannot be preserved in a flattened shape as a vector object, Illustrator will rasterize the shape instead. This will happen, for example, if two gradient objects with non-default transparency settings overlap. The resulting flattened shape would be rasterized in order to keep this complex area of transparency.

Vector shapes print with cleaner, higher quality color and crisper edges as compared to rasterized shapes. The Document Setup dialog box is used to control the percentage of flattened shapes that remain vectors versus the percentage of shapes that are rasterized. Choose File > **Document Setup**, then choose **Transparency** from the topmost pop-up menu **1**. Move the Raster/Vector Balance slider to control whether flattened shapes will remain as vectors or will be rasterized. The Raster/Vector Balance settings only apply to flattened shapes that represent transparency.

Higher values (to the right) produce a higher percentage of flattened shapes as vectors, though complex flattened areas may be rasterized. A higher percentage of vector shapes will result in higher quality output, but at the

(Continued on the following page)

Print and Export Transparency

465

expense of slower, more memory-demanding output processing.

The lowest value (to the left) won't necessarily produce poor output quality. In fact, if an illustration is very complex and contains a lot of transparency effects, this may be the only setting that produces adequate output. Low settings are usually used to produce fast output at a low resolution.

The rasterization process requires a resolution setting to determine output quality. To specify the resolution for areas that are rasterized, choose File > Document Setup, choose **Transparency** from the topmost pop-up menu, then enter a **Rasterization Resolution** value. As a rule of thumb, the resolution should equal twice the output device's line screen (lpi). The default is 300 ppi. For type, at least 600 ppi is required for good quality output.

➤ To control the flattening of a selection in a document, adjust the Raster/Vector Balance and Rasterization Resolution value (discussed above), but do it in the Object > **Flatten Transparency** dialog box.

Rasterization settings for effects

Some Effect menu commands must be rasterized when printed or exported. The default resolution setting is 72 ppi, a rather low setting that is suitable only for on-screen output.

To choose a higher resolution, choose Effect > **Document Raster Effects Settings** **1**, then click another resolution option or click Other and enter a custom resolution setting. The higher the resolution, the slower the output processing time.

➤ Leave the resolution for effects at the default 72 ppi while working on an illustration, then increase the resolution before printing or exporting the file. A new resolution setting will affect all objects with applied effects that will rasterize as well as resolution-dependent filters, such as Crystallize and Pointillize.

What gets rasterized

The Effect menu effects that will **rasterize** on export or output include all the effects below the dividing line on the menu: Artistic, Blur, Brush Strokes, Distort, Pixelate, Sharpen, Sketch, Stylize, Texture, and Video. The following effects on the Stylize submenu will also rasterize: Drop Shadow (if the Blur value is greater than 0), Inner Glow, Outer Glow, and Feather.

1 *The Raster Effects Settings dialog box*

Clipping complex regions

When an output file contains an object that is flattened into rasterized shapes next to vector shapes, there may be a visible discrepancy among the flattened shapes that share the same color. An example of this would be a complex, transparent, smaller object (which must be rasterized when flattened) overlapping a larger, solid color object. The solid color in the flattened vector shapes that represent the large solid color object may not perfectly match the background color of the flattened rasterized shape that represents the transparent object. This is called "stitching," and it is most likely to occur when the Raster/Vector Balance slider in Document Setup (Transparency) is between 1 and 30. At 0, the entire document is rasterized, and no stitching occurs.

Check Clip Complex Regions in File > **10.0!** Document Setup (Transparency) to make any boundaries between raster and vector flattened shapes fall on objects paths. This reduces the signs of stitching, but also produces complex paths that slow down printing.

For a fairly accurate preview of a flattened file, open the Flattening Preview palette, and click Refresh. Move the slider, if desired, check Options, then click Refresh again.

Flattening different types of objects

Text: Transparent text is flattened and preserved as a text object. Clipping and masking is used to preserve the look of transparency.

Text that is stroked, filled with a pattern, or used as a clipping mask will be converted to outlines. When strokes are converted to outlines, the filled "strokes" may be wider than the original stroke by one or two pixels. To **10.0!** prevent this thickening, move the Raster/Vector Balance slider to 100 (far right) or 0 (far left, causing all objects to be rasterized). Or enter a Rasterization Resolution value of 600 ppi or higher in File > Document Setup (Transparency).

Gradient mesh objects: When printed to a PostScript level 3 printer, mesh objects print as vectors. When mesh objects are printed

(Continued on the following page)

Print and Export Transparency

to a PostScript level 2 printer or saved to an EPS format that is PostScript Level 2 compatible, both vector data and rasterized data are saved in the file, allowing the output device to choose which set of data to use. Specify the resolution for the rasterized mesh object in the Gradient Mesh Resolution field **1** in File > Document Setup (Printing & Export).

10.0!

Placed or embedded images: When the Raster/Vector Balance slider is below 100, Illustrator rasterizes placed images at the resolution specified in the Rasterization Resolution field in File > Document Setup (Transparency). This value will be used only for portions of an image that overlap a transparent object; the remainder of the image will print at the image's original resolution. To keep things simple, always choose a Rasterization Resolution that's equal to or higher than the original resolution of the placed image.

For an EPS image that overlaps an object with transparency, embed the image into the Illustrator document via the Embed Image command on the Links palette menu. This will ensure an accurate printout of the image and the transparency effect.

Strokes: Strokes are converted into filled objects. The width of the object will equal the weight of the original stroke.

With the Raster/Vector Balance slider at 0, all strokes (and all objects, for that matter) will be rasterized. A high Rasterization Resolution ensures high quality output.

With the Raster/Vector Balance slider between 10 and 90, any strokes that overlap an object with transparency will be converted to outlines. Very thin strokes may be thickened slightly and may look noticeably different from parts of strokes that don't overlap transparency.

10.0!

Check Convert All Strokes to Outlines in File > Document Setup (Transparency) to convert all strokes in an illustration to outlines. This preserves the look of a stroke for its entire length, but results in a larger number of paths in the file. An alternative is to apply Object > Path > Outline Stroke to selected strokes.

1 *The Document Setup (Printing & Export) dialog box*

Exporting Illustrator files: A summary

The best way to save and export an Illustrator 10 file is by saving it in the Illustrator EPS format. In the Save As dialog box in the Mac OS, choose Compatibility: Illustrator 10. In Windows, choose Compatibility: Version 10. A file in this format can be reopened in Illustrator 10 at any time, and it can be edited and resaved with no loss of object data. For export to Adobe PageMaker or QuarkXPress, choose the EPS format.

For export to Adobe GoLive 5, Premiere 6, or After Effects 5.x, or InDesign, use the native Adobe Illustrator document format, Compatibility: Illustrator 10, and check Create PDF Compatible File.

To export to Adobe LiveMotion 1.0, Premiere 5, or After Effects 4.1, choose the native Adobe Illustrator document format, Compatibility: Illustrator 8.

When using the Clipboard to transfer Illustrator objects between Adobe applications, check the PDF and AICB options in Edit > Preferences > Files & Clipboard *10.0!* (Illustrator > Preferences > Files & Clipboard in Mac OSX). Doing so will allow the receiving application to choose its preferred format.

And finally, the Edit Original command in the latest versions of Premiere and After Effects launches Illustrator so you can make edits on Illustrator objects imported into those programs. The imported objects update automatically.

➤ An Illustrator file saved in the Illustrator EPS format will contain both unflattened Illustrator data and flattened EPS data. The unflattened data is read by Illustrator; the flattened EPS data is read by other programs the file is exported to.

Managing color

Problems with color can creep up on you when various hardware devices and software packages you use treat color differently. For example, if you open a graphic in several different imaging programs and in a Web browser, the colors in your image might look completely different in each case. And none of those programs may match the color of the picture you originally scanned in on your scanner. Print out the image, and you will probably find that your results are different again. In some cases, you might find these differences slight and unobjectionable. But in other circumstances, such color changes can wreak havoc with your design and turn a project into a disaster.

A color management system can solve most of these problems by acting as a color interpreter. A good system knows how each device and program understands color, and it can help you move your graphics among them by adjusting color so it looks the same in every program and device.

A color profile is a mathematical description of a device's color space. Illustrator uses ICC (International Color Consortium) profiles to tell your color management system how particular devices use color.

You can find most of Illustrator's color management controls in Edit > Color Settings. This dialog box includes a list of predefined management options for various publishing situations, including prepress output and Web output.

Illustrator also supports color management policies for RGB and CMYK color files. In a case where you, for example, import a graphic into an Illustrator document and that graphic does or does not have a color profile attached, these color management policies govern how Illustrator deals with color in such graphics.

➤ Consult with your prepress service provider, if you are using one, about color management to help ensure that your color management workflows will work together.

Learn it now

Illustrator's new color management features will probably seem complex to you at first. But it's well worth the investment of time to learn about them because those features have been adopted by the latest versions of other Adobe programs, such as Photoshop.

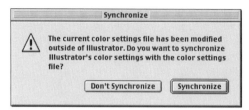

*The **Synchronize** alert box may open when Illustrator 10 is launched, if the current color settings have been modified in another Adobe program (e.g., Photoshop 5.5 or later). Click Synchronize to match Illustrator's Color Settings to the Color Settings from the other program.*

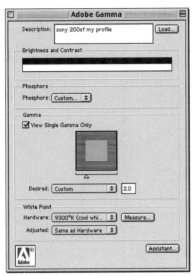

1 *The **Adobe Gamma** dialog box after choosing the Control Panel option*

➤ If you plan on using the same graphics for different purposes, such as for the Web and for printed material, you may benefit from using color management.

Calibration

The first step toward achieving color consistency is to calibrate your monitor. In this procedure, you will define the RGB color space your monitor can display using the Adobe Gamma control panel, which is installed automatically with Illustrator (and some other Adobe applications). You will adjust the contrast and brightness, gamma, color balance, and white point of your monitor.

The Adobe Gamma Control Panel creates an ICC profile, which Illustrator can use as its working RGB space to display the colors in your artwork accurately.

Note: You have to calibrate your monitor and save the settings as an ICC profile only once, and it applies to all applications.

To calibrate your monitor:

1. Give the monitor 30 minutes to warm up so the display is stabilized, and establish a level of room lighting that will remain constant.

2. Set the desktop pattern to light gray.

3. *Mac OS:* Choose Apple > Control Panels > Adobe Gamma.

   Windows: Choose Start menu > Settings > Control Panel > Adobe Gamma.

4. Click Step by Step (Assistant), which will walk you through the process.
   or
   Click Control Panel to choose settings from a single dialog box with no explanation **1**. (If the Adobe Gamma dialog box opens directly, you can skip this step.)

   Note: Click Next. If you're using the Assistant, click Next between dialog boxes.

5. Leave the default monitor ICC profile.
   or

   (Continued on the following page)

Click Load, then choose a profile that more closely matches your monitor.

6. Turn up your monitor's brightness and contrast settings; leave the contrast at maximum; and adjust the brightness to make the alternating gray squares in the top bar as dark as possible, but not black, while keeping the lower bar bright white.

7. For Phosphors, choose your monitor type or choose Custom and enter the Red, Green, and Blue chromaticity coordinates specified by your monitor manufacturer.

The gray square represents a combined grayscale reading of your monitor. Adjust the gamma using this slider until the smaller solid-color box matches the outer, stripey box. It helps to squint. You might find it easier to uncheck View Single Gamma Only and make separate adjustments based on the readings for Red, Green, and Blue.

For Desired, select the default for your system: 1.8 (Mac) or 2.2 (Windows), if this option is available.

For Hardware, select the white point the monitor manufacturer specifies, or click Measure and follow the instructions.

For Adjusted, choose Same as Hardware. Or if you know the color temperature at which your image will ultimately be viewed, you can choose it from the pop-up menu or choose Custom and enter it. *Note:* This option is not available for all monitors.

8. Close the Adobe Gamma window and save the profile. *Mac OS:* Save it in the System Folder > ColorSync Profiles folder. *Windows:* Save it in Windows > System > Color (extension, .icm). Illustrator can use this profile as its working RGB space in the Color Settings dialog box (see the following page).

Note: If you change your monitor's brightness and contrast settings or change the room lighting, you should recalibrate your monitor. Also keep in

Calibration

Point and learn!

The Color Settings dialog box provides a Description area **2** that displays valuable information on options the mouse is currently over. Make use of this great feature!

1 *The* Color Settings *dialog box with the* Web Graphics Defaults *setting chosen*

mind that this procedure is just a beginning. Professional calibration requires precise monitor measurement using expensive hardware devices such as colorimeters and spectrophotometers.

To choose a predefined color management setting:

1. Choose Edit > Color Settings.

2. Choose a configuration Option from the Settings pop-up menu **1**:

   Emulate Adobe Illustrator 6.0 uses the same color workflow used by Illustrator versions 6.0 and earlier. This option does not recognize or save color profiles.

   Color Management Off emulates the behavior of applications that do not support color management. This is a good choice for projects destined for video or onscreen presentation.

   U.S. Prepress Defaults manages color using settings based on common press conditions in the U.S. When the European or Japanese Prepress option is chosen, the CMYK Work Space changes to a press standard for that region.

   Web Graphics Defaults manages color for content that will be published on the Web.

   ColorSync Workflow (Mac OS only) manages color using the ColorSync 3.0 color management system. Profiles are based on those in the ColorSync control panel (including the monitor profile you may have created using the Adobe Gamma).

3. Click OK.

Choosing individual workspace settings

Colors output differently in different media. Color working spaces, which define the RGB and CMYK color profiles to be used in your document, control how colors in the illustration will be adjusted to output successfully in a particular output media's color range.

(Continued on the following page)

473

Color Settings

For CMYK settings, you should check with your service provider. For the RGB setting, the following profile choices are available:

Adobe RGB (1998)

This color space produces a wide range of colors, and is useful if you will be converting RGB images to CMYK images. This is not a good choice for Web work.

sRGB IEC61966-2.1

This is a good choice for Web work, as it reflects the settings on the average computer monitor. Many hardware and software manufacturers are using it as the default space for scanners, low-end printers, and software. sRGB IEC61966-2.1 should not be used for prepress work—Apple RGB, ColorMatch RGB, or Adobe RGB should be used instead.

Apple RGB

This space is useful for files that you plan to display on Mac monitors, as it reflects the characteristics of the older Standard Apple 13-inch monitors. It also is a good choice for working with older desktop publishing files, such as Adobe Photoshop 4.0 and earlier.

ColorMatch RGB

This space produces a smaller range of color than the Adobe RGB (1998) model, but it matches the color space of Radius Pressview monitors and is useful for print production work.

Monitor RGB (current monitor profile)

This choice sets the RGB working space to your monitor's profile. This is a useful setting if you know that other applications you will be using for your project do not support color management. Keep in mind that if you share this configuration with another user, the configuration will use that user's monitor profile as the RGB working space, and color consistency may be lost.

ColorSync RGB (Mac only)

Use this color space to match Illustrator's RGB space to the space specified in the Apple ColorSync 3.0 (or later) control panel. This can be the profile you created using Adobe Gamma. If you share this configuration with another user, it will utilize the ColorSync space specified by that user.

```
┌═══════════════ Color Settings ═══════════════┐
  Settings:  Custom                        [↕]
    ☐ Advanced Mode
  ┌─ Working Spaces ─────────────────────────┐
     RGB:  sRGB IEC61966-2.1          [↕]
     CMYK: U.S. Web Coated (SWOP) v2  [↕]
  └──────────────────────────────────────────┘
  ┌─ Color Management Policies ──────────────┐
     RGB:  Off                        [↕]
     CMYK: Off                        [↕]
     Profile Mismatches: ☑ Ask When Opening
                         ☐ Ask When Pasting
  └──────────────────────────────────────────┘
  Description:
  ┌──────────────────────────────────────────┐
   Policies specify how you want colors in a particular color model
   managed. Policies handle the reading and embedding of color
   profiles, mismatches between embedded color profiles and the
   working space, and the moving of colors from one document to
   another.
  └──────────────────────────────────────────┘
└══════════════════════════════════════════════┘
```

1 *Color Management Policies options are chosen from the middle portion of the* **Color Settings** *dialog box.*

You can choose a customized color management policy that will tell Illustrator how to deal with artwork that doesn't match the current color working space.

To customize your color management policies:

1. Choose Edit > Color Settings.

2. Choose any predefined setting from the Settings pop-up menu **1** other than Emulate Adobe Illustrator 6.

3. Choose a color management policy:

   If you choose **Off**, Illustrator will not color-manage imported or opened color files.

   Choose **Preserve Embedded Profiles** if you think you're going to be working with both color-managed and non-color-managed documents. This will tie each color file's profile to the individual file.

   Choose **Convert to Working Space** if you want all your documents to reflect the same color working space. This is usually the best choice for Web work.

   For Profile Mismatches, check **Ask When Opening** to have Illustrator display a message if the color profile in a file you are opening does not match either working space profile you've chosen. If you choose this option, you can override your color management policy when opening documents.

   Check **Ask When Pasting** to have Illustrator display a message when color profile mismatches occur as you paste color data into your document. If you choose this option, you can override your color management policy when pasting.

4. Click OK.

Color Settings

475

To customize your conversion options:

1. Choose Edit > Color Settings.

2. Check the Advanced Mode box **1**.

3. Under Conversion Options, choose a color management **Engine** that will be used to convert colors between color spaces: **Adobe (ACE)** uses Adobe's color management system and color engine; **Apple ColorSync** or **Apple CMM** uses Apple's color management system; and **Microsoft ICM** uses the system provided in the Windows 98 and Windows 2000 systems. Other CMMs can be chosen to fit into color workflows that use specific output devices.

4. Choose a rendering **Intent** to determine how colors will be changed as they are moved from one color space to another:

    Perceptual changes colors in a way that seems natural to the human eye, even though the color values actually do change; good for continuous-tone images.

    Saturation changes colors with the intent of preserving vivid colors, although it compromises the accuracy of the color; good for charts and business graphics.

    Absolute Colorimetric keeps colors that are inside the destination color gamut unchanged, but the relationships between colors outside this gamut are changed in an attempt to maintain color accuracy.

    Relative Colorimetric, the default intent for all predefined settings options, is the same as Absolute Colorimetric, except it compares the white point, or extreme highlight, of the source color space to the destination color space and shifts all colors accordingly. The accuracy of this intent depends on the accuracy of white point information in an image's profile.

    Note: Differences between rendering intents are visible only on a printout or a conversion to a different working space.

    Check **Use Black Point Compensation** if you would like to adjust for differences in black points among color spaces. When this option is chosen, the full dynamic

Save your settings

To save your custom settings for later use, click **Save** in the Color Settings dialog box. If you want your custom file to display on the Settings pop-up menu, save it in the Settings folder in the default location—that is, deeply nested in the System Folder (Mac OS)/Program Files folder (Win). When you're ready to reuse the saved settings, click **Load** in the Custom Settings dialog box, then locate your settings file.

1 *When Advanced Mode is checked in the* **Color Settings** *dialog box, the* **Conversion Options** *become available.*

Color Settings

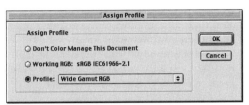

1 *Use the **Assign Profile** dialog box to change a file's color profile. (The Profile chosen here will also be listed as the Source Space in the Adobe Illustrator 10 pane of the File > Print dialog box.)*

range of the source color space is mapped into the full dynamic range of the destination color space. If you don't select this option, your blacks may appear as grays.

We recommend you check Use Black Point Compensation for RGB-to-CMYK or CMYK-to-CMYK conversions.

5. Click OK.

➤ When you save a file in a format that supports embedded profiles, such as the native Illustrator format, you can check Embed ICC Profile to save the profile in the document.

If you decide later that you want to change the color profile of a document or remove a profile, you can use the Assign Profile command to do so. For example, you may want to prepare a document for a specific output purpose, and you may need to adjust the profile accordingly. You also may want to use this option if you change your mind about your color management settings.

To change a document's color profile:

1. Choose Edit > Assign Profile **1**.

2. Click Don't Color Manage This Document to remove the color profile.
   or
   Click "Working [document color mode and the working space you're using]" to assign that particular working space to a document that uses no profile or that uses a profile that is different from the working space.
   or
   Click Profile to reassign a different profile to a color-managed document. Choose a profile from the pop-up menu.

3. Click OK.

➤ When you save a file in or export a file to a format that supports embedded profiles, you have the choice to select or deselect the Embed ICC Profile option. You should keep this option chosen unless you have a specific reason not to.

Assign Profile

477

Specifying a color management setup is all well and good, but sometimes all you want is to know how a document will look when it is printed out or viewed on a Windows or Mac monitor as part of a Web page. To do this, you can soft-proof your colors. While this method is less accurate than actually making a print or viewing your Web artwork on different monitors, it can give you a general idea of how your work will look in different settings.

To proof your colors:

1. From the View > Proof Setup submenu, choose which type of output display you want to simulate.

   Custom will allow you to create a proofing model for a specific output device using the Proof Setup dialog box. To do this, choose the color profile for your desired output device from the Profile pop-up menu, then check or uncheck Preserve Color Numbers. If you check this option, Illustrator will simulate how the colors will appear if they're not converted to the proofing space. If you uncheck this option, Illustrator will simulate how the colors will appear if they are converted, and you will need to specify a rendering intent as described on page 476 ("Customize your conversion options").
   or
   Choose **Macintosh RGB** or **Windows RGB** to soft-proof colors using a Mac or Windows monitor profile as the proofing space you wish to simulate.
   or
   Choose **Monitor RGB** to use your monitor profile as the space for proofing.

2. View > **Proof Color** will be checked automatically so the soft proof can be previewed. Uncheck this option to turn off proofing.

If Preserve Color Numbers is gray

The **Preserve Color Numbers** option is available only when the color mode of the current file is the same as that of the output device profile currently chosen in the Proof Setup dialog box. For example, if the document color mode is RGB and the chosen proofing profile is an RGB profile, then the Preserve Color Numbers option will be available.

Proof Setup

Chapter 26: Output/Export ◆ Study Guide

Learning Objectives

- Output to various types of printers.
- Troubleshoot common printing problems.
- Save a file in various formats for print or multimedia work.
- Export Illustrator files for animation.
- Understand the basics of color management.

Get Up and Running Exercises

- Set up color management on your workstation.
  - ▲ Calibrate and profile your monitor.
  - ▲ Choose a predefined color management setting that would be appropriate for prepress work.
- Open or create an Illustrator document and print successfully from the document. Objects should appear as you expect in the print, without error messages or unexpected results, such as being cut off at the edges.
- Open or create an Illustrator document and scale it so that it's larger than the current paper size. Set up the document so that it can be printed in pieces using the current paper size.
- Open or create a document that you will export to Flash format. Use a few features that aren't supported directly in Flash. After exporting the file, examine it closely to observe the results of exporting to the Flash format.

(Continued on the following page)

- Practice flattening. Open or create an Illustrator document that contains overlapping objects that use transparency. The document should also include objects that use effects.

  ▲ Install the Flattening Preview palette and use it to try different flattening settings. Zoom in on the palette preview and examine the results closely. Are there any problems with the results? If there are, can the problems be addressed by changing settings?

  ▲ Flatten a few selected objects. How is this method different than using the Flattening Preview palette?

  ▲ When you're satisfied with the flattening settings, save the document as a PDF (Acrobat 4 version, which doesn't support transparency). Examine the results in Acrobat.

Class Discussion Questions

- Can you briefly describe how color management works?

- What's the difference between flatness and flattening?

- What are some ways to identify and address general output issues related to document complexity?

- What are some ways to identify and address output issues related to patterned fills?

- What are some ways to identify and address output issues related to gradients?

- What are some ways to identify and address output issues related to transparency?

Review Questions

Multiple choice

1. Which statement about imagesetter output is true?

A. Higher resolutions require higher screen frequencies.

B. Higher resolutions produce lower screen frequencies.

C. Higher screen frequencies produce fewer levels of gray.

D. Higher screen frequencies produce more levels of gray.

2. Which RGB working space is a good choice for Web output and for exchanging files with other users, but should not be used for prepress work?

A. Adobe RGB (1998)

B. sRGB IEC61966-2.1

C. ColorMatch RGB

D. Monitor RGB

3. Which of the following program versions can import native Illustrator 10 files directly?

A. Adobe After Effects 4.1

B. Adobe GoLive 5.0

C. Adobe LiveMotion 1.0

D. QuarkXPress 5.0

4. What's the easiest way to find out if there are any clipping masks in an illustration?

A. Document Info palette

B. Info palette

C. Select All

D. Status bar

5. Which resolution option affects every object in the file at output time?

A. The Output Resolution option in the Document Setup dialog box

B. The Resolution option in the Document Raster Effects Settings dialog box

C. The Rasterization Resolution option in the Flatten Transparency dialog box

D. The Rasterization Resolution option in the Document Setup dialog box

Fill-in-the-blank

1. To remove crop marks, _____.

2. To proof the document by approximating colors that a specific printer would produce, _____.

3. Before creating your monitor profile, wait _____ minutes after turning the monitor on for colors to stabilize.

4. To evaluate the effects of the current flattening settings, use the _____.

5. If you could only keep one version of an Illustrator document, saving it in _____ format would provide the most editing flexibility in Illustrator and also the most compatibility with other programs.

6. When you change the color management rendering intent, the effect is visible only when you print the document or when you _____.

7. To print an illustration that's larger than the largest available paper size, use the _____ option together with the Page tool.

Definitions

1. What is an imagesetter?

2. What is the Clip Complex Regions in File option?

3. What is a color working space?

4. What is flatness?

5. What is a rendering intent?

This chapter covers the preparation of Illustrator files for the Web. Topics include choosing an appropriate export format; creating and using slices to achieve faster download speeds; choosing optimization settings using the Save for Web dialog box; and saving a file as SVG.

Illustrator's Save for Web

The file optimization features in Illustrator 10 are combined in the File > **Save for Web** dialog box **1**. There you'll find Original, Optimized, 2-Up, and 4-Up preview tabs at the top of the main window; a Color Table palette; and format, matte, quality, and other options. You'll also find Preview and Preview in [browser] menus in this dialog box.

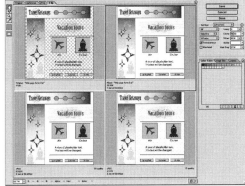

1 *Illustrator's Save for Web dialog box*

Exporting Web graphics

Illustrator excels at creating crisp, tidy graphics—the kind of graphics that are perfect for the Web. Thankfully, the latest version of the program boasts a number of tools that make preparing Web graphics much easier.

The basic formula for outputting a file for online viewing may seem straightforward: Design the illustration in RGB color mode and export it in GIF or JPEG format, which are the file formats used by Web servers and browsers (the applications that combine text, images, and HTML code into a viewable page on the World Wide Web). However, when you load and view an image via a Web browser, you may be disappointed to find that not all colors or blends display well on the Web. And an illustration with a large, placed image may take an unacceptably long time to download and render, due to its large storage size. If an image looks overly dithered (grainy and dotty), or was subject to unexpected color substitutions, or takes too long to view on a Web page, it means your design is not outputting well. Some of the key issues that you'll need to address for online output are discussed on the remaining pages of this chapter.

When you are preparing Web graphics, there are four important issues you'll need to address for online output: The pixel size of the image, the color palette, the color depth, and the file format (GIF, JPEG, PNG, Flash, or SVG).

Image size

In order to calculate the appropriate image size, you must know the monitor size and the modem speed of your intended viewers beforehand. In most cases, you should be designing your artwork for a 800 x 600-pixel viewing area, the most common monitor size, and a 56 Kbps modem, the most common modem speed (at least for the moment).

The Web browser window will display within these parameters, so your maximum image size will occupy only a portion of the browser window—about 8 inches high (570 pixels) by 7 inches wide (500 pixels). The image resolution needs to be only as high as the standard monitor resolution.

Saving a file in the GIF or JPEG file format reduces its storage size significantly because these formats have built-in compression schemes.

To determine a file's actual storage size:

Windows: Right-click the file in Windows Explorer and choose **Properties** from the pop-up menu.

Mac OS: Highlight the file name in the Finder, then choose File > **Get Info**.

If you know the exact size of the compressed image, you can then calculate how long it will take to transmit over the Web. If you use the Save for Web dialog box, you can find out exactly how large your JPEG, GIF, PNG-8, or PNG-24 file is and how long it will take to download **1**. Click the preview menu arrow in the upper right or Control-click/Right-click in an optimization window to choose a different modem speed to be used to calculate the download time.

The degree to which the GIF or JPEG file format compresses depends on how compressible the file is **2**. Both formats cause a small reduction in image quality, but it's worth the size-reduction tradeoff because your image will download faster on the Web. A file size of about 50K traveling on a 28.8 Kbps modem will take about 18 seconds to download, and half that time for a 56 Kbps modem. (No, this isn't a test question!)

Create a browser window layer

Take a screen shot of your browser window, Place the file into an Illustrator file, then drag it into the bottommost layer. Now you can design your layout for that specific browser window's dimensions.

1 *The current file's size and* **download time** *display in the Info annotation area in the lower left corner of the* **Save for Web** *dialog box.*

20K GIF from a 5-level posterized image

120K GIF from a continuous-tone image

2 *A comparison of* **GIFs** *of different sizes*

1 *GIF is a suitable optimization format for this illustration, because it has **flat** color shapes.*

2 *This **hybrid** illustration, which contains both a sharp-edged element (type) and a continuous-tone element (ducky), is also a good candidate for GIF optimization.*

A document with a solid background color and a few solid color shapes will compress a great deal (expect a file size in the range of 20 to 50K). A large file (over 100K) with many color areas, textures, or patterns won't compress nearly as much. Continuous-tone, photographic images may compress less than flat-color graphics when you use the GIF format. If you posterize a continuous-tone image down to somewhere between four and eight levels, the resulting file size will be similar to that of a flat-color graphic, but you will have lost the continuous color transitions in the bargain. JPEG is a better format choice for a photographic-type image.

To summarize, if the output image must be large (500 x 400 pixels or larger), ideally it should contain only a handful of large, solid-color shapes. If the output image is intricate in color or shape, restrict its size to only a portion of the Web browser window.

Instead of using the browser tiling method to create repetitive background shapes, use symbols to create repetitive elements on a Web page. Create a symbol set and place it behind other Illustrator objects. Use the symbolism tools to modify the symbol set, then export the entire Web page in SVG format.

Another way to handle larger illustrations is to slice them into smaller sections so they download faster. Read about slicing on pages 486–491.

GIF

GIF is an 8-bit file format, which means a GIF image can contain a maximum of 256 colors **1**–**2**. It's an older format that was developed when a majority of Web users had 8-bit monitors that could display a maximum of 256 colors. Today, most viewers' monitors display thousands or millions of colors. GIF is still a good choice for illustrations that contain solid-color areas and shapes with well-defined edges, such as type.

To save an illustration in the GIF format and to see how it will actually look when it's viewed via the browser, use File > Save for Web (we'll show you how in this chapter).

(Continued on the following page)

GIF

Your color choices for a GIF image should be based on what a Web browser palette can realistically display. Most browser palettes are 8-bit, which means they can display only 256 colors. Colors that aren't on the palette are simulated by dithering, a display technique that intermixes color pixels to simulate other colors.

To prevent unexpected dithering, consider optimizing your illustration using the Web palette in the Save for Web dialog box. Or Web Snap 30–50 percent of the colors using Save for Web and manually Web-shift the critical solid-color areas. (You'll read more about these methods later.) Color substitutions will be particularly noticeable in solid-color areas.

➤ If you want to apply a gradient fill to a large area of an illustration and you're going to use the GIF format, create a top-to-bottom gradient. Top-to-bottom gradients produce smaller file sizes than left-to-right or diagonal gradients.

Consider also creating a slice to define a gradient object and then optimize that slice for export in SVG format (see pages 502–503).

Color depth

If you lower the output file's color depth, you will reduce the actual number of colors it contains, which will in turn reduce its file size and speed up its download time on the Web. Color reduction may produce dithered edges and duller colors, but you'll get the reduction in file size that you need. You can reduce the number of colors in an 8-bit image to fewer than the 256 colors it originally contained using Illustrator's Save for Web dialog box.

➤ Always preview an image at 100% view to evaluate its color quality.

JPEG

The JPEG format may be a better choice for preserving color fidelity if your artwork is continuous tone (contains gradations of color or is photographic) and if your viewers have 24-bit monitors, which have the capacity to display millions of colors ∎.

Color depth

Number of colors	Bit depth
256	8
128	7
64	6
32	5
16	4
8	3
4	2
2	1

∎ *JPEG optimization is suitable for continuous-tone images like this one.*

JPEG isn't a great choice for optimizing sharp-edged graphics. Note the artifacts around the type.

The word "duck" looks crisper in this GIF.

A JPEG plus: It can take a 24-bit image and make it as small as the GIF format can make an 8-bit image.

JPEG shortcomings: First, a JPEG file has to be decompressed when it's downloaded for viewing on a Web page, which takes time.

Second, JPEG is not a good choice for flat-color graphics or type because its compression methods tend to produce artifacts along the well-defined edges of these types of objects.

And third, not all Web viewers use 24-bit monitors. A JPEG image will be dithered on an 8-bit monitor, though dithering in continuous-tone areas is less noticeable than in flat color areas. To preview what the image will look like in an 8-bit setting, you can lower your monitor's setting to 8-bit or choose Browser Dither from the Preview menu in the Save for Web dialog box. If it doesn't contain type or objects with sharp edges, the JPEG image will probably survive the conversion to 8-bit.

JPEG format files can now be optimized as Progressive JPEG, which is supported by both the Netscape Navigator and Internet Explorer browsers (versions 4 and up). A Progressive JPEG displays in increasing detail as it downloads onto a Web page.

If you choose JPEG as your output format, you can experiment in Illustrator's Save for Web dialog box by optimizing an illustration, then using the 4–Up option to preview several versions of it in varying degrees of compression. Decide which degree of compression is acceptable by weighing the file size versus diminished image quality. In Illustrator, you can save the optimized file separately and leave the original file intact to reserve it for potential future revision.

Each time an illustration is optimized using the JPEG format, some image data is lost. The greater the degree of compression, the greater the data loss. To prevent this data loss, use Illustrator's Save for Web feature to save an optimized version of the file. Then if you need to make changes later, go back to your original Illustrator file.

(Continued on the following page)

JPEG

Dithering

Dithering is the intermixing of two palette colors to create the impression of a third color. It's used to make images that contain a limited number of colors (256 or fewer) appear to have a greater range of colors and shades. Dithering is usually applied to continuous-tone images to increase their tonal range, but—argh, life is full of compromises—it can also make them look a bit dotty.

Dithering usually doesn't produce aesthetically pleasing results in flat-color graphics. This is because the browser palette will dither pixels to re-create any color that the palette doesn't contain. For flat-color graphics, it's better to create colors using the Web Safe RGB model on the Color palette with its Web Safe color ramp. Existing flat-color areas should also be selected and Web-shifted to make them Web-safe.

Continuous-tone imagery is, in a way, already dithered. Some continuous-tone imagery looks fine on a Web page with no dithering and 256 colors. However, color banding will result if you lower both the number of colors in the palette and the amount of dithering when an illustration is optimized. The Dither value is chosen in Illustrator's Save for Web dialog box. The higher the Dither value, the more seamless the color transitions will appear, but the more dotty the image may also appear **1**–**2**. You can decide which of these two evils appears lesser to your eye.

One more consideration: Dithering adds noise and additional colors to the file, so compression is less effective when dithering is turned on than when it's off. So, with dithering enabled, you may not be able to achieve your desired degree of file compression. As is the case with most Web output, you'll have to strike an acceptable balance between aesthetics and file size.

Alias versus anti-alias

Anti-aliasing blends the edge of an object with its background. It achieves this blending by adding pixels with progressively less opacity along an object's edge. When imagery is

1 *A closeup of an image with a **small** amount of **dithering***

2 *The same image with a **lot** of **dithering***

Dress down your bitmaps

One way to reduce the number of pixels and lessen the color complexity in a bitmap image before placing it is to use an image-editing program such as Photoshop to scale the image to the actual size needed for the Web page. You can also reduce the image resolution to 72 ppi.

You can also use Illustrator's Rasterize command to reduce the pixel resolution of a placed image (check the Anti-Alias option).

To reduce color complexity, try posterizing a continuous-tone image down to somewhere between four and eight levels in Photoshop, then place the image. The result will be a smaller file size—albeit with noticeable color transitions.

composited or montaged, anti-aliasing helps to smooth the transitions between shapes. With anti-aliasing turned off, the edges of an object will look sharp because no extra pixels will have been added.

If you create an object, save it for the Web, and later place it against a colored background, an unattractive fringe of pixels, sometimes called a halo, may be visible. To avoid halos, follow the instructions for creating a background matting for the GIF, PNG, and JPEG formats. This will determine how partially transparent pixels (the kind of pixels that are created by anti-aliasing) are treated.

PNG-8 and PNG-24

The two PNG formats can save partially transparent pixels (such as soft, feathered edges) using a method called alpha transparency. With alpha transparency, a pixel can have any one of 256 levels of opacity, ranging from totally transparent to totally opaque. The PNG-8 format is limited to a maximum of 256 colors in the optimized image, and is similar to the GIF format. The PNG-24 format allows for millions of colors in the optimized image and is similar to the JPEG format. The PNG formats use a lossless compression method (no data is lost).

There are a couple of drawbacks to using PNG: Animation cannot be done in the PNG format (animation can be done in the GIF format) and PNG-24 files are larger in size than equivalent JPEGs. However, PNG is now supported by all the major Web browsers (as of this writing, Internet Explorer versions 4.0 and later directly support PNG).

The SVG format is discussed on pages 502–505. The Flash format is discussed on pages 459–460.

PNG-8 and PNG-24

10.0! ## Slicing

Slicing is the division of areas in an illustration 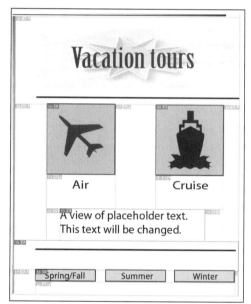. When exporting an illustration using the Save for Web dialog box, you can choose different optimization formats and settings for each slice in order to achieve faster download speeds. A separate export file will be generated for each slice containing the object or objects within the slice area. Slices also determine how the exported illustration will be translated into a valid HTML table for display as a Web page within a browser. Slices created in Illustrator can be edited in Adobe Photoshop or Adobe ImageReady, and Illustrator slices can be read by Adobe GoLive. Three types of slices can be created in Illustrator: object slices, text slices, and user slices.

An **object** slice is based on the size of a selected object's bounding box. If that object is moved or resized, the slice will automatically resize to accommodate the modified object. A group can also be made into an object slice, and as with an object, the slice will resize to accommodate changes made to the group.

A **text** slice is based on the bounding box of selected text. When a text slice is exported, the text is converted to HTML text with all its format and character settings intact.

A **user** slice is one that is created manually using the Slice tool. User slices can be moved and resized using the Slice Selection tool. Each user slice is listed as a separate <Slice> on the Layers palette.

To create an object or text slice:

1. Select an object, or multiple objects, or a group on the artboard.

2. Choose Object > Slice > Make **2**. A dark rectangle that matches the current bounding box will be created for the slice.

3. *Optional:* To create a text slice, follow steps 1–2 above, choose Object > Slice Options, then choose HTML Text from the Slice Type pop-up menu (read about Slice Options on pages 490–491).

Layer slices

You can also create layer slices. On the Layers palette, click the target circle to the right of a top-level layer name to target that layer, then choose Object > Slice > **Make**. The slice will contain all the objects on that layer and the slice's dimensions will match that of the layer's bounding box. If any changes are made on that layer, the slice will resize accordingly.

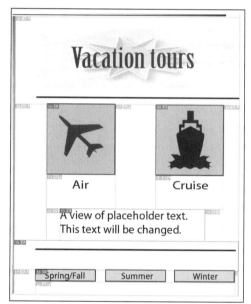
1 *An Illustrator file containing slices*

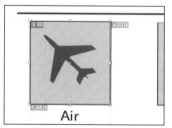
2 *An Object slice is created for the selected rectangular object.*

Automatic slices

Illustrator creates **automatic** slices that divide up the remaining rectangular areas around any object or user slices. This way a valid HTML table will be created for the exported illustration. Automatic slices cannot be selected or edited. They display as light lines and are redrawn and renumbered whenever an object or user slice is edited.

1 *Drag with the Slice tool over the area to be defined as a slice.*

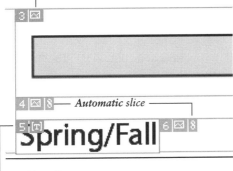

Object slice

Automatic slice

Text slice

2 *A sequence number displays on each slice. An icon also displays next to the number to signify what type of slice it is.*

3 *A selected user slice*

User slices are selected, moved, resized, divided, combined, duplicated, aligned, and restacked by way of the slice commands. (Object slices resize automatically if the objects inside them are resized or moved.)

To create a user slice: 10.0!

1. Choose the Slice tool.

2. Drag over the area of the artwork to be defined as a slice **1**.
   or
   Select an object, then choose Object > Slice > Create Slice from Selection.

   A rectangle will surround the selected object or area you marqueed.

➤ Shift-drag to constrain the slice to a square. Option/Alt-drag to create the slice from the center.

➤ If you want slices to be created from existing guides in the artwork, choose Slice > Create Slice from Guides. But beware, this command deletes all existing slices!

A rectangle surrounds each area or object that has been designated as a slice, and each slice has a sequence number in its upper left corner **2**. The slice in the upper left corner is assigned the number one, with the remaining slice numbers increasing in ascending order from left to right and top to bottom.

To show/hide slices: 10.0!

Choose View > Show Slices. To hide slices choose View > Hide Slices.

➤ To view slices in the Save for Web dialog box, click the Toggle Slice Visibility button 🔲 in the upper left corner. To hide slices, click the button again.

To select a slice: 10.0!

1. Choose the Slice Select tool 🔽 (it's on the Slice tool pop-out menu).

2. Click a user slice **3**. Shift-click if you want to select additional slices.

➤ Another way to select an object slice is to select the actual object.

Unlike object slices, user slices don't resize automatically when objects within the slice area are modified. If you modify or move objects inside a user slice, you can resize the slice afterward.

To resize a user slice:

1. Choose the Slice Select tool, then click a slice.

2. Position the pointer over a slice border or corner **1**. When the double-headed arrow displays, drag to resize **2**.

➤ The tip of the knife of the Slice Select tool pointer is the hot area for that tool.

To move a user slice:

1. Choose the Slice Select tool, then click a slice.

2. Position the pointer inside the slice, then drag to reposition it.

To duplicate a user slice:

1. Choose the Slice Select tool, then select a user slice.

2. Choose Object > Slice > Duplicate Slice. A copy of the slice will appear, offset from the original slice **3**–**4**.

➤ A selected slice can also be copied and pasted within the current document or into another document.

To combine two or more user slices into one:

1. Choose the Slice Select tool, then select two or more user slices. The selected slices can overlap each other, but they don't have to.

2. Choose Object > Slice > Combine Slices. One larger user slice will be created that encompasses the former selected slices **5**–**6**.

➤ To release the combined slices, choose Object > Slice > Release.

Align it

To align user slices precisely, select them, then apply any of the **Align** commands. This will help to streamline the overall layout of objects, eliminating any small, unnecessary slices that may have been generated automatically, and thus produce a simpler HTML table.

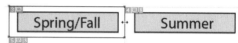

1 *Position the Slice Selection tool over the border of a selected slice...*

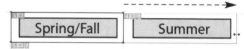

2 *...then drag with the tool to resize the slice.*

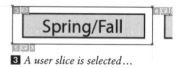

3 *A user slice is selected...*

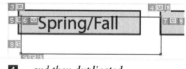

4 *...and then duplicated.*

5 *Several user slices are selected...*

Spring/Fall   Summer   Winter

6 *...and then combined into one slice.*

Resize, Move, Duplicate, Combine User Slices

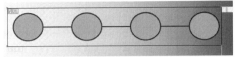

1 *A user slice is selected.*

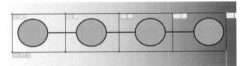

2 *The Divide Slice dialog box*

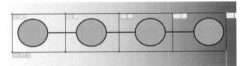

3 *The user slice is* **divided** *into four separate user slices.*

4 *A user slice is* **restacked** *using the Layers palette.*

To divide a user slice into smaller slices: 10.0!

1. Choose the Slice Select tool, then select a user slice **1**.
2. Choose Object > Slice > Divide Slices **2**.
3. Check Divide Horizontally Into and/or check Divide Vertically Into to specify where the division will occur, then for either or both options, click the first button and enter a value to divide the slice into evenly sized parts, or click the second button and enter an exact pixel size value for the divided parts.
4. Check Preview to preview the divisions.
5. Click OK **3**.

To restack a user slice: 10.0!

1. Choose the Slice Select tool, then select a user slice.
2. Locate the <Slice> you want to restack on the Layers palette, then drag it upward or downward **4**.
   or
   Choose a command from the Object > Arrange submenu.

The following commands apply to all kinds of slices.

To lock all slices: 10.0!

Choose View > Lock Slices. The Slice commands are not available when slices are locked.

To release a slice: 10.0!

1. Select any type of slice or select an object inside an object slice.
2. Choose Object > Slice > Release. Any object or user slices will be removed; the original artwork objects will remain.

Beware! If you delete an object slice, the artwork object within it will also be deleted.

To delete a user slice: 10.0!

1. Choose the Slice Select tool, then select a user slice.
2. Press Delete/Backspace.

➤ To remove all slices, choose Object > Slice > Delete All.

The Slice Options dialog box is used to categorize the content of a slice for browser viewing and to assign a URL and an Alt tag for the display of substitute text.

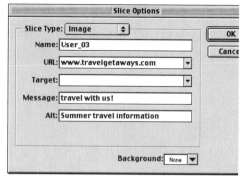
1 *The Slice Options dialog box with* **Image** *chosen as the* **Slice Type**

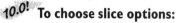
To choose slice options:

1. Choose Object > Slice Options.
or
Double-click a slice in the Save for Web dialog box.

2. Choose a category for the slice content from the Slice Type pop-up menu.

3. Follow the steps under the appropriate category below for the Slice Type you chose:

For the **Image** Slice Type **1**:

Leave the default slice name as is or enter a **Name** (with no spaces). This name will be used for the separate slice file.

Enter a **URL** or choose a previously used URL from the pop-up menu. The viewer will be linked to this URL if the slice area is clicked on in a browser.

Optional: Enter a frame **Target** or choose a standard frame from the pop-up menu. Linked content will load into the chosen frame target: _blank opens a new browser window for the link contents; _self loads the new link contents into the HTML frame for the current slice; _parent replaces the current HTML frames with the new link contents; and _top loads the new link contents into the entire browser window (this is similar to the _parent option). The Target field is only available when information is entered into the URL field.

Enter a **Message** to have text appear on the browser's status bar at the bottom of the browser window when the user's pointer is over that slice.

Enter **Alt** text to be used if a user's browser is set to not display images. This text is also spoken by browser-installed voice recognition software for visually impaired users.

Slice Options

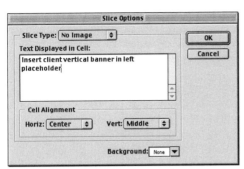

1 *The* **Slice Options** *dialog box with* **No Image** *chosen as the Slice Type*

2 *The* **Slice Options** *dialog box with* **HTML Text** *chosen as the Slice Type*

Choose a **Background** color to be displayed in the slice in a browser. (This color choice won't display in Illustrator.)
or
For the **No Image** Slice Type **1**:

Enter **text** to be displayed in the slice when viewed in a browser. (This text won't display in Illustrator.) Standard HTML formatting tags can be entered to control the text styling. The text you enter must fit within the slice area.

Under **Cell Alignment**, choose Horiz and/or Vert pop-up menu options to align the text inside the slice.

Choose a **Background** color to be displayed inside the slice in a browser. This color choice won't display in Illustrator.
or
For the **HTML Text** Slice Type **2**:

Under **Cell Alignment**, choose Horiz and/or Vert pop-up menu options to align the text within the slice.

Choose a **Background** color to be displayed in the slice in a browser. This color choice won't display in Illustrator.

4. Click OK.

➤ If text in a text object is changed, any text slice made for that object will resize to reflect those changes.

Slice Options

Optimization

Optimization is the process by which file format, storage size, and color parameters are chosen for an output image to preserve as much of its quality as possible while still enabling it to download quickly on the Web. Illustrator provides a variety of choices and options for optimization. In this section you will learn the basic steps. Your overall goal is to reduce the file size until the quality of the optimized image reaches its reduction limit (starts to degrade). Keep this goal in mind as you choose various palette options.

GIF and **JPEG** are the two most commonly used file formats for displaying graphics on the Web. GIF is recommended for optimized images that contain elements with sharp edges, such as solid-color areas, line art, or text. The PNG-8 format, which is similar to GIF, uses the same Optimize palette options, with practically the same results. An optimized GIF or PNG-8 file can contain up to 256 colors. You can view the color table for GIF and PNG-8 files and manipulate individual colors in the optimized image. Use the SVG format to output Illustrator objects as vectors (without rasterization) for viewing in a Web page.

If you know that your artwork is destined for the Web, then it's best to choose the **RGB Color mode** when you start a new document, as this is the color space you will eventually be using. You can change the document mode at any time via the File > Document Color Mode submenu.

One more thing to keep in mind. While you're working in Illustrator, your vector drawings will appear crisp and smooth. But if your illustration is saved for display on the Web as a GIF or JPEG, Illustrator will rasterize it at 72 ppi. Any rasterized objects that don't precisely align with the pixel grid will have edges that appear jagged or blurry due to **anti-aliasing**. You can preview how your illustration will look in a Web browser using the Pixel Preview command. Your artwork will display as if it had already been rasterized, allowing you to see the impact

Web color palette

If you've ever created an illustration with millions of colors and then viewed it on a monitor that can only display thousands—or just hundreds—of colors, then you have some idea how drastically colors can change and what Web-safe colors are all about.

No matter how few—or how many—colors a monitor is capable of displaying, all monitors that have at least eight bits of color can render **216** specific **colors** without dithering. This is because eight bits of color can be expressed as two to the eighth power, or 256 (each bit has one of two possible values). Subtract 40 for the colors that the Mac and Windows systems reserve for other uses, and you're left with 216 colors that you can use with confidence in your Web graphics.

But keep in mind that not even these 216 colors will display in the same way on every machine. Windows and Mac systems use different color gamma values, and each monitor may be calibrated somewhat differently. Since the Windows operating system uses a higher gamma value than the Macintosh operating system, an illustration created on a Mac will appear darker on a Windows system than on the Mac.

1 *View > Pixel Preview unchecked (off)*

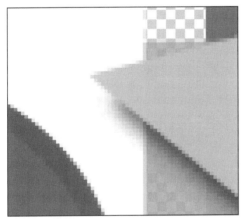

2 *View > Pixel Preview checked (on)*

of anti-aliasing. With Snap to Pixel selected, any artwork you create while your document is in Pixel Preview mode will automatically snap to a pixel grid that will prevent any horizontal and vertical edges in your artwork from being anti-aliased. To work in Pixel Preview mode, choose View > **Pixel Preview** **1**–**2**. Also choose View > Snap to Pixel—or deselect that option, if desired.

Transparent GIFs and JPEGs cannot preserve soft-edged shapes against transparency. If you want an optimized image to fade into a solid color background (as in a Drop Shadow effect, Outer Glow effect, or opacity mask), create two layers in your Illustrator document: a lower layer that contains a solid Web-safe color that will be used on the full Web page, and a layer above it that contains an overlapping object to which a soft, feathered effect (such as Drop Shadow) has been applied.

For a hybrid illustration that contains solid color areas or type combined with photographic imagery, the best approach is to create separate **slices** for the different elements in the illustration, then use the Save for Web dialog box to assign different optimization formats and settings to each slice. This way, the solid color areas will remain Web-safe and the continuous-tone areas will render reasonably well. Read about slicing on pages 486–491.

Pixel Preview

To optimize an illustration in the GIF or PNG-8 format:

1. Save your file, then choose File > Save for Web.

2. Click the 2-Up tab above the preview windows to display both the original and optimized previews of the image simultaneously. Pause for the previews to render. To optimize just a slice, select it now in the preview window.

3. Choose a named, preset combination of optimization settings from the Settings pop-up menu **1**, leave the preset as is, click Save, then save your file with a new name.
   or
   Follow the remaining steps to customize your optimization settings (**1**, next page).

4. From the next pop-up menu ("Optimized file format," if you use the Tool Tip), choose GIF or PNG-8.

5. For GIF only, drag the Lossy slider or enter a value to allow the compression scheme to eliminate pixels from the image, thus reducing file size. Note that you cannot use the Lossy option with the Interlaced option, or with the Noise or Pattern Dither algorithms.

6. Choose a palette option (color reduction algorithm) from the next pop-up menu (see the sidebar on the next page). The GIF and PNG-8 formats permit a maximum of only 256 colors. Perceptual, Selective, and Adaptive render the optimized image using colors from the original illustration, whereas Web shifts all colors to Web safe. Web is not the best choice if the illustration contains continuous-tone areas, blends, or gradients. Custom optimizes colors based on a palette that you have previously saved.

7. If you want to choose a specific number of colors, choose that value from the Colors pop-up menu; or enter a value in the field; or use the arrows to arrive at the number of colors.

8. From the next pop-up menu, choose a Dither method: No Dither, Diffusion,

No halos

When creating GIF or PNG-8 files, you can create a hard-edged transparency effect. This will cause all pixels that are more than 50% transparent to be fully transparent and pixels less than 50% transparent to be fully opaque. This type of transparency will eliminate the halo effect that can occur when the matte color is different from the background color in the original illustration.

To create hard-edged transparency:

1. Open an illustration that contains **transparency**.

2. Choose File > **Save for Web**, then choose **GIF** or **PNG-8**.

3. Check **Transparency**.

4. Choose **None** from the **Matte** pop-up menu.

5. Click **Save** to save the file.

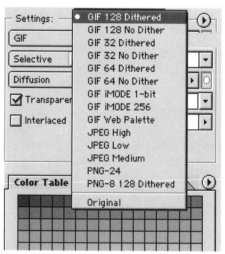

1 *You can choose from an assortment of preset optimization settings from the* **Settings** *pop-up menu in the* **Save for Web** *dialog box.*

Four of the GIF color palettes

Perceptual

Generates a color table based on the colors currently in the illustration, with particular attention paid to how people actually perceive colors. This table's strength is in preserving overall color integrity.

Selective

Generates a color table based on the colors currently in the illustration. The Perceptual and Selective options are similar, but the Selective option leans more toward preserving flat colors and Web-safe colors.

Adaptive

Generates a color table based on the part of the color spectrum that represents most of the color in the illustration. This choice produces a slightly larger optimized file.

➤ If you switch among the Perceptual, Selective, or Adaptive options, any Web-safe colors currently on the Color Table palette are preserved.

Web

Generates a color table by shifting image colors to colors that are available on the standard Web-safe palette. This choice produces the least number of colors and thus the smallest file size, though not necessarily the best image quality.

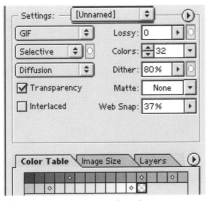

1 Use the **optimize** panel to choose custom settings for a GIF export.

Pattern, or Noise, then choose a dither value using the slider.

9. If the illustration contains transparency that you want to preserve, check the Transparency box. Fully transparent pixels will be preserved as transparent. Partially transparent pixels will be filled with the Matte color or will be converted to fully transparent or fully opaque pixels, depending on which Matte option you choose.

   If you don't check Transparency, both fully and partially transparent pixels will be filled with the Matte color.

10. To control how partially transparent pixels along the edges of the optimized image (such as the edges of anti-aliased or rasterized elements) will blend with the background of a Web page, choose a Matte option.

    Choose Other to set the Matte color to the color of the Web page background, if you happen to know what that color is. If the backgound color is unknown, set Matte to None (this will result in a hard, jagged edge). Both options eliminate halo effects along the edges of an optimized image when it's displayed on the Web. Any soft-edged effect (such as Drop Shadow or Feather) on top of transparency will be filled with the current Matte color.

11. Check Interlaced to have the GIF or PNG image display in successively greater detail as it downloads on the Web page.

12. To automatically shift colors to their closest Web palette equivalents, drag the Web Snap slider or enter a value. The higher the Web Snap value, the more colors will be shifted.

13. Click Save, then choose Format/Save as Type: "HTML and images." This format creates all the necessary files to use the image as a Web page. The appropriate file format extension will be appended to the file name. Change the name, if desired, then click Save again.

Optimize as GIF or PNG-8

To use the Save for Web previews:

Click the 4-Up tab on the main window to see an original view and three previews simultaneously. Illustrator will use the current optimize panel settings to generate the first preview, and then automatically generate ("autopopulate") the two other previews as variations based on the current optimization settings. You can click on any preview and change the optimize panel settings for just that preview. The optimized preview(s) will update every time a value or setting is changed on the optimize panel.

You can choose to repopulate your 4-Up view. This will create new optimized versions in each window based on the changes you make in the optimization settings. To do this, choose an optimized version of the illustration, make changes, click the arrow to the right of the Settings pop-up menu, then choose Repopulate Views. The original file and your selected optimization won't be affected, but Illustrator will generate smaller optimized versions for the other previews. If you're not happy with any particular optimization, choose Original from the Settings pop-up menu—the Original illustration will appear in that preview.

You can save your settings so that you can apply them to other files.

To save your Save for Web settings:

1. In the Save for Web dialog box, click the small arrowhead to display the Optimize menu (to the right of the Settings pop-up menu).

2. Choose Save Settings, then name the settings. By default, they are saved in the Adobe Illustrator 10 > Presets > Save for Web Settings > Optimize folder.

3. Click Save. Your new settings will appear on the Settings pop-up menu, if they were saved in the default location.

saving your settings

To save the current optimization settings to the current Illustrator file, click **Done** in the Save for Web dialog box. No export file will be generated.

1 *The **optimize** panel with settings chosen for a JPEG export*

JPEGs and Web-safe colors

JPEG compression adds compression arti-facts to an image. Because of this, Web-safe colors in a JPEG image are rendered non-Web-safe after compression. This is accept-able because the JPEG format is usually used to optimize continuous-tone imagery, and on this type of imagery, browser dither isn't objectionable. Don't try to match a color area in a JPEG file to a color area in a GIF file or on the background of a Web page, though, because the JPEG color will shift and dither when the artwork is compressed.

JPEG is the format of choice for optimizing continuous-tone imagery for display on the Web (photographs, paintings, gradients, blends, and the like). If you optimize to JPEG, the file's 24-bit color depth will be preserved, and these colors will be seen and enjoyed by any Web viewer whose monitor is set to mil-lions of colors (24-bit depth). Keep in mind, however, that JPEGs are optimized using a compression method that is lossy, which means it causes image data to be eliminated.

The PNG-24 format is similar to JPEG, except that PNG allows for multiple levels of transparency along edges and employs a lossless method of compression. PNG-24 files are larger than equivalent JPEGs.

To optimize an illustration in the JPEG format:

1. Open the original Illustrator file, choose File > Save for Web, then choose one of the JPEG settings from the Settings pop-up menu or choose JPEG from the next pop-up menu ("Optimized file format" pop-up menu, if you're using Tool Tips) **1**.

2. Click the 2-Up or 4-Up tab at the top of the main window to display the original and optimized previews of the illustration simultaneously. To optimize a slice, select it now in the preview window.

3. In the optimize panel, specify image quality by dragging the quality slider or by entering a value in the Quality box. *or*

(Continued on the following page)

Optimize as JPEG

Choose Low, Medium, High, or Maximum from the compression quality pop-up menu to the left. A higher setting preserves more color information, but makes the file size larger. Experiment with this setting to find the best balance between file size and file quality.

4. Check Progressive to create an optimized image that is rendered in stages in the browser. This feature isn't supported by all the browsers, but where it is, users will see a low-resolution version of your image before the highest resolution loads.

5. Increase the Blur value to lessen the visibility of JPEG artifacts that arise from JPEG's compression method and also reduce the file size. Be careful not to over-blur the image, though, or your details will soften too much. The Blur setting can be lowered later in order to reclaim image sharpness.

6. *Optional:* Check ICC Profile to embed an ICC Profile in the optimized image. To utilize this option, the document must have had a profile assigned to it in Illustrator (see the sidebar on this page).

7. Choose a Matte color to be used for areas of transparency found in the original illustration. If you choose "None," transparent areas will appear as white.

   Note: The JPEG format doesn't support transparency. To have the Matte color simulate transparency, choose Other and use the same solid color as the background of the Web page, if that color is known. Now soft edges will fade into the background color of the Web page.

8. *Optional:* Check Optimized to produce the smallest file size. *Beware!* Older browsers (version 3.0 or earlier) may not be able to read a JPEG that's saved with this option.

9. Click Save, then choose Format: "HTML and images." The appropriate file format extension will be appended to the file name. Change the name, if desired, then click Save once more.

Check your profiles

An embedded profile will slightly increase a file's size. As of this writing, Internet Explorer for Mac versions 4.01 and later support color profiles and ColorSync. On the Mac, ColorSync makes sure the browser and the operating system know the viewer's monitor profile. This helps to ensure consistent color between the monitor and JPEG files. As color management support and profile automation improve, and as soon as Navigator supports embedded profiles, embedded profiles will become standard. Windows has a bit of catching up to do in this area. For the moment, use your own judgment.

The optimize panel with settings chosen for a PNG-24 export

A highlighted *swatch*

Snap selected colors to Web palette button

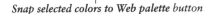

The Color Table pane in the Save for Web dialog box, with a color swatch highlighted

You can preserve multiple levels of transparency in PNG-24 images using a feature called alpha transparency. When a PNG is displayed in a browser that has a plug-in supporting alpha transparency, the PNG can display up to 256 levels of transparency.

To preserve multi-level transparency in PNG-24 images:

1. Open the Illustrator file, then choose File > Save for Web.

2. Choose PNG-24 from the file format pop-up menu ◼.

3. Check Interlaced to have the PNG image display in successively greater detail as it downloads on the Web page. This option increases the file size.

4. Check Transparency to preserve transparent pixels.
   or
   Uncheck Transparency to fill transparent pixels with the Matte color.

5. Click Save to save your file.

Let's say you have an illustration that you're going to optimize in the GIF format using the Perceptual, Selective, or Adaptive palette, but the illustration has solid color areas that aren't Web-safe. Before outputting the image online, you can make the solid color areas Web-safe.

To make solid color areas Web-safe:

1. Open the file and optimize it in the GIF format using File > Save for Web.

2. Choose the Eyedropper tool.

3. Click a solid color area to be made Web-safe.

4. Click the Color Table tab, if necessary. The color you just clicked on will now be the highlighted swatch ◼.

5. Click the "Snaps selected colors to Web palette" button 🔲 at the bottom of the palette. A diamond will display on the selected swatch to signify that the color was shifted to a Web-safe equivalent.

6. *Optional:* Click the Lock Selected Color button to preserve the currently selected

(Continued on the following page)

Optimize as PNG-24; Solid Color Areas

swatch even if the number of colors in the GIF palette is reduced.

➤ Shift-click with the Eyedropper tool on other areas in the Optimized preview to select more than one color, then Web-shift all the selected colors at once.

➤ Click a Web-shifted color swatch, then click the "Snaps selected colors to Web palette" button again to unshift the color out of the Web-safe range.

You can have Illustrator pick your optimization settings based on the desired file size.

To optimize to file size:
1. Open the Save for Web dialog box, then press the arrowhead in the circle and choose Optimize to File Size **1**.
2. Click a Start With option. Current Settings uses your current optimization settings; Auto Select GIF/JPEG tells Illustrator to choose either GIF or JPEG, depending on the program's analysis of your output image **2**.
3. Enter a value for the Desired File Size.
4. Click OK.

You can resize your output image directly in the Save for Web dialog box. *Note:* To make best use of this option, size your artboard before opening the Save for Web dialog box.

To resize your output image:
1. Open the File > Save for Web dialog box, then click the Image Size tab **3**.
2. Check Constrain Proportions if you want to maintain the relative width and height of your output image.
3. Enter a percent value if you want to make the new image a specific percentage of the original size.
   or
   Enter specific width and/or height values. If you clicked Constrain Proportions, the height will change as you change the width, and vice-versa.
4. To clip the exported illustration to the size of the document's current artboard size, choose Clip to Artboard. This can

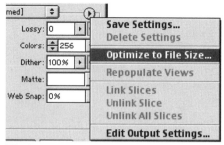

1 *Choose* Optimize to File Size *from the pop-up menu.*

2 *The* Optimize To File Size *dialog box*

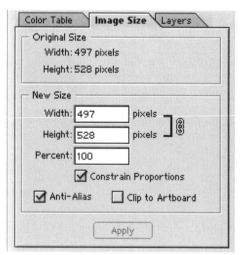

3 *The* Image Size *pane in the Save for Web dialog box*

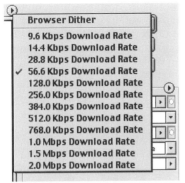

1 *Choose Browser Dither from the Preview menu.*

2 *An optimized image with Browser Dither unchecked*

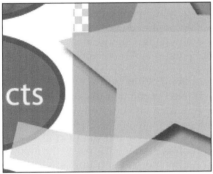

3 *An optimized image with Browser Dither checked:* Soft edges and transparent areas are dithered.

be useful for clipping artwork to an artboard that's the size of a banner ad.

5. Click Apply to preview the clipping effect on the image. (If you need to Undo Clip to Artboard, uncheck the option, then click Apply again.)

Most Web viewers use 16-bit monitors, which can display thousands of colors. On the few 8-bit, 256-color display monitors that are still in use, dithering is used to re-create any image colors that aren't on the browser palette. (Mac OS and Windows browsers use a color palette of 216 colors.) Follow the steps on this page to preview browser dithering in an image.

To preview potential browser dither in an optimized image:

1. With the illustration open, choose File > Save for Web, then click the 2-Up or 4-Up tab.

2. Click the Preview arrowhead and choose Browser Dither **1**–**3**.

When Illustrator optimizes an illustration, the application applies dithering to simulate gradients, gradient meshes, and semi-transparent colors from the original illustration that won't appear on the color palette of the optimized image. You can control the amount of dithering via the Dither field in the Save for Web dialog box. If you raise the **Dither** value, the optimized image will more closely color-match the original—but at the expense of a slightly larger file size.

The **Web Snap** value in the Save for Web dialog box also affects the amount of browser dithering in an optimized image. The higher the Web Snap, the less the optimized image will be dithered, and the smaller will be its file size. Some degree of dithering is acceptable in continuous-tone imagery, though, and it may be more pleasing than the color banding that a high Web Snap value can cause.

10.0! ## SVG

The SVG (Scalable Vector Graphics) format allows you to incorporate interactivity and scalability into an optimized image. Unlike the bitmap formats GIF, JPEG, and PNG, which save as large files that require large bandwidth for Web viewing, SVG is a vector format that is based on XML. Shapes, paths, text, SVG filter effects, and color quality support are stored in a small, efficient file size. Currently, Web surfers must download an SVG plug-in to view graphics in this format. Keep in mind that many people won't bother to do this and will miss out on your artwork.

SVG is now a native Illustrator format, which means Illustrator can open and save SVG files. We will look at several aspects of Illustrator and SVG: work guidelines that improve SVG performance; using Save for Web to optimize a file or a slice area as SVG; saving to the SVG format; and adding interactivity to SVG artwork.

Guidelines for using SVG effectively

Keep the following guidelines in mind when preparing illustrations for SVG format.

- Each layer in the illustration will become a group element in the SVG file; nested layers will become nested group elements. Plan your SVG groups by organizing your layers.

- Let each object have its own transparency setting. Don't set the transparency for the whole layer the objects are on.

- Any imported image in the illustration that does not have an alpha channel will be converted to JPEG format, and any image with an alpha channel will be converted to PNG format.

- All the commands below the horizontal dividing line on the Effects menu will produce a raster object in the SVG file. A gradient mesh object will also be rasterized in the SVG format. Rasterization will increase the file size and download time of the SVG file.

More about SVG

SVG format saves objects as vectors, and pre-serves gradients, animation, and SVG filter effects as efficient vector shapes. To display SVG files, the browser will require the SVG plug-in. An SVG file can be opened and displayed in Internet Explorer 5, in Netscape Navigator 4.6, or in any later version of either of those browsers.

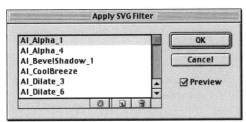

1 *The Apply SVG Filter dialog box*

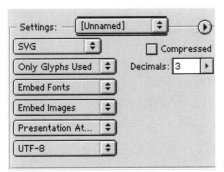

2 *The optimize panel in the Save for Web dialog box with settings chosen for SVG export*

When you use the SVG filter effects, you avoid the rasterization that the other Effect menu commands produce. SVG filter effects are rendered to the object in the browser, not in Illustrator, and this helps to reduce a file's download size. In Illustrator, you'll only see a preview of the SVG filter effect.

To apply an SVG filter effect to an 10.0! object:

1. Select an object.
2. Choose Effect > SVG Filters > Apply SVG Filter **1**.
3. Check Preview.
4. Choose a filter from the scroll list.
5. Click OK.

➤ To prevent an SVG effect from rasteriz-ing, an object's SVG filter must be listed at the bottom of the Appearance palette, just above the Transparency listing. Drag it downward to move it to the correct position, if necessary.

Optimize as SVG 10.0!

The Save for Web dialog box includes SVG as one of the available optimization formats for an Illustrator file destined for the Web. The SVG format can be applied to the entire file or to a selected slice within the illustration.

SVG format options display in the optimize panel of the Save for Web dialog box **2**. As listed in top to bottom order, the pop-up menu options are: File format, Font Subsetting, Font Location, Image Location, CSS Properties, and Character Encoding. On the right you'll see the Compressed checkbox for creating a compressed SVGZ file, as well as the Decimals option. These options are exactly the same as options found in the SVG Options dialog box. (The last three options and Decimals are found in the Advanced portion of the SVG Options dialog box.) You can read about these options on the following page.

10.0!

To save a file in SVG or SVGZ format:

1. Choose File > Save or Save As.

2. Choose a location and file name for the file.

3. Choose format/Save as Type: SVG (SVG) or SVG Compressed (SVGZ), then click Save.

4. In the SVG Options dialog box **1**, choose a Fonts Subsetting: option to embed the specific characters of the fonts you used in your document. All Glyphs includes every font character, including non-Roman characters; Common English or Common Roman includes only English or Roman characters. (These two options are also available with Glyphs Used in the file.) These choices allow for changes in text content in dynamic text (as in data-driven graphics for the Web). See the Description panel for information about the other Fonts Subsetting options.

5. Click a Fonts Location: Embed to embed the font sets in the document or choose Link to link the document to exported fonts from the Illustrator file.

6. Click an Images Location: Embed to embed rasterized images in the file or Link to link the file to the exported JPEG or PNG images from the Illustrator file.

7. Check Preserve Illustrator Editing Capabilities to include Illustrator-related data in the file. This permits the saved SVG file to be edited by designers even after a developer's code is added to it.

8. *Optional:* Click Advanced to choose
10.0! additional options, but only if you have a thorough understanding of the SVG format.

9. Click OK.

➤ Hold the cursor over each option to view descriptions for each in the Description panel, or read about these options in the Illustrator User Guide.

Link or embed?

Link a font or image if you're going to share the font or image file with multiple SVG files.

Embed a font or image to guarantee that the font or image will be available. This option increases the file size.

Worth the squeeze?

If you choose SVGZ in the Export dialog box, your file will be compressed. A compressed file cannot be edited using a text editor.

1 *The SVG Options dialog box*

Java what?

To learn more about JavaScript, we recommend **JavaScript for the World Wide Web:** Visual QuickStart Guide by Tom Negrino and Dori Smith (yup, you guessed it—Peachpit Press).

1 *Choose from the* **Event** *pop-up menu on the* **SVG Ineractivity** *palette.*

Using SVG, you can add JavaScript interactivity right in Illustrator and then export the result using the Export dialog box. For example, you can create a JavaScript action that will trigger an action if a Web user moves the cursor over part of an image.

To add interactivity to SVG artwork:

1. Select an object.

2. Choose Window > SVG Interactivity.

3. Choose an event from the Event pop-up menu **1**. This will determine when your action will take place. For example, if you choose "onclick," your action will occur when the user clicks on that object.

4. In the JavaScript field, type a JavaScript action **2**.

5. Press Return/Enter. The text now displays in the scroll window, and the event will now have a script routine that will run when the event occurs in a browser.

➤ To delete an event, highlight it, then click the Remove Selected Entry (trash) button or choose Delete Event from the SVG Interactivity palette menu.

2 *Then enter a* **JavaScript** *action here.*

10.0! **Export CSS layers**

CSS (Cascading Style Sheets) are used to put formatting information into separate layers for display in a browser. Each successively displayed layer will overwrite/replace the existing displayed layer in the browser. The Export as CSS Layers option in the Save for Web dialog box can be used to export each layer in an illustration as a separate file.

The exported CSS layer files can be used in a Web page creation program or with an interactive script to substitute in a given layer at an appropriate time for display on a Web page viewed in a browser.

To export Illustrator objects as CSS layers:

1. Use the Layers palette in Illustrator to arrange objects on separate layers, then choose File > Save for Web.

2. Click the Layers tab in the optimize panel **1**.

3. Check Export As CSS Layers.

4. Choose a layer from the Layer pop-up menu.

5. Click Visible, Hidden, or Do Not Export to determine how that layer's display will be handled in the exported HTML file.

6. Choose optimization settings from the optimize panel for the objects on the currently selected layer.

7. Choose another layer from the pop-up menu and repeat steps 5 and 6.

8. Click Save, then click Save again to export the layers as separate optimized files. The files will be collected in the folder name designated in the Output Settings dialog box under the Saving Files option. The default folder name is "images" (see sidebar on this page).

➤ Check Preview Only Selected Layer to preview only the layer chosen in step 4 in the Save for Web previews.

Where exported image files go

By default, when the Save for Web dialog box saves a Web page as a set of multiple image files, it places them in a new "**images**" folder in the same folder as the exported HTML file. To rename this folder, click Save in the Save for Web dialog box, click Output Settings, then choose Saving Files from the pop-up menu at top. In the Optimized Files area, change the folder name in the **Put Images in Folder:** field, then click OK.

1 *The Layers tab in the Save for Web dialog box*

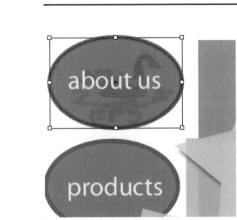

1 *Select the object to which you want to assign a URL...*

2 *...then enter a URL for the selected object on the **Attributes** palette.*

Image maps

Image maps can be created in Illustrator 10. In fact, any object you create can be linked to a URL.

To create an image map:

1. Select the object to which you want to attach a URL **1**.

2. Choose Window > Show Attributes.

3. From the Image Map pop-up menu, choose one of the following: Rectangular to create a rectangular image map around the object (the image map boundaries will be similar to the object's bounding box); or Polygon to create a map that follows the object's irregular contour. (Choose None if you don't want to create an image map.)

4. Type a URL into the URL field **2** or choose a URL from the pop-up menu. If you want more URL entries to display on the list, choose Palette Options from the palette menu, then enter a value (1–30).

5. You can check the URL location by clicking the Browser button on the palette to launch a browser (assuming you have one loaded on your system and your computer is currently connected to the Web).

6. When you're ready to export, use the Save for Web dialog box to optimize your artwork. Click Save when you're done, and in the Save Optimized As dialog box, choose Format: "HTML and images" to save the necessary HTML file, complete with the image map and URL links. The HTML-generated file and the optimized file containing the image map must be kept in the same folder when the image map is imported into your Web-page creation application. The HTML file contains the URLs, image name, dimensions, and necessary code in order for the image to display on a Web page.

Image Maps

10.0! Data-driven graphics

The **Variables** palette is not covered in this QuickStart Guide. This page contains a very brief synopsis of what it does. For more information, refer to *Real World Adobe Illustrator 10* by Deke McClelland (Peachpit Press) or the Illustrator documentation.

A Web server can connect with a database to send text and graphics to a Web page. Using Illustrator, a Web page designer can control which objects in the illustration can receive changes from a server. Each element the designer decides can be changed is assigned (bound) to a **variable** via the Variables palette **1**. Then, once the Illustrator object and a variable are bound together, they become dynamic and will update automatically whenever the server software accesses the database and downloads new data to the variable. Only objects bound to variables will change.

Illustrator's Variables palette is used to turn object attributes into variables. You can work with four types of variables: **Graph Data, Linked File, Text String,** and **Visibility**. A Graph Data variable updates a graph with new graph data; a Linked File variable replaces one placed image with another; and a Text String variable replaces text. The Visibility variable controls whether an object is visible, and can be changed for any object. The objects that are bound (to variables) serve merely as placeholders in the illustration, displaying whatever data the database and the server send down to that variable.

You can organize the changes that occur in one or more objects into sets, called **data sets**; each set is a collection of variables and their associated data. Each data set can contain the same variables, but with different object content. Sets are listed on the Data Set menu at the top of the Variables palette.

To edit the data associated with a variable, the object in the artwork to which that variable is bound is edited. A Visibility variable is edited by hiding or displaying its associated object via the Layers palette. After editing the objects that are bound to variables, the Variables palette is used to capture those edits to a new data set. You can switch between data sets on the Variables palette in order to preview how the changeable objects will look on the page.

Let's say you have a template for a Web page that displays a picture and text for a different car each week. It could contain several different data sets, with each set containing a Linked File variable bound to a picture of a car, and Text String variables that display text objects containing the text descriptions of each car. If you change the car images and text descriptions and capture those changes to a new data set, as you display each data set, the image and text content will update on the Web page.

Linked File variable ——
Visibility variable ——
Text String variable ——

1 *The Variables palette lists variables and the objects bound to them within each data set.*

Make Object Dynamic Make Visibility Dynamic Unbind Variable New Variable

Chapter 27: Web ◆ Study Guide

Learning Objectives

- Choose the best export format for various kinds of Web graphics.
- Create and edit slices.
- Create and edit image maps.
- Use the Save for Web command to optimize Web graphics.
- Save files as SVG.

Get Up and Running Exercises

- Practice optimizing Web graphics. Create or draw the following types of documents:

  - ▲ An illustration that includes gradual changes between colors, such as any combination of gradients, color blends, gradient meshes, and placed images, such as photographs.

  - ▲ An illustration that includes only solid colors, such as a simple logo or large display type.

  - ▲ An illustration that combines solid colors and continuous tones.

  - ▲ An illustration that includes only vector objects.

  Save optimized versions of the files, doing your best to balance image quality and file size. Which Web graphics format results in the most efficient combination of size and quality for each type of illustration?

- Build a fully functional Web page in Illustrator by exporting not only images, but HTML code as well. Create a page that incorporates objects you've drawn or imported, and view the page in a Web browser. Once it's working properly, add URL hyperlinks to it using slices and an image map. Finally, try to compress the file size of the Web page's graphics as far down as you can without compromising quality too much. Like a real-world Web designer, you may find yourself adjusting or even removing some of the bells and whistles on your page for the sake of good performance.

Class Discussion Questions

Basics

- How are Web graphics different than print graphics?

- What are four important issues you'll need to address for online output?

- What issues arise when using ICC profiles with Web graphics?

- How should you proof Web graphics?

Optimization

- Where are Web optimization controls located in Illustrator?

- What are the differences between the Perceptual, Selective, Adaptive, and Web-safe palettes?

Dividing Web graphics

- What are the differences between image maps and slices?

- How do you create and edit slices?

Compression

- What is the difference between lossless and lossy compression?

- GIF uses only lossless compression. How, then, is Illustrator able to provide a "lossy" GIF option?

- What are some things you can do to reduce the download time of a Web graphic?

Comparing GIF, JPEG, PNG, and SVG

- Compare how well Web browsers support the GIF, JPEG, PNG, and SVG file formats.

- Compare how GIF, JPEG, PNG, and SVG support color.

- Compare how GIF, JPEG, PNG, and SVG support data compression.

- Compare how GIF, JPEG, and PNG support transparency.

Review Questions

Multiple choice

1. Why is the GIF format generally preferred for Web type and solid-color graphics?

   A. Anti-aliasing routines are built in.

   B. Optimization options help minimize compression artifacts.

   C. Colors can be optimized to a 24-bit palette.

   D. Multiple levels of transparency are available.

2. Why is the JPEG format generally preferred for Web photographs?

   A. Its compression is lossless.

   B. Its colors are always Web-safe.

   C. Its palette can be optimized for photographic images.

   D. Its compression is efficient for continuous-tone images.

3. Which one of the following GIF color palettes contains the 216 colors common to Mac and Windows system color tables?

   A. Perceptual

   B. Selective

   C. Adaptive

   D. Web

4. Which one of the following GIF color palettes is designed to achieve a balance between preserving color integrity and preserving flat and Web-safe color areas?

   A. Perceptual

   B. Selective

   C. Mac OS

   D. Web

5. Which optimization option automatically shifts colors to their closest Web palette equivalents?

   A. Colors

   B. Dither

   C. Interlaced

   D. Web snap

6. When exporting SVG, when would you want to link a font or image instead of embedding it?

   A. You don't think the font or image will be available on the computer that reads the Web page.

   B. You'll use the font or image in multiple SVG files.

   C. You want to compress the SVG file.

   D. You want the SVG file to be compatible with non-Roman languages.

Fill-in-the-blank

1. When creating a new Illustrator document that will ultimately be used as a Web graphic, choose the _____ color mode.

2. To find out how much time a graphic will require to download over the Internet,

   _____.

3. The major difference between SVG and other Web graphics formats is that SVG primarily uses _____ graphics.

4. The difference between SVG and SVGZ is that SVGZ is _____.

5. The main reason graphics look different on Mac and Windows systems is the default _____ setting.

6. If a GIF graphic has a fringe or halo around it on a Web page, you probably need to change its _____.

7. If you want to slice an Illustrator document but you think you might need to reposition or resize image elements later, you may want to create _____ slices.

8. To let Illustrator determine compression settings, you can use the _____ feature.

Definitions

1. What is color depth?

2. What is anti-aliasing?

3. What is optimization?

4. What is dithering?

5. What is lossy compression?

6. What is an image map?

7. What is slicing?

8. What is a matte color?

Color separations (film output for process and spot color printing) can be produced directly from Illustrator files. This chapter contains a brief introduction to Illustrator's Separation Setup dialog box and an introduction to trapping, which helps to compensate for color misregistration on press.

©Chris Spollen

Color separation setup

Trapping and color separations are usually handled by a prepress provider—either a service bureau or a print shop. Talk with your print shop before producing color separations or building traps. They'll tell you what settings to use. Don't guess—this isn't the time to "wing it."

To print an illustration on press, unless your print shop uses direct-to-plate technology, you need to supply them with or have them produce black-and-white film output (color separations) from your Illustrator file—one sheet per process or spot color. Your print shop will use the film separations to produce plates to use on the press—one plate for each color.

In **process color** printing, four ink colors, Cyan (C), Magenta (M), Yellow (Y), and Black (K), are used to produce a multitude of colors. A document that contains color photographs or other continuous-tone images must be output as a four-color process job.

In **spot color** printing, a separate plate is produced for each spot color. PANTONE inks are the most commonly used spot color inks, at least in the U.S. Using Illustrator's Separation Setup, you can control which spot colors are converted into process colors and which will remain as spot colors, and you can specify which colors will output.

To prepare a file for separations:

1. Calibrate your monitor (see pages 471–473).

2. Choose File > Document Color Mode > CMYK Color.

3. Decide which colors in the illustration are to be overprinted (see "Overprinting," below).

4. Create traps, if needed (see pages 515–518).

5. Place any objects that you don't want to appear on the color separations on a separate layer and uncheck the Print option for that layer, or hide the layer altogether.

6. Create crop marks, if needed (see page 446).

7. Now have your service provider print the separations.

Overprinting

Normally, Illustrator automatically knocks out any color under an object so the object color won't mix with the color beneath it on press. If you check **Overprint Fill** or **Overprint Stroke** on the Attributes palette, the fill or stroke color will overprint colors underneath it instead—the inks will mix on press. Where colors overlap, a combination color will be produced. Turn the Overprint option on if you're building traps. Colors will overprint on a printing press, but not on a PostScript color composite printer.

Illustrator can show you how spot color objects, with the Overprint Fill or Overprint Stroke option checked (Attributes palette, see pages 515–516), will overprint underlying objects. To view overprinting, choose View > **Overprint Preview** 1–2. "Overprint Preview" is listed in the document window title bar when this option is checked. Also, any traps created with the Pathfinder Trap command will preview (see page 518). Now proceed with the instructions on the following page.

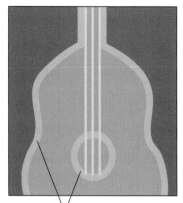

1 *Two objects with their strokes set to overprint*

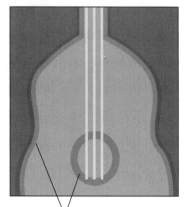

2 *With Overprint Preview checked, the overprint strokes simulate ink mixing with objects below.*

To use Separation Setup:

1. With your file in CMYK Color mode, choose File > Separation Setup. *Note:* To enable Separation Setup, a PostScript printer must be selected. To do this in the Mac OS, use the Chooser; in Windows, you can use Start menu > Settings > Printer.

2. You'll see a file preview window on the left and separation settings on the right. The dialog box will be grayed out until a PPD file is opened (the next step).

3. To open or change the current PPD file, click Open PPD on the right side of the dialog box, highlight the PPD file specified by your service bureau for your target printer or imagesetter, then click Open **1**. The PPD files should be located in the Printer Descriptions folder in the Mac OS System Folder > Extensions folder or the Windows > System subdirectory.

4. *Optional:* The white area in the preview window represents the page size. Separation Setup will automatically choose the default page size for the chosen printer definition. Choose a new size from the Page Size pop-up menu if your print shop requests that you do so.

For steps 5–8, ask your print shop for advice.

5. From the Orientation pop-up menu, choose Portrait to position the image vertically inside the imageable area of the separation **2**.
   or
   Choose Landscape to position the image horizontally inside the imageable area of the separation. The orientation of the image on the page will change; the orientation of the page on the film will not.

6. Choose Up (Right Reading) or Down (Right Reading) from the Emulsion pop-up menu.

7. Choose a combined Halftone screen ruling (lpi)/Device resolution (dpi) from the Halftone pop-up menu.

8. Choose Positive or Negative from the Image pop-up menu.

9. You can click OK at any time to save the current Separation Setup settings, and you can reopen the dialog box at a later time to make further changes. When you save your document, the separation settings will save with the document. Continue with the instructions on the next page.

Separation Setup

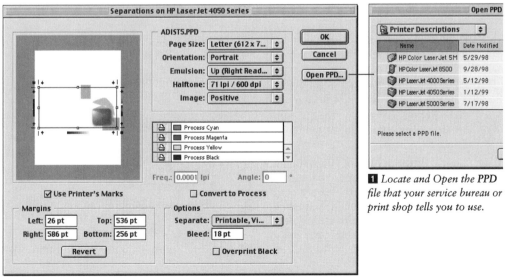

1 *Locate and Open the PPD file that your service bureau or print shop tells you to use.*

2 *The illustration will preview on the left side of the **Separations** dialog box. Choose the settings your print shop specifies from the right side of the dialog box.*

By default, Illustrator will create and print a separation for each process and spot color used in an illustration. Using the Separation Setup dialog box, you can turn printing on or off for individual colors or convert individual spot colors into process colors.

Choosing colors to print and/or convert to process

1. Choose File > Separation Setup if that dialog box isn't already open.

2. In the scroll window, you will see a listing for each color used in the illustration. For each process color you don't want to print, click the printer icon **1** next to the color name to hide the icon. (Click again to show the icon.)

3. Check Convert to Process to convert all spot colors in the document into process colors. This is the default setting.
   or
   Uncheck Convert to Process, then:
   Click in the box next to the spot color name until a four-color process icon appears for each spot color you want to convert into a process color and print.
   or
   Keep clicking until a printer icon appears to keep the color as a spot color and print it.
   or
   Keep clicking until the printer icon disappears to prevent a spot color from printing.

➤ Don't change the Freq. (Frequency) or Angle settings unless you're advised to do so by your print shop. These values are dependent on the type of output device to be used.

➤ Check Overprint Black if you want black fills and strokes to overprint background colors. You don't need to mix a process black (a black made from a mixture of C, M, Y, and K) to use this option. An alert box will appear, instructing you to use the Colors > Overprint Black filter when the file contains transparency (see page 517).

Proof it

There are several reasons to proof your computer artwork before it's printed. First, the RGB colors that you see on your computer screen won't match the printed CMYK colors unless your monitor is properly calibrated. Obtaining a proof will give you an opportunity to correct the color balance or brightness of a picture, or to catch output problems like banding in a gradient. And most print shops need a proof to refer to so they know what the printed piece is supposed to look like. **Digital** (direct-from-disk) **color proofs**—like IRIS or 3M prints—are inexpensive, but they're not perfectly reliable. An advantage of using an IRIS print, though, is that you can color correct your original electronic file and run another IRIS print before you order film.

A more accurate but more expensive proof is a **Chromalin** or **Matchprint**, which is produced from the actual film (color separations). Matchprint colors may be slightly more saturated than final print colors, though. The most reliable color proof—and the most expensive—is a **press proof**, which is produced in the print shop from your film negatives on the final paper stock.

Four-color process icon: This spot color will convert to process and print.

1 *Printer icon: This color will print as a separate plate.*

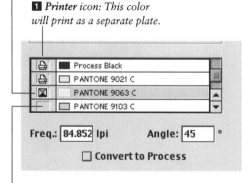

*A **blank** space (no icon): This color won't print.*

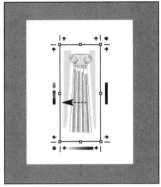

1 *Move the image in its printing bounding box.*

Creating crop marks for separations

If you haven't created crop marks for your document in Illustrator, the Separation Setup feature will, by default, create crop marks at the edge of the illustration's bounding box, which is the smallest rectangle that can encompass all the objects and direction lines in the illustration. It displays as a black rectangle in the preview window. Adobe recommends setting crop marks in Illustrator using Object > Crop Marks > Make, rather than using Separation Setup to set crop marks, so you can control more precisely the exact printable area of your illustration.

Separation Setup regards crop marks created using the Trim Marks filter as artwork. If your document contains Trim Marks, you can uncheck Use Printer's Marks to remove the default cropmarks. Unfortunately, this will also remove all printer's marks (crop marks, registration marks, and color bars). Check this box to restore printer's marks.

The printing bounding box defines the printable area around which Separation Setup places crop marks. You can resize the printing bounding box in the preview window so it surrounds a different part of the illustration, though it usually does not need to be adjusted. If you move or resize this printing bounding box, Separation Setup crop marks will move with the bounding box. You might need to move the image and/or resize the bounding box if the illustration contains objects that are outside the artboard and there are no Illustrator-generated crop marks, because Separation Setup will include off-the-page objects as part of the image to be printed. Follow the instructions below if you want to resize the printing bounding box (and thus re-crop the illustration).

Re-cropping the illustration in the printing bounding box

In the Separation Setup dialog box:

To move the illustration relative to the printing bounding box, position the pointer over the image in the preview window, then drag **1**.

or

(Continued on the following page)

Separation Setup

To move the black line printing bounding box and the image, position the pointer over any non-handle part of the line and drag the box **1**.
or
To resize the printing bounding box (the black line), drag any of its four corner or side handles **2**.

➤ To restore the default printing bounding box, click Revert. The original values will be reentered into the Left, Right, Top, and Bottom fields.

Specifying which layers in the illustration will separate

Choose one of these options from the Separate pop-up menu in the Separation Setup dialog box to control which layers will be color separated **3**:

Printable, Visible Layers, to separate only those visible layers for which the Print option was turned on. To use this option effectively, place any objects you don't want separated on a special non-printing layer. Separation Setup will place the crop marks correctly.

Visible Layers, to separate only those layers that aren't hidden.

All Layers, to separate all layers.

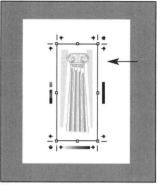

1 *Drag any part of the line except a handle to move the printing bounding box and the illustration together.*

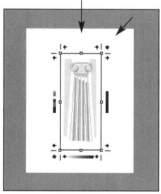

2 *Drag a side or corner handle to reshape the printing bounding box.*

Options		
Separate:	✓ **Printable, Visible Layers**	
Bleed:	**Visible Layers**	
	All Layers	
	☐ Overprint Black	

3 *The Separate pop-up menu in the Separation Setup dialog box*

Separation Setup

Scale, then trap

If you apply automatic trapping and then change an object's size, the trap width will change. You should apply trapping **after** you finalize the objects' dimensions.

Avoid the trap!

If all your colors have at least one component color in common (Cyan, Magenta, Yellow, or Black), you won't need to trap!

1 *Spread a lighter-colored foreground object.*

2 *Choke a darker-colored foreground object.*

The trap shrinks the darker-colored object.

3 *Check* **Overprint Stroke** *on the* **Attributes** *palette.*

Trapping

Trapping is the slight enlargement of a color area so it overlaps another color. The purpose of trapping is to compensate for gaps that might appear between printed colors due to misregistration on press.

There are two basic kinds of traps. A **spread** trap extends a lighter-colored object over a darker background color **1**. A **choke** trap extends a lighter background color over a darker-colored object **2**. In either case, the extending color overprints the object or background color, and a combination color is produced where they overlap.

In Illustrator, you can build traps automatically, or you can build them manually by specifying your own stroke width percentages. To turn on automatic trapping, see page 518.

Note: Ask your print shop for advice before building traps into your illustration.

To create a spread trap manually:

1. With your file in CMYK Color mode, select the lighter-colored foreground object.

2. Apply a stroke in the same color as the object's fill. The stroke weight should be **twice** the trap width that your print shop recommends for this object.

3. Open the Attributes palette, and check Overprint Stroke **3**. The foreground object will overlap the background object by half the thickness of the new stroke. The new stroke will blend with the background color via the Overprint option, and it will extend halfway inside and halfway outside the edge of the object.

Note: You'll be able to see the trap effect if you study the high-end output closely. To "proof" the overprinting effect on screen, use View > Overprint Preview.

Trapping

To create a choke trap manually:

1. Select the darker-colored foreground object.

2. Apply a stroke in the same color as the lighter background object's fill, in a weight that's twice the trap width your print shop recommends for this object.

3. Check the Overprint Stroke box on the Attributes palette. The lighter background color will now overlap the darker foreground object by half the width of the new stroke.

➤ A choke trap reduces the area of a darker object by half the stroke weight. Be careful when choking small type!

To trap a line manually:

1. Apply a stroke color and weight.

2. Choose Object > Path > Outline Stroke. The line becomes a filled object, the same width as the original stroke.

3. Apply a stroke to the modified line. If the line is lighter than the background color, apply the same color as the fill of the line. Otherwise, apply the lighter background color. Choose a stroke weight that is twice the trap width your print shop recommends for this object.

4. Check Overprint Stroke on the Attributes palette. The line will now overlap the background color by half the width of the new stroke 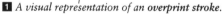. The stroke will blend with the background color when it overprints.

➤ If you're going to apply a choke trap to the line (where the stroke created in step 3 takes on the background color), the original outlined path will be reduced by the stroke weight. The stroke will reduce the path by half the stroke weight on each side of the path. To counteract this, create a line whose stroke weight is equal to the desired line weight plus the needed trap weight (see step 1, above). For example, let's say you have a 1 pt. line that needs a .2 pt. trap: Create a line with a 1.2 pt. weight stroke for step 1.

Strokes where you need 'em

You can use the **Outline** command (Pathfinder palette) to create trap strokes only where they're needed. To do this, create a new layer, then select the objects to be trapped. On the Layers palette, Option-drag/Alt-drag each object's selection square up to the new layer to copy it in its exact same x/y location to the new layer. Position the copies in the proper stacking order, then hide the original layer. Select the copied objects, click the Outline button on the Pathfinder palette to create strokes from those objects, then set the resulting strokes to overprint. Finally, using the Direct-selection tool, select and delete any stroke segments that you don't need, such as any strokes on a blank white background, then apply a stroke weight that's twice the trap amount your print shop specifies. Redisplay the original layer.

1 *A visual representation of an **overprint stroke**.*

Why the Overprint Black filter?

Normally, in PostScript color separations, objects on top knock out the color of objects underneath them so their ink colors don't inter-mix on press. When a color overprints, on the other hand, it prints right on top of the color beneath it and mixes with that color. Black is sometimes printed this way to eliminate the need for trapping. Using the **Overprint Black** filter, you can turn on overprinting or prevent overprinting in individual objects by exact per-centages of black. (Using the Separation Setup dialog box to specify overprinting instead would cause all black areas to overprint.)

Trapping type

Try not to use process colors on small type. Any misregistration on press will make the small type difficult to read. To trap type, make a copy of the type, choose Paste in Back, create a stroke for the copy, and set the stroke to overprint.

Type can also be converted into outlines. The resulting outline objects can be trapped like any other object.

A third way to prevent misregistration is to make the background a single process color, such as 100% black. This method is appropriate for newspaper printing.

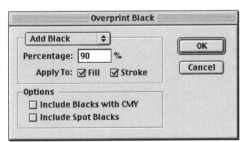

1 The *Overprint Black* dialog box

Before using this feature, read the sidebar at left and consult with your print shop.

To overprint a specified percentage of black:

1. Select an object(s) that contains black.

2. Choose Filter > Colors > Overprint Black.

3. Choose Add Black from the pop-up menu to turn the Overprint option on for the specified percentage you will enter **1**.
   or
   Choose Remove Black to turn the Overprint option off for the specified percentage you will enter.

4. Enter a Percentage value. Objects con-taining this black percentage will over-print or not overprint, depending on your choice for step 3.

5. Check Apply To: Fill to overprint black fills; check Stroke to overprint black strokes.

6. Check Options: Include Blacks with CMY to overprint any CMYK mixture contain-ing the specified percentage of black.

   Check Options: Include Spot Blacks to overprint any spot color containing the specified percentage of black.

   Note: To overprint a spot color, you must check both Options boxes.

7. Click OK.

➤ If you select more than one black object and then apply the Overprint Black filter, the filter will affect only those objects containing the specified percentage of black. The objects that are affected will remain selected after the filter is applied.

The Trap command creates traps automatically by determining which color object is lighter, and then spreading that color into the darker object. *Note:* The Trap command won't trap a placed image or any object that contains a gradient or pattern fill.

To create traps automatically:

1. With your document in CMYK Color mode, select two or more objects.

2. Choose Trap from the Pathfinder palette menu.

3. Enter the Thickness value your print shop specifies for the trap 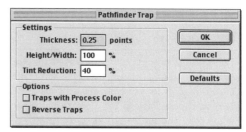.

Ask your print shop about optional steps 4–7.

4. Enter a Height/Width percentage to compensate for paper stretch on press (see the sidebar at right).

5. Enter a Tint Reduction percentage to prevent trap areas between light colors from printing too darkly.

6. Check Traps with Process Color to convert spot color traps in the selected objects into process colors, and thus prevent the creation of a separate plate just for traps.

7. Check Reverse Traps to trap darker colors into lighter colors.

8. Click OK. The trap shapes will become a new group on the currently active layer on the Layers palette.

The Trap filter doesn't always take the stroke color of a selected object into consideration. To overcome this limitation, convert the stroke into a filled object.

To create a trap on top of a fill and a stroke (a workaround):

1. Select an object that has a fill and a stroke, then choose Object > Path > Outline Stroke.

2. Apply the Trap command (see above).

Adjust trap height and width

Using the Trap command, you can adjust a trap to compensate for horizontal or vertical stretching of the paper on press. Enter a Height/Width percentage above 100% to widen the trap thickness for horizontal lines, or enter a Height/Width percentage below 100% to narrow the trap thickness for horizontal lines. Leave the percentage at 100 to have the same trap width apply to both horizontals and verticals.

1 *Choose the trap* **Thickness** *and other options in the* **Pathfinder Trap** *dialog box.*

Trapping

Chapter 28: Separations ◆ Study Guide

Learning Objectives

- Understand the basics of color reproduction.
- Understand the purpose and general operation of the Separation Setup dialog box.
- Understand the concepts behind trapping, including overprinting.

Get Up and Running Exercises

- Open or create a document containing process colors and one spot color. Suppose your print shop requires that all jobs be submitted with a laser proof so they can verify the final film output. Use a desktop printer to create a color-separated laser proof of the document. In the end, you should have five color-separated sheets, representing the five plates (four process inks and one spot ink).

- Open or create a document containing two overlapping objects. Fill the bottom object with PANTONE 1495M and fill the top object with PANTONE 2592M (both spot colors from the PANTONE Solid Matte swatch library). Set the stroke color of both objects to None. Duplicate the two objects so that you have three sets, then apply a different trapping method (below) to each set.

  ▲ Trap the first set of objects 0.25 points using a basic manual trap. What's the best way to view the results of your work?

  ▲ Trap the second set of objects by using the Trap command on the Pathfinder palette menu. How is the resulting trap different than the one applied to the previous set?

  ▲ For the third set, simply overprint the purple rectangle's fill. What's the difference between this method and method applied to the first set?

Class Discussion Questions

- How do you determine the proper settings for the Separation Setup dialog box?

- Why should you be wary of creating output from a job that uses 20 spot colors? Why wouldn't you have the same concern about creating output from a job that uses 20 process colors?

- Why is trapping applied to a document? How does trapping work?

- What's the difference between a spread trap and a choke trap?

- If you trap objects using strokes, how is it possible to trap a stroke, such as a line with a stroke but no fill?

Review Questions

Multiple choice

1. What is Illustrator's default method of color-separating adjacent colors?

   A. The color on top chokes the color underneath.

   B. The color on top knocks out the color underneath.

   C. The color on top overprints the color underneath.

   D. The color on top spreads the color underneath.

2. What is the most reliable and most expensive kind of color proof?

   A. Chromalin proof

   B. Digital IRIS proof

   C. Press proof

   D. Matchprint proof

3. When using the Trap command on the Pathfinder palette menu, which option traps darker colors into lighter colors?

   A. Reverse Traps

   B. Tint Reduction

   C. Thickness

   D. Traps with Process Color

4. When creating a spread trap manually, how much should you adjust the stroke weight based on the trap width your print shop recommends?

   A. Set the trap's stroke weight to the recommended trap width.

   B. Set the trap's stroke weight to half the recommended trap width.

   C. Set the trap's stroke weight to twice the recommended trap width.

   D. Set the trap's stroke weight to the object's stroke weight plus the recommended trap width.

Fill-in-the-blank

1. If the Separation Setup command is dimmed (unavailable) on the File menu, you need to _____.

2. To compensate for the stretching of paper on a press when using the Trap command, use the _____ option.

3. To see how overprinting would affect the document, use the _____ feature.

4. To precisely mark the printable area of a document, set _____.

5. If you don't overprint a color, the color will _____ any colors underneath it.

Definitions

1. What is color separation?
2. What is trapping?
3. What does it mean to knock out a color?
4. What is overprinting?
5. What is a PPD file?
6. What is a spread?
7. What is a choke?

KEYBOARD SHORTCUTS A

To assign custom shortcuts, see page 529

	Mac OS	Windows
Files		
New Document dialog box	Cmd-N	Ctrl-N
Open dialog box	Cmd-O	Ctrl-O
Close	Cmd-W	Ctrl-W
Save	Cmd-S	Ctrl-S
Save As dialog box	Cmd-Shift-S	Ctrl-Shift-S
Save a Copy dialog box	Cmd-Option-S	Ctrl-Alt-S
Document Setup dialog box	Cmd-Option-P	Ctrl-Alt-P
Quit/Exit Illustrator	Cmd-Q	Ctrl-Q
Tools		
Selection	V	V
Direct-selection	A	A
Magic Wand	Y	Y
Direct-select Lasso	Q	Q
Pen	P	P
Type	T	T
Line Segment	\	\
Rectangle	M	M
Ellipse	L	L
Paintbrush	B	B
Pencil	N	N
Rotate	R	R
Scale	S	S
Reflect	O	O
Warp	Shift-R	Shift-R
Free Transform	E	E
Symbol Sprayer	Shift-S	Shift-S
Column Graph	J	J
Mesh	U	U
Gradient	G	G
Eyedropper	I	I

	Mac OS	**Windows**
Paint Bucket	K	K
Blend	W	W
Slice	Shift-K	Shift-K
Scissors	C	C
Hand	H	H
Zoom	Z	Z
Add-anchor-point	+	+
Delete-anchor-point	-	-
Convert-anchor-point	Shift-C	Shift-C

Dialog boxes

Highlight next field/option	Tab	Tab
Highlight previous field/option	Shift-Tab	Shift-Tab
Cancel	Cmd . (period key) or Esc	Esc
OK	Return	Enter

Open/Save dialog boxes

Desktop	Cmd-D	
Up one folder level	Cmd-up arrow	

Palettes

Show/hide all palettes	Tab	Tab
Show/hide all palettes except Toolbox	Shift-Tab	Shift-Tab
Apply value in palette field	Return	Enter
Apply value in field, keep field selected	Shift-Return	Shift-Enter
Highlight next field (pointer in palette)	Tab	Tab
Highlight previous field (pointer in palette)	Shift-Tab	Shift-Tab
Highlight last-used field	Cmd-~	Ctrl-~

Views

Preview/Outline view toggle	Cmd-Y	Ctrl-Y
Pixel Preview view on/off	Cmd-Option-Y	Ctrl-Alt-Y
Overprint Preview view on/off	Cmd-Option-Shift-Y	Ctrl-Alt-Shift-Y
Use crosshair pointer (drawing tools)	Caps lock	Caps lock
Show/hide Edges	Cmd-H	Ctrl-H
Display entire artboard	Double-click Hand tool	Double-click Hand tool
Fit In Window	Cmd-0	Ctrl-0
Actual size	Double-click Zoom tool or Cmd-1	Double-click Zoom tool or Ctrl-1

	Mac OS	**Windows**
Zoom out (Zoom tool selected)	Option-click	Alt-click
Zoom in (any tool selected)	Cmd-Spacebar-click or Cmd-+	Ctrl-Spacebar-click or Ctrl-+
Zoom out (any tool selected)	Cmd-Option-Spacebar-click or Cmd- – (minus)	Ctrl-Alt-Spacebar-click or Ctrl- – (minus)
Adjust Zoom marquee position	Drag with Zoom tool, then Spacebar-drag	Drag with Zoom tool, then Spacebar-drag
Zoom in on specific area of artboard	Drag Zoom tool or Cmd-drag in Navigator palette	Drag Zoom tool or Ctrl-drag in Navigator palette
Use Hand tool (any tool selected)	Spacebar	Spacebar
Hide all unselected objects	Cmd-Option-Shift-3	Ctrl-Alt-Shift-3
Show All	Cmd-Option-3	Ctrl-Alt-3
Show/hide template(s)	Cmd-Shift-W	Ctrl-Shift-W
Show/hide bounding box	Cmd-Shift-B	Ctrl-Shift-B
Show/hide transparency grid	Cmd-Shift-D	Ctrl-Shift-D
Standard screen mode/Full screen mode with menu bar/Full screen mode	F	F

Undo/redo

	Mac OS	**Windows**
Undo last operation	Cmd-Z	Ctrl-Z
Redo last undone operation	Cmd-Shift-Z	Ctrl-Shift-Z

Create objects

	Mac OS	**Windows**
Draw object from center using Rectangle, Rounded Rectangle, or Ellipse tool	Option-drag	Alt-drag
Draw square with Rectangle or Rounded Rectangle tool; circle with Ellipse tool	Shift-drag	Shift-drag

Polygon, Star, Spiral tools

	Mac OS	**Windows**
Move object as you draw with Polygon, Star, or Spiral tool	Spacebar	Spacebar
Constrain orientation as you draw with Polygon, Star, or Spiral tool	Shift	Shift
Add or subtract sides as you draw with the Polygon tool, points as you draw with the Star tool, or segments as you draw with the Spiral tool	Up or down arrow	Up or down arrow
Align shoulders as you draw with Star tool	Option	Alt
Increase or decrease outer radius as you draw with Star tool or decay as you draw with Spiral tool	Cmd	Ctrl

	Mac OS	Windows
Select/copy		
Reselect (Select menu)	Cmd-6	Cmd-6
Use last-used selection tool (any non-selection tool chosen)	Cmd	Ctrl
Toggle between Selection tool and Direct-selection tool or Group-selection tool	Cmd-Ctrl-Tab	Ctrl-Tab
Toggle between Group-selection and Direct-selection tools	Option	Alt
Select All	Cmd-A	Ctrl-A
Deselect All	Cmd-Shift-A	Ctrl-Shift-A
Select an object hidden behind another object	Cmd-Option-[	Ctrl-Alt-[
Add to selection with either lasso tool	Shift-drag	Shift-drag
Subtract from selection with either lasso tool	Option-drag	Alt-drag
Move		
Open the Move dialog box (object selected)	Double-click Selection tool or Cmd-Shift-M	Double-click Selection tool or Ctrl-Shift-M
Drag copy of object	Option-drag	Alt-drag
Move selected object the current Keyboard Increment (Preferences > General)	Any arrow key	Any arrow key
Move selection 10x Keyboard Increment	Shift-arrow key	Shift-arrow key
Constrain movement to multiple of 45°	Shift	Shift
Clipboard		
Cut	Cmd-X	Ctrl-X
Copy	Cmd-C	Ctrl-C
Paste	Cmd-V	Ctrl-V
Paste In Front	Cmd-F	Ctrl-F
Paste In Back	Cmd-B	Ctrl-B
Transform		
Set origin, open dialog box (for any transform tool except Free Transform)	Option-click	Alt-click
Transform object along multiple of 45° (Shear, Reflect, Rotate tool)	Shift-drag	Shift-drag
Scale object uniformly (Scale, Free Transform tools)	Shift-drag	Shift-drag
Show/hide Attributes palette	F-11	F-11
Transform Again	Cmd-D	Ctrl-D
Transform pattern fill, not object (any transform tool)	~ drag	~ drag
Transform copy of object (any transform tool)	Start dragging, then Option-drag	Start dragging, then Alt-drag

	Mac OS	**Windows**
Transform copy of object (Transform palette)	Modify value, then press Option-Return	Modify value, then press Alt-Enter
Scale object uniformly (Transform palette)	Modify W or H value, then press Cmd-Return	Modify W or H value, then press Ctrl-Enter
Transform Each dialog box	Cmd-Option-Shift-D	Ctrl-Alt-Shift-D
Bounding box		
Scale object uniformly using bounding box (Free Transform or Selection tool)	Shift-drag handle	Shift-drag handle
Resize object from center using bounding box	Option-drag handle	Alt-drag handle
Blends		
Blend > Make	Cmd-Option-B	Ctrl-Alt-B
Blend > Release	Cmd-Option-Shift-B	Ctrl-Alt-Shift-B
Free Transform tool		
Transform from center	Option-drag a handle	Alt-drag a handle
Distort	Start dragging corner handle, then Cmd-drag	Start dragging corner handle, then Ctrl-drag
Skew	Start dragging side handle, then Cmd-drag	Start dragging side handle, then Ctrl-drag
Make Perspective	Start dragging corner handle, then Cmd-Option-Shift-drag	Start dragging corner handle, then Ctrl-Alt-Shift-drag

Drawing

Temporary Smooth tool (Pencil tool chosen)	Option	Alt
Close path while drawing with Pencil or Paintbrush tool	Drag, then Option-release	Drag, then Alt-release
Add to existing open path using Pencil tool	Cmd-click to select, then drag from endpoint	Ctrl-click to select, then drag from endpoint
Move anchor point while drawing with Pen	Spacebar	Spacebar

Reshape

Add-anchor-point and Delete-anchor-point tool toggle (either selected)	Option	Alt
Use Add-anchor-point tool (Scissors tool selected)	Option	Alt
Use Convert-anchor-point tool (Pen tool selected)	Option	Alt
Constrain direction line angle to multiple of 45° with Direct-selection or Convert-anchor-point tool	Shift-drag	Shift-drag
Join two selected endpoints	Cmd-J	Ctrl-J

	Mac OS	Windows
Average two selected endpoints	Cmd-Option-J	Ctrl-Alt-J
Average and Join two selected endpoints	Cmd-Option-Shift-J	Ctrl-Alt-Shift-J
Cut in a straight line with Knife tool	Option-drag	Alt-drag
Cut in 45° increment with Knife tool	Option-Shift	Alt-Shift

Fill & stroke

Show/hide Stroke palette	F-10	F-10
Default fill/stroke	D	D
Eyedropper and Paint Bucket tool toggle (either one selected)	Option	Alt
Fill/Stroke box toggle (Toolbox and Color palette)	X	X
Apply last-used solid color	<	<
Apply fill/stroke of None	/	/

Color palette

Show/hide Color palette	Cmd-I or F-6	Ctrl-I or F-6
Change fill color if Stroke box is active, or vice versa	Option-click or drag in color spectrum bar on Color palette	Alt-click or drag in color spectrum bar on Color palette
Cycle through color models	Shift-click color spectrum bar	Shift-click color spectrum bar
Swap fill/stroke	Shift-X	Shift-X

Swatches palette

Set options for new swatch	Option-click New Swatch button	Alt-click New Swatch button
Create new spot color	Cmd-click New Swatch button	Ctrl-click New Swatch button
Create new global process color	Cmd-Shift-click New Swatch button	Ctrl-Shift-click New Swatch button

Layers

Show/hide Layers palette	F-7	F-7
Expand/collapse all sublayers and groups in a layer	Option-click arrowhead	Alt-click arrowhead

Grouping

Group	Cmd-G	Ctrl-G
Ungroup	Cmd-Shift-G	Ctrl-Shift-G

Restacking (keyboard)

Bring To Front	Cmd-Shift-]	Ctrl-Shift-]
Send To Back	Cmd-Shift-[	Ctrl-Shift-[
Bring Forward	Cmd-]	Ctrl-]
Send Backward	Cmd-[	Ctrl-[

	Mac OS	**Windows**
Select		
Select layer, sublayer, group, or object	Click selection area or Option-click name	Click selection area or Alt-click name
Add to selection	Shift-click selection area	Shift-click selection area
Copy selection to new layer, sublayer, group	Option-drag square	Alt-drag-square
Views		
Hide/show all other layers	Option-click eye icon	Alt-click eye icon
View a layer in Outline/Preview view	Cmd-click eye icon	Ctrl-click eye icon
View all other layers in Outline/ Preview view	Cmd-Option-click eye icon	Ctrl-Alt-click eye icon
Lock/unlock all other layers	Option-click blank in second column	Alt-click blank box in second column
Create top-level layers		
Create layer above currently selected layer	Cmd-L	Ctrl-L
Create layer at top of list	Cmd-click New Layer button	Ctrl-click New Layer button
Create layer below currently selected layer	Cmd-Option-click New Layer button	Ctrl-Alt-click New Layer button
Create layer, open Layer Options dialog box	Option-click New Layer button	Alt-click New Layer button
Lock/unlock (keyboard)		
Lock (selected object)	Cmd-2	Ctrl-2
Lock all unselected objects	Cmd-Option-Shift-2	Ctrl-Alt-Shift-2
Unlock All	Cmd-Option-2	Ctrl-Alt-2
Type		
Show/hide Character palette	Cmd-T	Ctrl-T
Show/hide Paragraph palette	Cmd-M	Ctrl-M
Hard Return	Return	Enter
Soft Return	Shift-Return	Shift-Enter
Highlight font field on Character palette	Cmd-Option-Shift-M	Ctrl-Alt-Shift-M
Show/hide Tab Ruler palette	Cmd-Shift-T	Ctrl-Shift-T
Create Outlines	Cmd-Shift-O	Ctrl-Shift-O
Type tools		
Use Area Type tool (Type tool selected, over open path)	Option	Alt
Use Path Type tool (Type tool selected, over closed path)	Option	Alt
Switch to vertical/horizontal type tool equivalent as you create type	Shift with any type tool	Shift with any type tool
Switch to Type tool when selecting type block	Double-click with any selection tool	Double-click with any selection tool

525

Keyboard Shortcuts

	Mac OS	Windows
Selecting type		
Select a word	Double-click	Double-click
Select a paragraph	Triple-click	Triple-click
Select all the type in a block	Cmd-A	Ctrl-A
Move insertion pointer left/right one word	Cmd-left/right arrow	Ctrl-left/right arrow
Move insertion pointer up/down one line	Up/Down arrow	Up/Down arrow
Alignment		
Align left	Cmd-Shift-L	Ctrl-Shift-L
Align center	Cmd-Shift-C	Ctrl-Shift-C
Align right	Cmd-Shift-R	Ctrl-Shift-R
Justify	Cmd-Shift-J	Ctrl-Shift-J
Justify all lines	Cmd-Shift-F	Ctrl-Shift-F
Point size		
Increase point size	Cmd-Shift->	Ctrl-Shift->
Decrease point size	Cmd-Shift-<	Ctrl-Shift-<
Leading		
Increase leading	Option-down arrow	Alt-down arrow
Decrease leading	Option-up arrow	Alt-up arrow
Set leading to current font size	Double-click leading button on Character palette	Double-click leading button on Character palette
Horizontal scale		
Reset horizontal scale to 100%	Cmd-Shift-X	Ctrl-Shift-X
Kerning/tracking		
Highlight kerning field (cursor in text) or highlight tracking field (type object selected)	Cmd-Option-K	Ctrl-Alt-K
Increase kerning/tracking	Option-right arrow	Alt-right arrow
Decrease kerning/tracking	Option-left arrow	Alt-left arrow
Increase kerning/tracking 5x	Cmd-Option right arrow	Ctrl-Alt right arrow
Decrease kerning/tracking 5x	Cmd-Option left arrow	Ctrl-Alt left arrow
Reset kerning/tracking to 0	Cmd-Option-Q	Ctrl-Alt-Q
Baseline shift		
Increase baseline shift	Option-Shift up arrow	Alt-Shift up arrow
Decrease baseline shift	Option-Shift down arrow	Alt-Shift down arrow
Increase baseline shift 5x	Cmd-Option-Shift up arrow	Ctrl-Alt-Shift up arrow
Decrease baseline shift 5x	Cmd-Option-Shift down arrow	Ctrl-Alt-Shift down arrow

	Mac OS	**Windows**
Curly quotes		
'	Option Shift-]	Alt-0146
'	Option-]	Alt-0145
"	Option Shift-[	Alt-0148
"	Option-[	Alt-0147

Numeric keypad only (applies to the four Alt codes above)

Brushes

Show/hide Brushes palette	F-5	F-5

Combine paths

Compound Path > Make	Cmd-8	Ctrl-8
Compound Path > Release	Cmd-Option-8	Ctrl-Alt-8
Repeat last-used Pathfinder command	Cmd-4	Ctrl-4
Turn shape mode button into pathfinder	Option-click button	Alt-click button

Gradients

Show/hide Gradient palette	F-9	F-9
Reapply last-used gradient	> (period)	> (period)
Reset gradient palette to black and white	Cmd-click Gradient square on palette	Ctrl-click Gradient square on palette
Duplicate color stop	Option-drag	Alt-drag
Apply swatch color to active color stop	Option-click swatch	Alt-click swatch

Gradient meshes

Move mesh point along one of its lines	Shift-drag with Gradient Mesh tool	Shift-drag with Gradient Mesh tool
Add mesh point using adjacent mesh color	Shift-click with Gradient Mesh tool	Shift-click with Gradient Mesh tool
Remove mesh point	Option-click with Gradient Mesh tool	Alt-click with Gradient Mesh tool

Appearances

Add new fill	Cmd-/	Ctrl-/
Add new stroke	Cmd-Option-/	Ctrl-Alt-/
Sample style and append appearance of selected object	Option-Shift-click with Eyedropper	Alt-Shift-click with Eyedropper

Clipping masks

Clipping Mask > Make	Cmd-7	Ctrl-7
Clipping Mask > Release	Cmd-Option-7	Ctrl-Alt-7

Transparency

View only opacity mask in mask edit mode	Option-click mask thumbnail	Alt-click mask thumbnail
Disable opacity mask	Shift-click mask thumbnail	Shift-click mask thumbnail

Keyboard Shortcuts

	Mac OS	Windows
Change opacity in increments of 10 (for increments of 1, omit Shift)	Click field, then Shift-arrow	Click field, then Shift-arrow

Envelope distort

	Mac OS	Windows
Make with Warp	Cmd-Option-W	Ctrl-Alt-W
Make with Mesh	Cmd-Option-M	Ctrl-Alt-M
Make with Top Object	Cmd-Option-C	Ctrl-Alt-C

Effects & filters

	Mac OS	Windows
Apply Last Effect	Cmd-Shift-E	Ctrl-Shift-E
Last Effect (reopen last effect dialog box)	Cmd-Option-Shift-E	Ctrl-Alt-Shift-E
Apply Last Filter	Cmd-E	Ctrl-E
Last Filter (reopen last filter dialog box)	Cmd-Option-E	Ctrl-Alt-E

Precision tools

	Mac OS	Windows
Show/hide Rulers	Cmd-R	Ctrl-R
Show/hide Guides	Cmd- ;	Ctrl- ;
Make Guides	Cmd-5	Ctrl-5
Release Guides	Click selection area on Layers palette, then Cmd-Option-5	Click selection area on Layers palette, then Ctrl-Alt-5
Release a guide	Cmd-Shift-double-click guide	Ctrl-Shift-double-click guide
Convert guide between horizontal/vertical orientation	Option-drag new guide	Alt-drag new guide
Lock/Unlock Guides	Cmd-Option-;	Ctrl-Alt-;
Show/hide Grid	Cmd-"	Ctrl-"
Snap To Grid	Cmd-Shift-"	Ctrl-Shift-"
Snap To Point (Pixel Preview off); Snap To Pixel (Pixel Preview on)	Cmd-Option-"	Ctrl-Alt-"
Smart Guides	Cmd-U	Ctrl-U
Constrain Measure tool to multiple of 45°	Shift-drag with tool	Shift-drag with tool

Preferences

	Mac OS	Windows
General Preferences dialog box	Cmd-K	Ctrl-K

Export/print

	Mac OS	Windows
Save for Web	Cmd-Option-Shift-S	Ctrl-Alt-Shift-S
Page Setup/Print Setup dialog box	Cmd-Shift-P	Ctrl-Shift-P
Print dialog box	Cmd-P	Ctrl-P
Show/hide Info	F-8	F-8

Shortcuts/help

	Mac OS	Windows
Keyboard Shortcuts dialog box	Cmd-Option-Shift-K	Ctrl-Alt-Shift-K
Illustrator Help (online)	Cmd-Shift-?	F1

Reset keyset

To **reset** the keyboard shortcuts in the Keyboard Shortcuts dialog box at any time, Option-click/ Alt-click the Cancel (Reset) button.

Customizing shortcuts

If you don't like Illustrator's default shortcuts for commands and tools, you can assign your own. Shortcuts are organized into keysets.

To assign your own shortcuts:

1. Choose Edit menu > Keyboard Shortcuts (Cmd-Option-Shift-K/Ctrl-Alt-Shift-K).

2. To edit an existing keyset (set of shortcuts), choose a keyset name from the Set pop-up menu (**1**, next page). To create a new keyset, ignore this step (you'll create one later).

3. Choose Menu Commands or Tools from the next pop-up menu.

4. Click the command or tool name to which you want to assign a shortcut.

5. Press the shortcut key, then click on a blank area of the dialog box.

   If that key is already assigned to another command or tool, an alert message will appear in the dialog box, and the shortcut will be removed from the previous command or tool. To assign a new shortcut to the command or tool from which you just removed a shortcut, click Go To, then press a shortcut.
   or
   If you change your mind, click Undo in the dialog box. The shortcut will be reassigned to its original command or tool. To clear a shortcut altogether, click Clear.

6. *Optional:* In the Symbol column, enter the keyboard symbol you want to appear on the menu or tool tip for the command or tool.

7. Repeat steps 4–6 for any other shortcuts you want to assign.

8. As soon as one user-defined shortcut is entered in the dialog box, the word "Custom" appears on the Set pop-up menu. To create a new keyset to include your new shortcuts, click Save, type a name for the new keyset, click OK, then click OK again to exit the dialog box.

(Continued on the following page)

The new keyset name will appear on the
Set pop-up menu.
or
To save your changes to the currently
chosen keyset, click OK.

To choose, delete, or print a keyset:

1. Choose Edit menu > Keyboard Shortcuts
(Cmd-Option-Shift-K/Ctrl-Alt-Shift-K).

2. Choose a keyset from the Set pop-up
menu.

3. To use the chosen keyset, click OK.
or
To delete the chosen keyset, click Delete,
then click OK.
or
To print the chosen keyset, click Export
Text, type a name for the keyset, click
Save, then click OK to exit the dialog
box. Open the new SimpleText (Mac OS)/
Notepad (Win) file and print it.

INDEX

Index

Index

Index

Index

Index

Index

Index

Index

Index

Index

Index

Index

Index

Index

Index

Index

Index

Index

Index